'I cannot and I will not recant anything, for to
go against conscience is neither right nor safe.
Here I stand, I cannot do otherwise. God help
me. Amen.'

artin Luther refused to give way. From the
oment he had nailed his 95 theses to the
rch door in Wittenberg, he had been a
d man. His enemies accused him of
s books were burned, and he was
th excommunication and death.

biography by Roland Bainton gives
xciting picture of the man who
arch of his time upside down.

and inspiring story of a great
the crusader who spearheaded
formation. Excellent . . .
and eloquent.'
ork Times

HERE I STAND

ROLAND BAINTON

A LION PAPERBACK

Published by
Lion Publishing plc
Icknield Way, Tring, Herts, England
ISBN 0 85648 447 4
Albatross Books
PO Box 320, Sutherland, NSW 2232, Australia
ISBN 0 86760 459 X

First published by
Abingdon Press, Nashville, TN, USA
First UK edition 1983
Reprinted 1983, 1984

Printed and bound in Great Britain
by Richard Clay (The Chaucer Press) Ltd,
Bungay, Suffolk

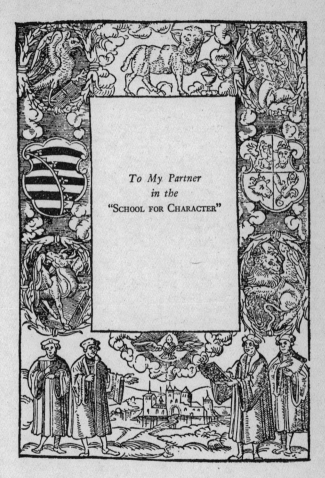

To My Partner
in the
"SCHOOL FOR CHARACTER"

ACKNOWLEDGMENTS

PORTIONS of this book have been delivered as the Nathaniel Taylor lectures at the Yale Divinity School, the Carew Lectures at the Hartford Seminary Foundation, and the Hein Lectures at the Wartburg Seminary and Capital University, as well as at the Bonebrake Theological Seminary, the Gettysburg Theological Seminary, and the Divinity School of Howard University. For many courtesies on the part of these institutions I am indebted.

I also thank the firm of J. C. B. Mohr at Tübingen for permission to reprint as Chapter XXI the article which appeared in the *Gerhard Ritter Festschrift*, and the Westminster Press for permission to use in condensed form certain portions from my *Martin Luther Christmas Book*.

Extensive travel and borrowing for this work have not been necessary because the Yale library is so richly supplied and so generous in acquiring new material. Especially to Mr. Babb, Mr. Wing, and Mr. Tinker hearty thanks are tendered by Martin Luther.

CONTENTS

CONTENTS

LIST OF ILLUSTRATIONS

LIST OF ILLUSTRATIONS

CHRONOLOGY

1483	November 10	Birth of Martin Luther at Eisleben
1484	early summer	Family moved to Mansfeld
1497	about Easter	Luther goes to school at Magdeburg
1498		Luther goes to school at Eisenach
1501	May	Matriculation at Erfurt
1502	September 29	Bachelor of Arts
1505	January 7	Master of Arts
	July 2	Thunderstorm and vow
	July 17	Enters Augustinian cloister at Erfurt
1507	May 2	First mass
1508	winter	Teaches one semester at Wittenberg
1509	October	Return to Erfurt
1510	November	Journey to Rome
1511	early April	Return to Erfurt; transfer to Wittenberg
1512	October 19	Doctor of Theology
1513	August 16	Lectures on Psalms begin
1515	April	Lectures on Romans begin
1516	September 7	Lectures on Romans end
	October 27	Lectures on Galatians begin
1517	October 31	Posting the ninety-five theses
1518	April 26	Disputation at Heidelberg
	July	Prierias attacks Luther
	August 5	Maximilian writes to the pope
	August 7	The pope cites Luther to Rome
	August 8	Luther appeals to Frederick
	August 25	Melanchthon arrives
	August 31	Luther's reply to Prierias
	September 26	Luther starts for Augsburg
	October 12-14	Interview with Cajetan
	October 20-21	Flight from Augsburg
	October 30	Back in Wittenberg
	November 8	The bull *Cum Postquam*
	November 28	Luther appeals to a general council

	December 2	Ready to go into exile
	December 18	Frederick will not banish Luther
1519	January 4-6	Interview of Luther with Miltitz
	January 12	Death of Emperor Maximilian
	June 28	Election of Charles V
	July 4-14	Leipzig debate between Luther and Eck
1520	January	Hutten and Sickingen offer Luther help
	May	*Sermon on Good Works*
	June 11	Offer of protection from one hundred knights; *The Papacy at Rome*
	June 15	*Exsurge Domine* gives Luther sixty days to submit
	August	*Address to the German Nobility*
	October 6	*Babylonian Captivity*
	October 10	Luther receives the pope's bull
	November 4	Charles at Cologne promises a hearing
	November 12	Burning of Luther's books at Cologne
	November	*Against the Execrable Bull of Antichrist; On the Freedom of the Christian Man*
	November 28	Luther invited to Worms
	December 10	Burning by Luther of the pope's bull
	December 17	Invitation to Worms rescinded
1521	January 3	The bull *Decet Romanum Pontificem* against Luther is ready
	January 5	Frederick arrives at Worms
	January 27	The diet of Worms opens
	February 10	The bull against Luther reaches Aleander
	February 13	Aleander's three-hour speech; the bull is sent back
	February 14	Glapion's attempts at mediation
	February 17	Draft of an edict against Luther
	February 19	Intense opposition
	February 22	Decision to summon Luther
	March 2	Second draft of an edict
	March 6	Invitation to Luther
	March 8	Edict for sequestration of Luther's books ready
	March 26	Edict issued
	April 10	Glapion reports failure of mission to Hutten and Sickingen

	April 16	Luther in Worms
	April 17	First hearing
	April 18	Second hearing
	April 19	The emperor announces his decision
	April 20	Diet requests a committee
	April 23-24	Hearings before the committee
	April 26	Luther leaves Worms
	May 4	Luther arrives at the Wartburg
	May 8	Edict of Worms ready
	May 26	Edict of Worms actually issued
	September 22	Melanchthon celebrates an evangelical Lord's Supper
	November 12	Thirteen monks leave the Augustinian cloister
	December 3-4	Tumult at Wittenberg; Luther's flying trip home and return
	December	Commencement of the New Testament translation; work on the Sermon Postils
	December 25	Carlstadt gives wine in the mass to laity
	December 27	Zwickau prophets in Wittenberg
1522	January 6	Disbanding of the Augustinian Congregation at Wittenberg
	February 26	Justus Jonas, minister of the Castle Church at Wittenberg, marries
	March 1-6	Luther's return to Wittenberg
	September–May, 1523	Sickingen's campaign against Trier
	September	Luther's German New Testament published
	September 14	Hadrian VI elected pope
1523	March 6	Edict of the Diet of Nürnberg deferring action
	March	*On Civil Government*
	Pentecost	*On the Order of Worship*
	July 1	Burning of the first martyrs of the Reformation at Brussels
	August 23	Death of Hutten
	September	Clement VII elected pope
1524		Hymnbook
	January–February	*To the Councilmen . . . Christian Schools*
	April 18	Edict of the second diet of Nürnberg
	September	Erasmus, *On the Freedom of the Will*

1525	January	*Against the Heavenly Prophets*
	March	Twelve articles of the peasants
	April 19	*Admonition to Peace*
	May 5	Death of Frederick the Wise
	May 5	*Against the Robbing and Murdering Hordes*
	May 15	Battle of Frankenhausen; capture of Müntzer
	May–June	Crushing of the peasants
	June 13	Luther's betrothal to Katherine von Bora
	July	*Open Letter Concerning the Hard Book Against the Peasants*
	before Christmas	*The German Mass*
	December	*On the Enslaved Will*
1526	June 25–August 27	Diet of Speyer defers action on the Edict of Worms
		Exposition of Jonah
1527	January	*Whether Soldiers Too May Be Saved*
	April	*Whether These Words: This Is My Body*
	summer	Sickness, intense depression
		Composition of "A Mighty Fortress"
1528	March 22	*Instruction for the Visitors*
	March 28	*Confession of the Lord's Supper*
1529	April 19	Protest at the Diet of Speyer
	October 1-4	Marburg Colloquy; German catechism
1530	April 16	Luther at the Coburg
	June 25	Presentation of the Augsburg Confession
		Exposition of the Eighty-Second Psalm (Death penalty for sedition and blasphemy)
1531		*Warning to His Beloved Germans*
1534		Publication of the complete German Bible
1536		Wittenberg Concord with the Swiss
		Outbreak of Anabaptists at Münster
		Melanchthon's memorandum on the death penalty for peaceful Anabaptists
1539		Bigamy of the Landgrave Philip
1543	January 4	*Against the Jews*
	July	Publication of the Genesis Commentary (lectures delivered from 1535-1545)
1545	March 25	*Against the Papacy at Rome Founded by the Devil*
1546	February 18	Luther's death at Eisleben

CHAPTER ONE

THE VOW

N A SULTRY DAY in July of the year 1505 a lonely traveler was trudging over a parched road on the outskirts of the Saxon village of Stotternheim. He was a young man, short but sturdy, and wore the dress of a university student. As he approached the village, the sky became overcast. Suddenly there was a shower, then a crashing storm. A bolt of lightning rived the gloom and knocked the man to the ground. Struggling to rise, he cried in terror, "St. Anne help me! I will become a monk."

The man who thus called upon a saint was later to repudiate the cult of the saints. He who vowed to become a monk was later to renounce monasticism. A loyal son of the Catholic Church, he was later to shatter the structure of medieval Catholicism. A devoted servant of the pope, he was later to identify the popes with Antichrist. For this young man was Martin Luther.

His demolition was the more devastating because it reinforced disintegrations already in progress. Nationalism was in process of breaking the political unities when the Reformation destroyed the religious. Yet this paradoxical figure revived the Christian consciousness of Europe. In his day, as Catholic historians all agree, the popes of the Renaissance were secularized, flippant, frivolous, sensual, magnificent, and unscrupulous. The intelligentsia did not revolt against the Church because the Church was so much of their mind and mood as scarcely to warrant a revolt. Politics were emancipated from any concern for the faith to such a degree that the Most Christian King of France and His Holiness the Pope did not disdain a military alliance with the Sultan against the Holy Roman Emperor. Luther changed all this. Religion became again a dominant factor even in politics for another century and a half. Men cared enough for the faith to die for it and to kill for it. If there is any sense remaining of Christian civilization in the West, this man Luther in no small measure deserves the credit.

Very naturally he is a controversial figure. The multitudinous portrayals fall into certain broad types already delineated in his own generation. His followers hailed him as the prophet of the Lord and the deliverer of Germany. His opponents on the Catholic side called him the son of perdition and the demolisher of Christendom. The agrarian agitators branded him as the sycophant of the princes, and the radical sectaries compared him to Moses, who led the children of Israel out of Egypt and left them to perish in the wilderness. But such judgments belong to an epilogue rather than a prologue. The first endeavor must be to understand the man.

One will not move far in this direction unless one recognizes at the outset that Luther was above all else a man of religion. The great outward crises of his life which bedazzle the eyes of dramatic biographers were to Luther himself trivial in comparison with the inner upheavals of his questing after God. For that reason this study may appropriately begin with his first acute religious crisis in 1505 rather than with his birth in 1483. Childhood and youth will be drawn upon only to explain the entry into the monastery.

AT HOME AND SCHOOL

The vow requires interpretation because even at this early point in Luther's career judgments diverge. Those who deplore his subsequent repudiation of the vow explain his defection on the ground that he ought never to have taken it. Had he ever been a true monk, he would not have abandoned the cowl. His critique of monasticism is made to recoil upon himself in that he is painted as a monk without vocation, and the vow is interpreted, not as a genuine call, but rather as the resolution of an inner conflict, an escape from maladjustment at home and at school.

A few sparse items of evidence are adduced in favor of this explanation. They are not of the highest reliability because they are  all taken from the conversation of the older Luther as recorded, often inaccurately, by his students; and even if they are genuine, they cannot be accepted at face value because the Protestant Luther was no longer in a position to recall objectively the motives of his Catholic period. Really there is only one saying which connects the taking of the cowl with resentment against parental discipline. Luther is reported to have said, "My mother caned me for stealing a nut, until the blood came. Such strict discipline drove me to the monastery, although she meant it well." This saying is reinforced by two others: "My father once whipped me so that I ran away and felt ugly toward him until he was at pains to win me back." "[At school] I was caned in a single morning fifteen times for nothing at all. I was required to decline and conjugate and hadn't learned my lesson."

Unquestionably the young were roughly handled in those days, and Luther may be correctly reported as having cited these instances in order to bespeak a more humane treatment, but there is no indication that such severity produced more than a flash of resentment. Luther was highly esteemed at home. His parents looked to him as a lad of brilliant parts who should become a

jurist, make a prosperous marriage, and support them in their old age.
When Luther became a Master of Arts, his father presented him with a
copy of the *Corpus Juris* and addressed him no longer with the
familiar *Du* but with the polite *Ihr*. Luther always exhibited an
extraordinary devotion to his father and was grievously disturbed
over parental disapproval of his entry into the monastery. When
his father died, Luther was too unnerved to work for several days.
The attachment to the mother appears to have been less marked;
but even of the thrashing he said that it was well intended, and he
recalled affectionately a little ditty she used to sing:

> If folk don't like you and me,
> The fault with us is like to be.

The schools also were not tender, but neither were they brutal.
The object was to impart a spoken knowledge of the Latin tongue.
The boys did not resent this because Latin was useful—the language

THE ASINUS

of the Church, of law, diplomacy, international relations, scholarship, and travel. The teaching was by drill punctuated with the rod. One scholar, called a *lupus* or wolf, was appointed to spy on the others and report lapses into German. The poorest scholar in the class every noon was given a donkey mask, hence called the *asinus*, which he wore until he caught another talking German. Demerits were accumulated and accounted for by birching at the end of the week. Thus one might have fifteen strokes on a single day.

But, despite all the severities, the boys did learn Latin and loved it. Luther, far from being alienated, was devoted to his studies and became highly proficient. The teachers were no brutes. One of them, Trebonius, on entering the classroom always bared his head in the presence of so many future burgomasters, chancellors, doctors, and regents. Luther respected his teachers and was grieved when they did not approve of his subsequent course.

Nor was he prevailingly depressed, but ordinarily rollicking, fond of music, proficient on the lute, and enamored of the beauty of the German landscape. How fair in retrospect was Erfurt! The woods came down to the fringes of the village to be continued by orchards and vineyards, and then the fields of blue-flowered flax, and the yellow wild saffron and German indigo which supplied the dye industry. Nestling within these brilliant rows lay the walls, the gates, the steeples of many-spired Erfurt. Luther called her a new Bethlehem.

RELIGIOUS DISQUIET

Yet Luther was at times severely depressed, and the reason lay not in any personal frictions but in the malaise of existence intensified by religion. This man was no son of the Italian Renaissance, but a German born in remote Thuringia, where men of piety still reared churches with arches and spires straining after the illimitable. Luther was himself so much a gothic figure that his faith may be called the last great flowering of the religion of the Middle Ages. And he came from the most religiously conservative element of

the population, the peasants. His father, Hans Luther, and his
mother, Margaretta, were sturdy, stocky, swarthy German *Bauern*.
They were not indeed actually engaged in the tilling of the soil
because as a son without inheritance Hans had moved from the
farm to the mines. In the bowels of the earth he had prospered
with the help of St. Anne, the patroness of miners, until he had

HANS LUTHER   MARGARETTA LUTHER

come to be the owner of half a dozen foundries; yet he was not
unduly affluent, and his wife had still to go to the forest and drag
home the wood. The atmosphere of the family was that of the
peasantry: rugged, rough, at times coarse, credulous, and devout.
Old Hans prayed at the bedside of his son, and Margaretta was a
woman of prayer.

Certain elements even of old German paganism were blended
with Christian mythology in the beliefs of these untutored folk.
For them the woods and winds and water were peopled by elves,
gnomes, fairies, mermen and mermaids, sprites and witches. Sinister

spirits would release storms, floods, and pestilence, and would seduce mankind to sin and melancholia. Luther's mother believed that they played such minor pranks as stealing eggs, milk, and butter; and Luther himself was never emancipated from such beliefs. "Many regions are inhabited," said he, "by devils. Prussia is full of them, and Lapland of witches. In my native country on the top of a high mountain called the Pubelsberg is a lake into which if a stone be thrown a tempest will arise over the whole region because the waters are the abode of captive demons."

The education in the schools brought no emancipation but rather reinforced the training of the home. In the elementary schools the children were instructed in sacred song. They learned by heart the *Sanctus*, the *Benedictus*, the *Agnus Dei*, and the *Confiteor*. They were trained to sing psalms and hymns. How Luther loved the *Magnificat!* They attended masses and vespers, and took part in the colorful processions of the holy days. Each town in which Luther went to school was full of churches and monasteries. Everywhere it was the same: steeples, spires, cloisters, priests, monks of the various orders, collections of relics, ringing of bells, proclaiming of indulgences, religious processions, cures at shrines. Daily at Mansfeld the sick were stationed beside a convent in the hope of cure at the tolling of the vesper bell. Luther remembered seeing a devil actually depart from one possessed.

The University of Erfurt brought no change. The institution at that time had not yet been invaded by Renaissance influences. The classics in the curriculum, such as Vergil, had always been favorites in the Middle Ages. Aristotelian physics was regarded as an exercise in thinking God's thoughts after him, and the natural explanations of earthquakes and thunderstorms did not preclude occasional direct divine causation. The studies all impinged on theology, and the Master's degree for which Luther was preparing for the law could have equipped him equally for the cloth. The entire training of home, school, and university was designed to instill fear of God and reverence for the Church.

In all this there is nothing whatever to set Luther off from his contemporaries, let alone to explain why later on he should have revolted against so much of medieval religion. There is just one respect in which Luther appears to have been different from other youths of his time, namely, in that he was extraordinarily sensitive and subject to recurrent periods of exaltation and depression of spirit. This oscillation of mood plagued him throughout his life. He testified that it began in his youth and that the depressions had been acute in the six months prior to his entry into the monastery. One cannot dismiss these states as occasioned merely by adolescence, since he was then twenty-one and similar experiences continued throughout his adult years. Neither can one blithely write off the case as an example of manic depression, since the patient exhibited a prodigious and continuous capacity for work of a high order.

The explanation lies rather in the tensions which medieval religion deliberately induced, playing alternately upon fear and hope. Hell was stoked, not because men lived in perpetual dread, but precisely because they did not, and in order to instill enough fear to drive them to the sacraments of the Church. If they were petrified with terror, purgatory was introduced by way of mitigation as an intermediate place where those not bad enough for hell nor good enough for heaven might make further expiation. If this alleviation inspired complacency, the temperature was advanced on purgatory, and then the pressure was again relaxed through indulgences.

Even more disconcerting than the fluctuation of the temperature of the afterlife was the oscillation between wrath and mercy on the part of the members of the divine hierarchy. God was portrayed now as the Father, now as the wielder of the thunder. He might be softened by the intercession of his kindlier Son, who again was delineated as an implacable judge unless mollified by his mother, who, being a woman, was not above cheating alike God and the Devil on behalf of her suppliants; and if she were remote, one could enlist her mother, St. Anne.

How these themes were presented is graphically illustrated in the most popular handbooks in the very age of the Renaissance. The theme was death; and the best sellers gave instructions, not on how to pay the income tax, but on how to escape hell. Manuals entitled *On the Art of Dying* depicted in lurid woodcuts the departing spirit surrounded by fiends who tempted him to commit the irrevocable sin of abandoning hope in God's mercy. To convince him that he was already beyond pardon he was confronted by the woman with whom he had committed adultery or the beggar he had failed to feed. A companion woodcut then gave encouragement by presenting the figures of forgiven sinners: Peter with his cock, Mary Magdalene with her cruse, the penitent thief, and Saul the persecutor, with the concluding brief caption, "Never despair."

FIENDS TEMPTING A DYING MAN TO ABANDON HOPE

If this conclusion ministered to complacency, other presentations invoked dread. A book strikingly illustrative of the prevailing mood is a history of the world published by Hartmann Schedel in Nürnberg in 1493. The massive folios, after recounting the history of mankind from Adam to the humanist Conrad Celtes, conclude with a meditation on the brevity of human existence accompanied by a woodcut of the dance of death. The final scene displays the day of judgment. A full-page woodcut portrays Christ the Judge sitting upon a rainbow. A lily extends from his right ear, signifying the redeemed, who below are being ushered by angels into paradise. From his left ear protrudes a sword, symbolizing the doom of the damned, whom the devils drag by the hair from the tombs and cast into the flames of hell. How strange, comments a modern editor, that a chronicle published in the year 1493 should end with the judgment day instead of the discovery of America! Dr. Schedel had finished his manuscript in June. Columbus had returned the previous March. The news presumably had not yet reached Nürnberg. By so narrow a margin Dr. Schedel missed this amazing scoop. "What an extraordinary value surviving copies of the Chronicle would have today if it had recorded the great event!"

So writes the modern editor. But old Dr. Schedel, had he known, might not have considered the finding of a new world worthy of record. He could scarcely have failed to know of the discovery of the Cape of Good Hope in 1488. Yet he never mentioned it. The reason is that he did not think of history as the record of humanity expanding upon earth and craving as the highest good more earth in which to expand. He thought of history as the sum of countless pilgrimages through a vale of tears to the heavenly Jerusalem. Every one of those now dead would some day rise and stand with the innumerable host of the departed before the judgment seat to hear the words, "Well done," or, "Depart from me into everlasting fire." The Christ upon the rainbow with the lily and the sword was a most familiar figure in the illustrated books of the period. Luther had seen pictures such as these and testified that he was utterly terror-stricken at the sight of Christ the Judge.

THE HAVEN OF THE COWL

Like everyone else in the Middle Ages he knew what to do about his plight. The Church taught that no sensible person would wait until his deathbed to make an act of contrition and plead for grace. From beginning to end the only secure course was to lay hold of every help the Church had to offer: sacraments, pilgrimages, indulgences, the intercession of the saints. Yet foolish was the man who relied solely on the good offices of the heavenly intercessors if he had done nothing to insure their favor!

CHRIST THE JUDGE SITTING UPON THE RAINBOW

And what better could he do than take the cowl? Men believed the end of the world already had been postponed for the sake of the Cistercian monks. Christ had just "bidden the angel blow his trumpet for the Last Judgment, when the Mother of Mercy fell at the feet of her Son and besought Him to spare awhile, 'at least

ERFURT

for my friends of the Cistercian Order, that they may prepare themselves.'" The very devils complained of St. Benedict as a robber who had stolen souls out of their hands. He who died in the cowl would receive preferential treatment in heaven because of his habit. Once a Cistercian in a high fever cast off his frock and so died. Arriving at the gate of Paradise he was denied entry by St. Benedict because of the lack of uniform. He could only walk around the walls and peep in through the windows to see how the brethren fared, until one of them interceded for him, and St. Benedict granted a reprieve to earth for the missing garment. All this was of course popular piety. However much such crude notions might be deprecated by reputable theologians, this was what the common man believed, and Luther was a common man. Yet even St. Thomas Aquinas himself declared the taking of the cowl to be second baptism, restoring the sinner to the state of innocence which he enjoyed when first baptized. The opinion was popular that if the monk should sin thereafter, he was peculiarly privileged because in his case repentance would bring restoration to the state of innocence. Monasticism was the way par excellence to heaven.

Luther knew all this. Any lad with eyes in his head understood what monasticism was all about. Living examples were to be seen on the streets of Erfurt. Here were young Carthusians, mere lads, already aged by their austerities. At Magdeburg, Luther looked upon the emaciated Prince William of Anhalt, who had forsaken the halls of the nobility to become a begging friar and walk the streets carrying the sack of the mendicant. Like any other brother he did the manual work of the cloister. "With my own eyes I saw him," said Luther. "I was fourteen years old at Magdeburg. I saw him carrying the sack like a donkey. He had so worn himself down by fasting and vigil that he looked like a death's-head, mere bone and skin. No one could look upon him without feeling ashamed of his own life."

Luther knew perfectly well why youths should make themselves old and nobles should make themselves abased. This life is only a brief period of training for the life to come, where the saved will enjoy an eternity of bliss and the damned will suffer everlasting torment. With their eyes they will behold the despair which can never experience the mercy of extinction. With their ears they will hear the moans of the damned. They will inhale sulphurous fumes and writhe in incandescent but unconsuming flame. All this will last forever and forever and forever.

These were the ideas on which Luther had been nurtured. There was nothing peculiar in his beliefs or his responses save their intensity. His depression over the prospect of death was acute but by no means singular. The man who was later to revolt against monasticism became a monk for exactly the same reason as thousands of others, namely, in order to save his soul. The immediate occasion of his resolve to enter the cloister was the unexpected encounter with death on that sultry July day in 1505. He was then twenty-one and a student at the University of Erfurt. As he returned to school after a visit with his parents, sudden lightning struck him to earth. In that single flash he saw the denouement of the drama of existence. There was God the all-terrible, Christ the inexorable, and all the leering fiends springing from their lurking places in pond and wood that with sardonic cachinnations they might seize his shock of curly hair and bolt him into hell. It was no wonder that he cried out to his father's saint, patroness of miners, "St. Anne help me! I will become a monk."

Luther himself repeatedly averred that he believed himself to have been summoned by a call from heaven to which he could not be disobedient. Whether or not he could have been absolved from his vow, he conceived himself to be bound by it. Against his own inclination, under divine constraint, he took the cowl. Two weeks were required to arrange his affairs and to decide what monastery to enter. He chose a strict one, the reformed congregation of the Augustinians. After a farewell party with a few friends he presented himself at the monastery gates. News was then sent to his father, who was highly enraged. This was the son, educated in stringency, who should have supported his parents in their old age. The father was utterly unreconciled until he saw in the deaths of two other sons a chastisement for his rebellion.

Luther presented himself as a novice. From no direct evidence but from the liturgy of the Augustinians we are able to reconstruct the scene of his reception. As the prior stood upon the steps of the altar, the candidate prostrated himself. The prior asked, "What seekest thou?" The answer came, "God's grace and thy mercy." Then the prior raised him up and inquired whether he was married, a bondsman, or afflicted with secret disease. The answer being negative, the prior described the rigors of the life to be undertaken: the renunciation of self-will, the scant diet, rough clothing, vigils by night and labors by day, mortification of the flesh, the reproach of poverty, the shame of begging, and the distastefulness of cloistered existence. Was he ready to take upon himself these burdens? "Yes, with God's help," was the answer, "and in so far as human frailty allows." Then he was admitted to a year of probation. As the choir chanted, the head was tonsured. Civilian clothes were exchanged for the habit of the novice. The initiate bowed the knee. "Bless thou thy servant," intoned the prior. "Hear, O Lord, our heartfelt pleas and deign to confer thy blessing on this thy servant, whom in thy holy name we have clad in the habit of a monk, that he may continue with thy help faithful in thy Church and merit eternal life through Jesus Christ our Lord. Amen." During the singing of the closing hymn Luther prostrated himself with arms extended in the form of a cross. He was then received into the convent by the brethren with the kiss of peace and again admonished by the prior with the words, "Not he that hath begun but he that endureth to the end shall be saved."

The meaning of Luther's entry into the monastery is simply this, that the great revolt against the medieval Church arose from a

SIXTEENTH-CENTURY MONKS IN A CHOIR

desperate attempt to follow the way by her prescribed. Just as Abraham overcame human sacrifice only through his willingness to lift the sacrificial knife against Isaac, just as Paul was emancipated from Jewish legalism only because as a Hebrew of the Hebrews he had sought to fulfill all righteousness, so Luther rebelled out of a more than ordinary devotion. To the monastery he went like others, and even more than others, in order to make his peace with God.

CHAPTER TWO

THE CLOISTER

 UTHER in later life remarked that during the first year in the monastery the Devil is very quiet. We have every reason to believe that his own inner tempest subsided and that during his novitiate he was relatively placid. This may be inferred from the mere fact that at the end of the year he was permitted to make his profession. The probationary period was intended to give the candidate an opportunity to test himself and to be tested. He was instructed to search his heart and declare any misgivings as to his fitness for the monastic calling. If his companions and superiors believed him to have no vocation, they would reject him. Since Luther was accepted, we may safely assume that neither he nor his brethren saw any reason to suppose that he was not adapted to the monastic life.

His days as a novice were occupied with those religious exercises designed to suffuse the soul with peace. Prayers came seven times daily. After eight hours of sleep the monks were awakened between one and two in the morning by the ringing of the cloister bell. At the first summons they sprang up, made the sign of the cross, and pulled on the white robe and the scapular without which the brother was never to leave his cell. At the second bell each came reverently to the church, sprinkled himself with holy water, and knelt before the high altar with a prayer of devotion to the Saviour of the world. Then all took their places in the choir. Matins lasted three quarters of an hour. Each of the seven periods of the day ended with the chanting by the cantor of the *Salve Regina:* "Save, O Queen, Thou Mother of mercy, our life, our delight, and our hope. To Thee we exiled sons of Eve lift up our cry. To Thee we sigh as we languish in this vale of tears. Be Thou our advocate. Sweet Virgin Mary, pray for us, Thou holy Mother of God." After the *Ave Maria* and the *Pater Noster* the brothers in pairs silently filed out of the church.

With such exercises the day was filled. Brother Martin was sure that he was walking in the path the saints had trod. The occasion of his profession filled him with joy that the brothers had found him worthy of continuing. At the foot of the prior he made his dedication and heard the prayer, "Lord Jesus Christ, who didst deign to clothe thyself in our mortality, we beseech thee out of thine immeasurable goodness to bless the habit which the holy fathers have chosen as a sign of innocence and renunciation. May this thy servant, Martin Luther, who takes the habit, be clothed also in thine immortality, O thou who livest and reignest with God the Father and the Holy Ghost, God from eternity to eternity. Amen."

THE COURTYARD OF THE AUGUSTINIAN CLOISTER

The solemn vow had been taken. He was a monk, as innocent as a child newly baptized. Luther gave himself over with confidence to the life which the Church regarded as the surest way of salvation. He was content to spend his days in prayer, in song, in meditation and quiet companionship, in disciplined and moderate austerity.

THE TERROR OF THE HOLY

Thus he might have continued had he not been overtaken by another thunderstorm, this time of the spirit. The occasion was the saying of his first mass. He had been selected for the priesthood by his superior and commenced his functions with this initial celebration.

The occasion was always an ordeal because the mass is the focal point of the Church's means of grace. Here on the altar bread and wine become the flesh and blood of God, and the sacrifice of Calvary is re-enacted. The priest who performs the miracle of transforming the elements enjoys a power and privilege denied even to angels. The whole difference between the clergy and the laity rests on this. The superiority of the Church over the state likewise is rooted here, for what king or emperor ever conferred upon mankind a boon comparable to that bestowed by the humblest minister at the altar?

Well might the young priest tremble to perform a rite by which God would appear in human form. But many had done it, and the experience of the centuries enabled the manuals to foresee all possible tremors and prescribe the safeguards. The celebrant must be concerned, though not unduly, about the forms. The vestments must be correct; the recitation must be correct, in a low voice and without stammering. The state of the priest's soul must be correct. Before approaching the altar he must have confessed and received absolution for all his sins. He might easily worry lest he transgress any of these conditions, and Luther testified that a mistake as to the vestments was considered worse than the seven deadly sins. But the manuals encouraged the trainee to regard no mistake as fatal because the efficacy of the sacrament depends only on the right intention to perform it. Even should the priest recall during the celebration a deadly sin unconfessed and unabsolved, he should not flee from the altar but finish the rite, and absolution would be forthcoming afterward. And if nervousness should so assail him that he could not continue, an older priest would be at his side to carry on. No insuperable difficulties faced the celebrant, and we have no reason to suppose that Luther approached his first mass with uncommon dread. The post-

THE MASS

ponement of the date for a month was not due to any serious misgivings.

The reason was rather a very joyous one. He wanted his father to be present, and the date was set to suit his convenience. The son and the father had not seen each other since the university days when old Hans presented Martin with a copy of the Roman law and addressed him in the polite speech. The father had been vehemently opposed to his entry into the monastery, but now he appeared to have overcome all resentment and was willing, like other parents, to make a gala day of the occasion. With a company of twenty horsemen Hans Luther came riding in and made a handsome contribution to the monastery. The day began with the chiming of the cloister bells and the chanting of the psalm, "O sing unto the Lord a new song." Luther took his place before the altar and began to recite the introductory portion of the mass until he came to the words, "We offer unto thee, the living, the true, the eternal God." He related afterward:

At these words I was utterly stupefied and terror-stricken. I thought to myself, "With what tongue shall I address such Majesty, seeing that all men ought to tremble in the presence of even an earthly prince? Who am I, that I should lift up mine eyes or raise my hands to the divine Majesty? The angels surround him. At his nod the earth trembles. And shall I, a miserable little pygmy, say 'I want this, I ask for that'? For I am dust and ashes and full of sin and I am speaking to the living, eternal and the true God."

The terror of the Holy, the horror of Infinitude, smote him like a new lightning bolt, and only through a fearful restraint could he hold himself at the altar to the end.

The man of our secularized generation may have difficulty in understanding the tremors of his medieval forebear. There are indeed elements in the religion of Luther of a very primitive character, which hark back to the childhood of the race. He suffered from the savage's fear of a malevolent deity, the enemy of men, capricious, easily and unwittingly offended if sacred places be violated or magical formulas mispronounced. His was the fear of ancient Israel before the ark of the Lord's presence. Luther felt similarly toward the sacred host of the Saviour's body; and when it was carried in procession, panic took hold of him. His God was the God who inhabited the storm clouds brooding on the brow of Sinai, into whose presence Moses could not enter with unveiled face and live. Luther's experience, however, far exceeds the primitive and should not be so unintelligible to the modern man who, gazing upon the uncharted nebulae through instruments of his own devising, recoils with a sense of abject littleness.

Luther's tremor was augmented by the recognition of unworthiness. "I am dust and ashes and full of sin." Creatureliness and imperfection alike oppressed him. Toward God he was at once attracted and repelled. Only in harmony with the Ultimate could he find peace. But how could a pigmy stand before divine Majesty; how could a transgressor confront divine Holiness? Before God the high and God the holy Luther was stupefied. For such an experience he had a word which has as much right to be carried over into English as *Blitzkrieg*. The word he used was *Anfechtung*, for which there is no English equivalent. It may be a trial sent by God to test man, or an assault by the Devil to destroy man. It is all the doubt, turmoil, pang, tremor, panic, despair, desolation, and desperation which invade the spirit of man.

Utterly limp, he came from the altar to the table where his father and the guests would make merry with the brothers. After shuddering at the unapproachableness of the heavenly Father he now craved some word of assurance from the earthly father. How his heart would be warmed to hear from the lips of old Hans that his resentment had entirely passed, and that he was now cordially in accord with his son's decision! They sat down to meat together, and Martin, as if he were still a little child, turned and said, "Dear father, why were you so contrary to my becoming a monk? And perhaps you are not quite satisfied even now. The life is so quiet and godly."

This was too much for old Hans, who had been doing his best to smother his rebellion. He flared up before all the doctors and the masters and the guests, "You learned scholar, have you never read in the Bible that you should honor your father and your mother? And here you have left me and your dear mother to look after ourselves in our old age."

Luther had not expected this. But he knew the answer. All the manuals recalled the gospel injunction to forsake father and mother, wife and child, and pointed out the greater benefits to be conferred in the spiritual sphere. Luther answered, "But, father, I could do you

"And When I Saw Him, I Fell at His Feet as Dead"

more good by prayers than if I had stayed in the world." And then he must have added what to him was the clinching argument, that he had been called by a voice from heaven out of the thunder cloud.

"God grant," said the old Hans, "it was not an apparition of the Devil."

There was the weak spot of all medieval religion. In this day of skepticism we look back with nostalgia to the age of faith. How fair it would have been to have lived in an atmosphere of naïve assurance, where heaven lay about the infancy of man, and doubt had not arisen to torment the spirit! Such a picture of the Middle Ages is sheer romanticism. The medieval man entertained no doubt of the supernatural world, but that world itself was divided. There were saints, and there were demons. There was God, and there was the Devil. And the Devil could disguise himself as an angel of light. Had Luther, then, been right to follow a vision which might after all have been of the arch fiend, in preference to the plain clear word of Scripture to honor father and mother? The day which began with the ringing of the cloister chime and the psalm "O sing unto the Lord a new song" ended with the horror of the Holy and doubt whether that first thunderstorm had been a vision of God or an apparition of Satan.

THE WAY OF SELF-HELP

This second upheaval of the spirit set up in Luther an inner turmoil which was to end in the abandonment of the cowl, but not until after a long interval. In fact he continued to wear the monastic habit for three years after his excommunication. Altogether he was garbed as a monk for nineteen years. His development was gradual, and we are not to imagine him in perpetual torment and never able to say mass without terror. He pulled himself together and went on with the appointed round and with whatever new duties were assigned. The prior, for example, informed him that he should resume his university studies in order to qualify for the post of lector in the Augustinian order. He took all such assignments in stride.

But the problem of the alienation of man from God had been renewed in altered form. Not merely in the hour of death but daily at the altar the priest stood in the presence of the All High and the All Holy. How could man abide God's presence unless he were himself holy? Luther set himself to the pursuit of holiness. Monasticism constituted such a quest; and while Luther was in the world, he had looked upon the cloister in any form as the higher righteousness. But after becoming a monk he discovered levels within monasticism itself. Some monks were easygoing; some were strict. Those Carthusian lads prematurely old; that prince of Anhalt, mere animated bones—these were not typical examples. They were the rigorists, heroic athletes, seeking to take heaven by storm. Whether Luther's call to the monastery had been prompted by God or the Devil, he was now a monk, and a monk he would be to the uttermost. One of the privileges of the monastic life was that it emancipated the sinner from all distractions and freed him to save his soul by practicing the counsels of perfection—not simply charity, sobriety, and love, but chastity, poverty, obedience, fastings, vigils, and mortifications of the flesh. Whatever good works a man might do to save himself, these Luther was resolved to perform.

He fasted, sometimes three days on end without a crumb. The seasons of fasting were more consoling to him than those of feasting. Lent was more comforting than Easter. He laid upon himself vigils and prayers in excess of those stipulated by the rule. He cast off the blankets permitted him and well-nigh froze himself to death. At times he was proud of his sanctity and would say, "I have done nothing wrong today." Then misgivings would arise. "Have you fasted enough? Are you poor enough?" He would then strip himself of all save that which decency required. He believed in later life that his austerities had done permanent damage to his digestion.

I was a good monk, and I kept the rule of my order so strictly that I may say that if ever a monk got to heaven by his monkery it was I. All my brothers in the monastery who knew me will bear me out. If I had kept on any longer, I should have killed myself with vigils, prayers, reading, and other work.

All such drastic methods gave no sense of inner tranquillity. The purpose of his striving was to compensate for his sins, but he could never feel that the ledger was balanced. Some historians have therefore asserted that he must have been a very great sinner, and that  in all likelihood his sins had to do with sex, where offenses are the least capable of any rectification. But Luther himself declared that this was not a particular problem. He had been chaste. While at Erfurt he had never even heard a woman in confession. And later at Wittenberg he had confessed only three women, and these he had not seen. Of course he was no wood carving, but sexual temptation beset him no more than any other problem of the moral life.

The trouble was that he could not satisfy God at any point. Commenting in later life on the Sermon on the Mount, Luther gave searching expression to his disillusionment. Referring to the precepts of Jesus he said:

This word is too high and too hard that anyone should fulfil it. This is proved, not merely by our Lord's word, but by our own experience and feeling. Take any upright man or woman. He will get along very nicely with those who do not provoke him, but let someone proffer only the slightest irritation and he will flare up in anger, . . . if not against friends, then against enemies. Flesh and blood cannot rise above it.

Luther simply had not the capacity to fulfill the conditions.

THE MERITS OF THE SAINTS

But if he could not, others might. The Church, while taking an individualistic view of sin, takes a corporate view of goodness. Sins must be accounted for one by one, but goodness can be pooled; and there is something to pool because the saints, the Blessed Virgin, and the Son of God were better than they needed to be for their own salvation. Christ in particular, being both sinless and God, is possessed of an unbounded store. These superfluous merits of the righteous constitute a treasury which is transferable to those whose accounts are in arrears. The transfer is effected through the Church and, particularly, through the pope, to whom as the successor of St. Peter have been committed the keys to bind and loose. Such a transfer of credit was called an indulgence.

Precisely how much good it would do had not been definitely defined, but the common folk were disposed to believe the most extravagant claims. No one questioned that the pope could draw on the treasury in order to remit penalties for sin imposed by himself on earth. In fact one would suppose that he could do this by mere fiat without any transfer. The important question was whether or not he could mitigate the pangs of purgatory. During the decade in which Luther was born a pope had declared that the efficacy of indulgences extended to purgatory for the benefit of the living and the dead alike. In the case of the living there was no assurance of avoiding purgatory entirely because God alone knew the extent of the unexpiated guilt and the consequent length of the sentence, but the Church could tell to the year and the day by how much the term could be reduced, whatever it was. And in the case of those already dead and in purgatory, the sum of whose wickedness was complete and known, an immediate release could be offered. Some bulls of indulgence went still further and applied not merely to reduction of penalty but even to the forgiveness of sins. They offered a plenary remission and reconciliation with the Most High.

There were places in which these signal mercies were more accessible than in others. For no theological reason but in the interest of advertising, the Church associated the dispensing of the merits of the saints with visitation upon the relics of the saints. Popes frequently specified precisely how much benefit could be derived from viewing each holy bone. Every relic of the saints in Halle, for example, was endowed by Pope Leo X with an indulgence for the reduction of purgatory by four thousand years. The greatest storehouse for such treasures was

Rome. Here in the single crypt of St. Callistus forty popes were buried and 76,000 martyrs. Rome had a piece of Moses' burning bush and three hundred particles of the Holy Innocents. Rome had the portrait of Christ on the napkin of St. Veronica. Rome had the chains of St. Paul and the scissors with which Emperor Domitian clipped the hair of St. John. The walls of Rome near the Appian gate showed the white spots left by the stones which turned to snowballs when hurled by the mob against St. Peter before his time was come. A church in Rome had the crucifix which leaned over to talk to St. Brigitta. Another had a coin paid to Judas for betraying our Lord. Its value had greatly increased, for now it was able to confer an indulgence of fourteen hundred years. The amount of indulgences to be obtained between the Lateran and St. Peter's was greater than that afforded by a pilgrimage to the Holy Land. Still another church in Rome possessed the twelve-foot beam on which Judas hanged himself. This, however, was not strictly a relic, and doubt was permitted as to its authenticity. In front of the Lateran were the *Scala Sancta*, twenty-eight stairs, supposedly those which once stood in front of Pilate's palace. He who crawled up them on hands and knees, repeating a *Pater Noster* for each one, could thereby release a soul

 from purgatory. Above all, Rome had the entire bodies of St. Peter and St. Paul. They had been divided to distribute the benefits among the churches. The heads were in the Lateran, and one half of the body of each had been deposited in their respective churches. No city on earth was so plentifully supplied with holy relics, and no city on earth was so richly endowed with spiritual indulgences as Holy Rome.

THE TRIP TO ROME

Luther felt himself to be highly privileged when an opportunity presented itself to make a trip to the Eternal City. A dispute had arisen in the Augustinian order calling for settlement by the pope. Two brothers were sent to the holy city to represent the chapter at Erfurt.

One of the brothers was Martin Luther. This was in the year 1510.

The trip to Rome is very revealing of the character of Martin Luther. What he saw, and what he did not care to see, throw light upon him. He was not interested in the art of the Renaissance. Of course, the great treasures were not yet visible. The piers of the new basilica of

St. Peter's had only just been laid, and the Sistine Chapel was not yet completed. But the frescoes of Pinturicchio were in view and might have awakened his admiration had he not been more interested in a painting of the Virgin Mary attributed to Luke the Evangelist than in all the Madonnas of the Renaissance. Again, the ruins of antiquity evoked no enthusiasm but served only to point the moral that the city founded on fratricide and stained with the blood of martyrs had been overthrown by divine justice like the Tower of Babel.

Neither the Rome of the Renaissance nor the Rome of antiquity interested Luther so much as the Rome of the saints. The business of the order would not be too time-consuming to prevent taking advantage of the unusual opportunities to save his soul. Luther's mood was that of a pilgrim who at the first sight of the Eternal City cried, "Hail, holy Rome!" He would seek to appropriate for himself and his relatives all the enormous spiritual benefits available only there. He had but a month in which to do it. The time was strenuously spent. He must of course perform the daily devotions of the Augustinian cloister in which he was lodged, but there remained sufficient hours to enable him to say the general confession, to celebrate mass at sacred shrines, to visit the catacombs and the basilicas, to venerate the bones, the shrines, and every holy relic.

Disillusionments of various sorts set in at once. Some of them were irrelevant to his immediate problem but were concomitants in his total distress. On making his general confession he was dismayed by the incompetence of the confessor. The abysmal ignorance, frivolity, and levity of the Italian priests stupefied him. They could rattle through six or seven masses while he was saying one. And when he was only at the Gospel, they had finished and would say to him, "*Passa! Passa!*"—"Get a move on!" The same sort of thing Luther could have discovered in Germany if he had emerged from the cloister to visit mass priests, whose assignment it was to repeat a specified number of masses a day, not for communicants but in behalf of the dead. Such a practice lent itself to irreverence. Some of the Italian clergy, however, were flippantly unbelieving and would address the sacrament saying, "Bread art thou and bread thou wilt remain, and wine art thou and wine thou wilt remain." To a devout believer from the unsophisticated Northland such disclosures were truly shocking. They need not have made him despondent in regard to the validity of his own quest because the Church had long taught that the efficacy of the sacraments did not depend on the character of the ministrants.

By a like token the stories that came to Luther's ears of the immorality of the Roman clergy should not logically have undermined his faith in the capacity of Holy Rome to confer spiritual benefits. At the same time he was horrified to hear that if there were a hell Rome was built upon it. He need not have been a scandalmonger to know that the district of ill fame was frequented by ecclesiastics. He heard there were those who considered themselves virtuous because they confined themselves to women. The unsavory memory of Pope Alexander VI was still a stench. Catholic historians recognize candidly the scandal of the Renaissance popes, and the Catholic Reformation was as greatly concerned as the Protestant to eradicate such abuses.

Yet all these sorry disclosures did not shatter Luther's confidence in the genuine goodness of the faithful. The question was whether they had any superfluous merit which could be conveyed to him or to his family, and whether the merit was so attached to sacred places that visits would confer benefit. This was the point at which doubt overtook him. He was climbing Pilate's stairs on hands and knees repeating a *Pater Noster* for each one and kissing each step for good measure in the hope of delivering a soul from purgatory. Luther regretted that his own father and mother were not yet dead and in purgatory so that he might confer on them so signal a favor. Failing that, he had resolved to release Grandpa Heine. The stairs were climbed, the *Pater Nosters* were repeated, the steps were kissed. At the top Luther raised himself and exclaimed, not as legend would have it, "The just shall live by faith!"—he was not yet that far advanced. What he said was, "Who knows whether it is so?"

That was the truly disconcerting doubt. The priests might be guilty of levity and the popes of lechery—all this would not matter so long as the Church had valid means of grace. But if crawling up the very stairs on which Christ stood and repeating all the prescribed prayers would be of no avail, then another of the great grounds of hope had proved to be illusory. Luther commented that he had gone to Rome with onions and had returned with garlic.

CHAPTER THREE

THE GOSPEL

ETURNING from Rome, Luther came under new influences due to a change of residence. He was transferred from Erfurt to Wittenberg, where he was to pass the remainder of his days. In comparison with Erfurt, Wittenberg was but a village with a population of only 2,000 to 2,500. The whole length of the town was only nine tenths of a mile. Contemporaries variously described it as "the gem of Thuringia" and "a stinking sand dune." It was built on a sand belt and for that reason was called the White Hillock, *Witten-Berg*. Luther never rhapsodized over the place, and he addressed to it this ditty:

> Little land, little land,
> You are but a heap of sand.
> If I dig you, the soil is light;
> If I reap you, the yield is slight.

But as a matter of fact it was not unproductive. Grain, vegetables, and fruit abounded, and the near-by woods provided game. The river Elbe flowed on one side, and a moat surrounded the town on the other. Two brooks were introduced by wooden aqueducts through the walls on the upper side and flowed without a covering down the two main streets of the town until they united at the mill. Open sluggish water was at once convenient and offensive. Luther lived in the Augustinian cloister at the opposite end from the Castle Church.

The chief glory of the village was the university, the darling of the elector, Frederick the Wise, who sought in this newly founded academy to rival the prestige of the century-old University of Leipzig. The new foundation had not flourished according to hope, and the elector endeavored to secure better teachers by inviting the Augustinians and Franciscans to supply three new professors. One of them was Luther. This was in 1511.

By reason of the move he came to know well a man who was to exercise a determinative influence upon his development, the vicar of the Augustinian order, Johann von Staupitz. No one better could have been found as a spiritual guide. The vicar knew all the cures prescribed by the schoolmen for spiritual ailments, and besides had a warm religious life of his own with a sympathetic appreciation of the distresses of another. "If it had not been for Dr. Staupitz," said Luther, "I should have sunk in hell."

Luther's difficulties persisted. A precise delineation of their course eludes us. His tremors cannot be said to have mounted in unbroken crescendo to a single crisis. Rather he passed through a series of crises

WITTENBERG IN 1627

to a relative stability. The stages defy localization as to time, place, or logical sequence. Yet this is clear. Luther probed every resource of contemporary Catholicism for assuaging the anguish of a spirit alienated from God. He tried the way of good works and discovered that he could never do enough to save himself. He endeavored to avail himself of the merits of the saints and ended with a doubt, not a very serious or persistent doubt for the moment, but sufficient to destroy his assurance.

THE FAILURE OF CONFESSION

He sought at the same time to explore other ways, and Catholicism had much more to offer. Salvation was never made to rest solely nor even primarily upon human achievement. The whole sacramental system of the Church was designed to mediate to man God's help and favor. Particularly the sacrament of penance afforded solace, not to saints but to sinners. This only was required of them, that they should confess all their wrongdoing and seek absolution. Luther endeavored unremittingly to avail himself of this signal mercy. Without confession, he testified, the Devil would have devoured him long ago. He confessed frequently, often daily, and for as long as six hours on a single occasion. Every sin in order to be absolved was to be confessed. Therefore the soul must be searched and the memory ransacked and the motives probed. As an aid the penitent ran through the seven deadly sins and the Ten Commandments. Luther would repeat a confession and, to be sure of including everything, would review his entire life until the confessor grew weary and exclaimed, "Man, God is not angry with you. You are angry with God. Don't you know that God commands you to hope?"

This assiduous confessing certainly succeeded in clearing up any major transgressions. The leftovers with which Luther kept trotting in appeared to Staupitz to be only the scruples of a sick soul. "Look here," said he, "if you expect Christ to forgive you, come in with something to forgive—parricide, blasphemy, adultery—instead of all these peccadilloes."

But Luther's question was not whether his sins were big or little, but whether they had been confessed. The great difficulty which he encountered was to be sure that everything had been recalled. He learned from experience the cleverness of memory in protecting the ego, and he was frightened when after six hours of confessing he could still go out and think of something else which had eluded his most conscientious scrutiny. Still more disconcerting was the discovery that some of man's misdemeanors are not even recognized, let alone remembered. Sinners often sin without compunction. Adam and Eve, after tasting of the fruit of the forbidden tree, went blithely for a walk in the cool of the day; and Jonah, after fleeing from the Lord's commission, slept soundly in the hold of the ship. Only when each was confronted by an accuser was there any consciousness of guilt. Frequently, too, when man is reproached he will still justify himself like Adam, who replied, "The woman whom thou gavest to be with me"—as if to say to God, "She tempted me; you gave her to me; you are to blame."

There is, according to Luther, something much more drastically wrong with man than any particular list of offenses which can be enumerated, confessed, and forgiven. The very nature of man is corrupt. The penitential system fails because it is directed to particular lapses. Luther had come to perceive that the entire man is in need of forgiveness. In the course of this quest he had wrought himself into a state of emotional disturbance passing the bounds of objectivity. When, then, his confessor said that he was magnifying his misdemeanors, Luther could only conclude that the consultant did not understand the case and that none of the proffered consolations was of any avail.

In consequence the most frightful insecurities beset him. Panic invaded his spirit. The conscience became so disquieted as to start and tremble at the stirring of a wind-blown leaf. The horror of nightmare gripped the soul, the dread of one waking in the dusk to look into the eyes of him who has come to take his life. The heavenly champions all withdrew; the fiend beckoned with leering summons to the impotent soul. These were the torments which Luther repeatedly testified were far worse than any physical ailment that he had ever endured.

His description tallies so well with a recognized type of mental malady that again one is tempted to wonder whether his disturbance should be regarded as arising from authentic religious difficulties or from gastric or glandular deficiencies. The question can better be faced when more data become available from other periods of his life. Suffice it for the moment to observe that no malady ever impaired his stupendous capacity for work; that the problems with which he wrestled were not imaginary but implicit in the religion on which he had been reared; that his emotional reactions were excessive, as he would himself recognize after emerging from a depression; that he did make headway in exhausting one by one the helps proffered by medieval religion.

He had arrived at a valid impasse. Sins to be forgiven must be confessed. To be confessed they must be recognized and remembered. If they are not recognized and remembered, they cannot be confessed. If they are not confessed, they cannot be forgiven. The only way out is to deny the premise. But that Luther was not yet ready to do. Staupitz at this point offered real help by seeking to divert his attention from individual sins to the nature of man. Luther later on formulated what he had learned by saying that the physician does not need to probe each pustule to know that the patient has smallpox, nor is the disease to be cured scab by scab. To focus on particular offenses is a counsel of despair. When Peter started to count the waves, he sank. The whole nature of man needs to be changed.

THE MYSTIC LADDER

This was the insight of the mystics. Staupitz was a mystic. Although the mystics did not reject the penitential system, their way of salvation was essentially different, directed to man as a whole. Since man is weak, let him cease to strive; let him surrender himself to the being and the love of God.

The new life, they said, calls for a period of preparation which consists in overcoming all the assertiveness of the ego, all arrogance, pride, self-seeking, everything connected with the I, the me, and the my. Luther's very effort to achieve merit was a form of assertiveness. Instead of striving he must yield and sink himself in God. The end of the mystic way is the absorption of the creature in the creator, of the drop in the ocean, of the candle flame in the glare of the sun. The struggler overcomes his restlessness, ceases his battering, surrenders himself to the Everlasting, and in the abyss of Being finds his peace.

Luther tried this way. At times he was lifted up as if he were amid choirs of angels, but the sense of alienation would return. The mystics knew this too. They called it the dark night of the soul, the dryness, the withdrawing of the fire from under the pot until it no longer bubbles. They counseled waiting until exaltation would return. For Luther it did not return because the enmity between man and God is too great. For all his impotence, man is a rebel against his Maker.

The acuteness of Luther's distress arose from his sensitivity at once to all the difficulties by which man has ever been beset. Could he have taken them one at a time, each might the more readily have been assuaged. For those who are troubled by particular sins the Church offers forgiveness through the penitential system, but pardon is made contingent upon conditions which Luther found unattainable. For those too weak to meet the tests there is the mystic way of ceasing to strive and of losing oneself in the abyss of the Godhead. But Luther could not envisage God as an abyss hospitable to man the impure. God is holy, majestic, devastating, consuming.

Do you not know that God dwells in light inaccessible? We weak and ignorant creatures want to probe and understand the incomprehensible majesty of the unfathomable light of the wonder of God. We approach; we prepare ourselves to approach. What wonder then that his majesty overpowers us and shatters!

So acute had Luther's distress become that even the simplest helps of religion failed to bring him heartsease. Not even prayer could quiet his tremors; for when he was on his knees, the Tempter would come and say, "Dear fellow, what are you praying for? Just see how quiet it is about you here. Do you think that God hears your prayer and pays any attention?"

Staupitz tried to bring Luther to see that he was making religion altogether too difficult. There is just one thing needful, and that is to love God. This was another favorite counsel of the mystics, but the intended word of comfort pierced like an arrow. How could anyone love a God who is a consuming fire? The psalm says, "Serve the Lord with fear." Who, then, can love a God angry, judging, and damning? Who can love a Christ sitting on a rainbow, consigning the damned souls to the flames of hell? The mere sight of a crucifix was to Luther like a stroke of lightning. He would flee, then, from the angry Son to the merciful Mother. He would appeal to the saints—twenty-one of them he had selected as his especial patrons, three for each day of the week. All to no avail, for of what use is any intercession if God remains angry?

The final and the most devastating doubt of all assailed the young man. Perhaps not even God himself is just. This misgiving arose in two forms, depending on the view of God's character and behavior. Basic to both is the view that God is too absolute to be conditioned by considerations of human justice. The late scholastics, among whom Luther had been trained, thought that God is so unconditioned that he is bound by no rules save those of his own making. He is under no obligation to confer reward on man's achievements, no matter how meritorious. Normally God may be expected to do so, but there is no positive certitude. For Luther this meant that God is capricious and man's fate is unpredictable. The second view was more disconcerting because it held that man's destiny is already determined, perhaps adversely. God is so absolute that nothing can be contingent. Man's fate has been decreed since the foundation of the world, and in large measure also man's character is already fixed. This view commended itself all the more to Luther because it had been espoused by the founder of his order, St. Augustine, who, following Paul, held that God has already chosen some vessels for honor and some for dishonor, regardless of their deserts. The lost are lost, do what they can; the saved are saved, do what they may. To those who think they are saved this is an unspeakable comfort, but to those who think they are damned it is a hideous torment.

Luther exclaimed:

Is it not against all natural reason that God out of his mere whim deserts men, hardens them, damns them, as if he delighted in sins and in such torments of the wretched for eternity, he who is said to be of such mercy and goodness? This appears iniquitous, cruel, and intolerable in God, by which very many have been offended in all ages. And who would not be? I was myself more than once driven to the very abyss of despair so that I wished I had never been created. Love God? I hated him!

The word of blasphemy had been spoken. And blasphemy is the supreme sin because it is an offense against the most exalted of all beings, God the majestic. Luther reported to Staupitz, and his answer was, "*Ich verstehe es nicht!*"—"I don't understand it!" Was, then, Luther the only one in all the world who had been so plagued? Had Staupitz himself never experienced such trials? "No," said he, "but I think they are your meat and drink." Evidently he suspected Luther of thriving on his disturbances. The only word of reassurance he could give was a reminder that the blood of Christ was shed for the remission of sins. But Luther was too obsessed with the picture of Christ the avenger to be consoled with the thought of Christ the redeemer.

Staupitz then cast about for some effective cure for this tormented spirit. He recognized in him a man of moral earnestness, religious sensitivity, and unusual gifts. Why his difficulties should be so enormous and so persistent was baffling. Plainly argument and consolation did no good. Some other way must be found. One day under the pear tree in the garden of the Augustinian cloister—Luther always treasured that pear tree—the vicar informed Brother Martin that he should study for his doctor's degree, that he should undertake preaching and assume the chair of Bible at the university. Luther gasped, stammered out fifteen reasons why he could do nothing of the sort. The sum of it all was that so much work would kill him. "Quite all right," said Staupitz. "God has plenty of work for clever men to do in heaven."

Luther might well gasp, for the proposal of Staupitz was audacious if not reckless. A young man on the verge of a nervous collapse over religious problems was to be commissioned as a teacher, preacher, and counselor to sick souls. Staupitz was practically saying, "Physician, cure thyself by curing others." He must have felt that Luther was fundamentally sound and that if he was entrusted with the cure of souls he would be disposed for their sakes to turn from threats to promises, and some of the grace which he would claim for them might fall also to himself.

Staupitz knew likewise that Luther would be helped by the subject matter of his teaching. The chair designed for him was the one which Staupitz himself had occupied, the chair of Bible. One is tempted to surmise that he retired in order unobtrusively to drive this agonizing brother to wrestle with the source book of his religion. One may wonder why Luther had not thought of this himself. The reason is not that the Bible was inaccessible, but that Luther was following a prescribed course and the Bible was not the staple of theological education.

Yet anyone who seeks to discover the secret of Christianity is inevitably driven to the Bible, because Christianity is based on something which happened in the past, the incarnation of God in Christ at a definite point in history. The Bible records this event.

THE EVANGELICAL EXPERIENCE

Luther set himself to learn and expound the Scriptures. On August 1, 1513, he commenced his lectures on the book of Psalms. In the fall of 1515 he was lecturing on St. Paul's Epistle to the Romans. The Epistle to the Galatians was treated throughout 1516-17. These studies proved to be for Luther the Damascus road. The third great religious crisis which resolved his turmoil was as the still small voice compared to the earthquake of the first upheaval in the thunderstorm at Stotternheim and the fire of the second tremor which consumed him at the saying of his first mass. No *coup de foudre*, no heavenly apparition, no religious ceremony, precipitated the third crisis. The place was no lonely road in a blinding storm, nor even the holy altar, but simply the study in the tower of the Augustinian monastery. The

Biblia: das ist:
Die gantze Heilige
Schrifft: Deudsch
Auffs New zugericht.

D. Mart. Luth.

Begnadet mit Kur-
fürstlicher zu Sachsen Freiheit.

Gedruckt zu Wittem-
berg / Durch Hans Lufft.

M·D·XLI·

Luther's Bible

solution to Luther's problems came in the midst of the performance of the daily task.

His first lectures were on the book of Psalms. We must bear in mind his method of reading the Psalms and the Old Testament as a whole. For him, as for his time, it was a Christian book foreshadowing the life and death of the Redeemer.

The reference to Christ was unmistakable when he came to the twenty-second psalm, the first verse of which was recited by Christ as he expired upon the cross. "My God, my God, why hast thou forsaken me?" What could be the meaning of this? Christ evidently felt himself to be forsaken, abandoned by God, deserted. Christ too had *Anfechtungen*. The utter desolation which Luther said he could not endure for more than a tenth of an hour and live had been experienced by Christ himself as he died. Rejected of men, he was rejected also of God. How much worse this must have been than the scourging, the thorns, the nails! In the garden he sweat blood as he did not upon the cross. Christ's descent into hell was nothing other than this sense of alienation from God. Christ had suffered what Luther suffered, or rather Luther was finding himself in what Christ had suffered, even as Albrecht Dürer painted himself as the Man of Sorrows.

Why should Christ have known such desperations? Luther knew perfectly well why he himself had had them: he was weak in the presence of the Mighty; he was impure in the presence of the Holy; he had blasphemed the Divine Majesty. But Christ was not weak; Christ was not impure; Christ was not impious. Why then should he have been so overwhelmed with desolation? The only answer must be that Christ took to himself the iniquity of us all. He who was without sin for our sakes became sin and so identified himself with us as to participate in our alienation. He who was truly man so sensed his solidarity with humanity as to feel himself along with mankind estranged from the All Holy. What a new picture this is of Christ! Where, then, is the judge, sitting upon the rainbow to condemn sinners? He is still the judge. He must judge, as truth judges error and light darkness; but in judging he suffers with those whom he must condemn and feels himself with them subject to condemnation. The judge upon the rainbow has become the derelict upon the cross.

A new view also of God is here. The All Terrible is the All Merciful too. Wrath and love fuse upon the cross. The hideousness of sin cannot be denied or forgotten; but God, who desires not that a sinner should die but that he should turn and live, has found the reconciliation in the pangs of bitter death. It is not that the Son by his sacrifice has placated the irate Father; it is not primarily that the Master by his self-abandoning goodness has made up for our deficiency. It is that in some inexplicable way, in the utter desolation of the forsaken Christ, God was able to reconcile the world to himself. This does not mean that all the mystery is clear. God is still shrouded at times in thick darkness. There are almost two Gods, the inscrutable God whose ways are past finding out and the God made known to us in Christ. He is still a consuming fire, but he burns that he may purge and chasten and heal. He is not a God of idle whim, because the cross is not the last word. He who gave his Son unto death also raised him up and will raise us with him, if with him we die to sin that we may rise to newness of life.

Who can understand this? Philosophy is unequal to it. Only faith can grasp so high a mystery. This is the foolishness of the cross which is hid from the wise and prudent. Reason must retire. She cannot understand that "God hides his power in weakness, his wisdom in folly, his goodness in severity, his justice in sins, his mercy in anger."

How amazing that God in Christ should do all this; that the Most High, the Most Holy should be the All Loving too; that the ineffable Majesty should stoop to take upon himself our flesh, subject to hunger and cold, death and desperation. We see him lying in the feedbox of a donkey, laboring in a carpenter's shop, dying a derelict under the sins of the world. The gospel is not so much a miracle as a marvel, and every line is suffused with wonder.

What God first worked in Christ, that he must work also in us. If he who had done no wrong was forsaken on the cross, we who are truly alienated from God must suffer a deep hurt. We are not for that reason to upbraid, since the hurt is for our healing.

Repentance which is occupied with thoughts of peace is hypocrisy. There must be a great earnestness about it and a deep hurt if the old man is to be put off. When lightning strikes a tree or a man, it does two things at once—it rends the tree and swiftly slays the man. But it also turns the face of the dead man and the broken branches of the tree itself toward heaven. . . . We seek to be saved, and God in order that he may save rather damns. . . . They are damned who flee damnation, for Christ was of all the saints the most damned and forsaken.

The contemplation of the cross had convinced Luther that God is neither malicious nor capricious. If, like the Samaritan, God must first pour into our wounds the wine that smarts, it is that he may thereafter use the oil that soothes. But there still remains the problem of the justice of God. Wrath can melt into mercy, and God will be all the more the Christian God; but if justice be dissolved in leniency, how can he be the just God whom Scripture describes? The study of the apostle Paul proved at this point of inestimable value to Luther and at the same time confronted him with the final stumbling block because Paul unequivocally speaks of the justice of God. At the very expression Luther trembled. Yet he persisted in grappling with Paul, who plainly had agonized over precisely his problem and had found a solution. Light broke at last through the examination of exact shades of meaning in the Greek language. One understands why Luther could never join those who discarded the humanist tools of scholarship. In the Greek of the Pauline epistles the word "justice" has a double sense, rendered in English by "justice" and "justification." The former is a strict enforcement of the law, as when a judge pronounces the appropriate sentence. Justification is a process of the sort which sometimes takes place if the judge suspends the sentence, places the prisoner on parole, expresses confidence and personal interest in him, and thereby instills such resolve that the man is reclaimed and justice itself ultimately better conserved than by the exaction of a pound of flesh. Similarly the moral improvement issuing from the Christian experience of regeneration, even though it falls far short of perfection, yet can be regarded as a vindication of the justice of God.

But from here on any human analogy breaks down. God does not condition his forgiveness upon the expectation of future fulfillment. And man is not put right with God by any achievement, whether present or foreseen. On man's side the one requisite is faith, which means belief that God was in Christ seeking to save; trust that God will keep his promises; and commitment to his will and way. Faith is not an achievement. It is a gift. Yet it comes only through the hearing and study of the Word. In this respect Luther's own experience was made normative. For the whole process of being made new Luther took over from Paul the terminology of "justification by faith."

These are Luther's own words:

I greatly longed to understand Paul's Epistle to the Romans and nothing stood in the way but that one expression, "the justice of God," because I took it to mean that justice whereby God is just and deals justly in punishing the unjust. My situation was that, although an impeccable monk, I stood before God as a sinner troubled in conscience, and I had no confidence that my merit would assuage him. Therefore I did not love a just and angry God, but rather hated and murmured against him. Yet I clung to the dear Paul and had a great yearning to know what he meant.

Night and day I pondered until I saw the connection between the justice of God and the statement that "the just shall live by his faith." Then I grasped that the justice of God is that righteousness by which through grace and sheer mercy God justifies us through faith. Thereupon I felt myself to be reborn and to have gone through open doors into paradise. The whole of Scripture took on a new meaning, and whereas before the "justice of God" had filled me with hate, now it became to me inexpressibly sweet in greater love. This passage of Paul became to me a gate to heaven. . . .

If you have a true faith that Christ is your Saviour, then at once you have a gracious God, for faith leads you in and opens up God's heart and will, that you should see pure grace and overflowing love. This it is to behold God in faith that you should look upon his fatherly, friendly heart, in which there is no anger nor ungraciousness. He who sees God as angry does not see him rightly but looks only on a curtain, as if a dark cloud had been drawn across his face.

Luther had come into a new view of Christ and a new view of God. He had come to love the suffering Redeemer and the God unveiled on Calvary. But were they after all powerful enough to deliver him from all the hosts of hell? The cross had resolved the conflict between the wrath and the mercy of God, and Paul had reconciled for him the inconsistency of the justice and the forgiveness of God, but what of the conflict between God and the Devil? Is God lord of all, or is he himself impeded by demonic hordes? Such questions a few years ago would have seemed to modern man but relics of medievalism, and fear of demons was dispelled simply by denying their existence. Today so much of the sinister has engulfed us that we are prone to wonder whether perhaps there may not be malignant forces in the heavenly places. All those who have known the torments of mental disorder well understand the imagery of satanic hands clutching to pull them to their doom. Luther's answer was not scientific but religious. He did not dissipate the demons by turning on an electric light, because for him they had long ago been routed when the veil of the temple was rent and the earth quaked and darkness descended upon the face of the land. Christ in his utter anguish had fused the wrath and the mercy of God, and put to flight all the legions of Satan.

In Luther's hymns one hears the tramp of marshaled hordes, the shouts of battle, and the triumph song.

> In devil's dungeon chained I lay
>   The pangs of death swept o'er me.
> My sin devoured me night and day
>   In which my mother bore me.
> My anguish ever grew more rife,
> I took no pleasure in my life
>   And sin had made me crazy.

> Then was the Father troubled sore
>   To see me ever languish.
> The Everlasting Pity swore
>   To save me from my anguish.
> He turned to me his father heart
> And chose himself a bitter part,
>   His Dearest did it cost him.

66

Thus spoke the Son, "Hold thou to me,
   From now on thou wilt make it.
I gave my very life for thee
   And for thee I will stake it.
For I am thine and thou art mine,
And where I am our lives entwine,
   The Old Fiend cannot shake it."

CHAPTER FOUR

THE ONSLAUGHT

LUTHER'S new insights contained already the marrow of his mature theology. The salient ideas were present in the lectures on Psalms and Romans from 1513 to 1516. What came after was but commentary and sharpening to obviate misconstruction. The center about which all the petals clustered was the affirmation of the forgiveness of sins through the utterly unmerited grace of God made possible by the cross of Christ, which reconciled wrath and mercy, routed the hosts of hell, triumphed over sin and death, and by the resurrection manifested that power which enables man to die to sin and rise to newness of life. This was of course the theology of Paul, heightened, intensified, and clarified. Beyond these cardinal tenets Luther was never to go.

His development lay rather on the positive side in the drawing of practical inferences for his theory of the sacraments and the Church, and on the negative side by way of discovering discrepancies from contemporary Catholicism. At the start Luther envisaged no reform other than that of theological education with the stress on the Bible rather than on the decretals and the scholastics. Not that he was indifferent to the evils of the Church! In his notes for the lectures on Romans he lashed out repeatedly against the luxury, avarice, ignorance, and greed of the clergy and upbraided explicitly the chicanery of that warrior-pope Julius II. Yet whether these strictures were ever actually delivered is doubtful; for no record of them appears in the student notes on the lectures. Luther was, in fact, less impelled to voice a protest against immoral abuses in the Church than were some of his contemporaries.

For one reason he was too busy. In October, 1516, he wrote to a friend:

I could use two secretaries. I do almost nothing during the day but write letters. I am a conventual preacher, reader at meals, parochial preacher, director of studies, overseer of eleven monasteries, superintendent of the fish pond at Litzkau, referee of the squabble at Torgau, lecturer on Paul, collector of material for a commentary on the Psalms, and then, as I said, I am overwhelmed with letters. I rarely have full time for the canonical hours and for saying mass, not to mention my own temptations with the world, the flesh, and the Devil. You see how lazy I am.

But out of just such labors arose his activities as a reformer.

As a parish priest in a village church he was responsible for the spiritual welfare of his flock. They were procuring indulgences as he had once done himself. Rome was not the only place in which such favors were available, for the popes delegated to many churches in Christendom the privilege of dispensing indulgences, and the Castle Church at Wittenberg was the recipient of a very unusual concession granting full remission of all sins. The day selected for the proclamation was the first of November, the day of All Saints, whose merits provided the ground of the indulgences and whose relics were then on display. Frederick the Wise, the elector of Saxony, Luther's prince, was a man of simple and sincere piety who had devoted a lifetime to making Wittenberg the Rome of Germany as a depository of sacred relics. He had made a journey to all parts of Europe, and diplomatic negotiations were facilitated by an exchange of relics. The king of Denmark, for example, sent him fragments of King Canute and St. Brigitta.

The collection had as its nucleus a genuine thorn from the crown of Christ, certified to have pierced the Saviour's brow. Frederick so built up the collection from this inherited treasure that the catalogue illustrated by Lucas Cranach in 1509 listed 5,005 particles, to which

FREDERICK THE WISE ADORING THE VIRGIN AND CHILD

were attached indulgences calculated to reduce purgatory by 1,443 years. The collection included one tooth of St. Jerome, of St. Chrysostom four pieces, of St. Bernard six, and of St. Augustine four; of Our Lady four hairs, three pieces of her cloak, four from her girdle, and seven from the veil sprinkled with the blood of Christ. The relics of Christ included one piece from his swaddling clothes, thirteen from his crib, one wisp of straw, one piece of the gold brought by the Wise Men and three of the myrrh, one strand of Jesus' beard, one of the nails driven into his hands, one piece of bread eaten at the Last Supper, one piece of the stone on which Jesus stood to ascend into heaven, and one twig of Moses' burning bush. By 1520 the collection had mounted to 19,013 holy bones. Those who viewed these relics on the designated day and made the stipulated contributions might receive from the pope indulgences for the reduction of purgatory, either for themselves or others, to the extent of 1,902,202 years and 270 days. These were the treasures made available on the day of All Saints.

Three times during his sermons of the year 1516 Luther spoke critically of these indulgences. The third of these occasions was Halloween, the eve of All Saints. Luther spoke moderately and without certainty on all points. But on some he was perfectly assured. No one, he declared, can know whether the remission of sins is complete, because complete remission is granted only to those who exhibit worthy contrition and confession, and no one can know whether contrition and confession are perfectly worthy. To assert that the pope can deliver souls from purgatory is audacious. If he can do so, then he is cruel not to release them all. But if he possesses this ability, he is in a position to do more for the dead than for the living. The purchasing of indulgences in any case is highly dangerous and likely to induce complacency. Indulgences can remit only those private satisfactions imposed by the Church, and may easily militate against interior penance, which consists in true contrition, true confession, and true satisfaction in spirit.

Luther records that the elector took this sermon amiss. Well he might, because indulgences served not merely to dispense the merits

of the saints but also to raise revenues. They were the bingo of the
sixteenth century. The practice grew out of the crusades. At first
indulgences were conferred on those who sacrificed or risked their
lives in fighting against the infidel, and then were extended to those
who, unable to go to the Holy Land, made contributions to the enterprise. The device proved so lucrative that it was speedily extended
to cover the construction of churches, monasteries, and hospitals.
The gothic cathedrals were financed in this way. Frederick the Wise
was using an indulgence to reconstruct a bridge across the Elbe. Indulgences, to be sure, had not degenerated into sheer mercenariness.
Conscientious preachers sought to evoke a sense of sin, and presumably only those genuinely concerned made the purchases. Nevertheless, the Church today readily concedes that the indulgence traffic
was a scandal, so much so that a contemporary preacher phrased the
requisites as three: contrition, confession, and contribution.

A cartoon by Holbein makes the point that the handing over of
the indulgence letter was so timed as not to anticipate the dropping of
the money into the coffer. We see in this cartoon a chamber with

the pope enthroned. He is probably Leo X because the arms of the Medici appear frequently about the walls. The pope is handing a letter of indulgence to a kneeling Dominican. In the choir stalls on either side are seated a number of church dignitaries. On the right one of them lays his hand upon the head of a kneeling youth and with a stick points to a large ironbound chest for the contributions, into which a woman is dropping her mite. At the table on the left various Dominicans are preparing and dispensing indulgences. One of them repulses a beggar who has nothing to give in exchange, while another is carefully checking the money and withholding the indulgences until the full amount has been received. In contrast he shows on the left the true repentance of David, Manasseh, and a notorious sinner, who address themselves only to God.

The indulgences dispensed at Wittenberg served to support the Castle Church and the university. Luther's attack, in other words, struck at the revenue of his own institution. This first blow was certainly not the rebellion of an exploited German against the mulcting of his country by the greedy Italian papacy. However much in after years Luther's followers may have been motivated by such considerations, his first onslaught was not so prompted. He was a priest responsible for the eternal welfare of his parishioners. He must warn them against spiritual pitfalls, no matter what might happen to the Castle Church and the university.

THE INDULGENCE FOR ST. PETER'S

In 1517, the year following, his attention was called to another instance of the indulgence traffic fraught with far-reaching ramifications. The affair rose out of the pretensions of the house of Hohenzollern to control the ecclesiastical and civil life of Germany. An accumulation of ecclesiastical benefices in one family was an excellent expedient, because every bishop controlled vast revenues, and some bishops were princes besides. Albert of Brandenburg, of the house of Hohenzollern, when not old enough to be a bishop at all, held already the sees of Halberstadt and Magdeburg, and aspired to the archbishopric of Mainz, which would make him the primate of Germany.

He knew that he would have to pay well for his office. The installation fee was ten thousand ducats, and the parish could not afford it, being already depleted through the deaths of three archbishops in a decade. One of them apologized for dying after an incumbency of only four years, thereby so soon involving his flock in the fee for his successor. The diocese offered the post to Albert if he would discharge the fee himself. He realized that he would have to pay the pope in addition for the irregularity of holding three sees at once and probably still more to counteract the pressures of the rival house of Hapsburg on the papacy.

Yet Albert was confident that money would speak, because the pope needed it so badly. The pontiff at the moment was Leo X, of the house of Medici, as elegant and as indolent as a Persian cat. His chief pre-eminence lay in his ability to squander the resources of the Holy See on carnivals, war, gambling, and the chase. The duties of his holy office were seldom suffered to interfere with sport. He wore long hunting boots which impeded the kissing of his toe. The resources of three papacies were dissipated by his profligacy: the goods of his predecessors, himself, and his successor. The Catholic historian Ludwig von Pastor declared that the ascent of this man in an hour of crisis to the chair of St. Peter, " a man who scarcely so much as understood the obligations of his high office, was one of the most severe trials to which God ever subjected his Church."

Leo at the moment was particularly in need of funds to complete a project commenced by his predecessor, the building of the new St. Peter's. The old wooden basilica, constructed in the age of Constantine, had been condemned, and the titanic Pope Julius II had overawed the consistory into approving the grandiose scheme of throwing a dome as large as the Pantheon over the remains of the apostles Peter

ALBERT OF BRANDENBURG

and Paul. The piers were laid; Julius died; the work lagged; weeds sprouted from the pillars; Leo took over; he needed money.

The negotiations of Albert with the pope were conducted through the mediation of the German banking house of Fugger, which had a monopoly on papal finances in Germany. When the Church needed funds in advance of her revenues, she borrowed at usurious rates from the sixteenth-century Rothschilds or Morgans. Indulgences were issued in order to repay the debts, and the Fuggers supervised the collection.

Knowing the role they would ultimately play, Albert turned to them for the initial negotiations. He was informed that the pope demanded twelve thousand ducats for the twelve apostles. Albert offered seven thousand for the seven deadly sins. They compromised on ten thousand, presumably not for the Ten Commandments. Albert had to pay the money down before he could secure his appointment, and he borrowed the sum from the Fuggers.

Then the pope, to enable Albert to reimburse himself, granted the privilege of dispensing an indulgence in his territories for the period of eight years. One half of the return, in addition to the ten thousand ducats already paid, should go to the pope for the building of the new St. Peter's; the other half should go to reimburse the Fuggers.

These indulgences were not actually offered in Luther's parish because the Church could not introduce an indulgence without the consent of the civil authorities, and Frederick the Wise would not grant permission in his lands because he did not wish the indulgence of St. Peter to encroach upon the indulgences of All Saints at Wittenberg. Consequently the vendors did not enter electoral Saxony, but they came close enough so that Luther's parishioners could go over the border and return with the most amazing concessions.

In briefing the vendors Albert reached the pinnacle of pretensions as to the spiritual benefits to be conferred by indulgences. He made no reference whatever to the repayment of his debt to the Fuggers. The instructions declared that a plenary indulgence had been issued by His Holiness Pope Leo X to defray the expenses of remedying the sad state of the blessed apostles Peter and Paul and the innumerable martyrs and saints whose bones lay moldering, subject to constant desecration from rain and hail. Subscribers would enjoy a plenary and perfect remission of all sins. They would be restored to the state of innocence which they enjoyed in baptism and would be relieved of all the pains of purgatory, including those incurred by an offense to the Divine Majesty. Those securing indulgences on behalf of the dead already in purgatory need not themselves be contrite and confess their sins.

Then let the cross of Christ, continued the instructions, and the arms of the pope be planted at preaching stations that all might contribute according to their capacity. Kings and queens, archbishops and bishops, and other great princes were expected to give twenty-five gold florins. Abbots, cathedral prelates, counts, barons, and other great nobles and their wives were put down for twenty. Other prelates and lower nobility should give six. The rate for burghers and merchants was three. For those more moderately circumstanced, one.

And since we are concerned for the salvation of souls quite as much as for the construction of this building, none shall be turned empty away.

HAWKING INDULGENCES

So much money is going into the coffer of the vendor that new coins have to be minted on the spot.

The very poor may contribute by prayers and fastings, for the Kingdom of Heaven belongs not only to the rich but also to the poor.

The proclamation of this indulgence was entrusted to the Dominican Tetzel, an experienced vendor. As he approached a town, he was met by the dignitaries, who then entered with him in solemn procession. A cross bearing the papal arms preceded him, and the pope's bull of indulgence was borne aloft on a gold-embroidered velvet cushion. The cross was solemnly planted in the market place, and the sermon began.

THE VENDOR

Listen now, God and St. Peter call you. Consider the salvation of your souls and those of your loved ones departed. You priest, you noble, you merchant, you virgin, you matron, you youth, you old man, enter now into your church, which is the Church of St. Peter. Visit the most holy cross erected before you and ever imploring you. Have you considered that you are lashed in a furious tempest amid the temptations and dangers of the world, and that you do not know whether you can reach the haven, not of your mortal body, but of your immortal soul? Consider that all who are contrite and have confessed and made contribution will receive complete remission of all their sins. Listen to the voices of your dear dead relatives and friends, beseeching you and saying, "Pity us, pity us. We are in dire torment from which you can redeem us for a pittance." Do you not wish to? Open your ears. Hear the father saying to his son, the mother to her daughter, "We bore you, nourished you, brought you up, left you our fortunes, and you are so cruel and hard that now you are not willing for so little to set us free. Will you let us lie here in flames? will you delay our promised glory?"

Remember that you are able to release them, for

> As soon as the coin in the coffer rings,
> The soul from purgatory springs.

Will you not then for a quarter of a florin receive these letters of indulgence through which you are able to lead a divine and immortal soul into the fatherland of paradise?

Such harangues were not being delivered in Wittenberg because of the prohibition of Frederick the Wise, but Tetzel was just over the border, not too far away for Luther's parishioners to make the journey and return with the pardons. They even reported Tetzel to have said that papal indulgences could absolve a man who had violated the Mother of God, and that the cross emblazoned with the papal arms set up by the indulgence sellers was equal to the cross of Christ. A cartoon published somewhat later by one of Luther's followers showed the cross in the center empty of all save the nail holes and the crown of thorns. More prominent beside it stood the papal arms with the balls of the Medici, while in the foreground the vendor hawked his wares.

THE NINETY-FIVE THESES

This was too much. Again on the eve of All Saints, when Frederick the Wise would offer his indulgences, Luther spoke, this time in writing, by posting in accord with current practice on the door of the Castle Church a printed placard in the Latin language consisting of ninety-five theses for debate. Presumably at the time Luther did not know all the sordid details of Albert's transaction. He must have known that Albert would get half the returns, but he directed his attack solely against Tetzel's reputed sermon and Albert's printed instructions, which marked the apex of unbridled pretensions as to the efficacy of indulgences. Sixtus IV in 1476 had promised immediate release to souls in purgatory. Tetzel's jingle thus rested on papal authority. And Leo X in 1513 had promised crusaders plenary remission of all sins and reconciliation with the Most High. Albert assembled the previous pretensions and in addition dispensed explicitly with contrition on the

THE CASTLE CHURCH

part of those who purchased on behalf of the dead in purgatory.

Luther's *Theses* differed from the ordinary propositions for debate because they were forged in anger. The ninety-five affirmations are crisp, bold, unqualified. In the ensuing discussion he explained his meaning more fully. The following summary draws alike on the *Theses* and the subsequent explications. There were three main points: an objection to the avowed object of the expenditure, a denial of the powers of the pope over purgatory, and a consideration of the welfare of the sinner.

The attack focused first on the ostensible intent to spend the money in order to shelter the bones of St. Peter beneath a universal shrine of Christendom. Luther retorted:

The revenues of all Christendom are being sucked into this insatiable basilica. The Germans laugh at calling this the common treasure of Christendom. Before long all the churches, palaces, walls, and bridges of Rome will be built out of our money. First of all we should rear living temples, next local churches, and only last of all St. Peter's, which is not necessary for us. We Germans cannot attend St. Peter's. Better that it should never be built than that our parochial churches should be despoiled. The pope would do better to appoint one good pastor to a church than to confer indulgences upon them all. Why doesn't the pope build the basilica of St. Peter out of his own money? He is richer than Croesus. He would do better to sell St. Peter's and give the money to the poor folk who are being fleeced by the hawkers of indulgences. If the pope knew the exactions of these vendors, he would rather that St. Peter's should lie in ashes than that it should be built out of the blood and hide of his sheep.

This polemic would evoke a deep *Ja wohl* among the Germans, who for some time had been suffering from a sense of grievance against the venality of the Italian *curia* and often quite overlooked the venality of the German confederates. Luther lent himself to this distortion by accepting Albert's picture of the money going all to Rome rather than to the coffers of the Fuggers. Yet in a sense Albert's picture was right. He was only being reimbursed for money which had already gone to Rome. In any case, however, the financial aspect was the least in Luther's eyes. He was ready to undercut the entire practice even though not a gulden left Wittenberg.

His second point denied the power of the pope over purgatory for the remission of either sin or penalty. The absolution of sin is given to the contrite in the sacrament of penance.

Papal indulgences do not remove guilt. Beware of those who say that indulgences effect reconciliation with God. The power of the keys cannot make attrition into contrition. He who is contrite has plenary remission of guilt and penalty without indulgences. The pope can remove only those penalties which he himself has imposed on earth, for Christ did not say, "Whatsoever I have bound in heaven you may loose on earth."

The penalties of purgatory the pope cannot reduce because these have been imposed by God, and the pope does not have at his disposal a treasury of credits available for transfer.

The saints have no extra credits. Every saint is bound to love God to the utmost. There is no such thing as supererogation. If there were any superfluous credits, they could not be stored up for subsequent use. The Holy Spirit would have used them fully long ago. Christ indeed had merits, but until I am better instructed I deny that they are indulgences. His merits are freely available without the keys of the pope.

Therefore I claim that the pope has no jurisdiction over purgatory. I am willing to reverse this judgment if the Church so pronounces. If the pope does have the power to

FORGIVENESS FROM CHRIST OUTWEIGHS
INDULGENCES FROM THE POPE

release anyone from purgatory, why in the name of love does he not abolish purgatory by letting everyone out? If for the sake of miserable money he released uncounted souls, why should he not for the sake of most holy love empty the place? To say that souls are liberated from purgatory is audacious. To say they are released as soon as the coin in the coffer rings is to incite avarice. The pope would do better to give away everything without charge. The only power which the pope has over purgatory is that of making intercession on behalf of souls, and this power is exercised by any priest or curate in his parish.

Luther's attack thus far could in no sense be regarded as heretical or original. Even though Albert's instructions rested on papal bulls, there had as yet been no definitive pronouncement, and many theologians would have endorsed Luther's claims.

But he had a more devastating word:

Indulgences are positively harmful to the recipient because they impede salvation by diverting charity and inducing a false sense of security. Christians should be taught that he who gives to the poor is better than he who receives a pardon. He who spends his money for indulgences instead of relieving want receives not the indulgence of the pope but the indignation of God. We are told that money should be given by preference to the poor only in the case of extreme necessity. I suppose we are not to clothe the naked and visit the sick. What is extreme necessity? Why, I ask, does natural humanity have such goodness that it gives itself freely and does not calculate necessity but is rather solicitous that there should not be any necessity? And will the charity of God, which is incomparably kinder, do none of these things? Did Christ say, "Let him that has a cloak sell it and buy an indulgence"? Love covers a multitude of sins and is better than all the pardons of Jerusalem and Rome.

Indulgences are most pernicious because they induce complacency and thereby imperil salvation. Those persons are damned who think that letters of indulgence make them certain of salvation. God works by contraries so that a man feels himself to be lost in the very moment when he is on the point of being saved. When God is about to justify a man, he damns him. Whom he would make alive he must first kill. God's favor is so communicated in the form of wrath that it seems farthest when it is at hand. Man must first cry out that there is no health in him. He must be consumed with horror. This is the pain of purgatory. I do not know where it is located, but I do know that it can be experienced in this life. I know a man who has gone through such pains that had they lasted for one tenth of an hour he would have been reduced to ashes. In this disturbance salvation begins. When a man believes himself to be utterly lost, light breaks. Peace comes in the word of Christ through faith. He who does not have this is lost even though he be absolved a million times by the pope, and he who does have it may not wish to be released from purgatory, for true contrition seeks penalty. Christians should be encouraged to bear the cross. He who is baptized into Christ must be as a sheep for the slaughter. The merits of Christ are vastly more potent when they bring crosses than when they bring remissions.

Luther's *Ninety-Five Theses* ranged all the way from the complaints of aggrieved Germans to the cries of a wrestler in the night watches. One portion demanded financial relief, the other called for the crucifixion of the self. The masses could grasp the first. Only a few elect spirits would ever comprehend the full import of the second, and yet in the second lay all the power to create a popular revolution. Complaints of financial extortion had been voiced for over a century without visible effect. Men were stirred to deeds only by one who regarded indulgences not merely as venal but as blasphemy against the holiness and mercy of God.

Luther took no steps to spread his theses among the people. He was merely inviting scholars to dispute and dignitaries to define, but others surreptitiously translated the theses into German and gave them to the press. In short order they became the talk of Germany. What Karl Barth said of his own unexpected emergence as a reformer could be said equally of Luther, that he was like a man climbing in the darkness a winding staircase in the steeple of an ancient cathedral. In the blackness he reached out to steady himself, and his hand laid hold of a rope. He was startled to hear the clanging of a bell.

CHAPTER FIVE

THE SON OF INIQUITY

ENERAL dissemination was not in Luther's mind when he posted the theses. He meant them for those concerned. A copy was sent to Albert of Mainz along with the following letter:

Father in Christ and Most Illustrious Prince, forgive me that I, the scum of the earth, should dare to approach Your Sublimity. The Lord Jesus is my witness that I am well aware of my insignificance and my unworthiness. I make so bold because of the office of fidelity which I owe to Your Paternity. May Your Highness look upon this speck of dust and hear my plea for clemency from you and from the pope.

Luther then reports what he had heard about Tetzel's preaching that through indulgences men are promised remission, not only of penalty but also of guilt.

God on high, is this the way the souls entrusted to your care are prepared for death? It is high time that you looked into this matter. I can be silent no longer. In fear and trembling we must work out our salvation. Indulgences can offer no security but only the remission of external canonical penalties. Works of piety and charity are infinitely better than indulgences. Christ did not command the preaching of indulgences but of the gospel, and what a horror it is, what a peril to a bishop, if he never gives the gospel to his people except along with the racket of indulgences. In the instructions of Your Paternity to the indulgence sellers, issued without your knowledge and consent [Luther offers him a way out], indulgences are called the inestimable gift of God for the reconciliation of man to God and the emptying of purgatory. Contrition is declared to be unnecessary. What shall I do, Illustrious Prince, if not to beseech Your Paternity through Jesus Christ our Lord to suppress utterly these instructions lest someone arise to confute this book and to bring Your Illustrious Sublimity into obloquy, which I dread but fear if something is not done speedily? May Your Paternity accept my faithful admonition. I, too, am one of your sheep. May the Lord Jesus guard you forever. Amen.

WITTENBERG, 1517, on the eve of All Saints

If you will look over my theses, you will see how dubious is the doctrine of indulgences, which is so confidently proclaimed.

MARTIN LUTHER, Augustinian Doctor of Theology

Albert forwarded the theses to Rome. Pope Leo is credited with two comments. In all likelihood neither is authentic, yet each is revealing. The first was this: "Luther is a drunken German. He will feel different when he is sober." And the second: "Friar Martin is a brilliant chap. The whole row is due to the envy of the monks."

Both comments, wherever they originated, contain a measure of truth. If Luther was not a drunken German who would feel different when sober, he was an irate German who might be amenable if mollified. If at once the pope had issued the bull of a year later, clearly defining the doctrine of indulgences and correcting the most glaring abuses, Luther might have subsided. On many points he was not yet fully persuaded in his own mind, and he was prompted by no itch for controversy. Repeatedly he was ready to withdraw if his opponents would abandon the fray. During the four years while his case was pending his letters reveal surprisingly little preoccupation with the public dispute. He was engrossed in his duties as a professor and a parish priest, and much more concerned to find a suitable incumbent for the chair of Hebrew at the University of Wittenberg than to knock a layer from the papal tiara. Prompt and straightforward action might have allayed the outburst.

But the pope preferred to extinguish the friar with a clandestine snuffer and appointed a new general of the Augustinians that he might "quench a monk of his order, Martin Luther by name, and thus smother the fire before it should become a conflagration." The first opportunity came the next May at the regular triennial gathering of the chapter, meeting in that year at Heidelberg. Luther was scheduled to report on the completion of his term as vicar and was likewise to defend the theology of the father of the order, St. Augustine, concerning human depravity. The question of indulgences was not on the docket, but the Augustinian theology had provided the ground for Luther's attack.

He had reason to fear the occasion. Warnings of danger came from many sources. His enemies were boasting, some that he would be burned within a month, some within two weeks. He was warned of the possibility of assassination on the road to Heidelberg. "Nevertheless," wrote Luther, "I will obey. I am going on foot. Our Prince [Frederick the Wise] quite unsolicited has undertaken to see that under no circumstances I shall be taken to Rome." Yet as a precaution Luther traveled incognito. After four days of tramping he wrote back, "I am properly contrite for going on foot. Since my contrition is perfect, full penance has already been done, and no indulgence is needed."

To his amazement he was received at Heidelberg as a guest of honor. The Count Palatine invited him, along with Staupitz and others, to dinner and personally conducted them on a tour to see the ornaments of the chapel and the armor. Before the chapter Luther defended the Augustinian view that even outwardly upright acts may be mortal sins in the eyes of God.

"If the peasants heard you say that, they would stone you," was the frank comment of one hearer, but the company roared. Acrimonious letters against Luther were presented before the chapter, but there were no repercussions. The older men did no more than shake their heads, and the younger were enthusiastic. "I have great hope," Luther said, "that as Christ, when rejected by the Jews, went over to the Gentiles, so this true theology, rejected by opinionated old men, will pass over to the younger generation." Among those young men were several later to be prominent as leaders in the Lutheran movement.

There were John Brenz, the reformer of Wuerttemberg, and Martin Bucer, the leader at Strassburg. He was a Dominican who was permitted to attend the public session. "Luther," he reported, "has a marvelous graciousness in response and unconquerable patience in listening. In argument he shows the acumen of the apostle Paul. That which Erasmus insinuates he speaks openly and freely."

Far from being shunned by the brothers Luther was invited to ride home with the Nürnberg delegation until their ways diverged. Then he was transferred to the wagon of the Erfurters, where he found himself beside his old teacher, Dr. Usingen. "I talked with him," said Luther, "and tried to persuade him, but I do not know with what success. I left him pensive and dazed." On the whole Luther felt that he was returning from a triumph. He summed it all up with the comment, "I went on foot. I came back in a wagon."

THE DOMINICAN ASSAULT

The Augustinians were conceivably the more loath to suppress their obstreperous brother because their rivals, the Dominicans, were pressing him hard. This is the truth of the second comment attributed to Pope Leo. The Dominicans rallied to the aid of Tetzel, who was granted a doctor's degree that he might be in a position to publish. At his promotion he roundly defended the jingle,

> As soon as the coin in the coffer rings,
> The soul from purgatory springs.

His theses were printed. The students at Wittenberg by theft or purchase collected eight hundred copies and, unbeknown to the elector, the university, or to Luther, committed them to a bonfire. Luther was highly embarrassed by their impetuosity. To Tetzel he did not deign a reply.

But he did feel constrained to declare himself more fully to the general public. The *Ninety-Five Theses* had been given by the printer to all Germany, though intended only for professional theologians. The many bald assertions called for explanation and clarification, but Luther could never confine himself to a mere reproduction or explication of what he had said previously. The sermons written out by request on Monday do not correspond to the notes taken by hearers on Sunday. Ideas were so churning within him that new butter always came out of the vat. The *Resolutions Concerning the Ninety-Five Theses* contain some new points. Luther had made the discovery that the biblical text from the Latin Vulgate, used to support the sacrament of penance, was a mistranslation. The Latin for Matt. 4:17 read *penitentiam agite*, "do penance," but from the Greek New Testament of Erasmus, Luther had learned that the original meant simply "be penitent." The literal sense was "change your mind." "Fortified with this passage," wrote Luther to Staupitz in the dedication of the *Resolutions*, "I venture to say they are wrong who make more of the act in Latin than of the change of heart in Greek." This was what Luther himself called a "glowing" discovery. In this crucial instance a sacrament of the Church did not rest on the institution of Scripture.

In a very casual way Luther threw off another remark for which he was to be severely pressed. "Suppose," said he, "that the Roman Church were as once it was before the days of Gregory I, when it was not above the other churches, at least not above the Greek." This was to say that the primacy of the Roman Church was a historical development due rather to the exigencies of history than to divine ordination reaching back to the very founding of the Church.

Declarations of such sweeping import soon raised the controversy far above a mere strife of the orders, and every fresh stage served to elicit the radicalism implicit in Luther's presuppositions. He was soon prompted to deny not only the pope's power to release from, but also his ability to consign to, purgatory. Hearing that he was under the ban, Luther had the temerity to preach on the ban, declaring, according to the reports of hostile hearers, that excommunication and reconciliation affect only the external fellowship of the Church on earth and not the grace of God. Bishops are impious who excommunicate over money matters, and they should be disobeyed. These alleged statements were printed by opponents and shown at the imperial diet to the papal legates, who were rumored to have sent them to Rome. Luther was informed that they had done him inestimable damage. To put himself in the clear he wrote out for the press what he could remember of the sermon, but his attempt to conciliate was hardly felicitous. If Mother Church errs in her censures, said he, we should still honor her as Christ honored Caiaphas, Annas, and Pilate. Excommunications apply only to the outward communion of the sacraments, to burial, and to public prayers. The ban does not commit a man to the Devil unless he is already consigned. Only God can sever spiritual communion. No creature can separate us from the love of Christ. We need not fear to die in a state of excommunication. If the sentence is just, the condemned man, if contrite, can still be saved; and if it is unjust, he is blessed.

The printed sermon was not off the press until the end of August. In the meantime the more provocative version of his critics took effect. The pope would no longer dally. From the un-co-operative Augustinians he turned to the Dominicans. Sylvester Prierias, of the Order of St. Dominic, Master of the Sacred Palace at Rome, was commissioned to draft a reply to Luther. He produced it in short order. The opening paragraph shifted the focus from indulgences to the ban and the prerogatives of the pope. Prierias declared that the universal Church is virtually the Roman Church. The Roman Church consists representatively in the cardinals, but virtually in the pope. Just as the universal Church cannot err on faith and morals, nor can a true council, neither can the Roman Church nor the pope when speaking in his official capacity. Whoever does not accept the doctrine of the Roman Church and of the Roman pontiff as the infallible rule of faith from which sacred Scripture derives strength and authority is a heretic, and he who declares that in the matter of indulgences the Roman Church cannot do what actually it does is a heretic. Then Prierias proceeded to refute Luther's errors, describing him on the way as a leper with a brain of brass and a nose of iron.

Luther retorted:

I am sorry now that I despised Tetzel. Ridiculous as he was, he was more acute than you. You cite no Scripture. You give no reasons. Like an insidious devil you pervert the Scriptures. You say that the Church consists virtually in the pope. What abominations will you not have to regard as the deeds of the Church? Look at the ghastly shedding of blood by Julius II. Look at the outrageous tyranny of Boniface VIII, who, as the proverb declares, "came in as a wolf, reigned as a lion, and died as a dog." If the Church consists representatively in the cardinals, what do you make of a general council of the whole Church? You call me a leper because I mingle truth with error. I am glad you admit there is some truth. You make the pope into an emperor in power and violence. The Emperor Maximilian and the Germans will not tolerate this.

The radicalism of this tract lies not in its invective but in its affirmation that the pope might err and a council might err and that only Scripture is the final authority. Prior to the appearance of this declaration the pope had already taken action. On the seventh of August, Luther received a citation to appear at Rome to answer to charges of heresy and contumacy. He was given sixty days in which to make his appearance. On the following day Luther wrote to the elector to remind him of his previous assurance that the case would not be taken to Rome. Then began a tortuous series of negotiations culminating in Luther's hearing before the Diet of Worms. The significance of that occasion is that an assembly of the German nation came to function as a council of the Catholic Church. The popes were doing their best to stifle or control councils. The result was that a secular assembly assumed conciliar functions, but not until after many other devices had first been tried.

THE CASE TRANSFERRED TO GERMANY

The initial step toward a hearing before a German diet was the transfer of Luther's trial from Rome to Germany. To this end on August 8 he besought the intervention of the elector. The plea was addressed not directly to him but to the court chaplain, George Spalatin, who from now on played a large role as the intermediary between the professor and the prince. Frederick was eager that his right hand might plausibly claim ignorance of the left, and was very chary of appearing to endorse Luther's opinions or of backing his person beyond the due of any subject. The elector protested not to have spoken with Luther more than twenty words in all his life. Now in response to the plea transmitted by Spalatin, Frederick opened negotiations with Cardinal Cajetan, the papal legate, to give Luther a personal hearing in connection with the forthcoming meeting of the imperial diet at Augsburg. The hearing was to be private and not before the diet, but would at least be on German soil. The gain on this score was offset, however, by the competence and character of Cardinal Cajetan, a high papalist of integrity and erudition. He could scarcely tolerate Luther's *Reply to Prierias* or the *Sermon on the Ban*, and would be less inclined to moderation because Emperor Maximilian had been incensed by the excerpts from the reputed

SPALATIN

sermon and had himself taken the initiative on the fifth of August in writing to the pope "to set a stop to the most perilous attack of Martin Luther on indulgences lest not only the people but even the princes be seduced." With the emperor, the pope, and the cardinal against him Luther had but slender hope of escaping the stake.

He started for Augsburg with grave misgiving. The danger was vastly greater than three years later when he went to Worms as the champion of an aroused nation. At this time he was only an Augustinian eremite suspected of heresy. He saw ahead the stake and said to himself, "Now I must die. What a disgrace I shall be to my parents!" On the road he contracted an intestinal infection and well-nigh fainted. Even more disconcerting was the recurring doubt whether

the taunt of his critics might after all be right, "Are you alone wise
and all the ages in error?" Luther's friends had advised him not to
enter Augsburg without a safe conduct, and Frederick at length obtained one from Emperor Maximilian. Cajetan, on being consulted,
was incensed. "If you don't trust me," he said, "why do you ask my
opinion, and if you do why is a safe conduct necessary?"

But the cardinal was in a much more complacent mood than Luther had reason to know. The diet was already over, and during its
course he had learned much. His mission had been to rally the north
for a great new crusade against the Turk. The Bohemian heretics
should be reconciled in order that they might participate in the enterprise; a tax should be levied for the purpose; important persons were
to be enlisted by emoluments and distinctions. The Archbishop of
Mainz was to be elevated to the purple, and Emperor Maximilian to
be decorated with a helmet and dagger as the Protector of the Faith.
Incidentally the tares were to be weeded from the vineyard of the
Lord.

The diet opened with characteristic medieval pageantry and
etiquette. All due deference was shown to the cardinal. Albert of
Mainz received the purple with becoming blushes, and the emperor
accepted the dagger without demur. But when the business began,
the princes were not ready to fight the Turk under the auspices
of the Church. They were through with crusades and averred their
inability to raise a tax after being so exploited by the Church. The
grievances of the German nation were presented, as on many previous
occasions, but this time with fangs. The document declared:

These sons of Nimrod grab cloisters, abbeys, prebends, canonates, and
parish churches, and they leave these churches without pastors, the
people without shepherds. Annates and indulgences increase. In cases
before the ecclesiastical courts the Roman Church smiles on both sides
for a little palm grease. German money in violation of nature flies over
the Alps. The pastors given to us are shepherds only in name. They care
for nothing but fleece and batten on the sins of the people. Endowed
masses are neglected, the pious founders cry for vengeance. Let the
Holy Pope Leo stop these abuses.

Cajetan failed in all his large objectives. The crusade and the tax had been rejected. Could he succeed better with the weed in the vineyard of the Lord? He sensed that he must tread warily, but he was shackled by papal instructions which allowed him only to reconcile Luther to the Church in case he recanted, and, in case he did not, to send him bound to Rome. The aid of the secular arm should be invoked, particularly of Emperor Maximilian, whose remonstrance may well have prompted the pope's instructions.

The genuineness of this papal document was first impugned by Luther and subsequently by modern historians on the ground that the pope would not take such summary action before the expiration of the sixty days allowed in the citation. But the pope had merely given Luther sixty days in which to appear, and had made no promises in case he did not. Besides, as Cardinal de Medici wrote to Cajetan on the seventh of October, "In cases of notorious heresy no further ceremony or citation needs to be observed."

The genuineness of these instructions cannot be absolutely established because the original is not extant. The Vatican archives contain, however, the manuscript of another letter written on the very same day by the pope to Frederick, which is no less peremptory.

Beloved son, the apostolic benediction be upon you. We recall that the chief ornament of your most noble family has been devotion to the faith of God and to the honor and dignity of the Holy See. Now we hear that a son of iniquity, Brother Martin Luther of the Augustinian eremites, hurling himself upon the Church of God, has your support. Even though we know it to be false, we must urge you to clear the reputation of your noble family from such calumny. Having been advised by the Master of the Sacred Palace that Luther's teaching contains heresy, we have cited him to appear before Cardinal Cajetan. We call upon you to see that Luther is placed in the hands and under the jurisdiction of this Holy See lest future generations reproach you with having fostered the rise of a most pernicious heresy against the Church of God.

THE INTERVIEWS WITH CAJETAN

In the light of this letter the instructions to Cajetan need not be doubted on the score of the content. Obviously they curtailed his freedom, and a fresh memorandum limited him to inquiry as to Luther's teaching. There should be no discussion. Three interviews took place—on Tuesday, Wednesday, and Thursday the twelfth through the fourteenth of October, 1518. Staupitz was among those present. On the first day Luther prostrated himself in all humility,

The Interview with Cajetan

and the cardinal raised him up in all paternity and then informed him that he must recant. Luther answered that he had not made the arduous journey to Augsburg to do what he could have done quite as well at Wittenberg. He would like to be instructed as to his errors.

The cardinal replied that the chief was the denial of the Church's treasury of merit clearly enunciated in the bull *Unigenitus* of Pope Clement VI in the year 1343. "Here," said Cajetan, "you have a statement by the pope that the merits of Christ are a treasure of indulgences." Luther, who knew the text well, answered that he would recant if it said so. Cajetan chuckled, leafed through the page to the spot where it said that Christ by his sacrifice acquired a treasure. "Oh, yes," said Luther, "but you said that the merits of Christ *are* a treasure. This says he *acquired* a treasure. To *be* and to *acquire* do not mean the same thing. You need not think we Germans are ignorant of grammar."

The reply was both rude and irrelevant. Luther blustered because he was cornered. Any unprejudiced reader would have said that the cardinal correctly paraphrased the sense of the decretal which declares that Christ by his sacrifice acquired a treasure which through the power of the keys has been placed at the disposal of Peter and his successors in order to release the faithful from temporal penalties. This treasure has been increased by the merits of the Blessed Virgin and the saints. The pope dispenses this store as a treasury to those who visit Rome in the jubilee year 1350, when to those penitent and confessed may be given full remission of all their sins.

The whole concept of the treasury of the surplus merits of Christ and the saints is unmistakably here, but Luther was trapped because he must recant or reject the decretal or interpret it in an acceptable sense. He tried the latter and, realizing the delicacy of the task, requested to be allowed to submit a statement in writing, remarking *en passant* that they had "wrangled quite enough." The cardinal was nettled, for he realized that he had gone beyond his instructions in debating with Luther. "My son," he snapped, "I did not wrangle with you. I am ready to reconcile you with the Roman Church." But since reconciliation was possible only through recantation, Luther protested that he ought not to be condemned unheard and unrefuted. "I am not conscious," said he, "of going against Scripture, the fathers, the decretals, or right reason. I may be in error. I will submit to the judgment of the universities of Basel, Freiburg, Louvain, and, if need be, of Paris." This was a most undiplomatic attempt to evade the cardinal's jurisdiction.

The written statement was only a more ingenious and labored effort to place a favorable construction on the decretal. Cajetan must have impressed this upon Luther, for he shifted ground and came out with a blunt rejection of the decretal and of the authority of the pope who formulated it. "I am not so audacious that for the

sake of a single obscure and ambiguous decretal of a human pope
I would recede from so many and such clear testimonies of divine
Scripture. For, as one of the canon lawyers has said, 'in a matter
of faith not only is a council above a pope but any one of the faithful,
if armed with better authority and reason.'" The cardinal reminded
Luther that Scripture has itself to be interpreted. The pope is the
interpreter. The pope is above a council, above Scripture, above
everything in the Church. "His Holiness abuses Scripture," retorted
Luther. "I deny that he is above Scripture." The cardinal flared up
and bellowed that Luther should leave and never come back unless
he was ready to say, "*Revoco*"—"I recant."

Luther wrote home that the cardinal was no more fitted to handle
the case than an ass to play on a harp. The cartoonists before long
took up the theme and pictured the pope himself in this pose.

Cajetan promptly cooled off and had dinner with Staupitz, urging
him to induce Luther to recant and insisting that Luther had no
better friend than he. Staupitz answered,
"I have often tried, but I am not equal
to him in ability and command of Scripture. You are the pope's representative.
It is up to you."

THE POPE AS AN ASS
PLAYING BAGPIPES

"I am not going to talk with him any
more," said the cardinal. "His eyes are as
deep as a lake, and there are amazing
speculations in his head."

Staupitz released Luther from his vow
of obedience to the order. He may have
wished to relieve the Augustinians of
the onus, or he may have sought to un-
fetter the friar, but Luther felt that he
had been disclaimed. "I was excommunicated three times," he said later, "first
by Staupitz, secondly by the pope, and thirdly by the emperor."

He waited until the next week in Augsburg to see whether he
would be summoned further, then posted an appeal from Cajetan

to the pope, pointing out that since the doctrine of indulgences had never been officially declared, a debate on dubious questions should not be regarded as heresy, especially on points unessential for salvation. Luther com-

plained of the citation to Rome which would submit him to the Dominicans. Besides, Rome would not be a safe place even with a safe conduct. In Rome not even Pope Leo himself was safe. The reference was to a conspiracy, lately disclosed, among the very cardinals to poison His Holiness. In any case Luther as a mendicant had no funds for the journey. He had been gra-

THE CARDINAL-FOOL

ciously received by Cajetan, but instead of being allowed to debate had been given only an opportunity to recant. The proposal to submit the case to the universities had been spurned. "I feel that I have not had justice because I teach nothing save what is in Scripture. Therefore I appeal from Leo badly informed to Leo better informed."

Rumor then reached Luther that the cardinal was empowered to arrest him. The gates of the city were being guarded. With the connivance of friendly citizens Luther escaped by night, fleeing in such haste that he had to ride horseback in his cowl without breeches, spurs, stirrups, or a sword. He arrived in Nürnberg and there was shown the pope's instructions to Cajetan. Luther questioned the authenticity but at the same time contemplated an appeal from the pope to a general council. On the thirtieth day of October he was back in Wittenberg.

THREATENING EXILE

His tenure there became highly precarious. Cajetan sent his report of the interview to Frederick the Wise, declaring that what Luther had said with regard to the papal decretal was not fit to put on paper. Let Frederick either send Luther bound to Rome or else banish him from his territories. The elector showed this to Luther, who made the matter still more difficult for his prince by publishing a version of the interview with Cajetan strengthened by subsequent reflection. There was no longer any attempt to explain the papal decretal in a favorable sense. Instead it was called emphatically false. The ambiguous decretal of a mortal pope was contrasted with the clear testimonies of holy Scripture. Luther continued:

You are not a bad Christian if you deny the decretal. But if you deny the gospel, you are a heretic. I damn and detest this decretal. The Apostolic Legate opposed me with the thunder of his majesty and told me to recant. I told him the pope abused Scripture. I will honor the sanctity of the pope, but I will adore the sanctity of Christ and the truth. I do not deny this new monarchy of the Roman Church which has arisen in our generation, but I deny that you cannot be a Christian without being subject to the decrees of the Roman pontiff. As for that decretal, I deny that the merits of Christ are a treasure of indulgences because his merits convey grace apart from the pope. The merits of Christ take away sins and increase merits. Indulgences take away merits and leave sins. These adulators put the pope above Scripture and say that he cannot err. In that case Scripture perishes, and nothing is left in the Church save the word of man. I resist those who in the name of the Roman Church wish to institute Babylon.

On the twenty-eighth of November, Luther lodged with a notary an appeal from the pope to a general council, declaring that such a council, legitimately called in the Holy Spirit, represents the Catholic Church and is above the pope, who, being a man, is able to err, sin, and lie. Not even St. Peter was above this infirmity. If the pope orders anything against divine mandates, he is not to be obeyed.

Therefore from Leo badly advised and from his excommunication, suspension, interdict, censures, sentences, and fines, and whatsoever denunciations and declarations of heresy and apostasy, which I esteem as null, nay, as iniquitous and tyrannical, I appeal to a general council in a safe place.

Luther had the appeal printed and requested that all the copies be committed to him to be released only if he was actually banned, but the printer disregarded the injunction and gave them at once to the public. This put Luther in a most exposed position because Pope Julius II had ruled that an appeal without papal consent to a council would itself constitute heresy.

Frederick the Wise was doubly embarrassed. He was a most Catholic prince, addicted to the cult of relics, devoted to indulgences, quite sincere in his claim that he was not in a position to judge Luther's teaching. On such matters he craved guidance. That was why he had founded the University of Wittenberg and why he so often turned to it for advice on matters juristic and theological. Luther was one of the doctors of that university, commissioned to instruct his prince in matters of faith. Was the prince to believe that his doctor of Holy Scripture was in error? Of course, if the pope declared him to be a heretic, that would settle the matter, but the pope had not yet passed sentence. The theological faculty at Wittenberg had not repudiated Luther. Many scholars throughout Germany believed him to be right. If Frederick should take action prior to papal condemnation, might he not be resisting the word of God? On the other hand, the pope had urged that Luther be taken into custody and had called him a "son of iniquity." Might not a refusal to comply mean the harboring of a heretic? Such questions troubled Frederick. He differed from other princes of his time in that he never asked how to extend his boundaries nor even how to preserve his dignities. His only question was, "What is my duty as a Christian prince?" At this juncture he was gravely disturbed and would take no action beyond writing on the nineteenth of November beseeching the emperor either to drop the case or to grant a hearing before unimpeachable judges in Germany.

Luther wrote to the elector:

I am sorry that the legate blames you. He is trying to bring the whole House of Saxony into disrepute. He suggests that you send me to Rome or banish me. What am I, a poor monk, to expect if I am banished? Since I am in danger enough in your territory, what would it be outside?

But lest Your Honor suffer on my account I will gladly leave your dominions.

To Staupitz, Luther wrote:

The prince opposed the publication of my version of the interview but has at length given his consent. The legate has asked him to send me to Rome or banish me. The prince is very solicitous for me, but he would be happier if I were somewhere else. I told Spalatin if the ban came I would leave. He dissuaded me from precipitant flight to France.

When at Augsburg one of the Italians had asked Luther where he would go if abandoned by the prince, he had answered, "Under the open sky."

On the twenty-fifth of November he sent word to Spalatin:

I am expecting the curses of Rome any day. I have everything in readiness. When they come, I am girded like Abraham to go I know not where, but sure of this, that God is everywhere.

Staupitz wrote Luther from Salzburg in Austria:

The world hates the truth. By such hate Christ was crucified, and what there is in store for you today if not the cross I do not know. You have few friends, and would that they were not hidden for fear of the adversary. Leave Wittenberg and come to me that we may live and die together. The prince [Frederick] is in accord. Deserted let us follow the deserted Christ.

Luther told his congregation that he was not saying good-by; but if they should find him gone, then let this be his farewell. He entertained a few friends at supper. In another two hours he would have left had not a letter come from Spalatin saying that the prince wished him to stay. Precisely what had happened we shall never know. Years afterward Luther declared that the prince had in mind a plan to hide him, but a few weeks after the event Luther wrote, "At first the prince would have been willing not to have me here." Two years later Frederick justified himself before Rome for taking no action against Luther on the ground that he had been ready to accept Luther's offer to leave when word came from the papal nuncio advising that Luther would be much less dangerous under surveillance than at large. Frederick of course might have said this after the event, even though secretly he had entertained the design of spiriting Luther to some hide-out. Yet it is equally possible that for a moment Frederick was ready to yield but delayed until after the pope had made his move. At any rate on the eighteenth of December, Frederick sent to Cajetan the only document he ever addressed to the Roman *curia* on Luther's behalf:

We are sure that you acted paternally toward Luther, but we understand that he was not shown sufficient cause to revoke. There are learned men in the universities who hold that his teaching has not been shown to be unjust, unchristian, or heretical. The few who think so are jealous of his attainments. If we understood his doctrine to be impious or untenable, we would not defend it. Our whole purpose is to fulfill the office of a Christian prince. Therefore we hope that Rome will pronounce on the question. As for sending him to Rome or banishing him, that we will do only after he has been convicted of heresy. His offer to debate and submit to the judgment of the universities ought to be considered. He should be shown in what respect he is a heretic and not condemned in advance. We will not lightly permit ourselves to be drawn into error nor to be made disobedient to the Holy See. We wish you to know that the Univeristy of Wittenberg has recently written on his behalf. A copy is appended.

Luther commented to Spalatin:

I have seen the admirable words of our Most Illustrious Prince to our Lord the Legate of Rome. Good God, with what joy I read them and read them over again!

CHAPTER SIX

THE SAXON HUS

RESUMABLY the shift in papal policy was due in part to the discerning reports of Cardinal Cajetan. He well knew that a man may be a vexation without being a heretic, because heresy involves a rejection of the established dogma of the Church, and the doctrine of indulgences had not yet received an official papal definition. The pope must first speak; and only then, if Luther refused to submit, could he properly be placed under the ban. A papal declaration was at last forthcoming, composed in all likelihood by Cajetan himself. On November 9, 1518, the bull *Cum Postquam* definitely clarified many of the disputed points. Indulgences were declared to apply only to penalty and not to guilt, which must first have been remitted through the sacrament of penance. Not the eternal pains of hell but only the temporal penalties of earth and purgatory might be diminished. Over the penalties imposed on earth by himself, the pope of course exercised complete jurisdiction by virtue of the power of absolution. But in the case of the penalties of purgatory he could do no more than present to God the treasury of the superfluous merits of Christ and the saints by way of petition. This decretal terminated some of the worst abuses.

Had it appeared earlier, the controversy might conceivably have been terminated, but in the interim Luther had attacked not only the papal power to loose but also the power to bind through the ban. He had further declared the pope and councils to be capable of error. He had undercut the biblical text used to support the sacrament of penance and had rejected a portion of the canon law as incompatible with Scripture. The Dominicans had called him a notorious heretic, and the pope had referred to him as a son of iniquity.

But how was he to be handled? The conciliatory policy commenced in December, 1518, was prompted by considerations of politics. The pope knew that the plan for a crusade had been repudiated, that the tax had been refused, that the grievances of the German nation were recriminatory. There was a more serious consideration. Emperor Maximilian died on the twelfth of January. An election to the office of Holy Roman Emperor was thereby precipitated, and for some time earlier Maximilian was known to have been scheming to ensure the election of his grandson Charles as his successor.

The empire was a waning but still imposing legacy from the Middle Ages. The office of emperor was elective, and any European prince was eligible. The electors were, however, preponderantly German and preferred a German. Yet they were realistic enough to perceive that no German had sufficient strength in his own right to sustain the office. For that reason they were ready to accept the head of one of the great powers, and the choice lay between Francis of France and Charles of Spain. The pope objected, however, to either because an accretion of power on one side or the other would destroy that balance on which papal security depended. When the Germans despaired of a German, the pope threw his support to Frederick the Wise. Under such circumstances his wishes with regard to Martin Luther could not lightly be disregarded. The situation of course was altered when Frederick, sensible of his inadequacy, defeated himself by voting for the Hapsburg who on June 28, 1519, was chosen as Charles V of the Holy Roman Empire. Yet the situation did not so greatly alter, because for fully a year and a half thereafter Charles was too occupied in Spain to concern himself with Germany, and Frederick remained the pivotal figure. The pope still could not afford to alienate him unduly over Luther.

Papal policy became conciliatory; and Cajetan was assigned an assistant, a German related to Frederick the Wise, Carl von Miltitz by name, whose assignment was to curry the favor of the elector and to keep Luther quiet until the election was settled. For these ends Miltitz was equipped with every arrow in the quiver of the Vatican, from indulgences to interdicts. In order to soften Frederick he brought new privileges for the Castle Church at Wittenberg, whereby to those who made appropriate contributions purgatory might be reduced by a hundred years for every bone of the saints in Frederick's famous collection. He was further honored by a long-coveted distinction, the gift of a golden rose from the hand of the pope. In conferring this honor Leo X wrote to him:

Beloved son, the most holy golden rose was consecrated by us on the fourteenth day of the holy fast. It was anointed with holy oil and sprinkled with fragrant incense with the papal benediction. It will be presented to you by our most beloved son, Carl von Miltitz, of noble blood and noble manners. This rose is the symbol of the most precious blood of our Saviour, by which we are redeemed. The rose is a flower among flowers, the fairest and most fragrant on earth. Therefore, dear son, permit the divine fragrance to enter the innermost heart of Your Excellency, that you may fulfill whatever the aforementioned Carl von Miltitz shall show you.

No little delay occurred in the delivery of the rose, because it was deposited for safekeeping in the bank of the Fuggers at Augsburg.

Frederick suggested another reason for the delay. "Miltitz," he said, "may refuse to give me the golden rose unless I banish the monk and pronounce him a heretic." Luther heard that Miltitz was armed with a papal brief which made the gift of the rose conditional on his extradition, but that Miltitz was deterred from taking this course by the prudence of a cardinal who exclaimed, "You are a pack of fools if you think you can buy the monk from the prince." Miltitz was most certainly preceded by letters from the pope and the *curia* to Frederick urging all to assist against that "child of Satan, son of perdition, scrofulous sheep, and tare in the vineyard, Martin Luther." Brother Martin fully expected to be arrested, and Miltitz may have started out with that intent. "I learned afterwards," wrote Luther to Staupitz, "at the court of the prince, that Miltitz came armed with seventy apostolic briefs, that he might take me to the Jerusalem which kills the prophets, the purple Babylon." Miltitz boasted in Germany that he had the friar in his pocket, but he was made quickly aware that too peremptory a course would not be discreet. In the inns on the way he questioned the people and discovered that for every one in favor of the pope there were three for Luther. He frankly confessed that no case had so plagued the Church in a thousand years, and Rome would gladly pay ten thousand ducats to have it out of the way. The *curia* was prepared to do even more than that. Frederick the Wise was given to understand that if he were compliant he might be permitted to name a cardinal. He took this to mean that the dignity might be conferred on Luther.

Miltitz arrived full of blandishments. In one interview he said to Luther, "We'll have it all fixed up in no time." He asked of Luther that he should subscribe to the new papal decretal on indulgences. Luther replied that there was not a word in it from Scripture. Then Miltitz required of him but one thing, that he should refrain from debate and publication if his opponents would observe the same condition. Luther promised. Miltitz wept. "Crocodile tears," commented Luther.

Tetzel was made the scapegoat. Miltitz summoned him to a hearing and charged that he was extravagant in traveling with two horses and a carriage, and that he had two illegitimate children. Tetzel retired to a convent to die of chagrin. Luther wrote to him, "Don't take it too hard. You didn't start this racket. The child had another father." The elector in the meantime took advantage of his singular position to use Miltitz for a plan of his own. Let Luther's case be referred to a commission of German ecclesiastics under the chairmanship of the Archbishop of Trier, Richard of Greiffenklau, who might please the Germans because he was an elector, the pope because he was an archbishop, and Luther because in the election he was opposing the papal candidate. Cajetan was won for the scheme, and Richard expressed his willingness. Frederick arranged with him that the hearing take place at the forthcoming meeting of the Diet of Worms

But the pope neither authorized nor disavowed the proposal, and for the moment nothing came of it.

Luther in the meantime became involved in further debate. He had agreed to refrain from controversy only if his opponents also

PHILIP MELANCHTHON

observed the truce, and they did not. The universities were becoming involved. The University of Wittenberg was coming to be regarded as a Lutheran institution. Prominent among the faculty were Carlstadt and Melanchthon. The former was Luther's senior and had conferred on him the doctor's hood. Carlstadt was erudite but devoid of the caution which learning sometimes induces. He was sensitive, impressionable, impetuous, and at times tumultuous. His espousal of Luther's teachings prompted him to indulge in such blasts against critics that Luther himself was prone at times to wince.

Melanchthon was gentler, younger—only twenty-one—a prodigy of learning, enjoying already a European reputation. In appearance he was not prepossessing, as he had an impediment of speech and a hitch in the shoulder when he walked. Luther once, when asked how he envisaged the appearance of the apostle Paul, answered with an affectionate guffaw, "I think he was a scrawny shrimp like Melanchthon." But when the stripling opened his mouth, he was like the boy Jesus in the temple. He came as professor of Greek, not of theology, and without any commitment to Luther; but soon he succumbed to his spell. His conversion stemmed from no travail of spirit but from agreement with Luther's interpretation of the apostle Paul. These were the leaders of the Wittenberg phalanx.

THE GAUNTLET OF ECK

The Goliath of the Philistines who stepped forth to taunt Israel was a professor from the University of Ingolstadt, John Eck by name. On the appearance of Luther's theses he had leveled against them an attack under the title *Obelisks*, the word used to designate interpolations in Homer. Luther replied with *Asterisks*. Eck's attack was galling to Luther because he was an old friend, not a mendicant but a humanist, not "a perfidious Italian" but a German, and not the least because he was formidable. Despite his butcher's face and bull's voice he was a man of prodigious memory, torrential fluency, and uncanny acumen—a professional disputant who would post to Vienna or Bologna to debate the works of the Trinity, the substance of angels, or the contract of usury. Particularly exasperating was his propensity for clothing the opprobrious with plausibility and driving an opponent to incriminating conclusions.

Eck succeeded in inducing, not his own institution, but the University of Leipzig to enter the lists as the challenger of Wittenberg. Thereby old jealousies were brought into alignment with the new conflict, because Wittenberg and Leipzig represented the rival sections of electoral and ducal Saxony. Eck approached the patron of Leipzig, Duke George the Bearded—all the Saxon princes were bearded, but George left it to the others to be known as the Wise, the Steadfast, and the Magnanimous. He agreed that Eck should debate at Leipzig with Carlstadt, who in Luther's defense had already launched at Eck a virulent attack. But Eck had no mind to fence with the second. He openly baited Luther by challenging his alleged assertions

JOHN ECK

that the Roman Church in the days of Constantine was not above the others, and that the occupant of the see of Peter had not always been recognized as the successor of Peter and the vicar of Christ—in other words, that the papacy was of recent and therefore of human origin. Luther retorted:

Let it be understood that when I say the authority of the Roman pontiff rests on a human decree I am not counseling disobedience. But we cannot admit that all the sheep of Christ were committed to Peter. What, then, was given to Paul? When Christ said to Peter, "Feed my sheep," he did not mean, did he, that no one else can feed them without Peter's permission? Nor can I agree that the Roman pontiffs cannot err or that they alone can interpret Scripture. The papal decretal by a new grammar turns the words of Christ, "Thou art Peter" into "Thou art the primate." By the decretals the gospel is extinguished. I can hardly restrain myself against the most impious and perverse blasphemy of this decretal.

Plainly the debate was between Eck and Luther, but to bring a man stigmatized by the pope as a "son of iniquity" out into the open in a public debate under the auspices of the orthodox University of Leipzig was daring. The bishop of the region interposed a prohibition. But Duke George rallied. He was later to become Luther's most implacable opponent, but at the moment he really wanted to know whether

> As soon as the coin in the coffer rings,
> The soul from purgatory springs.

He reminded the bishop: "Disputations have been allowed from ancient times, even concerning the Holy Trinity. What good is a soldier if he is not allowed to fight, a sheep dog if he may not bark, and a theologian if he may not debate? Better spend money to support old women who can knit than theologians who cannot discuss." Duke George had his way. Luther was given a safe conduct to debate at Leipzig. "If that isn't the very devil!" commented Tetzel from his enforced retirement.

Luther set himself to prepare for the debate. Since he had asserted that only in the decretals of the previous four hundred years could the claims of papal primacy be established, he must devote himself to a study of the decretals. As he worked, his conclusions grew ever more radical. To a friend he wrote in February:

Eck is fomenting new wars against me. He may yet drive me to a serious attack upon the Romanists. So far I have been merely trifling.

In March, Luther confided to Spalatin:

I am sending Eck's letters in which he already boasts of having won the Olympic. I am studying the papal decretals for my debate. I whisper this in your ear, "I do not know whether the pope is Antichrist or his apostle, so does he in his decretals corrupt and crucify Christ, that is, the truth."

The reference to Antichrist was ominous. Luther was to find it easier to convince men that the pope was Antichrist than that the just shall live by faith. The suspicion which Luther did not yet dare breathe in the open links him unwittingly with the medieval sectaries who had revived and transformed the theme of Antichrist, a figure invented by the Jews in their captivity to derive comfort from calamity on the ground that the coming of Messiah is retarded by the machinations of an Anti-Messiah, whose raging must reach a peak before the Saviour should come. The gloomiest picture of the present thus became the most encouraging for the future. The book of Revelation made of the Anti-Messiah an Antichrist and added the details that before the end two witnesses must testify and suffer martyrdom. Then would appear Michael the Archangel and a figure with eyes of flame upon a white horse to cast the beast into the abyss. How the theme was handled in Luther's day is graphically shown in a woodcut from the *Nürnberg Chronicle*. Below on the left a very plausible Antichrist beguiles the people, while on the right the two witnesses from a pulpit instruct the throng. The hillock in the center is the Mount of Olives, from which Christ ascended into heaven and from which Antichrist is to be cast into hell. At the top Michael smites with his sword.

Antichrist at the top is smitten by Michael and dragged by devils toward hell. The hillock is the Mount of Olives, from which Christ ascended into heaven and from which Antichrist is cast down. In the foreground at the left Antichrist with a devil speaking into his ear is beguiling the people. On the right the two witnesses give their testimony.

The theme became very popular in the late Middle Ages among the Fraticelli, Wycliffites, and Hussites, who identified the popes with the Antichrist soon to be overthrown. Luther was unwittingly in line with these sectaries, with one significant difference, however. Whereas they identified particular popes, because of their evil lives, with Antichrist, Luther held that every pope was Antichrist even though personally exemplary, because Antichrist is collective: an institution, the papacy, a system which corrupts the truth of Christ. That was why Luther could repeatedly address Leo X in terms of personal respect only a week or so after blasting him as Antichrist. But all this was yet to come. On the eve of the Leipzig debate Luther was frightened by his own thoughts. To one who had been so devoted to the Holy Father as the vicar of Christ the very suggestion that he might be, after all, the great opponent of Christ was ghastly. At the same time the thought was comforting, for the doom of Antichrist was sure. If Luther should fall like the two witnesses, his assailant would early be demolished by the hand of God. It was no longer a fight merely with men, but against the principalities and the powers and the world ruler of this darkness in the heavenly places.

THE LEIPZIG DEBATE

The debate was held in Leipzig in the month of July. Eck came early and strode in a chasuble in the *Corpus Christi* procession. The Wittenbergers arrived a few days later, Luther, Carlstadt, Melanchthon, and other doctors with two hundred students armed with battle-axes. Eck was provided by the town council with a bodyguard of seventy-six men to protect him day and night from the Wittenbergers and the Bohemians whom he believed to be among them. Morning and evening a guard marched with streaming banners to fife and drum, and stationed themselves at the castle gate. The debate had been scheduled to be held in the aula of the university; but so great was the concourse of abbots, counts, Knights of the Golden Fleece, learned and unlearned, that Duke George placed at their disposal the auditorium of the castle. Chairs and benches were decorated with tapestries, those of the Wittenbergers with the emblem of St.

Martin and Eck's with the insigne of the dragon killer, St. George.

On the opening day the assembly attended mass at six in the morning in St. Thomas Church. The liturgy was sung by a choir of twelve voices under the leadership of George Rhaw, later to be the printer of Luther's music at Wittenberg. The assembly then transferred itself to the castle. The session was opened with a Latin address of two hours by Duke George's secretary on the proper mode of conducting a theological discussion with decorum. "A grand address," said Duke George, "though I marvel that theologians should need such advice." Then the choir rendered the *Veni, Sancte Spiritus* while the town piper blew lustily. By then it was dinnertime. Duke George had an eye for the delicacies of the table. To Eck he sent a deer, to Carlstadt a roe, and wine all round.

In the afternoon began the preliminary skirmish over the rules of the tournament. The first question was whether to have stenographers. Eck said no, because taking them into account would chill the passionate heat of the debate. "The truth might fare better at a lower temperature," commented Melanchthon. Eck lost. The next question was whether to have judges. Luther said no. Frederick was arranging to have his case heard by the Archbishop of Trier, and he did not wish at this juncture to give the appearance of interjecting a rival plan. But Duke George was insistent. Luther lost. The universities of Erfurt and Paris were chosen. This was a reversion to the method several times previously proposed for the handling of his case. When Paris accepted, Luther demanded that the entire faculty be invited and not merely the theologians, whom he had come to distrust. "Why then," blurted Eck, "don't you refer the case to shoemakers and tailors?" The third question was whether to admit any books to the arena. Eck said no. Carlstadt, he charged, on the opening days lugged in tomes and read the audience to sleep. The Leipzigers in particular had to be awakened for dinner. Carlstadt accused Eck of wishing to befuddle the audience by a torrent of erudition. Carlstadt lost. By common consent the notes of the debate were not to be published until after the judges had submitted their verdict. The discussion proper then began.

An eyewitness has left us a description of the contestants.

Martin is of middle height, emaciated from care and study, so that you can almost count his bones through his skin. He is in the vigor of manhood and has a clear, penetrating voice. He is learned and has the Scripture at his fingers' ends. He knows Greek and Hebrew sufficiently to judge of the interpretations. A perfect forest of words and ideas stands at his command. He is affable and friendly, in no sense dour or arrogant. He is equal to anything. In company he is vivacious, jocose, always cheerful and gay no matter how hard his adversaries press him. Everyone chides him for the fault of being a little too insolent in his reproaches and more caustic than is prudent for an innovator in religion or becoming to a theologian. Much the same can be said of Carlstadt, though in a lesser degree. He is smaller than Luther, with a complexion of smoked herring. His voice is thick and unpleasant. He is slower in memory and quicker in anger. Eck is a heavy, square-set fellow with a full German voice supported by a hefty chest. He would make a tragedian or town crier, but his voice is rather rough than clear. His eyes and mouth and his whole face remind one more of a butcher than a theologian.

THE LEIPZIG DEBATE

After Carlstadt and Eck had wrestled for a week over the depravity of man, Luther entered to discuss the antiquity of the papal and the Roman primacy, together with the question whether it was of human or divine institution. "What does it all matter," inquired Duke George, "whether the pope is by divine right or by human right? He remains the pope just the same." "Perfectly right," said Luther, who insisted that by denying the divine origin of the papacy he was not counseling a withdrawal of obedience. But Eck saw more clearly than Luther the subversiveness of his assertions. The claim of the pope to unquestioning obedience rests on the belief that his office is divinely instituted. Luther revealed how lightly after all he esteemed the office when he exclaimed, "Even if there were ten popes or a thousand popes there would be no schism. The unity of Christendom could be preserved under numerous heads just as the separated nations under different sovereigns dwell in concord."

"I marvel," sniffed Eck, "that the Reverend Father should forget the everlasting dissension of the English and the French, the inveterate hatred of the French for the Spaniards, and all the Christian blood spilled over the Kingdom of Naples. As for me, I confess one faith, one Lord Jesus Christ, and I venerate the Roman pontiff as Christ's vicar."

But to prove that Luther's views were subversive was not to prove that they were false. The contestants had to come to grips with history. Eck asserted that the primacy of the Roman see and the Roman bishop as the successor of Peter went back to the very earliest days of the Church. By way of proof he introduced letters ascribed to a bishop of Rome in the first century affirming, "The Holy Roman and Apostolic Church obtained the primacy not from the apostles but from our Lord and Saviour himself, and it enjoys pre-eminence of power above all of the churches and the whole flock of Christian people"; and again, "The sacerdotal order commenced in the period of the New Testament directly after our Lord Christ, when to Peter was committed the pontificate previously exercised in the Church by Christ himself." Both of these statements had been incorporated into the canon law.

"I impugn these decretals," cried Luther. "No one will ever persuade me that the holy pope and martyr said that." Luther was right. They are today universally recognized by Catholic authorities as belonging to the spurious Isidorian decretals. Luther had done an excellent piece of historical criticism, and without the help of Lorenzo Valla, whose work he had not yet seen. Luther pointed out that actually in the early centuries bishops beyond Rome were not confirmed by nor subject to Rome, and the Greeks never accepted the Roman primacy. Surely the saints of the Greek Church were not on that account to be regarded as damned.

THE ENDORSEMENT OF HUS

"I see," said Eck, "that you are following the damned and pestiferous errors of John Wyclif, who said, 'It is not necessary for salvation to believe that the Roman Church is above all others.' And you are espousing the pestilent errors of John Hus, who claimed that Peter neither was nor is the head of the Holy Catholic Church."

"I repulse the charge of Bohemianism," roared Luther. "I have never approved of their schism. Even though they had divine right on their side, they ought not to have withdrawn from the Church, because the highest divine right is unity and charity."

Eck was driving Luther onto ground especially treacherous at Leipzig, because Bohemia was near by, and within living memory the Bohemian Hussites, the followers of John Hus, burned for heresy at Constance, had invaded and ravaged the Saxon lands. The assembly took time out for lunch. Luther availed himself of the interlude to go to the university library and read the acts of the Council of Constance, by which Hus had been condemned. To his amazement he discovered among the reproved articles the following: "The one holy universal Church is the company of the predestined," and again, "The universal Holy Church is one, as the number of the elect is one." The second of these statements he recognized as deriving directly from St. Augustine. When the assembly reconvened at two o'clock, Luther declared, "Among the articles of John Hus, I find many which are plainly Christian and evangelical, which the universal Church cannot condemn." Duke George at these words jabbed his elbows into his ribs and muttered audibly, "The plague!" His mind conjured up the Hussite hordes ravaging the Saxon lands. Eck had scored.

Luther continued. "As for the article of Hus that 'it is not necessary for salvation to believe the Roman Church superior to all others' I do not care whether this comes from Wyclif or from Hus. I know that innumerable Greeks have been saved though they never heard this article. It is not in the power of the Roman pontiff or of the Inquisition to construct new articles of faith. No believing Christian can be coerced beyond holy writ. By divine law we are forbidden to believe anything which is not established by divine Scripture or manifest revelation. One of the canon lawyers has said that the opinion of a single private man has more weight than that of a Roman pontiff or an ecclesiastical council if grounded on a better authority or reason. I cannot believe that the Council of Constance would condemn these propositions of Hus. Perhaps this section in the acts has been interpolated."

"They are recorded," stated Eck, "in the reliable history of Jerome of Croatia, and their authenticity has never been impugned by the Hussites."

"Even so," replied Luther, "the council did not say that all the articles of Hus were heretical. It said that 'some were heretical, some erroneous, some blasphemous, some presumptuous, some seditious, and some offensive to pious ears respectively.' You should differentiate and tell us which were which."

"Whichever they were," retorted Eck, "none of them was called most Christian and evangelical; and if you defend them, then you are heretical, erroneous, blasphemous, presumptuous, seditious, and offensive to pious ears respectively."

"Let me talk German," demanded Luther. "I am being misunderstood by the people. I assert that a council has sometimes erred and may sometimes err. Nor has a council authority to establish new articles of faith. A council cannot make divine right out of that which by nature is not divine right. Councils have contradicted each other, for the recent Lateran Council has reversed the claim of the councils of Constance and Basel that a council is above a pope. A simple layman armed with Scripture is to be believed above a pope or a council without it. As for the pope's decretal on indulgences I say that neither the Church nor the pope can establish articles of faith. These must come from Scripture. For the sake of Scripture we should reject pope and councils."

"But this," said Eck, "is the Bohemian virus, to attach more weight to one's own interpretation of Scripture than to that of the popes and councils, the doctors and the universities. When Brother Luther says that this is the true meaning of the text, the pope and councils say, 'No, the brother has not understood it correctly.' Then I will take the council and let the brother go. Otherwise all the heresies will be renewed. They have all appealed to Scripture and have believed their interpretation to be correct, and have claimed that the popes and the councils were mistaken, as Luther now does. It is rancid to say that those gathered in a council, being men, are able to err. This is horrible, that the Reverend Father against the holy Council of Constance and the consensus of all Christians does not fear to call certain articles of Hus and Wyclif most Christian and evangelical. I tell you, Reverend Father, if you reject the Council of Constance, if you say a council, legitimately called, errs and has erred, be then to me as a Gentile and a publican."

Luther answered, "If you won't hold me for a Christian, at least listen to my reasons and authorities as you would to a Turk and infidel."

Eck did. They went on to discuss purgatory. Eck cited the famous passage from II Maccabees 12:45, "Wherefore he made the propitiation for them that had died, that they might be released from their sin." Luther objected that the book of II Maccabees belongs to the Apocrypha and not to the canonical Old Testament, and is devoid of authority. This was the third time during the debate that he had impugned the relevance of the documentary buttresses of papal claims.

LUTHER AND HUS ADMINISTER THE BREAD AND WINE TO THE
HOUSE OF SAXONY

First he had denied the genuineness of papal decretals of the first century, and he was right. Next he questioned the acts of the Council
of Constance, and he was wrong. This time he rejected the authority
of the Old Testament Apocrypha, which is, of course, a matter of
judgment.

Then they took up indulgences, and there was scarcely any debate. Eck declared that if Luther had not assailed the papal primacy,

their differences could easily have been composed. On the subject of penance, however, Eck kept pressing Luther with the query, "Are you the only one that knows anything? Except for you is all the Church in error?"

"I answer," replied Luther, "that God once spoke through the mouth of an ass. I will tell you straight what I think. I am a Christian theologian; and I am bound, not only to assert, but to defend the truth with my blood and death. I want to believe freely and be a slave to the authority of no one, whether council, university, or pope. I will confidently confess what appears to me to be true, whether it has been asserted by a Catholic or a heretic, whether it has been approved or reproved by a council."

The debate lasted eighteen days and "might have gone forever," said a contemporary, "had not Duke George intervened." He had not learned much about what happens when the coin in the coffer rings, and he needed the assembly hall for the entertainment of the Margrave of Brandenburg, on his way home from the imperial election. Both sides continued the controversy in a pamphlet war. The agreement to wait for the judgment of the universities before publishing the notes was not observed, because Erfurt never reported at all, and Paris not for two years.

Before leaving the debate a minor incident is worth recording because it is so revealing of the coarseness and insensitivity of that whole generation. Duke George had a one-eyed court fool. A comic interlude in the disputation was staged when Eck and Luther debated whether this fool should be allowed a wife, Luther pro and Eck con. Eck was so opprobrious that the fool took offense; and whenever subsequently Eck entered the hall, the fool made grimaces. Eck retaliated by mimicking the blind eye, at which the fool ripped out a volley of bitter profanity. The audience roared.

After the debate Eck came upon a new fagot for Luther's pyre. "At any rate," he crowed, "no one is hailing me as the Saxon Hus." Two letters to Luther had been intercepted, from John Paduška and Wenzel Roždalowski, Hussites of Prague, in which they said, "What

Hus was once in Bohemia you, Martin, are in Saxony. Stand firm." When these letters did reach Luther, they were accompanied by a copy of Hus's work *On the Church*. "I agree now," said Luther, "with more articles of Hus than I did at Leipzig." By February, 1520, he was ready to say, "We are all Hussites without knowing it." By that time Eck was in Rome informing the pope that the son of iniquity was also the Saxon Hus.

CHAPTER SEVEN

THE GERMAN HERCULES

IN THE early years of the Reform a cartoon appeared portraying Luther as "the German Hercules." The pope is suspended in derision from his nose. Beneath his hand cowers the inquisitor Hochstraten, and about him sprawl the scholastic theologians. The caption reveals that Luther had become a national figure. Such prominence came to him only after the Leipzig debate. Why the debate should of itself have so contributed to his reputation is puzzling. He had said very little at Leipzig which he had not said before, and the partial endorsement of Hus might rather have brought opprobrium than acclaim. Perhaps the very fact that an insurgent heretic had been allowed to debate at all was what attracted public notice.

A more important factor, however, may have been the dissemination of Luther's writings. John Froben, that hardy printer of Basel, had collected and brought out in a single edition the *Ninety-Five Theses*, the *Resolutions*, the *Answer to Prierias*, the sermon *On Penitence*, and the sermon *On the Eucharist*. In February, 1519, he was able to report to Luther that only ten copies were left, and that no issue from his press had ever been so quickly exhausted. The copies had gone not only to Germany but also to other lands, making of Luther not only a national but also an international figure. Six hundred had been sent to France and to Spain, others to Brabant and England. Zwingli, the reformer of Switzerland, ordered several hundred in

From a cartoon attributed to Holbein and assigned to the year 1522. The pope is suspended from Luther's nose. Jakob von Hochstraten, the inquisitor, is under his hand. Among the vanquished are St. Thomas, Duns Scotus, Robert Holcot, William of Occam, Nicholas of Lyra, Aristotle, and Peter Lombard in the immediate foreground with the title of his Sentences upside down. The devil disguised as a monk is fleeing in the background.

order that a colporteur on horseback might circulate them among the people. Even from Rome came a letter to Luther written by a former fellow student, informing him that disciples at the peril of their lives were spreading his tracts under the shadow of the Vatican. He deserved a statue as the father of his country.

Such acclaim speedily made Luther the head of a movement which has come to be known as the Reformation. As it took on shape, it was bound to come into relation with the two other great movements of the day, the Renaissance and nationalism.

The Renaissance was a many-sided phenomenon in which a central place was occupied by the ideal commonly called Humanism. It was basically an attitude to life, the view that the proper interest of mankind is man, who should bring every area of the earth within his compass, every domain of knowledge within his ken, and every discipline of life within his rational control. War should be reduced to strategy, politics to diplomacy, art to perspective, and business to bookkeeping. The individual should seek to comprise within his grasp all the exploits and all the skills of which man is capable. The *uomo universale*, the universal man, should be courtier, politician, explorer, artist, scientist, financier, and quite possibly divine as well. The literature and languages of classical antiquity were pursued with avidity as a part of the quest for universal knowledge, and because the Hellenic attitude to life had been similar.

This program entailed no overt breach with the Church, since the secularized popes of the Renaissance became its patrons, and because a synthesis between the classical and the Christian had already been achieved by St. Augustine. At the same time a menace to Christianity was implicit in the movement because it was centered on man, because the quest for truth in any quarter might lead to relativity, and because the philosophies of antiquity had no place for the distinctive tenets of Christianity: the Incarnation and the Cross.

Yet only one overt clash occurred between the Humanists and the Church. The issue was over freedom of scholarship, and the scene was Germany. Here a fanatical Jewish convert, Pfefferkorn by name, sought to have all the Hebrew books destroyed. He was resisted by the great German Hebraist, Reuchlin, the great-uncle of Melanchthon. The obscurantists enlisted the aid of the inquisitor Jacob von Hochstraten, who in the cartoon lies beneath Luther's hand, and of Sylvester Prierias as the prosecutor. The upshot was a compromise. Reuchlin was permitted to continue his teaching, though saddled with the costs of the trial. Essentially he had won.

At several points Humanism and the Reformation could form an alliance. Both demanded the right of free investigation. The Humanists included the Bible and the biblical languages in their program of the revival of antiquity, and Luther's battle for the right understanding of Paul appeared to them and to Luther himself as a continuation of the Reuchlin affair. The opponents were the same, Hochstraten and Prierias; and the aim was the same, unimpeded inquiry. The Humanist of Nürnberg, Willibald Pirkheimer, lampooned Eck by portraying him as unable to secure a doctor in the Humanist cities of Augsburg and Nürnberg and under the necessity, therefore, of turning to Leipzig, the scene of his recent "triumph" over Luther. The message was sent by a witch who, to make her goat mount the air, pronounced the magic words *Tartshoh Nerokreffefp*, which in reverse give the names of the principals in the Reuchlin case, Pfefferkor(e)n and Ho(c)hstrat(en).

Luther's exposure of the spuriousness of papal documents appeared to the Humanists as to him to be entirely on a par with Lorenzo Valla's demonstration that the *Donation of Constantine* was a forgery. For different reasons Humanism as well as the Reformation attacked indulgences. What the one called blasphemy the other ridiculed as silly superstition.

The deepest affinity appeared at that point where Renaissance man was not sure of himself, when he began to wonder whether his valor might not be thwarted by the goddess Fortuna or whether his destiny had not already been determined by the stars. Here was Luther's problem of God the capricious and God the adverse. Renaissance man, confronted by this enigma and having no deep religion of his own, was commonly disposed to find solace less in

Luther's stupefying irrationalities than in the venerable authority of the Church.

But reactions were diverse. Many early admirers of Luther, like Pirkheimer, recoiled and made their peace with Rome. Three examples well illustrate the varied courses taken by others: Erasmus passed from discriminating support of Luther to querulous opposition; Melanchthon became the most devoted and the most disconcerting of colleagues; Dürer might have become the artist of the Reformation had not death intervened not too long after his crisis of the spirit.

THE HUMANISTS: ERASMUS

Erasmus was closer to Luther than many another figure of the Renaissance because he was so Christian. The major portion of his literary labors was devoted, not to the classics, but to the New Testament and the Fathers. His ideal, like that of Luther, was to revive the Christian consciousness of Europe through the dissemination of the sacred writings, and to that end Erasmus first made available in print the New Testament in the original Greek. From the press of Froben in 1516 was issued a handsome volume, the Greek type reminiscent of manuscripts, the text accompanied by a literal translation and illumined by annotations. The volume reached Wittenberg as Luther was lecturing on the ninth chapter of Romans, and thereafter became his working tool. From the accompanying translation he learned the inaccuracy of the Vulgate rendering of "do penance" instead of "be penitent." Erasmus throughout his life continued to improve the tools of biblical scholarship. Luther prized his efforts and in his lectures on Galatians in 1519 declared that he would have been happier to have waited for a commentary from the pen of Erasmus. The first letter of Luther to Erasmus was adulatory. The prince of the Humanists was called "Our delight and our hope. Who has not learned from him?" In the years 1517-1519 Luther was so sensible of his affinity with the Humanists as to adopt their fad of Hellenizing vernacular names. He called himself Eleutherius, the free man.

Luther and Erasmus did have much in common. Both insisted that the Church of their day had relapsed into the Judaistic legalism castigated by the apostle Paul. Christianity, said Erasmus, has been made to consist not in loving one's neighbor but in abstaining from butter and cheese during Lent. What are pilgrimages, he demanded, but outward feats, often at the expense of family responsibility? What good are indulgences to those who do not mend their ways? The costly votive offerings which bedeck the tomb of St. Thomas at Canterbury might better be devoted to the charity dear to the saint. Those who never in their lives endeavored to imitate St. Francis desire to die in his cowl. Erasmus scoffed at those who to forfend the fiends trusted to a garment incapable of killing lice.

Both men had a quarrel with the pope, Luther because the pontiffs imperiled the salvation of souls, Erasmus because they fostered external ceremonies and impeded at times free investigation. Erasmus went out of his way to interpolate in new editions of his works passages which could scarcely be interpreted other than as abetting Luther. The *Annotations on the New Testament* in the edition of 1519 introduced this passage:

By how many human regulations has the sacrament of penitence and confession been impeded? The bolt of excommunication is ever in readiness. The sacred authority of the Roman pontiff is so abused by absolutions, dispensations, and the like that the godly cannot see it without a sigh. Aristotle is so in vogue that there is scarcely time in the churches to interpret the gospel.

Again, the edition of the *Ratio Theologiae* in 1520 inserted this interpolation:

There are those who, not content with the observance of confession as a rite of the Church, superimpose the dogma that it was instituted not merely by the apostles but by Christ himself, nor will they suffer one sacrament to be added or subtracted from the number of the seven although they are perfectly willing to commit to one man the power to abolish purgatory. Some assert that the universal body of the Church has been contracted into a single Roman pontiff, who cannot err on faith and morals, thus ascribing to the pope more than he claims for himself, though they do not hesitate to dispute his judgment if he interferes with their purses or their prospects. Is not this to open the door to tyranny in case such power were wielded by an impious and pestilent man? The same may be said of vows, tithes, restitutions, remissions, and confessions by which the simple and superstitious are beguiled.

During the years after the attack on indulgences and before the assault on the sacraments Erasmus and Luther appeared to contemporaries to be preaching so nearly the same gospel that the first apology for Luther issued in the German tongue and composed in 1519 by the Humanist secretary of Nürnberg, Lazarus Spengler, lauded him as the emancipator from rosaries, psalters, pilgrimages, holy water, confession, food and fast laws, the misuse of the ban, and the pomp of indulgences. Erasmus could have said every word of that.

But there were differences; and the most fundamental was that Erasmus was after all a man of the Renaissance, desirous of bringing religion itself within the compass of man's understanding. He sought to do so, not like the scholastics by rearing an imposing edifice of rationally integrated theology, but rather by relegating to the judgment day the discussion of difficult points and couching Christian teaching in terms simple enough to be understood by the Aztecs, for whom his devotional tracts were translated. His patron saint was ever the penitent thief because he was saved with so little theology.

For another reason also Erasmus was diffident of unreserved support to Luther. Erasmus was nostalgic for the vanishing unities of Europe. His dream was that Christian Humanism might serve as a check upon nationalism. In dedicating his commentary on the four Gospels to four sovereigns of the new national states—Henry of England, Francis of France, Charles of Spain, and Ferdinand of Austria—he voiced the hope that as their names were linked with the evangelists, so might their hearts be welded by the evangel. The threat of division and war implicit in the Reformation frightened him.

Most decisive of all was his own inner need. That simple philosophy of Christ which he so vaunted did not allay ultimate doubts, and that very program of scholarship which he trusted to redeem the world was not immune to wistful scoffing. Why inflict upon oneself pallor, invalidism, sore eyes, and premature age in the making of books when perchance wisdom lies with babes? He who could so query the utility of his life's endeavor needed anchorage—if not with Luther, then with Rome.

Such a man simply could not give Luther unqualified endorsement without a violation of his own integrity. Erasmus chose his course with circumspection and held to it with more tenacity and courage than are usually credited to him. He would defend the man rather than the opinions. If he endorsed an idea, it would be as an idea and not as Luther's. He would champion the right of the man to speak and to be heard. Erasmus pretended even not to know what Luther was saying. There had been no time, he affirmed, to read Luther's books, save perhaps a few lines of the Latin works, and of the German nothing at all, through ignorance of the language—though two letters of Erasmus to Frederick the Wise in German are extant. After such disclaimers he would then over and over again betray acquaintance even with the German works. But his point was sound enough. He was confining the defense to questions of civil and religious liberty. Luther was a man of irreproachable life. He was ready to submit to correction. He had asked for impartial judges. He should be accorded a hearing, and a real hearing, to determine whether his interpretation of Scripture was sound. The battle was for freedom of investigation. Even if Luther was mistaken, he should be corrected fraternally and not by bolts from Rome. Erasmus was by conviction a neutral in an age intolerant of neutrality.

MELANCHTHON AND DÜRER

Others among the Humanists went over to Luther unreservedly, among them Melanchthon, who as a Humanist scholar had been convinced that Luther correctly interpreted the apostle Paul. Melanchthon therefore became the colleague and the ally. Yet he continued to occupy a position at once so mediating and so ambiguous as to provoke questioning to this day whether he was the defender or the perverter of Luther's gospel. The fact that to the end Melanchthon preserved the unbroken friendship of Erasmus would not of itself be particularly significant were it not that he was ever ready to place upon Luther's teaching an alien nuance. After Luther's death Melanchthon translated the Augsburg Confession into Greek for the patriarch at Constantinople and in so doing actually transmuted Luther's teaching of justification by faith into the Greek concept of the deification of man through sacramental union with the incorruptible Christ. Humanism was a dubious ally.

One wonders whether Luther was not better understood by that German Humanist who in his early years was the typical Renaissance figure. The artist Albrecht Dürer was a fine example of the *uomo universale*, experimenting with all techniques and seeking to comprehend all mysteries in esoteric symbolism; given sometimes to a touch of levity, as in the "Madonna of the Parrot"; subject also to profound disquiet over the futility of all human endeavor. Those exuberant horsemen of the Renaissance reined up before the chasms of destiny. Their plight is poignantly displayed in Dürer's *Melancolia*. There sits a winged woman of high intelligence in torpid idleness amid all the tools and symbols of man's highest skills. Unused about her lie the compass of the draftsman, the scales of the chemist, the plane of the carpenter, the inkwell of the author; unused at her belt the keys of power, the purse of wealth; unused beside her the ladder of construction. The perfect sphere and the chiseled rhomboid inspire no new endeavor. Above her head the sands in the hourglass sink, and the magic square no matter how computed yields no larger sum. The bell above is ready to toll. Yet in sable gloom she broods, because the issues of destiny strive in the celestial sphere. In the sky the rainbow arches, sign of the covenant sworn by God to Noah, never to bring again the waters upon the earth; but within the rainbow glimmers a comet, portent of impending disaster. Beside Melancolia, perched upon a millstone, sits a scribbling cherub alone active because insouciant of the forces at play. Is the point again, as with Erasmus, that wisdom lies with the simplicity of childhood, and man might better lay aside his skills until the gods have decided the issues of the day?

What a parallel have we here in quite other terms to Luther's agonizing quest for the ultimate meaning of life! His language was different; his symbols were different; but the Renaissance could encompass a shift of symbols. When Dürer heard that man is saved by faith, he comprehended that the comet had been drawn into the rainbow, and desired with God's help to see Martin Luther and to engrave his portrait "as a lasting memorial of the Christian man who has helped me out of great anxiety." Thereafter Dürer's art abandoned the secular for the evangelical. From "scintillating splendor" he passed to a "forbidding yet strangely impassioned austerity."

THE NATIONALISTS: HUTTEN AND SICKINGEN

The second great movement to relate itself to the Reformation was German nationalism. The movement was itself inchoate in Luther's day because Germany was retarded in national unification as compared with Spain, France, and England. Germany had no centralized government. The Holy Roman Empire no more than approximated a German national state because it was at once too large, since any European prince was eligible to the highest office, and too small,

LUTHER AND HUTTEN AS COMPANIONS IN ARMS

because actually the Hapsburg dynasty was dominant. Germany was segmented into small and overlapping jurisdictions of princes and bishops. The free cities twinkled in the murky way of entangling alliances. The knights were a restive class seeking to arrest the waning of their power, and the peasants were likewise restive because desirous of a political role commensurate with their economic importance. No government, and no class, was able to weld Germany into one. Dismembered and retarded, she was derided by the Italians and treated by the papacy as a private cow. Resentment against Rome was more intense than in countries where national governments curbed papal exploitation.

HUTTEN AND LUTHER BOWLING
AGAINST THE POPE

The representatives of German nationalism who for several years in some measure affected Luther's career were Ulrich von Hutten and Franz von Sickingen. Hutten was himself both a knight and a Humanist, fond of parading both in armor and laurel. He illustrates again the diversities of Humanism, which could be international in Erasmus and national in him. Hutten did much to create the concept of German nationalism and to construct the picture of the ideal German, who should repel the enemies of the fatherland and erect a culture able to vie with the Italian.

The first enemy to be repulsed was the Church, responsible so often for the division and the mulcting of Germany. Hutten wielded the pen of the Humanist to blast the *curia* with the most virulent invective. In a tract called *The Roman Trinity* he catalogued in a crescendo of triplets all the sins of Rome: "Three things are sold in Rome: Christ, the priesthood, and women. Three things are hateful to Rome: a general council, the reformation of the church, and the opening of German eyes. Three ills I pray for Rome: pestilence, famine, and war. This be my trinity."

The man who wrote this did not at first applaud Luther. In the opening stages of the skirmish with Eck, Hutten looked on the controversy as a squabble of monks and rejoiced that they would devour each other, but after the Leipzig debate he perceived that Luther's words had the ring of his own. Luther, too, resented the fleecing of Germany, Italian chicanery and superciliousness. Luther wished that St. Peter's might lie in ashes rather than that Germany should be despoiled. Hutten's picture of the romantic German could be

THE EBERNBURG

enriched by Luther's concept of a mystical depth in the German soul exceeding that of other peoples. In 1516 Luther had discovered an anonymous manuscript emanating from the Friends of God and had published it under the title of *A German Theology*, declaring in the preface that he had learned from it more than from any writing save the Bible and the works of St. Augustine. These words imply no narrow nationalism, for St. Augustine was a Latin, but certainly Luther meant that the Germans should be rated above those by whom they were despised. The similarity between Hutten and Luther became all the more marked when Hutten grew evangelical and shifted his idiom from Athens to Galilee.

The practical question for Hutten was how to implement his program for the emancipation of Germany. He looked first to Emperor Maximilian to curb the Church and consolidate the nation, but Maximilian died. Next Hutten hoped that Albert of Mainz, as the primate of Germany, might be induced to head a genuinely national church, but Albert owed too much to Rome.

One class alone in Germany responded to Hutten's pleas, and that was his own, the knights. Among them the most outstanding figure was Franz von Sickingen, who did so much to effect the imperial election by throwing his troops around Frankfurt. Sickingen was trying to obviate the extinction of his class by giving to Germany a system of justice after the manner of Robin Hood. He announced himself as the vindicator of the oppressed, and since his troops lived off the land, he was always seeking more oppressed to vindicate. Hutten saw a chance to enlist him for the vindication alike of Germany and Luther. During the warless winter Hutten established himself at Sickingen's castle called the Ebernburg, and there the poet laureate of Germany read to the illiterate swordsman from the German works of the Wittenberg prophet. Sickingen's foot and fist stamped assent, as he resolved to champion the poor and the sufferers for the gospel. Popular pamphlets began to picture him as the vindicator of the peasants and of Martin Luther. In one of these manifestoes a peasant, having paid half of his fine to the Church, cannot produce the remainder. Sickingen advises him that he should not have paid the first half and cites the word of Christ to the disciples to take neither scrip nor purse. The peasant inquires where these words are to be found, and Sickingen replies, "In Matthew 10, also in Mark 6, and Luke 9 and 10."

"Sir Knight," exclaims the astonished peasant, "how did you learn so much Scripture?"

Sickingen answers that he learned from Luther's books as read to him by Hutten at the Ebernburg.

The picture of Sickingen as the vindicator of the oppressed was not altogether fantastic. He did permit himself to be enlisted by Hutten to embark on a minor crusade for Humanism and the Reform. Reuchlin was thereby relieved of his fine, and fugitives for the gospel were harbored at the Ebernburg. Among them was that young Dominican, Martin Bucer, who had been so enthusiastic about Luther at the Heidelberg conference and now, having abandoned his own cowl, had fled to the gentlemen of the greenwood tree. Luther was made to know that he, too, would be welcome. What he replied we do not know, but we can infer his answer from the response to a similar overture on the part of a knight who informed him that, should the elector fail, one hundred knights could be mustered for his protection, so long as he was not confuted by irreproachable judges. To such offers Luther was noncommittal. "I do not despise them," he confided to Spalatin, "but I will not make use of them unless Christ, my protector, be willing, who has perhaps inspired the knight."

But Luther was ready to utilize the letters he had received for diplomatic purposes, and instructed Spalatin if it was not improper to show them to Cardinal Riario. Let the *curia* know that if by their fulminations he was expelled from Saxony, he would not go to Bohemia but would find an asylum in Germany itself, where he might be more obnoxious than when under the surveillance of the prince and fully occupied with the duties of teaching. The mood of the letter was truculent. "For me the die is cast," he said. "I despise alike Roman fury and Roman favor. I will not be reconciled nor communicate with them. They damn and burn my books. Unless

I am unable to get hold of a fire, I will publicly burn the whole canon law."

In August, 1520, Luther intimated that because he had been delivered by these knights from the fear of men he would attack the papacy as Antichrist. But he had already done that; and while the assurance of protection undoubtedly heartened and emboldened him, the source of his courage was not to be found in a sense of immunity. One of his friends was fearful that Luther might retreat before the impending danger. He answered:

You ask how I am getting on. I do not know. Satan was never so furious against me. I can say this, that I have never sought goods, honor, and glory, and I am not cast down by the hostility of the masses. In fact, the more they rage the more I am filled with the spirit. But, and this may surprise you, I am scarcely able to resist the smallest wave of inner despair, and that is why the least tremor of this kind expels the greatest of the other sort. You need not fear that I shall desert the standards.

The most intrepid revolutionary is the one who has a fear greater than anything his opponents can inflict upon him. Luther, who had so trembled before the face of God, had no fear before the face of man.

As the issue became more plainly drawn, it was clear that he would have no violence either for himself or for the gospel. To Spalatin he wrote in January, 1521:

You see what Hutten asks. I am not willing to fight for the gospel with bloodshed. In this sense I have written to him. The world is conquered by the Word, and by the Word the Church is served and rebuilt. As Antichrist arose without the hand of man, so without the hand of man will he fall.

CHAPTER EIGHT

THE WILD BOAR
IN THE VINEYARD

ECAUSE Luther relied at long last on the arm of the Lord outstretched from heaven, he was not for that reason remiss in doing what might be done on earth. The delay of a year and a half in his trial gave him an opportunity to elaborate his views and to declare his findings. His theology, as we have seen, was already mature before the breach with Rome as to the essential nature of God and Christ and as to the way of salvation. On these points Luther had been brought to see that he was in some respects at variance with the Church. But he had not as yet thought through the practical implications of his theology for the theory of the Church, her rites, her composition, and her relation to society. Neither had he addressed himself to the problems of moral conduct. The interlude during which he was unmolested, from the conference with Cajetan in October of 1518 to the arrival of the papal bull in October of 1520, provided the opportunity. Luther availed himself feverishly of the respite, not knowing of course how long it would last. During the summer of 1520 he delivered to the printer a sheaf of tracts which are still often referred to as his primary works: *The Sermon on Good Works* in May, *The Papacy at Rome* in June, and *The Address to the German Nobility* in August, *The Babylonian Captivity* in September, and *The Freedom of the Christian Man* in November.

The latter three pertain more immediately to the controversy and will alone engage us for the moment.

The most radical of them all in the eyes of contemporaries was the one dealing with the sacraments, entitled *The Babylonian Captivity*, with reference to the enslavement of the sacraments by the Church. This assault on Catholic teaching was more devastating than anything that had preceded; and when Erasmus read the tract, he ejaculated, "The breach is irreparable." The reason was that the pretensions of the Roman Catholic Church rest so completely upon the sacraments as the exclusive channels of grace and upon the prerogatives of the clergy, by whom the sacraments are exclusively administered. If sacramentalism is undercut, then sacerdotalism is bound to fall. Luther practically reduced the number of the sacraments from seven to two. Confirmation, marriage, ordination, penance, and extreme unction were eliminated. The Lord's Supper and baptism alone remained. The principle which dictated this reduction was that a sacrament must have been directly instituted by Christ and must be distinctively Christian.

The removal of confirmation and extreme unction was not of tremendous import save that it diminished the control of the Church over youth and death. The elimination of penance was much more serious because this is the rite of the forgiveness of sins. Luther in this instance did not abolish it utterly. Of the three ingredients of penance he recognized of course the need for contrition and looked upon confession as useful, provided it was not institutionalized. The drastic point was with regard to absolution, which he said is only a declaration by man of what God has decreed in heaven and not a ratification by God of what man has ruled on earth.

The repudiation of ordination as a sacrament demolished the caste system of clericalism and provided a sound basis for the priesthood of all believers, since according to Luther ordination is simply a rite of the Church by which a minister is installed to discharge a particular office. He receives no indelible character, is not exempt from the jurisdiction of the civil courts, and is not empowered by ordination to perform the other sacraments. At this point what the priest does any

Christian may do, if commissioned by the congregation, because all Christians are priests. The fabrication of ordination as a sacrament

was designed to engender implacable discord whereby the clergy and the laity should be separated farther than heaven and earth, to the incredible injury of baptismal grace and to the confusion of evangelical fellowship. This is the source of that detestable tyranny over the laity by the clergy who, relying on the external anointing of their hands, the tonsure and the vestments, not only exalt themselves above lay Christians, anointed by the Holy Spirit, but even regard them as dogs, unworthy to be included with them in the Church. . . . Here Christian brotherhood has expired and shepherds have become wolves. All of us who have been baptized are priests without distinction, but those whom we call priests are ministers, chosen from among us that they should do all things in our name and their priesthood is nothing but a ministry. The sacrament of ordination, therefore, can be nothing other than a certain rite of choosing a preacher in the Church.

But Luther's rejection of the five sacraments might even have been tolerated had it not been for the radical transformation which he effected in the two which he retained. From his view of baptism he was to infer a repudiation of monasticism on the ground that it is not a second baptism, and no vow should ever be taken beyond the baptismal vow.

Most serious of all was Luther's reduction of the mass to the Lord's Supper. The mass is central for the entire Roman Catholic system because the mass is believed to be a repetition of the Incarnation and the Crucifixion. When the bread and wine are transubstantiated, God again becomes flesh and Christ again dies upon the altar. This wonder can be performed only by priests empowered through ordination. Inasmuch as this means of grace is administered exclusively by their hands, they occupy a unique place within the Church; and because the Church is the custodian of the body of Christ, she occupies a unique place in society.

Luther did not attack the mass in order to undermine the priests. His concerns were always primarily religious and only incidentally ecclesiastical or sociological. His first insistence was that the sacrament of the mass must be not magical but mystical, not the performance of a rite but the experience of a presence. This point was one of several discussed with Cajetan at the interview. The cardinal complained of Luther's view that the efficacy of the sacrament depends upon the faith of the recipient. The teaching of the Church is that the sacraments cannot be impaired by any human weakness, be it the unworthiness of the performer or the indifference of the receiver. The sacrament operates by virtue of a power within itself *ex opere operato*. In Luther's eyes such a view made the sacrament mechanical and magical. He, too, had no mind to subject it to human frailty and would not concede that he had done so by positing the necessity of faith, since faith is itself a gift of God, but this faith is given by God when, where, and to whom he will and even without the sacrament is efficacious; whereas the reverse is not true, that the sacrament is of efficacy without faith. "I may be wrong on indulgences," declared Luther, "but as to the need for faith in the sacraments I will die before I will recant." This insistence upon faith diminished the role of the priest who may place a wafer in the mouth but cannot engender faith in the heart.

The second point made by Luther was that the priest is not in a position to do that which the Church claims in the celebration of the mass. He does not "make God," and he does not "sacrifice Christ." The simplest way of negating this view would have been to say that God is not present and Christ is not sacrificed, but Luther was ready to affirm only the latter. Christ is not sacrificed because his sacrifice was made once and for all upon the cross, but God is present in the elements because Christ, being God, declared, "This is my body." The repetition of these words by the priest, however, does not transform the bread and wine into the body and blood of God, as the Catholic Church holds. The view called transubstantiation was that the elements retain their accidents of shape, taste, color, and so on, but lose their substance, for which is substituted the substance of God. Luther rejected this position less on rational than on biblical grounds. Both Erasmus and Melanchthon before him had pointed out that the concept of substance is not biblical but a scholastic sophistication.

For that reason Luther was averse to its use at all, and his own view should not be called consubstantiation. The sacrament for him was not a chunk of God fallen like a meteorite from heaven. God does not need to fall from heaven because he is everywhere present throughout his creation as a sustaining and animating force, and Christ as God is likewise universal, but his presence is hid from human eyes. For that reason God has chosen to declare himself unto mankind at three loci of revelation. The first is Christ, in whom the Word was made flesh. The second is Scripture, where the Word uttered is recorded. The third is the sacrament, in which the Word is manifest in food and drink. The sacrament does not conjure up God as the witch of Endor but reveals him where he is.

To the degree that the powers of the priest were diminished, his prerogatives also were curtailed. In Catholic practice one of the distinctions between the clergy and the laity is that only the priest drinks the wine at the mass. The restriction arose out of the fear that the laity in clumsiness might spill some of the blood of God. Luther felt no less reverence for the sacrament, but he would not safeguard it at the expense of a caste system within the Church. Despite the risk, the cup should be given to all believers. This pronouncement in his day had an uncommon ring of radicalism because the chalice for the laity was the cry of the Bohemian Hussites. They justified their practice on the ground that Christ said, "Drink ye all of it." Catholic interpreters explain these words as addressed only to the apostles, who were all priests. Luther agreed, but retorted that all believers are priests.

THE SACRAMENTS AND THE THEORY OF THE CHURCH

Such a view was fraught with far-reaching consequences for the theory of the Church, and Luther's own view of the Church was derivative from his theory of the sacraments. His deductions, however, were not clear-cut in this area, because his view of the Lord's Supper pointed in one direction and his view of baptism in another. That is why he could be at once to a degree the father of the congregationalism of the Anabaptists and of the territorial church of the later Lutherans.

His view of the Lord's Supper made for the gathered church of convinced believers only, because he declared that the sacrament depends for its efficacy upon the faith of the recipient. That must of necessity make it highly individual because faith is individual. Every soul, insisted Luther, stands in naked confrontation before its Maker. No one can die in the place of another; everyone must wrestle with the pangs of death for himself alone. "Then I shall not be with you, nor you with me. Everyone must answer for himself." Similarly, "The mass is a divine promise which can help no one, be applied for no one, intercede for no one, and be communicated to none save him only who believes with a faith of his own. Who can accept or apply for another the promise of God which requires faith of each individually?"

Here we are introduced to the very core of Luther's individualism. It is not the individualism of the Renaissance, seeking the fulfillment of the individual's capacities; it is not the individualism of the late scholastics, who on metaphysical grounds declared that reality consists only of individuals, and that aggregates like Church and state are not entities but simply the sum of their components. Luther was not concerned to philosophize about the structure of Church and state; his insistence was simply that every man must answer for himself to God. That was the extent of his individualism. The faith requisite for the sacrament must be one's own. From such a theory the obvious inference is that the Church should consist only of those possessed of a warm personal faith; and since the number of such persons is never large, the Church would have to be a comparatively small conventicle. Luther not infrequently spoke precisely as if this were his meaning. Especially in his earlier lectures he had delineated a view of the Church as a remnant because the elect are few. This must be so, he held, because the Word of God goes counter to all the desires of the natural man, abasing pride, crushing arrogance, and leaving all human pretensions in dust and ashes. Such a work is unpalatable, and few will receive it. Those who do will be stones rejected by the builders. Derision and persecution will be their lot. Every Abel is bound to have his Cain, and every Christ his Caiaphas. Therefore the true Church will be despised and rejected of men and will lie hidden in the midst of the world. These words of Luther might readily issue in the substitution for the Catholic monastery of the segregated Protestant community.

But Luther was not willing to take this road because the sacrament of baptism pointed for him in another direction. He could readily enough have accommodated baptism to the preceding view, had he been willing, like the Anabaptists, to regard baptism as the outward sign of an inner experience of regeneration appropriate only to adults and not to infants. But this he would not do. Luther stood with the Catholic Church on the score of infant baptism because children must be snatched at birth from the power of Satan. But what then becomes of his formula that the efficacy of the sacrament depends upon the faith of the recipient? He strove hard to retain it by the figment of an implicit faith in the baby comparable to the faith of a man in sleep. But again Luther would shift from the faith of the child to the faith of the sponsor by which the infant is undergirded. Birth for him was not so isolated as death. One cannot die for another, but one can in a sense be initiated for another into a Christian community. For that reason baptism rather than the Lord's Supper is the sacrament which links the Church to society. It is the sociological sacrament. For the medieval community every child outside the ghetto was by birth a citizen and by baptism a Christian. Regardless of personal conviction the same persons constituted the state and the Church. An alliance of the two institutions was thus natural. Here was a basis for a Christian society. The greatness and the tragedy of Luther was that he could never relinquish either the individualism of the eucharistic cup or the corporateness of the baptismal font. He would have been a troubled spirit in a tranquil age.

PROSECUTION RESUMED

But his age was not tranquil. Rome had not forgotten him. The lifting of the pressure was merely opportunist; and as the time approached when the Most Catholic Emperor would come from Spain to Germany, the papacy was prepared to resume the prosecution. Even before the publication of the assault on the sacraments, which in the eyes of Erasmus made the breach irreparable, Luther had said quite enough to warrant drastic action. The assertions of the indulgence controversy had been augmented by the more devastating attack upon the divine origin and rule of the papacy at the Leipzig debate. His offense was so glaring that a member of the *curia* deprecated waiting until the arrival of the emperor. Then came Eck to Rome, armed not only with the notes on Leipzig but also with condemnations of Luther's teaching by the universities of Cologne and Louvain. When Erfurt had declined and Paris had failed to report on the disputation between Luther and Eck, these two other universities stepped unsolicited into the breach. The judgment of Cologne, dominated by the Dominicans, was more severe. Louvain was slightly tinctured with Erasmianism. Both were agreed in condemning Luther's views on human depravity, penance, purgatory, and indulgences. Louvain was silent with regard to the attack on the papacy, whereas Cologne complained of heretical notions as to the primacy and derogation from the power of the keys.

Luther retorted that neither cited against him any proof from the Scripture.

Why do we not abolish the gospel and turn instead to them? Strange that handworkers give sounder judgments than theologians! How seriously should one take those who condemned Reuchlin? If they burn my books, I will repeat what I have said. In this I am so bold that for it I will suffer death. When Christ was filled with scorn against the Pharisees and Paul was outraged by the blindness of the Athenians, what, I beg you, shall I do?

Nothing further of the prosecution is on record until March, when the attempt was resumed to suppress Luther quietly through the Augustinian order. The general wrote to Staupitz:

The order, never previously suspected of heresy, is becoming odious. We beg you in the bonds of love to do your utmost to restrain Luther from speaking against the Holy Roman Church and her indulgences. Urge him to stop writing. Let him save our order from infamy.

Staupitz extricated himself by resigning as vicar.

Another approach was made through Frederick the Wise. Cardinal Riario, lately pardoned for his complicity in an attempt on the life of the pope, wrote to Frederick:

Most illustrious noble lord and brother, when I recall the splendor of your house and the devotion ever displayed by your progenitors and yourself toward the Holy See, I think it the part of friendship to write to you concerning the common good of Christendom and the everlasting honor of yourself. I am sure you are not ignorant of the rancor, contempt, and license with which Martin Luther rails against the Roman pontiff and the whole *curia*. Wherefore I exhort you, bring this man to reject his error. You can if you will; with just one little pebble the puny David killed the mighty Goliath.

Frederick replied that the case had been referred to his most dear friend, the Archbishop of Trier, Elector of the Holy Roman Empire, Richard of Greiffenklau.

In May dallying ended. Four meetings of the consistory were held, on May 21, 23, 26, and June 1. The pope on the evening of the twenty-second retired to his hunting lodge at Magliana, *a soliti piaceri*. The cardinals, the canonists, and the theologians carried on. There may have been some forty in attendance. Eck was the only German. The three great monastic orders were represented, the Dominicans, the Franciscans, and the Augustinians. No longer could one speak of a monk's squabble. Luther's own general was there, not to mention his old opponents Prierias and Cajetan. Three questions were to be settled: what to do with Luther's opinions, what to do with his books, and what to do with his person. Lively differences of opinion ensued. Some in the first session questioned the expediency of issuing a bull at all in view of the exacerbated state of Germany. The theologians were for condemning Luther outright. The canonists contended that he should be given a hearing like Adam, for even though God knew him to be guilty he gave him an opportunity to defend himself when he said, "Where art thou?" A compromise was reached whereby Luther was not to have a hearing but should be given sixty days in which to make his submission.

With regard to his teaching there were debates, though by whom and about what can only be surmised. Reports at second or third hand suggest the differences within the consistory. The Italian Cardinal Accolti is said to have called Tetzel a "*porcaccio*" and to have given Prierias a *rabbuffo* for composing in three days a reply to Luther which might better have taken three months. Cajetan is reported to have sniffed on Eck's arrival in Rome, "Who let in that beast?" Spanish Cardinal Carvajal, a conciliarist, is said to have opposed vehemently the action against Luther. In the end unanimity was attained for the condemnation of forty-one articles. The previous strictures of Louvain and Cologne were combined and amplified.

THE BULL "EXSURGE"

Anyone acquainted with Luther's mature position will feel that the bull was exceedingly sparse in its reproof. Luther's views on the mass were condemned only at the point of the cup to the laity. No other of the seven sacraments received notice, save penance. There was nothing about monastic vows, only a disavowal of Luther's desire that princes and prelates might suppress the sacks of the mendicants. There was nothing about the priesthood of all believers. The articles centered on Luther's disparagement of human capacity even after baptism, on his derogation from the power of the pope to bind and loose penalties and sins, from the power of the pope and councils to declare doctrine, from the primacy of the pope and of the Roman Church. At one point the condemnation of Luther conflicted with the recent pronouncement of the pope on indulgences. Luther was reproved for reserving the remission of penalties imposed by divine justice to God alone, whereas the pope himself had just declared that in such cases the treasury of merits could be applied only by way of intercession, not of jurisdiction. The charge of Bohemianism against Luther had plainly lodged, because he was condemned on the score of introducing certain of the articles of John Hus. Two characteristical-

THE BULL AGAINST LUTHER

ly Erasmian tenets received strictures, that to burn heretics is against the will of the Spirit and that war against the Turks is resistance to God's visitation. The forty-one articles were not pronounced uniformly heretical but were condemned as "heretical, or scandalous, or false, or offensive to pious ears, or seductive of simple minds, or repugnant to Catholic truth, respectively." Some suspected at the time that this formula was adopted because the consistory was not able to make up its mind which were which, and therefore, like the triumvirs, proscribed the enemies of each though they might be friends of the rest. One may doubt, however, whether this was the case, because the formula was stereotyped and had been used in the condemnation of John Hus.

The completed bull was presented to the pope for a preface and conclusion. In keeping with the surroundings of his hunting lodge at Magliana he commenced:

Arise, O Lord, and judge thy cause. A wild boar has invaded thy vineyard. Arise, O Peter, and consider the case of the Holy Roman Church, the mother of all churches, consecrated by thy blood. Arise, O Paul, who by thy teaching and death hast and dost illumine the Church. Arise, all ye saints, and the whole universal Church, whose interpretation of Scripture has been assailed. We can scarcely express our grief over the ancient heresies which have been revived in Germany. We are the more downcast because she was always in the forefront of the war on heresy. Our pastoral office can no longer tolerate the pestiferous virus of the following forty-one errors. [They are enumerated.] We can no longer suffer the serpent to creep through the field of the Lord. The books of Martin Luther which contain these errors are to be examined and burned. As for Martin himself, good God, what office of paternal love have we omitted in order to recall him from his errors? Have we not offered him a safe conduct and money for the journey? [Such an offer never reached Luther.] And he has had the temerity to appeal to a future council although our predecessors, Pius II and Julius II, subjected such appeals to the penalties of heresy. Now therefore we give Martin sixty days in which to submit, dating from the time of the publication of this bull in his district. Anyone who presumes to infringe our excommunication and anathema will stand under the wrath of Almighty God and of the apostles Peter and Paul.

Dated on the 15th day of June, 1520.

This bull is known by its opening words, which are *Exsurge Domine*. A few weeks later the pope wrote to Frederick the Wise:

Beloved son, we rejoice that you have never shown any favor to that son of iniquity, Martin Luther. We do not know whether to credit this the more to your sagacity or to your piety. This Luther favors the Bohemians and the Turks, deplores the punishment of heretics, spurns the writings of the holy doctors, the decrees of the ecumenical councils, and the ordinances of the Roman pontiffs, and gives credence to the opinions of none save himself alone, which no heretic before ever presumed to do. We cannot suffer the scabby sheep longer to infect the flock. Wherefore we have summoned a conclave of venerable brethren. The Holy Spirit also was present, for in such cases he is never absent from our Holy See. We have composed a bull, sealed with lead, in which out of the innumerable errors of this man we have selected those in which he perverts the faith, seduces the simple, and relaxes the bonds of obedience, continence, and humility. The abuses which he has vaunted against our Holy See we leave to God. We exhort you to induce him to return to sanity and receive our clemency. If he persists in his madness, take him captive.

Given under the seal of the Fisherman's ring on the 8th of July, 1520, and in the eighth year of our pontificate.

THE BULL SEEKS LUTHER

The papal bull took three months to find Luther, but there were early rumors that it was on the way. Hutten wrote to him on June 4, 1520:

You are said to be under excommunication. If it be true, how mighty you are! In you the words of the psalm are fulfilled, "They have condemned innocent blood, but the Lord our God will render to them their iniquity and destroy them in their malice." This is our hope; be this our faith. There are plots against me also. If they use force, they will be met with force. I wish they would condemn me. Stand firm. Do not waver. But why should I admonish you? I will stand by, whatever come. Let us vindicate the common liberty. Let us liberate the oppressed fatherland. God will be on our side; and if God is with us, who can be against us?

This was the time when renewed offers came from Sickingen and from a hundred knights besides. Luther was not unmoved, yet he

148

scarcely knew whether to rely on the arm of man or solely on the Lord. During that summer of 1520, when the papal bull was seeking him throughout Germany, his mood fluctuated between the incendiary and the apocalyptic. In one unguarded outburst he incited to violence. A new attack by Prierias lashed Luther to rage. In a printed reply he declared:

It seems to me that if the Romanists are so mad the only remedy remaining is for the emperor, the kings, and princes to gird themselves with force of arms to attack these pests of all the world and fight them, not with words, but with steel. If we punish thieves with the yoke, highwaymen with the sword, and heretics with fire, why do we not rather assault these monsters of perdition, these cardinals, these popes, and the whole swarm of the Roman Sodom, who corrupt youth and the Church of God? Why do we not rather assault them with arms and wash our hands in their blood?

Luther explained afterwards that he really did not mean what the words imply.

I wrote "*If* we burn heretics, why do we not rather attack the pope and his followers with the sword and wash our hands in their blood?" Since I do not approve of burning heretics nor of killing any Christian—this I well know does not accord with the gospel—I have shown what they deserve *if* heretics deserve fire. There is no need to attack you with the sword.

Despite this disclaimer Luther was never suffered to forget his incendiary blast. It was quoted against him in the Edict of the Diet of Worms.

The disavowal was genuine. His prevailing mood was expressed in a letter of October to a minister who was prompted to leave his post. Luther wrote:

Our warfare is not with flesh and blood, but against spiritual wickedness in the heavenly places, against the world rulers of this darkness. Let us then stand firm and heed the trumpet of the Lord. Satan is fighting, not against us, but against Christ in us. We fight the battles of the Lord. Be strong therefore. If God is for us, who can be against us?

You are dismayed because Eck is publishing a most severe bull against Luther, his books, and his followers. Whatever may happen, I am not moved, because nothing can happen save in accord with the will of him who sits upon the heaven directing all. Let not your hearts be troubled. Your Father knows your need before you ask him. Not a leaf from a tree falls to the ground without his knowledge. How much less can any of us fall unless it be his will.

If you have the spirit, do not leave your post, lest another receive your crown. It is but a little thing that we should die with the Lord, who in our flesh laid down his life for us. We shall rise with him and abide with him in eternity. See then that you do not despise your holy calling. He will come, he will not tarry, who will deliver us from every ill. Fare well in the Lord Jesus, who comforts and sustains mind and spirit. Amen.

CHAPTER NINE

THE APPEAL TO CAESAR

T ONE point Luther was perfectly clear. Whoever helped or did not help him, he would make his testimony.

"For me the die is cast. I despise alike Roman fury and Roman favor. I will not be reconciled or communicate with them. Let them damn and burn my books. I for my part, unless I cannot find a fire, will publicly damn and burn the whole canon law."

Neither did Luther neglect his defense. He had appealed in vain to the pope and in vain to a council. There was one more recourse, the appeal to the emperor. During the month of August Luther addressed Charles V in these words:

It is not presumptuous that one who through evangelical truth has ascended the throne of Divine Majesty should approach the throne of an earthly prince, nor is it unseemly that an earthly prince, who is the image of the Heavenly, should stoop to raise up the poor from the dust. Consequently, unworthy and poor though I be, I prostrate myself before your Imperial Majesty. I have published books which have alienated many, but I have done so because driven by others, for I would prefer nothing more than to remain in obscurity. For three years I have sought peace in vain. I have now but one recourse. I appeal to Caesar. I have no desire to be defended if I am found to be impious or heretical. One thing I ask, that neither truth nor error be condemned unheard and unrefuted.

Luther asked of Caesar, however, more than that he should hear a man. He was also to vindicate a cause. The Church was desperately in need of reform, and the initiative would have to come, as Hutten contended, from the civil power. A mighty program of reformation was delineated by Luther in the *Address to the German Nobility*. The term "nobility" was broadly used to cover the ruling class in Germany, from the emperor down. But by what right, the modern reader may well inquire, might Luther call upon them to reform the Church? The question has more than an antiquarian interest, because some contend that in this tract Luther broke with his earlier view of the Church as a persecuted remnant and laid instead the basis for a church allied with and subservient to the state. Luther adduced three grounds for his appeal. The first was simply that the magistrate was the magistrate, ordained of God to punish evildoers. All that Luther demanded of the magistrate as magistrate was that he should hale the clergy before the civil courts, protect citizens against ecclesiastical extortion, and vindicate the state in the exercise of civil functions from clerical interference. This was the sense in which Luther often asserted that no one in a thousand years had so championed the civil state as he. The theocratic pretensions of the Church were to be repulsed.

The *Address to the German Nobility*, however, goes far beyond a mere circumscribing of the Church to her proper sphere. Luther was much less concerned for the emancipation of the state than for the purification of the Church. The stripping away of temporal power and inordinate wealth was designed to emancipate the Church from worldly cares that she might better perform her spiritual functions. The basis of the right of the magistrate to undertake this reform is stated in Luther's second reason, namely, "The temporal authorities are baptized with the same baptism as we." This is the language of the Christian society, built upon the sociological sacrament administered to every babe born into the community. In such a society, Church and state are mutually responsible for the support and correction of each other.

In a third passage Luther gave the additional ground, that the magistrates were fellow Christians sharing in the priesthood of all believers,

An den Christlichenn
Adel teutscher Nation:
von des Christlichen
standes besserung:
D. Martinus
Luther.

Durch yhn selbs ge,
mehret vnd corrigirt.

Vuittemberg.

from which some modern historians have inferred that Luther would concede to the magistrate the role of Church reformer only if he were himself a convinced Christian, and then only in an emergency. But no such qualification is stated in this tract. The priesthood of all believers itself was made to rest upon the lower grade of faith implicit in the baptized infant. Luther's whole attitude to the reformatory role of the magistrate is essentially medieval. What sets it off from so many other attempts at the redress of grievances is its deeply religious tone. The complaints of Germany were combined with the reform of the Church, and the civil power itself was directed to rely less on the arm of flesh than upon the hand of the Lord.

The program began with religious premises. Three walls of Rome must tumble down like the walls of Jericho. The first was that the spiritual power is above the temporal. This claim Luther countered with the doctrine of the priesthood of all believers. "We are all alike Christians and have baptism, faith, the Spirit, and all things alike. If a priest is killed, a land is laid under an interdict. Why not in the case of a peasant? Whence comes this great distinction between those who are called Christians?" The second wall was that the pope alone might interpret Scripture. This assertion was met, not so much by the vindication of the rights of Humanist scholarship against papal incompetence, as by the claims of lay Christianity to understand the mind of Christ. "Balaam's ass was wiser than the prophet himself. If God then spoke by an ass against a prophet, why should he not be able even now to speak by a righteous man against the pope?" The third wall was that the pope alone could call a council. Here again the priesthood of all believers gave the right to anyone in an emergency, but peculiarly to the civil power because of its strategic position.

Then follow all the proposals for the reforms to be instituted by a council. The papacy should return to apostolic simplicity, with no more triple crown and no toe kissing. The pope should not receive the sacrament seated, proffered to him by a kneeling cardinal through a golden reed, but should stand up like any other "stinking sinner." The cardinals should be reduced in number. The temporal possessions and claims of the Church should be abandoned that the pope might devote himself only to spiritual concerns. The income of the Church should be curtailed—no more annates, fees, indulgences, golden years, reservations, crusading taxes, and all the rest of the tricks by which the "drunken Germans" were despoiled. Litigation in Church courts involving Germans should be tried in Germany under a German primate. This suggestion looked in the direction of a national church. For Bohemia it was definitely recommended.

The proposals with regard to monasticism and clerical marriage went beyond anything Luther had said previously. The mendicants should be relieved of hearing confession and preaching. The number of orders should be reduced, and there should be no irrevocable vows. The clergy should be permitted to marry because they need housekeepers, and to place man and woman together under such circumstances is like setting straw beside fire and expecting it not to burn.

Miscellaneous recommendations called for the reduction of Church festivals and a curb on pilgrimages. Saints should be left to canonize themselves. The state should inaugurate legal reform and undertake sumptuary legislation. This program was comprehensive and for the most part would evoke hearty applause in Germany.

Underlying it all was a deep indignation against the corruption of the Church. Again and again the pope was shamed by a comparison with Christ. This theme went back through Hus to Wyclif. An illustrated work in Bohemian on the disparity of Christ and the pope was in the library of Frederick the Wise. A similar work was later issued in Wittenberg with annotations by Melanchthon and woodcuts by Cranach. The idea was already present in the *Address to the German Nobility*, where reference was made to Christ on foot, the pope in a palanquin with a retinue of three or four thousand mule drivers; Christ washing the disciples' feet, the pope having his feet kissed; Christ enjoining keeping faith even with an enemy, the pope declaring that no faith is to be kept with him who has no faith, and that promises to heretics are not binding. Still worse, constraint against them is employed. "But heretics should be vanquished with books, not with burnings. O Christ my Lord, look down. Let the day of thy judgment break and destroy the devil's nest at Rome!"

On the left Christ is washing the disciples' feet. On the right Antichrist, the pope, is having his toes kissed by monarchs.

PUBLICATION OF THE BULL

In the meantime the bull *Exsurge Domine* was being executed at Rome. Luther's books were burned in the Piazza Navona. The bull was printed, notarized, and sealed for wider dissemination. The task of its publication in the north was committed to two men who were named papal nuncios and special inquisitors for the purpose. One of them was John Eck. The other, Jerome Aleander, was a distinguished Humanist, master of three languages—Latin, Greek, and Hebrew—a former rector of the University of Paris. He had some acquaintance with German affairs through his youth in the Low Countries. His irregularities in private morals gave no offense in the days of the unreformed papacy. The field was divided between the two men, partly along geographical lines. Eck was to take the east, Franconia and Bavaria. Aleander should cover the Low Countries and the Rhine.

There was a further division of function in that Aleander should address himself to the emperor and his court and to the high magnates, lay and clerical, whereas Eck should go rather to the bishops and the universities. The two men were enjoined to act in perfect accord. Aleander's instructions told him first of all to deliver the bull "To our beloved son Charles, Holy Roman Emperor and Catholic King of Spain." At that moment all parties were looking to Charles. He was young and had not yet declared himself. The pope expected him to follow the example of his grandmother, Isabella the Catholic. The Germans saw in him the heir of his grandfather, Maximilian the German. Aleander was advised in case Luther should demand a hearing before the court of the emperor to reply that the case was being handled solely by Rome. This is the first suggestion that Luther might ask to have his case referred to a secular tribunal. The secretary who composed this memorandum was singularly clairvoyant, because the instructions were drafted prior to Luther's appeal to Caesar. Eck received a secret commission, unknown to Aleander, permitting the inclusion in the condemnation of more names than Luther's, according to discretion.

Neither man relished his assignment, which each undertook at the risk of his life. Eck made his task vastly more difficult by adding names at his indiscretion, six of them: three from Wittenberg, including Carlstadt; and three from Nürnberg, including Spengler and Pirkheimer. He could not have chosen a more inopportune moment to attack the leaders of German Humanism, who were never more united. Aleander likewise in the Netherlands was confronted with many Luther sympathizers. There was Erasmus, who said, "The inclemency of this bull ill comports with the moderation of Leo." And again, "Papal bulls are weighty, but scholars attach more weight to books with good arguments drawn from the testimony of divine Scripture, which does not coerce but instructs." In Antwerp the Marrani, Spaniards and Portuguese of Jewish extraction, were printing Luther in Spanish. German merchants were disseminating his ideas. Albrecht Dürer was executing commissions in Antwerp while looking to Luther and Erasmus to purify the Church. In the Rhine valley there were rumors that

Sickingen might vindicate Luther, as he had done Reuchlin, by force of arms.

Eck met with the most unexpected opposition. Duke George held back on the ground that his locality had not been specifically named. Frederick the Wise was expected to obstruct, but he did so in the most disconcerting way by reporting that he had learned from Aleander that Eck had no authorization to include anyone save Luther. Eck then was forced to produce his secret instructions. On one ground or another the very bishops held back, some of them for six months, before publishing the bull. The University of Vienna declined to act without the bishop, and the University of Wittenberg protested the impropriety of entrusting the publication of the bull to a party in the dispute. "The goat should not be permitted to be a gardener, nor the wolf a shepherd, nor John Eck a papal nuncio." Not only the University of Wittenberg but even the Duke of Bavaria expressed fear that publication of the bull would produce disorder. There was some reason for such concern. At Leipzig, Eck had to hide for his life in a cloister. At Erfurt, when he had the bull reprinted, the students dubbed it a "bulloon" and threw all the copies in the river to see whether they would float. At Torgau it was torn down and besmeared. The only easy successes were with the bishops of Brandenburg, Meissen, and Merseburg, who permitted the publication of the bull on September 21, 25, and 29 respectively. Eck, in honor of this triumph, erected a votive tablet in the church at Ingolstadt: "John Eck, *professor ordinarius* of theology and university chancellor, papal nuncio and apostolic protonotary, having published in accord with the command of Leo X the bull against Lutheran doctrine in Saxony and Meissen, erects this tablet in gratitude that he has returned home alive."

Aleander found his task complicated because the bull leaked to Germany before its publication, and in a form discrepant from his own. He was well received, however, at the imperial court at Antwerp, and His Majesty promised to stake his life on the protection of the Church and the honor of the pope and the Holy See. He was perfectly ready to execute the bull in his hereditary domains, and Aleander was able therefore to institute an auto-da-fé of Lutheran books at Louvain on

October 8. When the fire was started, however, students threw in works of scholastic theology and a medieval handbook for preachers entitled *Sleep Well*. A similar burning took place at Liége on the seventeenth. The mendicants and the conservatives of the university faculty at Louvain were incited to make life intolerable for Erasmus. The Counter Reformation, aided by the imperial arm, was already begun.

FROM TITLE PAGE OF HUTTEN'S PROTEST "AGAINST THE BURNING OF LUTHER'S BOOKS AT MAINZ"

But in the Rhineland it was different. The emperor there ruled only by virtue of his election. When at Cologne on November 12 Aleander tried to have a bonfire, though the archbishop had given his consent, the executioner refused to proceed without an express imperial mandate. The archbishop asserted his authority, and the books were burned. At Mainz the opposition was more violent. The executioner, before applying the torch, turned to the assembled onlookers and inquired whether these books had been legally condemned. When with one voice the throng boomed back "No!" the executioner stepped down and refused to act. Aleander appealed to Albert, the archbishop, and secured from him authorization to destroy a few books on the following day. The order was carried out on the twenty-ninth of November, not by the public executioner, but by a gravedigger, and with no witnesses save a few women who had brought their geese to market. Aleander was pelted with stones, and he declared that except for the intervention of the abbot he would not have come off with his life. His word might be doubted had we no other evidence, for he magnified his danger to enhance his achievements.

But in this instance there is independent corroboration. Ulrich von Hutten came out in verse with an invective both in Latin and in German:

> O God, Luther's books they burn.
> Thy godly truth is slain in turn.
> Pardon in advance is sold,
> And heaven marketed for gold.
> The German people is bled white
> And is not asked to be contrite.
> To Martin Luther wrong is done—
> O God, be thou our champion.
> My goods for him I will not spare,
> My life, my blood for him I dare.

On October 10 the bull reached Luther. The following day he commented to Spalatin:

This bull condemns Christ himself. It summons me not to an audience but to a recantation. I am going to act on the assumption that it is spurious, though I think it is genuine. Would that Charles were a man and would fight for Christ against these Satans. But I am not afraid. God's will be done. I do not know what the prince should do unless to dissemble. I am sending you a copy of the bull that you may see the Roman monster. The faith and the Church are at stake. I rejoice to suffer in so noble a cause. I am not worthy of so holy a trial. I feel much freer now that I am certain the pope is Antichrist. Erasmus writes that the imperial court is overrun with mendicants, and there is no hope from the emperor. I am on the way to Lichtenburg for a conference with Miltitz. Farewell and pray for me.

The game of obstruction had already begun. Frederick the Wise played the instructions of Aleander and the commission of Miltitz against John Eck. Miltitz had never been recalled by the pope and now said frankly that Eck had no business to publish the bull while friendly negotiations were still in progress. Frederick resolved to keep them going, and therefore arranged for a new interview between Luther and Miltitz, and of course the Archbishop of Trier was still in the picture as an arbiter. For that reason Luther impugned the genuineness of the bull on the ground that Rome would not make monkeys of two electors by taking the case out of their hands. "Therefore I will not believe in the authenticity of this bull until I see the original lead and wax, string, signature, and seal with my own eyes."

For a time Luther reckoned with the double possibility that the bull might be either true or false. In that sense he came out with a vehement assault, apparently at the instance of Spalatin, to whom he wrote:

It is hard to dissent from all the pontiffs and princes, but there is no other way to escape hell and the wrath of God. If you had not urged, I would leave everything to God and do no more than I have done. I have put out a reply to the bull in Latin, of which I am sending you a copy. The German version is in the press. When since the beginning of the world did Satan ever so rage against God? I am overcome by the magnitude of the horrible blasphemies of this bull. I am almost persuaded by many and weighty arguments that the last day is at the threshold. The Kingdom of Antichrist begins to fall. I see an insuppressible insurrection coming out of this bull, which the Roman *curia* deserves.

AGAINST THE EXECRABLE BULL OF ANTICHRIST

The reply to which he referred was entitled *Against the Execrable Bull of Antichrist*. Luther wrote:

I have heard that a bull against me has gone through the whole earth before it came to me, because being a daughter of darkness it feared the light of my face. For this reason and also because it condemns manifestly Christian articles I had my doubts whether it really came from Rome and was not rather the progeny of that man of lies, dissimulation, errors, and heresy, that monster John Eck. The suspicion was further increased when it was said that Eck was the apostle of the bull. Indeed the style and the spittle all point to Eck. True, it is not impossible that where Eck is the apostle there one should find the kingdom of Antichrist. Nevertheless in the meantime I will act as if I thought Leo not responsible, not that I may honor the Roman name, but because I do not consider myself worthy to suffer such high things for the truth of God. For who before God would be happier than Luther if he were condemned from so great and high a source for such manifest truth? But the cause seeks a worthier martyr. I with my sins merit other things. But whoever wrote this bull, he is Antichrist. I protest before God, our Lord Jesus, his sacred angels, and the whole world that with my whole heart I dissent from the damnation of this bull, that I curse and execrate it as sacrilege and blasphemy of Christ, God's Son and our Lord. This be my recantation, O bull, thou daughter of bulls.

Having given my testimony I proceed to take up the bull. Peter said that you should give a reason for the faith that is in you, but this bull condemns me from its own word without any proof from Scripture, whereas I back up all my assertions from the Bible. I ask thee, ignorant Antichrist, dost thou think that with thy naked words thou canst prevail against the armor of Scripture? Hast thou learned this from Cologne and Louvain? If this is all it takes, just to say, "I dissent, I deny," what fool, what ass, what mole, what log could not condemn? Does not thy meretricious brow blush that with thine inane smoke thou withstandest the lightning of the divine Word? Why do we not believe the Turks? Why do we not admit the Jews? Why do we not honor the heretics if damning is all that it takes? But Luther, who is used to *bellum*, is not afraid of *bullam*. I can distinguish between inane paper and the omnipotent Word of God.

They show their ignorance and bad conscience by inventing the adverb "respectively." My articles are called "respectively some heretical, some erroneous, some scandalous," which is as much as to say, "We don't know which are which." O meticulous ignorance! I wish to be instructed, not respectively, but absolutely and certainly. I demand that they show absolutely, not respectively, distinctly and not confusedly, certainly and not probably, clearly and not obscurely, point by point and not in a lump, just what is heretical. Let them show where I am a heretic, or dry up their spittle. They say that some articles are heretical, some erroneous, some scandalous, some offensive. The implication is that those which are heretical are not erroneous, those which are erroneous are not scandalous, and those which are scandalous are not offensive. What then is this, to say that something is not heretical, not scandalous, not false, but yet is offensive? So then, you impious and insensate papists, write soberly if you want to write. Whether this bull is by Eck or by the pope, it is the sum of all impiety, blasphemy, ignorance, impudence, hypocrisy, lying— in a word, it is Satan and his Antichrist.

Where are you now, most excellent Charles the Emperor, kings, and Christian princes? You were baptized into the name of Christ, and can you suffer these Tartar voices of Antichrist? Where are you, bishops? Where, doctors? Where are you who confess Christ? Woe to all who live in these times. The wrath of God is coming upon the papists, the enemies of the cross of Christ, that all men should resist them. You then, Leo X, you cardinals and the rest of you at Rome, I tell you to your faces: "If this bull has come out in your name, then I will use the power which has been given me in baptism whereby I became a son of God and co-heir with Christ, established upon the rock against which the gates of hell cannot prevail. I call upon you to renounce your diabolical blasphemy and audacious impiety, and, if you will not, we shall all hold your seat as possessed and oppressed by Satan, the damned seat of Antichrist, in the name of Jesus Christ, whom you persecute." But my zeal carries me away. I am not yet persuaded that the bull is by the pope but rather by that apostle of impiety, John Eck.

Then follows a discussion of the articles. The tract concludes:

If anyone despise my fraternal warning, I am free from his blood in the last judgment. It is better that I should die a thousand times than that I should retract one syllable of the condemned articles. And as they excommunicated me for the sacrilege of heresy, so I excommunicate them in the name of the sacred truth of God. Christ will judge whose excommunication will stand. Amen.

THE FREEDOM OF THE CHRISTIAN MAN

Two weeks after the appearance of this tract another came out so amazingly different as to make one wonder whether it could be by the same man, or if by the same author, how he could pretend to any semblance of sincerity. It was entitled *Freedom of the Christian Man* and commenced with a deferential address to Leo X. This little work was the fruit of the interview with Miltitz, who reverted to his old principle of mediation by asking Luther to address to the pope a disclaimer of personal abusiveness and a statement of faith. Luther could respond in all integrity. He was not fighting a man but a system. Within a fortnight he could blast the papacy as Antichrist and yet address the pope with deference.

Most blessed father, in all the controversies of the past three years I have ever been mindful of you, and although your adulators have driven me to appeal to a council in defiance of the futile decrees of your predecessors, Pius and Julius, I have never suffered myself because of their stupid tyranny to hold your Beatitude in despite. To be sure, I have spoken sharply against impious doctrine, but did not Christ call his adversaries a generation of vipers, blind guides, and hypocrites? And did not Paul refer to his opponents as dogs, concision, and sons of the Devil? Who could have been more biting than the prophets? I contend with no one about his life, but only concerning the Word of Truth. I look upon you less as Leo the Lion than as Daniel in the lions' den of Babylon. You may have three or four learned and excellent cardinals, but what are they among so many? The Roman *curia* deserves not you but Satan himself. What under heaven is more pestilent, hateful, and corrupt? It is more impious than the Turk. But do not think, Father Leo, that when I scathe this seat of pestilence I am inveighing against your person. Beware of the sirens who would make you not simply a man but half a god. You are a servant of servants. Do not listen to those who say that none can be Christians without your authority, who make you the lord of heaven, hell, and purgatory. They err who put you above a council and the universal Church. They err who make you the sole interpreter of Scripture. I am sending you a tract as an auspice of peace, that you may see the sort of thing with which I could and would more fruitfully occupy myself if your adulators would leave me alone.

Then followed Luther's canticle of the freedom of the Christian man. If Luther supposed that this letter and tract would mollify the pope, he was exceedingly naïve. The deferential letter itself denied the primacy of the pope over councils, and the treatise asserted the priesthood of all believers. The pretense that the attack was directed, not against the pope, but against the *curia* is the device commonly employed by constitutionally-minded revolutionaries who do not like to admit to themselves that they are rebelling against the head of a government. The English Puritans similarly for some time claimed that they were not fighting Charles I but only the "Malignants" by whom he was surrounded. As conflicts continue, such fictions soon become too transparent to be useful. Luther was early driven to abandon the distinction, for the bull had been issued in the name of the pope and had never been disclaimed from the Vatican. It demanded recantation. That Luther would never accord. On the twenty-ninth of November he came out with the *Assertion of All the Articles*

Wrongly Condemned in the Roman Bull. The tone may be inferred from the two following:

No. 18. The proposition condemned was that "indulgences are the pious defrauding of the faithful." Luther commented:

I was wrong, I admit it, when I said that indulgences were "the pious defrauding of the faithful." I recant and I say, "Indulgences are the most impious frauds and imposters of the most rascally pontiffs, by which they deceive the souls and destroy the goods of the faithful.

No. 29. The proposition condemned was "that certain articles of John Hus condemned at the Council of Constance are most Christian, true, and evangelical, which the universal Church cannot condemn." Luther commented:

I was wrong. I retract the statement that certain articles of John Hus are evangelical. I say now, "Not some but all the articles of John Hus were condemned by Antichrist and his apostles in the synagogue of Satan." And to your face, most holy Vicar of God, I say freely that all the condemned articles of John Hus are evangelical and Christian, and yours are downright impious and diabolical.

This came out on the day Luther's books were burned at Cologne. There were rumors that the next bonfire would be at Leipzig. The sixty days of grace would soon expire. The count was usually reckoned from the day the citation was actually received. The bull had reached Luther on the tenth of October. On the tenth of December, Melanchthon on Luther's behalf issued an invitation to the faculty and students of the university to assemble at ten o'clock at the Elster gate, where, in reprisal for the burning of Luther's

LUTHER BURNING THE PAPAL BULL

pious and evangelical books, the impious papal constitutions, the canon law, and works of scholastic theology would be given to the flames. Luther himself threw in the papal bull for good measure. The professors went home, but the students sang the *Te Deum* and paraded about the town in a wagon with another bull affixed to a pole, and an indulgence on the point of a sword. The works of Eck and other opponents of Luther were cremated.

Luther publicly justified what he had done.

Since they have burned my books, I burn theirs. The canon law was included because it makes the pope a god on earth. So far I have merely fooled with this business of the pope. All my articles condemned by Antichrist are Christian. Seldom has the pope overcome anyone with Scripture and with reason.

Frederick the Wise undertook to excuse Luther's course to the emperor. To one of the counselors he wrote:

After I left Cologne, Luther's books were burned, and again at Mainz. I regret this because Dr. Martin has already protested his readiness to do everything consistent with the name of Christian, and I have constantly insisted that he should not be condemned unheard, nor should his books be burned. If now he has given tit for tat, I hope that His Imperial Majesty will graciously overlook it.

Frederick had never before gone so far as this. He boasted that in his whole life he had not exchanged more than twenty words with Luther. He claimed to pass no judgment on his teachings but to demand only that he be given an impartial hearing. Frederick could still say that he was not defending Luther's views but merely excusing his act. The ground was not theology but law. Luther's books had been illegally burned. He ought not, indeed, to have retaliated, but the emperor should wink at the affront in view of the provocation. Frederick was saying that a German, subject to a miscarriage of justice, should be excused for burning not only a papal bull but the entire canon law, the great legal code which even more than the civil law in the Middle Ages had provided the legal basis for European civilization.

CHAPTER TEN

HERE I STAND

REDERICK was well advised to turn to the emperor. The case at Rome was settled, and a formal ban was inevitable. The question was whether any additional penalty would be inflicted by the state. That question the state itself would have to decide. Obviously Luther could do no more than preach, teach, and pray, and wait for others to determine the disposition to be made of his case.

Six months were required for the answer. That does not seem a long time in comparison with the four years of dallying on the part of the Church. Yet one might have supposed that since the emperor was imbued with the orthodoxy of Spain he would brook no delay. The emperor was not in the position, however, to do as he pleased. The pageantry of his coronation did not excuse him from the necessity of appending his signature to the imperial constitution, and two clauses of that constitution have been supposed by some to have been inserted by Frederick the Wise in order to safeguard Luther. One stipulated that no German of any rank should be taken for trial outside Germany, and the other that none should be outlawed without cause and without a hearing. That these provisions were really meant to protect the rights of a monk accused of heresy is extremely dubious, and in no extant document did Frederick or Luther ever appeal to them. At the same time the emperor was a constitutional monarch; and whatever his own convictions, he would not find it expedient to govern Germany by arbitrary fiat.

He confronted a divided public opinion. Some were for Luther, some against, and some in between. Those who were for him were numerous, powerful, and vocal. Aleander, the papal nuncio in Germany, reported that nine tenths of the Germans cried, "Luther," and the other one tenth, "Death to the pope." This was unquestionably an exaggeration. Yet Luther's following was not contemptible. His supporters were powerful. Franz von Sickingen from his fortress on the Ebernburg controlled the Rhine valley and might well prevent the emperor, who came to Germany without Spanish troops, from taking action. Luther's supporters were also vocal, and notably Ulrich von Hutten, who, scorning submission to Rome in order to obviate excommunication, fulminated from the Ebernburg against the *curia* and curdled the blood of Aleander with successive manifestoes. The bull *Exsurge* was reprinted with stinging annotations, and in a tract Hutten portrayed himself as the "Bull Killer." He appealed to the emperor to shake off the rabble of priests. Threats of violence were addressed to Albert of Mainz. Aleander, the papal nuncio, was urged to heed the groans of the German people and to accord a fair trial, which should not be denied to a parricide. "Do you suppose," demanded Hutten, "that through an edict extracted by guile from the

TITLE PAGE OF HUTTEN'S "SATIRE ON
THE BULL AGAINST LUTHER"

emperor you will be able to separate Germany from liberty, faith, religion, and truth? Do you think you can intimidate us by burning books? This question will not be settled by the pen but by the sword."

The most influential of Luther's supporters was Frederick the Wise. He had gone so far as to excuse the burning of the papal bull. At the Diet of Worms he permitted Fritz, his court fool, to mimic the cardinals. Frederick had refused to be wooed by the golden rose, the indulgences for the Castle Church at Wittenberg, and a benefice for his natural son. The most clear-cut confession of Luther's cause on his part comes to us only at third hand. Aleander claimed to have heard from Joachim of Brandenburg that Frederick had said to him, "Our faith has long lacked this light which Martin has brought to it." The remark must be discounted because both narrators were eager to smear Frederick with adherence to Luther. The elector himself repeatedly insisted that he was not espousing Dr. Martin's opinions but merely demanding a fair hearing. If the friar was properly heard and condemned, Frederick would be the first to do his duty against him as a Christian prince. Yet Frederick's notion of a fair hearing meant that Luther should be convicted out of the Scriptures. Frederick was often murky as to the issues; but when clear, he was dogged.

On the opposite side were the papalists, men like Eck who took their cue from Rome. The *curia* reiterated pleas to root out the tare, expel the scabby sheep, cut away the putrid member, and throw overboard the rocker of the bark of St. Peter. The representative of Rome throughout the trial was Aleander, whose objective was to have the case settled arbitrarily by the emperor without consulting the German estates, which were known to be divided. Above all else Luther should not receive a hearing before a secular tribunal. He had already been condemned by the Church, and the laity should simply implement the Church's decision and not re-examine the grounds of condemnation.

Then there was the middle party, headed personally by Erasmus, who, despite his statement that the breach was irreparable, did not desist from efforts at mediation and even fathered a memorandum proposing the appointment by the emperor and the kings of England and Hungary of an impartial tribunal. The Erasmians as a party sensed less than their leader the depth of the cleavage between Luther and the Church and between Luther and themselves.

With opinion thus divided delays in settling Luther's case were inevitable. The Lutheran party deliberately resorted to filibustering.

Curiously some of the greatest obstructionists were at the Vatican because the pope had seen his worst fears realized in the election of Charles as emperor, and was now disposed to curb his power by supporting France. But whenever a move was made in that direction, Charles, for all his orthodoxy, intimated that Luther could be used as a weapon. Even the greatest activists on the scene were less active than might have been expected. Hutten was restrained by hope, because he believed that history would inevitably repeat itself and in due time any German emperor would clash with the temporal pretensions of the pope. Beguiled by these expectations he deferred his priests' war until a fellow Humanist taunted him with emitting only froth. But at the same time Aleander was intimidated by Hutten's fulminations; and when the pope sent a bull of excommunication against both Luther and Hutten, Aleander withheld the publication and sent the bull back to Rome to have the name of Hutten first expunged. Such communications of themselves took months, and thus by reason of Aleander's timidity Luther came actually to be outlawed by the empire before he had been formally excommunicated by the Church.

A HEARING PROMISED AND RECALLED

Where, how, and by whom his case should be handled was the problem which faced Charles. A decision on the point was reached on the fourth of November, 1520, when Charles after his coronation at Aachen went to confer with "Uncle Frederick," marooned by the gout at Cologne. All knew that important decisions were pending. The Lutherans placarded the city with the appeal to Caesar. For the papalists Aleander hastened to interview Frederick the Wise and urged him to commit the case to the pope. Frederick instead called in Erasmus, the leader of the moderates, and asked his judgment. Erasmus pursed his lips. Frederick strained forward for the weighty answer. "Two crimes Luther has committed," came the verdict. "He has attacked the crown of the pope and the bellies of the monks." Frederick laughed.

Thus fortified Frederick conferred with the emperor and secured a promise that Luther should not be condemned without a hearing. On what grounds Charles was persuaded we do not know, nor what

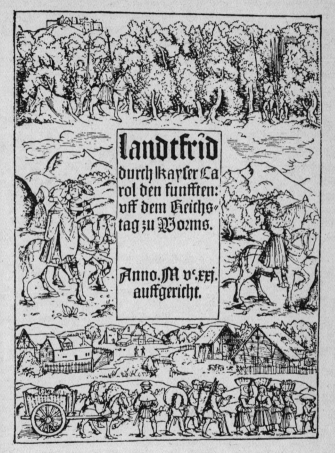

landtfrid durch Kayser Carol den funfften: vff dem Reichstag zu Worms.

Anno. M v^c. xxj. auffgericht.

THE DIET OF WORMS AND THE PUBLIC PEACE

sort of hearing he had in mind. The University of Wittenberg promptly pointed to a hearing before the forthcoming diet of the German nation soon to be assembled at the city of Worms. Frederick transmitted the proposal to the emperor's counselors and received from His Majesty a reply dated November 28 and addressed to his "beloved Uncle Frederick: We are desirous that you should bring the above-mentioned Luther to the diet to be held at Worms, that there he may be thoroughly investigated by competent persons, that no injustice be done nor anything contrary to law." He does not say what law, nor by whom the investigation should be conducted, nor whether Luther would be at liberty to defend his views. Luther should come, that was all. The appeal to Caesar had been heard. This invitation on the twenty-eighth of November marked an amazing reversal of policy. The Defender of the Faith, who had been burning the books, now invited the author of those very books to some sort of hearing. Had the emperor been won over to the policy of Erasmus? Had some disquieting political news disposed him for a moment to bait the pope and cultivate the Germans? Was he fearful of popular insurrection? His motives elude us. This only we know, that the invitation was issued.

That was in November, but Luther did not actually appear at the diet until April of the next year. In the interim the invitation was rescinded and reissued. All the strife of the parties centered on this point: Should Luther be permitted to appear before a secular tribunal to be examined as to the faith? "Never," was the resolve of Aleander.

As for myself, I would gladly confront this Satan, but the authority of the Holy See should not be prejudiced by subjection to the judgment of the laity. One who has been condemned by the pope, the cardinals, and prelates should be heard only in prison. The laity, including the emperor, are not in a position to review the case. The only competent judge is the pope. How can the Church be called the ship of Peter if Peter is not at the helm? How can she be the ark of Noah if Noah is not the captain? If Luther wants to be heard, he can have a safe conduct to Rome. Or His Majesty might send him to the inquisitors in Spain. He can perfectly well recant where he is and then come to the diet to be forgiven. He asks for a place which is not suspect. What place to him is not suspect, unless it be Germany? What judges would he accept unless Hutten and the poets? Has the Catholic Church been dead for a thousand years to be revived only by Martin? Has the whole world gone wrong and Martin only has the eyes to see?

The emperor was impressed. On the seventeenth of December he rescinded the invitation to bring Luther to the diet. The reason assigned was that the sixty days had expired and in consequence if Luther were to come to Worms the city would find itself under an interdict. One may doubt whether this was the real reason. The motives of the emperor for recalling the invitation are as elusive as his motives for issuing it, for Luther was not yet formally under the ban; and even if he were, a papal dispensation could be secured. Charles may have been persuaded by Aleander, irritated by Luther's burning of the bull, depressed by news from Spain, and desirous of placating the *curia*. Whatever his reasons, he might have spared himself the onus of a public reversal had he but waited, because Frederick the Wise declined the invitation on the ground that the case appeared to be prejudged by the burning of Luther's books, for which he was sure the emperor was not responsible. Frederick might well entertain a doubt because on the very day of the burning at Mainz the emperor had issued the invitation to Luther. Frederick was determined to drive Charles to a clarification of his position and to an assumption of full responsibility.

For that reason the elector inquired of Luther whether he would be willing to come in case he was invited directly by the emperor himself. He answered:

ALEANDER

You ask me what I shall do if I am called by the emperor. I will go even if I am too sick to stand on my feet. If Caesar calls me, God calls me. If violence is used, as well it may be, I commend my cause to God. He lives and reigns who saved the three youths from the fiery furnace of the king of Babylon, and if He will not save me, my head is worth nothing compared with Christ. This is no time to think of safety. I must take care that the gospel is not brought into contempt by our fear to confess and seal our teaching with our blood.

His mood is more fully revealed in letters to Staupitz.

This is not the time to cringe, but to cry aloud when our Lord Jesus Christ is damned, reviled, and blasphemed. If you exhort me to humility, I exhort you to pride. The matter is very serious. We see Christ suffer. If hitherto we ought to have been silent and humble, I ask you whether now, when the blessed Saviour is mocked, we should not fight for him. My father, the danger is greater than many think. Now applies the word of the gospel, "He who confesses me before men, him will I confess in the presence of my father, and he who denies me before men, him will I deny." I write this candidly to you because I am afraid you hesitate between Christ and the pope, though they are diametrically contrary. Let us pray that the Lord Jesus will destroy the son of perdition with the breath of his mouth. If you will not follow, permit me to go. I am greatly saddened by your submissiveness. You seem to me to be a very different Staupitz from the one who used to preach grace and the cross. . . . Father, do you remember when we were at Augsburg you said to me, "Remember, brother, you started this in the name of the Lord Jesus." I have never forgotten that, and I say it now to you. I burned the pope's books at first with fear and trembling, but now I am lighter in heart than I have ever been in my life. They are so much more pestilent than I supposed.

LUTHER WITH A DOVE ABOVE HIS HEAD

THE EMPEROR ASSUMES RESPONSIBILITY

Aleander, unaware of the new approaches to Luther, thought the occasion propitious to present an edict which the emperor should issue without consulting the diet. The emperor answered that he could not act alone. The Archbishop of Mainz had not yet arrived; and when he came, he opposed the edict, even though a month earlier he had himself authorized the burning of Luther's books. The Elector of Saxony also had not yet arrived. His entry coincided with the Feast of the Three Kings, and he rode into Worms like one of the Wise Men bearing gifts for the young emperor, from whom he secured another reversal of policy. Charles promised to assume responsibility for Luther's case. Luther being informed replied to Frederick, "I am heartily glad that His Majesty will take to himself this affair, which is not mine but that of all Christianity and the whole German nation."

But Charles by this promise evidently did not mean that Luther was to have a public hearing before the diet. Instead a committee was appointed to handle the case, and Aleander was permitted to address it. He bungled his advantage at the very beginning by undertaking to demonstrate that Luther was an abominable heretic, whereas in all consistency he ought to have pleaded that a lay committee had no jurisdiction. Instead he sought to demonstrate from a medieval manuscript that the papacy was at least as old as Charlemagne. All of this would have been pertinent enough at the Leipzig debate, but the time for such discussion had gone by. In the meantime the pope had spoken; and the diet was being invited, not to ratify, but simply to implement the papal verdict. The committee listened and said they would have to wait.

The delays served to feed the mood of popular violence in the city. The reports which we have from opposing sides indicate that religious war lay in the offing. Aleander, in the mood of a martyr, reported:

Martin is pictured with a halo and a dove above his head. The people kiss these pictures. Such a quantity have been sold that I was not able to obtain one. A cartoon has appeared showing Luther with a book in his hand, accompanied by Hutten in armor with a sword under the caption, "Champions of Christian Liberty." Another sheet portrays Luther in front and Hutten behind carrying a chest on which are two chalices with the inscription, "The Ark of the True Faith." Erasmus, in front, is playing the harp as David. In the background is John Hus, whom Luther has recently proclaimed his saint. In another part of the picture the pope and the cardinals are being bound by the soldiers of the guard. I cannot go out on the streets but the Germans put their hands to their swords and gnash their teeth at me. I hope the pope will give me a plenary indulgence and look after my brothers and sisters if anything happens to me.

The disturbances are described from the other side in a letter of a Humanist at Worms to Hutten:

A Spaniard tore up your edition of the bull and trampled it in the mud. A chaplain of the emperor and two Spaniards caught a man with sixty copies of *The Babylonian Captivity*. The people came to the rescue, and the assailants had to take refuge in the castle. A mounted Spaniard pursued one of our men, who barely escaped through a door. The Spaniard reined up so suddenly that he fell off his horse and could not rise until a German lifted him. Every day two or three Spaniards gallop on their mules through the market place, and the people have to make way for them. This is our freedom.

Overt violence was continually incited by the dissemination of defamatory pamphlets. Aleander claimed that a wagon would not hold the scurrilous tracts with which Worms was deluged, such as a parody on the Apostles' Creed:

I believe in the pope, binder and looser in heaven, earth, and hell, and in Simony, his only son our lord, who was conceived by the canon law and born of the Romish church. Under his power truth suffered, was crucified, dead and buried, and through the ban descended to hell, rose again through the gospel and Paul and was brought to Charles, sitting at his right hand, who in future is to rule over spiritual and worldly things. I believe in the canon law, in the Romish church, in the destruction of faith and of the communion of saints, in indulgences both for the remission of guilt and penalty in purgatory, in the resurrection of the flesh in an Epicurean life, because given to us by the Holy Father, the pope. Amen.

The emperor was irritated. When on February 6 Luther's appeal was handed to him, he tore it up and trampled on it. But he was quick to recover his composure and summoned a plenary session of the diet on the thirteenth of February. The plan was to present a new version of the edict, to be issued in the name of the emperor but with the consent of the diet. Aleander was given an opportunity to prepare their minds in a three-hour speech. Once again he allowed the opportunity to slip through his fingers. He was now in a position to correct the mistake he had made in addressing the committee. Two days previously the papal bull excommunicating Luther had come into his hands. He had only to produce it to allay the objection that the diet was being asked to outlaw a man not yet banned by the Church. This was the time when Aleander held back because the bull named not only Luther but Hutten. The document was not produced. The diet proceeded to examine a case of heresy, and Aleander himself rather than Luther was responsible for turning a secular assembly into a church council.

Aleander unquestionably made a very good case against Luther, a very much better case than did the bull, which simply incorporated the earlier condemnation of *Exsurge Domine*, with no fresh examination of the more subversive tracts of the summer of 1520. Aleander had memorized whole sections of these works and set out again to prove that Luther was

a heretic who brought up John Hus from hell and endorsed not some but all of his articles. In consequence he must endorse also Wyclif's denial of the real presence [which he did not], and Wyclif's claim that no Christian can bind another by law. This point Luther claimed to have asserted in his *Freedom of the Christian Man* [which he did not]. He rejects monastic vows. He rejects ceremonies. He appeals to councils and rejects the authority of councils. Like all heretics he appeals to Scripture and yet rejects Scripture when it does not support him. He would throw out the Epistle of James because it contains the proof text for extreme unction [which certainly was not Luther's reason]. He is a heretic and an obstinate heretic. He asks for a hearing, but how can a hearing be given to one who will not listen to an angel from heaven? He is also a revolutionary. He claims that the Germans should wash their hands in the blood of the papists. [The reference is obviously to Luther's unbridled outburst against Prierias.]

No more damaging case could have been made against Luther before the diet, which was now asked to endorse the imperial edict proclaiming Luther a Bohemian heretic and a revolutionary who would soon be formally excommunicated by the pope. (The bull, of course, had been held back.) Unless absolved, he should be imprisoned and his books eradicated. Non-co-operators with the edict would be guilty of lese majesty. The presentation of this edict precipitated a storm. The electors of Saxony and Brandenburg had to be separated on the floor of the diet by Cardinal Lang. The Elector Palatinate, ordinarily taciturn, bellowed like a bull. The estates demanded time, and on the nineteenth answered that Luther's teaching was already so firmly rooted among the people that a condemnation without a hearing would occasion grave danger of insurrection. He should be brought to the diet under safe conduct, to be examined by learned men. He should be brought to answer, not to argue. If he would renounce what he had said against the faith, other points could be discussed. If he refused, then the diet would support the edict.

INVITATION TO LUTHER RENEWED

The emperor thereupon reverted to his earlier agreement that Luther should come. The edict was subjected to dentistry. The penalties for lese majesty were dropped. The edict should be issued in the name of the estates rather than of the emperor alone, and Luther should be brought to the diet for examination. The emperor then composed a new invitation for Luther. It was dated the sixth, although not sent until the eleventh, because in the meantime another attempt was made to induce Frederick to assume responsibility for bringing the accused. But again he passed the onus directly back to the emperor, who at last sent the missive addressed to "Our noble, dear, and esteemed Martin Luther." "Zounds!" exclaimed Aleander when he saw it, "that's no way to address a heretic." The letter continued: "Both we and the diet have decided to ask you to come under safe conduct to answer with regard to your books and teaching. You shall have twenty-one days in which to arrive." There is no clear statement that discussion would be precluded. The invitation was delivered at the hands, not of the common postman, but of the imperial herald, Caspar Sturm.

Would Luther come? There was real doubt. To Spalatin he wrote:

I will reply to the emperor that if I am being invited simply to recant I will not come. If to recant is all that is wanted, I can do that perfectly well right here. But if he is inviting me to my death, then I will come. I hope none but the papists will stain their hands in my blood, Antichrist reigns. The Lord's will be done.

To another he wrote:

This shall be my recantation at Worms: "Previously I said the pope is the vicar of Christ. I recant. Now I say the pope is the adversary of Christ and the apostle of the Devil."

Evidently Luther had decided to go.

On the way he learned of an edict for the sequestration of his books. Its publication had been delayed, perhaps through fear that if he saw it he would infer that the case was settled and would not come. But his comment was, "Unless I am held back by force, or Caesar revokes his invitation, I will enter Worms under the banner of Christ against the gates of hell." He had no illusions as to the probable outcome. After an ovation at Erfurt he commented, "I have had my Palm Sunday. I wonder whether this pomp is merely a temptation or whether it is also the sign of my impending passion."

While his coming was awaited, another lampoon was published in Worms, entitled the *Litany of the Germans:*

Christ hear the Germans; Christ hear the Germans. From evil counselors deliver Charles, O Lord. From poison on the way to Worms deliver

Martin Luther, preserve Ulrich von Hutten, O Lord. Suffer not thyself, Lord, to be crucified afresh. Purge Aleander, O Lord. The nuncios working against Luther at Worms, smite from heaven. O Lord Christ, hear the Germans.

The Catholic moderates, however, desired that the case might be disposed of out of court. The leader of this party was Glapion, the emperor's confessor. Whether he was a sincere Erasmian or a son of duplicity is debatable, but he certainly began his negotiations before there could be any suspicion that he was trying to divert Luther from Worms until after the expiration of the safe conduct. Glapion had previously approached Frederick the Wise with a very engaging argument. Luther's earlier works, he claimed, had warmed his heart. He thoroughly agreed with the attack on indulgences and saw in *The Freedom of the Christian Man* a wonderful Christian spirit. But when he had read *The Babylonian Captivity*, he was simply aghast. He could not believe that Luther would acknowledge the book. It was not in his usual style. If he had written it, he must have done so in a fit of passion. In that case he should be ready to have it interpreted in the sense of the Church. If he would comply, he would have many supporters. The matter should be settled in private, else the Devil would stir up contention, war, and insurrection. No good could come of public controversy, and only the Devil would profit from Luther's appearance at Worms.

The appeal was most ingratiating because it was so true. Had Luther been willing to abandon the attack on the sacraments, he might have rallied a united German nation for the reduction of papal power and extortion. The diet might have wrung from the pope the sort of concessions already granted to the strong national states of France, Spain, and England. Schism might have been avoided, and religious war could have been averted. To a man like Frederick the Wise this must have been a most appealing proposal, but he was resolved to make no overtures which would give the emperor an opportunity to evade his responsibility.

Glapion then turned to another quarter. Why not work through

Sickingen and Hutten? First, engage Hutten with a pension from the emperor; then let Luther be invited to Sickingen's castle at the Ebernburg for a conference. Glapion had the courage to go in person and beard Hutten and Sickingen in their eagle's nest. He was so sympathetic toward Luther and made the emperor appear so favorable that Hutten accepted the pension (subsequently to be declined), and Sickingen sent his chaplain, Martin Bucer, to intercept Luther on the way to Worms and to extend the invitation. But Luther had set his face to go up to Jerusalem and would not be turned aside. He would enter Worms though there were as many devils as tiles on the roofs. Hutten was moved. "It is as clear as day," he wrote Pirkheimer, "that he was directed by divine guidance. He disregarded all human considerations and threw himself utterly upon God." And to Luther, "Here is the difference between us. I look to men. You, who are already more perfect, trust everything to God."

LUTHER BEFORE THE DIET

On the sixteenth of April, Luther entered Worms in a Saxon two-wheeled cart with a few companions. The imperial herald preceded, wearing the eagle upon his cloak. Although it was the dinner hour, two thousand turned out to conduct Luther to his lodging. On the following day at four o'clock Luther was waited upon by the herald and the imperial marshal, who conducted him furtively, to avoid the crowds, to a meeting of the emperor, the electors, and a portion of the estates. The monk stood before the monarch, who exclaimed, "That fellow will never make a heretic of me."

The scene lends itself to dramatic portrayal. Here was Charles, heir of a long line of Catholic sovereigns—of Maximilian the romantic, of Ferdinand the Catholic, of Isabella the orthodox—scion of the house of Hapsburg, lord of Austria, Burgundy, the Low Countries, Spain, and Naples, Holy Roman Emperor, ruling over a vaster domain than any save Charlemagne, symbol of the medieval unities, incarnation of a glorious if vanishing heritage; and here before him a simple monk, a miner's son, with nothing to sustain him save his own faith in the Word of God. Here the past and the future were met. Some would see at this point the beginning of modern times. The contrast is real enough. Luther himself was sensible of it in a measure. He was well aware that he had not been reared as the son of Pharaoh's daughter, but what overpowered him was not so much that he stood in the presence of the emperor as this, that he and the emperor alike were called upon to answer before Almighty God.

Luther was examined by an official of the Archbishop of Trier, Eck by name, not of course the Eck of the Leipzig debate. Luther was confronted with a pile of his books and asked whether they were

LUTHER'S FIRST HEARING AT WORMS

his. The very question reopened the overture of Glapion. Luther might now repudiate *The Babylonian Captivity* and invite discussion of the financial and political pretensions of the papacy. This was his opportunity to rally a united Germany. In a voice barely audible he answered, "The books are all mine, and I have written more."

The door was closed, but Eck opened it again. "Do you defend them all, or do you care to reject a part?"

Luther reflected aloud, "This touches God and his Word. This affects the salvation of souls. Of this Christ said, 'He who denies me before men, him will I deny before my father.' To say too little or too much would be dangerous. I beg you, give me time to think it over."

The emperor and the diet deliberated. Eck brought the answer. He expressed amazement that a theological professor should not be ready at once to defend his position, particularly since he had come for that very purpose. He deserved no consideration. Nevertheless, the emperor in his clemency would grant him until the morrow.

Eck's amazement has been so shared by some modern historians as to prompt the suggestion that Luther's request was preconcerted, a part of the stalling tactic of Frederick the Wise. But anyone who recalls Luther's tremors at his first mass will scarcely so interpret this hesitation. Just as then he wished to flee from the altar, so now he was too terrified before God to give an answer to the emperor. At the same time we must admit that Luther's tremor before the Divine Majesty served actually to bring him before a plenary session of the diet. On the following day, the eighteenth, a larger hall was chosen and was so crowded that scarcely any save the emperor could sit. The terror of the Holy conspired to give Luther a hearing before the German nation.

He had been summoned for four o'clock on the afternoon of the morrow, but the press of business delayed his appearance until six. This time his voice was ringing. Eck reiterated the question of the previous day. Luther responded: "Most serene emperor, most illustrious princes, most clement lords, if I have not given some of you your proper titles I beg you to forgive me. I am not a courtier, but a monk. You asked me yesterday whether the books were mine and whether I would repudiate them. They are all mine, but as for the second question, they are not all of one sort."

This was a skillful move. By differentiating his works Luther won for himself the opportunity of making a speech instead of answering simply yes or no.

He went on: "Some deal with faith and life so simply and evangelically that my very enemies are compelled to regard them as worthy of Christian reading. Even the bull itself does not treat all my books as of one kind. If I should renounce these, I would be the only man on earth to damn the truth confessed alike by friends and foes. A second class of my works inveighs against the desolation of the Christian world by the evil lives and teaching of the papists. Who can deny this when the universal complaints testify that by the laws of the popes the consciences of men are racked?"

"No!" broke in the emperor.

Luther, unruffled, went on to speak of the "incredible tyranny" by which this German nation was devoured. "Should I recant at this point, I would open the door to more tyranny and impiety, and it will be all the worse should it appear that I had done so at the instance of the Holy Roman Empire." This was a skillful plea to German nationalism, which had a strong following in the diet. Even Duke George the Catholic took the fore in presenting grievances.

"A third class," continued Luther, "contains attacks on private individuals. I confess I have been more caustic than comports with my profession, but I am being judged, not on my life, but for the teaching of Christ, and I cannot renounce these works either, without increasing tyranny and impiety. When Christ stood before Annas, he said, 'Produce witnesses.' If our Lord, who could not err, made this demand, why may not a worm like me ask to be convicted of error from the prophets and the Gospels? If I am shown my error, I will be the first to throw my books into the fire. I have been reminded of the dissensions which my teaching engenders. I can answer only in the words of the Lord, 'I came not to bring peace but a sword.' If our God is so severe, let us beware lest we release a deluge of wars, lest the reign of this noble youth, Charles, be inauspicious. Take warning from the examples of Pharaoh, the king of Babylon, and the kings of Israel. God it is who confounds the wise. I must walk in the fear of the Lord. I say this not to chide but because I cannot escape my duty to my Germans. I commend myself to Your Majesty. May you not suffer my adversaries to make you ill disposed to me without cause. I have spoken."

Eck replied: "Martin, you have not sufficiently distinguished your works. The earlier were bad and the latter worse. Your plea to be heard from Scripture is the one always made by heretics. You do nothing but renew the errors of Wyclif and Hus. How will the Jews, how will the Turks, exult to hear Christians discussing whether they have been wrong all these years! Martin, how can you assume that you are the only one to understand the sense of Scripture? Would you put your judgment above that of so many famous men and claim that you know more than they all? You have no right to call into question the most holy orthodox faith, instituted by Christ the perfect lawgiver, proclaimed throughout the world by the apostles, sealed by the red blood of the martyrs, confirmed by the sacred councils, defined by the Church in which all our fathers believed until death and gave to us as an inheritance, and which now we are forbidden by the pope and the emperor to discuss lest there be no end of debate. I ask you, Martin—answer candidly and without horns—do you or do you not repudiate your books and the errors which they contain?" Luther replied, "Since then Your Majesty and your lordships desire a simple reply, I will answer without horns and without teeth. Unless I am convicted by Scripture and plain reason—I do not accept the authority of popes and councils, for they have contradicted each other—my conscience is captive to the Word of God. I cannot and I will not recant anything, for to go against conscience is neither right nor safe. God help me. Amen."

The earliest printed version added the words: "Here I stand, I cannot do otherwise." The words, though not recorded on the spot, may nevertheless be genuine, because the listeners at the moment may have been too moved to write.

Luther had spoken in German. He was asked to repeat in Latin. He was sweating. A friend called out, "If you can't do it, Doctor, you have done enough." Luther made again his affirmation in Latin, threw up his arms in the gesture of a victorious knight, and slipped out of the darkened hall, amid the hisses of the Spaniards, and went to his lodging. Frederick the Wise went also to his lodging and remarked, "Dr. Martin spoke wonderfully before the emperor, the princes, and the estates in Latin and in German, but he is too daring for me." On the following day Aleander heard the report that all six of the electors were ready to pronounce Luther a heretic. That would include Frederick the Wise. Spalatin says that Frederick was indeed much troubled to know whether Luther had or had not been convicted from the Scriptures.

THE EDICT OF WORMS

The emperor called in the electors and a number of the princes to ask their opinions. They requested time. "Very well," said the emperor, "I will give you my opinion," and he read to them a paper which he had written out himself in French. This was no speech composed by a secretary. The young Hapsburg was confessing his faith:

I am descended from a long line of Christian emperors of this noble German nation, and of the Catholic kings of Spain, the archdukes of Austria, and the dukes of Burgundy. They were all faithful to the death to the Church of Rome, and they defended the Catholic faith and the honor of God. I have resolved to follow in their steps. A single friar who goes counter to all Christianity for a thousand years must be wrong. Therefore I am resolved to stake my lands, my friends, my body, my blood, my life, and my soul. Not only I, but you of this noble German nation, would be forever disgraced if by our negligence not only heresy but the very suspicion of heresy were to survive. After having heard yesterday the obstinate defense of Luther, I regret that I have so long delayed in proceeding against him and his false teaching. I will have no more to do with him. He may return under his safe conduct, but without preaching or making any tumult. I will proceed against him as a notorious heretic, and ask you to declare yourselves as you promised me.

Many of the emperor's hearers took on the hue of death. On the following day the electors declared themselves fully in accord with the emperor, but out of six only four signed. The dissenters were

LUTHER'S SECOND HEARING AT WORMS

In handwriting: Intitulentur libri—*"Let them read the titles," the words called out by Luther's lawyer; and* Hie stehe ich/ich kan nicht anders/Got helffe mir. Amen.—*"Here I stand. I cannot do otherwise. God help me. Amen."*

Ludwig of the Palatinate and Frederick of Saxony. He had come into the clear.

The emperor felt now that he had sufficient backing to proceed with the edict, but during the night there was posted on the door of the town hall and elsewhere in Worms a placard stamped with the *Bundschuh.* This was the symbol of the peasants' revolt, the sandal clog of the workingman in contrast to the high boot of the noble. For a century Germany had been distraught by peasant unrest. This poster strongly implied that if Luther were condemned, the peasants would rise. Where the poster came from could only be guessed.

Hutten surmised that it had been placarded by the papalists in order to discredit the Lutherans, but Aleander was equally innocent of the source. Whoever did it, Albert of Mainz was in a panic. At dawn he rushed to the lodging of the emperor, who laughed at him. But Albert would not be put off, and enlisted his brother Joachim, the most ardent opponent of Luther. At the instance of these two the estates petitioned the emperor to permit Luther to be examined again. The emperor replied that he would have nothing to do with it himself, but that they might have three days.

Then began the attempt to break Luther down through a committee. The ordeal, though less dramatic, was more crucial than the public appearance. He who is able to give a ringing No before a public assembly may find it harder, if he is at all sensitive, to resist the kindly remonstrances of men concerned to prevent the disruption of Germany and the disintegration of the Church. The committee was headed by Richard of Greiffenklau, the Archbishop of Trier, the custodian of the seamless robe of Christ, whom Frederick the Wise had so long been proposing as the arbiter. With him were associated some of Luther's friends and some of his foes, among them Duke George.

In a slightly different form the attempt of Glapion to secure a partial revocation was renewed. Luther's attack on the indulgence sellers was again declared to have been warranted, and his denunciation of Roman corruption was heart-warming. He had written well about good works and the Ten Commandments, but *The Freedom of the Christian Man* would prompt the masses to reject all authority. One observes that this time the attack centered not on the demolition of the sacramental system in *The Babylonian Captivity* but on the alleged threat to public tranquillity in the tract on Christian liberty. Luther replied that he intended nothing of the sort and would counsel obedience even to evil magistrates. Trier besought him not to rend the seamless robe of Christendom. He answered with the counsel of Gamaliel, to wait and see whether his teaching was of God or of man. Luther was reminded that if he went down, Melanchthon would be pulled after him. At this his eyes welled with tears; but when asked to name a judge whom he would accept, he stiffened and replied that he would name a child of eight or nine years. "The pope," he declared, "is no judge of matters pertaining to God's Word and faith, but a Christian man must examine and judge for himself." The committee reported failure to the emperor.

On the sixth of May, His Majesty presented to a diminishing diet the final draft of the Edict of Worms, prepared by Aleander. Luther was charged with attacking the seven sacraments after the manner of the damned Bohemians.

He has sullied marriage, disparaged confession, and denied the body and blood of our Lord. He makes the sacraments depend on the faith of the recipient. He is pagan in his denial of free will. This devil in the habit of a monk has brought together ancient errors into one stinking puddle and has invented new ones. He denies the power of the keys and encourages the laity to wash their hands in the blood of the clergy. His teaching makes for rebellion, division, war, murder, robbery, arson, and the collapse of Christendom. He lives the life of a beast. He has burned the decretals. He despises alike the ban and the sword. He does more harm to the civil than to the ecclesiastical power. We have labored with him, but he recognizes only the authority of Scripture, which he interprets in his own sense. We have given him twenty-one days, dating from April the 25th. We have now gathered the estates. Luther is to be regarded as a convicted heretic [although the bull of excommunication still had not been published]. When the time is up, no one is to harbor him. His followers also are to be condemned. His books are to be eradicated from the memory of man.

Aleander brought the edict to the emperor for his signature. He took up the pen. "Then," says Aleander, "I haven't the ghost of a notion why, he laid it down and said he must submit the edict to the diet." The emperor knew why. The members were going home. Frederick the Wise had left, Ludwig of the Palatinate had left. Those who remained were a rump ready to condemn Luther. Although the edict was dated as of the sixth of May, it was not issued until the twenty-sixth. By that time the diet was sufficiently reduced to consent. The emperor then signed. Aleander recorded:

His Majesty signed both the Latin and the German with his own blessed hand, and smiling said, "You will be content now." "Yes," I answered, "and even greater will be the contentment of His Holiness and of all Christendom." We praise God for giving us such a religious emperor. May God preserve him in all his holy ways, who has already acquired perpetual glory, and with God eternal reward. I was going to recite a paean from Ovid when I recalled that this was a religious occasion. Therefore blessed be the Holy Trinity for his immense mercy.

The Edict of Worms, passed by a secular tribunal entrusted with a case of heresy at the instance of Lutherans and against the opposition of the papalists, was at once repudiated by the Lutherans as having been passed by only a rump, and was sponsored by the papalists because it was a confirmation of the Catholic faith. The Church of Rome, which had so strenuously sought to prevent turning the Diet of Worms into an ecclesiastical council, became in the light of the outcome the great vindicator of the pronouncement of a secular tribunal on heresy.

CHAPTER ELEVEN

My Patmos

ontemporaries deemed Luther's trial at Worms a re-enactment of the passion of Christ. Albrecht Dürer on the seventeenth of May recorded in his diary this prayer: "O Lord, who desirest before thou comest to judgment that as thy Son Jesus Christ had to die at the hands of the priests and rise from the dead and ascend to heaven, even so should thy disciple Martin Luther be made conformable to him." The secularized twentieth century is more shocked by such a comparison than the sixteenth, when men walked in a perpetual Passion play. Some anonymous pamphleteer did not hesitate to narrate the proceedings at Worms in the very language of the Gospels, identifying Albert with Caiaphas, Lang with Annas, Frederick with Peter, and Charles with Pilate. Our sole account of the burning of Luther's books at Worms is from this document and reads:

Then the governor [Charles in the role of Pilate] delivered to them the books of Luther to be burned. The priests took them; and when the princes and the people had left, the diet made a great pyre in front of the high priest's palace, where they burned the books, placing on the top a picture of Luther with this inscription, "This is Martin Luther, the Doctor of the Gospel." The title was read by many Romanists because the place where Luther's books were burned was not far from the bishop's court. Now this title was written in French, German, and in Latin.

Then the high priests and the Romanists said to the governor, "Write not, 'A Doctor of evangelical truth,' but that he said, 'I am a Doctor of evangelical truth.'"

But the governor answered, "What I have written I have written."

And with him two other doctors were burned, Hutten and Carlstadt, one on the right and one on the left. But the picture of Luther would not burn until the soldiers had folded it and put it inside a vessel of pitch, where it was reduced to ashes. As a count beheld these things which were done, he marveled and said, "Truly he is a Christian." And all the throng present, seeing these things which had come to pass, returned beating their breasts.

The following day the chief priests and the Pharisees, together with the Romanists, went to the governor and said, "We recall that this seducer said he wished later to write greater things. Make an order, therefore, throughout the whole earth that his books be not sold, lest the latest error be worse than the first."

But the governor said, "You have your own guard. Go publish bulls, as you know how, through your false excommunication." They then went away and put forth horrible mandates in the name of the Roman pontiff and of the emperor, but to this day they have not been obeyed.

This picture of Charles as Pilate yielding only reluctantly to the churchmen does not of course fit the facts. In his private domains the Counter Reformation, already begun, was pursued in earnest. Aleander returned to the Netherlands, and the burning of books went on merrily. As a certain friar was supervising a bonfire, a bystander said to him, "You would see better if the ashes of Luther's books got into your eyes." He was a bold man who dared to say so much. Erasmus, at Louvain, to escape the constant harassment to which he would be subject were he not willing to be turned into an inquisitor, transferred his residence to Basel.

Albrecht Dürer in the Netherlands received the word that Luther's passion was complete. He reflected in his diary:

I know not whether he lives or is murdered, but in any case he has suffered for the Christian truth. If we lose this man, who has written more clearly than any other in centuries, may God grant his spirit to another. His books should be held in great honor, and not burned as the emperor commands, but rather the books of his enemies. O God, if Luther is dead, who will henceforth explain to us the gospel? What might he not have written for us in the next ten or twenty years?

AT THE WARTBURG

Luther was not dead. His friends began to receive letters "From the Wilderness," "From the Isle of Patmos." Frederick the Wise had decided to hide him, and gave instructions to court officials to make the arrangements without divulging the details, even to himself, that he might truthfully feign innocence. Spalatin, however, might know.

Luther and one companion were apprised of the plan. Luther was not very happy over it. He had set his face to return to Wittenberg, come what might. With a few companions in a wagon he was entering the woods on the outskirts of the village of Eisenach when armed horsemen fell upon the party and with much cursing and show of

THE WARTBURG

violence dragged Luther to the ground. The one companion, privy to the ruse, played his part and roundly berated the abductors. They placed Luther upon a horse and led him for a whole day by circuitous roads through the woods until at dusk, loomed up against the sky, the massive contours of Wartburg Castle. At eleven o'clock in the night the party reined up before the gates.

This ancient fortress was already the symbol of a bygone day, when German knighthood was in flower and sanctity unquestioned as the highest end of man. Here monarchs and minstrels, knights and fools, had had their assemblage, and here St. Elizabeth had left the relics of her holiness. But Luther was of no mind for historic reveries. As he laid him down in the chamber of the almost untenanted bastion, and the owls and bats wheeled about in the darkness, it seemed to him that the Devil was pelting nuts at the ceiling and rolling casks down the stairs. More insidious than such pranks of the Prince of Darkness was the unallayed question, "Are you alone wise? Have so many centuries gone wrong? What if you are in error and are taking so many others with you to eternal damnation?" In the morning he threw open the casement window and looked out on the fair Thuringian hills. In the distance he could see a cloud of smoke rising from the pits of the charcoal burners. A gust of wind lifted and dissipated the cloud. Even so were his doubts dispelled and his faith restored.

LUTHER AS JUNKER GEORGE AT THE WARTBURG

But only for a moment. The mood of Elijah at Horeb was upon him. The priests of Baal indeed were slain, but Jezebel sought the prophet's life, and he cried, "It is enough! Now, O Lord, take away my life!" Luther passed from one self-incrimination to another. If he had not been in error, then had he been sufficiently firm in the defense of truth? "My conscience troubles me because at Worms I yielded to the importunity of my friends and did not play the part of Elijah. They would hear other things from me if I were before them again." And when he contemplated the sequel, he could not well feel encouraged. "What an abominable spectacle is the kingdom of the Roman Antichrist," he wrote to Melanchthon. "Spalatin writes of the most cruel edicts against me."

Yet all the outward peril was as nothing to the inner struggles. "I can tell you in this idle solitude there are a thousand battles with Satan. It is much easier to fight against the incarnate Devil—that is, against men—than against spiritual wickedness in the heavenly places. Often I fall and am lifted again by God's right hand." Solitude and idleness increased his distress. To Spalatin he wrote, "Now is the time to pray with our might against Satan. He is plotting an attack on Germany, and I fear God will permit him because I am so indolent in prayer. I am mightily displeasing to myself, perhaps because I am alone." He wasn't quite alone. There were the warden and two serving boys, but they were hardly the sort to whom he could unburden himself as to Staupitz of old. He had been warned not to seek out company and not to become confidential lest he betray himself. The monk's cowl was laid aside. He dressed as a knight and grew a long beard. The warden did his best to provide a diversion, and included Luther in a hunting party. But he was revolted. "There is some point," he reflected, "in tracking down bears, wolves, boars, and foxes, but why should one pursue a harmless creature like a rabbit?" One ran up his leg to escape the dogs, but they bit through the cloth and killed it. "Just as the pope and the Devil treat us," commented the inveterate theologian.

He was idle, so he said. At any rate he was removed from the fracas. "I did not want to come here," he wrote. "I wanted to be in the fray." And again, "I had rather burn on live coals than rot here."

To loneliness and lack of public activity were added physical ills which were not new but were greatly accentuated by the circumstances. While still at Worms he had been overtaken by acute attacks of constipation, due perhaps to nervous depletion after the crucial days. The restricted diet and the sedentary ways at the Wartburg made the case worse. He was minded to risk his life by forsaking his concealment in order to procure medical assistance at Erfurt. Complaints continued from May until October, when Spalatin was able to send in laxatives.

The other malady was insomnia. It began in 1520 through attempts to make up arrears in saying the canonical hours. All through his controversy with Rome he was still a monk, obligated to say matins, tierce, nones, vespers, and complin. But when he became a professor at the university, a preacher in the village church, and the director of eleven monasteries, he was simply too busy to keep up. He would stack his prayers for a week, two weeks, even three weeks, and then would take off a Sunday or, on one occasion, three whole days without food or drink until he was "prayed up." After such an orgy in 1520 his head reeled. For five days he could get no sleep, and lay on his bed as one

LUTHER AS THE EVANGELIST MATTHEW
TRANSLATING THE SCRIPTURES

dead, until the doctor gave him a sedative. During convalescence the prayer book revolted him, and he fell in arrears a quarter of a year. Then he gave up. This was one of the stages in his weaning from monasticism. The permanent residue of the experience was insomnia.

Luther found one cure for depressions at the Wartburg, and that was work. "That I may not be idle in my Patmos," he said, in dedicating a tract to Sickingen, "I have written a book of Revelation." He wrote not one, but closer to a dozen. To a friend at Strassburg he explained:

It would not be safe to send you my books, but I have asked Spalatin to see to it. I have brought out a reply to Catharinus and another to Latomus, and in German a work on confession, expositions of Psalms 67 and 36, a commentary on the Magnificat, and a translation of Melanchthon's reply to the University of Paris. I have under way a volume of sermons on the lessons from the epistles and Gospels. I am attacking the Cardinal of Mainz and expounding the ten lepers.

On top of all this he translated the entire New Testament into his mother tongue. This was his stint for the year. One wonders whether his depressions were anything more than the rhythm of work and fatigue.

THE REFORMATION AT WITTENBERG. MONASTICISM

Nor was he actually removed from the fray. The reformation at Wittenberg moved with disconcerting velocity, and he was kept abreast of it in so far as tardy communication and the conditions of his concealment permitted. His opinion was continually solicited, and his answers affected the developments, even though he was not in a position to take the initiative. Leadership fell to Melanchthon, professor of Greek at the university; to Carlstadt, professor and archdeacon at the Castle Church; and to Gabriel Zwilling, a monk of Luther's own order, the Augustinians. Under the lead of these men the reformation for the first time assumed a form distinctly recognizable to the common man.

Nothing which Luther had done hitherto made any difference to the ways of ordinary folk, except of course the attack on indulgences, but that had not as yet proved especially effective. While at the Wartburg, Luther learned that Cardinal Albert of Mainz was continuing the old traffic at Halle. On the first of December, 1521, Luther informed His Grace that he was quite mistaken if he thought Luther dead.

You may think me out of the fray, but I will do what Christian love demands, without regard to the gates of hell, let alone unlearned popes, cardinals, and bishops. I beg you, show yourself not a wolf but a bishop. It has been made plain enough that indulgences are rubbish and lies. See what conflagration has come from a despised spark, so that now the pope himself is singed. The same God is still alive, and he can resist the Cardinal of Mainz though he be upheld by four emperors. This is the God who breaks the cedars of Lebanon and humbles the hardened Pharaohs. You need not think Luther is dead. I will show the difference between a bishop and a wolf. I demand an immediate answer. If you do not reply within two weeks, I will publish a tract against you.

The cardinal replied that the abuses had already been suppressed. He confessed himself to be a stinking sinner, ready to receive correction.

That was something. Yet Luther was not able to say while at the Wartburg that indulgences had been discontinued in his own parish of Wittenberg. Then during his absence in 1521 and 1522 one innovation followed another with disconcerting rapidity. Priests married, monks married, nuns married. Nuns and monks even married each other. The tonsured permitted their hair to grow. The wine in the mass was given to the laity, and they were suffered to take the elements into their own hands. Priests celebrated the sacrament without vestments, in plain clothes. Portions of the mass were recited in the German tongue. Masses for the dead were discontinued. Vigils ceased, vespers were altered, images were smashed. Meat was eaten on fast days. Endowments were withdrawn by patrons. The enrollment in universities declined because students were no longer supported by ecclesiastical stipends. All this could not escape the eye of Hans and Gretel. Doctrine might go over their heads, but liturgy was a part of their daily religious life. They realized now that the reformation meant something, and this began to worry Luther. The glorious liberty of the sons

Wie gar gfarlich sey. So

Ain Priester kain Eeweyb hat. Wye Vn
christlich. vnd schedlich aim gmainen
Nutz die menschen seynd. Welche
hindern die Pfaffen Am Ee-
lichen stand. Durch
Johan Eberlin Von Güntzburg. Anno.

MARRIAGE OF BISHOPS, MONKS, AND NUNS

of God was in danger of becoming a matter of clothes, diet, and haircuts. But he applauded the changes at the start.

First came the marriage of priests. Luther had said in *The Babylonian Captivity* that the laws of men cannot annul the commands of God; and since God has ordained marriage, the union of a priest and his wife is a true and indissoluble union. In the *Address to the Nobility* he declared that a priest must have a housekeeper, and that to put man and woman thus together is like bringing fire to straw and expecting nothing to happen. Marriage should be free to priests, though the whole canon law go to pieces. Let there be an end of unchaste chastity. Luther's advice was being put into practice. Three priests married in 1521 and were arrested by Albert of Mainz. Luther sent him a warm protest. Albert consulted the University of Wittenberg. Carlstadt answered with a work on celibacy, in which he went so far as to assert not only that a priest might marry but that he must, and should also be the father of a family. For obligatory celibacy he would substitute obligatory matrimony and paternity. And he got married himself. The girl was described as of a noble family, neither pretty nor rich, appearing to be about fifteen years of age. Carlstadt sent an announcement to the Elector.

Most noble prince, I observe that in Scripture no estate is so highly lauded as marriage. I observe also that marriage is allowed to the clergy, and for lack of it many poor priests have suffered sorely in the dungeons of the Devil. Therefore if Almighty God permits, I am going to marry Anna Mochau on St. Sebastian's Eve, and I hope Your Grace approves.

Luther did. "I am very pleased over Carlstadt's marriage," he wrote. "I know the girl."

Yet he had no mind to do the like himself because he was not only a priest but also a monk. At first he was aghast when Carlstadt attacked also monastic celibacy. "Good heavens!" wrote Luther, "will our Wittenbergers give wives to monks? They won't give one to me!" But under the fiery preaching of Gabriel Zwilling the Augustinian monks began to leave the cloister. On November 30, fifteen withdrew. The prior reported to the Elector:

It is being preached that no monk can be saved in a cowl, that cloisters are in the grip of the Devil, that monks should be expelled and cloisters demolished. Whether such teaching is grounded in the gospel I greatly doubt.

But now should such monks be forced to go back? And if not, should they be allowed to marry? Melanchthon consulted Luther. "I wish I could talk this over with you," he replied.

The case of a monk seems to me to be different from that of a priest. The monk has voluntarily taken vows. You argue that a monastic vow is not binding because it is incapable of fulfillment. By that token you would abrogate all the divine precepts. You say that a vow entails servitude. Not necessarily. St. Bernard lived happily under his vows. The real question is not whether vows can be kept, but whether they have been enjoined by God.

To find the answer Luther set himself to search the Scriptures. He was not long in making up his mind, and soon sent to Wittenberg some theses about vows. When they were read to the circle of the Wittenberg clergy and professors, Bugenhagen, priest at the Castle Church, pronounced the judgment, "These propositions will upset public institutions as Luther's doctrine up to this point would not have done." The theses were shortly followed by a treatise *On Monastic Vows*. In a preface addressed to "my dearest father" Luther professed now to discern the hand of Providence in making him a monk against his parents' will in order that he might be able to testify from experience against monasticism. The monk's vow is unfounded in Scripture and in conflict with charity and liberty. "Marriage is good, virginity is better, but liberty is best." Monastic vows rest on the false assumption that there is a special calling, *a vocation*, to which superior Christians are invited to observe the counsels of perfection while ordinary Christians fulfill only the commands; but there simply is no special religious vocation, declared Luther, since the call of God comes to each man at the common tasks. "This is the work," said Jonas, "which emptied the cloisters." Luther's own order in Wittenberg, the Augustinians, at a meeting in January, instead of disciplining the apostate monks, ruled that thereafter any member should be free to stay or leave as he might please.

Next came the reform of the liturgy, which touched the common man more intimately because it altered his daily devotions. He was being invited to drink the wine at the sacrament, to take the elements into his own hands, to commune without previous confession, to hear the words of institution in his own tongue, and to participate extensively in sacred song.

Luther laid the theoretical groundwork for the most significant changes. His principle was that the mass is not a sacrifice but a thanksgiving to God and a communion with believers. It is not a sacrifice in the sense of placating God, because he does not need to be placated; and it is not an oblation in the sense of something offered, because man cannot offer to God, but only receive. What then should be done with such expressions in the mass as "this holy sacrifice," "this oblation," "these offerings"? In *The Babylonian Captivity*, Luther had interpreted them figuratively, but at the Wartburg he came to the more drastic conclusion: "The words in the canon are plain; the words of Scripture are plain. Let the canon yield to the gospel." The liturgy then would have to be revised.

A particular form of the mass rested exclusively upon its sacrificial character. This was the private mass for the benefit of departed spirits, for whom the priest offered a sacrifice; and since they could not possibly be present, he communed alone. This form of the mass was called private because privately endowed. It was also privately conducted. Luther objected first to the principle of sacrifice and second to the absence of the congregation. In *The Babylonian Captivity* he had been willing to tolerate such masses as private devotions on the part of the priest, provided of course that they were conducted in a devotional spirit and not rattled through to complete the quota for the day. At the Wartburg he reached a more pronounced position. To Melanchthon he wrote on the first of August, "I will never again celebrate a private mass in eternity." Luther concluded a tract on the abolition of private masses with an appeal to Frederick the Wise to emulate the crusade of Frederick Barbarossa for the liberation of the Holy Sepulchre. Let Frederick liberate the gospel at Wittenberg by abolishing all the masses which he had privately endowed. Incidentally, a staff of twenty-five priests was employed for the saying of such masses at the Castle Church.

On the old question raised by the Hussites, whether the wine as well as the bread should be given to the laity, Luther and the Wittenbergers were agreed in desiring to restore the apostolic practice. As to fasting and confession prior to communion Luther was indifferent. There was variance as to whether the priest should hold aloft the elements. Carlstadt viewed the act as the presentation of a sacrifice to be rejected, whereas Luther saw only a mark of reverence to be retained.

THE OUTBREAK OF VIOLENCE

The agreement was certainly sufficient to warrant action, and Melanchthon made a beginning on September 29 by administering communion in both kinds to a few students in the parish church. In the Augustinian cloister Zwilling delivered impassioned pleas to the brothers to refuse to celebrate unless the mass was reformed. The prior responded that he would rather have no mass than to have it mutilated. Consequently the mass ceased in the Augustinian cloister on October 23. In the Castle Church on All Saints' Day, November 1, the very day for the exhibition of the relics and the dispensing of indulgences, Justus Jonas branded indulgences as rubbish and clamored for the abolition of vigils and private masses. In future he would refuse to celebrate unless communicants were present. Popular violence commenced. Students and townsmen so intimidated the old believers that the faithful Augustinians feared for their own safety and for that of their cloister. The elector was disturbed. As a prince he was responsible for the public peace. As a Christian he was concerned for the true faith. He wished to be enlightened as to the meaning of Scripture, and appointed a committee. But the committee could not agree. No group in Wittenberg could agree, neither the university, nor the

Augustinians, nor the chapter at the Castle Church. "What a mess we are in," said Spalatin, "with everybody doing something else."

The old order argued that God would not have suffered his Church so long to be deceived. Changes should wait at least until unanimity had been achieved, and the clergy should not be molested. Frederick the Wise pointed out, moreover, to the innovators that masses were endowed; and if the masses ceased, the endowments would cease. He could not see how a priest could expect to get married, stop saying mass, and still draw his stipend. The alteration of the mass concerned all Christendom, he argued; and if a little town like Wittenberg could not make up its mind, the rest of the world would not be impressed. Above all, let there be no division and tumult. The Evangelicals replied by pointing to the example of Christ and the apostles, who, though but a handful, were not deterred from reform by the fear of tumult. As for the ancestors who endowed the masses, if they could return to life and receive better instruction, they would be glad to have their money used to further the faith in a better way. The old believers rebutted, "You need not think because you are a handful that therefore you are in the position of Christ and the apostles."

Luther's sympathies for the moment were with the handful, and he was distressed because events were moving too slowly. He had sent Spalatin the manuscripts of his tracts entitled *On Monastic Vows, On the Abolition of Private Masses*, and *A Blast Against the Archbishop of Mainz*. None of them had appeared. Luther resolved to make a trip incognito to Wittenberg to find the reason why.

CHAPTER TWELVE

THE RETURN OF THE EXILE

ITH BEARD SUFFICIENT to deceive his mother the exile from the Wartburg appeared on the streets of Wittenberg on the fourth of December, 1521. He was immensely pleased with all that his associates had lately introduced by way of reform, but irate because his recent tracts had not been published. If Spalatin had withheld them from the printer, let him note that worse would replace them. Spalatin thereupon released the treatises on vows and private masses but still retained the blast against Albert, which never did appear. Luther let it be known in Wittenberg that he was contemplating a blast also against Frederick if he did not disperse his collection of relics and contribute to the poor fund all the gold and silver in which they were encased. At this moment Luther was distinctly for speeding up the reformation.

But not by violence. The day before he arrived in Wittenberg there had been a riot. Students and townsfolk, with knives under their cloaks, invaded the parish church, snatched the mass books from the altar, and drove out the priests. Stones were thrown against those saying private devotions to the Virgin Mary. On the morrow, the very day of Luther's arrival, the Franciscans were intimidated. This was not the worst of it. Luther might perhaps have excused this tumult as a student prank, but on the sortie from and back to the Wartburg he sensed among the people a revolutionary temper. He hastened, therefore, to bring out a warning against recourse to violence. "Remember," he warned, "that Antichrist, as Daniel said, is to be broken without the hand of man. Violence will only make him stronger. Preach, pray, but do not fight. Not that all constraint is ruled out, but it must be exercised by the constituted authorities."

But in the meantime at Wittenberg the constituted authority was inhibitive. Elector Frederick issued an order on December 19 in which he said that discussion might continue, but there could be no changes in the mass until unanimity was reached. Carlstadt thereupon undertook to defy the elector and announced that when his turn came to say mass at New Year's he would give communion in both kinds to the whole town. The elector interposed, but Carlstadt forestalled him by trading his turn for Christmas and by issuing the public invitation only the night before. The populace was stirred, and Christmas Eve was celebrated by rioting. The mob invaded the parish church, smashed the lamps, intimidated the priests, sang through the church, "My maid has lost her shoe," and then from the courtyard caterwauled against the choir. Finally they went to the Castle Church and as the priest was giving the benediction wished him pestilence and hell-fire.

TURMOIL

On Christmas Day 2,000 people assembled in the Castle Church—"the whole town," said a chronicler. And it very nearly was, for the total population was only 2,500. Carlstadt officiated without vestments in a plain black robe. In his sermon he told the people that in preparation for the sacrament they had no need of fasting and confession. If they felt that they must first be absolved, then they lacked faith in the sacrament itself. Faith alone is needed, faith and heartfelt longing and deep contrition. "See how Christ makes you a sharer in his blessedness if you believe. See how he has cleansed and hallowed you through his promise. Still better, see that Christ stands before you. He takes from you all your struggle and doubt, that you may know that through his word you are blessed."

Then Carlstadt recited the mass in Latin, in very abbreviated form omitting all the passages on sacrifice. At the consecration and distribution of the elements, both the bread and the wine, he passed from

Latin into German. For the first time in their lives the 2,000 assembled people heard in their own tongue the words, "This is the cup of my blood of the new and eternal testament, spirit and secret of the faith, shed for you to the remission of sins." One of the communicants so trembled that he dropped the bread. Carlstadt told him to pick it up;

Klagrede der armen verfolgten Götzen vnd Tempelpilder/über so vngleich vrtayl vnd straffe.

A CARTOON AGAINST THE IMAGE BREAKERS

With a very graphic illustration of the saying on the mote and the beam in the background.

but he who had had the courage to come forward and take the sacred morsel into his own hand from the plate, when he saw it desecrated on the floor was so overcome by all the terror of sacrilege to the body of God that he could not bring himself to touch it again.

Under Carlstadt's leading the town council at Wittenberg issued the first city ordinance of the Reformation. Mass was to be conducted about as Carlstadt had done it. Luther's ideas on social reform were implemented. Begging was forbidden. Those genuinely poor should be maintained from a common fund. Prostitutes should be banned. And then came quite a new point: images should be removed from the churches.

The question of images, pictures, and statues of the saints and the Virgin, and crucifixes, had been greatly agitated during the preceding weeks. Zwilling had led an iconoclastic riot, overturning altars and smashing images and pictures of the saints. The author of the idea was Carlstadt. He took his stand squarely upon Scripture: "Thou shalt not make unto thee any graven image, or any likeness of any thing that is in heaven above, or that is in the earth beneath, or that is in the water under the earth." Scripture was reinforced by his own experience. He had been so deeply attached to images as to be diverted by them from true worship. "God is a spirit" and must be worshiped only in spirit. Christ is a spirit, but the image of Christ is wood, silver, or gold. One who contemplates a crucifix is reminded only of the physical suffering of Christ rather than of his spiritual tribulations.

Coupled with this attack on art in religion went an attack also on music in religion. "Relegate organs, trumpets, and flutes to the theater," said Carlstadt.

Better one heart-felt prayer than a thousand cantatas of the Psalms. The lascivious notes of the organ awaken thoughts of the world. When we should be meditating on the suffering of Christ, we are reminded of Pyramus and Thisbe. Or, if there is to be singing, let it be no more than a solo.

While Wittenberg was thus convulsed by iconoclasm, three laymen arrived from Zwickau near the Bohemian border, claiming to be prophets of the Lord and to have had intimate conversations with the Almighty. They had no need of the Bible but relied on the Spirit. If the Bible were important, God would have dropped it directly from heaven. They repudiated infant baptism and proclaimed the speedy erection of the kingdom of the godly through the slaughter of the ungodly, whether at the hands of the Turks or of the godly themselves. Melanchthon listened to them agape. He wrote to the Elector:

I can scarcely tell you how deeply I am moved. But who shall judge them, other than Martin, I do not know. Since the gospel is at stake, arrangements should be made for them to meet with him. They wish it. I would not have written to you if the matter were not so important. We must beware lest we resist the Spirit of God, and also lest we be possessed of the Devil.

But such a disputation with Martin appeared dangerous for him and disturbing for Wittenberg. She had already enough on her plate, was the opinion of Spalatin.

Luther in his letters rejected the prophets on religious grounds, because they talked too glibly.

Those who are expert in spiritual things have gone through the valley of the shadow. When these men talk of sweetness and of being transported to the third heaven, do not believe them. Divine Majesty does not speak directly to men. God is a consuming fire, and the dreams and visions of the saints are terrible. . . . Prove the spirits; and if you are not able to do so, then take the advice of Gamaliel and wait.

In another letter he added:

I am sure we can restrain these firebrands without the sword. I hope the Prince will not imbrue his hands in their blood. I see no reason why on their account I should come home.

Frederick the Wise was harassed by one eruption after another. Next came a blow from the right. The noise of the doings at Wittenberg reached Duke George over the border, and the confessional cleavage coalesced with the ancient rivalry between the two houses of Saxony. Luther was soon able to complete his trinity of opposition as the pope, Duke George, and the Devil. At the moment the duke was the most active of the three. He was at the Diet of Nürnberg and persuaded the estates to send both to Frederick the Wise and to the Bishop of Meissen, who had ecclesiastical jurisdiction over the Wittenberg region, the following instructions:

We have heard that priests celebrate mass in lay habit, omitting essential portions. They consecrate the holy sacrament in German. The recipients are not required to have made prior confession. They take the elements into their own hands and in both kinds. The blood of our Lord is served not in a chalice but in a mug. The sacrament is given to children. Priests are dragged from the altars by force. Priests and monks marry, and the common people are incited to frivolity and offense.

In response to this communication the Bishop of Meissen requested of Frederick the Wise permission to conduct a visitation throughout his domains, and Frederick consented, although making no promises to discipline offenders. Then on February 13 Frederick issued instructions of his own to the university and to the chapter at the Castle Church.

We have gone too fast. The common man has been incited to frivolity, and no one has been edified. We should have consideration for the weak. Images should be left until further notice. The question of begging should be canvassed. No essential portion of the mass should be omitted. Moot points should be discussed. Carlstadt should not preach any more.

This document can scarcely be described as a complete abrogation of the reforms. Frederick simply called a halt and invited further consideration, but he did emphatically abrogate the city ordinance of January. If there were to be reforms, he was determined they should not be by towns but by territories, as in the later German pattern. Carlstadt submitted and agreed not to preach. Zwilling left Wittenberg.

THE INVITATION TO COME BACK

But the town council resolved to defy the elector by inviting Martin Luther to come home. An invitation was sent to him in the name of "The Council and the entire City of Wittenberg." If the elector nullified their ordinance, then they would bring back the author of the whole movement. Probably they expected Luther to exert a moderating influence. Carlstadt and Zwilling were smoldering firebrands. Melanchthon was in a dither, thought of leaving to escape the radicals, and frankly said, "The dam has broken, and I cannot stem the waters." The council knew nowhere to look for leadership save to the Wartburg, and without consulting or even informing the elector invited Luther to return.

He was not unwilling to come, for he had said as early as December that he had no intention of remaining in hiding longer than Easter. He would stay until he had finished a volume of sermons and the translation of the New Testament. Then he proposed to turn to the translation of the Old Testament and to settle somewhere in the neighborhood of Wittenberg in order that he might engage the collaboration of colleagues better versed than he in Hebrew. At the time these scholarly concerns motivated him rather than any desire to take the wheel at Wittenberg.

But when a direct invitation came from the town and congregation, that was to him a call from God.

FREDERICK THE WISE

Luther had the courtesy to notify the elector of his intention. Frederick replied that he realized he had perhaps not done enough. But what should he do? He did not wish to go counter to the will of God, nor to provoke disorder. The Diet of Nürnberg and the Bishop of Meissen threatened intervention. If Luther should return and the pope and the emperor should step in to harm him, the elector would take it amiss. But if the elector should resist, there would be great disturbance in the land. So far as his person was concerned, the elector was prepared to suffer, but he would like to know for what. If he knew that the cross was from God, he would bear it, but at Wittenberg no one knew who was the cook and who the waiter. A new meeting of the diet would take place soon. In the meantime let Luther lie low. Time might change things greatly.

Luther answered:

I wrote for your sake, not for mine. I was disturbed that the gospel was brought into disrepute at Wittenberg. If I were not sure that the gospel is on our side, I would have given up. All the sorrow I have had is nothing compared to this. I would gladly have paid for this with my life, for we can answer neither to God nor to the world for what has happened. The Devil is at work in this. As for myself, my gospel is not from men. Concessions bring only contempt. I cannot yield an inch to the Devil. I have done enough for Your Grace by staying in hiding for a year. I did not do it through cowardice. The Devil knows I would have gone into Worms though there were as many devils as tiles on the roof, and I would ride into Leipzig now, though it rained Duke Georges for nine days.

I would have you know that I come to Wittenberg with a higher protection than that of Your Grace. I do not ask you to protect me. I will protect you more than you will protect me. If I thought you would protect me, I would not come. This is not a case for the sword but for God, and since you are weak in the faith you cannot protect me. You ask what you should do, and think you have done too little. I say you have done too much, and you should do nothing but leave it to God. You are excused if I am captured or killed. As a prince you should obey the emperor and offer no resistance. No one should use force except the one who is ordained to use it. Otherwise there is rebellion against God. But I hope you will not act as my accuser. If you leave the door open, that is enough. If they try to make you do more than that, I will then tell you what to do. If Your Grace had eyes, you would see the glory of God.

THE RETURN TO WITTENBERG

The return to Wittenberg was incomparably brave. Never before had Luther stood in such peril. At the interview with Cajetan and at Worms he had not been under the ban of Church and empire, and Frederick had been ready to provide asylum. But this time Luther was made to know that he could count on no protection in case of extradition by the diet or the emperor. At Worms there had been a second line of defense in Sickingen, Hutten, and the knights. This wall was fast crumbling. Sickingen had had the indiscretion after Worms to embark on an adventure designed to arrest the doom of German knighthood at the expense of the territorial princes and bishops. The attack was focused on the prince bishop, Richard of Greiffenklau, elector and archbishop of Trier. A number of knights who had earlier proffered help to Luther joined Sickingen, but his campaign was doomed at the outset, because victims of his former depredations rallied to Trier and corralled Sickingen in one of his own castles, where he died of wounds. Hutten had been unable to accompany him on this campaign because he was ill of syphilis at the Ebernburg. But in intervals of health he had engaged in a foray on his own, a priests' war he called it, consisting mainly in the sacking of cloisters. When Sickingen failed, he fled to Switzerland to sizzle out his meteoric career on an island of Lake Zurich. The knights who had shared in Sickingen's exploit suffered the confiscation of their estates. Had Luther relied upon them, they would have proved a broken reed. But he had long since resolved to trust only to the Lord of Hosts, who does not always deliver his children from the mouth of the lion.

A detail of Luther's homeward journey is recorded by a Swiss chronicler who apologetically introduced into a cryptic history of the times a leisurely description of an experience of his own when with a companion on the way to Wittenberg he pulled up late one night out of the storm at the portal of the Black Bear Inn of a Thuringian village. The host brought the bedraggled travelers into a room where sat a knight with a bushy black beard clad in a scarlet cloak and woolen tights, his hands resting on the hilt of a sword as he engaged in reading. The knight rose and hospitably invited the muddy wayfarers to sit and share with him a glass. They noticed that his book was in Hebrew. They asked him whether he knew if Luther were in Wittenberg. "I know quite positively that he is not," said he, "but he will be." Then he inquired what the Swiss thought of Luther. The host, observing that the pair were well disposed to the reformer, confided to one that the knight was Luther himself. The Swiss could not believe his ears, thought he must have mistaken the name for Hutten. On parting the next morning they let the knight know that they took him for Hutten. "No, he is Luther," interposed the host. The knight laughed. "You take me for Hutten. He takes me for Luther. Maybe I am the Devil." Within a week they were to meet him again in Wittenberg.

Luther's first concern there was to restore confidence and order. With stalwart presence and mellifluous voice he mounted the pulpit to preach patience, charity, and consideration for the weak. He reminded his hearers that no man can die for another, no man can believe for another, no man can answer for another. Therefore every man should be fully persuaded in his own mind. No one can be intimidated into belief. The violence of those who demolish altars, smash images, and drag priests by the hair was to Luther a greater blow than any ever dealt him by the papacy. He was beginning to realize that perhaps after all he was closer to Rome than to his own sectaries. He was deeply cut because the predictions of his assailants that he would be the occasion of "division, war, and insurrection" were being all too abundantly fulfilled. He pleaded:

Give men time. I took three years of constant study, reflection, and discussion to arrive where I now am, and can the common man, untutored in such matters, be expected to move the same distance in three months? Do not suppose that abuses are eliminated by destroying the object which is abused. Men can go wrong with wine and women. Shall we then prohibit wine and abolish women? The sun, the moon, and stars have been worshiped. Shall we then pluck them out of the sky? Such haste and violence betray a lack of confidence in God. See how much he has been able to accomplish through me, though I did no more than pray and preach. The Word did it all. Had I wished I might have started a conflagration at Worms. But while I sat still and drank beer with Philip and Amsdorf, God dealt the papacy a mighty blow.

In response to these appeals Zwilling agreed to give up celebrating the Lord's Supper with feathers in his beret, and Luther cordially recommended him to a pastorate at Altenburg, one of the villages of Electoral Saxony. Carlstadt took over a congregation in the neighboring Orlamünde. Wittenberg was in hand.

Luther then turned to deal with the elector, who desired from him a statement to be submitted to the Diet at Nürnberg, exculpating the prince from any complicity in the return from the Wartburg. Luther gladly complied but in the course of the letter remarked that things are settled differently in heaven than in Nürnberg. Frederick suggested that the words "on earth" be substituted for "in Nürnberg." Luther again complied.

CHAPTER THIRTEEN

NO OTHER FOUNDATION

 XTERNALLY speaking, Luther had reached the turning point of his career. The leader of the opposition was called to be the head of the government, albeit in a very restricted area. The demolisher was summoned to build. The change of course was not absolute because he had been constructive all along, and to the end he never ceased to flay the papacy. Nevertheless the change was vast between the role of railing against "the execrable bull of Antichrist" and that of providing a new pattern of Church, state, and society, a new constitution for the Church, a new liturgy, and a new Scripture in the vernacular.

In the accomplishment of this task there were two considerations. The first had to do with principles which Luther sought to realize in the concrete, and the second with the people who constituted the field in which these ideas were to be realized. Luther's views were for the most part already mature by the time of his return to Wittenberg. Controversy was to sharpen the emphases. Practical experience dictated the lines of advance or retrenchment, while long years in the pulpit and classroom afforded occasion for copious illustration.

Luther's principles in religion and ethics alike must constantly be borne in mind if he is not at times to appear unintelligible and even petty. The primary consideration with him was always the pre-eminence of religion. Into a society where the lesser breed were given to gaming, roistering, and wenching—the Diet of Worms was called a veritable Venusberg—at a time when the choicer sort were glorying in the accomplishments of man, strode this Luther, entranced by the song of angels, stunned by the wrath of God, speechless before the wonder of creation, lyrical over the divine mercy, a man aflame with God. For such a person there was no question which mattered much save this: How do I stand before God? Luther would never shirk a mundane task such as exhorting the elector to repair the city wall to keep the peasants' pigs from rooting in the villagers' gardens, but he was never supremely concerned about pigs, gardens, walls, cities, princes, or any and all of the blessings and nuisances of this mortal life. The ultimate problem was always God and man's relationship to God. For this reason political and social forms were to him a matter of comparative indifference. Whatever would foster the understanding, dissemination, and practice of God's Word should be encouraged, and whatever impeded must be opposed. This is why it is futile to inquire whether Luther was a democrat, aristocrat, autocrat, or anything else. Religion was for him the chief end of man, and all else peripheral.

And the religion which he had in mind was of course the Christian religion. Everyone in his age would have said that, if for no other reason than out of national or European pride. But Luther so spoke because he had experienced a sheer impasse in any other approach to God than through his own self-disclosure in Jesus Christ. "No other foundation is laid than has been laid in Jesus Christ our Lord."

NATURE, HISTORY, AND PHILOSOPHY

Nature cannot reveal God. Nature is indeed very wonderful, and every particle of creation reveals the handiwork of God, if one has the eyes to see. But that is precisely the difficulty. If one already believes in the beneficence of God, then one is overcome with amazement and joy at the trembling of the dawn when night is not yet day and day is not night but light imperceptibly dispels darkness. How amazing are the clouds sustained without pillars and the firmament of heaven upheld without columns! How fair are the birds of heaven and the lilies of the field! "If thou couldst understand a single grain of wheat, thou wouldst die for wonder." God is in all this. He is in every creature, inwardly and outwardly, through and through, over and under, behind and before, so that nothing can be more inward and hidden in any creature than God. "In him we live, and move, and have our being." Without him is naught. God fills all the world, but by the world he is not contained. "Whither shall I flee from thy presence? If I ascend up into heaven, thou art there: if I make my bed in hell, behold, thou art there." But who sees all this? Only faith and spirit. The trouble with Erasmus is that he is not stupefied with wonder at the child in the womb. He does not contemplate marriage with reverent amazement, nor praise and thank God for the marvel of a flower or the bursting of a peach stone by the swelling seed. He beholds these wonders like a cow staring at a new door. The deficiency of faith is made evident by a lack of wonder, for nature is a revelation only to those to whom God has already been revealed.

It is no better with history, which also cannot reveal God, for the whole of history appears at first glance to be nothing but a commentary on the text, "He hath put down the mighty from their seats, and exalted them of low degree." God suffers the mighty empires to strut for a time upon the stage—Assyria, Babylon, Persia, Greece, and Rome. Then when each becomes too overweening, God places the sword in the hand of another and releases him to cast down the braggart, only in turn after his swaggering to be brought low. Here again we meet with an Augustinian theme, save that for Augustine history is an illustration of man's lust for domination and of the justice of God in abasing the arrogant. But Luther wonders whether God is amusing himself with a puppet show.

Even more disconcerting is the recognition that all too often God does not cast down the mighty and does not exalt those of low degree. But he leaves them in their squalor, unrequited and unavenged. Throughout history it is the saints who are despised and rejected, maltreated, abused, and trodden under the feet of man. Joseph, for example, for no adequate reason was seized by his brethren, cast into the well, sold to the Ishmaelites, and carried as a slave into Egypt. And there precisely because he was honorable he was besmirched with the accusation of adultery and thrown into prison. And the Virgin Mary, after being informed by the angel Gabriel that she was to be the mother of the Most High, had to suffer the suspicion of her own husband. Joseph's situation is understandable, for they had not yet come together, and she had been three months absent with her cousin Elisabeth. He could not well put a good construction upon her condition until the angel instructed him in a dream. But why did God wait to disabuse him until after Mary had been put to shame?

Some of the afflictions which fall upon the just were, in Luther's view, the work of the Devil, and here he was following the familiar Augustinian dualism of the eternal conflict between the City of God and the earthly city through which Satan operates. Luther could in this way take comfort in tumult because the Devil is bound to assail the faith, and tumult is the proof that faith is present and under attack. But it is not always the Devil who is responsible. God is a God who works through contraries. The Virgin had to be put to shame before she could come into glory. Joseph had to be humiliated by false accusation before he could become the prime minister and savior of Egypt. In such moments God appears hidden. Joseph must have had a fearful struggle. He would say, "Oh, if I could only get back to my father," and then he would grip himself and say, "Hold fast. If only I could find the way out of this dungeon. Hold fast. What if I die in disgrace in this prison? Hold fast." Such alternations of anguish and consolation assailed him until he was able to discern the hand of God.

There is no escaping from the horrors of darkness because God is such a God "that before he can be God he must first appear to be the Devil. We cannot reach heaven until we first descend into hell. We cannot be God's children unless first we are the Devil's children. Again before the world can be seen to be a lie it must first appear to be the truth."

It must seem so. Yet God has not really deserted us, but he is hidden, and by direct searching we cannot find him out. Why God wishes to hide himself from us we do not know; but this we know: our nature cannot attain unto his majesty. "David did not speak with the absolute God, whom we must fear if we would not perish, because human nature and the absolute God are implacable enemies. And it cannot but be that human nature should be oppressed by such majesty. Therefore David does not talk with the absolute God but with God clothed and mantled in the Word."

Neither can philosophy reveal God. In making this assertion Luther was in part echoing the language of the late scholastics, on whose works he had been reared. The Occamists had wrecked the synthesis of Thomas Aquinas whereby nature and reason lead through unbroken stages to grace and revelation. Instead between nature and grace, between reason and revelation, these theologies introduced a great gulf. So much so indeed that philosophy and theology were compelled to resort to two different kinds of logic and even two different varieties of arithmetic. The classic illustration was the doctrine of the Trinity, which asserts that three persons are one God. According to human arithmetic this is preposterous, and yet according to divine arithmetic it must be believed. Luther at this point outdid his teachers and asserted that whereas by the standard of human reason two and five equal seven, yet if God should declare them to be eight, one must believe against reason and against feeling. All this Luther could say with his teachers, but such conundrums gave him little concern.

The inadequacy of philosophy was to him the more apparent and the more depressing at those points where his master, St. Augustine, had accentuated the cleavage between the natural man and the redeemed man, and had thereby widened at the same time the breach between natural and revealed religion. Augustine freely conceded that in some respects man still resembles God, in whose image he was created. The fall of Adam did not obliterate all the vestiges, but their meaning is unintelligible to one who is not acquainted with the original pattern. The late scholastics heightened the point that as cow tracks in a meadow bespeak a cow only to one who has previously seen a cow, so the trinitarian structure of man, with intellect, memory, and will, bespeaks the trinitarian structure of God only to one to whom the doctrine has already been revealed.

Luther took over this whole manner of thinking and applied it in a much more drastic and poignant way, because for him the problems were not so much metaphysical as religious. The crucial point was not as to the structure of God but as to the character of God. His structure remains an insoluble mystery into which we were wiser not to pry, but we must ask, Is he good? Is he just? Is he good *to me?* Augustine's heart was no longer restless after he had received the yoke that is easy. But Luther never ceased to revolve these old tormenting queries.

CHRIST THE SOLE REVEALER

For his answer he was driven to seek God where he has chosen to make himself known, namely in the flesh of Jesus Christ our Lord, who is the sole revealer of God.

The prophet Isaiah said, "The people that walked in darkness have seen a great light." Don't you think that this is an inexpressible light which enables us to see the heart of God and the depth of the Godhead? And that we may also see the thoughts of the Devil and what sin is and how to be freed from it and what death is and how to be delivered. And what man is, and the world, and how to conduct oneself in it. No one before was sure what God is or whether there are devils, what sin and death are, let alone how to be delivered. This is all the work of Christ, and in this passage he is called Mighty and Wonderful.

He is the sole redeemer of man from the thralldom of sin and the gates of death. He alone is the hope of any enduring society upon earth. Where men do not know Bethlehem's babe they rave and rage and strive. The angels proclaimed peace on earth, and so shall it be to those who know and receive this Babe. For what is it like where Jesus Christ is not? What is the world if not a perfect hell with nothing but lying, cheating, gluttony, guzzling, lechery, brawling, and murder. That is the very Devil himself. There is no kindliness nor honor. No one is sure of another. One must be as distrustful of friends as of enemies, and sometimes more. This is the kingdom of the world where the Devil reigns and rules. But the angels show in their song that those who know and accept the Child Jesus not only give honor to God but treat their fellow men as if they were gods, with peaceable demeanor, glad to help and counsel any man. They are free from envy and wrangling, for the Christian way is quiet and friendly in peace and brotherly love where each gladly does the best he can for another.

All then would seem to be simple. "Believe on the Lord Jesus Christ, and thou shalt be saved," but faith in Christ is far from simple and easy because he is an astounding king, who, instead of defending his people, deserts them. Whom he would save he must first make a despairing sinner. Whom he would make wise he must first turn into a fool. Whom he would make alive he must first kill. Whom he would bring to honor he must first bring into dishonor. He is a strange king who is nearest when he is far and farthest when he is near.

The attempt of Erasmus to make Christianity simple and easy was to Luther utterly vain because Christ must so deeply offend. Man's corruption must be assailed before ever his eyes can be opened. One of Luther's students recorded:

On Christmas eve of 1538 Dr. Martin Luther was very jocund. All his words and songs and thoughts were of the incarnation of our Lord. Then with a sigh he said, "Oh, we poor men that we should be so cold and indifferent to this great joy which has been given us. This indeed is the greatest gift, which far exceeds all else that God has created. And we believe so feebly even though the angels proclaim and preach and sing, and their song is fair and sums up the whole Christian religion, for 'glory to God in the highest' is the very heart of worship. This they wish for us and bring to us in Christ. For the world, since Adam's fall, knows neither God nor his creatures. Oh, what fine, fair, happy thoughts would man have had-were he not fallen! How he would have meditated upon God in all creatures, that he should see in the smallest and meanest flower God's omnipotent wisdom and goodness! Every tree and branch would have been more esteemed than if it were gold or silver. And properly considered every green tree is lovelier than gold and silver. Surely the contemplation of the whole creation, and especially of the simplest grasses of the fields and the adornment of the earth, proves that our Lord God is an artist like unto none. Adam and his children would have gloried in all this, but now since the pitiable fall the Creator is dishonored and reviled. That is why the dear angels summon fallen men once more to faith in Christ and to love that they may give to God alone the honor and may dwell in this life in peace with God and one another."

The reason why faith is so hard and reason so inadequate is a problem far deeper than logic. Luther often railed at reason, and he has been portrayed in consequence as a complete irrationalist in religion. This is quite to mistake his meaning. Reason in the sense of logic he employed to the uttermost limits. At Worms and often elsewhere he asked to be instructed from Scripture and reason. In this sense reason meant logical deduction from known premises; and when Luther railed against the harlot reason, he meant something else. Common sense is perhaps a better translation. He had in mind the way in which man ordinarily behaves, feels, and thinks. It is not what God says that is a foreign tongue, but what God does that is utterly incomprehensible.

When I am told that God became man, I can follow the idea, but I just do not understand what it means. For what man, if left to his natural promptings, if he were God, would humble himself to lie in the feedbox of a donkey or to hang upon a cross? God laid upon Christ the iniquities of us all.

This is that ineffable and infinite mercy of God which the slender capacity of man's heart cannot comprehend and much less utter—that unfathomable depth and burning zeal of God's love toward us. And truly the magnitude of God's mercy engenders in us not only a hardness to believe but also incredulity itself. For I hear not only that the omnipotent God, the creator and maker of all things, is good and merciful, but also that the Supreme Majesty was so concerned for me, a lost sinner, a son of wrath and of everlasting death, that he spared not his own Son but delivered him to the most ignominious death, that, hanging between two thieves, he might be made a curse and sin for me, a cursed sinner, that I might be made just, blessed, a son and heir of God. Who can sufficiently declare this exceeding great goodness of God? Therefore the holy Scripture speaks of far other than philosophical or political matters, namely of the unspeakable and utterly divine gifts, which far surpass the capacity both of men and of angels.

In God alone can man ever find peace. God can be known only through Christ, but how lay hold on Christ when his ways are likewise so incredible? The answer is not by sight but by faith which walks gaily into the darkness. Yet once again, how shall one come by this faith? It is a gift of God. By no act of will can it be induced.

THE WORD AND THE SACRAMENTS

No, but man is not left entirely without recourse. He can expose himself to those channels of self-disclosure which God has ordained. They are all summed up in the *Word*. It is not to be equated with Scripture nor with the sacraments, yet it operates through them and not apart from them. The *Word* is not the Bible as a written book because "the gospel is really not that which is contained in books and composed in letters, but rather an oral preaching and a living word, a voice which resounds throughout the whole world and is publicly proclaimed." This Word must be heard. This Word must be pondered. "Not through thought, wisdom, and will does the faith of Christ arise in us, but through an incomprehensible and hidden operation of the Spirit, which is given by faith in Christ only at the hearing of the Word and without any other work of ours." More, too, than mere reading is required. "No one is taught through much reading and thinking. There is a much higher school where one learns God's Word. One must go into the wilderness. Then Christ comes and one becomes able to judge the world."

Likewise faith is given to those who avail themselves of those outward rites which again God has ordained as organs of revelation, the sacraments.

For although he is everywhere and in all creatures and I may find him in stone, fire, water, or rope, since he is assuredly there, yet he does not wish me to seek him apart from the Word, that I should throw myself into fire or water or hang myself with a rope. He is everywhere, but he does not desire that you should seek him everywhere but only where the Word is. There if you seek him you will truly find, namely in the Word. These people do not know and see who say that it doesn't make sense that Christ should be in bread and wine. Of course Christ is with me in prison and the martyr's death, else where should I be? He is truly present there with the Word, yet not in the same sense as in the sacrament, because he has attached his body and blood to the Word and in bread and wine is bodily to be received.

These were Luther's religious principles: that religion is paramount, that Christianity is the sole true religion to be apprehended by faith channeled through Scripture, preaching, and sacrament.

The practical deductions from such a view are obvious. All institutions must accord to religion the right of way. The study of Scripture must be cultivated in church and school. In church the pulpit and the altar must each sustain the other.

Still further consequences of a less tangible sort were implicit. If religion is so central, then all human relations must be conditioned by it. Alliances, friendships, and matings will be secure only if grounded in a common faith. Contemporaries were sometimes appalled that Luther would disrupt human relations or churchly unities over a single point of doctrine. To which he replied that he might as well be told it was unreasonable to sever friendship over the single point of strangling his wife or child. To deny God in one point is to attack God in all.

Again the exclusiveness which Luther assigned to Christianity was bound to entail a sentence of rejection upon other religions such as Judaism. He might or he might not be charitable to the worshipers of false gods, but their error he could never condone. Neither could he feel leniently disposed toward those who disparaged or in his judgment misinterpreted the Scripture and the sacraments.

THE MENACE TO MORALS

In the field of morals many felt that his preoccupation with religion was dangerous. Particularly his insistence that upright conduct constitutes no claim upon God was believed to undercut the most potent motive for good behavior. The same retort was given to Luther as to Paul. If we are saved not by merit but by mercy, "let us then sin that grace may abound." Both Paul and Luther answered, "God forbid." And anyone who had followed Luther closely would have known that he was far from indifferent to morality. Nevertheless the charge was not altogether perverse. Luther did say things at times which emphatically sounded subversive to morals. The classic example is the notorious *pecca fortiter*, "Sin for all you are worth.

God can forgive only a lusty sinner." To make this the epitome of
Luther's ethic is grossly unfair because it was a piece of uproarious
chaffing of the anemic Melanchthon, who was in a dither over scruples
of conscience. Luther's counsel was essentially the same as that given
to him by Staupitz, who told him that before coming so frequently
to the confessional he should go out and commit a real sin like parricide. Staupitz was certainly not advising Luther to murder his father,
and Luther well knew that his jest would not induce the impeccable
Melanchthon to jettison the Ten Commandments. Luther was saying
merely that it might do him good for once to spoil his record.

This is a point which Luther did make at times, that one sin is needed
as medicine to cure another. An unblemished record engenders the
worst of all sins, pride. Hence a failure now and then is conducive
to humility. But the only sins which Luther actually recommended
as record spoilers were a little overeating, overdrinking, and oversleep-
ing. Such controlled excesses might be utilized as the antidote to arrogance.

He did say something else with an unethical ring, however, namely,
that good works without faith "are idle, damnable sins." Erasmus was
horrified to hear integrity and decency so stigmatized. But Luther
never meant to say that from the social point of view decency is no
better than indecency. What he meant was that the decency of the
man who behaves himself simply for fear of damaging his reputation
is in the eyes of God an idle, damnable sin, and far worse than the indecency of the contrite offender. Luther's statement is nothing more
than a characteristically paradoxical version of the parable of the
penitent publican.

But perhaps the deepest menace of Luther to morals lay in his
rescue of morals. He would suffer no attenuation of the appalling
demands of the New Testament. Christ said, "Give away your cloak,
take no thought for the morrow, when struck turn the other cheek,
sell all and give to the poor, forsake father and mother, wife and
child." The Catholic Church of the Middle Ages had several devices
for attenuating the inexorable. One was to make a distinction between
Christians and to assign only to heroic souls the more arduous injunc-

tions of the gospel. The counsels of perfection were consigned to monasticism. Luther closed this door by abolishing monasticism. Another distinction was between the continuous and the customary. Strenuous Christians should love God and the neighbor uninterruptedly, but ordinary Christians only ordinarily. Luther was scornful of all such casuistry; and when reminded that without it the precepts of the gospel are impossible, he would retort, "Of course they are. God commands the impossible." But then comes again the old question, If the goal cannot be reached, why make the effort?

Here one must be clear as to precisely how much Luther meant by calling the goal unattainable. He very clearly meant that the noblest human achievement will fall short in the eyes of God. All men are sinners. But they are not for that reason all rascals. A certain level of morality is not out of reach. Even the Jews, the Turks, and the heathen are able to keep the natural law embodied in the Ten Commandments.

"Thou shalt not steal" should be placed by the miller on his sack, the baker on his bread, the shoemaker on his last, the tailor on his cloth, and the carpenter on his ax.

Temptations of course cannot be avoided, but because we cannot prevent the birds from flying over our heads, there is no need that we should let them nest in our hair.

There is then a wide basis for genuine moral conduct even apart from Christianity.

But once more the danger to ethics arises because all this is not enough. God demands not only acts but attitudes. He is like the mother who asks her daughter to cook or to milk the cow. The daughter may comply gaily or grudgingly. Not only does God require that we refrain from adultery, but he exacts purity of thought and restraint within marriage. These are the standards to which we cannot attain. "A horse can be controlled with a golden bit, but who can control himself at those points where he is vitally touched?" Even our very quest for God is a disguised form of self-seeking. The pursuit of perfection is all the more hopeless because the goal is recessive. Every act of goodness opens the door for another; and if we do not enter in, we have failed. Hence all righteousness of the moment is sin with respect to that which must be added in the following instant. Even more disconcerting is the discovery that we are guilty of sins of which we are not aware. Luther had learned in the confessional the difficulty of remembering or recognizing his shortcomings. The very recognition that we are sinners is an act of faith. "By faith alone it must be believed that we are sinners, and indeed more often than not we seem to know nothing against ourselves. Wherefore we must stand by God's judgment and believe his words by which he calls us unrighteous."

THE GROUND OF GOODNESS

Once again Luther's critics arise to inquire whether if man in the end has no standing with God he should make the effort to be good. Luther's answer is that morality must be grounded somewhere else than in self-help and the quest for reward. The paradox is that God must destroy in us all illusions of righteousness before he can make us righteous. First we must relinquish all claim to goodness. The way to eliminate feelings of guilt is to admit guilt. Then there is some hope for us. "We are sinners and at the same time righteous"—which is to say that however bad we are, there is a power at work in us which can and will make something out of us.

This is wonderful news to believe that salvation lies outside ourselves. I am justified and acceptable to God, although there are in me sin, unrighteousness, and horror of death. Yet I must look elsewhere and see no sin. This is wonderful, not to see what I see, not to feel what I feel. Before my eyes I see a gulden, or a sword, or a fire, and I must say, "There is no gulden, no sword, no fire." The forgiveness of sins is like this.

And the effect of it is that the forgiven, unpretentious sinner has vastly more potentialities than the proud saint.

The righteousness of the sinner is no fiction. It must and it will produce good works, but they can never be good if done for their own sake. They must spring from the fount of the new man. "Good works do not make a man good, but a good man does good works."

Von der freyheyt
eynes Christen
menschen.

Martinus Luther.

Czu Vuittenberg: Im
XX.iar.

TITLE PAGE OF "ON THE FREEDOM OF THE CHRISTIAN MAN"

Luther variously described the ground of goodness. Sometimes he would say that all morality is gratitude. It is the irrepressible expression of thankfulness for food and raiment, for earth and sky, and for the inestimable gift of redemption. Again morality is the fruit of the spirit dwelling in the heart of the Christian. Or morality is the behavior becoming the nature of one united with Christ as the bride with the bridegroom. As there is no need to tell lovers what to do and say, so is there no need for any rules to those who are in love with Christ. The only word that covers all this is faith. It removes all the inhibitions arising from worry and sets man in such a relationship to God and Christ that all else will come of itself.

Nowhere does Luther set forth his views in more rugged and glowing words than in the canticle *On the Freedom of the Christian Man.*

The soul which with a firm faith cleaves to the promises of God is united with them, absorbed by them, penetrated, saturated, inebriated by their power. If the touch of Christ was healing, how much more does that most tender touch in the spirit, that absorption in the Word convey to the soul all the qualities of the Word so that it becomes trustworthy, peaceable, free, full of every good, a true child of God. From this we see very easily why faith can do so much and no good work is like unto it, for no good work comes from God's Word like faith. No good work can be within the soul, but the Word and faith reign there. What the Word is that the soul is, as iron becomes fire-red through union with the flame. Plainly then faith is enough for the Christian man. He has no need for works to be made just. Then is he free from the law.

But he is not therefore to be lazy or loose. Good works do not make a man good, but a good man does good works. A bishop is not a bishop because he consecrates a church, but he consecrates a church because he is a bishop. Unless a man is already a believer and a Christian, his works have no value at all. They are foolish, idle, damnable sins, because when good works are brought forward as ground for justification, they are no longer good. Understand that we do not reject good works, but praise them highly. The apostle Paul said, "Let this mind be in you which was also in Christ Jesus, who being on an equality with God emptied himself, taking the form of a servant, and becoming obedient unto death." Paul means that when Christ was fully in the form of God, abounding in all things, so that he had no need of any work or any suffering to be saved, he was not puffed up, did not arrogate to himself power, but rather in suffering, working, enduring, and dying made himself like other men, as if he needed all things and were not in the form of God. All this he did to serve us. When God in his sheer mercy and without any merit of mine has given me such unspeakable riches, shall I not then freely, joyously, wholeheartedly, unprompted do everything that I know will please him? I will give myself as a sort of Christ to my neighbor as Christ gave himself for me.

This is the word which ought to be placarded as the epitome of Luther's ethic, that a Christian must be a Christ to his neighbor. Luther goes on to explain what this entails.

I must even take to myself the sins of others as Christ took mine to himself. Thus we see that the Christian man lives not to himself but to Christ and his neighbor through love. By faith he rises above himself to God and from God goes below himself in love and remains always in God and in love.

Where will one find a nobler restoration of ethics, and where will one find anything more devastating to ethics? The Christian man is so to identify himself with his neighbor as to take to himself sins that he has not personally committed. The parents assume the sins of the children, the citizens the sins of the state. Luther's scorn was directed against making the chief end of man to keep the record clean. The Christian, like Christ, must in some sense become sin with and for the sinner, and like Christ share in the alienation of those who through sin are separated from God.

CHAPTER FOURTEEN

REBUILDING THE WALLS

HE REBUILDING of the walls of Jerusalem by Ezra and Nehemiah is quaintly illustrated in Luther's German Bible by a woodcut in which the theme is from the Old Testament and the scenery from Saxony. The rebuilders of the walls are the Jews returned from Babylon. The stones, mortar, logs, saws, wheelbarrows, inclined planes, and derricks are precisely those employed to repair the walls of Wittenberg. Very similar was Luther's application of Christian principles to the reconstruction of society. The pre-eminence of religion, the sole sufficiency of Christianity, the obligation of the Christian to be a Christ to the neighbor —these were the principles. The applications were conservative. Luther came not to destroy, but to fulfill, and against all misconception of his teaching sought to make plain that the traditional Christian ethic remained intact. *The Sermon on Good Works* is built, not around the Beatitudes, but around the Ten Commandments, the core of the law of Moses equated with the law of nature. Like those before him Luther extended the command to honor father and mother to include reverence for all in authority, such as bishops, teachers, and magistrates. His domestic ethic was Pauline and patriarchal, the economic ethic Thomistic and mainly agrarian, the political ethic Augustinian and small town.

THE CALLINGS

In one respect Luther was more conservative than Catholicism because he abolished monasticism and thus eliminated a selected area for the practice of the higher righteousness. In consequence the gospel could be exemplified only in the midst of secular callings, except that Luther refused to call them secular. As he had extended the priesthood of all believers, so likewise he extended the concept of divine calling, vocation, to all worthy occupations.

Our expression "vocational guidance" comes directly from Luther. God has called men to labor because he labors. He works at common occupations. God is a tailor who makes for the deer a coat that will last for a thousand years. He is a shoemaker also who provides boots that the deer will not outlive. God is the best cook, because the heat of the sun supplies all the heat there is for cooking. God is a butler who sets forth a feast for the sparrows and spends on them annually more than the total revenue of the king of France. Christ worked as a carpenter. "I can just imagine," said Luther from the pulpit, "the people of Nazareth at the judgment day. They will come up to the Master and say, 'Lord, didn't you build my house? How did you come

REBUILDING THE WALLS OF JERUSALEM

to this honor?'" The Virgin Mary worked, and the most amazing example of her humility is that after she had received the astonishing news that she was to be the mother of the Redeemer, she did not vaunt herself but went back and milked the cows, scoured the kettles, and swept the house like any housemaid. Peter worked as a fisherman and was proud of his skill, though not too proud to take a suggestion from the Master when he told him to cast on the other side. Luther commented:

I would have said, "Now look here, Master. You are a preacher, and I am not undertaking to tell you how to preach. And I am a fisherman, and you need not tell me how to fish." But Peter was humble, and the Lord therefore made him a fisher of men.

The shepherds worked. They had a mean job watching their flocks by night, but after seeing the babe they went back.

Surely that must be wrong. We should correct the passage to read, "They went and shaved their heads, fasted, told their rosaries, and put on cowls." Instead we read, "The shepherds returned." Where to? To their sheep. The sheep would have been in a sorry way if they had not.

As God, Christ, the Virgin, the prince of the apostles, and the shepherds labored, even so must we labor in our callings. God has no hands and feet of his own. He must continue his labors through human instruments. The lowlier the task the better. The milkmaid and the carter of manure are doing a work more pleasing to God than the psalm singing of a Carthusian. Luther never tired of defending those callings which for one reason or another were disparaged. The mother was considered lower than the virgin. Luther replied that the mother exhibits the pattern of the love of God, which overcomes sins just as her love overcomes dirty diapers.

Workers with brawn are prone to despise workers with brain, such as city secretaries and schoolteachers. The soldier boasts that it is hard work to ride in armor and endure heat, frost, dust, and thirst. But I'd like to see a horseman who could sit the whole day and look into a book. It is no great trick to hang two legs over a horse. They say writing is just pushing a feather, but I notice that they hang swords on their hips and feathers in high honor on their hats. Writing occupies not just the fist

Wes sich ein Haußvatter mit seiner
Arbeit das Jar über/Alle Monat in sonderheit/
halten soll.

A FATHER OF A HOUSEHOLD AT WORK

or the foot while the rest of the body can be singing or jesting, but the whole man. As for schoolteaching, it is so strenuous that no one ought to be bound to it for more than ten years.

Luther preferred to center his social thinking around the callings and to deal with men where they were in their stations, but he could not well treat all occupations in a purely personal way without regard to wider contexts. Luther recognized three broad areas of human relations, all of them good because instituted by God at the creation prior to the fall of man. These three are the ecclesiastical, the political, and the domestic, including the economic, which Luther conceived primarily in terms of raising a family. Among these only the ecclesiastical engaged his theoretical thinking in any detail. The state was for him ordinarily simply the magistrate, though he did envisage the state as an association for mutual benefit, and in view of the fall of man as that institution which is peculiarly invested with the exercise of coercive power. In the realm of economics he considered less abstract laws of supply and demand than the personal relations of buyer and seller, debtor and creditor. His views with regard to marriage and the family will be considered later.

ECONOMICS

In the economic sphere Luther was as conservative in the same sense as in the theological. In both he charged the Church of his day with innovation and summoned his contemporaries to return to the New Testament and to the early Middle Ages. The new Europe after the barbarian invasions had been agrarian, and the Church had bestowed the highest esteem on agriculture, next on handicraft, and last of all on commerce. This too was Luther's scale of values. He was not hospitable to the changes introduced by the Crusades, which recovered the Mediterranean for Christian trade and thus gave an immense stimulus to commerce. The altered situation greatly affected the propriety of lending at interest. When a loan was of food stuffs in a famine of the early Middle Ages, any replacement in excess of the goods consumed appeared to be extortion. But in a commercial venture for profit the case was different. St. Thomas saw this and sanctioned a sharing in profit by the lender provided there was

FROM TITLE PAGE OF LUTHER'S TRACT
"ON USURY"

also a sharing in loss. A contract of mutual risk was acceptable but not a contract of fixed return which would give to Shylock his ducats even though the ships of Antonio were on the rocks. In the age of the Renaissance, however, adventurers preferred a higher stake and bankers a more assured though lower return. The Church was ready to accommodate them both because she herself was so intimately involved in the whole process of the rise of capitalism, with banking, bookkeeping, credit, and loans. The Fuggers were not begrudged the services of the theologian John Eck to defend for a subsidy all the casuistic devices for evading the medieval and Thomistic restrictions on interest.

Luther on the other hand became the champion of the precapitalist economy. How agrarian was his thinking is vividly exemplified in a cartoon on the title page of his tract on usury, in which a peasant is shown in the act of returning not only the goose which he had borrowed but also the eggs. Luther took his stand on the Deuteronomic prohibition of usury and the Aristotelian theory of the sterility of money. One gulden, said Luther, cannot produce another. The only way to make money is to work. Monastic idleness is a stench. If Adam had never fallen, he would still have worked at tilling and hunting. Begging should be abolished. Those who cannot protect themselves should be maintained by the community and the rest should work. There is but one exception. The aged with available funds may loan at interest not in excess of 5 per cent or less, depending on the success of the enterprise. That is, Luther retained the contract of mutual risk. Otherwise loans for him came under the head of charity; and Luther, despite his contempt for the Franciscan vow of poverty, was himself Franciscan in the prodigality of his giving.

Obviously Luther was opposed to the spirit of capitalism, and naïvely attributed the rise of prices to the rapacity of the capitalists. At the same time he contributed himself unwittingly to the developments which he deplored. The abolition of monasticism and the expropriation of ecclesiastical goods, the branding of poverty as either a sin or at least a misfortune if not a disgrace, and the exaltation of work as the imitation of God stimulated distinctly the spirit of economic enterprise.

POLITICS

With regard to the state one must bear in mind that Luther was not primarily interested in politics, but in his position he could not avoid politics. Concrete situations pressed upon him, and he offered prompt comments. Emperor Charles forbade his New Testament—intolerable! Elector Frederick protected his cause and his person—admissible! The papacy deposed heretical rulers—usurpation! The Church fomented crusades—abomination! The sectaries rejected all government—the very devil! When Luther came to construct a theory of government, he relied, as in theology, on Paul and Augustine.

The point of departure for all Christian political thinking has been the thirteenth chapter of Romans, where obedience is enjoined to the higher powers because they are ordained of God and bear not the sword in vain that as ministers of God they may execute wrath upon evildoers. Luther was perfectly clear that coercion can never be eliminated because society can never be Christianized.

The world and the masses are and always will be unchristian, although they are baptized and nominally Christian. Hence a man who would venture to govern an entire community or the world with the gospel would be like a shepherd who should place in one fold wolves, lions, eagles, and sheep. The sheep would keep the peace, but they would not last long. The world cannot be ruled with a rosary.

The sword to which Luther referred meant for him the exercise of restraint in preserving the peace both within and without the state. The police power in his day was not differentiated from war, and the soldier had a dual function.

In the use of the sword the ruler and his men act as the instruments of God. "Those who sit in the office of magistrate sit in the place of God, and their judgment is as if God judged from heaven." "If the emperor calls me," said Luther when invited to Worms, "God calls me." This would seem to settle the question that a Christian can serve as magistrate, but not necessarily, because God can make use of the worst sinners as his instruments, just as he employed the Assyrian as the rod of his anger. And in any case Christianity is not necessary for a sound political administration because politics belongs to the sphere of nature. Luther combined a denial of man's perfectibility with a sober faith in man's essential decency. It is perfectly true that men if unrestrained will devour each other like fishes, but equally is it true that all men recognize by the light of reason that murder, theft, and adultery are wrong. The propriety of gradations within society appeared to Luther equally obvious. "I do not need the Holy Spirit to tell me that the Archbishop of Mainz sits higher than the Bishop of Brandenburg." Reason in its own sphere is quite adequate to tell a man how to tend cows, build houses, and govern states. It is even "reported that there is no better government on earth than under the Turks, who have neither civil nor canon law but only the Koran." The natural man can be trusted to recognize and administer justice provided he operates within the framework of law and government and does not seek to vindicate himself. In that case he cannot be trusted. "If the magistrate allows any private feeling to enter in, then he is the very devil. He has a right to seek redress in an orderly way, but not to avenge himself by using the keys of his office."

But if under such conditions the non-Christian may perfectly well administer the state, why should a Christian be a statesman? And if the state is ordained because of sin, why not let sinners run it while the saints as a whole adopt the code of monks and renounce all exercise of the sword? To these questions Luther replied that if the Christian is involved for himself alone, he should suffer himself to be despoiled, but he has no right to make the same renunciation for his neighbor. This sounds as if Luther were saying that the ethical code of the Christian community should be set by the weaker members. The Christian who for himself would renounce protection must ensure justice to others. If the Christian abstains, the government may not be strong enough to afford the necessary protection. Not for himself then, but out of love for the neighbor the Christian accepts and upholds the office of the sword.

Is he not then involved in a double ethic? The charge has been leveled against Luther that he relegated the Christian ethic to private life and turned over the state to the Devil. This is a gross misunderstanding of his position. His distinction was not between private and public, but between individual and corporate. The point was that a man cannot act so blithely when responsible for wife, child, pupils, parishioners, and subjects as if involved only for himself. One has no right to forego rights if they are other people's rights. The line was not between the state and all other institutions, because Luther placed the family on the side of the state and classed the father with the magistrate as equally bound to exercise severity, however much the methods might differ. One can say that Luther consigned the literal observance of the Sermon on the Mount to individual relations. He would not have the private man defend himself. Perhaps by a miracle one could do so in a disinterested spirit, but the course is very hazardous. Further must it be recognized that the distinction between individual and corporate does not exhaust Luther's categories. The minister also might not use the sword, not for himself or anybody else because of a different office. The magistrate uses the sword, the father uses the fist, the minister uses the tongue. In other words, there are varying codes of behavior according to the callings. In all this, Luther was drawing from and simplifying St. Augustine, who in his ethic of war had posited four categories: that of the magistrate, who determines the justice of the cause and declares hostilities; that of the private citizen, who wields the sword only at the magistrate's behest; that of the minister, who abstains from the sword because of his service at the altar; and that of the monk, who abstains because dedicated to the counsels of perfection. Luther accepted these categories with the omission of the monk.

But for all the codes there must be only one disposition. The unifying factor is the attitude of Christian love. This is the sense in which the Sermon on the Mount applies in all relations, even in war, because the killing of the body in the eyes of Augustine and Luther was not incompatible with love. Slaying and robbing in war are to be compared to the amputation of a limb to save a life. Since the exercise of the sword is necessary for the maintenance of peace, war may be regarded as a small misfortune designed to prevent a greater. But then Luther would shift the problem from man to God.

When a magistrate condemns to death a man who has done him no harm, he is not his enemy. He does this at God's behest. There should be no anger or bitterness in the man's heart, but only the wrath and sword of God. Also in war, where in defense one has to hew, stab, and burn, there is sheer wrath and vengeance, but it does not come from the heart of man but from the judgment and command of God.

Luther's problem was thus ultimately theological. He believed that God had drowned the whole human race in a flood, had wiped out Sodom with fire, and had extinguished lands, peoples, and empires. God's behavior forces one to conclude that he is almighty and frightful. But this is the hidden God, and faith holds that at the last his severities will appear as mercies. "Therefore the civil sword out of great mercy must be unmerciful and out of sheer goodness must exercise wrath and severity." The dualism does not lie in any outward sphere but in the heart of God and man. Hence the office of the magistrate must be fraught with sadness. "The godly judge is distressed by the condemnation of the guilty and is truly sorry for the death which justice brings upon them." "The executioner will say, 'Dear God, I kill a man unwillingly, for in thy sight I am no more godly than he.'"

CHURCH AND STATE

With regard to the relations of Church and state, the matter is complicated because Luther introduced two other entities not to be equated with either. He called them the Kingdom of Christ and the Kingdom of the World. Neither actually exists on earth. They are rather contrary principles, like Augustine's City of God and City of the Earth. The Kingdom of Christ is the way men behave when actuated by the spirit of Christ, in which case they have no need for laws and swords. Such a society, however, is nowhere in evidence, not even in the Church itself, which contains the tares along with the wheat. And the Kingdom of the World is the way men behave when not restrained by law and government. But as a matter of fact they are so restrained. Church and state, then, are not to be identified with the Kingdom of Christ and the Kingdom of the World, but Church and state are both rent by the tugging of the demonic and the divine.

The demarcation of the spheres of Church and state corresponds in a rough way to dualisms running through the nature of God and man. God is wrath and mercy. The state is the instrument of his wrath, the Church of his mercy. Man is divided into outward and inward. Crime is outward and belongs to the state. Sin is inward and belongs to the Church. Goods are outward and fall to the state. Faith is inward and falls to the Church, because

faith is a free work to which no one can be forced. Heresy is a spiritual matter and cannot be prevented by constraint. Force may avail either to strengthen alike faith and heresy, or to break down integrity and turn a heretic into a hypocrite who confesses with his lips what he does not believe in his heart. Better to let men err than to drive them to lie.

The most important distinction for Luther's political thought was between the lower and the higher capacities of man, corresponding to nature and reason on the one hand and to grace and revelation on the other. The natural man, when not involved for himself, has enough integrity and insight to administer the state in accord with justice, equity, and even magnanimity. These are the civil virtues. But the Church inculcates humility, patience, long-suffering, and charity—the Christian virtues—attainable even approximately only by those endowed with grace, and consequently not to be expected from the masses. That is why society cannot be ruled by the gospel. And that is why theocracy is out of the question. Then again there are different levels involved. The God of the state is the God of the Magnificat, who exalts the lowly and abases the proud. The God of the Church is the God of Gethsemane, who suffered at the hands of men without retaliation or reviling and refused the use of the sword on his behalf.

These distinctions all point in the direction of the separation of

Church and state. But on the other hand Luther did not split God and did not split man. And if he did not contemplate a Christianized society, he was not resigned to a secularized culture. The Church must run the risk of dilution rather than leave the state to the cold light of reason, unwarmed by tenderness. Of course if the magistrate were not a Christian, separation would be the obvious recourse. But if he were a convinced church member, the Church should not disdain his help in making the benefits of religion accessible to the whole populace. The magistrate should be the nursing father of the Church. Such a parallelism is reminiscent of the dream of Dante, never actually realized in practice, because, where Church and state are allied, one always dominates, and the outcome is either theocracy or caesaropapism. Luther declined to separate Church and state, repudiated theocracy, and thereby left the door open for caesaropapism, however remote this was from his intent.

He has been accused of fostering political absolutism, of leaving the citizen without redress against tyranny, of surrendering conscience to the state, and of making the Church servile to the powers that be. These accusations rest upon a modicum of truth, because Luther did inculcate reverence for government and discountenanced rebellion. He was the more emphatic because he was accused by the papists of subversiveness to government. He countered with characteristic exaggeration which left him open on the other side to the charge of subservience. "The magistracy," said he, "has never been so praised since the days of the apostles as by me"—by which he meant that none had so stoutly withstood ecclesiastical encroachments. Christ himself, affirmed Luther, renounced any theocratic intentions by allowing himself to be born when a decree went out from Augustus Caesar. In most unqualified terms Luther repudiated rebellion because if the mob breaks loose, instead of one tyrant there will be a hundred. At this point he was endorsing the view of St. Thomas that tyranny is to be ended by insurrection only if the violence will presumably do less damage than the evil which it seeks to correct.

All of which is not to say that Luther left the oppressed without recourse. They had prayer, which Luther did not esteem lightly, and they had the right of appeal. Feudal society was graded, and every lord had his overlord. If the common man was wronged, he might address himself against the lord to the overlord, all the way up to the emperor. When, for example, Duke Ulrich of Württemberg murdered a Hutten and took his wife, the Hutten clan appealed to the empire, and the duke was expelled. The emperor in turn was subject to check by the electors. If one inquire as to the attitude of Luther to democracy, one must bear in mind that democracy is a complex concept. A widely extended franchise commended itself to none in his generation, except in Switzerland, but a responsiveness of government to the will and welfare of the people may have been better exemplified in the intimate patriarchalism of his feudal society than in the unwieldy modern democracies.

Neither was conscience surrendered to the state. The illegitimacy of rebellion did not exclude civil disobedience. This was not a right, but a duty on two counts: "In case the magistrate transgresses the first three of the Ten Commandments relating to religion, say to him, 'Dear lord, I owe you obedience with life and goods. Command me within the limits of your power on earth, and I will obey. But to put away books [referring to Luther's New Testament] I will not obey, for in this you are a tyrant.'" Secondly, the prince is not to be obeyed if he requires service in a war manifestly unjust, as when Joachim of Brandenburg enlisted soldiers, ostensibly against the Turk but really against the Lutherans. They deserted with Luther's hearty approval. "Since God will have us leave father and mother for his sake, certainly he will have us leave lords for his sake."

Servility on the part of the Church to the magistrate was repugnant to Luther. The minister is commissioned to be the mentor of the magistrate.

We should wash the fur of the magistrate and clean out his mouth whether he laughs or rages. Christ has instructed us preachers not to withhold the truth from the lords but to exhort and chide them in their injustice. Christ did not say to Pilate, "You have no power over me." He said that Pilate did have power, but he said, "You do not have this power from yourself. It is given to you from God." Therefore he upbraided Pilate. We do the same. We recognize the authority, but we must rebuke our Pilates in their crime and self-confidence. Then they say to us, "You are reviling the majesty of God," to which we answer, "We will suffer what you do to us, but to keep still and let it appear that you do right when you do wrong, that we cannot and will not do." We must confess the truth and rebuke the evil. There is a big difference between suffering injustice and keeping still. We should suffer. We should not keep still. The Christian must bear testimony for the truth and die for the truth. But how can he die for the truth if he has not first confessed the truth? Thus Christ showed that Pilate did exercise authority from God and at the same time rebuked him for doing wrong.

Here Luther was returning to the theme of the calling. The magistrate has his calling; the minister has his calling. Each must serve God according to his office. One calling is not better than another. One is not easier than another. There are temptations peculiar to each. The husband is tempted to lust, the merchant to greed, the magistrate to arrogance. And if the duty is faithfully performed, all the more will there be crosses.

If the burgomaster does his duty, there will scarcely be four who will like him. If the father disciplines his son, the lad will be ugly. It is true everywhere. The prince has nothing for his pains. One is tempted to say, "Let the Devil be burgomaster. Let Lucifer preach. I will go to the desert and serve God there." It is no light task to love your neighbor as yourself. The more I live, the more vexation I have. But I will not grumble. So long as I have my job I will say, "I did not start it for myself, and I will not end it. It is for God and those who want to hear the gospel, and I will not pass by on the other side."

But the spirit of work should not be grim. Let the birds here teach us a lesson.

If you say, "Hey, birdie, why are you so gay? You have no cook, no cellar," he will answer, "I do not sow, I do not reap, I do not gather into barns. But I have a cook, and his name is Heavenly Father. Fool, shame on you. You do not sing. You work all day and cannot sleep for worry. I sing as if I had a thousand throats."

The sum of it all is this, that at certain points Luther's attitudes on economic and political problems could be predicted in advance. He would tolerate no wanton disturbance of the ancient ways. Rebellion was to him intolerable; but since religion alone is the paramount concern of man, the forms of the external life are indifferent and may be left to be determined by circumstance.

CHAPTER FIFTEEN

THE MIDDLE WAY

 ᴘᴇʀsᴏɴs committed to his ideals were plainly necessary if Luther's program was to be implemented. At one time the hope did not appear unrealistic that all Europe could be enlisted for the reform. Luther naïvely supposed that the pope himself, when abuses were called to his attention, would promptly correct them. With the waning of this hope expectancy turned to the nobility of the German nation, including the emperor, but this dream also proved to be illusory; and when Luther returned to Wittenberg, he was under the ban of both the Church and the empire.

Yet even under those circumstances hope for a widespread reform did not appear altogether chimerical when a change occurred in the character of the papacy. The flippant popes of the Renaissance were succeeded by one of the austere popes of the Counter Reformation, a pope as much concerned as Luther for the correction of the moral and financial abuses. Such a pope was Hadrian VI, a Hollander reared in the tradition of the Brethren of the Common Life. If his brief pontificate did not suffice to cleanse the Augean stables of the papacy, it might have been enough to inaugurate a new policy with regard to Luther. But quite on the contrary the struggle was only intensified. This was, in Luther's eyes, precisely as it should be. All along he had declared that the contest was over the faith and not over the life, and that if the morals were amended the teaching would still be unsound. The verdict of Erasmus remained true that the breach was irreparable because even if the reformed popes had conceded clerical marriage as

FREDERICK AND LUTHER

the Church does to the Uniats, and communion in both kinds as on occasion to the Hussites, and a national church under Rome as in Spain and France, and even justification by faith properly guarded as at Trent—even so they could scarcely have suffered the reduction of the number of the sacraments, the emasculation of the mass, the doctrine of the priesthood of all believers, let alone the rejection of papal infallibility, even though as yet it had not been formally promulgated.

HOSTILITY OF THE REFORMED PAPACY

And Luther did nothing to placate them. His work of reconstruction commenced with further demolition. Indulgences were still being proclaimed in Wittenberg. Luther addressed to the elector a demand that they be discontinued in so far as they rested on his patronage. Frederick was not hard to persuade, probably because indulgences had become so unpopular that the very preacher who announced them on All Saints'

Day of 1522 declared them to be rubbish, and the crowds greeted the relics with booing. Frederick did not repeat the attempt on All Saints' Day of 1523.

When asked whether in that case he desired the annual exhibition of relics, he replied in the negative. Their whole purpose had been to advertise the indulgences. Yet he could not quite bring himself to destroy or dissipate the collection amassed during a lifetime. A few of the choicest relics should be placed upon the altar and the rest stored in the sacristy to be shown on request to foreign visitors. The elector who had traveled to the Orient and negotiated with monarchs and ecclesiastical dignitaries for one more holy bone renounced his cherished avocation and relinquished the most lucrative revenue of the Castle Church and the university.

Luther's next attack centered on the endowed masses in the Castle Church, where twenty-five priests were employed to celebrate for the souls of the departed members of the House of Saxony. These private sacrifices had come to be in Luther's eyes idolatry, sacrilege, and blasphemy. Part of his indignation was aroused by the immorality of the priests, for he estimated that out of the twenty-five not over three were not fornicators. But this was not the primary ground for his attack. He always insisted that he differed from previous reformers in that they attacked the life and he the doctrine. Certainly Frederick should as patron suppress this scandal, but that might have been done by dismissing the offenders and securing better recruits. Luther in that case would not have been satisfied. The mass must go. Frederick obviously would have to be persuaded. Preferably the clergy also should concur. But Luther was ready to move, either in accord with both or without either. The essential was always the reform, whether instituted by the prince without the clergy or by the clergy without the prince. Universal acquiescence was desirable but not imperative. The plea of weakness might become a cloak for wickedness. "Not all the priests of Baal under Josiah believed their rites to be impious, but Josiah paid no attention to that. It is one thing to tolerate the weak in nonessentials, but to tolerate in matters clearly impious is itself impious." The mob smashed the windows of the deanery. When the recalcitrants were down to three, Luther reproached them with a sectarian spirit in holding out against the unity of the universal Church—as if Wittenberg were Christendom. This obviously sounds incredibly naïve, but Luther was not thinking either of numbers or of centuries, but of the Church founded upon the Word of God as he understood it. The town council was more abrupt. They informed the priests that the celebration of the mass was an offense worthy of death. The clergy at length unanimously declared themselves convinced. By the beginning of 1525 the mass was at an end in Wittenberg. One cannot say precisely that it had been suppressed by force, but certainly the pressure was acute, though not inordinately hurried. The mass had continued for two and one half years after Luther's return from the Wartburg.

Such changes aroused in the papists intense antagonism, and Pope Hadrian addressed to Frederick the Wise a veritable manifesto of the Counter Reformation.

Beloved in Christ, we have endured enough and more than enough. Our predecessors exhorted you to desist from corrupting the Christian faith through Martin Luther, but the trumpet has sounded in vain. We have been moved by mercy and paternal affection to give you a fatherly admonition. The Saxons have ever been defenders of the faith. But now who has bewitched you? Who has wasted the vineyard of the Lord? Who but a wild boar? We have you to thank that the churches are without people, the people without priests, the priests without honor, and Christians without Christ. The veil of the temple is rent. Be not beguiled because Martin Luther appeals to Scripture. So does every heretic, but Scripture is a book sealed with seven seals which cannot be so well opened by one carnal man as by all the holy saints. The fruits of this evil are evident. For this robber of churches incites the people to smash images and break crosses. He exhorts the laity to wash their hands in the blood of the priests. He has rejected or corrupted the sacraments, repudiated the expunging of sins through fasts, and rejects the daily celebration of the mass. He has committed the decretals of the holy Fathers to the flames. Does this sound to you like Christ or Antichrist? Separate yourself from Martin Luther and put a muzzle on his blasphemous tongue. If you will do this, we will rejoice with all the angels of heaven over one sinner that is saved. But if you refuse, then in the name of Almighty God and Jesus Christ our Lord, whom we represent on earth, we tell you that you will not escape punishment on earth and eternal fire hereafter. Pope Hadrian and Emperor Charles are in accord. Repent therefore before you feel the two swords.

Frederick replied:

Holy Father, I have never and do not now act other than as a Christian man and an obedient son of the holy Christian Church. I trust that God Almighty will give me his grace that for the few years I have left I may strengthen his holy word, service, peace, and faith.

But the fate of Luther and his reform rested not with the pope, the emperor, or the elector alone, but with the German diet meeting at Nürnberg. Like the Diet of Worms it was divided. The Catholic party was rallied by the papal legate, who freely conceded abuses but blamed them all on the deceased Leo and called for obedience to his noble

DUKE GEORGE

successor. Leadership among the laity fell in the absence of the emperor to his brother Ferdinand of Austria, who in his brief week of attendance tried to enforce the edict of Worms on his own authority and was promptly repulsed by the diet. Thereupon a coterie of Catholic princes formed the nucleus of the subsequent league. There was Joachim of Brandenburg, eager by zeal against Lutheranism to appease the emperor for having voted against his election. There was Cardinal Lang, spokesman of the Hapsburgs. The Bavarians were consistently Catholic, and the Palatinate was swinging over. This of course was not the definitive alignment.

Frederick the Wise with his bland obstructionism certainly did not speak the common mind of Catholic laity. There were other princes who gladly heeded the admonitions of the pope. Chief among them was Duke George, whose zeal against heresy was enough to set the Rhine on fire. Luther had felt a twinge of uneasiness over his blasts against the duke and made a gesture of reconciliation but was repulsed. George said:

I write not in hate but to bring you to yourself. As a layman I am unable to put on the armor of Saul and dispute Scripture with you, but I can see that you have offended against your neighbor. You have reviled not only me but the emperor. You have made Wittenberg an asylum for escaped monks and nuns. The fruit of your gospel is blasphemy of God and the sacrament, and rebellion against government. When has there been more corrupting of cloisters? When more breach of marriages than since you began to preach? No, Luther, keep your gospel. I will stay by the gospel of Christ with body and soul, goods and honor. But God is merciful. He will forgive you if you return, and I will then try to obtain for you a pardon from the emperor.

Henry VIII was another Catholic prince to have a tilt with Luther, and he was hardly mollified by the reply which referred to Martin Luther as "minister at Wittenberg by the grace of God" and to "Henry, King of England by the disgrace of God." Even though Luther made a subsequent gesture of reconciliation, Henry continued to regard him as a preacher of "unsatiate liberty." Plainly the "papists," whether clerical or lay, were Sanballats who would impede the building of the walls.

RECOIL OF THE MODERATE CATHOLICS: ERASMUS

The Catholic moderates might conceivably react differently—the Erasmians, the Humanists who had constituted the middle party at Worms. And indeed their stand might have been different had not the pressures been so intense as to leave no room for neutrality. Reluctantly the mediators were driven to enter one camp or the other. They went in both directions. Some very outstanding persons returned to Rome, among them Pirkheimer of Nürnberg. The deepest offense to Luther lay in the stand taken by Erasmus of Rotterdam. His position had not essentially changed. He still felt that Luther had done much good, and that he was no heretic. This Erasmus openly said in a colloquy published as late as 1524. But he deplored the disintegration of Christendom. His dream of European concord had been shattered by the outbreak of war between France and the empire before the close of the Diet of Worms. Coincidently the ecclesiastical division had rent the seamless robe of Christ. Erasmus preferred the role of mediator, but he was unremittingly pushed by prominent persons whom he esteemed—kings, cardinals, and his old friend Pope Hadrian—to declare himself. At last he yielded and consented to state at what point he differed from Luther. It was not indulgences. It was not the mass. It was the doctrine of man. Erasmus brought out a tract entitled *On the Freedom of the Will.*

Luther thanked him for centering the discussion at this point. "You alone have gone to the heart of the problem instead of debating the papacy, indulgences, purgatory, and similar trifles. You alone have gone to the core, and I thank you for it." Luther's fundamental break with the Catholic Church was over the nature and destiny of man, and much more over the destiny than the nature. That was why he and Erasmus did not come altogether to grips. Erasmus was interested primarily in morals, whereas Luther's question was whether doing right, even if it is possible, can affect man's fate. Erasmus succeeded in diverting Luther from the course by asking whether the ethical precepts of the Gospels have any point if they cannot be fulfilled. Luther countered with characteristic controversial recklessness that man is like a donkey ridden now by God and now by the Devil, a statement which certainly seems to imply that man has no freedom whatever to decide for good or ill. This certainly was not Luther's habitual thought. He was perfectly ready to say that even the natural man can practice the civil virtues as a responsible husband, an affectionate father, a decent citizen, and an upright magistrate. Man is capable of the integrity and valor displayed by the Romans of old or the Turks of today. Most of the precepts of the gospel can be outwardly kept. But in the eyes of God "there is none righteous, no, not one." Motives are never pure. The noblest acts are vitiated by arrogance, self-love, the desire of the eye and the lust of power. From the religious point of view man is a sinner. He has therefore no claim upon God. If man is not irretrievably lost, it can only be because God deigns to favor him beyond his desert.

The problem then shifts from man to God. Erasmus was concerned for morality in God as well as in man. Is it not unjust that God should create man incapable of fulfilling the conditions for salvation and then at whim save or damn for what cannot be helped? "Of course this is a stumbling block," answered Luther.

Common sense and natural reason are highly offended that God by his mere will deserts, hardens, and damns, as if he delighted in sins and in such eternal torments, he who is said to be of such mercy and goodness. Such a concept of God appears wicked, cruel, and intolerable, and by it many men have been revolted in all ages. I myself have more than once been cast down to the very depth of the abyss of desperation, so that I wished I had never been created. There is no use trying to get away from this by ingenious distinctions. Natural reason, however much it is offended, must admit the consequences of the omniscience and omnipotence of God.

But this was precisely what the natural reason of Erasmus would not concede. He perceived that the conflict lay between the power and goodness of God. He would rather limit the power than forfeit the goodness; Luther the reverse. At any rate Erasmus would not assert more than he had to. Difficulties he recognized—that some men, for example, are born morons, and God is responsible for their condition—but why project these riddles of life into eternity and transfix paradoxes into dogmas? "They are not my paradoxes," retorted Luther. "They are God's paradoxes." Erasmus inquired how Luther could know this, and he countered by citing the statement of the apostle Paul that the fates of Jacob and Esau were settled before they emerged from the womb. Erasmus rejoined that other passages of Scripture bear a different sense, and the matter is therefore not clear. If it were, why should debates over it have continued for centuries? Scripture needs to be interpreted, and the claim of the

Lutherans to have the Spirit by which to interpret is not confirmed by the fruits of the Spirit in their behavior.

Luther's answer to Erasmus was to impute to him a spirit of skepticism, levity, and impiety. Tranquil discussion of man's destiny of itself betrays insensitivity to God's majesty. The craving of Erasmus to confine himself to the clear and simple spelled for Luther the abandonment of Christianity, for the reason that Christianity cannot be simple and obvious to the natural man.

Show me a single mortal in the whole universe, no matter how just and saintly, to whose mind it would have ever occurred that this should be the way of salvation to believe in him who was both God and man, who died for our sins, who rose and sits at the right hand of the Father. What philosopher ever saw this? Who among the prophets? The cross is a scandal to the Jews and a folly to the Gentiles. . . . If it is difficult to believe in God's mercy and goodness when he damns those who do not deserve it, we must recall that if God's justice could be recognized as just by human comprehension, it would not be divine. Since God is true and one, he is utterly incomprehensible and inaccessible to human reason. Therefore his justice also must be imcomprehensible. "O the depth of the riches both of the wisdom and knowledge of God! how unsearchable are his judgments!"

They are hidden to the light of nature and revealed only to the light of glory. "Erasmus, who does not go beyond the light of nature," said Luther, "may like Moses die in the plains of Moab without entering into the promised land of those higher studies which pertain to piety."

Erasmus characterized his own position in these words: "The wise navigator will steer between Scylla and Charybdis. I have sought to be a spectator of this tragedy." Such a role was not permitted to him, and between the confessional millstones his type was crushed. Where again does one find precisely his blend of the cultivated Catholic scholar: tolerant, liberal, dedicated to the revival of the classical Christian heritage in the unity of Christendom? The leadership of Protestantism was to pass to the Neo-Scholastics and of the Catholics to the Jesuits.

Luther for all his bluster was not untouched by the reproach that his acrimony ill comported with the spirit of the apostles. He had angered Henry VIII, infuriated Duke George, estranged Erasmus. Had he perhaps hurt also old Dr. Staupitz, who had not written for some time? Luther inquired, and Staupitz answered:

My love for you is unchanged, passing the love of women . . . , but you seem to me to condemn many external things which do not affect justification. Why is the cowl a stench in your nostrils when many in it have lived holy lives? There is nothing without abuse. My dear friend, I beseech you to remember the weak. Do not denounce points of indifference which can be held in sincerity, though in matters of faith be never silent. We owe much to you, Martin. You have taken us from the pigsty to the pasture of life. If only you and I could talk for an hour and open the secrets of our hearts! I hope you will have good fruit at Wittenberg. My prayers are with you.

Shortly after the receipt of this letter Luther received the news that Dr. Staupitz was dead. So it was then in the Catholic camp: the pope implacable, Henry VIII railing, Duke George raging, Erasmus refuting, Staupitz dead.

DEFECTION OF THE PURITANS: CARLSTADT

Obviously, then, the walls could be rebuilt only by those who had definitely broken with Rome. And then came the next blow, vastly more stunning than the first. Those who had broken with Rome were not themselves united. Partly through defections from Lutheranism and partly through the independent rise of variant forms of Evangelicalism the pattern of diversity was displayed. Luther was stung. The initial disorders at Wittenberg had already dealt him a more severe stroke than any he had ever received from the papacy, and he had already begun to perceive that he was closer to Rome than to the radicals. At any rate he was in between. "I take," said he, "the middle road." He found himself now in the position formerly occupied by the Erasmians at Worms. When they were driven to the wall, the Lutherans emerged as the middle group between the papists to the right and the sectaries to the left.

One of the most curious aspects of the whole shift is that in many respects the radicals were the heirs of Erasmus, who saw the great abuse in Catholicism, not as did Luther in the exaltation of man, but in the externalization of religion. The degree to which the sectaries stressed the inward and spiritual led to drastic consequences for the theory and life of the Church. The spirit was set in opposition to the letter of Scripture, as already by the Zwickau prophets. The spirit was considered able to dispense with all external aids, whether of art or music, as Carlstadt had just been saying, or even of the sacraments as the outward channels of invisible grace. The experience of the spirit was made the necessary qualification for Church membership. Infant baptism was consequently rejected, if not indeed all baptism, on the ground that outward water "profiteth nothing." The idea of a national or territorial church was discarded because the total population of any given district never meets so exacting a test. The Church of the spirit is of necessity a sect which may seek to preserve its integrity by segregation from society, or may attempt to dominate the world through the reign of the saints. Here is the concept of all the Protestant theocracies. Within the religious community leadership falls to the spirit-filled, be they clerical or lay, and the outcome may well be the abolition of a professional ministry.

Another Erasmian idea, not altogether consonant with the first, is that of the restitution of primitive Christianity. The details selected for restoration were commonly those in accord with the religion of the spirit, but the very attempt to restore lent itself readily to a new externalism and legalism.

This whole pattern of ideas was alien to Luther. He could not separate spirit and flesh because man is a whole. Therefore art, music, and sacrament are the appropriate expressions of religion. The attempt to build the Church on a selective basis did intrigue him, and his fury against the sectaries was in large measure intensified by the conflict within himself. But the notion of a Protestant theocracy was to him as abhorrent as the papal monarchy. The effort to restore the minutiae of New Testament practice wore for him the air of a new legalism and externality against which he employed the very slogans of the radicals and became himself the champion of the spirit against the letter.

The first attempt to give concretion to many of the elements in this pattern occurred in Luther's own circle and might be regarded as defection from his ranks. The environs of Wittenberg provided the terrain, and the leaders were Andrew Carlstadt again and Thomas Müntzer. This was unfortunate because, although both were sensitive and gifted, neither was balanced and stable. If Luther had met such ideas first in Zwingli and the sober Anabaptists, he might not have been so devoid of understanding and so implacable in opposition.

Carlstadt's most serious radicalism developed after he had retired to the parish of Orlamünde. There he added to his prior attack on images and church music a further denial of the real presence of Christ in the sacrament of the altar. The objection in all three instances was to the use of the physical as a means of communion with the divine. God is a spirit, and he cannot be in bread and wine. Christ said only, "This do in remembrance of me." Hence the bread and wine are merely reminders, not even symbols, let alone channels. Carlstadt interpreted the words of Christ, "This is my body, this is my blood," to mean, "This is the body which will be broken. This is the blood which will be shed." Luther countered that if this passage was in the least ambiguous there was another text which reads, "The cup . . . , is it not the communion of the blood of Christ? The bread . . . , is it not the communion of the body of Christ?" (I Cor. 10:16.) "This is the thunderclap from which there is no escape. If five years ago I could have been convinced of Carlstadt's position, I should have been grateful for such a mighty weapon against the papacy, but the Scripture was too strong for me." One wonders whether Scripture was really determinative. The roles of Luther and Carlstadt were reversed when they passed from the question of images to the Lord's Supper. Carlstadt was the literalist on the words of Moses, "Thou shalt not make unto thee any graven image," and Luther on the words of Christ, "This is my body." The real question was whether the physical is an aid or an impediment to religion. Carlstadt's Biblicism was in evidence mainly in restraining him from rejecting the Lord's Supper entirely, as did the Quakers. He retained the rite because Christ said, "This do in remembrance of me."

He rejected likewise infant baptism. The Zwickau prophets had done this before him, and the Anabaptists were to make this the cardinal tenet of their sect. The essential point was the necessity of an adult experience of religious conviction. There was with Carlstadt the added point that outward physical water is of no efficacy and is often destructive, as when the hosts of Pharaoh were swallowed in the Red Sea. One wonders again why he did not reject all baptism. His emphasis on Sabbatarianism was designed to give men relief from mundane tasks that they might have quiet times for the cultivation of the inner life.

His greatest eccentricities in Luther's eyes arose from his efforts to achieve a lay ministry. Luther had proclaimed the priesthood of all believers. The corollary might be, as with the Quakers, that there should be no professional minister at all. So far Carlstadt would not go, but he wished as a minister to be set off in no way from his fellows. The parishioners were not to call him *Herr Doktor* or *Herr Pfarrer*, but simply "good neighbor" or "Brother Andreas." He gave up any distinctive garb and wore only a plain gray coat, declined to be supported by the congregation, undertaking instead to earn his living at the plow.

Luther was completely without feeling for this whole program. He cared nothing indeed for the falderal of academic degrees, but he cared mightily for a trained ministry and perceived that if Carlstadt's plan prevailed the outcome would assuredly be not that the peasant would know as much as the preacher, but that the preacher would know no more than the peasant. He twitted Carlstadt for reeling off Hebrew quotations in a peasant's smock. As for the plain cloak and the "Brother Andreas," these appeared, if not as an affectation, then as a neomonastic attempt to win the favor of heaven by spectacular renunciations. As to the earning of one's bread at the plow, Luther was willing enough to support himself by manual labor if expelled from his ministry, but voluntarily to withdraw from a parish to a farm savored to him of an evasion of responsibility. "What would I not give to get away from a cantankerous congregation and look into the friendly eyes of animals?"

Other points in Carlstadt's program—such as Sabbatarianism, obligatory clerical matrimony, and the rejection of images—appeared to Luther as a new legalism. Carlstadt, he claimed, reversed the relation of inward and outward. By making absolute rules for days, dress, and status he was attaching altogether too much importance to the exterior. Here the spirit should decide. Plainly there were other notes in Carlstadt's religion than the stress on the spiritual. He was consumed by a passion for holiness and a concern for the renunciation of privilege with a degree of social leveling. At these points Luther would accord a wider latitude. And he might have been willing to grant latitude also to Carlstadt had it not been for the insurgence of a much more sinister figure.

THE REVOLUTIONARY SAINTS: MÜNTZER

Thomas Müntzer came from Zwickau and revived some of the ideas of the prophets from that town, but with much greater

THOMAS MÜNTZER

allure because of his learning, ability, and intense enthusiasm. Müntzer gave a much more radical turn than Carlstadt to the cleavage of spirit and flesh by rejecting not only infant baptism, but all baptism, and by applying this dualism to the spirit versus the letter of Scripture. Those who rely on the letter, said he, are the scribes against whom Christ inveighed. Scripture as a mere book is but paper and ink. "Bible, Babel, bubble!" he cried. Behind this virulence was a religious concern. Müntzer had not been troubled like Luther as to how to get right with God, but as to whether there is any God to get right with. The Scripture as a mere written record did not reassure him because he observed that it is convincing only to the convinced. The Turks are acquainted with the Bible but remain completely alienated. The men who wrote the Bible had no Bible at the time when they wrote. Whence, then, did they derive their assurance? The only answer can be that God spoke to them directly, and so must he speak to us if we are so much as to understand the Bible. Müntzer held, with the Catholic Church, that the Bible is inadequate without a divinely inspired interpreter, but that interpreter is not the Church nor the pope but the prophet, the new Elijah, the new Daniel, to whom is given the key of David to open the book sealed with seven seals.

Müntzer was readily able to find support for his view of the spirit in the Scripture itself, where it is said that "the letter killeth, but the spirit giveth life" (II Cor. 3:6). Luther replied that of course the letter without the spirit is dead, but the two are no more to be divorced than the soul is to be separated from the body. The real menace of Müntzer in Luther's eyes was that he destroyed the uniqueness of Christian revelation in the past by his elevation of revelation in the present. Luther for himself had had absolutely no experience of any contemporary revelation, and in times of despondency the advice to rely upon the spirit was for him a counsel of despair, since within he could find only utter blackness.

In such moments he must have assurance in tangible form in a written record of the stupendous act of God in Christ. Luther freely avowed his weakness and his need of historic revelation. Therefore he would not listen to Müntzer though "he had swallowed the Holy Ghost, feathers and all." At this point lies much of the difference not only between Müntzer and Luther, but between modern liberal Protestantism and the religion of the founders.

Had Müntzer drawn no practical consequences from his view, Luther would have been less outraged, but Müntzer proceeded to use the gift of the Spirit as a basis for the formation of a church.

He is the progenitor of the Protestant theocracies, based not as in Judaism primarily on blood and soil, nor as in Catholicism on sacramentalism, but rather on inward experience of the infusion of the Spirit. Those who are thus reborn can recognize each other and can join in a covenant of the elect, whose mission it is to erect God's kingdom. Such a role for the Church was to Luther completely repugnant. Müntzer did not expect the elect to enter into their inheritance without a struggle. They would have to slaughter the ungodly. At this point Luther was horrified because the sword is given to the magistrate, not to the minister, let alone to the saints. In the struggle Müntzer well recognized that many of the godly would fall, and he was constantly harping on suffering and cross bearing as a mark of the elect. Luther was taunted as "Dr. Easychair and Dr. Pussyfoot," basking in the favor of the princes. His reply was that the outward cross is neither to be sought nor evaded. The constant cross is suffering within. Once again the tables were turned, and Luther appeared as the champion of the inward.

BANISHMENT OF THE AGITATORS

In 1523 Müntzer succeeded in having himself elected as minister in the Saxon town of Alstedt. As many as two thousand outsiders flocked to his preaching. He was able to report thirty units ready to slaughter the ungodly. The only overt act, however, was the burning of a chapel dedicated to the Virgin Mary. This was in March, 1524.

Luther thereupon addressed the princes of Saxony:

These Alstedters revile the Bible and rave about the spirit, but where do they show the fruits of the spirit, love, joy, peace, and patience? Do not interfere with them so long as they confine themselves to the office of the Word. Let the spirits fight it out, but when the sword is drawn you must step in, be it they or we who take it. You must banish the offender from the land. Our office is simply preaching and suffering. Christ and the apostles did not smash images and churches, but won hearts with God's Word. The Old Testament slaughter of the ungodly is not to be imitated. If these Alstedters want to wipe out the ungodly, they will have to bathe in blood. But you are ordained of God to keep the peace, and you must not sleep.

The young prince John Frederick, nephew and heir apparent to Frederick the Wise, was already being associated with his uncle and his father in the administration of Saxony. To a subordinate he wrote in August, 1524:

I am having a terrible time with the Satan of Alstedt. Kindliness and letters do not suffice. The sword which is ordained of God to punish the evil must be used with energy. Carlstadt also is stirring up something, and the Devil wants to be Lord.

Here Carlstadt and Müntzer are linked together. For Carlstadt this was both unjust and unfortunate. He had written to Müntzer that he would have nothing to do with his covenant, nor with bloodshed. But the iconoclastic riots in Orlamünde and Alstedt appeared to be of one stripe. Carlstadt was summoned to Jena for an interview with Luther and convinced him of the injustice of the charge of rebellion. When, however, Luther himself visited Orlamünde and observed the revolutionary temper of the congregation, he came to question the sincerity of the disclaimer and acquiesced in the banishment of Carlstadt, who was compelled to quit Saxony, leaving his pregnant wife and their child to join him later. He departed claiming in the very words of Luther after Worms that he had been condemned "unheard and unconvicted," and that he had been expelled by his former colleague who was twice a papist and a cousin of Antichrist.

Müntzer, having been summoned to preach at Weimar in the presence of Frederick the Wise and his brother Duke John, had the temerity to seek to enlist them for his program. He took his text from Daniel's interpretation of the dream of King Nebuchadnezzar and began by saying that the Church was an undefiled virgin until corrupted by the scribes who murder the Spirit and assert that God no longer reveals himself as of old. He declared further:

But God does disclose himself in the inner word in the abyss of the soul. The man who has not received the living witness of God knows really nothing about God, though he may have swallowed 100,000 Bibles. God comes in dreams to his beloved as he did to the patriarchs, prophets, and apostles. He comes especially in affliction. That is why Brother Easychair rejects him. God pours out his Spirit upon all flesh, and now the Spirit reveals to the elect a mighty and irresistible reformation to come. This is the fulfilment of the prediction of Daniel about the fifth monarchy. You princes of Saxony, you need a new Daniel to disclose unto you this revelation and to show you your role. Think not that the power of God will be realized if your swords rust in the scabbard. Christ said that he came not to bring peace but a sword, and Deuteronomy says "You are a holy people. Spare not the idolators, break down their altars, smash their images and burn them in the fire." The sword is given to you to wipe out the ungodly. If you decline, it will be taken from you. Those who resist should be slaughtered without mercy as Elijah smote the priests of Baal. Priests and monks who mock the gospel should be killed. The godless have no right to live. May you like Nebuchadnezzar appoint a Daniel to inform you of the leadings of the Spirit.

The Saxon princes were of no mind to appoint Müntzer to such a post. Instead they referred the case to a committee. Müntzer did not wait for the report but by night escaped over the walls of Alstedt and fled from Saxony. Latitude had been vindicated at the expense of liberty. The regime of Carlstadt would have been rigoristic and the reign of Müntzer's saints intolerant of the godless. Yet the fact could not be gainsaid that the agitators had been expelled by the sword of the magistrate. Luther ruefully pondered the gibe that instead of being a martyr he was making martyrs.

CHAPTER SIXTEEN

BEHEMOTH, LEVIATHAN, AND THE GREAT WATERS

 COPE FOR rebuilding was further reduced by the rise independently of rival forms of Evangelicalism, namely Zwinglianism and Anabaptism. These were Luther's Behemoth and Leviathan. Then came the conjunction of the religious ferment with a vast social revolt when the waters were unloosed in the Peasants' War. The outcome was at once a restriction of Luther's sphere of operations and a waning of his trust in humankind.

The new movements were largely independent but not wholly unrelated to the recent disturbances in Wittenberg. Carlstadt expelled from Saxony went to the south German cities. Luther shortly thereafter received letters from the ministers of Strassburg. "We are not yet persuaded by Carlstadt, but many of his arguments are weighty. We are disturbed because you have driven out your old colleague with such inhumanity. At Basel and Zurich are many who agree with him." "From the Lord's Supper, the symbol of love, arise such hatreds."

Basel was the residence of Erasmus, who both repudiated and abetted the inferences drawn from his premises by impetuous disciples. He would not concede, because the flesh of Christ in the sacrament profits nothing, that therefore the flesh is not present. At the same time he confided to a friend that were it not for the authority of the Church he would agree with the innovators.

RIVALS: ZWINGLI AND THE ANABAPTISTS

Zurich was the seat of a new variety of the Reformation which was to be set over against that of Wittenberg and characterized as the Reformed. The leader was Ulrich Zwingli. He had received a Humanist training and as a Catholic priest divided his parsonage into a parish house on the ground floor and a library of the classics on the second. On the appearance of Erasmus' New Testament he committed the epistles to memory in Greek, and affirmed in consequence that Luther had been able to teach him nothing about the understanding of Paul. But what Zwingli selected for emphasis in Paul was the text, "The letter killeth, but the spirit giveth life," which he coupled with a Johannine verse, "The flesh profiteth nothing." Flesh was taken by Zwingli in the Platonic sense of body, whereas Luther understood it in the Hebraic sense of the evil heart which may or may not be physical. Zwingli made a characteristic deduction from his disparagement of the body that art and music are inappropriate as the handmaids of religion—and this, although he was himself a musician accomplished on six instruments. The next step was easy: to deny the real presence in the sacrament, which was reduced to a memorial of the death of Christ as the Passover was a commemoration of the escape of Israel from Egypt. When Luther appealed to the words, "This is my body," Zwingli countered that in the Aramaic tongue spoken by Jesus the copulative verb was omitted, so that what he said was simply, "This—my body." (In the Greek of the Lukan version the companion verse reads, "This cup the new testament.") And in this phrase one may with perfect right supply not "is" but "signifies." Luther sensed at once the affinity of Zwingli's view with that of Carlstadt, on whom he was not dependent, and with that of Erasmus, in whom he was steeped. The familiar reproach against Erasmus was hurled at Zwingli that he did not take religion seriously. "How does he know?" retorted Zwingli. "Can he read the secrets of our hearts?"

A similarity to Müntzer also impressed Luther because Zwingli was politically minded and not averse to the use of the sword even for religion. Zwingli was always a Swiss patriot, and in translating the Twenty-third Psalm rendered the second verse "He maketh me to lie down in an Alpine meadow." And there he could find no still waters. The evangelical issue threatened to disrupt his beloved confederation. For the Catholics turned to the traditional enemy, the House of Hapsburg. Ferdinand of Austria was instrumental in the calling of the assembly of Baden to discuss Zwingli's theory of the sacrament. This was his Diet of Worms, and the sequel convinced him that the gospel could be saved in Switzerland and the confederation conserved only if the Catholic League with Austria were countered by an evangelical league with the German Lutherans, ready if need be to use the sword. But the very notion of a military alliance for the defense of the gospel savored for Luther of Thomas Müntzer.

Then arose in Zwingli's circle a party at the opposite pole of the political question. These were the Anabaptists. Their point of departure was another aspect of the Erasmian program, dear also to Zwingli. This was the restoration of primitive Christianity, which they took to mean the adoption of the Sermon on the Mount as a literal code for all Christians, who should renounce oaths, the use of the sword whether in war or civil government, private possessions, bodily adornment, reveling and drunkenness. Pacifism, religious communism, simplicity, and temperance marked their communities. The Church should consist only of the twice-born, committed to the covenant of discipline. Here again we meet the concept of the elect, discernible by the two tests of spiritual experience and moral achievement. The Church should rest not on baptism administered in infancy, but on regeneration, symbolized by baptism in mature years. Every member should be a priest, a minister, and a missionary prepared to embark on evangelistic tours. Such a Church, though seeking to convert the world, could never embrace the unconverted community. And if the state comprised all the inhabitants, then Church and state would have to be separated. In any case religion should be free from constraint. Zwingli was aghast to see the medieval unity shattered and in panic invoked the arm of the state. In 1525 the Anabaptists in Zurich were subjected to the death penalty. Luther was not yet ready for such savage expedients. But he too was appalled by what to him appeared to be a reversion to the monastic attempt to win salvation by a higher righteousness. The leaving of families for missionary expeditions was in his eyes a sheer desertion of domestic responsibilities, and the repudiation of the sword prompted him to new vindications of the divine calling alike of the magistrate and of the soldier.

RELIGION AND SOCIAL UNREST

Then came the fusion of a great social upheaval with the ferment of the Reformation in which Luther's principles were to his mind perverted and the radicalism of the sectaries contributed to a state of anarchy. Nothing did so much as the Peasants' War to make Luther recoil against a too drastic departure from the pattern of the Middle Ages.

The Peasants' War did not arise out of any immediate connection with the religious issues of the sixteenth century because agrarian unrest had been brewing for fully a century. Uprisings had occurred all over Europe, but especially in south Germany, where particularly the peasants suffered from changes which ultimately should have ministered to their security and prosperity. Feudal anarchy was being superseded through the consolidation of power. In Spain, England, and France this had taken place on a national scale, but in Germany only on a territorial basis; and in each political unit the princes were endeavoring to integrate the administration with the help of a bureaucracy of salaried court officials. The expenses were met by increased levies on the land. The peasant paid the bill. The law was being unified by displacing the diverse local codes in favor of Roman law, whereby the peasant again suffered, since the Roman law knew only private property and therefore imperiled the commons—the woods, streams, and meadows shared by the community in old Germanic tradition. The Roman law knew also only free men, freedmen, and slaves; and did not have a category which quite fitted the medieval serf.

Another change, associated with the revival of commerce in cities after the crusades, was the substitution of exchange in coin for exchange in kind. The increased demand for the precious metals enhanced their value; and the peasants, who were at first benefited by the payment of a fixed sum of money rather than a percentage in kind, found themselves hurt by deflation. Those who could not meet the imposts sank from freeholders to renters, and from renters to serfs. The solution which at first suggested itself to the peasants was simply resistance to the changes operative in their society and a return to the good old ways. They did not in the beginning demand the abolition of serfdom but only the prevention of any further extension of peonage. They clamored rather for free woods, waters, and meadows as in the former days, for the reduction of imposts and the reinstatement of the ancient Germanic law and local custom. The methods to be used for the attainment of these ends were at first conservative. On the occasion of a special grievance the peasants would assemble in thousands in quite unpremeditated fashion and would present their petitions to the rulers with a request for arbitration. Not infrequently the petition was met in a patriarchal way and the burdens in some measure eased, yet never sufficiently to forestall recurrence.

On the other hand the peasant class was not uniformly impoverished; and the initiative for the redress of grievances came not from the downtrodden, but rather from the more prosperous and enterprising, possessed themselves of lands and a respectable competence. Inevitably their demands began to go beyond economic amelioration to political programs designed to insure for them an influence commensurate with and even exceeding their economic importance. The demands likewise changed as the movement worked north into the region around the big bend of the Rhine where peasants were also townsmen, since artisans were farmers. In this section urban aspirations were added to the agrarian. Farther down the Rhine the struggle became almost wholly urban, and the characteristic program called for a more democratic complexion in the town councils, a less restrictive membership in the guilds, the subjection of the clergy to civil burdens, and uncurtailed rights for citizens to engage in brewing.

Many of the tendencies coalesced in a movement in Alsace just prior to the Reformation. This uprising used the symbol characteristic of the great Peasants' War of 1525, the *Bundschuh*. The name came from the leather shoe of the peasant. The long thong with which it was laced was called a *Bund*. The word had a double meaning because a *Bund* was also an association, a covenant. Müntzer had used this word for his covenant of the elect. Before him the peasants had adopted the term for a compact of revolution. The aims of this *Bundschuh* centered not so much on economics as on politics. The ax should be laid to the root of the tree and all government abolished save that of the pope and the emperor. These were the two traditional swords of Christendom, the joint rulers of a universal society. To them the little men had always turned for protection against overlords, bishops, metropolitans, knights, and princes. The *Bundschuh* proposed to complete the process by wiping out all the intermediate grades and leaving only the two great lords, Caesar and Peter.

Prior to the Peasants' War of 1525 this movement was often anticlerical but not anti-Catholic. Bishops and abbots were resented as exploiters, but "Down with the bishop" did not mean "Down with the pope" or "Down with the Church." The banners of the *Bundschuh* often carried, besides the shoe, some religious symbol, such as a picture of Mary, a crucifix, or a papal tiara. The accompanying woodcut shows the crucifix resting upon a black shoe. On the right a group of peasants are swearing allegiance. Above them other peasants are tilling the soil, and Abraham is sacrificing Isaac as a sign of the cost to be paid by the members of the *Bund*.

LUTHER AND THE PEASANTS

A movement so religiously-minded could not but be affected by the Reformation. Luther's freedom of the Christian man was purely religious but could very readily be given a social turn. The priesthood of believers did not mean for him equalitarianism, but Carlstadt took it so. Luther certainly had blasted usury and in 1524 came out with another tract on the subject, in which he scored also the subterfuge of annuities, a device whereby capital was loaned in perpetuity for an annual return. His attitude on monasticism likewise admirably suited peasant covetousness for the spoliation of cloisters. The peasants with good reason felt themselves strongly drawn to Luther. A cartoon displayed Luther surrounded by peasants as he expounded the Word of God to the ecclesiastics, and when the great upheaval came in 1524-25 a Catholic retorted by portraying Luther in armor seated before a fire greasing a *Bundschuh*. The Catholic princes never ceased to hold Luther responsible for the uprising, and the Catholic historian Janssen has in modern times endeavored to prove that Luther was actually the author of the movement which he so vehemently repudiated. Such an explanation hardly takes into account the century of agrarian unrest by which the Reformation had been preceded.

SWEARING ALLEGIANCE TO THE BUND

One intangible contributory factor was utterly foreign to Luther's way of thinking, and that was astrology. Melanchthon dabbled in it but Luther never. Astrological speculation may well explain why so many peasant uprisings coincided in the fall of 1524 and the spring of 1525. It was in the year 1524 that all the planets were in the constellation of the Fish. This had been foreseen twenty years previously, and great disturbances had been predicted for that year. As the time approached, the foreboding was intense. In the year 1523 as many as fifty-one tracts appeared on the subject. Woodcuts like the one below displayed the Fish in the heavens and upheavals upon earth. The peasants with their banners and flails watch on one side; the emperor, the pope, and the ecclesiastics on the other. Some in 1524 held back in the hope that the emperor would call a diet and redress the grievances. The diet was not called, and the great Fish unloosed the waters.

With all this the Reformation had nothing to do. At the same time a complete dissociation of the reform from the Peasants' War is not de-

Practica vber die grossen vnd ma=

nigfeltigen Conuunction der Planeten/die im
jar M. D. XXiiij. erscheinen/vñ vnge=
zweiffelt vil wunderparlicher
ding geperen werden.

Auß Rö.Kay.May.Gnaden vnd Freihaiten/hüt sich menigklich/diese meine Pra=
ctica in zwayen jaren nach zütrucken bey verlierung. 4.Marck lötigs Golts.

PROPHECY OF CONVULSION IN 1524

fensible. The attempt to enforce the Edict of Worms through the arrest of Lutheran ministers was not infrequently the immediate occasion for the assembly of peasant bands to demand their release, and Luther was regarded as a friend. When some of the peasants were asked to name persons whom they would accept as arbiters, the first name on the list was that of Martin Luther. No formal court was ever established, and no legal judgment was ever rendered. But Luther did pronounce a verdict on the demands of the peasants as couched in the most popular of their manifestoes, *The Twelve Articles*. These opened with phrases reminiscent of Luther himself. "To the Christian reader, peace and the grace of God through Christ. . . . The gospel is not a cause of rebellion and disturbance." Rather those who refuse such reasonable demands are themselves the disturbers. "If it be the will of God to hear the peasants, who will resist His Majesty? Did he not hear the children of Israel and deliver them out of the hand of Pharaoh?" The first articles have to do with the Church. The congregation should have the right to appoint and remove the minister, who is obligated to "preach the Holy Gospel without human addition," which sounds very much like Luther. Ministers are to be supported on a modest scale by the congregations out of the so-called great tithe on produce. The surplus should go to relieve the poor and to obviate emergency taxation in war. The so-called little tithe on cattle should be abolished, "for the Lord God created cattle for the free use of man." The main articles embodied the old agrarian program of common fields, forests, waters. The farmer should be free to hunt, to fish, and to protect his lands against game. Under supervision he might take wood for fire and for building. Death dues, which impoverished the widow and orphan by requisitioning the best cloak or the best cow, were to be abolished. Rents should be revised in accord with the productivity of the land. New laws should not displace the old, and the community meadows should not pass into private hands. The only article which exceeded the old demands was the one calling for the total abolition of serfdom. Land should be held on lease with stipulated conditions. If any labor in excess of the agreement was exacted by the lord, he should pay for it on a wage basis. *The Twelve Articles* conceded that any demand not consonant with the Word of God should be null. The whole program was conservative, in line with the old feudal economy. There was notably no attack on government.

The evangelical ring of the articles pleased Luther, but in addressing the peasants he disparaged most of their demands. As to the right of the congregation to choose its own minister, that depends upon whether they pay him. Even if they do and the princes will not tolerate them, they should rather emigrate than rebel. The abolition of tithes is highway robbery, and the abrogation of serfdom is making Christian liberty into a thing of the flesh. Having thus criticized the program, Luther then turned to the means employed for its realization. Under no circumstances must the common man seize the sword on his own behalf. If each man were to take justice into his own hands, then there would be "neither authority, government, nor order nor land, but only murder and bloodshed." But all this was not intended to justify the unspeakable wrongs perpetrated by the rulers. To the princes Luther addressed an appeal in which he justified many more of the peasant demands than he had done when speaking to them. The will of the congregation should be regarded in the choice of a minister. The demands of the peasants for redress of their grievances were fair and just. The princes had none but themselves to thank for these disorders, since they had done nothing but disport themselves in grandeur while robbing and flaying their subjects. The true solution was the old way of arbitration.

But that way neither side was disposed to take, and the prediction of Luther was all too abundantly fulfilled, that nothing would ensue but murder and bloodshed. Luther had long since declared that he would never support the private citizen in arms, however just the cause, since such means inevitably entailed wrong to the innocent. He could not envisage an orderly revolution. And how there could have been one in the sixteenth century is difficult to conceive, since the facilities were inadequate for the forging of a united front by either persuasion or force. A minority could not then seize the machinery of the state and by technological warfare impose its will upon the community, nor were modern means of propaganda available.

The Peasants' War lacked the cohesion of the Puritan revolution because there was no clear-cut program and no coherent leadership. Some groups wanted a peasant dictatorship, some a classless society, some a return to feudalism, some the abolition of all rulers save the pope and the emperor. The chiefs were sometimes peasants, sometimes sectaries, sometimes even knights. The separate bands were not co-ordinated. There was not even unity of religion because Catholics and Protestants were on both sides. In Alsace, where the program called for the elimination of the pope, the struggle took on the complexion of a religious war; and the duke and his brother the cardinal hunted the peasants as "unbelieving, divisive, undisciplined Lutherans, ravaging like Huns and Vandals." There can be no question that the hordes were undisciplined, interested mainly in pillaging castles and cloisters, raiding game, and depleting fish ponds.

The drawing below of the plundering of a cloister is typical of the Peasants' War. Observe the group in the upper left with a net in

PEASANTS PLUNDERING A CLOISTER

the fish pond. Some are carrying off provisions. The bloodshed is inconsiderable. One man only has lost a hand. At various points peasants are guzzling and vomiting, justifying the stricture that the struggle was not so much a peasants' war as a wine war.

Another glimpse of their behavior is afforded by a letter of an abbess who says that her cloister was raided till not an egg or a pat of butter was left. Through their windows the nuns could see the populace abused and the smoke rising from burning castles. When the war ended, 70 cloisters had been demolished in Thuringia, and in Franconia 270 castles and 52 cloisters. When the Palatinate succumbed to the peasants, the disorder was so great that their own leaders had to invite the former authorities to return to assist in the restoration of order. But the authorities preferred to wait until the peasants had first been beaten.

Could it have been otherwise? Was there any person who could have conceived and carried through a constructive plan for adjusting the peasant to the new political and economic order? The most

PEASANTS ABOUT TO TAKE OVER A CLOISTER

276

strategic person would have been an emperor, but no emperor would essay the role. There was only one other who was sufficiently known and trusted throughout Germany to have done it. That man was Martin Luther, and he refused. For him as a minister to take the sword and lead the peasants would have been to forsake his office as he conceived it. He had not demolished the papal theocracy to set up in its place a new theocracy of saints or peasants. The magistrate should keep the peace. The magistrate should wield the sword. Not for Luther the role of a Ziska at the head of the Hussite hordes, or of a Cromwell leading the Ironsides.

MÜNTZER FOMENTS REBELLION

Yet Luther would never have condemned the peasants quite so savagely had it not been that someone else essayed the very role which he abhorred. In Saxony there would have been no Peasants' War without Thomas Müntzer. Banished, he had gone to Bohemia, then had returned and insinuated himself into a Saxon village, won control over the government, and now at last in the peasants discovered the *Bund* of the elect who should slaughter the ungodly and erect the kingdom of the saints. The point was not the redress of economic grievance, which in Saxony was not acute since serfdom had long since been abolished. Müntzer was interested in economic amelioration only for the sake of religion, and he did have the insight to see what no one else in his generation observed, that faith itself does not thrive on physical exhaustion. He exclaimed:

Luther says that the poor people have enough in their faith. Doesn't he see that usury and taxes impede the reception of the faith? He claims that the Word of God is sufficient. Doesn't he realize that men whose every moment is consumed in the making of a living have no time to learn to read the Word of God? The princes bleed the people with usury and count as their own the fish in the stream, the bird of the air, and the grass of the field, and Dr. Liar says, "Amen!" What courage has he, Dr. Pussyfoot, the new pope of Wittenberg, Dr. Easychair, the basking sycophant? He says there should be no rebellion because the sword has been committed by God to the ruler, but the power of the sword belongs to the whole community. In the good old days the people stood by when judgment was rendered lest the ruler pervert justice, and the rulers have perverted justice. They shall be cast down from their seats. The fowls of the heavens are gathering to devour their carcasses.

In such a mood Müntzer came to Mülhausen, and there he was responsible for fomenting a peasants' war. In front of the pulpit he unfurled a long, silk banner, emblazoned with a rainbow and the motto, "The Word of the Lord Abideth Forever." "Now is the time," he cried. "If you be only three wholly committed unto God, you need not fear one hundred thousand. On! On! On! Spare not! Pity not the godless when they cry. Remember the command of God to Moses to destroy utterly and show no mercy. The whole countryside is in commotion. Strike! Clang! Clang! On! On!"

The countryside was indeed in commotion. The peasants had been thoroughly aroused. And Frederick the Wise was weary and at the point of death. To his brother John he wrote: "Perhaps the peasants have been given just occasion for their uprising through the impeding of the Word of God. In many ways the poor folk have been wronged by the rulers, and now God is visiting his wrath upon us. If it be his will, the common man will come to rule; and if it be not his will, the end will soon be otherwise. Let us then pray to God to forgive our sins, and commit the case to him. He will work it out according to his good pleasure and glory." Brother John yielded to the peasants the right of the government to collect tithes. To Frederick he wrote, "As princes we are ruined."

Luther tried to dike the deluge by going down into the midst of the peasants and remonstrating. They met him with derision and violence. Then he penned the tract, *Against the Murderous and Thieving Hordes of Peasants*. To his mind hell had been emptied because all the devils had gone into the peasants, and the archdevil was in Thomas Müntzer, "who does nothing else but stir up robbery, murder, and bloodshed." A Christian ruler like Frederick the Wise should, indeed, search his heart and humbly pray for help against the Devil, since our "warfare is not with flesh and blood but with spiritual wickedness." The prince, moreover, should exceed his duty in offer-

Wider die Mördischen
vnd Reubischen Rotten der Bawren.

Psalm. vij.
Seyne tück werden jn selbs treffen/
Vnd seyn mütwill/ wirdt vber jn außgeen.
1 5 2 5.
Martinus Luther. Wittemberg.

TITLE PAGE OF LUTHER'S TRACT "AGAINST THE MURDEROUS
AND THIEVING HORDES OF PEASANTS"

ing terms to the mad peasants. If they decline, then he must quickly grasp the sword. Luther had no use for the plan of Frederick the Wise to sit still and leave the outcome to the Lord. Philip of Hesse was more to his taste, who said, "If I hadn't been quick on my toes, the whole movement in my district would have been out of hand in four days."

Luther said:

If the peasant is in open rebellion, then he is outside the law of God, for rebellion is not simply murder, but it is like a great fire which attacks and lays waste a whole land. Thus, rebellion brings with it a land full of murders and bloodshed, makes widows and orphans, and turns everything upside down like a great disaster. Therefore, let everyone who can, smite, slay, and stab, secretly or openly, remembering that nothing can be more poisonous, hurtful, or devilish than a rebel. It is just as when one must kill a mad dog; if you don't strike him, he will strike you, and the whole land with you.

Some of the princes were only too ready to smite, stab, and slay; and Thomas Müntzer was only too prompt to provoke them. Duke George and Landgrave Philip, among others, were quick enough on their toes. Müntzer and the peasants were drawn up near Frankenhausen. They sent word to the princes that they sought nothing but the righteousness of God and desired to avoid bloodshed. The princes replied, "Deliver up Thomas Müntzer. The rest shall be spared." The offer was tempting, but Müntzer loosed his eloquence: "Fear not. Gideon with a handful discomfited the Midianites, and David slew Goliath." Just at that moment a rainbow appeared in the sky, the very symbol on Müntzer's banner. He pointed to it as a sign. The peasants rallied. But the princes took advantage of a truce to surround them. Only six hundred were taken prisoner. Five thousand were butchered. Müntzer escaped, but was caught, tortured, and beheaded. The princes then cleaned up the countryside.

THE DEBACLE AND THE EFFECT ON THE REFORMATION

Other bands fared no better. The forces of the Swabian League were led by a general who when outnumbered would have recourse to diplomacy, duplicity, strategy, and at last combat. He managed to isolate the bands and destroy them one at a time. The peasants were tricked and finally outnumbered. It was claimed that 100,000 were liquidated. On the day when Bishop Conrad rode in triumph into Würzburg, the event was celebrated with the execution of 64 citizens and peasants. Then the bishop made a tour of his diocese, accompanied by his executioner, who took care of 272 persons. Excessive fines were imposed, yet the peasants as a class were not exterminated; the nobles could not afford to wipe out the tillers of the soil. Neither was their prosperity destroyed, for they were able to pay the fines, but their hope for a share in the political life of Germany was at an end. For three centuries they became hornless oxen.

Unhappily Luther's savage tract was late in leaving the press and appeared just at the time when the peasants were being butchered. He tried to counteract the effect by another pamphlet in which he still said that the ears of the rebels must be unbuttoned with bullets, but he had no mind to decry mercy to captives. All the devils, he declared, instead of leaving the peasants and returning to hell, had now entered the victors, who were simply venting their vengeance.

But this tract was not noticed, and that one sentence of Luther's, "smite, slay, and stab," brought him obloquy never to be forgotten. He was reproached by the peasants as a traitor to their cause, though he never ceased to be held responsible by the Catholic princes for the entire conflagration. The peasants in consequence tended to find their religious home in Anabaptism, though this point must not be overdone. The ultimate agrarian complexion of the Anabaptist movement is not by any means wholly the result of the Peasants' War but much more of the persecution which could more readily purge the cities than the farms. Neither did the peasants secede en masse, and to the end of his life Luther's congregation consisted largely of the farmers around about Wittenberg. Nevertheless, Luther's stand was contributory to the alienation of the peasants.

At the same time the Catholic princes held Luther responsible for the whole outbreak, and color was lent to the charge by the participation on the peasants' side of hundreds of Lutheran ministers,

SURRENDER OF THE UPPER SWABIAN PEASANTS. UPPER LEFT: *arrival of the ar*

TER: *slaughter of peasants.* BOTTOM: *surrender.*

THREE VIEWS OF LUTHER AND THE PEASANTS
1. FRIENDLY: LUTHER INSTRUCTS THE PEASANTS

whether voluntarily or under constraint. The rulers in Catholic lands thereafter used the utmost diligence to exclude evangelical preachers, and the persistent Catholicism of Bavaria and Austria dates not so much from the Counter Reformation as from the Peasants' War.

The deepest hurt was to Luther's own spirit. He became so fearful that religious extravagances would lead to social disorders as to become at times hard and undiscriminating.

The sphere, then, of Luther's activity was being constantly curtailed. The Catholics, whether clerical or lay, were obdurate. The Swiss, the south German Protestant cities, and the Anabaptists had developed divergent forms. Even Wittenberg had experienced insurgent movements and might not be free from new infiltrations of the sectaries. But in the areas remaining Luther was resolved to build.

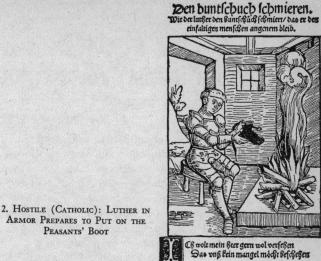

Den buntschuch schmieren.

Wie der luther den buntschuch schmiert/ das er den
einfaltigen menschen angenem bleib.

Ich wolt mein herr gern wol versehen
Das vnß kein mangel möcht beschehen

**2. Hostile (Catholic): Luther in
Armor Prepares to Put on the
Peasants' Boot**

Luther.   Paur.

**3. Hostile (Peasant Side): Peasant Taxes Luther
as Double-Tongued**

CHAPTER SEVENTEEN

THE SCHOOL FOR CHARACTER

 AFFLED, rebuffed, curtailed, restricted, Luther did what he could. The most unpremeditated and dramatic witness to his principles was his own marriage. If he could not reform all Christendom, at any rate he could and he did establish the Protestant parsonage. He had no thought of doing anything of the sort; and when the monks began to marry during his stay at the Wartburg, he had exclaimed, "Good heavens! They won't give me a wife." After the event he said that if anyone had told him at Worms that in six years he would have a wife he would not have believed him.

But a practical situation arose out of his teaching which caused a change of mind. Not only monks but also nuns were leaving the cloisters. Some sisters in a neighboring village sought his counsel as to what they should do in view of their evangelical persuasion. He took it upon himself to arrange their escape. This was hardy because the abduction of nuns was a capital offense, and Duke George exacted the penalty. Frederick the Wise might not be so severe, but he did not relish open violation of the law. Luther clandestinely enlisted the aid of a respected burgher of Torgau, Leonard Kopp, sixty years of age, a merchant who from time to time delivered barrels of herring to the convent. On the Eve of the Resurrection in 1523 he bundled twelve nuns into his covered wagon as if they were empty barrels. Three returned to their own homes. The remaining nine arrived in Wittenberg. A student reported to a friend, "A wagon load of vestal virgins has just come to town, all more eager for marriage than for life. God grant them husbands lest worse befall."

Luther felt responsible to find for them all homes, husbands, or positions of some sort. An obvious solution was that he should dispose of one case by marrying himself. Someone suggested it. His comment on November 30, 1524, was that he had no such intention, not because he was a sexless stone, nor because he was hostile to marriage, but because he expected daily the death of a heretic. Five months later Spalatin had apparently renewed the suggestion. He answered:

As for what you write about my marrying, do not be surprised that I do not wed, even if I am so famous a lover. You should be more surprised when I write so much about marriage and in this way have so much to do with women that I do not turn into a woman, let alone marry one. Although if you want my example you have it abundantly, for I have had three wives at once and have loved them so hard as to lose two to other husbands. The third I hold barely with my left hand, and she is perhaps about to be snatched from me. You are really the timid lover who do not dare to marry even one.

The jocular reference to the three wives was of course to the three last nuns waiting to be placed.

KATHERINE VON BORA

In the end all were provided for save one, Katherine von Bora. Two years after the escape she was still in domestic service, where incidentally she received excellent training, but she was awaiting a better solution and had been intended for a young patrician of Nürnberg, studying at Wittenberg. On his return home his family presumably objected. Katherine was disconsolate and asked Luther to find out how things stood. The outcome was that the Nürnberger married someone else. Then Luther made another selection and picked for Katherine a certain Dr. Glatz, whom she would accept on no terms. But her position was delicate. She knew well that the whole affair had been a trial to Luther, doubly so that it fell in the midst of the Peasants' War, and her case had been the most protracted. In those days of early marriages a girl of twenty-six might begin to think of herself as verging on the upper limits of eligibility. In her embarrassment she bespoke the good offices of a visitor in Wittenberg, Dr. Amsdorf of Magdeburg. Would he please tell Luther that she could not abide Glatz but she was not unreasonable? She would take Amsdorf himself or Luther. These two were named presumably because they were out of the question, since beyond the customary age for marriage. Luther was forty-two.

He did not respond seriously to the suggestion until he went home to visit his parents. What he related, probably as a huge joke, was taken by his father as a realistic proposal. His desire was that his son should pass on the name. The suggestion began to commend itself to Luther for quite another reason. If he was to be burned at the stake within a year, he was hardly the person to start a family. But by marriage he could at once give a status to Katherine and a testimony to his faith. In May of 1525 he intimated that he would marry Katie before he died. And early in June, when Albert of Mainz contemplated secularizing his bishopric after the example of his cousin in Brandenburg, Luther wrote, "If my marrying will strengthen him, I am ready. I believe in marriage, and I intend to get married before I die, even though it should be only a betrothal like Joseph's." This was no love match. "I am not infatuated," said Luther, "though I cherish my wife." On another occasion he declared, "I would not exchange Katie for France or for Venice, because God has given her to me and other women have worse faults." He summed up by giving three reasons for his marriage: to please his father, to spite the pope and the Devil, and to seal his witness before martyrdom.

When once the resolve was taken, marriage followed speedily to scotch rumor and protest. "All my best friends," said Luther, "exclaimed, 'For heaven's sake, not this one.'" A jurist predicted that "the world and the Devil would laugh and Luther's work would be undone." Curiously at that very juncture Spalatin asked Luther what he thought of long engagements. He replied, "Don't put off till tomorrow! By delay Hannibal lost Rome. By delay Esau forfeited his birthright. Christ said, 'Ye shall seek me, and ye shall not find.' Thus

Scripture, experience, and all creation testify that the gifts of God must be taken on the wing." That was on the tenth of June. On the thirteenth Luther was publicly betrothed to Katherine and, in the

A Wedding Party in Front of the Church

This is not the betrothal, which established the legal bond, but the public declaration. The party first paraded through the streets to the sound of the pipers.

eyes of the law, was thereby already a married man. The public ceremony which followed was only an announcement party.

This was the social event. It was set for the twenty-seventh, and Luther sent out letters of invitation: To Spalatin, "You must come to my wedding. I have made the angels laugh and the devils weep." To another, "Undoubtedly the rumor of my marriage has reached you. I can hardly believe it myself, but the witnesses are too strong. The wedding will be next Thursday in the presence of my father and mother. I hope you can bring some game and come yourself." To

Amsdorf, who had mediated for Katie, "The rumor of my marriage is correct. I cannot deny my father the hope of progeny, and I had to confirm my teaching at a time when many are so timid. I hope you will come." To a Nürnberger, "My tract has greatly offended the peasants. I'd be sorry if it had not. While I was thinking of other things, God has suddenly brought me to marriage with Katherine. I invite you and absolve you from any thought of a present." To Leonard Kopp, who organized the escape of the nuns, "I am going to get married. God likes to work miracles and to make a fool of the world. You must come to the wedding." Curiously there is a second invitation to Kopp. The editor of the letters in the Weimar edition questions the authenticity. It reads, "I am to be married on Thursday. My lord Katie and I invite you to send a barrel of the best Torgau beer, and if it is not good you will have to drink it all yourself."

On the appointed day at ten o'clock in the morning Luther led Katherine to the sound of bells through the streets of Wittenberg to the parish church, where at the portal in the sight of all the people the religious ceremony was observed. Then came a banquet in the Augustinian cloister, and after dinner a dance at the town hall. In the evening there was another banquet. At eleven all the guests took their departure on pain of being sent home by the magistrates.

DOMESTICITY

Marriage brought many changes to Luther's way of living. "Before I was married the bed was not made for a whole year and became foul with sweat. But I worked so hard and was so weary I tumbled in without noticing it." Katie cleaned house. There were other adjustments to be made. "There is a lot to get used to in the first year of marriage," reflected Luther. "One wakes up in the morning and finds a pair of pigtails on the pillow which were not there before." He soon discovered that a husband must take the wishes of his wife into account. The fears and tears of Katie restrained him from attending Spalatin's wedding, in view of the danger of violence from peasants on the way. If Martin referred jocularly to his wife as "my rib," he called her quite as often "my lord." Sometimes he even punned

KATHERINE VON BORA AND MARTIN LUTHER
IN THE YEAR OF THEIR MARRIAGE

upon the name Katie and turned it in German into *Kette*, meaning "chain."

Marriage also brought new financial responsibilities, because neither of them started with a cent. Katherine's mother died when she was a baby. Her father consigned her to a convent and married again. He did nothing for her now. Luther had only his books and his clothes. He was not entitled to the revenues of the cloister, since he had abandoned the cowl. He took never a penny from his books, and his university stipend was not enough for matrimony. In 1526 he installed a lathe and learned woodworking that in case of need he might be able to support his family. But one may doubt whether he ever took this thought very seriously. He was minded to give himself exclusively to the service of the Word, and he trusted that the heavenly Father would provide. The angel Gabriel must have been kept rather busy making suggestions to men of substance in Luther's entourage. The elector made over the Augustinian cloister to Luther and his bride, doubled his salary, and frequently sent game, clothes, and wine. And the Archbishop of Mainz, Albert of Brandenburg, presented Katie with twenty gold gulden which her husband was disposed to decline.

If marriage brought new responsibilities for Luther, vastly more was this the case for Katie. Keeping house for so improvident a husband was no light task. His giving was so prodigal that Lucas Cranach, the artist and banker, refused to honor his draft. Luther's comment was, "I do not believe I can be accused of niggardliness." He was irritatingly blithe. "I do not worry about debts," he said, "because when Katie pays one, another comes." She watched him, and she needed to watch him. In one letter he says to a friend, "I am sending you a vase as a wedding present. P.S. Katie's hid it." At one point he was of real help. He took care of the garden, which produced lettuce, cabbage, peas, beans, melons, and cucumbers. Katie looked after an orchard beyond the village, which supplied them with apples, grapes, pears, nuts, and peaches. She had also a fish pond from which she netted trout, carp, pike, and perch. She looked after the barnyard with hens, ducks, pigs, and cows, and did the slaughtering herself. Luther gives a glimpse into her activities in a letter of 1535: "My lord Katie greets you. She plants our fields, pastures and sells cows, *et cetera* [how much does that *et cetera* cover?]. In between she has started to read the Bible. I have promised her 50 gulden [where did he expect to get them?] if she finishes by Easter. She is hard at it and is at the end of the fifth book of Moses." In later years he acquired a farm at Zulsdorf, which Katie managed, spending there some weeks out of the year. Luther wrote her on such occasions: "To the rich lady of Zulsdorf, Mrs. Dr. Katherine Luther, who lives in the flesh at Wittenberg but in the spirit at Zulsdorf," and again, "To my beloved wife, Katherine, Mrs. Dr. Luther, mistress of the pig market, lady of Zulsdorf, and whatsoever other titles may befit thy Grace."

Looking after him was the more of a task because he was so often sick. He suffered at one time or another from gout, insomnia, catarrh, hemorrhoids, constipation, stone, dizziness, and ringing in the ears like all the bells of Halle, Leipzig, Erfurt, and Wittenberg. Katie was a master of herbs, poultices, and massage. Her son Paul, who became a doctor, said his mother was half one. She kept Luther from wine and gave him beer, which served as a sedative for insomnia and a solvent for the stone. And she brewed the beer herself. When he was away from home, how he appreciated her ministrations! After a year of marriage he wrote to a friend, "My Katie is in all things so obliging and pleasing to me that I would not exchange my poverty for the riches of Croesus." He paid her the highest tribute when he called St. Paul's epistle to the Galatians "my Katherine von Bora." He began to be a trifle worried over his devotion: "I give more credit to Katherine than to Christ, who has done so much more for me."

CHILDREN AND TABLE TALK

Katie had soon more than Luther to think about. On October 21, 1525, Luther confided to a friend, "My Katherine is fulfilling Genesis 1:28." On May 26, 1526, he wrote to another, "There is about to be born a child of a monk and a nun. Such a child must have a great lord for godfather. Therefore I am inviting you. I cannot be precise as to the time." On the eighth of June went out the news, "My dear Katie brought into the world yesterday by God's grace at two o'clock a little son, Hans Luther. I must stop. Sick Katie calls me." When the baby was bound in swaddling clothes, Luther said, "Kick, little fellow. That is what the pope did to me, but I got loose." The next entry in Hans's *curriculum vitae* was this: "Hans is cutting his teeth and beginning to make a joyous nuisance of himself. These are the joys of marriage of which the pope is not worthy." On the arrival of a daughter Luther wrote to a prospective godmother, "Dear lady, God has produced from me and my wife Katie a little heathen. We hope you will be willing to become her spiritual mother and help make her a Christian." There were six children in all. Their names and birthdays are as follows: Hans, June 7, 1526; Elizabeth, December 10, 1527; Magdalena, December 17, 1529; Martin, November 9, 1531; Paul, January 28, 1533; Margaretha, December 17, 1534.

And besides the children there were all those whom the Luthers took in. On the very night of the wedding, when the guests had departed by eleven o'clock, another guest unbeknown to the magistrate appeared. It was Carlstadt, fleeing from the Peasants' War and asking for shelter; and Luther, who had done so much to put him out of Saxony, took him into his own home on his wedding night. Carlstadt of course did not stay indefinitely, but others arrived. And since the cloister was large and suited for a hospital, the sick also were taken in. Furthermore the Luthers brought up four orphaned children from among relatives, in addition to their own six. To eke out the finances they had recourse to a device familiar in professional families of opening a pension for student boarders. The household would number as many as twenty-five.

Katie of course could not do all the labor for such an establishment. There were maidservants and manservants, but she had to superintend everything. Perhaps the hardest part of her position, however, was that she was invariably overshadowed by her famous husband. She expected it and did not resent it. She always called him Doctor, and used the polite form *Ihr* rather than the familiar *Du*. Yet at times she must have been a trifle disquieted because he was on every

THE LUTHER HOUSEHOLD AT TABLE
There is an unpardonable omission. Katie is not there.

294

occasion the center of the conversation. It was not altogether his fault. The student boarders regarded mealtime as an opportunity to continue their education, and sat at table with notebooks to scribble down every nugget and every clod from his voluble mouth. Katie thought he should have charged them for it. Luther was himself irritated at times, though he never put a stop to it. At one point he was responsible for stepping in front of the lights. He talked a great deal about his bouts with Satan until to have experienced none placed one in a lower category. Katie was not to be outdone. One day she arose from the table, retired to her room, fainted, and afterwards reported that she had experienced *multa perniciosa*, and she announced it in Latin. From then on Katie qualified.

Luther's *Table Talk* would deserve a notice if for no other reason than its sheer volume. There are 6,596 entries, and it is among the better known of his works because his students after his death culled, classified, and produced a handy volume adorned with a woodcut of Luther at the table with his family. The classification obscures the lush profusion and unpredictable variety of the original. Luther ranged from the ineffable majesty of God the Omnipotent to the frogs in the Elbe. Pigs, popes, pregnancies, politics, and proverbs jostle one another. Some random samples may convey a faint impression:

The monks are the fleas on God Almighty's fur coat.

When asked why he was so violent, Luther replied, "A twig can be cut with a bread knife, but an oak calls for an ax."

God uses lust to impel men to marriage, ambition to office, avarice to earning, and fear to faith.

The only portion of the human anatomy which the pope has had to leave uncontrolled is the hind end.

Printing is God's latest and best work to spread the true religion throughout the world.

I am a pillar of the pope. After I am gone he will fare worse.

Birds lack faith. They fly away when I enter the orchard, though I mean them no ill. Even so do we lack faith in God.

There are rumors that the world will end in 1532. I hope it won't be long. The last decade seems like a new century.

A cartoon has appeared of me as a monster with seven heads. I must be invincible because they cannot overcome me when I have only one.

A dog is a most faithful animal and would be more highly prized if less common.

A melancholic claimed to be a rooster and strutted about crowing. The doctor said he, too, was a rooster and for several days crowed with him. Then he said, "I am not a rooster any more, and you are changed too." It worked.

Germany is the pope's pig. That is why we have to give him so much bacon and sausages.

What lies there are about relics! One claims to have a feather from the wing of the angel Gabriel, and the Bishop of Mainz has a flame from Moses' burning bush. And how does it happen that eighteen apostles are buried in Germany when Christ had only twelve?

I cannot think what we shall find to do in heaven, mused Luther. "No change, no work, no eating, no drinking, nothing to do. I suppose there will be plenty to see." "Yes," said Melanchthon, " 'Lord, show us the Father, and it sufficeth us.' " "Why, of course," responded Luther, "that sight will give us quite enough to do."

The ark of Noah was 300 ell long, 50 wide, and 30 high. If it were not in Scripture, I would not believe it. I would have died if I had been in the ark. It was dark, three times the size of my house, and full of animals.

They are trying to make me into a fixed star. I am an irregular planet.

An officer in the Turkish war told his men that if they died in battle they would sup with Christ in Paradise. The officer fled. When asked why he did not wish to sup with Christ, he said he was fasting that day.

In 1538 on May the 26th there was a big rain. Luther said, "Praise God. He is giving us one hundred thousand gulden worth. It is raining corn, wheat, barley, wine, cabbage, onions, grass, and milk. All our goods we get for nothing. And God sends his only begotten Son, and we crucify him."

"I am the son of a peasant," said Luther, "and the grandson and the great-grandson. My father wanted to make me into a burgomaster. He went to Mansfeld and became a miner. I became a baccalaureate and a master. Then I became a monk and put off the brown beret. My father didn't like it, and then I got into the pope's hair and married an apostate nun. Who could have read that in the stars?"

The above selections speak well enough for themselves, but a word of comment is in order with regard to Luther's vulgarity, be-

Sieben köpffe Martini Luthers
Vom Hochwürdigen Sacrament des Altars / Durch
Doctor Jo. Cocleus.

Doctor — Martinus — Luther — Ecclesiast — Schwirmer — Visitirer — Barrabas

Martinus Luther
Siebenkopff.

LUTHER AS A SEVEN-HEADED MONSTER
One head is a fanatic with wasps in his hair.

cause he is often represented as inordinately coarse, and the *Table Talk* is cited by way of example. There is no denying that he was not fastidious, nor was his generation. Life itself stank. One could not walk around Wittenberg without encountering the odors of the pigsty, offal, and the slaughterhouse. And even the most genteel were not reticent about the facts of daily experience. Katie, when asked about the congregation on a day when Luther was unable to attend, replied, "The church was so full it stank." "Yes," said Luther, "they had manure on their boots." Erasmus did not hesitate to compose a colloquy in which the butcher and the fishmonger celebrated the offensiveness of each other's wares. Luther delighted less in muck than many of the literary men of his age; but if he did indulge, he excelled in this as in every other area of speech. The volume of coarseness, however, in his total output is slight. Detractors have sifted from the pitchblende of his ninety tomes a few pages of radioactive vulgarity. But there are whole volumes which contain nothing more offensive than a quotation from the apostle Paul, who "suffered the loss of all things," and counted them but dung, that he might win Christ.

A word may be said at this point also about Luther's drinking. He imbibed and took some pride in his capacity. He had a mug around which were three rings. The first he said represented the Ten Commandments, the second the Apostles' Creed, and the third the Lord's Prayer. Luther was highly amused that he was able to drain the glass of wine through the Lord's Prayer, whereas his friend Agricola could not get beyond the Ten Commandments. But Luther is not recorded ever to have exceeded a state of hilarity.

VIEWS OF MARRIAGE

But to return to marriage. The Luther who got married in order to testify to his faith actually founded a home and did more than any other person to determine the tone of German domestic relations for the next four centuries. We may conveniently at this point consider his views on marriage. Here as elsewhere he walked in the steps of Paul and Augustine. His position with regard to marriage was tinctured throughout by patriarchalism. According to Luther the man is the head of the wife because he was created first. She is to give him not only love but also honor and obedience. He is to rule her with gentleness, but he is to rule. She has her sphere, and she can do more with the children with one finger than he with two fists. But she is to confine herself to her sphere. If Luther did not say that children, church, and kitchen are the province of women, he did say that women have been created with large hips in order that they should stay at home and sit on them. Children are subject to parents and especially to the father, who exercises in the household the same sort of authority as does the magistrate in the state. Disrespect for parents is a breach of the Ten Commandments. On one occasion Luther refused to forgive his son for three days, although the boy begged his pardon and Katie and others interceded. The point was that the boy in disobeying his father had offended the majesty of God. If only Luther could have left God out of it now and then, he would have been more humane. Yet it must be remembered that in his judgment the apple should always lie alongside of the rod.

The whole institution of marriage was set by Luther within the framework of family relationships. There was no room left for the exercise of unbridled individualism. Matings should be made by families; and whereas parents should not force children to repulsive unions, children in turn should not, because of infatuations, resist reasonable choices on the part of their elders. This whole picture was carried directly over from the Middle Ages, in which Catholic sacramentalism and agrarian society tended to make of marriage an institution for the perpetuation of families and the preservation of properties. The romantic revolution of the Courts of Love in France was at first extramatrimonial, and the combination of romance and marriage was effected only during the Renaissance.

To these currents Luther was entirely a stranger. His ideal was Rebecca, who accepted the mate selected for her by the family. Jacob was reprehensible in his eyes because after receiving Leah, who bore him children, he worked yet seven other years out of infatuation for the pretty face of Rachel. Luther was glad, however, of this failing because it proved that he was saved by faith and not by works. But if in this respect Luther followed the medieval view, on other counts he broke with it, and notably in the rejection of virginity as an ideal. By this move the way was open for the romanticizing and refinement of marriage. But its immediate effect was rather the contrary. In Luther's early polemic, marriage was reduced to the most elemental physical level because in order to repulse ecclesiastical interference Luther insisted that sexual intercourse is as necessary and inevitable as eating and drinking. Those not gifted with chastity must find gratification. To refuse them is to prefer fornication to wedlock. In interpreting these words, however, one must be careful. Luther did not really mean that external chastity is impossible, but merely that without sexual satisfaction many will be tormented by desire, and for that reason marriage is a purer state than monasticism. The controversial tracts, however, up to 1525 are certainly unguarded in creating the impression that the sole object of marriage is to serve as a remedy for sin.

But after his own wedding the emphasis shifted, and he began to portray marriage as a school for character. In this sense it displaces the monastery, which had been regarded by the Church as the training ground of virtue and the surest way to heaven. Luther in rejecting all earning of salvation did not exclude exercise in fortitude, patience, charity, and humility. Family life is exacting. The head of the house has the lifelong worry over daily bread. The wife has the bearing of children. During pregnancy she suffers from dizziness, headache, nausea, toothache, and swelling of the legs. In travail her husband may comfort her by saying, "Think, dear Greta, that you are a woman and your work is pleasing to God. Rejoice in his will. Bring forth the child. Should you die, it is for a noble work and in obedience to God. If you were not a woman, you should wish to be one, that you might suffer and die in so precious and noble a work of God." The rearing of children is a trial for both parents. To one of his youngsters Luther said, "Child, what have you done that I should love you so? You have disturbed the whole household with your bawling." And when a baby cried for an hour and the parents were at the end of their resources, he remarked, "This is the sort of thing that has caused the Church fathers to vilify marriage. But God before the last day has brought back marriage and the magistracy to their proper esteem." The mother of course has the brunt of it. But the father may have to hang out the diapers, to the neighbors' amusement. "Let them laugh. God and the angels smile in heaven."

There are vexations between the married couple. "Good God," ejaculated Luther, "what a lot of trouble there is in marriage! Adam has made a mess of our nature. Think of all the squabbles Adam and Eve must have had in the course of their nine hundred years. Eve would say, 'You ate the apple,' and Adam would retort, 'You gave it to me.' "

Luther once at the table was expatiating with gusto in response to student questions. When he paused, Katie broke in, "Doctor, why don't you stop talking and eat?"

"I wish," snapped Luther, "that women would repeat the Lord's Prayer before opening their mouths." The students tried to get him on the track again, but he was derailed for that meal.

On occasion Katie could have well returned the compliment. Once she was praying out loud for rain, and Luther broke in, "Yes, why not, Lord? We have persecuted thy Word and killed thy saints. We have deserved well of thee."

Part of the difficulty was that the rhythm of work and rest did not coincide for Luther and his wife. After a day with children, animals, and servants, she wanted to talk with an equal; and he, after preaching four times, lecturing and conversing with students at meals, wanted to drop into a chair and sink into a book. Then Katie would start in, "Herr Doktor, is the prime minister of Prussia the Duke's brother?"

"All my life is patience," said Luther. "I have to have patience with the pope, the heretics, my family, and Katie." But he recognized that it was good for him.

Nor should it be for a moment supposed that he excluded love from marriage. Of course the Christian should love his wife, said Luther. He is bound to love his neighbor as himself. His wife is his nearest neighbor. Therefore she should be his dearest friend. And Luther signed himself to Katie, *Dir lieb und treu.* The greatest grace of God is when love persists in marriage. "The first love is drunken. When the intoxication wears off, then comes the real married love." The couple should study to be pleasing to each other. In the old days this sound advice was given to the bride: "My dear, make your husband glad to cross his threshold at night"; and to the groom, "Make your wife sorry to have you leave." "The dearest life is to live with a godly, willing, obedient wife in peace and unity." "Union of the flesh does nothing. There must also be union of manners and mind." "Katie, you have a husband that loves you. Let someone else be empress."

When Katie was ill, Luther exclaimed, "Oh, Katie, do not die and leave me."

When he was ill and thought he was about to die, he turned to his wife. "My dearest Katie, if it be God's will accept it. You are mine. You will rest assured of that, and hold to God's word. I did want to write another book on baptism, but God's will be done. May he care for you and Hans."

Katie answered, "My dear Doctor, if it is God's will I would rather have you with our Lord than here. But I am not thinking just of myself and Hans. There are so many people that need you. But don't worry about us. God will take care of us."

CONSOLATIONS OF HOME

Luther thoroughly enjoyed his home. Once his colleague Jonas remarked that he saw the blessing of God in fruit and for that reason had hung a cherry bough above his table. Luther said, "Why don't you think of your children? They are in front of you all the time, and you will learn from them more than from a cherry bough." But there was no sentimentality in what Luther expected him to learn. "O dear God, how Adam must have loved Cain, and yet he turned out to be the murderer of his brother." When Luther looked at his family in 1538, he remarked, "Christ said we must become as little children to enter the kingdom of heaven. Dear God, this is too much. Have we got to become such idiots?" One wonders whether the children were ever minded to wonder who was the idiot when Luther cut up Hans's pants to mend his own. Yet what child would not cheerfully forgive a father who wrote to him a letter like this? On August 22, 1530, Luther wrote to Hans, then four years old:

My dearest son:

I am glad to know that you learn well and pray hard. Keep on, my lad, and when I come home, I'll bring you a whole fair.

I know a lovely garden where many children in golden frocks gather rosy apples under the trees, as well as pears, cherries, and plums. They sing, skip, and are gay. And they have fine ponies with golden bridles and silver saddles. I asked the gardener who were these children, and he said, "They are the children who like to pray and learn and be good." And I said, "Good man, I too have a son, and his name is Hans Luther. Couldn't he come into the garden, too, and eat the rosy apples and the pears and ride a fine pony and play with these children?" And the man said, "If he likes to pray and learn and be good, he too may come into the garden, and Lippus and Jost [the sons of Melanchthon and Jonas] as well; and when they all come together, they shall have golden whistles and drums and fine silver crossbows." But it was early, and the children had not yet had their breakfasts, so I couldn't wait for the dance. I said to the man, "I will go at once and write all this to my dear son Hans that he may work hard, pray well, and be good, so that he too may come into this garden. But he has an Aunt Lena he'll have to bring too." "That will be all right," said he. "Go and write this to him."

So, my darling son, study and pray hard and tell Lippus and Jost to do this too, so that you may all come together into the garden. May the dear God take care of you. Give my best to Auntie Lena and give her a kiss for me.

Your loving father,
MARTIN LUTHER

Luther reveled in household festivities and may well have composed for Hans and Lenchen the Christmas pageant *Vom Himmel Hoch* with its delightful, childlike quality. Equally charming is this brief carol:

> Our little Lord, we give thee praise
> That thou has deigned to take our ways.
> Born of a maid a man to be,
> And all the angels sing to thee.

The eternal Father's Son he lay
Cradled in a crib of hay.
The everlasting God appears
In our frail flesh and blood and tears.

What the globe could not enwrap
Nestled lies in Mary's lap.
Just a baby, very wee,
Yet Lord of all the world is he.

When Magdalena was fourteen years old, she lay upon her deathbed. Luther prayed, "O God, I love her so, but thy will be done." And turning to her, "*Magdalenchen,* my little girl, you would like to stay with your father here and you would be glad to go to your Father in heaven?"

And she said, "Yes, dear father, as God wills."

And Luther reproached himself because God had blessed him as no bishop had been blessed in a thousand years, and yet he could not find it in his heart to give God thanks. Katie stood off, overcome by grief; and Luther held the child in his arms as she passed on. When she was laid away, he said, "*Du liebes Lenichen,* you will rise and shine like the stars and the sun. How strange it is to know that she is at peace and all is well, and yet to be so sorrowful!"

CHAPTER EIGHTEEN

THE CHURCH TERRITORIAL

owever much Luther's activity may have been curtailed by defections, he did found a church. Feverish missionary activity was to win most of northern Germany within a decade for the Reform. This success was achieved through a wave of propaganda unequaled hitherto and in its precise form never repeated. The primary tools were the tract and the cartoon. The number of pamphlets issued in Germany in the four years 1521 through 1524 exceeds the quantity for any other four years of German history until the present. This is not to say, of course, that there was more reading than after the introduction of the newspaper and periodical, but only that the tracts were more numerous. In all this Luther himself took the lead, and his own pamphlets in the vernacular run into the hundreds; but a vast cohort assisted him, and the printers who brought out these highly controversial materials were an intrepid breed who risked their establishments and their lives. The cohesiveness and adroitness of this underground is strikingly exemplified in the case of a press which issued, without any identifying marks, an attack on the Bishop of Constance for tolerating and taxing priests' bastards. Two hundred other works can be traced by the paper and the type to this press, and yet its identity has never yet been disclosed. The Catholics of course retaliated in kind, though by no means in equal volume.

DISSEMINATION OF THE REFORM

A brief glance at the content of this pamphleteering is revealing alike for the methods and the selection of themes for popular dissemination. All the external abuses of the Roman Church were easy to lampoon. The familiar theme of the contrast between Christ and the pope was exploited. Christ in a skit is made to say, "I have not where to lay my head." The pope comments, "Sicily is mine. Corsica is mine. Assisi is mine. Perugia is mine." Christ: "He who believes and is baptized will be saved." Pope: "He who contributes and receives indulgences will be absolved." Christ: "Feed my sheep." Pope: "I shear mine." Christ: "Put up your sword." Pope: "Pope Julius killed sixteen hundred in one day." In a cartoon the pope in armor on a war horse accompanied by a devil drops his lance on seeing Christ on a donkey carrying a large cross.

Monasticism, images, and magic received many gibes. "Three finches in a birdhouse praise God more joyfully than one hundred monks in a cloister." A pamphleteer describes an image of the Virgin with the head hollowed out and needle holes in the eyes, through which water could be squirted to make her weep. A Catholic mother in Swabia had sent to her son studying at Wittenberg a little wax lamb marked *Agnus Dei* to protect him against mishap. His reply to her was printed in 1523.

THREE POLEMICAL CARTOONS
1. CHRIST DISARMS THE POPE

Luthers vnd Lutsbers

eintrechtige vereinigung/ so in xxij

eygenschafften sindt allenthalben gleychförmig verfüget/
Durch M. pet. Sylvium der Christenheyt zu seliger warnung trewlich
beschriben/vnd mit Götlicher schrifft vnwidersprechlich ergrün=
det/ wie es am letzten blat ist volkomlicher berürt.

2. LUTHER AND LUCIFER IN LEAGUE

Liebe Mutter:

You should not be upset over Dr. Martin Luther's teaching, nor worried about me. It is safer here than in Swabia. I am grateful to you for sending me the little wax *Agnus Dei*, to protect me against being shot, cut, and

3. The Devil Delivers a Declaration of War to Luther

from falling, but honestly it won't do me any good. I cannot set my faith on it because God's Word teaches me to trust only in Jesus Christ. I am sending it back. We'll try it out on this letter and see whether it is protected from tampering. I don't thank you one bit less, but I pray God you won't believe any more in sacred salt and holy water and all this devil's tomfoolery. I hope you won't give the wax lamb to my brother. And dearest mother, I hope father will let me stay longer in Wittenberg. Read Dr. Martin Luther's New Testament. It is on sale at Leipzig. I am going to buy a brown hat at Wittenberg. Love to my dear father and brother and sisters.

The tracts did not forget to extol Luther. In one of the pamphlets a peasant, meeting a resplendent figure, inquires whether he is God. "No," comes the answer, "I am a fisher of men, Peter by name, and I have just come from Wittenberg, where in God's good pleasure my fellow apostle Martin Luther has arisen to tell the people the truth that I never was the bishop of Rome, nor was I ever a bloodsucker of the poor, for I had neither silver nor gold."

The Devil was called in to assist both sides. A Catholic cartoon shows him whispering into the ear of his confidant, Martin Luther. On the other hand a Reformation cut depicts Luther at his desk when the Devil breaks in with a letter which reads:

We Lucifer, lord of eternal darkness and ruler of all the kingdoms of the world, declare to you, Martin Luther, our wrath and displeasure. We have learned from our legates, Cardinals Campeggio and Lang, the damage you have done in that you have revived the Bible which at our behest has been little used for the last four hundred years. You have persuaded monks and nuns to leave the cloisters in which formerly they served us well, and you are yourself an apostate from our service. Therefore we will persecute you with burning, drowning, and beheading. This is a formal declaration of war, and you will receive no other notice. Sealed with our hellish seal in the City of Damnation on the last day of September, 1524.

The drama reinforced the tract. A play disclosed a conspiracy to overthrow the kingdom of Christ through the erection of the papacy with such success that Satan invited the pope and his satellites to a banquet. When they were sated with roast princes and sausages made from the blood of the poor, a messenger broke in with the news that justification by faith was being preached at Wittenberg. Hell was thrown into confusion, and Christ took over.

These examples illustrate the attack on Romish abuses. Luther's positive teaching was less graphic and more difficult to popularize;

but Hans Sachs, the shoemaker poet of Nürnberg, succeeded not badly in rhyming couplets on Luther as "The Wittenberg Nightingale":

> Luther teaches that we all
> Are involved in Adam's fall.
> If man beholds himself within,
> He feels the bite and curse of sin.
> When dread, despair, and terror seize,
> Contrite he falls upon his knees.
> Then breaks for him the light of day.
> Then the gospel may have sway.
> Then sees he Christ of God the Son,
> Who for us all things has done.
> The law fulfilled, the debt is paid,
> Death overcome, the curse allayed,
> Hell destroyed, the devil bound,
> Grace for us with God has found.
> Christ, the Lamb, removes all sin.
> By faith alone in Christ we win.

By such simple summaries Luther's teaching was taken to the common man in every walk of life. When Luther was reproached for making his appeal to the laity, one of the pamphleteers replied:

You subtle fools, I tell you there are now at Nürnberg, Augsburg, Ulm, in Switzerland, and in Saxony wives, maidens, and maids, students, handworkers, tailors, shoemakers, bakers, knights, nobles, and princes such as the Elector of Saxony, who know more about the Bible than all the schools of Paris and Cologne and all the papists in the world.

PRACTICAL CHURCH PROBLEMS

But this very dissemination of the gospel raised many practical problems as to the organization of the Church. Luther's views on that subject had never been clarified. The true Church for him was always the Church of the redeemed, known only to God, manifest here and there on earth, small, persecuted and often hidden, at any rate scattered and united only in the bond of the spirit. Such a view could scarcely issue in anything other than a mystical fellowship devoid of any concrete form. This was what Luther meant by the kingdom of Christ. He did not pretend that it could be actualized, but he was not prepared to leave the Church disembodied. The next possibility was to gather together such ardent souls as could be assembled in a particular locality, and Luther came close to forming such an association in 1522 when he instructed those who desired communion in both kinds to receive it apart from the rest. After such communion became the common practice, he still desired to gather true believers into an inner fellowship, but not at the price of abandoning the church comprising the community. He would rather form a cell within the structure of the comprehensive body. The practical difficulties, however, in his judgment were insuperable, and by 1526 he declared his dream to be impossible. On that score he was mistaken, because the Anabaptists succeeded, but they did so by making a clean break with the church territorial. Luther's dilemma was that he wanted both a confessional church based on personal faith and experience, and a territorial church including all in a given locality. If he were forced to choose, he would take his stand with the masses, and this was the direction in which he moved.

To do so required some efforts in the direction of organization. By 1527 the whole of electoral Saxony could be regarded as evangelical. At many points the abandonment of the old ways had produced confusion. Notably was this the case at the point of ecclesiastical properties and finances. Cloisters had been abandoned. What then should become of their endowments and revenues? The donors in some instances had been dead for centuries, and the heirs were beyond identification. The lands were in danger of expropriation by powerful neighbors, and revenues in any case declined because the peasants were indisposed to surrender the produce after the object had been altered. Secondly, the liturgical reforms had engendered chaos, because Luther was so averse to uniformity. Each village and even each church had its own variety. Soon within the very same city the several churches exhibited diversity, and even a single church might vary in its practice. To those whose sense of religious security depended upon hallowed usage, such variety and unpredictability were genuinely disturbing. Luther began to feel that uniformity would have to be established, at least within the limits of each town.

Worst of all, differences in doctrine imperiled the public peace. Remnants of Catholicism survived, and Zwinglianism and Anabaptism were infiltrating. Such was the public temper that positive strife ensued. For this Luther saw no solution other than that one religion only should be publicly celebrated in a given locality. How to bring this to pass was by no means clear in his mind, because he was impelled by conflicting principles. He regarded the mass as idolatry and blasphemy, but he would compel no one to the faith. He was driven to the recognition of the rights of rival confessions. The outcome was the territorial church, in which the confession was that of the majority in a given locality, and the minority were free to migrate to favorable terrain. Whether this principle should apply only to the Catholics or also to the sectaries was another question.

But who should take the initiative in terminating the confusion? Hitherto Luther had been inclined to congregationalism and had stoutly objected to the dismissal of Zwilling from Altenburg by a patron against the wishes of the people. But independent local congregations were not in a position to cope with problems affecting several areas. These would have been handled by the bishops, but the bishops had not embraced the reform; and even if they had, Luther would not have accorded to them their ancient functions because he had come to be persuaded that in the New Testament every pastor was a bishop. Hence in more than jest he referred to his colleagues as "the bishop of Lochau or the bishop of Torgau." Some substitute, then, would have to be devised for the bishop. The answer was to create the office of superintendent, but how and by whom should he be chosen? If by the churches, who could call them together?

THE GODLY PRINCE

To all these questions Luther saw no answer other than for the time being to call upon the prince. He should act not as a magistrate, but as a Christian brother advantageously situated to serve as an emergency bishop. All the church property should temporarily at least be vested in him that he might redirect the revenues for the support of ministers, teachers, and the poor. As to uniformity in liturgy and faith, if the will of the majority was to be determinative the situation called for a survey. Let Saxony be investigated. Visitations in the old days had been conducted by the bishops. Now let the elector appoint a commission for the purpose. This was done; and Visitors, including theologians with Luther at the head, and jurists to handle financial matters were appointed. Melanchthon composed the visitation articles to be presented in print to each of the clergy. Luther's preface stressed the provisional nature of the whole plan, but the elector referred to the commissioners as "My Visitors," and Melanchthon's instructions were less a questionnaire than a program to be instituted. Luther had unwittingly started down the road which was to lead to the territorial church under the authority of the prince.

The Visitors in two months investigated thirty-eight parishes inquiring into finances, behavior, forms of worship, and the faith. In the matter of finances they discovered great confusion and neglect. Parsonages were in a deplorable condition. One minister complained that four gulden worth of books had been ruined through a leaky roof. The Visitors decided to hold the parishioners responsible for repairs. Morals were not too shocking. The liturgy required standardization within limits. With regard to the faith, the determinative point was the evangelical complexion of all Saxony. The implementation of the reform therefore could not be regarded as an imposition of faith on a majority of the citizens. But there were dissenters, and in the interests of the public peace two religions could not be permitted to exist side by side. For that reason remnants of Catholicism must disappear. Priests who declined to accept the reform were dismissed. If young, they were left to fend for themselves. If old, they were pensioned. One minister on the arrival of the Visitors married his cook. He was asked why he had not done so earlier, and he replied that he expected her to die soon and he could then marry someone younger. He was adjudged to be popish and was deposed. A case was discovered in which a minister served two parishes, one in Catholic and one in evangelical territory, and ministered to each according to its respective rites. This arrangement was deemed unacceptable.

A sharp eye was kept on the sectaries, whether Zwinglian or Anabaptist. But Luther was not yet willing to treat the Anabaptists as the Zwinglians had already done in subjecting them to the death penalty. As late as June, 1528, Luther replied to an inquiry as follows:

You ask whether the magistrate may kill false prophets. I am slow in a judgment of blood even when it is deserved. In this matter I am terrified by the example of the papists and the Jews before Christ, for when there was a statute for the killing of false prophets and heretics, in time it came about that only the most saintly and innocent were killed. . . . I cannot admit that false teachers are to be put to death. *It is enough to banish.*

But even banishment required some adjustment of theory. Luther still held stoutly to his objection to any compulsion to faith. But this did not preclude restriction of the public profession of faith. The outward manifestations of religion, he held, may be subjected to regulation in the interests of orderliness and tranquillity. In all this Luther never dreamed that he was subordinating the Church to the state. The system later introduced in England which made the king the head of the Church was hardly to his taste. But Christian princes in his view were certainly responsible for fostering the true religion. Luther's concern was always that the faith be unimpeded. Anyone might help; no one might hinder. If the prince would render assistance, let it be accepted. If he interfered, then let him be disobeyed. This remained Luther's principle to the end of his life. Nevertheless the sharp line of demarcation which he had delineated between the spheres of the Church and the state in his tract *On Civil Government* in 1523 was already in process of being blurred.

THE PROTEST

This was all the more the case because the evangelical cause was menaced in the political terrain, and inevitably the defense fell to the lay leaders. From now on the electors, princes, and delegates of the free cities rather than the theologians were called upon to say, "Here I stand." Luther himself was not so much the confessor as the mentor of confessors. It was his to encourage, chide, guide, counsel, and warn against undue concessions or unworthy means.

The fortunes of Lutheranism depended upon the decisions of the German diets in conjunction with the emperor or his deputy Ferdinand. A brief review is in order of the struggle of Lutheranism for recognition and of the part played by Luther in the events from the Diet of Worms through the Diet of Augsburg.

After the Diet of Worms each succeeding gathering of the German estates had been forced to occupy itself with the Lutheran question. First came the Diet of Nürnberg in 1522. It differed from the Diet of Worms in that the middle party was gone and the implacables confronted the intransigents. A Catholic group began to form in terms even of political alignment. Duke George of Saxony was the most militant and to inflame his colleagues took it upon himself to copy with his own hand the most offensive passages from Luther's successive works. Joachim of Brandenburg, the Hapsburgs, and the Bavarians constituted the core.

On the other side the free imperial cities were strong for the reform. Augsburg and Strassburg, despite their bishops, were infected with heresy. Nürnberg, where the diet was in session, declared that though the pope had three more layers on his tiara he could not induce them to abandon the Word. Frederick the Wise pursued his usual discreet course, refrained from suppressing the mass in the Castle Church at Wittenberg until the diet was over, but declined equally to banish Luther.

Each side overestimated the other. Ferdinand reported to the emperor that in Germany not one in a thousand was untainted by Lutheranism. But Frederick's delegate reported that he was in danger of being subjected to economic sanctions. With the forces so evenly matched, even though there was no middle party, compromise was the only possible solution. And the Catholics were the readier to concede it because they could not gainsay the word of Frederick's delegate that Luther had actually become a bulwark against disorder, that without him his followers were quite unmanageable, and that his return to Wittenberg against the wishes of his prince had been quite imperative to allay chaos.

The diet at its session of March 6, 1523, contented itself with the ambiguous formula that until the meeting of a general council Luther and his followers should refrain from publishing and that nothing should be preached other than the holy gospel in accord with the interpretation of the writings approved by the Christian Church. When the assembly reconvened the following year, again at Nürnberg, the accession of a new pope, Clement VII, a Medici quite as secular as Leo X, made under the circumstances no difference. The formula adopted on April 18, 1524, was: "The gospel should be preached in accord with the interpretation of the universal Church. Each prince in his own territory should enforce the Edict of Worms in so far as he might be able." Here in germ was the principle of *cuius regio eius religio*, that each region should have its own religion.

Everyone knew that this was only a respite, and the Peasants' War of 1525 intensified the conflict because the Catholic princes hanged Lutheran ministers in batches. In consequence a new brand of Lutheranism began to emerge, political in complexion. The genius of the movement was a recent convert, Philip of Hesse. He was young, impetuous, and always active. He it was who had been on his toes in the Peasants' War when the Saxon princes were for leaving the outcome to God. Philip was guided by three principles: he would compel none to the faith; he would fight rather than suffer compulsion for himself; and he would make an alliance with those of another faith. He was now eager to demonstrate his attachment to the gospel. When the diet of the empire reassembled at Speyer in 1526, Philip marched in with two hundred horsemen and Lutheran preachers, who, being denied the pulpits, stood upon balconies of the inns and addressed throngs of four thousand. Philip made evident his faith by serving an ox on Friday. A representative from Strassburg wished that he had chosen a more significant testimony than staging a barbecue on a fast day. Such flagrant flaunting of ancient usage would never have been tolerated by the emperor had he been free. But having defeated France in 1525, he was subsequently embroiled with the pope and unable to attend the diet. The outcome was another temporizing measure. Each member was left on the religious question to act "as he would have to answer to God and the emperor." This was practically a recognition of the territorial principle.

This respite lasted for three years, during which time most of northern Germany became Lutheran, and in the south the cities of Strassburg, Augsburg, Ulm, and Nürnberg. Constance embraced the reform, severed connections with the Hapsburgs, and joined the Swiss. Basel came over to the reform in 1529.

This was the year of the Second Diet of Speyer. The significance of this gathering is that it solidified the confessions and divided Germany into two camps. On the eve of the diet such was by no means the case. The Evangelicals were divided alike on faith and tactics. Philip of Hesse, duped into believing that the Catholics meditated an attack, had negotiated with France and Bohemia, the traditional enemies of the House of Hapsburg, to the horror of the Saxon princes who had no mind to dismember the empire. The Catholics were divided on policy. The emperor was for the gloved hand, his brother Ferdinand for the mailed fist. The Diet of Speyer brought clarification, because Ferdinand chose to suppress the instructions of his brother Charles, who again was absent, and demanded the extirpation of heresy. His attempt, even though but moderately successful, solidified the Evangelicals. The time appeared propitious for their suppression, because France, the pope, and the Turk were at the moment either in hand or less menacing. But the diet was not too amenable to Ferdinand's wishes, and the decree was far less severe than it might have been. The Edict of Worms was reaffirmed only for Catholic territories. Provisionally until the meeting of the general council Lutheranism was to be tolerated in those regions where it could not be suppressed without tumult. In Lutheran lands the principle of religious liberty for Catholics must be observed, whereas in Catholic lands the same liberty would not be extended to the Lutherans. Against this invidious arrangement the Evangelicals protested, whence the origin of the name Protestant. They contended that the majority of one diet could not rescind the unanimous action of the previous assembly. They questioned whether this was the intent of the emperor, and on that score they were correct. They affirmed that they could not have two religions side by side in their territories without menace to the public peace, and if their plea was not heard, then "they must protest and testify publicly before God that they could consent to nothing contrary to his Word."

Their stand has been variously misrepresented. In the Protestant camp the emphasis has been all too much on the first word, "protest," rather than on the second, "testify." Above all else they were confessing their faith. On the Catholic side the misrepresentation has been flagrant. The historian Janssen said that they were protesting against religious liberty. In a sense of course they were. Neither side was tolerant, but the objection was to the inequality of the arrangement which demanded liberty for Catholics and denied it to Protestants. In this protest the Zwinglians and Lutherans were joined.

PROTESTANT ALLIANCE: THE MARBURG COLLOQUY

Philip of Hesse believed that the time had come to go further. The rescript of this diet also was only provisional. The Protestants then should protect themselves by a common confession and a common confederation. His hope was to unite the Lutherans, the Swiss, and the Strassburgers, who took an intermediate position on the Lord's Supper. But Luther was of no mind for a political confederation. "We cannot in conscience," said he, "approve such a league inasmuch as bloodshed or other disaster may be the outcome, and we may find ourselves so involved that we cannot withdraw even though we would. Better be ten times dead than that our consciences should be burdened with the insufferable weight of such disaster and that our gospel should be the cause of bloodshed, when we ought rather to be as sheep for the slaughter and not avenge or defend ourselves."

The common confession was another matter, and Luther with some misgivings accepted an invitation to assemble with a group of German and Swiss theologians in Philip's picturesque castle on a hillock overlooking the slender Lahn and the towers of Marburg. A notable company assembled. Luther and Melanchthon represented Saxony, Zwingli came from Zurich, Oekolampadius from Basel, Bucer from Strassburg, to name only the more outstanding. All earnestly desired a union. Zwingli rejoiced to look upon the faces of Luther and Melanchthon, and declared with tears in his eyes that there were none with whom he would be more happy to be in accord. Luther likewise exhorted to unity. The discussion commenced inauspiciously, however, when Luther drew a circle with chalk upon the table and wrote within it the words, "This is my body." Oekolampadius insisted that these words must be taken metaphorically, because the flesh profits nothing and the body of Christ has ascended into heaven. Luther inquired why the ascent should not also be metaphorical. Zwingli went to the heart of the matter when he affirmed that flesh and spirit are incompatible. Therefore the presence of Christ can only be spiritual. Luther replied that flesh and spirit can be conjoined, and the spiritual, which no one denied, does not exclude the physical. They appeared to have arrived at a deadlock, but actually they had made substantial gains, because Zwingli advanced from his view that the Lord's Supper is only a memorial to the position that Christ is spiritually present. And Luther conceded that whatever the nature of the physical presence, it is of no benefit without faith. Hence any magical view is excluded.

This approximation of the two positions offered hope for agreement, and the Lutherans took the initiative in proposing a formula of concord. They confessed that hitherto they had misunderstood the Swiss. For themselves they declared "that Christ is truly present,

319

that is, substantively, essentially, though not quantitatively, qualitatively, or locally." The Swiss rejected this statement as not clearly safeguarding the spiritual character of the Lord's Supper, because they could not understand how something could be present but not locally present. Luther told them that geometrical conceptions cannot be used to describe the presence of God.

The common confession had failed. But then the Swiss proposed that despite the disagreement intercommunion be practiced, and to this "Luther momentarily agreed." This we know on the testimony of Bucer, "until Melanchthon interposed out of regard for Ferdinand and the emperor." This statement is extremely significant. It means that Luther did not play the role of utter implacability commonly ascribed to him, and was disposed to join with the Swiss until Melanchthon made him aware that to coalesce with the left would estrange the right. Melanchthon still entertained a hope for the reform of all Christendom and the preservation of the larger medieval unities through a reconciliation of the Lutherans and the Catholics. The alignment of Speyer did not seem to him definitive, but he sensed that the price would be the repudiation of the sectaries. Luther was far less sanguine as to the Catholics and preferred a consolidated Protestantism, but he yielded to Melanchthon, the one friend who was ever able to deflect him from an intransigent course. Luther's judgment was ultimately to be confirmed; and when Melanchthon had exhausted his efforts at conciliation with the Catholics, the line dropped at Marburg was resumed and issued in the Wittenberg Concord.

A united confession had failed. Intercommunion had failed. But the confederation ought nevertheless to be possible, argued Philip of Hesse. People can unite to defend the right of each to believe what he will even though they are not altogether of the same persuasion. His pleas were very plausible. They were referred for consideration not only to the theologians but also to the lay leaders of Saxony. If Luther is reproached for his willingness to accept so much help from the state, we must recall that the statesmen of that day were Christian believers who were ready to stake everything upon their convictions, and with much more to lose than Luther himself. It was the

Ioannes Oecolampadius S

Huldrychus Zwinglius

Martinus Bucerus

Caspar Hedio

Martinus Luther

Justus Jonas.

Philippus Melanchthon

Andreas Osiander

Stephanus agricola

Joannes Brentius

THE SIGNATURES AT THE MARBURG COLLOQUY

Joannes Oecolampadius, Huldrychus Zwinglius, Martinus Bucerius,
Caspar Hedio, Martinus Luther, Justus Jonas, Philippus Melanchthon,
Andreas Osiander, Stephanus Agricola, Joannes Brentius

chancellor of Saxony who composed the answer to Philip of Hesse. The chancellor was not like Luther averse to any political alliance, nor like Philip indifferent to a confessional basis. The arguments on both sides were reviewed. In favor of the confederation it might be said that among the Zwinglians were doubtless many good Christians who did not agree with Zwingli, and in any case a political alliance could be made even with the heathen. To this the reply was that an alliance with the heathen would be more defensible than an alliance with apostates. The faith is supreme. Therefore the considerable assistance which might be rendered by the Swiss must be renounced and the outcome left entirely in the hands of God.

This left the Swiss to take care of themselves. In the second Kappel War in 1531 Zwingli fell sword in hand on the field of battle. Luther considered his death a judgment upon him because as a minister he wielded the sword.

THE AUGSBURG CONFESSION

The Lutherans were left also to take care of themselves. In 1530 Emperor Charles was at last free to come to Germany. Having humbled France and the pope, he approached Germany with a gracious invitation that each should declare himself on the score of religion, but with the intent not to spare severe measures should the milder fail. Luther was not permitted to attend the diet. For six months he was again "in the wilderness" as he had been at the Wartburg, this time in another castle called the Feste Coburg. He was not quite so lonely because he was attended by his secretary, from whose pen we have a little glimpse of the doctor in a report sent to his wife.

Dear and gracious Mrs. Luther:

Rest assured that your lord and we are hale and hearty by God's grace. You did well to send the doctor the portrait [of his daughter Magdalena], for it diverts him from his worries. He has nailed it on the wall opposite the table where we eat in the elector's apartment. At first he could not quite recognize her. "Dear me," said he, "Lenchen is too dark." But he likes the picture now, and more and more comes to see that it is Lenchen. She is strikingly like Hans in the mouth, eyes, and nose, and in fact in the whole face, and will come to look even more like him. I just had to write you this.

Do not be concerned about the doctor. He is in good trim, praise God. The news of his father's death shook him at first, but he was himself again after two days. When the letter came, he said, "My father is dead." He took his psalter, went to his room, and wept so that he was incapacitated for two days, but he has been all right since. May God be with Hans and Lenchen and the whole household.

As at the Wartburg, Luther devoted himself to biblical studies and likewise to admonitions and advice to those who were conducting the defense of the evangelical cause at Augsburg. His absence and their success were the manifest proof that the movement could survive without him. The great witness was borne this time not by the monk of Wittenberg or even by the ministers and theologians, but by the lay princes who stood to lose their dignities and their lives. When the Holy Roman Emperor, Charles the Fifth, approached the city of Augsburg, the dignitaries went out to receive him. As the notables knelt, bareheaded, for the benediction of Cardinal Campeggio, the Elector of Saxony stood bolt upright. On the following day came one of the most colorful processions in the history of medieval pageantry. In silk and damask, with gold brocade, in robes of crimson and the colors appropriate to each house, came the electors of the empire followed by the most exalted of their number, John of Saxony, carrying in accord with ancient usage the glittering naked sword of the emperor. Behind him marched Albert, the Archbishop of Mainz, the Bishop of Cologne, King Ferdinand of Austria, and his brother the emperor. They marched to the cathedral, where the emperor and all the throng knelt before the high altar. But Elector John of Saxony and the landgrave, Philip of Hesse, remained standing. On the morrow the emperor took the Lutheran princes aside. John and Philip were of course among them, and also the aged George, the margrave of Brandenburg. The emperor told them that their ministers must not preach in Augsburg. The princes refused. The emperor insisted that at any rate the ministers must not preach polemical sermons. The princes again refused. The emperor informed them that the following day would see the *Corpus Christi* procession, in which they would be expected to march. The princes once more refused. The emperor continued to insist, when the margrave stepped forward and said, "Before I let anyone take from me the Word of God and ask me to deny my God, I will kneel and let him strike off my head."

The emperor, despite all these rebuffs, was willing to let the Protestants state their case. The commission fell to Melanchthon. He was still hopeful for the emperor and for the moderates in the Catholic camp, led now by Albert, the Archbishop of Mainz, who had once sent Luther a wedding present. To be sure Eck and Campeggio were raving and disseminating lies and all manner of misrepresentation, but after all they were not the whole Catholic Church.

Melanchthon himself had a deep streak of the Erasmian. He wished neither to deny the faith of Martin Luther nor to be the man to remove the keystone and let fall the arch of Christendom. He sat in his room and wept. At the same time he explored every avenue of conciliation and even went so far as to say that the differences between the Lutherans and the Catholics were no more serious than the use of German in the mass.

Luther was exceedingly concerned and wrote to him that the difference between them was that Melanchthon was stout and Luther yielding in personal disputes, but the reverse was true on public controversies. Luther was thinking of the discussion at Marburg when he had been concessive, Melanchthon obdurate. Now Melanchthon was for recognizing even the pope, whereas Luther felt that there could be no peace with the pope unless he abolished the papacy. The real point was not between personal and public controversies, but in their respective judgments of the left and of the right. Melanchthon in his efforts to conciliate the Catholics was in danger of emasculating the reform.

But he did not. The Augsburg Confession was his work, and in the end it was as stalwart a confession as any made by the princes. Luther was immensely pleased with it and thought its moderate tone better than anything he could have achieved. In the first draft the Augsburg Confession spoke only in the name of electoral Saxony, but in the final draft it confessed the faith of a united Lutheranism. Even Philip of Hesse signed, despite his leanings to the Swiss. But the statement on the Lord's Supper was such that the Swiss declined and submitted a statement of their own. The Strassburgers also refused to sign, and they too brought in another confession. In all there were three Protestant statements of faith submitted at Augsburg. The Anabaptists of course received no hearing at all. Yet despite these divergences in the Evangelical ranks, the Augsburg Confession did much to consolidate Protestantism and to set it over against Catholicism. One might take the date June 25, 1530, the day when the Augsburg Confession was publicly read, as the death day of the Holy Roman Empire. From this day forward the two confessions stood over against each other, poised for conflict. Charles V allowed the Evangelicals until April, 1531, to make their submission. If at that time they declined, they would then feel the edge of the sword.

Against this threat Luther addressed an appeal for moderation to the leader of the conciliatory party in the Roman camp, his old opponent and friend, Albert the Archbishop of Mainz, in the following words:

Inasmuch as there is now no hope of unanimity in the faith, I humbly beseech your Grace that you will endeavor to have the other side keep the peace, believing as they will and permitting us to believe this truth which has been confessed and found blameless. It is well known that no one, be he pope or emperor, should or can force others to believe, for God himself has never yet seen fit to drive anyone by force to believe. How then shall his miserable creatures presume to coerce men not only to faith but to that which they themselves must regard as lies? Would to God that your Grace or anyone else would be a new Gamaliel to commend this counsel of peace.

Luther's counsel was taken not on principle but by reason of necessity, for the emperor was not to find himself again in a position to intervene for another fifteen years.

CHAPTER NINETEEN

THE CHURCH TUTORIAL

ISITATION had established the outward form of the Church, but Luther well knew that the Church of the spirit cannot be engendered by the arm of the magistrate. The true Christian Church is the work of the Word communicated by every available means. Early Luther sensed the need for a new translation of the Scriptures from the original tongues into idiomatic German. There must be likewise a body of instructional material for the young. The liturgy would have to be revised to eliminate popish abuses and to enlighten the people. Congregational singing should be cultivated alike to inspire and instruct. The Bible, the catechism, the liturgy, and the hymnbook thus constituted the needs, and all four were to be met by Luther himself.

THE BIBLE TRANSLATION

For the translation of the Bible, Luther availed himself of the enforced leisure at the Wartburg to produce in three months a rendering of the complete New Testament. The Old Testament came later. The German Bible is Luther's noblest achievement, unfortunately untranslatable because every nation has its own direct version. For the Germans, Luther's rendering was incomparable. He leaped beyond the tradition of a thousand years. There had been translations before him of the Scripture into German, reaching back to the earliest transcription of the Gothic tongue by Ulfilas. There were even portions of the Bible translated not from the Latin Vulgate, but from the Hebrew and the Greek. But none had the majesty of diction, the sweep of vocabulary, the native earthiness, and the religious profundity of Luther. "I endeavored," said he, "to make Moses so German that no one would suspect he was a Jew."

The variety of German chosen as a basis was the court tongue of electoral Saxony, enriched from a number of dialects with which Luther had gained some familiarity in his travels. He went to incredible pains to find words. The initial translation did not satisfy him. His New Testament was first published in September, 1522, but he was revising it to the day of his death in 1546. The last printed page on which he ever looked was the proof of the latest revision. The Old Testament was commenced after his return from the Wartburg. The complete translation of the entire Bible did not appear until 1534. This, again, was subject to constant reworking in collaboration with a committee of colleagues.

Luther on occasion achieved the most felicitous rendering at the first throw. At other times he had to labor. In that case he would first make a literal translation in the word order of the original. Then he would take each word separately and gush forth a freshet of synonyms. From these he would select those which not only best suited the sense but also contributed to balance and rhythm. All of this would then be set aside in favor of a free rendering to catch the spirit. Finally the meticulous and the free would be brought together. Sometimes he was at a loss for terms and would set out in quest of words. In order to name the precious stones in the twenty-first chapter of Revelation he examined the court jewels of the elector of Saxony. For the coins of the Bible he consulted the numismatic collections in Wittenberg. When he came to describe the sacrifices of Leviticus and needed terms for the inward parts of goats and bullocks, he made repeated trips to the slaughterhouse and inquired of the butcher. The birds and beasts of the Old Testament proved a hard knot. To Spalatin he wrote:

I am all right on the birds of the night—owl, raven, horned owl, tawny owl, screech owl—and on the birds of prey—vulture, kite, hawk, and sparrow hawk. I can handle the stag, roebuck, and chamois, but what in the Devil am I to do with the taragelaphus, pygargus, oryx, and camelopard [names for animals in the Vulgate]?

Another problem was the translation of idioms. Here Luther insisted that the idiom of one language must be translated into the equivalent idiom of the other. He was scornful of the Vulgate translation, "Hail, Mary, full of grace." "What German would understand that if translated literally? He knows the meaning of a purse full of gold or a keg full of beer, but what is he to make of a girl full of grace? I would prefer to say simply, '*Liebe Maria*.' What word is more rich than that word, '*liebe*'?"

There is no doubt that it is a rich word, but its connotations are not precisely the same as "endowed with grace," and Luther did not use the word in his official version. Here is the problem of the translator. Should he use always an indigenous word which may have a particular local connotation? If the French call a centurion a gendarme, and the Germans make a procurator into a burgomaster, Palestine has moved

CRANACH'S "JACOB WRESTLING WITH THE ANGEL"

west. And this is what did happen to a degree in Luther's rendering. Judea was transplanted to Saxony, and the road from Jericho to Jerusalem ran through the Thuringian forest. By nuances and turns of expression Luther enhanced the graphic in terms of the local. When he read, "There is a river, the streams whereof shall make glad the city of God," he envisaged a medieval town begirt with walls and towers, surrounded by a moat through which coursed a living stream laving with laughter the massive piers.

What the word could not do at this point, the pictures supplied. The Luther Bibles were copiously illustrated, particularly for the earlier portion of the Old Testament and for the book of Revelation in the New Testament. The restriction of illustrations to these portions of the Bible had become a convention in Germany. The Gospels and the epistles were adorned only with initial letters. Why this should have

LEMBERGER'S "JACOB WRESTLING WITH THE ANGEL"

been the case is difficult to see. Certainly there was no objection to illustrating the Gospels; witness Dürer's "Life of Mary," or the woodcuts of the Passion, or Schongauer's nativities. Within the conventional limits Luther's Bible was richly illustrated. In the various editions to appear during his lifetime there were some five hundred woodcuts. They were not the choicest expressions of the art, but they did Germanize the Bible. Moses and David might almost be mistaken for Frederick the Wise and John Frederick.

An interesting development is to be observed in the illustrations from one artist to another in the successive editions of the Luther Bible, notably from Cranach to Lemberger. One senses something of the transition from the Renaissance to baroque. Compare their renderings of the wrestling of Jacob with the angel. Cranach has a balance of spaces, with decorative background. Lemberger displays strains in tension, with even the trees participating in the struggle.

Unfortunately the illustrations for the book of Revelation were made all too contemporary. The temptation was too strong to identify the pope with Antichrist. In the first edition of the New Testament in September, 1522, the scarlet woman sitting on the seven hills wears the papal tiara. So also does the great dragon. The beast out of the abyss has a monk's cowl. Fallen Babylon is plainly Rome. There is no mistaking the Belvedere, the Pantheon, and the Castelo de St. Angelo. Duke George was so enraged by these pictures that he sent a warm protest to Frederick the Wise. In consequence, in the issue of December, 1522, the tiaras in the woodcuts were chiseled down to innocuous crowns of a single layer, but other details were left unchanged and attracted so little notice that Emser, Luther's Catholic opponent, actually borrowed the blocks from Cranach to illustrate his own Bible. In the New Testament of 1530 Luther introduced an annotation explaining that the frogs issuing from the mouth of the dragon were his opponents, Faber, Eck, and Emser. In the completed edition of the whole Bible in 1534, after Frederick the Wise was dead, the woodcuts were done over and the papal tiaras restored.

DOCTRINAL PROBLEMS IN TRANSLATION

The most difficult task in translating consisted not in making vivid the scenes but in capturing the moods and ideas. "Translating is not an art that everyone can practice. It requires a right pious, faithful, diligent, God-fearing, experienced, practical heart." Luther did not think to add that it requires an instructed head, but he had his ideas about the Bible which in some measure affected alike what he did and what he left undone. He did not attempt any minor harmonization of discrepancies, because trivial errors gave him no concern. If on occasion he could speak of every iota of Holy Writ as sacred, at other times he displayed blithe indifference to minor blemishes, such as an error in quotation from the Old Testament in the New Testament. The Bible for him was not strictly identical with the Word of God. God's Word is the work of redemption in Christ which became concrete in Scripture as God in Christ became incarnate in the flesh; and as Christ by the incarnation was not denuded of human characteristics, so the Scripture as the medium of the Word was not divested of human limitations. Hence Luther was not subject to the slightest temptation to accommodate a gospel citation from the prophets to the text of the Old Testament. No more was he concerned to harmonize the predictions of Peter's denial with the accounts of the denial itself.

But when doctrinal matters were involved, the case was different. Luther read the New Testament in the light of the Pauline message that the just shall live by faith and not by works of the law. That this doctrine is not enunciated with equal emphasis throughout the New Testament and appears to be denied in the book of James did not escape Luther, and in his preface to the New Testament of 1522 James was stigmatized as "an epistle of straw." Once Luther remarked that he would give his doctor's beret to anyone who could reconcile James and Paul. Yet he did not venture to reject James from the canon of Scripture, and on occasion earned his own beret by effecting a reconciliation. "Faith," he wrote, "is a living, restless thing. It cannot be inoperative. We are not saved by works; but if there be no works, there must be something amiss with faith." This was simply to put a

RIGHT: *In the New Testament of September, 1522, she is shown wearing the papal tiara.*

Pauline construction upon James. The conclusion was a hierarchy of values within the New Testament. First Luther would place the Gospel of John, then the Pauline epistles and First Peter, after them the three other Gospels, and in a subordinate place Hebrews, James, Jude, and Revelation. He mistrusted Revelation because of its obscurity. "A revelation," said he, "should be revealing."

These presuppositions affected the translation but slightly. Yet occasionally an overly Pauline turn is discernible. There is the famous example where Luther rendered "justification by faith" as "justification by faith alone." When taken to task for this liberty, he replied that he was not translating words but ideas, and that the extra word was necessary in German in order to bring out the force of the original.

LEFT: *The papal tiara elicited such a vigorous remonstrance from Duke George to Frederick the Wise that he interposed, and in the issue of December, 1522, the tiara was reduced to an innocuous single layer.*

BELOW: *In the Bible of 1534 after Frederick's death the cut was done over and the tiara restored.*

Throughout all the revisions of his lifetime he would never relinquish that word "alone." In another instance he was more flexible. In 1522 he had translated the Greek words meaning "by the works of the law" with German words meaning "by the merit of works." In 1527 he substituted a literal rendering. That must have hurt. He was an honest workman, and successive revisions of the New Testament were marked by a closer approximation to the original. And yet there were places where Luther's peculiar views, without any inaccuracy, lent a nuance to the rendering. In the benediction, "The peace of God, which passeth all understanding," Luther translated, "The peace which transcends all reason." One cannot exactly quarrel with that. He might better have said, "which surpasses all comprehension," but he was so convinced of the inadequacy of human reason to scale the heavenly heights that he could not but see here a confirmation of his supreme aversion.

If the New Testament was for Luther a Pauline book, the Old Testament was a Christian book. Only the ceremonial law of the Jews was abrogated. The moral law was still valid because it was in accord with the law of nature. But more significant than the ethic was the theology. The Old Testament foreshadowed the drama of redemption. Adam exemplified the depravity of man. Noah tasted the wrath of God, Abraham was saved by faith, and David exhibited contrition. The pre-existent Christ was working throughout the Old Testament, speaking through the mouths of the prophets and the psalmist. A striking witness to the Christological interpretation of the Old Testament current in Luther's day is to be found in the illustrations of his Bible. Among the hundreds of woodcuts the only portrayal of the nativity of Jesus is located not in the Gospels, where one would expect to find it, but on the title page to Ezekiel. Reading the Old Testament in this fashion Luther could not well escape Christianizing shades of meaning. The "lovingkindness of the Lord" became "grace"; the "Deliverer of Israel" became "the Saviour"; and "life" was rendered "eternal life." That was why Bach could treat the Sixteenth Psalm as an Easter hymn.

Luther's liberties were greatest with the Psalms because here he was so completely at home. They were the record of the spiritual struggles through which he was constantly passing. The favorite words of his *Anfechtungen* could not be excluded. Where the English version of Ps. 90 speaks of "secret sins" Luther has "unrecognized sins." He was thinking of his fruitless efforts in the cloister to recall every wrongdoing, that it might be confessed and pardoned. Where the English translates, "So teach us to number our days, that we may apply our hearts unto wisdom," Luther is blunt: "Teach us so to reflect on death that we may be wise."

Luther so lived his way into the Psalms that he improved them. In the original the transitions are sometimes abrupt and the meaning not always plain. Luther simplified and clarified. When he came to a passage which voiced his wrestlings in the night watches, he was free to paraphrase. Take his conclusion to the Seventy-third Psalm.

My heart is stricken and my bones fail, that I must be a fool and know nothing, that I must be as a beast before thee. Nevertheless I will ever cleave to thee. Thou holdest me by thy right hand and leadest me by thy counsel. Thou wilt crown me at last with honor. If only I have that, I will not ask for earth or heaven. When body and soul fail me, thou art ever God, my heart's comfort and my portion.

The Bible, just as it stood in Luther's rendering, was a great educational tool; but more was needed, obviously for children but also for adults, who were almost equally ignorant. The children should be taught at church, at school, and at home; and to that end pastors, teachers, and parents should receive prior training. Hence Luther's plea that Catholic schools be replaced by municipal schools with a system of compulsory education including religion. "The Scripture cannot be understood without the languages," argued Luther, "and the languages can be learned only in school. If parents cannot spare their children for a full day, let them send them for a part. I would wager that in half of Germany there are not over four thousand pupils in school. I would like to know where we are going to get pastors and teachers three years from now."

The mere training of pastors, teachers, and parents would, however, not suffice. They must in turn be provided with a body of religious literature adapted to children. The Middle Ages supplied little by way of models because the catechisms had been for adults. The Humanists had made a beginning, as in the *Colloquies of Erasmus*, and the Bohemian Brethren had a question book for children; but the material was so scant that one can without exaggeration ascribe to the Reformation the creation of the first body of religious literature for the young. Luther was so exceedingly busy that he attempted to delegate this assignment to others, and they undertook it with zest. In the seven years between his return to Wittenberg and the appearance of his own catechisms his collaborators had produced materials comprising five goodly volumes in a modern reprint.

For the most part they were crude and boiled down to about this: "You are a bad child. You deserve to be punished forever in hell; but since God has punished his Son Jesus Christ in your place, you can be forgiven if you will honor, love, and obey God." That *if* bothered Luther, because it restored the merit of man as in the penitential system. Even Melanchthon moralized too much, for his manual was a compilation of the ethical portions of the New Testament with the maxims of the pagan sages. Some catechisms pitted the inner against the outer word of Scripture, and some even spiritualized the sacraments. In other words the radicals were appropriating the catechetical method. High time that Luther undertook the task himself!

He produced two catechisms in the year 1529: the Large Catechism for adults, with a long section on marriage, scarcely suitable for the young; and the Small Catechism for children. Both were built about five points: the Ten Commandments as a mirror of sin, the Apostles' Creed as a proclamation of forgiveness, the Lord's Prayer as an acceptance of mercy, and the two sacraments of baptism and the Lord's Supper as channels of grace.

In the Large Catechism the exposition was comparatively full and the tone at times polemical. The command to worship only the Lord gave an opportunity to upbraid the Catholic cult of the saints, whereas the sections on the sacraments called for a refutation of the radicals. The Small Catechism for children is devoid of all polemic, an inimitable affirmation of faith. The section on the death of Christ stresses not the substitution of penalty but the triumph over all the forces of darkness.

I believe in Jesus Christ . . . , who when I was lost and damned saved me from all sin and death and the power of the Devil, not with gold and silver but with his own precious, holy blood and his sinless suffering and death, that I might belong to him and live in his kingdom and serve him forever in goodness, sinlessness, and happiness, just as he is risen from the dead and lives and reigns forever. That is really so.

Luther said that he would be glad to have all his works perish except the reply to Erasmus and the catechism.

Do not think the catechism is a little thing to be read hastily and cast aside. Although I am a doctor, I have to do just as a child and say word for word every morning and whenever I have time the Lord's Prayer and the Ten Commandments, the Creed and the Psalms. I have to do it every day, and yet I cannot stand as I would. But these smart folk in one reading want to be doctors of doctors. Therefore I beg these wise saints to be persuaded that they are not such great doctors as they think. To be occupied with God's Word helps against the world, the flesh, and the Devil, and all bad thoughts. This is the true holy water with which to exorcise the Devil.

Luther's intention was that the catechism should be used in church as a basis for sermons, but more particularly in the home. The father should check up on the children at least once a week and also on the servants. If the children would not learn, they should not eat; if the servants declined, they should be dismissed.

The catechisms were enlivened with quaint woodcuts of episodes from the Bible suitable to each point. "I believe in God the Father Almighty" naturally called for a view of the creation. "Hallowed be thy name" was illustrated by a preaching scene. "Remember the Sabbath day" showed a devout group inside a church while outside a man

Our Father

Hallowed Be Thy Name

Remember the Sabbath Day

Thou Shalt Not Covet Thy
Neighbor's Wife

was gathering wood. Luther was, however, no rigid sabbatarian, and incidentally he did not select these pictures. Excessively modest is the cut accompanying the sixth commandment, where David with his harp is seduced by the sight of Bathsheba having her feet washed. At the close of the catechetical hour Luther suggested the singing of a psalm or a hymn.

LITURGY

Another of Luther's great contributions lay in the field of public worship, which he revised first in the interests of purity and then as a medium of instruction. While still at the Wartburg he had come to realize that some changes in the liturgy were imperative, and had applauded Carlstadt's initial endeavors. Yet Luther himself was very conservative in such matters and desired to alter the beloved mass as little as possible. The main point was that all pretension to human merit should be excluded. Luther undertook in 1523 to make the minimal revisions essential to evangelical doctrine. His *Formula Missae* was in Latin. The canon of the mass disappeared because this was the portion in which the reference to sacrifice occurred. Luther restored the emphasis of the early Church upon the Lord's Supper as an act of thanksgiving to God and of fellowship through Christ with God and with each other. This first Lutheran mass was solely an act of worship in which true Christians engaged in praise and prayer, and were strengthened in the inner man.

But speedily Luther came to the recognition that an act of worship was not possible for many in the congregation without explanation. The Church embraced the community, and the congregation consisted of the townsfolk of Wittenberg and of the peasants from the villages round about. How much would these peasants understand of his revision of the Latin mass? They would of course recognize the change involved in giving to them the wine as well as the bread, and they would sense that something had altered when the inaudible portions were discontinued. But since it was still all in a foreign tongue they would hardly perceive that the idea of sacrifice was gone. The mass therefore would have to be in German. Others had felt this earlier than Luther, and Müntzer had prepared a German mass which Luther liked so long as he did not know it was Müntzer's. Gradually Luther came to the conclusion that he must undertake the revision himself. In 1526 he came out with the German mass.

Everything was in German save for the Greek refrain, "Kyrie eleison." The changes left intact the essential structure; and a Swiss visitor in 1536, accustomed to simpler services, felt that the Lutherans had retained many elements of popery: genuflections, vestments, veerings to the altar or the audience, lectern and pulpit on opposite sides. Even the elevation of the elements was retained until 1542. To Luther all such points were indifferent. He would not substitute a new formalism for an old and allowed very wide latitude and variation in liturgical matters. The main point was that in the German as in the Latin the canon of the mass was gone. In its place there was a simple exhortation to receive communion. But the whole tone of the service was altered in two respects: there was more of the scriptural and more of the instructional. With the canon removed the Gospel and Epistle assumed a more prominent position; the words of institution were given in German; the sermon occupied a larger place, and not infrequently the notices were as long as the sermon. The church thus became not only the house of prayer and praise but also a classroom.

MUSIC

The most far-reaching changes in the liturgy were with regard to the music, and those at three points: the chants intoned by the priest, the chorals rendered by the choir, and the hymns sung by the congregation. Luther set himself to revise all three. He was competent, if not to execute, at least to direct and inspire, since he could play the lute and sing even though he did not regard himself as skilled in composition. Modern specialists are not agreed as to how many of the musical settings to his hymns may be his own. Ten are commonly ascribed to him. Certainly he knew how to compose simple melodies, to harmonize and arrange. Above all else he was able to inspire, because his enthusiasm for music was so great. He said:

Music is a fair and lovely gift of God which has often wakened and moved me to the joy of preaching. St. Augustine was troubled in conscience whenever he caught himself delighting in music, which he took to be sinful. He was a choice spirit, and were he living today would agree with us. I have no use for cranks who despise music, because it is a gift of God. Music drives away the Devil and makes people gay; they forget thereby all wrath, unchastity, arrogance, and the like. Next after theology I give to music the highest place and the greatest honor. I would not exchange what little I know of music for something great. Experience proves that next to the Word of God only music deserves to be extolled as the mistress and governess of the feelings of the human heart. We know that to the devils music is distasteful and insufferable. My heart bubbles up and overflows in response to music, which has so often refreshed me and delivered me from dire plagues.

Perhaps the fact that Dürer was old and Luther young when each embraced the reform may explain in a measure why in German Lutheranism pictorial art declined in favor of the musical expression of the faith.

The first melodic portion of the liturgy to be reformed was the part intoned by the priest, including the Epistle and Gospel. Since Luther was so desirous that every word of Scripture should be distinctly heard and understood, one wonders why he did not discontinue the music entirely in favor of reading in a natural voice. The answer lies in the architectural structure, which was more conducive to the word sung than to the word spoken. But Luther did employ every device to bring out the meaning. Only one note should be used for one syllable, and the organ accompaniment should not obscure the words. Throughout the service the organ was used only antiphonally. The Gospel texts should not be conflated, and the seven words of Christ from the cross were not to be blended from all four Gospels. The Lutheran tradition explains why Bach should write a *St. Matthew's Passion*. The meaning should be further emphasized by dramatic coloring. The Gregorian chants for the Epistle and the Gospel were monotone save for the lowering of the voice at the end. Luther introduced different registers for the narrative of the evangelist, the words of Christ, and the words of the apostles. The mean register he set high because his own voice was tenor, but he explained that he was offering only suggestions and each celebrant should discover and adapt the musical setting to suit his own liturgical range. Again the modes should be varied: the sixth should be used for the Gospel because Christ was joyful, and the eighth for the Epistle because Paul was more somber. This terminology calls for a word of explanation. Today we have a number of keys and only two modes, the major and minor. The intervals in all keys are those of C, conserved by the use of accidentals in transposing. In the sixteenth century eight modes were in vogue with different intervals formed by starting on each note of the octave and ascending without accidentals. The attention which Luther in all these respects devoted to musical settings for the prose text of the Scripture in the vernacular prepared the way for the oratorios.

The degree to which he was assisted in his task appears in an account by his collaborator Walther, who wrote:

When Luther forty years ago wanted to prepare his German mass, he requested of the Elector of Saxony and Duke John that Conrad Rupff and I be summoned to Wittenberg, where he might discuss music and the nature of the eight Gregorian psalm modes. He prepared the music for the Epistles and Gospels, likewise for the words of institution of the true body and blood of Christ; he chanted these for me and asked me to express my opinion of his efforts. At that time he kept me in Wittenberg for three weeks; we discussed how the Epistles and Gospels might properly be set. I spent many a pleasant hour singing with him and often found that he seemingly could not weary of singing or even get enough of it; in addition he was always able to discuss music eloquently.

The second element to be revised was the choral for the choir. Here a rich background was available in the polyphonic religious music of the Netherlands which Luther admired above all other. The melody of the Gregorian chant was taken as a base, and about it three, four, or more voices rotated in counterpoint with elaborate embellishments. Luther himself in the preface to the musical work of 1538 gathered into a single passage all of his praises of music together with the most apt description ever penned of the Netherlandish polyphonic choral:

To all lovers of the liberal art of music Dr. Martin Luther wishes grace and peace from God the Father and our Lord Jesus Christ. With all my heart I would extol the precious gift of God in the noble art of music, but I scarcely know where to begin or end. There is nothing on earth which has not its tone. Even the air invisible sings when smitten with a staff. Among the beasts and the birds song is still more marvelous. David, himself a musician, testified with amazement and joy to the song of the birds. What then shall I say of the voice of man, to which naught else may be compared? The heathen philosophers have striven in vain to explain how the tongue of man can express the thoughts of the heart in speech and song, through laughter and lamentation. Music is to be praised as second only to the Word of God

because by her are all the emotions swayed. Nothing on earth is more mighty to make the sad gay and the gay sad, to hearten the downcast, mellow the overweening, temper the exuberant, or mollify the vengeful. The Holy Spirit himself pays tribute to music when he records that the evil spirit of Saul was exorcised as David played upon his harp. The fathers desired that music should always abide in the Church. That is why there are so many songs and psalms. This precious gift has been bestowed on men alone to remind them that they are created to praise and magnify the Lord. But when natural music is sharpened and polished by art, then one begins to see with amazement the great and perfect wisdom of God in his wonderful work of music, where one voice takes a simple part and around it sing three, four, or five other voices, leaping, springing round about, marvelously gracing the simple part, like a square dance in heaven with friendly bows, embracings, and hearty swinging of the partners. He who does not find this an inexpressible miracle of the Lord is truly a clod and is not worthy to be considered a man.

Not the least merit of music, according to Luther, is that it is not contentious. He was never controversial in song. The great polyphonic chorals of the Netherlands were Catholic, but Luther did not for that reason cease to love and draw from them. Again, when the dukes of Bavaria became so much his violent enemies that to receive a letter from him might endanger one in their territories, he ventured nevertheless to write to the Bavarian composer Senfl: "My love for music leads me also to hope that my letter will not endanger you in any way, for who even in Turkey would reproach one who loves the art and lauds the artist? At any rate I laud your Bavarian dukes even though they dislike me, and I honor them above all others because they cultivate and honor music." Erasmus sought to preserve the European unities in politics; Luther conserved them in music.

The polyphonic choral called for a choir. Luther was very assiduous in his efforts on behalf of trained choirs. George Rhaw, the cantor of Duke George and conductor of the twelve-part singing at the Leipzig debate, was brought to Wittenberg to serve alike as the cantor of the court choir and to the church. The choirs supported by the German princes are worthy of note because they provided ready to hand bodies of trained singers. Luther was greatly distressed when John Frederick economized by discontinuing the choir long maintained through the bounty of Frederick the Wise. By way of compensation choral societies were formed in the cities, and above all the children were trained thoroughly in the schools.

The last and greatest reform of all was in congregational song. In the Middle Ages the liturgy was almost entirely restricted to the celebrant and the choir. The congregation joined in a few responses in the vernacular. Luther so developed this element that he may be considered the father of congregational song. This was the point at which his doctrine of the priesthood of all believers received its most concrete realization. This was the point and the only point at which Lutheranism was thoroughly democratic. All the people sang. Portions of the liturgy were converted into hymns: the Creed and the *Sanctus*. The congregation sang not, "I believe," but, "We believe in one God." The congregation sang how the prophet Isaiah saw the Lord high and lifted up and heard the seraphim intone, Holy, Holy, Holy.

HYMNBOOK

In addition in 1524 Luther brought out a hymnbook with twenty-three hymns of which he was the author and perhaps in part the composer. Twelve were free paraphrases from Latin hymnody. Six were

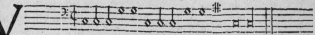

QVINTA VOX. BASSVS.
PRIMA PARS.

Viue Luthere, Viue Melanthon,
Viuite noſtræ Lumina terræ,
Characȝ Chriſto Pectora, per vos
Inclyta nobis Dogmata Chriſti   **Amen.**
Reddita, veſtro Munere, pulſis
Nubibus atris, Prodȵt ortu
Candidiore   Dogma ſalutis,
Viuite longos Neſtoris annos.

versifications of the Psalms. His own experiences of anguish and deliverance enabled him in such free renderings to invest the Psalms with a very personal feeling. "Out of the depths" became "In direst need." That great battle hymn of the Reformation, "A Mighty Fortress," appeared only in a later hymnbook. Here if anywhere we have both Luther's words and music, and here more than elsewhere we have the epitome of Luther's religious character. The hymn is based on the Vulgate version of the Forty-sixth Psalm, for Luther in his personal devotions continued to use the Latin on which he had been reared. Whereas in this psalm the Hebrew reads "God is our refuge," The Latin has "Our God is a refuge." Similarly Luther begins, "A mighty fortress is *our* God." Though the Forty-sixth Psalm is basic, it is handled with exceeding freedom and interwoven with many reminiscences of the Pauline epistles and the Apocalypse. Richly quarried, rugged words set to majestic tones marshal the embattled hosts of heaven. The hymn to the end strains under the overtones of cosmic conflict as the Lord God of Sabaoth smites the prince of darkness grim and vindicates the martyred saints.

Luther's people learned to sing. Practices were set during the week for the entire congregation, and in the home after the catechetical hour singing was commended to the family. A Jesuit testified that "the hymns of Luther killed more souls than his sermons." How the songs were carried to the people is disclosed in this excerpt from a chronicle of the city of Magdeburg:

On the day of St. John between Easter and Pentecost, an old man, a weaver, came through the city gate to the monument of Kaiser Otto and there offered hymns for sale while he sang them to the people. The burgomaster, coming from early mass and seeing the crowd, asked one of his servants what was going on. "There is an old scamp over there," he answered, "who is singing and selling the hymns of the heretic Luther." The burgomaster had him arrested and thrown into prison; but two hundred citizens interceded and he was released.

Among the hymns which he was singing through the streets of Magdeburg was Luther's *Aus tiefer Not*:

> I cry to thee in direst need.
>   O God, I beg thee hear me.
> To my distress I pray give heed.
>   O Father, draw thou near me.
> If thou shouldst wish to look upon
> The wrong and wickedness I've done,
>   How could I stand before thee?
>
> With thee is naught but untold grace
>   Evermore forgiving.
> We cannot stand before thy face,

Not by the best of living.
No man boasting may draw near.
All the living stand in fear.
    Thy grace alone can save them.

Therefore in God I place my trust,
    My own claim denying.
Believe in him alone I must,
    On his sole grace relying.
He pledged to me his plighted word.
My comfort is in what I heard.
    There will I hold forever.

CHAPTER TWENTY

THE CHURCH MINISTERIAL

 ISTINGUISHED alike in the translation of the Bible, the composition of the catechism, the reform of the liturgy, and the creation of the hymnbook, Luther was equally great in the sermons preached from the pulpit, the lectures delivered in the class hall, and the prayers voiced in the upper room. His versatility is genuinely amazing. No one in his own generation was able to vie with him.

PREACHING

The Reformation gave centrality to the sermon. The pulpit was higher than the altar, for Luther held that salvation is through the Word and without the Word the elements are devoid of sacramental quality, but the Word is sterile unless it is spoken. All of this is not to say that the Reformation invented preaching. In the century preceding Luther, for the single province of Westphalia ten thousand sermons are in print, and though they are extant only in Latin they were delivered in German. But the Reformation did exalt the sermon. All the educational devices described in the preceding chapter found their highest utilization in the pulpit. The reformers at Wittenberg undertook an extensive campaign of religious instruction through the sermon. There were three public services on Sunday: from five to six in the morning on the Pauline epistles, from nine to ten on the Gospels, and in the afternoon at a variable hour on a continuation of the theme of the morning or on the catechism. The church was not locked during

348

the week, but on Mondays and Tuesdays there were sermons on the catechism, Wednesdays on the Gospel of Matthew, Thursdays and Fridays on the apostolic letters, and Saturday evening on John's Gospel. No one man carried this entire load. There was a staff of the clergy, but Luther's share was prodigious. Including family devotions he spoke often four times on Sundays and quarterly undertook a two-week series four days a week on the catechism. The sum of his extant sermons is 2,300. The highest count is for the year 1528, for which there are 195 sermons distributed over 145 days.

His pre-eminence in the pulpit derives in part from the earnestness with which he regarded the preaching office. The task of the minister is to expound the Word, in which alone are to be found healing for life's hurts and the balm of eternal blessedness. The preacher must die daily through concern lest he lead his flock astray. Sometimes from the pulpit Luther confessed that gladly like the priest and the Levite would he pass by on the other side. But Luther was constantly repeating to himself the advice which he gave to a discouraged preacher who complained that preaching was a burden, his sermons were always short, and he might better have stayed in his former profession. Luther said to him:

Contrast of the Evangelical service, where devout hearers listen with reverent attention and signs of contrition. The girl on the left is reading the Scriptures. And the Catholic service, where the people lightheartedly tell their beads. The man behind the pillar is pointing in both directions.

If Peter and Paul were here, they would scold you because you wish right off to be as accomplished as they. Crawling is something, even if one is unable to walk. Do your best. If you cannot preach an hour, then preach half an hour or a quarter of an hour. Do not try to imitate other people. Center on the shortest and simplest points, which are the very heart of the matter, and leave the rest to God. Look solely to his honor and not to applause. Pray that God will give you a mouth and to your audience ears. I can tell you preaching is not a work of man. Although I am old [he was forty-eight] and experienced, I am afraid every time I have to preach. You will most certainly find out three things: first, you will have prepared your sermon as diligently as you know how, and it will slip through your fingers like water; secondly, you may abandon your outline and God will give you grace. You will preach your very best. The audience will be pleased, but you won't. And thirdly, when you have been unable in advance to pull anything together, you will preach acceptably both to your hearers and to yourself. So pray to God and leave all the rest to him.

Luther's sermons followed the course prescribed by the Christian year and the lessons assigned by long usage to each Sunday. In this area he did not innovate. Because he commonly spoke at the nine o'clock service, his sermons are mostly on the Gospels rather than upon his favorite Pauline epistles. But the text never mattered much to him. If he did not have before him the Pauline words, "The just shall live by faith," he could readily extract the same point from the example of the paralytic in the Gospels, whose sins were forgiven before his disease was cured. Year after year Luther preached on the same passages and on the same great events: Advent, Christmas, Epiphany, Lent, Easter, Pentecost. If one now reads through his sermons of thirty years on a single theme, one is amazed at the freshness with which each year he illumined some new aspect. When one has the feeling that there is nothing startling this time, then comes a flash. He is narrating the betrayal of Jesus. Judas returns the thirty pieces of silver with the words, "I have betrayed innocent blood," and the priest answers, "What is that to us?" Luther comments that there is no loneliness like the loneliness of a traitor since even his confederates give him no sympathy. The sermons cover every theme from the sublimity of God to the greed of a sow. The conclusions were often abrupt because the sermon was followed by the announcements, themselves frequently as long as the sermon because all the events of the coming week were explained with appropriate or inappropriate exhortations and castigations. A few samples from the sermons and announcements will have to suffice.

The first example shows how he would pass directly from the sermon to the announcements. The financial difficulties to which he refers had not been solved by the intervention of the prince, and each member of the congregation was therefore urged to give four pennies. Luther points out that personally he is not affected because he receives his stipend as a university professor from the prince. The following excerpts are of course exceedingly condensed.

The sermon on the 8th of November, 1528, was on the lord who forgave his servant: This lord, said Luther, is a type of the Kingdom of God. The servant was not forgiven because he had forgiven his fellow servant. On the contrary he received forgiveness before he had done anything whatever about his fellow servant. From this we see that there are two kinds of forgiveness. The first is that which we receive from God; the second is that which we exercise by bearing no ill will to any upon earth. But we must not overlook the two administrations, the civil and the spiritual, because the prince cannot and should not forgive. He has a different administration than Christ, who rules over crushed and broken hearts. The Kaiser rules over scoundrels who do not recognize their sins and mock and carry their heads high. That is why the emperor carries a sword, a sign of blood and not of peace. But Christ's kingdom is for the troubled conscience. He says, "I do not ask of you a penny, only this, that you do the same for your neighbor." And the lord in the parable does not tell the servant to found a monastery, but simply that he should have mercy on his fellow servants.

But now what shall I say to you Wittenbergers? It would be better that I preach to you the *Sachsenspiegel* [the imperial law], because you want to be Christians while still practicing usury, robbing and stealing. How do people who are so sunk in sins expect to receive forgiveness? The sword of the emperor really applies here, but my sermon is for crushed hearts who feel their sins and have no peace. Enough for this gospel.

I understand that this is the week for the church collection, and many of you do not want to give a thing. You ungrateful people should be ashamed of yourselves. You Wittenbergers have been relieved of schools and hospitals, which have been taken over by the common chest, and now you want to know why you are asked to give four pennies. They are for the ministers, schoolteachers, and sacristans. The first labor for your salvation, preach to you the precious treasure of the gospel, administer the sacraments, and visit you at great personal risk in the plague. The second train children to be good magistrates, judges, and ministers. The third care for the poor. So far the common chest has cared for these, and now that you are asked to give four miserable pennies you are up in arms. What does this mean if not that you do not want the gospel preached, the children taught, and the poor helped? I am not saying this for myself. I receive nothing from you. I am the prince's beggar. But I am sorry I ever freed you from the tyrants and the papists. You ungrateful beasts, you are not worthy of the treasure of the gospel. If you don't improve, I will stop preaching rather than cast pearls before swine.

And now another point: couples to be blessed by the curate before a wedding should come early. There are stated hours: in summer, mornings at eight and afternoons at three; in winter, mornings at nine and afternoons at two. If you come later, I will bless you myself, and you won't thank me for it. And the invited guests should prepare themselves in good time for the wedding and let not Miss Goose wait for Mrs. Duck.

On January 10th, 1529, the lesson was the wedding at Cana of Galilee. This passage, said Luther, is written in honor of marriage. There are three estates: marriage, virginity, and widowhood. They are all good. None is to be despised. The virgin is not to be esteemed above the widow, nor the widow above the wife, any more than the tailor is to be esteemed above the butcher. There is no estate to which the Devil is so opposed as to marriage. The clergy have not wanted to be bothered with work and worry. They have been afraid of a nagging wife, disobedient children, difficult relatives, or the dying of a pig or a cow. They want to lie abed until the sun shines through the window. Our ancestors knew this and would say, "Dear child, be a priest or a nun and have a good time." I have heard married people say to monks, "You have it easy, but when we get up we do not know where to find our bread." Marriage is a heavy cross because so many couples quarrel. It is the grace of God when they agree. The Holy Spirit declares there are three wonders: when brothers agree, when neighbors love each other, and when a man and a wife are at one. When I see a pair like that, I am as glad as if I were in a garden of roses. It is rare.

SERMON ON THE NATIVITY

Luther is at his best and most characteristic in his sermons on the Nativity. The entire recital appears utterly artless, but by way of preparation he had steeped himself in the interpretations of the story by Augustine, Bernard, Tauler, and Ludwig of Saxony, the author of a life of Christ. All that thus had preceded was infused by Luther with the profundities of his theology and vitalized by his graphic imagination. Here is an example:

How unobtrusively and simply do those events take place on earth that are so heralded in heaven! On earth it happened in this wise: There was a poor young wife, Mary of Nazareth, among the meanest dwellers of the town, so little esteemed that none noticed the great wonder that she carried. She was silent, did not vaunt herself, but served her husband, who had no man or maid. They simply left the house. Perhaps they had a donkey for Mary to ride upon, though the Gospels say nothing about it, and we may well believe that she went on foot. The journey was certainly more than a day from Nazareth in Galilee to Bethlehem, which lies on the farther side of Jerusalem. Joseph had thought, "When we get to Bethlehem, we shall be among relatives and can borrow everything."

"The Nativity" from Luther's Bible of 1534

On the left is Luther's seal. He desired that the cross be black for mortification, the rose white for the joy of faith, the field blue for the joy of heaven, and the ring gold for eternal blessedness.

A fine idea that was! Bad enough that a young bride married only a year could not have had her baby at Nazareth in her own house instead of making all that journey of three days when heavy with child! How much worse that when she arrived there was no room for her! The inn was full. No one would release a room to this pregnant woman. She had to go to a cow stall and there bring forth the Maker of all creatures because nobody would give way. Shame on you, wretched Bethlehem! The inn ought to have been burned with brimstone, for even though Mary had been a beggar maid or unwed, anybody at such a time should have been glad to give her a hand. There are many of you in this congregation who think to yourselves: "If only I had been there! How quick I would have been to help the Baby! I would have washed his linen. How happy I would have been to go with the shepherds to see the Lord lying in the manger!" Yes, you would! You say that because you know how great Christ is, but if you had been there at that time you would have done no better than the people of Bethlehem. Childish and silly thoughts are these! Why don't you do it now? You have Christ in your neighbor. You ought to serve him, for what you do to your neighbor in need you do to the Lord Christ himself. The birth was still more pitiable. No one regarded this young wife bringing forth her first-born. No one took her condition to heart. No one noticed that in a strange place she had not the very least thing needful in childbirth. There she was without preparation: no light, no fire, in the dead of night, in thick darkness. No one came to give the customary assistance. The guests swarming in the inn were carousing, and no one attended to this woman. I think myself if Joseph and Mary had realized that her time was so close she might perhaps have been left in Nazareth. And now think what she could use for swaddling clothes—some garment she could spare, perhaps her veil—certainly not Joseph's breeches, which are now on exhibition at Aachen.

Think, women, there was no one there to bathe the Baby. No warm water, nor even cold. No fire, no light. The mother was herself midwife and the maid. The cold manger was the bed and the bathtub. Who showed the poor girl what to do? She had never had a baby before. I am amazed that the little one did not freeze. Do not make of Mary a stone. For the higher people are in the favor of God, the more tender are they.

Let us, then, meditate upon the Nativity just as we see it happening in our own babies. Behold Christ lying in the lap of his young mother. What can be sweeter than the Babe, what more lovely than the mother! What fairer than her youth! What more gracious than her virginity! Look at the Child, knowing nothing. Yet all that is belongs to him, that your conscience should not fear but take comfort in him. Doubt nothing. To me there is no greater consolation given to mankind than this, that Christ became man, a child, a babe, playing in the lap and at the breasts of his most gracious mother. Who is there whom this sight would not comfort? Now is overcome the power of sin, death, hell, conscience, and guilt, if you come to this gurgling Babe and believe that he is come, not to judge you, but to save.

EXPOSITION OF JONAH

As Luther's sermons were often didactic, so were his lectures commonly sermonic. He was always teaching, whether in the classroom or the pulpit; and he was always preaching, whether in the pulpit or the classroom. His lectures on Jonah are even more of a sermon than many preached in the Castle Church. Luther handled Jonah as he did every other biblical character—as a mirror of his own experience. Here is a digest of the exposition.

Jonah was sent to rebuke the mighty king of Assyria. That took courage. If we had been there, we should have thought it silly that one single man should attack such an empire. How silly it would seem for one of us to go on such a mission to the Turks. And how ridiculous often it has appeared that a single man should rebuke the pope. But God's work always appears as folly.

"And Jonah took ship for Tarshish." The godless think they can get away from God by going to a town where he is not recognized. Why did Jonah refuse? First because the assignment was very great. No prophet had ever been chosen to go to the heathen. Another reason was that he felt the enmity of Nineveh. He thought God was only the God of the Jews, and he would rather be dead than proclaim the grace of God to the heathen.

Then God sent a great wind. Why should he have involved the other passengers in Jonah's punishment? We are not the ones to lay down rules for God, and for that matter the other persons on the boat were not innocent. We have all transgressed. The storm must have been very sudden because the people felt that it must have an unusual cause. Natural reason taught the sailors that God is God. The light of reason is a great light, but it fails in that it is ready to believe that God is God, but not to believe that God is God *to you*. These people called on God. This proves that they believed he was God, that is to others, but they did not really believe he would help them, otherwise they would not have thrown Jonah overboard. They did their uttermost to save the ship like the papists who try to be saved by works.

Jonah was asleep in the hold. Men are like that when they have sinned. They feel no compunction. If God had forgotten his sin, Jonah would never have given it another thought. But when he was awakened and saw the state of the ship he recognized his guilt. His conscience became active. Then he felt the sting of death and the anger of God. Not only the ship but the whole world was too small for him. He admitted his fault and cleared all the others. This is what contrition does. It makes all the world innocent and yourself only a sinner. But Jonah was not yet ready to make a public acknowledgment. He let the sailors wrestle until God made it plain that they would all perish with him. No one would confess. They had to cast lots. Wounds cannot be healed until they are revealed, and sins cannot be forgiven until they are confessed. Some say that they sinned in casting lots, but I cannot see that lot-casting is forbidden in Scripture.

Then Jonah said, "I am a Hebrew. I fear the God who made heaven and earth." The weight of sin and conscience is made greater if confessed. Then faith begins to burn, albeit weakly. When God's wrath overtakes us there are always two things, sin and anxiety. Some allow the sin to stand and center on the anxiety. That won't do. Reason does this when faith and grace are not present.

Jonah confessed his sin to be all the greater when he said, "I am a Hebrew and a worshiper of the true God." This made him all the more inexcusable. And Jonah said, "Throw me into the sea." The sailors thought confession was enough, and they set to work again on the oars. Jonah had to plumb the shame which was a thousand times greater because it was against God. For such a one there is no corner into which he may creep, no, not even in hell. He did not foresee his deliverance. God takes all honor and all comfort away and leaves only shame and desolation.

Then came death, for the sting of death is sin. Jonah pronounced his own sentence, "Throw me into the sea." We must always remember that Jonah could not see to the end. He saw only death, death, death. The worst of it was that this death was due to God's anger. It would not be so bad to die as a martyr, but when death is a punishment it is truly horrible. Who does not tremble before death, even though he does not feel the wrath of God? But if there be also sin and conscience, who can endure shame before God and the world? What a struggle must have taken place in Jonah's heart. He must have sweat blood. He had to fight against sin, against his own conscience, the feeling of his heart, against death, and against God's anger all at once.

As if the sea were not enough, God prepared a great fish. As the monster opened its frightful jaws, the teeth were jagged like mountain peaks. The waves rushed in and swept Jonah into the belly. What a picture is this of *Anfechtung*. Just so the conscience wilts before the wrath of God, death, hell, and damnation. "And Jonah was three days and three nights in the belly of the whale." Those were the longest three days and three nights that ever happened under the sun. His lungs and liver pounded. He would hardly have looked around to see his habitation. He was thinking, "When, when, when will this end?"

How could anyone imagine that a man could be three days and three nights in the belly of a fish without light, without food, absolutely alone, and come out alive? Who would not take this for a fairy tale if it were not in Scripture?

But God is even in hell.

"And Jonah prayed unto the Lord from the belly of the whale." I do not believe he could compose such a fine psalm while he was down there, but this shows what he was thinking. He was not expecting his salvation. He thought he must die, yet he prayed, "I cried by reason of mine affliction unto the Lord." This shows that we must always pray to God. If you can just cry, your agony is over. Hell is not hell any more if you can cry to God. But no one can believe how hard this is. We can understand wailing, trembling, sighing, doubting, but to cry out, this is what we cannot do. Conscience, sin, and the wrath of God are about our necks. Nature cannot cry out. When Jonah reached the point that he could cry, he had won. Cry unto the Lord in your anguish, and it will be milder. Just cry and nothing else. He does not ask about your merit. Reason does not understand this, and always wants to bring in something to placate God. But there just is nothing to bring. Reason does not believe that all that is needed to quiet God's anger is a cry.

"All thy waves and thy billows are gone over me." Observe that Jonah calls them *thy* waves. If a wind-blown leaf can affright a host, what must not the sea have done to Jonah? And what will not the majesty of God at the judgment day do to all angels and all creatures? "My soul melted within me, and I thought of the Lord." This is to turn from the God of judgment to God the Father. But this does not lie in the power of man. "I will sacrifice unto thee with the voice of thanksgiving, I will pay that I had vowed." "And the Lord spake unto the fish, and it cast Jonah forth upon the dry land." The instrument of death is become the agency of life.

PRAYER

Luther was above all else a man of prayer, and yet of his prayers we have less than of his sermons and conversations because he succeeded in keeping his students out of the secret chamber. There are the collects which he composed for the liturgy, the prayer for the sacristy, and a prayer reputed to have been overheard by his roommate at Worms. We are on safer ground in the following excerpts from his exposition of the Lord's Prayer:

Luther instructs his readers to say: O Heavenly Father, dear God, I am not worthy that I should lift up mine eyes or my hands to thee in prayer, but since thou hast commanded us to pray and hast taught us how through Jesus Christ our Lord, I will say, "Give us this day our daily bread." O dear Lord Father, give us thy blessing in this earthly life. Give us graciously thy peace and spare us from war. Grant to our Kaiser wisdom and understanding that he may govern his earthly kindom in peace and blessedness. Give to all kings, princes, and lords good counsel that they may direct their lands in quietness and justice, and especially guard the ruler of our dear land. Protect him from malignant tongues, and instill into all subjects grace to serve in fidelity and obedience. Bestow on us good weather and the fruits of the earth. We commend unto thee house, grounds, wife, and child. Help that we may govern, nourish, and rear. Ward off the Corrupter and the evil angels who impede these things. Amen.

"Forgive us our trespasses, as we forgive those who trespass against us." Dear Lord and Father, enter not into judgment with us, since before thee is no man living justified. Reckon not unto us our transgressions and that we are so ungrateful of all thy unspeakable mercies of the spirit and of the body, and that we daily fail more than we know or are aware. Mark not how good or evil we be, but vouchsafe to us thy unmerited mercy through Jesus Christ, thy dear Son. Forgive also all our enemies and all who have hurt and done us wrong as we also forgive them from our hearts, for they do themselves the greatest wrong in that they kindle thee against them. But we are not helped by their loss and would much rather that they be blessed. Amen. (And if anyone here feels that he cannot forgive, let him pray for grace that he may. But that is a point which belongs to preaching.)

CHAPTER TWENTY ONE

THE STRUGGLE FOR FAITH

 LWAYS more intimately personal than his teaching and preaching was Luther's pastoral counseling. Neither in the classroom nor in the pulpit was the personal ever wholly absent. But when the physician was engaged in the cure of souls, he drew almost exclusively on that which he had himself discovered to be good for like ailments. For that reason any consideration of what he did for others by way of allaying spiritual distress must take the form of the further analysis of his own maladies and of the remedies which he found to be of avail alike for himself and for others.

LUTHER'S PERSISTENT STRUGGLE

At the outset the recognition is inescapable that he had persistent maladies. This man who so undergirded others with faith had for himself a perpetual battle for faith. Perhaps the severest upheaval of his whole life came in the year 1527. The recurrence of these depressions raises for us again the question whether they may have had some physical basis, and the question really cannot be answered. The attempt to discover a correlation between his many diseases and the despondencies has proved unsuccessful, and one must not forget in this connection that his spiritual ailments were acute in the monastery before the physical had begun. To discover a connection with outward events is more plausible. Crises were precipitated by a thunderstorm, by the saying of the first mass, and in 1527 by the total impact of the radicals, coupled with the fact that Luther was still sleeping in his own bed while his followers were dying for the faith. As he came out from under the state of shock which overtook him, he was wrestling with the self-reproach of being still alive. "I was not worthy," he was saying, "to shed my blood for Christ as many of my fellow confessors of the gospel have done. Yet this honor was denied to the beloved disciple, John the Evangelist, who wrote a much worse book

MARTYRDOM OF HEINRICH OF ZUETPHEN

against the papacy than ever I did." Although outward events affected him, the very nature of the dark night of the soul is that it may be occasioned by nothing tangible whatever. Physical debilitation was more often the effect than the cause.

The content of the depressions was always the same, the loss of faith that God is good and that he is good *to me*. After the frightful *Anfechtung* of 1527 Luther wrote, "For more than a week I was close to the gates of death and hell. I trembled in all my members. Christ was wholly lost. I was shaken by desperation and blasphemy of God." His agony in the later years was all the more intense because he was a physician of souls; and if the medicine which he had prescribed for himself and for them was actually poison, how frightful was his responsibility. The great problem for him was not to know where his depressions came from, but to know how to overcome them. In the course of repeated utterances on the subject he worked out a technique for himself and for his parishioners.

The first comfort which he offered was the reflection that intense upheavals of the spirit are necessary for valid solutions of genuine religious problems. The emotional reactions may be unduly acute, for the Devil always turns a louse into a camel. Nevertheless the way of man with God cannot be tranquil.

If I live longer, I would like to write a book about *Anfechtungen*, for without them no man can understand Scripture, faith, the fear or the love of God. He does not know the meaning of hope who was never subject to temptations.

David must have been plagued by a very fearful devil. He could not have had such profound insights if he had not experienced great assaults.

Luther verged on saying that an excessive emotional sensitivity is a mode of revelation. Those who are predisposed to fall into despondency as well as to rise into ecstasy may be able to view reality from an angle different from that of ordinary folk. Yet it is a true angle; and when the problem or the religious object has been once so viewed, others less sensitive will be able to look from a new vantage point and testify that the insight is valid.

HIS DEPRESSIONS

Luther felt that his depressions were necessary. At the same time they were dreadful and by all means and in every way to be avoided and overcome. His whole life was a struggle against them, a fight for faith. This is the point at which he interests us so acutely, for we too are cast down and we too would know how to assuage our despondency. Luther had two methods: the one was a head-on attack, the other an approach by way of indirection. Sometimes he would engage in direct encounter with the Devil. This particular *mise en scène* may amuse the modern reader and incline him not to take Luther seriously; but it is noteworthy that what the Devil says to Luther is only what one says to oneself in moments of introspection, and, what is still more significant, only the minor difficulties were referred to the Devil. In all the major encounters, God himself was the assailant. The Devil was something of a relief. Luther relished, by comparison, the personification of his enemy in the form of a being whom he could bait without danger of blasphemy. He describes with gusto some of these bouts:

When I go to bed, the Devil is always waiting for me. When he begins to plague me, I give him this answer: "Devil, I must sleep. That's God's command, 'Work by day. Sleep by night.' So go away." If that doesn't work and he brings out a catalog of sins, I say, "Yes, old fellow, I know all about it. And I know some more you have overlooked. Here are a few extra. Put them down." If he still won't quit and presses me hard and accuses me as a sinner, I scorn him and say, "St. Satan, pray for me. Of course you have never done anything wrong in your life. You alone are holy. Go to God and get grace for yourself. If you want to get me all straightened out, I say, 'Physician, heal thyself.'"

Sometimes Luther had the temerity to undertake also the greater encounter with God himself. "I dispute much with God with great impatience," said he, "and I hold him to his promises." The Canaanite woman was a source of unending wonder and comfort to Luther because she had the audacity to argue with Christ. When she asked him to come and cure her daughter, he answered that he was not sent but to the lost sheep of the house of Israel, and that it was not meet to take the children's bread and give it to the dogs. She did not dispute his judgment. She agreed that she was a dog. She asked no more than that which befits a dog, to lick up the crumbs which fall from the children's table. She took Christ at his own words. He then treated her not as a dog but as a child of Israel.

All this is written for our comfort that we should see how deeply God hides his face and how we must not go by our feeling but only by his Word. All Christ's answers sounded like no, but he did not mean no. He had not said that she was not of the house of Israel. He had not said that she was a dog. He had not said no. Yet all his answers were more like no than yes. This shows how our heart feels in despondency. It sees nothing but a plain no. Therefore it must turn to the deep hidden yes under the no and hold with a firm faith to God's word.

THE WAY OF INDIRECTION

At times, however, Luther advised against any attempt to wrestle one's way through. "Don't argue with the Devil," he said. "He has had five thousand years of experience. He has tried out all his tricks on Adam, Abraham, and David, and he knows exactly the weak spots." And he is persistent. If he does not get you down with the first assault, he will commence a siege of attrition until you give in from sheer exhaustion. Better banish the whole subject. Seek company and discuss some irrelevant matter as, for example, what is going on in Venice. Shun solitude. "Eve got into trouble when she walked in the garden alone. I have my worst temptations when I am by myself." Seek out some Christian brother, some wise counselor. Undergird yourself with the fellowship of the church. Then, too, seek convivial company, feminine company, dine, dance, joke, and sing. Make yourself eat and drink even though food may be very distasteful. Fasting is the very worst expedient. Once Luther gave three rules for dispelling despondency: the first is faith in Christ; the second is to get downright angry; the third is the love of a woman. Music was especially commended. The Devil hates it because he cannot endure gaiety. Luther's physician relates that on one occasion he came with some friends for a musical soiree only to find Luther in a swoon; but when the others struck up the song, he was soon one of the party. Home life was a comfort and a diversion. So also was the presence of his wife when the Devil assaulted him in the night watches. "Then I turn to my Katie and say, 'Forbid me to have such temptations, and recall me from such vain vexations.'" Manual labor was a relief. A good way, counseled Luther,

DEVIL AND DEATH HARASS A SOUL

to exorcise the Devil is to harness the horse and spread manure on the fields. In all this advice to flee the fray Luther was in a way prescribing faith as a cure for the lack of faith. To give up the argument is of itself an act of faith akin to the *Gelassenheit* of the mystics, an expression of confidence in the restorative power of God, who operates in the subconscious while man occupies himself with extraneous things.

This explains why Luther liked to watch those who take life blithely, such as birds and babies. When he saw his little Martin nursing, he remarked, "Child, your enemies are the pope, the bishops, Duke George, Ferdinand, and the Devil. And there you are sucking unconcernedly."

When Anastasia, then four years old, was prattling of Christ, angels, and heaven, Luther said, "My dear child, if only we could hold fast to this faith."

"Why, papa," said she, "don't you believe it?"

Luther commented:

Christ has made the children our teachers. I am chagrined that although I am ever so much a doctor, I still have to go to the same school with

Hans and Magdalena, for who among men can understand the full meaning of this word of God, "Our Father who art in heaven"? Anyone who genuinely believes these words will often say, "I am the Lord of heaven and earth and all that is therein. The Angel Gabriel is my servant, Raphael is my guardian, and the angels in my every need are ministering spirits. My Father, who is in heaven, will give them charge over me lest I dash my foot against a stone." And while I am affirming this faith, my Father suffers me to be thrown into prison, drowned, or beheaded. Then faith falters and in weakness I cry, "Who knows whether it is true?"

WRESTLING WITH THE ANGEL

Merely watching children could not answer that question. The encounter had to be resumed on the direct level. If Luther was disturbed about the state of the world and the state of the Church, he could gain reassurance only through the recognition that as a matter of plain fact the situation was not bad. Despite the many pessimistic judgments of his later years Luther could say, "I entertain no sorry picture of our Church, but rather that of the Church flourishing through pure and uncorrupted teaching and one increasing with excellent ministers from day to day."

At other times the depression was with regard to himself. One recalls his oscillation of feeling at the Wartburg as to whether he had been brash or craven. The answer in his own case could never be that he had any claim on God, and then the question forever recurred whether God would then be gracious. When one is assailed by this doubt, where shall one turn? Luther would say that one never knows where, but always somewhere. To inquire after the starting point of Luther's theology is futile. It begins where it can. Christ himself appears variable, sometimes as a good Shepherd and sometimes as the avenging Judge. If then Christ appeared hostile, Luther would turn to God and would recall the first commandment, "I am the Lord thy God." This very pronouncement is at the same time a promise, and God must be held to his promises.

In such a case we must say, "Let go everything in which I have trusted. Lord, thou alone givest help and comfort. Thou hast said that thou wouldst help me. I believe thy word. O my God and Lord, I have heard

Des lutters gestalt mag wol verderbenn
Sein cristlich gemuet wirt nymer sterben
D · XXIII · D

from thee a joyful and comforting word. I hold to it. I know thou wilt not lie to me. No matter how thou mayest appear, thou wilt keep what thou hast promised, that and nothing else."

On the other hand, if God hides himself in the storm clouds which brood over the brow of Sinai, then gather about the manger, look upon the infant Jesus as he leaps in the lap of his mother, and know that the hope of the world is here. Or again, if Christ and God alike are unapproachable, then look upon the firmament of the heavens and marvel at the work of God, who sustains them without pillars. Or take the meanest flower and see in the smallest petal the handiwork of God.

All the external aids of religion are to be prized. Luther attached great importance to his baptism. When the Devil assailed him, he would answer, "I am baptized." In his conflicts with the Catholics and the radicals he reassured himself similarly by making appeal to his doctorate. This gave him authority and the right to speak.

THE ROCK OF SCRIPTURE

But always and above all else the one great objective aid for Luther was the Scriptures, because this is the written record of the revelation of God in Christ. "The true Christian pilgrimage is not to Rome or Compostela, but to the prophets, the Psalms, and the Gospels." The Scriptures assumed for Luther an overwhelming importance, not primarily as a source book for antipapal polemic, but as the one ground of certainty. He had rejected the authority of popes and councils, and could not make a beginning from within as did the prophets of the inward word. The core of his quarrel with them was that in moments of despondency he could find nothing within but utter blackness. He was completely lost unless he could find something without on which to lay hold. And this he found in the Scriptures.

He approached them uncritically, from our point of view, but not with credulity. Nothing so amazed him in all the biblical record as the faith of the participants: that Mary credited the annunciation of the angel Gabriel; that Joseph gave credence to the dream which allayed his misgivings; that the shepherds believed the opening of the heavens and the angels' song; that the Wise Men were ready to go to Bethlehem at the word of the prophet. There were three miracles of the Nativity: that God became man, that a virgin conceived, and that Mary believed. And the greatest of these was the last. When the Wise Men relied upon their judgment and went straight to Jerusalem without consulting the star, God lifted it out of heaven and left them bewildered to make inquiry of Herod, who then called his wise men and they searched the Scriptures. And that is what we must do when we are bereft of the star.

But this is just the point where some in our day find Luther's lead elusive. They can feel with him in the description of his distress but cannot follow his prescriptions for the cure. They are acquainted with the findings of modern biblical criticism and are unable to turn to the Scripture with Luther's simplicity. Here a word of Luther may help, after all, for he declared that the gospel is not so much a miracle as a marvel, *non miracula sed mirabilia.* There is no better way to feel the wonder than to take Luther as guide. Let him portray for us, with all his power and poignancy, the spiritual despondencies of the biblical characters and the way in which they were able to find the hand of the Lord.

We have already seen an example in the case of his treatment of Jonah. By way of further illustration let us take his portrayal of the sacrifice of Isaac by Abraham. Save for the initial assumption that God commanded the sacrifice and that the angel intervened in the end, all else is the record of an inner struggle which is not hard to translate into the story of an emerging insight or an unfolding revelation. Hear Luther as he expounds the tale:

Abraham was told by God that he must sacrifice the son of his old age by a miracle, the seed through whom he was to become the father of kings and of a great nation. Abraham turned pale. Not only would he lose his son, but God appeared to be a liar. He had said, "In Isaac shall be thy seed," but now he said, "Kill Isaac." Who would not hate a God so cruel and contradictory? How Abraham longed to talk it over with someone! Could he not tell Sarah? But he well knew that if he mentioned it to anyone he would be dissuaded and prevented from carrying out the behest. The spot designated for the sacrifice, Mount Moriah, was some distance away; "and Abraham rose up early in the morning, and saddled his ass, and took two of his young men with him, and Isaac his son, and clave the wood for the burnt-offering." Abraham did not leave the saddling of the ass to others. He himself laid on the beast the wood for the burnt offering. He was thinking all the time that these logs would consume his son, his hope of seed. With these very sticks that he was picking up the boy would be burned. In such a terrible case should he not take time to think it over? Could he not tell Sarah? With what inner tears he suffered! He girt the ass and was so absorbed he scarcely knew what he was doing.

He took two servants and Isaac his son. In that moment everything died in him: Sarah, his family, his home, Isaac. This is what it is to sit in sackcloth and ashes. If he had known that this was only a trial, he would not have been tried. Such is the nature of our trials that while they last we cannot see to the end. "Then on the third day Abraham lifted up his eyes, and saw the place afar off." What a battle he had endured in those three days! There Abraham left the servants and the ass, and he laid the wood upon Isaac and himself took the torch and the sacrificial knife. All the time he was thinking, "Isaac, if you knew, if your mother knew that you are to be sacrificed." "And they went both of them together." The whole world does not know what here took place. They two walked together. Who? The father and the dearest son—the one not knowing what was in store but ready to obey, the other certain that he must leave his son in ashes. Then said Isaac, "My father." And he said, "Yes, my son." And Isaac said, "Father, here is the fire and here the wood, but where is the lamb?" He called him father and was solicitous lest he had overlooked something, and Abraham said, "God will himself provide a lamb, my son."

When they were come to the mount, Abraham built the altar and laid on the wood, and then he was forced to tell Isaac. The boy was stupefied. He must have protested, "Have you forgotten: I am the son of Sarah by a miracle in her age, that I was promised and that through me you are to be the father of a great nation?" And Abraham must have answered that God would fulfill his promise even out of ashes. Then Abraham bound him and laid him upon the wood. The father raised his knife. The boy bared his throat. If God had slept an instant, the lad would have been dead. I could not have watched. I am not able in my thoughts to follow. The lad was as a sheep for the slaughter. Never in history was there such obedience, save only in Christ. But God was watching, and all the angels. The father raised his knife; the boy did not wince. The angel cried, "Abraham, Abraham!" See how divine majesty is at hand in the hour of death. We say, "In the midst of life we die." God answers, "Nay, in the midst of death we live."

Luther once read this story for family devotions. When he had finished, Katie said, "I do not believe it. God would not have treated his son like that."

"But, Katie," answered Luther, "he did."

Hear Luther also as he describes the passion of Christ. The narrative is placed on a most human level. We are reminded that the death of Christ was of all the most terrible because it was an execution. This means death at a known moment for one who is fully aware of what is involved. In old age the angel of death often muffles his wings and permits us to slip peacefully away. Jesus went to his death in full possession of his faculties. He suffered even more than did the malefactors. A robber was simply crucified, not at the same time reviled. To Christ were spoken words of raillery, "If you are the Son of God, come down." As if to say, "God is just. He would not suffer an innocent man to die upon a cross." Christ at this point was simply a man, and it was for him as it is for me when the Devil comes and says, "You are mine." After the reviling of Christ, the sun was darkened and the earth trembled. If a troubled conscience shudders at the rustling of a wind-blown leaf, how much more terrible must it have been when the sun was blotted out and the earth was shaken. Christ was driven to a cry of desperation. The words are recorded in the original tongue that we may sense the stark desolation: *Eli, Eli, lama sabachthani?* "My God, my God, why hast thou forsaken me?" But note this, the prayer of the forsaken began, *"My* God." The cry of despair was a confession of faith.

What wonder then that Luther, in the year of his deepest depression, composed these lines:

> A mighty bulwark is our God
> A doughty ward and weapon.

"A Mighty Fortress" in Luther's Hand

He helps us clear from every rod
  By which we now are smitten.
Still our ancient foe
Girds him to strike a blow.
Might and guile his gear.
His armor striketh fear.
  On earth is not his equal.

By our own strength is nothing won.
  We court at once disaster.
There fights for us the Champion
  Whom God has named our Master.
Would you know his name?
Jesus Christ the same
  Lord Sabaoth is he.

No other God can be.
　The field is his to hold it.

　And though the fiends on every hand
　　Were threatening to devour us,
We would not waver from our stand.
　They cannot overpower us.
This world's prince may rave.
However he behave,
He can do no ill.
God's truth abideth still.
　One little word shall fell him.

That word they never can dismay.
　However much they batter,
For God himself is in the fray
　And nothing else can matter.
Then let them take our life,
Goods, honor, children, wife.
We will let all go.
They shall not conquer so,
　For God will win the battle.

CHAPTER TWENTY-TWO

THE MEASURE OF THE MAN

HE LAST sixteen years of Luther's life, from the Augsburg Confession in 1530 to his death in 1546, are commonly treated more cursorily by biographers than the earlier period, if indeed they are not omitted altogether. There is a measure of justification for this comparative neglect because the last quarter of Luther's life was neither determinative for his ideas nor crucial for his achievements. His own verdict in 1531 was more than a grim jest, namely, "Should the papists by their devouring, biting, tearing help me to put off this sinful carcass and should the Lord not wish this time to deliver me as he has so often done before, then may he be praised and thanked. I have lived long enough. Not until I am gone will they feel Luther's full weight." He was right; his ideas were matured; his church was established; his associates could carry on, as indeed in the public sphere they were compelled to do because for the remainder of his life he was under the ban of Church and state.

THE BIGAMY OF THE LANDGRAVE

This exile from the public scene chafed him the more because the conflicts and the labors of the dramatic years had impaired his health and made him prematurely an irascible old man, petulant, peevish, unrestrained, and at times positively coarse. This is no doubt another reason why biographers prefer to be brief in dealing with this period. There are several incidents over which one would rather draw the veil, but precisely because they are so often exploited to his discredit they are not to be left unrecorded. The most notorious was his attitude toward the bigamy of the landgrave, Philip of Hesse. This prince had been given in marriage with no regard to his own affections—that is, for purely political reasons—at the age of nineteen to the daughter of Duke George. Philip, unable to combine romance with marriage, found his satisfaction promiscuously on the outside. After his conversion his conscience so troubled him that he dared not present himself at the Lord's Table. He believed that if he could have one partner to whom he was genuinely attached he would be able to keep himself within the bounds of matrimony. There were several ways in which his difficulty could have been solved. If he had remained a Catholic, he might have been able to secure an annulment on the grounds of some defect in the marriage; but since he had become a Lutheran, he could expect no consideration from the pope. Nor would Luther permit recourse to the Catholic device. A second solution would have been divorce and remarriage. A great many Protestant bodies in the present day would countenance this method, particularly since Philip had been subjected in his youth to a loveless match. But Luther at this point interpreted the Gospels rigidly and held to the word of Christ as reported by Matthew that divorce is permissible only for adultery. But Luther did feel that there should be some remedy, and he discovered it by a reversion to the mores of the Old Testament patriarchs, who had practiced bigamy and even polygamy without any manifestation of divine displeasure. Philip was given the assurance that he might in good conscience take a second wife. Since, however, to do so would be against the law of the land, he should keep the union a secret. This the new bride's mother declined to do; and then Luther counseled a lie on the ground that his advice had been given as in the confessional, and to guard the secrets of the confessional a lie is justified. But the secret was out, and the disavowal was ineffective. Luther's final comment was that if anyone thereafter should practice bigamy, let the Devil give him a bath in the abyss of hell.

The whole episode had disastrous political consequences for the Protestant movement because Philip, in order to secure pardon from the emperor, had to dissociate himself from a military alliance with the Protestants. The scene of Philip abjectly seeking grace from His Imperial Majesty has a certain irony because Charles deposited illegitimate children all over Europe, whom the pope legitimatized in order that they might occupy high offices of state. Luther's solution of the problem can be called only a pitiable subterfuge. He should first have directed his attack against the evil system of degrading marriage to the level of a political convenience, and he might well have adopted the later Protestant solution of divorce.

ATTITUDE TO THE ANABAPTISTS

The second development of those later years was a hardening toward sectaries, notably the Anabaptists. Their growth constituted a very real problem to the territorial church, since despite the decree of death visited upon them at the Diet of Speyer in 1529 with the concurrence of the Evangelicals, the intrepidity and irreproachable lives of the martyrs had enlisted converts to the point of threatening to depopulate the established churches. Philip of Hesse observed more improvement of life among the sectaries than among the Lutherans, and a Lutheran minister who wrote against the Anabaptists testified that they went in among the poor, appeared very lowly, prayed much, read from the Gospel, talked especially about the outward life and good works, about helping the neighbor, giving and lending, holding goods in common, exercising authority over none, and living with all as brothers and sisters. Such were the people executed by Elector John in Saxony. But the blood of the martyrs proved again to be the seed of the church.

Luther was very much distraught over the whole matter. In 1527 he wrote with regard to the Anabaptists:

It is not right, and I am deeply troubled that the poor people are so pitifully put to death, burned, and cruelly slain. Let everyone believe what he likes. If he is wrong, he will have punishment enough in hell fire. Unless there is sedition, one should oppose them with Scripture and God's Word. With fire you won't get anywhere.

This obviously did not mean, however, that Luther considered one faith as good as another. Most emphatically he believed that the wrong faith would entail hell-fire; and although the true faith cannot

THE ANABAPTIST PREACHER

be created by coercion, it can be relieved of impediments. The magistrate certainly should not suffer the faith to be blasphemed. In 1530 Luther advanced the view that two offenses should be penalized even with death, namely sedition and blasphemy. The emphasis was thus shifted from incorrect belief to its public manifestation by word and deed. This was, however, no great gain for liberty, because Luther construed mere abstention from public office and military service as sedition and a rejection of an article of the Apostles' Creed as blasphemy.

In a memorandum of 1531, composed by Melanchthon and signed by Luther, a rejection of the ministerial office was described as insufferable blasphemy, and the disintegration of the Church as sedition against the ecclesiastical order. In a memorandum of 1536, again composed by Melanchthon and signed by Luther, the distinction between the peaceful and the revolutionary Anabaptists was obliterated. Philip of Hesse had asked several cities and universities for advice as to what he should do with some thirty Anabaptists whom he was holding under arrest. He had steadfastly refused to inflict the death penalty and had resorted to no more than banishment. But this was ineffective because the Anabaptists argued that the earth is the Lord's and refused to stay away. Of all the replies which Philip received those from the Lutherans were the most severe. Melanchthon this time argued that even the passive action of the Anabaptists in rejecting government, oaths, private property, and marriages outside of the faith was itself disruptive of the civil order and therefore seditious. The Anabaptist protest against the punishment of blasphemy was itself blasphemy. The discontinuance of infant baptism would produce a heathen society and separation from the Church, and the formation of sects was an offense against God.

Luther may not have been too happy about signing these memoranda. At any rate he appended postscripts to each. To the first he said, "I assent. Although it seems cruel to punish them with the sword, it is crueler that they condemn the ministry of the Word and have no well-grounded doctrine and suppress the true and in this way seek to subvert the civil order." Luther's addition to the second document was a plea that severity be tempered with mercy. In 1540 he is reported in his *Table Talk* to have returned to the position of Philip of Hesse that only seditious Anabaptists should be executed; the others should be merely banished. But Luther passed by many an opportunity to speak a word for those who with joy gave themselves as sheep for the slaughter. One would have thought that he might have been moved by the case of Fritz Erbe, who died at the Wartburg after sixteen years of incarceration. As to the effectiveness of such severity Luther might have pondered had he learned that the steadfastness of Erbe had converted one half of the populace of Eisenach to Anabaptism.

For the understanding of Luther's position one must bear in mind that Anabaptism was not in every instance socially innocuous. The year in which Luther signed the memorandum counseling death even for the peaceful Anabaptists was the year in which a group of them ceased to be peaceful. Goaded by ten years of incessant persecution, bands of fanatics in 1534 received a revelation from the Lord that they should no more be as sheep for the slaughter but rather as the angel with the sickle to reap the harvest. By forcible measures they took over the city of Münster in Westphalia and there inaugurated the reign of the saints, of which Thomas Müntzer had dreamed. Catholics and Protestants alike conjoined to suppress the reign of the new Daniels and Elijahs. The whole episode did incalculable damage to the reputation of the Anabaptists, who before and after were peaceable folk. But this one instance of rebellion engendered the fear that sheep's clothing concealed wolves who might better be dealt with before they threw off the disguise. In Luther's case it should further be remembered that the leading Anabaptist in Thuringia was Melchior Rink, and he had been with Thomas Müntzer at the battle of Frankenhausen. Yet when all of these attenuating considerations are adduced, one cannot forget that Melanchthon's memorandum justified the eradication of the peaceful, not because they were incipient and clandestine revolutionaries, but on the ground that even a peaceful renunciation of the state itself constituted sedition.

The other point to remember alike in the case of Luther and Melanchthon is that they were quite as much convinced as was the church of the inquisition that the truth of God can be known, and being known lays supreme obligations upon mankind to preserve it unsullied. The Anabaptists were regarded as the corrupters of souls. Luther's leniency toward them is the more to be remarked than his severity. He did insist to the end that faith is not to be forced, that in private a man may believe what he will, that only open revolt or public attack on the orthodox teaching should be penalized—in his own words, that only sedition and blasphemy rather than heresy should be subject to constraint.

ATTITUDE TO THE JEWS

Another dissenting group to attract Luther's concern was the Jews. He had early believed that they are a stiff-necked people to have rejected Christ, but contemporary Jews could not be blamed for the sins of their fathers and might readily be excused for their rejection of Christianity by reason of the corruptions of the papacy. He said:

If I were a Jew, I would suffer the rack ten times before I would go over to the pope.

The papists have so demeaned themselves that a good Christian would rather be a Jew than one of them, and a Jew would rather be a sow than a Christian.

What good can we do the Jews when we constrain them, malign them, and hate them as dogs? When we deny them work and force them to usury, how can that help? We should use toward the Jews not the pope's but Christ's law of love. If some are stiff-necked, what does that matter? We are not all good Christians.

Luther was sanguine that his own reform, by eliminating the abuses of the papacy, would accomplish the conversion of the Jews. But the converts were few and unstable. When he endeavored to proselytize some rabbis, they undertook in return to make a Jew of him. The rumor that a Jew had been suborned by the papists to murder him was not received with complete incredulity. In Luther's latter days, when he was often sorely frayed, news came that in Moravia, Christians were being induced to Judaize. Then he came out with a vulgar blast in which he recommended that all the Jews be deported to Palestine. Failing that, they should be forbidden to practice usury, should be compelled to earn their living on the land, their synagogues should be burned, and their books including the Bible should be taken away from them.

One could wish that Luther had died before ever this tract was written. Yet one must be clear as to what he was recommending and why. His position was entirely religious and in no respect racial. The supreme sin for him was the persistent rejection of God's revelation of himself in Christ. The centuries of Jewish suffering were themselves a mark of the divine displeasure. The territorial principle should be applied to the Jews. They should be compelled to leave and go to a land of their own. This was a program of enforced Zionism. But if it were not feasible, then Luther would recommend that the Jews be compelled to live from the soil. He was unwittingly proposing a return to the condition of the early Middle Ages, when the Jews had been in agriculture. Forced off the land, they had gone into commerce and, having been expelled from commerce, into money lending. Luther wished to reverse the process and thereby inadvertently would accord the Jews a more secure position than they enjoyed in his day. The burning of the synagogues and the confiscation of the books was, however, a revival of the worst features of Pfefferkorn's program. One other word must be added: if similar tracts did not appear in England, France, and Spain in Luther's day, it was because the Jews had already been completely expelled from these countries. Germany, disorganized in this as in so many other respects, expelled the Jews from certain localities and tolerated them in others, such as Frankfurt and Worms. The irony of the situation was that Luther justified himself by appealing to the ire of Jehovah against those who go awhoring after other gods. Luther would not have listened to any impugning of the validity of this picture of God, but he might have recalled that Scripture itself discountenances human imitation of the divine vengeance.

THE PAPISTS AND THE EMPEROR

The third group toward whom Luther became more bitter was the papists. His railing against the pope became perhaps the more vituperative because there was so little else that could be done. Another public appearance such as that at Worms, where an ampler confession could be made, was denied Luther, and the martyrdom which came to others also passed him by. He compensated by hurling vitriol. Toward the very end of his life he issued an illustrated tract with outrageously vulgar cartoons. In all of this he was utterly unrestrained.

The case was different in his attitude toward the emperor. Here Luther entertained his last great illusion. Even in 1531 he lauded Charles for his previous clemency and could not be persuaded that the emperor would yield to the goading of the papists. But should he do so and should he take up arms to suppress the gospel, then

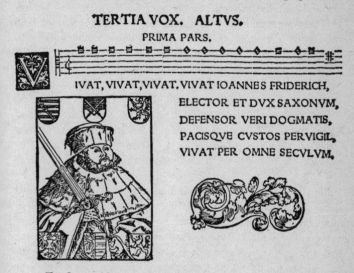

TERTIA VOX. ALTVS.
PRIMA PARS.

IVAT, VIVAT, VIVAT. VIVAT IOANNES FRIDERICH,
ELECTOR ET DVX SAXONVM,
DEFENSOR VERI DOGMATIS,
PACISQVE CVSTOS PERVIGIL,
VIVAT PER OMNE SECVLVM.

THE LOWER MAGISTRATE: JOHN FREDERICK, ELECTOR OF SAXONY

his subjects should do no more than refuse to serve under his banners, and for the rest should leave the outcome to the Lord, who delivered Lot from Sodom. Should God not intervene to preserve his own, yet would he be the Lord God, and under no circumstances should subjects take up arms against the powers ordained. The next year, however, Luther was brought to observe that the word used by the apostle Paul, namely "powers," is in the plural, and that although the common man may not take the sword which is committed only to the "power," yet one power may legitimately exercise a check even by the sword upon another. In other words, one department of the government may employ force to restrain the injustice of another. The Holy Roman Empire was a constitutional monarchy, and the emperor had sworn at his coronation that no German subject should be outlawed unheard and uncondemned. Although this clause had not been invoked to protect a monk accused of heresy, yet when princes and electors came to be involved the case was altered. If Charles were faithless to that oath, then he might be resisted even in arms by the lower magistrates. The formula thus suggested to Luther by the jurists was destined to have a very wide and extended vogue. The Lutherans employed it only until they gained legal recognition in 1555. Thereafter the Calvinists took up the slogan and equated the lower magistrates with the lesser nobility in France. Subsequently the Puritans in England made the same identification with Parliament. Later historians are so accustomed to regard Lutheranism as politically subservient and Calvinism as intransigent that they would do well to recall the origin of this doctrine on Lutheran soil.

But it was not the invention of Luther, even though he accepted its validity, never, however, without a measure of misgiving and such qualification as to make one uncertain whether his conditions were ever actually fulfilled. The emperor, he felt, might be forcibly resisted, not in case he should reintroduce the mass, but only in case he endeavored to force the Lutherans to attend the mass. This the emperor did only after Luther's death when Philip of Hesse was captured and required to be present at the celebration. Whether in that instance Luther would have felt the time had come for the legitimate use of the sword we shall never know. He was always ready to disobey, but exceedingly loath to raise a hand against the Lord's anointed.

Such were the public questions which engaged the later years, but in none of them could Luther do much more than write a memorandum. He must devote his labors to more restricted tasks, and that he did by preference. "A cow," said he, "does not get to heaven by giving milk, but that is what she is made for," and by the same token he would say that Martin Luther by his ministry could not settle the fate of Europe, but for the ministry he was made. To all the obligations of university and parish he gave himself unremittingly. To the end he was preaching, lecturing, counseling, and writing. However much the superb defiance of the earlier days might degenerate into the peevishness of one racked by disease, labor, and discouragement, yet a case of genuine need would always restore his sense of proportion and bring him into the breach. The closing events of his life are an example. He was in such a panic of disgust because the girls at Wittenberg were wearing low necks that he left home declaring that he would not return. His physician brought him back. Then came a request from the counts of Mansfeld for a mediator in a dispute. Melanchthon was too sick to go. Luther was too sick to live. He went, reconciled the counts, and died on the way home.

Luther's later years are, however, by no means to be written off as the sputterings of a dying flame. If in his polemical tracts he was at times savage and coarse, in the works which constitute the real marrow of his life's endeavor he grew constantly in maturity and artistic creativity. The biblical translation was improved to the very end. The sermons and the biblical commentaries reached superb heights. The delineation of the sacrifice of Isaac, already quoted, comes from the year 1545. Some of the passages

LUTHER IN THE YEAR OF HIS DEATH

cited throughout this book to illustrate Luther's religious and ethical principles are also from the later period.

THE MEASURE OF THE MAN

When one comes to take the measure of the man, there are three areas which naturally suggest themselves. The first is his own Germany. He called himself the German prophet, saying that against the papist asses he must assume so presumptuous a title, and he addressed himself to his beloved Germans. The claim is frequent that no man did so much to fashion the character of the German people. Their indifference to politics and their passion for music were already present in him. Their language was so far fashioned by his hand that the extent of their indebtedness is difficult to recognize. If a German is asked whether a passage of Luther's Bible is not remarkable, he may answer that this is precisely the way in which any German would speak. But the reason is simply that every German has been reared on Luther's version. The influence of the man on his people was deepest in the home. In fact the home was the only sphere of life which the Reformation profoundly affected. Economics went the way of capitalism and politics the way of absolutism. But the home took on that quality of affectionate and godly patriarchalism which Luther had set as the pattern in his own household. The most profound impact of Luther on his people was in their religion. His sermons were read to the congregations, his liturgy was sung, his catechism was rehearsed by the father with the household, his Bible cheered the fainthearted and consoled the dying. If no Englishman occupies a similar place in the religious life of his people, it is because no Englishman had anything like Luther's range. The Bible translation in England was the work of Tyndale, the prayer book of Cranmer, the catechism of the Westminster divines. The sermonic style stemmed from Latimer; the hymnbook came from Watts. And not all of these lived in one century. Luther did the work of more than five men. And for sheer richness and exuberance of vocabulary and mastery of style he is to be compared only with Shakespeare.

The Germans naturally claim such a German for themselves. Yet when one begins to look over the centuries for those whom one would most naturally compare with this man, not a single one of his stature proves to be a German. In fact a German historian has said that in the course of three hundred years only one German ever really understood Luther, and that one was Johann Sebastian Bach. If one would discover parallels to Luther as the wrestler with the Lord, then one must turn to Paul the Jew, Augustine the Latin, Pascal the Frenchman, Kierkegaard the Dane, Unamuno the Spaniard, Dostoevski the Russian, Bunyan the Englishman, and Edwards the American.

And that is why in the second great area, that of the Church, Luther's influence extends so far beyond his own land. Lutheranism took possession of Scandinavia and has an extensive following in the United States, and apart from that his movement gave the impetus which sometimes launched and sometimes helped to establish the other varieties of Protestantism. They all stem in some measure from him. And what he did for his own people to a degree, he did also for others. His translation, for example, affected the English version. Tyndale's preface is taken from Luther. His liturgical reforms likewise had an influence on the *Book of Common Prayer*. And even the Catholic Church owes much to him. Often it is said that had Luther never appeared, an Erasmian reform would have triumphed, or at any rate a reform after the Spanish model. All of this is of course conjectural, but it is obvious that the Catholic Church received a tremendous shock from the Lutheran Reformation and a terrific urge to reform after its own pattern.

The third area is of all the most important and the only one which to Luther mattered much, and that is the area of religion. Here it is that he must be judged. In his religion he was a Hebrew, not a Greek fancying gods and goddesses disporting themselves about some limpid pool or banqueting upon Olympus. The God of Luther, as of Moses, was the God who inhabits the storm clouds and rides on the wings of the wind. At his nod the earth trembles, and the people before him are as a drop in the bucket. He is a God of majesty and power, inscrutable, terrifying, devastating, and consuming in his anger. Yet the All Terrible is the All Merciful too. "Like as a father pitieth his children, so the Lord . . . " But how shall we know this? In Christ, only in Christ. In the Lord of life, born in the squalor of a cow stall and dying as a malefactor under the desertion and the derision of men, crying unto God and receiving for answer only the trembling of the earth and the blinding of the sun, even by God forsaken, and in that hour taking to himself and annihilating our iniquity, trampling down the hosts of hell and disclosing within the wrath of the All Terrible the love that will not let us go. No longer did Luther tremble at the rustling of a wind-blown leaf, and instead of calling upon St. Anne he declared himself able to laugh at thunder and jagged bolts from out the storm. This was what enabled him to utter such words as these: "Here I stand. I cannot do otherwise. God help me. Amen."

REFERENCES

KEY TO ABBREVIATIONS

AD—Aleander Depeschen (Kalkoff, ed.)

Ann—Annales

ARG—Archiv für Reformationsgeschichte

Bd—Buchwald, *Luthers Predigten*

BDF—Briefe, Depeschen und Berichte (see Kalkoff)

Bibel—Bible in *WA*

BR—Briefwechsel in *WA*

CR—Corpus reformatorum

Dok (K)—*Dokumente zum Ablassstreit von 1517* (Walther Koehler, ed., 1902)

Dok (S)—*Dokumente zu Luthers Entwicklung* (Otto Scheel, ed., 1929)

EA—Erlangen Ausgabe

EE—Erasmi epistolae

Ep—Epistolae Ulrichi Huttenis

F—Forschungen

JLG—Jahrbuch der Luthergesellschaft

LJ—Luther Jahrbuch

QFRG—Quellen und Forschungen zur Reformationsgeschichte

ova—Opera varii argumenti in *EA*

RA—Deutsche Reichstagsakten

SVRG—Schriften des Vereins für Reformationsgeschichte

TR—Tischreden in *WA*

VLG—Vierteljahrschrift der Luthergesellschaft

W—Walch ed. of Luther's works

WA—Weimar Ausgabe, ordinarily referred to simply by volume and page

ZHT—Zeitschrift für die historische Theologie

ZKG—Zeitschrift für Kirchengeschichte

ZST—Zeitschrift für systematische Theologie

PAGE LINE

CHAP. I

23   21   *TR*, 3566 A (1537)
23   25   *TR*, 1559 (1532)
23   29   *TR*, 5571 (1543)
24   12   XXXVIII, 338
25   14   Scheel, 1, 290, n. 13
26   12   Boehmer, *JL*, p. 24
27   9   *TR*, 3841
28   9   *TR*, 3593, p. 439
29   23   Gerke, *Th.Bl.*, XI, 320
30   9   Bullen, p. XXV
30   24   *Dok* (S), Nos. 346, 358, 381
32   7   Coulton, 1, 92
32   15   Coulton, III, 17
33   13   *Dok* (S), No. 371

PAGE LINE

33   22   Scheel, 1, 95, n. 65
34   3   Buchwald, *LL*, p. 6
34   14   *Dok* (S), under *Eintritt*
35   18   Scheel, 1, 261-62

CHAP. II

37   3   *Dok* (S), No. 50
38   6   Scheel, II, 35-36
38   17   *Ibid.*, II, 62
39   2   *Dok* (S), No. 35
39   29   *Ibid.*, Nos. 24, 477
41   19   *Ibid.*, under *Primitz*
41   29   *Ibid.*, No. 201
44   5   *Ibid.*, Nos. 286, 303, 343, 508, 536

REFERENCES

PAGE LINE

93 12 BR, 105
93 16 Archivio stor. ital., XXIV (1876), 23
93 32 ova, II, 352-53; cf. Kolde, ZKG, II, 472-80
94 2 Kalkoff, F, 59
95 3 BR, 99
95 13 Dok (S), No. 10
96 11 BR, 99-110; Acta Aug. WA, II
96 13 BR, 100
96 21 BR, 99
96 25 W, XV, 208
96 27 Koestlin-Kawerau, 211
96 33 TR, 225, 409
96 35 II, 17; BR, 1, 242
97 22 II, 27-33
97 24 BR, I, 242; II, 17
97 27 TR, 5349, p. 78
97 31 BR, 105
98 3 BR, 110
98 24 II, 18-22 = ova, 1, 386-92
98 35 II, 39-40
99 4 BR, 124
99 30 W, XV, No. 247
100 2 BR, 110 = I, 245
100 8 BR, 114
100 11 TR, 5349, p. 79
100 15 BR, 112
100 22 BR, 119
100 24 BR, 118
100 27 BR, 116
100 28 TR, 1203
100 30 BR, 121, p. 271
101 24 BR, I, 250
101 28 BR, 124

CHAP. VI

102 11 II, 447
102 21 ova, II, 423-32
104 7 Kalkoff, F, 184-87
104 19 W, XV, No. 311
104 24 Smith, Corr., No. 108
104 28 BR, 205, cf. 196; TR, 156; TR, 3413
104 31 W, XV, Nos. 249-53
105 2 BR, 152
105 3 BR, 196
105 6 W, XIV, p. 445
105 9 BR, 140
105 12 RA, I, 824; BR, No. 122, p. 274

105 14 BR, 204
105 16 BR, 134, 136
105 19 BR, 140
105 26 Smith, Corr., I, 570
106 2 W, XV, Nos. 284, 297-99, 302, 306-8, 321-27
106 23 BR, 82, 249
106 30 TR, 1245
107 34 BR, 151
108 4 W, XVIII, No. 32
108 15 II, 180-239
108 29 W, XV, 393
108 32 BR, 167
109 6 BR, 141
109 12 BR, 161
111 24 W, XV, Nos. 392, 396
111 26 BR, I, 442, n. 9
111 28 W, XV, No. 396
112 1 Ibid., No. 392, cf. No. 396 and BR, I, 442, n. 9
112 13 W, XV, Nos. 390, 392
112 24 W, XV, Nos. 395, 393
112 27 BR, I, pp. 477, 498
112 30 BR, 187; W, XV, No. 396
112 31 Ibid., No. 392
112 34 BR, I, 428-30
113 19 W, XV, p. 1201; Smith, Corr., I, 262; Loescher, Analecta, III; 248
114 6 II, 400
114 15 II, 313-14
114 21 II, 316
114 35 Decret., pt. I, dist. 22, c.2; dist. 21, c.21
115 10 II, 265, 276, 279, 285; BR, I, p. 422; Koehler, LKG
115 19 II, 275
116 2 Ibid., 279, 287
116 3 W, XV, No. 392, p. 1207
117 1 II, 280-308
117 4 II, 400; BR, I, 471
117 5 II, 649; BR, I, 391
117 7 II, 427
117 8 BR, No. 192, p. 472
117 11 II, 282
117 17 W, XV, p. 1318
117 21 II, 283
117 24 II, 311
117 27 II, 406
117 33 II, 324
119 1 BR, I, 422
119 12 II, 404
119 18 W, XV, p. 1199

Page Line

119 30 *Ibid.*, p. 1215
119 32 *BR*, I, 451
120 1 *BR*, 185, 186
120 4 II, 702
120 5 *BR*, 254

Chap. VII

121 24 *BR*, 146
123 2 Farner, *Zwingli*, 315
123 5 *BR*, 213
123 21 *Eccius Dedolatus*
125 28 II, 449
125 30 *BR*, 163 = *EE*, 932
125 33 *BR*, 50
126 3 *Op.*, IV, 474
126 12 *Op.*, I, 870
126 25 *Op.*, VI, 64 D-E
126 6 *Ausg. Werke*, 205-6
126 15 Spengler, *Schutzrede*
128 5 *Op.*, IV, 459-60
128 28 *EE*, Nos. 939, 967, 1033, 1167
129 10 Benz
130 12 Panofsky, *Dürer*, I, 198-99
132 2 *Op.*, IV, 262-64
132 6 *Op.*, I, 167
133 6 I, 378-79
133 30 *BR*, 360
134 8 Schade, II, 1-59
134 17 *BR*, 281
134 21 *BR*, 298
134 24 *BR*, 287
135 2 *BR*, 310
135 5 *BR*, 323
135 16 *BR*, 282
135 28 *BR*, 368

Chap. VIII

137 4 VI, 497-573
137 8 *EE*, 1203
138 16 VI, 563-64
139 17 *W*, XV, No. 238, p. 640; cf. *BR*, 110, p. 237
139 35 Koehler, *ZL*, 50-52
140 12 Bornkamm, *LgW*, Chap. V
141 10 X, 3, 1
141 14 VI, 521
142 1 III, 304; Seeberg, I, 133-41
143 19 *ova*, IV, 172-85
143 28 VI, 181-95
144 2 Kolde, *ZKG*, II, 460-70
144 3 *BR*, 285
144 15 Kalkoff, *ZKG*, XXV, 589-91

Page Line

144 18 *Ibid.*, 593
144 21 Sanuto, *Diarii*, XXVIII, col. 549
145 9 *BR*, 122
145 11 Kalkoff, *ZKG*, XXV, 115, n. 2; Schubert, *Spengler*, 220, n. 2
145 12 *ova*, IV, 310-14 = Ferguson, *E Op.*, 322
147 6 *ova*, IV, 283
147 10 *ova*, IV, 312 = Ferguson, *E Op.*, 325
148 1 *ova*, IV, 269, 290, 293
148 21 *ova*, V, 10-12
148 28 Ps. 91:21, 24
148 34 *BR*, 295
149 15 VI, 347
149 23 VII, 645-46
150 13 *BR*, 333, p. 189

Chap. IX

151 9 *BR*, 310
151 24 *BR*, 332
156 5 Kalkoff, *ZKG*, XXV, 129-30
157 7 Balan, No. 3
157 14 *Ibid.*, No. 4
157 19 Schubert, *Spengler*, 241
157 26 *EE*, No. 1167, p. 409
157 35 Kalkoff, *Anfänge*
158 8 Schubert, *Spengler*, 232, 241
158 10 Wiedemann, *Eck*, 156-65
158 14 Schubert, *Vorgeschichte*, 21
158 16 *W*, XV, No. 466
158 20 *BR*, 340, 348, 351, 352
158 23 *W*, XV, No. 340
158 28 Wiedemann, *Eck*, 165
159 10 Kalkoff, *Anfänge*
160 1 Beatus Rhenanus, *BR*, No. 194; Pacquier, *Aléandre*, 172-73; cf. *AD*, 17; *RA*, II, 472
160 13 *Hutteni Op.*, III, 455-59
160 26 *BR*, 341
161 3 *W*, XV, No. 442, sec. 39-42
161 17 *BR*, 351
163 18 VI, 597-612
164 20 VII, 42-49
165 8 *Ibid.*, 125
165 18 *Ibid.*, 135
166 3 *Ibid.*, 183
166 7 *Ibid.*, 184-85; *BR*, 361; *W*, XV, No. 486

Page Line

166 13 VII, 161-82
166 21 W, XV, No. 519

Chap. X

167 16 RA, II, 90-94
168 5 AD, 48
168 28 Ep. 229, cf. Op. IV, 309-31; Ep. 233-34
169 1 Kalkoff, WR, 213, n. 3
169 7 AD, 182
169 14 RA, II, 471
169 19 Balan, Nos. 13, 32, 34, 52
169 31 Ferguson, E Op., 334-35; cf. 336-37, 352-61
170 6 AD, p. 92
170 10 Ep, 230
170 11 Ep, 247
170 15 W, XV, No. 526 and Balan, p. 18
170 24 BR, 349; WA, VI, 477-80
170 30 Spalatin, Ann., p. 29; Seckendorf, I, 126; RA, II, 464, n. 1
170 32 EE, 1166, p. 399
172 3 W, XV, 1585
172 9 RA, II, No. 61
172 35 Balan, No. 34, pp. 85-86
173 1 AD, p. 34
173 5 Balan, No. 35, p. 90
173 10 RA, II, No. 62
173 20 Ibid., No. 63
174 9 BR, 365
174 39 BR, 376
175 4 AD, p. 36
175 13 BR, 371, p. 254
175 26 AD, pp. 35-36
176 11 AD, pp. 30, 40, 55-57, 82
176 22 Hutten, Ep., 247, p. 63; Kalkoff, BDB, p. 6
176 25 AD, p. 56
177 2 Schade, II, 177
177 4 RA, II, 476, n. 3
177 14 AD, p. 169
178 5 RA, II, 496-505
178 12 RA, II, No. 68
178 15 AD, p. 73
178 23 RA, II, No. 69
178 28 Ibid., No. 72
178 33 Ibid., No. 74
179 2 AD, p. 101
179 5 RA, II, No. 73
179 14 BR, 389
179 18 BR, 391

Page Line

179 25 BR, 395, 396
179 28 BR, 395
180 4 Hutteni Op., II, 52-53; cf. AD, pp. 183, 198
180 23 RA, II, No. 66
181 9 RA, II, No. 78
181 11 Spalatin, Ann., p. 38; W. XV, No. 554
181 15 Op., II, 62, 55
181 19 W, XV, No. 557
181 24 AD, p. 170
183 4 RA, II, p. 851
183 17 RA, II, pp. 548-49, 574
183 27 Kalkoff, BDB, 52
183 32 Ibid., Note 112; RA, II, No. 209, p. 885
184 16 AD, p. 152
185 7 RA, II, pp. 551-55
185 24 VII, 836-38
185 33 RA, II, p. 555
186 6 AD, p. 153; RA, p. 558
186 9 Spalatin, Ann., 49-50
186 10 RA, II, p. 867
186 13 Spalatin, Ann., 50-51
186 33 RA, II, pp. 595-96
187 4 Ibid., II, p. 596, n. 3
188 2 Op., II, 61
188 3 AD, 158
188 9 AD, 160; RA, II, No. 84
188 29 RA, II, No. 86; pp. 617, 621
188 33 Ibid., No. 85, pp. 603, 610
188 35 RA, II, p. 631
189 5 BR, 404, p. 325
189 26 RA, II, No. 92
190 8 AD, pp. 221-24

Chap. XI

191 9 Dürer, Briefe, 121
192 17 Clemen, Beiträge, III, 10-15; Bainton, Dürer
192 24 Kalkoff, Anfänge, II, 22
192 27 Opera (Louvain), X, 166 C; EE IV, 599, and X, No. 2792
192 36 Dürer, Briefe, 119-22
193 23 BR, 408; TR, 5353
193 30 VIII, 211
193 32 TR, 6816, p. 209
194 1 VIII, 412, 483; XXXVI, 476
194 5 VIII, 139
194 12 I Kings 19:4
194 23 BR, 429
194 28 BR, 407
194 33 BR, 435

REFERENCES

Page Line

221 10 XIX, 154
221 36 *TR*, 4201
223 14 *TR*, 5015
223 32 XL, 1, 455
224 11 XXVII, 154
224 15 V, 550
224 19 IX, 610
224 34 XIX, 492
226 1 BR, 424
227 8 *Dok* (S), 672, 755; BR, 428, p. 383
227 18 *Bd*, I, 99
227 21 BR, 1593
227 27 *Bd*, I, 88
227 29 *Ibid.*, I, 90
227 31 *Ibid.*, I, 249
227 32 LVI, 304, 361
228 2 IV, 324, 364
228 10 LVI, 231
228 18 II, 496
228 26 *Bd*, II, 25
231 8 VII, 53, 59-64

Chap. XIV

233 11 *TR*, 2223
233 13 *TR*, 2123*b*
234 1 *TR*, 5360
234 5 VII, 575
234 12 LII, 399-400
234 18 XXXII, 292-94
234 24 *Bd*, II, 518, 528; *WA*, VII, 244
234 28 *TR*, 437
235 5 XXX, 2, 570-75
235 6 *TR*, 5252
237 26 XV, 321
238 23 II, 252
238 23 XVIII, 389
238 30 XXVIII, 525
238 32 BR, 365
239 12 XXIX, 355
239 13 XL, 1, 292
239 15 VI, 459
239 21 XLI, 747
239 35 II, 254-61
240 16 *Ibid.*, II, 261
241 2 XIX, 625-26
241 9 XLI, 746-47
241 12 XXVIII, 699
241 17 XVIII, 391
241 21 VI, 267
241 22 XVI, 474
242 17 XI, 268-69

243 25 *TR*, 433
243 29 XXVII, 515-17
243 30 VIII, 680
244 22 XI, 267
244 26 *TR*, 3263*b*
244 27 XIX, 657
244 32 Pauls, 69; LII, 189; XXXVII, 319
245 13 XXVIII, 360-61; Matthes, 143
245 20 *Bd*, I, 147
245 29 *Bd*, I, 555-56
246 2 *Bd*, I, 572

Chap. XV

249 1 N. Müller, *WB*, No. 25, pp. 62-63
249 2 Kalkoff, *Ablass*, 85
249 13 *Ibid.*, 115-16
249 20 BR, 558, 566
249 31 BR, 572, 586, 678, 748
249 35 BR, 648
250 3 BR, 799
250 13 Bainton, *Development*, 113-14
251 4 *W*, XV, No. 716
251 9 *Ibid.*, No. 717
251 14 Planitz, No. 121, p. 271
251 22 *Ibid.*, No. 153
252 4 *Ibid.*, No. 29
252 17 BR, 956
252 21 X, 2, 227
252 22 BR, 914
252 23 Smith, *Corr.*, No. 737
253 14 *Op.*, IX, 1215-48
254 20 XVIII, 719
255 14 *Ibid.*, 758-59
255 21 *Ibid.*, 784-85
255 26 BR, 626
255 29 *Op.*, X, 1251, 1257-58
256 15 BR, 726
256 30 XV, 392
258 24 *W*, XX, Nos. 6, 7; XV, 391-96
258 28 XV, 394
260 3 XLII, 157-58
261 30 XVII, 1, 361-62
262 23 XV, 199-200
263 2 *Ibid.*, 210-11
263 10 BR, 754
263 14 Boehmer-Kirn, No. 56
264 19 Brandt, *Muentzer*, 148-63
264 28 BR, 785

REFERENCES

CHAP. XVIII

303 29 *BR*, 1595
304   8 XXXV, 434-35
304 21 *TR*, 5494, pp. 190-91
305 23 Clemen, *Flugschriften*, IV, 278-80
306 11 *Ibid.*, II, 133-34
306 13 *Ibid.*, I, 69
306 16 *Ibid.*, II, 147
306 18 *Ibid.*, II, 142
309   2 *Ibid.*, I, 10-17
309   9 *Ibid.*, III, 201-3
309 24 *Ibid.*, III, 362-63
309 31 Berger, V, 260-61
310 19 Sachs, *Werke*, I, 8-24
310 27 Clemen, *Flugschriften*, II, 172; cf. Berger, II, 286
311   8 *BR*, 465
311 14 XIX, 75; Holl L, 360; Bainton, *Development*, 130-31
312 29 Cf. Clemen, *Flugschriften*, I, 53-54
313 19 Holl, I, 326-80
314   5 Berbig, *ARG*, III, 376
314   9 Winter, 301
314 20 *BR*, No. 1294, pp. 498-99
315 30 *RA*, III, p. 386; Planitz, *No.* 133
316   3 *RA*, III, No. 242
316   4 Planitz, Nos. 200, 206, 209; *RA*, III, p. 385
316 11 Planitz, No. 121, p, 273
316 16 *RA*, III, No. 84
316 23 *RA*, IV, No. 149
317   7 Friedensburg, 161-62
317 12 *Ibid.*, 188
318   7 *RA*, VII, pp. 1142-43
318 11 *Ibid.*, No. 72
318 15 *Ibid.*, No. 137, p. 1286
319   5 *BR*, 1496
320   2 Koehler, *Marburg*, 131
320 11 *Ibid.*, 139
322 11 Reu, *AC*, No. 13
323   8 *BR*, 1595
323 19 Schirrmacher, 55
324   5 *CR*, II, 107, 115
324 23 *BR*, No. 1611, p. 412
324 34 *BR*, 1621
325 30 XXX, 2, 397-412

CHAP. XIX

327   4 *TR*, 2771*a*
327 26 *BR*, 492
327 30 Reu, *Bible*, 160, 187
328   2 *BR*, 556
328 10 XXX, 2, 632-33
329   8 Cf. Schmidt
330 33 Grisar, *L Studien*, III; Schramm; *WA, Bibel* II, 625
331   4 XXX, 2, 632-33
331 27 *EA*, LXXIII, 115
331 29 *TR*, 3292*a*
331 33 VIII, 361
332   6 Cf. Fullerton
332 10 XXX, 2, 637
334   2 *Bibel*, VII, *ad loc.*
335 33 XXX, 2, 550
337 11 XXX, 1, 249
337 23 *Ibid.*, 126-27
339   6 *Ibid.*, 132
341 14 *TR*, 4441, 7034, 968; *Op. Lat.*, VII, 591, 554; *BR*, 1727
342 26 Buszin, *Music. Q.*, 95-96
343 38 L, 368-73
343 40 *TR*, 1300, 2362
344 10 *BR*, 1727
346   9 *Bd*, I, 539-40
346 11 Buszin, *Mus. Heritage*, 116
346 21 Koehler, "Lutherthum," *SVRG*, LI, 43
347 11 XXXV, 419-21; cf. 97-109

CHAP. XX

349   8 Cf. Kiessling
349 13 *TR*, 272
349 15 *Bd*, I, 555
350 17 *TR*, 2606*a-b*
350 35 LII, 774
352 22 *Bd*, I, No. 4
352 40 *Bd*, I, No. 28
355   7 X, 1, 62-63; XLI, 480; XVII, 2, 302; LII, 38; XVII, 2, 303; X, 1, 65-66; XXXII, 253-55; IX, 439-46
357 40 XIX, 185-251
358 35 XXXVIII, 360-62

CHAP. XXI

361   1 Reiter, II, 578
361 10 *BR*, 1126

PAGE LINE

361 20 *TR*, 1289, 1113; XXVII, 96
361 25 *TR*, 4777
361 27 *TR*, 199
362 27 *TR*, 1557
362 30 *TR*, 3558b
363 14 XVII, 2, 202
363 17 *TR*, 4329
363 18 *TR*, 590
363 21 *BR*, 1670
363 22 *TR*, 1089
363 24 *TR*, 4857
363 25 *TR*, 122, p. 52
363 27 *BR*, 1670
363 29 *TR*, 1349
363 31 *TR*, 833; cf. *BR*, 1670
363 32 *TR*, 194
364 1 Ratzeberger, 58
364 5 *TR*, 1557
364 9 XLVI, 210
364 26 *TR*, 1631
364 30 *TR*, 660
365 9 *TR*, 2047
365 18 Enders, XV, 172
365 21 *BR*, 429
365 28 XXVII, 64
367 3 XXI, 111
367 7 IX, 440-41
367 9 *BR*, 1675
367 11 XXIII, 133-34
367 14 Bühler, 100-101
367 16 Preuss, *ML Prophet*, 96-97
367 20 *TR*, 3588
367 32 XII, 459
368 1 XXVII, 482-84
368 2 XXXVII, 241

PAGE LINE

368 3 X, 1, 612-13
368 5 IX, 517-19
368 10 XVII, 2, 364-65
370 5 XLIII, 200-220
370 9 *TR*, 1032, 1033, 2754b
370 15 Stamge
370 28 XVII, 1, 67-68
370 30 V, 607
372 20 XXXV, 455-57

CHAP. XXII

373 14 XXX, 3, 279
375 11 Rockwell, *Doppelehe*
375 16 *RA*, VII, 1299, 1264
375 19 Wappler, *Kursachsen*, 21
375 25 Menius, *Wiedertäufer*, 307a
376 2 XXVI, 145-46
376 14 XXXI, 1, 208
376 18 *CR*, IV, 739-40
377 14 L, 6-14
377 23 *CR*, IV, 740
377 27 *TR*, 5232b
377 34 Wappler, *Kursachsen*, 41, 94
378 19 Menius, *Wiedertäufer*, 316b
379 8 *TR*, 2912a
379 11 XI, 314
379 16 XI, 336
379 29 LIII, 417-18
382 28 K. Müller, *Wiederstand*, and Waldeck
382 33 *Bd*, 1, 468
383 10 *BR*, 4158
383 15 Smith, *ML*, 416-22

SOURCES OF ILLUSTRATIONS

SOURCES OF ILLUSTRATIONS

INDEX

401

INDEX

Luther, Martin—cont'd

Luther, Martin—cont'd

INDEX

Netherlands. *See* Low Countries
New Testament, 125-26, 197, 226, 257,
   312, 327, 329, 331-32, 334, 336
Nimrod, 92
Ninety-Five Theses, 79-84, 87, 121
Nineveh, 355
Noah, 129, 172, 296, 334
Nonresistance, 135, 149, 212, 274, 381
Novitiate, 37
Nürnberg, 29, 87, 97, 109, 124, 127, 157,
   252, 287, 290, 310, 315, 317

Oaths, 267
Obelisks, 107
Occam, William, 122, 219
Oecolampadius, John, 319, 321
Old Testament, 62, 117, 232, 262, 326-
   27, 331, 334, 374
Ordination, 137-38
Orlamünde, 214, 258, 263
Osiander, Andreas, 321
Ovid, 190

Pacifism, 267. *See also* Nonresistance
Paduška, John, 119
Palatinate, 178, 187, 189, 251, 276
Palestine, 328, 379
Palm Sunday, 179
Pamphleteering, 305
Pantheon, 75, 330
Papacy
   antiquity, 98, 108, 114-15, 175
   infallibility, 89, 98, 126-27, 248
   primacy, 114-15, 164
Papacy at Rome, The, 136
Paradise, 32, 78, 296, 368
Paradox, 254
Paris, 95, 112, 143, 156, 197, 310
Pascal, Blaise, 385
Passion of Christ, 191, 330, 370
Pastor, Ludwig von, 75
Pater Noster, 38, 48, 50. *See also*
   Lord's Prayer
Patmos, 191, 193, 197
Paul, St., 48, 58, 60, 64, 75, 76, 87, 106,
   108, 124, 128, 143, 147, 164, 176,
   225, 232, 238, 254, 266, 298, 331-32,
   334, 349, 350, 381, 385
Peasants, 26, 86, 131-33, 186, 311, 339
Peasants' War, 265, 268-85, 287, 293,
   316
Pecca Fortiter, 225
Penance, 54, 57, 81, 86, 88, 102-3, 118,
   137, 143

Penitence, On, 121
Pentecost, 346, 350
Perfection, unattainable, 46, 227, 239,
   254
Persia, 217
Perugia, 306
Peter, Epistle of, 332
Peter, St., 29, 48, 56, 75-78, 80, 98,
   108, 114, 147, 162, 169, 172, 191,
   233, 270, 331, 349, 350
Peter's, St., basilica of, 48-49, 74-77,
   80, 132
Pfefferkorn, John, 123-24, 380
Pharaoh, 182, 185, 198, 259, 273
Pharisees, 143, 192
Philip of Hesse, 280, 316-20, 322-25,
   373-75, 382
Philosophy, 63, 219
Pilate, 48, 50, 89, 191-92, 245
Pilgrimages, 30, 48-49, 126-27, 155, 367
Pinturicchio, 49
Pirkheimer, Willibald, 124-25, 157, 181,
   252
Pius II, 147, 163
Political theory, 239-45, 380-82. *See
   also* Magistrate, Resistance, Non-
   resistance, Liberty, Revolution
Poor relief, 207, 210
Pope
   authority of, 89-90, 95-96, 102, 108,
      114, 126, 367
   contrasted with Christ, 155
   see also Papacy
Portuguese, 157
Prague, 119
Prayer, 57-58, 195, 206, 358
Preaching, 349-58, 383
Predestination, 115, 253-55. *See also*
   Free will
Prierias, Sylvester, 89, 91, 93, 121, 124,
   144, 145, 149
Priesthood of all believers, 137, 145,
   152-54, 248, 270
Protestants, 255, 257, 261-62, 286, 318,
   324-25, 375
Protestation at Speyer, 318
Prussia, 27, 301
Psalms, 60-62, 68, 197, 208, 267, 335,
   337, 345-46, 367
Pubelsberg, 27
Purgatory, 28, 47, 50, 71, 76, 78-83,
   88, 102, 104, 108, 117, 143, 176,
   368

Praise for *Devil's Peak*

'A fascinating portrayal . . . a black, assegai-wielding former freedom fighter who turns into a vigilante and goes on a killing spree; a high-class tart; and a policeman who drinks to drown the screaming that's waiting inside his head . . . gripping, shocking . . . Highly recommended.'   *Literary Review*

'With Deon Meyer you can't go wrong. He's a writer whose work I admire, wait for and then devour.'
                                                    Michael Connelly

'One of the sharpest and most perceptive thriller writers around . . . Think of Meyer in the way that you might have regarded a bottle of Cape red a dozen years ago – dark, strong with an unusual but beguilingly moreish taste'   *The Times*

'Meyer is a gifted writer . . . believable and disturbing'
                                                    Tangled Web

'Tough in-your-face crime writing that spares nothing in language, visceral scenes of blood and mayhem (for Meyer is adroit at choreographing descriptions of slaughter), and never wavers from the compelling pace of the story. It also has a mean line in humour that comes through in the snappy dialogue.'
                                                    Sunday Independent

'Deon Meyer, who writes in Afrikaans, portrays a world of terrifying uncertainty, in which those who fought for liberation from apartheid are having to come to terms with the knowledge that freedom is not enough to wipe out cruelty. A thoughtful and exciting novel'   *Times Literary Supplement*

Deon Meyer lives and works in Melkbosstrand on the South African West Coast with his wife and four children. Other than his family, Deon's big passions are motorcycling, music, reading, cooking and rugby. He has recently retired from his day job as a consultant on brand strategy for BMW Motorrad, and is now a full time author.

Deon Meyer's books have attracted worldwide critical acclaim and a growing international fanbase. Originally written in Afrikaans, they have now been translated into several languages, including English, French, Italian, Spanish, German, Dutch, Bulgarian, Czech, Danish and Norwegian.

Devil's Peak won South Africa's ATKV Prose Prize in 2004.

Also by Deon Meyer

Dead Before Dying
Dead at Daybreak
Heart of the Hunter

Devil's Peak

Deon Meyer

Translated by K L Seegers

HODDER

First published in Great Britain in 2007 by Hodder & Stoughton
An Hachette Livre UK company

First published in paperback in 2008

5

A CIP catalogue record for this title is available from the British Library.

ISBN 978 0 340 82266 1

Typeset in Plantin Light by Hewer Text UK Ltd, Edinburgh
Printed and bound by Clays Ltd, St Ives plc

Hodder & Stoughton policy is to use papers that are natural,
renewable and recyclable products and made from wood grown in
sustainable forests. The logging and manufacturing processes are expected
to conform to the environmental regulations of the country of origin.

Hodder & Stoughton Ltd
338 Euston Road
London NW1 3BH

www.hodder.co.uk

PART ONE
Christine

I

The moment before the clergyman folded back the carton flaps the world stood still and she saw everything with a greater clarity. The robust man in his middle years had a diamond-shaped birthmark on his cheek that looked like a distorted pale rose teardrop. His face was angular and strong, his thinning hair combed back, his hands massive and rough, like those of a boxer. The books behind him covered the whole wall in a mosaic of alternating colours. The late afternoon Free State sun threw a shaft of light onto the desktop, a magic sunbeam across the box.

She pressed her hands lightly against the coolness of her bare knees. Her hands were perspiring, her eyes searching for clues in the slightest shift of his expression, but she saw only calm, perhaps some suppressed, benign curiosity about the content of the carton. In the moment before he lifted the flaps, she tried to see herself as he saw her – evaluate the impression she was trying to create. The shops in town had been no help; she had to use what she had. Her hair was long, straight and clean, the multicoloured blouse sleeveless; a shade too tight, perhaps, for this occasion, for him? A white skirt that had shifted up to just above her knees as she sat down. Her legs were smooth and lovely. White sandals. Little gold buckles. Her toenails unpainted, of that she had made sure. Just a single ring, a thin gold band on her right hand. Her make-up was light, delicately downplaying the fullness of her mouth.

Nothing to betray her. Apart from her eyes and her voice.

He lifted the flaps, one after the other, and she realised she was sitting on the edge of the armchair, leaning forward. She wanted to lean back, but not now, she must wait for his reaction.

The last flap was folded back, the box open.

'*Liewe Genade*,' he said in Afrikaans and half rose to his feet. *Sweet Mercy.*

He looked at her, but he seemed not to see her and his attention returned to the contents of the box. He thrust one of his big hands in, took something out and held it up to the sun.

'Sweet mercy,' he repeated with his hands in front of him. His fingers felt for authenticity.

She sat motionless. She knew his reaction would determine everything. Her heart thumped, she could even hear it.

He replaced the object in the carton, retracted his hands, leaving the flaps open. He sat again, taking a deep breath as if he wanted to compose himself and then looked up at her. What was he thinking? What?

Then he pushed the carton to one side, as if he didn't want it to come between them.

'I saw you yesterday. In church.'

She nodded. She had been there – to take his measure. To see if she would be recognised. But it was impossible, since she had attracted so much attention anyway – strange young woman in a small town church. He preached well, with compassion, with love in his voice, not so dramatic and formal as the ministers of her youth. When she walked out of the church she was certain it was right to come here. But now she wasn't so sure . . . He seemed upset.

'I . . .' she said, her thoughts scrambling for the right words.

He leaned towards her. He needed an explanation; that she well understood. His arms and hands made a straight line on the edge of the desk, from elbow to interlinked fingers flat on the desk. He was wearing a formal shirt unbuttoned at the neck, light blue with a faint red stripe. His sleeves were rolled up, forearms hairy where the sun caught them. From outside came the sounds of a weekday afternoon in a small town – the Sotho people greeting one another across the breadth of the street, the municipal tractor accelerating duh-duh-duh up to the garage, the cicadas, the clanging beat of a hammer alternating with the mindless barking of two dogs.

'There's a lot I have to tell you,' she said, and her voice sounded small and lost.

At last he moved, his hands folded open.

'I hardly know where to start.'

'Begin at the beginning,' he said softly, and she was grateful for the empathy.

'The beginning,' she approved, voice gaining strength. Her fingers gathered the long blonde hair from where it hung over her shoulder and tossed it back with a rhythmic, practised motion.

2

It began for Thobela Mpayipheli late on a Saturday afternoon at a filling station in Cathcart.

Pakamile was seated beside him, eight years old, bored and tired. The long road from Amersfoort lay behind them, seven dreary hours of driving. When they turned in at the garage the child sighed. 'Still sixty kilometres?'

'Only sixty kilometres,' he said consolingly. 'Do you want a cold drink?'

'No thanks,' said the boy and lifted up the 500-ml Coca Cola bottle that had been lying at his feet. It was not yet empty.

Thobela stopped at the pumps and climbed out of the pick-up. There was no attendant in sight. He stretched his limbs, a big black man in jeans, red shirt and running shoes. He walked around his vehicle, checked that the motorbikes on the load bed were still firmly strapped down – Pakamile's little KX 65 and his big BMW. They had been learning to ride off-road that weekend, an official course through sand and gravel, water, hills, humps, gullies and valleys. He had seen the boy's self-confidence grow with every hour, the enthusiasm that glowed within him like an ember with every 'Look, Thobela, watch me!'

His son . . .

Where were the petrol attendants?

There was another car at the pumps, a white Polo – the engine idled, but there was no one in the car. Strange. He called out, 'Hello!' and saw movement in the building. They must be coming now.

He turned around to unlatch the pick-up bonnet, glancing at the western horizon where the sun was going down . . . soon it would be dark. Then he heard the first shot. It reverberated through the quiet of the early evening and he jumped in fright and dropped instinctively to his haunches. 'Pakamile!' he screamed. 'Get down!' But his last words were deafened by another shot, and another, and he saw them coming out of the door – two of them, pistols in hand, one carrying a white plastic bag, eyes wild. They spotted him, shot. Bullets slammed against the pump, against the pick-up.

He shouted, a guttural roar, leapt up, jerked open the pick-up door and dived in, trying to shield the boy from the bullets. He felt the little body shiver. 'Okay,' he said, and heard the shots and the lead whining over them. He heard one car door slam, then another and screeching tyres. He looked up – the Polo was moving towards the road. Another shot. The glass of an advertising display above him shattered and rained down on the pick-up. Then they were in the road, the Volkswagen's engine revving too high and he said, 'It's okay, okay,' and felt the wet on his hand and Pakamile had stopped shivering and he saw the blood on the child's body and he said: 'No, God, no.'

That is where it began for Thobela Mpayipheli.

He sat in the boy's room, on his bed. The document in his hand was his last remaining proof.

The house was as quiet as the grave, for the first time since he could remember. Two years ago Pakamile and he had pushed open the door and looked at the dusty interior, the empty rooms. Some of the light fittings were hanging askew from the ceiling, kitchen cupboard doors were broken or just ajar, but all they saw was potential, the possibilities of their new house overlooking the Cata River and the green fields of the farm in high summer. The boy had run through the house leaving footprints in the dust. 'This is my room, Thobela,' he had called down the passage. When he reached the master bedroom he had expressed his awe at the vast space in a long whistle. Because all he knew was a cramped four-room house in the Cape Flats.

That first night they slept on the big veranda. First they had watched the sun disappear behind the storm clouds and the twilight deepen over the yard, watched the shadows of the big trees near the gate blend with the darkness, and the stars magically open their silver eyes in the firmament. He and the boy, squeezed up against each other with their backs against the wall.

'This is a wonderful place, Thobela.'

There was a deep sense of comfort in Pakamile's sigh and Thobela was eternally relieved, because it was only a month since the boy's mother had died and he had not known how they would adjust to the change of environment and circumstance.

They spoke of the cattle they would buy, a milk cow or two, a few fowls ('. . . and a dog, Thobela, please, a big old dog'). A vegetable garden at the back door. A patch of lucerne down by the riverbank. They had dreamed their dreams that night until Pakamile's head had dropped against his shoulder and he had laid the boy down softly on the bedding on the floor. He had kissed him on the forehead and said, 'Good night, my son.'

Pakamile was not of his own blood. The son of the woman he had loved, the boy had become his own. Very quickly he had come to love the boy like his own flesh and blood, and in the months since they had moved here he had begun the long process of making it official – writing letters, filling in forms and being interviewed. Slow bureaucrats with strange agendas had to decide whether he was suitable to be a parent, when the whole world could see that the bond between them had become unbreakable. But, at last, after fourteen months, the registered documents had arrived; in the long-winded, clumsy language of state officialdom, these put the seal on his adoption.

And now these pages of yellow-white paper were all he had. These, and a heap of new ground under the pepper trees by the river. And the minister's words, meant to comfort: 'God has a purpose with everything.'

Lord, he missed the boy.

He could not accept that he would never hear that chuckling laugh again. Or the footsteps down the passage. Never slow, always in a rush, as if life were too short for walking. Or the boy calling his name from the front door, voice loaded with excitement over some new discovery. Impossible to accept that he would never feel Pakamile's arms around him again. That, more than anything – the contact, the absolute acceptance, the unconditional love.

It was his fault.

There was never an hour of the day or night that he did not relive the events at the garage with the fine-tooth comb of self-reproach. He should have realised, when he saw the empty Polo idling at the pumps. He should have reacted more swiftly when he heard the first shot, he should have thrown himself over the child then, he should have been a shield, he should have taken the bullet. He should. It was his fault.

The loss was like a heavy stone in him, an unbearable burden. What would he do now? How would he live? He could not even see tomorrow, neither the sense nor the possibility. The phone rang in the sitting room, but he did not want to get up – he wanted to stay here with Pakamile's things.

He moved sluggishly, feeling the emotion pressing against him. Why could he not weep? The telephone rang. Why would the grief not break out?

Inexplicably, he was standing with the instrument in his hand and the voice said: 'Mr Mpayipheli?' and he said: 'Yes.'

'We've got them, Mr Mpayipheli. We've caught them. We want you to come and identify them.'

Later he unlocked the safe and placed the document carefully on the topmost shelf. Then he reached for his firearms, three of them: Pakamile's airgun, the .22 and the hunting rifle. He took the longest one and walked to the kitchen.

As he cleaned it with methodical concentration he slowly became aware that guilt and loss were not all that lay within him.

'I wonder if he believed,' she said, the minister's full attention on her now. His eyes no longer strayed to the box.

'Unlike me.' The reference to herself was unplanned and she wondered for a moment why she said it. 'Maybe he didn't go to church or such, but he might have believed. And perhaps he could not understand why the Lord gave to him and then took away. First his wife, and then his child on the farm. He thought he was being punished. I wonder why that is? Why we all think that when something bad happens? I do too. It's weird. I just could never work out what I was being punished for.'

'As an unbeliever?' asked the minister.

She shrugged. 'Yes. Isn't it strange? It's like the guilt is here inside us. Sometimes I wonder if we are being punished for the things we are going to do in the future. Because my sins only came later, after I was punished.'

The minister shook his head and took a breath as if to answer, but she didn't want to be sidetracked now; didn't want to break the rhythm of her story.

They were out of reach. There were eight men behind the one-way glass, but he could only focus on the two for whom his hate burned. They were young and devil-may-care, their mouths stretched in the same 'so-what' smirks, their eyes staring a challenge at the window. For a moment he considered the possibility of saying he recognised none of them and then waiting outside the police station with the hunting rifle . . . But he wasn't prepared, hadn't studied the exits and streets outside. He lifted his finger like a rifle barrel and said to the superintendent: 'There they are, numbers three and five.' He did not recognise the sound of his own voice; they were the words of a stranger.

'You are sure?'

'Dead sure,' he said.

'Three and five?'

'Three and five.'

'That's what we thought.'

They asked him to sign a statement. Then there was nothing more he could do. He walked to his pick-up, unlocked the door and got in, conscious of the rifle behind the seat and the two men somewhere inside the building. He sat and wondered what the superintendent would do if he asked for a few moments alone with them, because he felt the compulsion to thrust a long blade into their hearts. His eyes lingered a moment on the front door of the police station and then he turned the key and drove slowly away.

3

The public prosecutor was a Xhosa woman and her office was filled with the pale yellow dossiers of her daily work. They were everywhere. The desk was overloaded and the heaps overflowed to the two tables and the floor, so they had to pick their way to the two chairs. She had a sombre quality and a vague absence, as if her attention was divided between the countless documents, as if the responsibility of her work was sometimes too heavy to bear.

She explained. She was the one who would lead the state prosecution. She had to prepare him as a witness. Together they must convince the judge that the accused were guilty.

That would be easy, he said.

It is never easy, she replied, and adjusted her large gold-rimmed spectacles with the tips of her thumb and index finger, as if they could never be wholly comfortable. She questioned him about the day of Pakamile's death, over and over, until she could see the event through his eyes. When they had finished, he asked her how the judge would punish them.

'If they are found guilty?'

'When they are found guilty,' he replied with assurance.

She adjusted her spectacles and said one could never predict these things. One of them, Khoza, had a previous conviction. But it was Ramphele's first offence. And he must remember that it was not their intent to murder the child.

'Not their intent?'

'They will attest that they never even saw the child. Only you.'

'What sentence will they get?'

'Ten years. Fifteen? I can't say for sure.'

For a long moment he just stared at her.

'That is the system,' she said with an exonerating shrug.

A day before the court case was to begin he drove his pick-up to Umtata because he needed to buy a couple of ties, a jacket and black shoes.

He stood in his new clothes before the long mirror. The shop assistant said, 'That looks *sharp*,' but he did not recognise himself in the reflection – the face was unfamiliar and the beard which had appeared on his cheeks since the boy's death grew thick and grey on the chin and cheeks. It made him look harmless, and wise, like a stalwart.

The eyes mesmerised him. Were they his? They reflected no light, as if they were empty and dead inside.

From the late afternoon he lay on his hotel bed, arms behind his head, motionless.

He remembered: Pakamile in the shed above the house milking a cow for the first time, all thumbs, in too much of a hurry. Frustrated that the teats would not respond to the manipulation of his small fingers. And then, at last, the thin white stream shooting off at an angle to spray the shed floor and the triumphant cry from the boy: 'Thobela! Look!'

The small figure in school uniform that waited every afternoon for him, socks at half-mast, shirt-tails hanging, the backpack disproportionately big. The joy every day when he drew up. If he came on the motorbike, Pakamile would first look around to see which of his friends was witness to this exotic event, this unique machine that only he had the right to ride home on.

Sometimes his friends slept over; four, five, six boys tailing Pakamile around the farmyard. 'My father and I planted all these vegetables.' 'This is my father's motorbike and this is mine.' 'My father planted all this lucerne himself, hey.' A Friday night . . . everyone in a Christmas bed in the sitting room, jammed in like sardines in a flat tin. The house had vibrated with life. The house was full. Full.

The emptiness of the room overwhelmed him. The silence, the contrast. A part of him asked the question: what now? He tried to banish it with memories, but still it echoed. He thought long about it, but he knew in an unformulated way that Miriam and Pakamile had been his life. And now there was nothing.

He got up once to relieve himself and drink water and went back to lie down. The air conditioner hissed and blew under the window. He stared at the ceiling, waited for the night to pass so the trial could begin.

The accused sat alongside each other: Khoza and Ramphele. They looked him in the eyes. Beside them the advocate for the defence stood up: an Indian, tall and athletically lean, flamboyant in a smart black suit and purple tie.

'Mr Mpayipheli, when the state prosecutor asked you what your profession was, you said you were a farmer.'

He did not answer, because it was not a question.

'Is that correct?' The Indian had a soothing voice, as intimate as if they were old friends.

'It is.'

'But that is not the whole truth, is it?'

'I don't know what . . .'

'How long have you been a so-called farmer, Mr Mpayipheli?'

'Two years.'

'And what was your profession before you began farming?'

The state prosecutor, the serious woman with the gold-rimmed spectacles, stood up. 'Objection, Your Honour. Mr Mpayipheli's work history is irrelevant to the case before the court.'

'Your Honour, the background of the witness is not only relevant to his reliability as a witness, but also to his behaviour at the filling station. The defence has serious doubts about Mr Mpayipheli's version of the events.'

'I shall allow you to continue,' said the judge, a middle-aged white man with a double chin and a red complexion. 'Answer the question, Mr Mpayipheli.'

'What was your profession before you went farming?' repeated the advocate.

'I was a gofer at a motorbike retailer.'

'For how long?'

'Two years.'

'And before that?'

His heart began to race. He knew he must not hesitate, nor look unsure.

'I was a bodyguard.'

'A bodyguard.'

'Yes.'

'Let us go one step further back, Mr Mpayipheli, before we return to your answer. What did you do before you, as you say, became a bodyguard?'

Where had the man obtained this information? 'I was a soldier.'

'A soldier.'

He did not answer. He felt hot in his suit and tie. He felt sweat trickle down his back.

The Indian shuffled documents on the table before him and came up with a few sheets of paper. He walked to the state prosecutor and gave her a copy. He repeated the process with the judge and placed one before Thobela.

'Mr Mpayipheli, would it be accurate to say you tend towards euphemism?'

'Objection, Your Honour, the defence is intimidating the witness and the direction of questioning is irrelevant.' She had glanced at the document and began to look uncomfortable. Her voice had reached a higher note.

'Overruled. Proceed.'

'Mr Mpayipheli, you and I can play evasion games all day but I have too much respect for this court to allow that. Let me help you. I have here a newspaper report' – he waved the document in the air – 'that states, and I quote: "Mpayipheli, a former Umkhonto We Sizwe soldier who received specialist training in Russia and the former East Germany, was connected until recently to a drugs syndicate on the Cape Flats . . ." End of quote. The article refers to a certain Thobela Mpayipheli who was wanted by the authorities two years ago in connection with the disappearance of, and I quote once more, "government intelligence of a sensitive nature".'

Just before the prosecutor leapt up, she glanced fiercely at Thobela, as if he had betrayed her. 'Your Honour, I must protest. The witness is not on trial here . . .'

'Mr Singh, are you going somewhere with this argument?'

'Absolutely, Your Honour. I ask for just a moment of the court's patience.'

'Proceed.'

'Is that what this newspaper article is referring to, Mr Mpayipheli?'

'Yes.'

'Excuse me, I can't hear you.'

'Yes.' Louder.

'Mr Mpayipheli, I put it to you that your version of the events at the filling station is just as evasive and euphemistic as your description of your background.'

'That is . . .'

'You are a highly trained military man, schooled in the military arts, urban terrorism and guerrilla warfare . . .'

'I object, Your Honour – that is not a question.'

'Overruled. Let the man finish, madam.'

She sat down, shaking her head, with a deep frown behind the gold-rimmed spectacles. 'As it pleases the court,' she said, but her tone said otherwise.

'And a "bodyguard" for the drug syndicate in the Cape for two years. A *bodyguard*. That is not what the newspapers say . . .'

The state prosecutor stood up, but the judge pre-empted her: 'Mr Singh, you are testing the patience of the court. If you wish to lead evidence, please await your turn.'

'My sincere apologies, Your Honour, but it is an affront to the principles of justice for a witness under oath to fabricate a story—'

'Mr Singh, spare me. What is your question?'

'As it pleases the court, Your Honour. Mr Mpayipheli, what was the specific purpose of your military training?'

'That was twenty years ago.'

'Answer the question, please.'

'I was trained in counter-espionage activities.'

'Did this include the use of firearms and explosives?'

'Yes.'

'Hand-to-hand combat?'

'Yes.'

'The handling of high-pressure situations?'

'Yes.'

'Elimination and escape.'

'Yes.'

'And at the filling station you say, and I quote: "I ducked behind the petrol pump," when you heard the shots?'

'The war was over ten years ago. I was not there to fight, I was there to fill up . . .'

'The war was not over for you ten years ago, Mr Mpayipheli. You took the war to the Cape Flats with your training in death and injury. Let us discuss your role as bodyguard . . .'

The prosecutor's voice was high and plaintive. 'Your Honour, I object in the strongest—'

At that moment Thobela saw the faces of the accused; they were laughing at him.

'Objection sustained. Mr Singh, that is enough. You have made your point. Do you have any specific questions about the events at the filling station?'

Singh's shoulders sagged, as if wounded. 'As it pleases the court, Your Honour, I have.'

'Then get on with it.'

'Mr Mpayipheli, did you forget that it was *you* who attacked the accused when they left the filling station?'

'I did not.'

'You did not forget?'

'Your Honour, the defence . . .'

'Mr Singh!'

'Your Honour, the accused . . . excuse me, the witness is evading the question.'

'No, Mr Singh, it is you who are leading the witness.'

'Very well. Mr Mpayipheli, you say you did not charge at the accused in a threatening manner?'

'I did not.'

'You did not have a wheel spanner or some tool . . .'

'I object, Your Honour, the witness has already answered the question.'

'Mr Singh . . .'

'I have no further questions for this liar, Your Honour . . .'

4

'I think he believed he could make things right. Anything,' she said in the twilit room. The sun had dropped behind the hills of the town and the light entering the room was softer. It made the telling easier, she thought, and wondered why.

'That is the thing that I admired most. That somebody stood up and did something that the rest of us were too afraid to do, even if we wanted to. I never had the guts. I was too scared to fight back. And then I read about him in the papers and I began to wonder: maybe I could also . . .'

She hesitated a fraction and then asked with bated breath: 'Do you know about Artemis, Reverend?'

He did not react at first, sitting motionless, tipped slightly forward, engrossed in the story she was telling. Then he blinked, his attention refocused.

'Artemis? Er, yes . . .' he said tentatively.

'The one the papers wrote about.'

'The papers . . .' He seemed embarrassed. 'Some things pass me by. Something new every week. I don't always keep up.'

She was relieved about that. There was an imperceptible shift in their roles – he the small-town minister, she the wordly-wise one, the one in the know. She slipped her foot out of its sandal and folded it under her, shifting to a more comfortable position in the chair. 'Let me tell you,' she said with more self-assurance.

He nodded.

'I was in trouble when I read about him for the first time. I was in the Cape. I was . . .' For a fraction of a second she hesitated and wondered if it would upset him. 'I was a call girl.'

*   *   *

At half-past eleven that night he was still awake on his hotel bed when someone knocked softly on his door, apologetically.

It was the public prosecutor, her eyes magnified behind the spectacles.

'Sorry,' she said, but she just looked tired.

'Come in.'

She hesitated a moment and he knew why: he was just in his shorts, his body glistening with perspiration. He turned around and picked up his T-shirt, motioning her to take the single arm-chair. He perched on the end of the bed.

She sat primly on the chair; her hands folded the dark material of her skirt over her plump legs. She had an officious air, as if she had come to speak of weighty things.

'What happened today in court?' he asked.

She shrugged.

'He wanted to blame *me*. The Indian.'

'He was doing his job. That's all.'

'His job?'

'He has to defend them.'

'With lies?'

'In law there are no lies, Mr Mpayipheli. Just different versions of the truth.'

He shook his head. 'There is only one truth.'

'You think so? And what one truth is there about you? The one where you are a farmer? A father? A freedom fighter? Or a drug dealer? A fugitive from the state?'

'That has nothing to do with Pakamile's death,' he said, anger creeping into his words.

'The moment Singh brought it up in court, it became part of his death, Mr Mpayipheli.'

Rage flooded over him, reliving the day of frustration: 'All that Mister, Mister, so polite, and objections and playing little legal games ... And those two sitting there and laughing.'

'That is why I have come,' she said. 'To tell you: they have escaped.'

He did not know how long he sat there, just staring at her.

'One of them overpowered a policeman. In the cells, when he brought him food. He had a weapon, a knife.'

'Overpowered,' he said, as if tasting the word.

'The police . . . They are short of manpower. Not everyone turned up on shift.'

'They both got away.'

'There are roadblocks. The station commander said they won't get far.'

The rage inside him took on another face that he did not wish her to see. 'Where would they go?'

She shrugged once more, as if she was beyond caring. 'Who knows?'

When he did not respond, she leaned forward in the chair. 'I wanted to tell you. You have the right to know.'

She stood up. He waited for her to pass him, then stood up and followed her to the door.

There was doubt in the minister's face. He had shifted his large body back and cocked his head sideways, as if waiting for her to qualify her statement, to complete the sentence with a punch line.

'You don't believe me.'

'I find it . . . unlikely.'

Somewhere she felt emotion. Gratitude? Relief? She did not mean to show it but her voice betrayed her. 'My professional name was Bibi.'

His voice was patient as he responded. 'I believe you. But I look at you and I listen to you and I can't help wondering why. Why was that necessary for you?'

This was the second time she had been asked that. Usually they asked 'How?' For them she had a story to fit expectations. She wanted to use it now – it lay on her tongue, rehearsed, ready.

She drew a breath to steady herself. 'I could tell you I was always a sex addict, a nymphomaniac,' she said with deliberation.

'But that is not the truth,' he said.

'No, Reverend, it is not.'

He nodded as if he approved of her answer. 'It's getting dark,' he said, standing up and switching on the standard lamp in the corner. 'Can I offer you something to drink? Coffee? Tea?'

'Tea would be lovely, thank you.' Did he need time to recover, she wondered?

'Excuse me a moment,' he said, and opened the door diagonally behind her.

She remained behind, alone, wondering what was the worst thing he had heard in this study. What small-town scandals? Teenage pregnancies? Affairs? Friday night domestics?

What made someone like him stay here? Perhaps he liked the status, because doctors and ministers were important people in the rural areas, she knew. Or was he running away like she was? As he had run off just now; as if there was a certain level of reality that became too much for him.

He came back, shutting the door behind him. 'My wife will bring the tea soon,' he said and sat down.

She did not know how to begin. 'Did I upset you?'

He pondered a while before he answered, as if he had to gather the words together. 'What upsets me is a world – a society – that allows someone like you to lose the way.'

'We all lose our way sometimes.'

'We don't all become sex workers,' he motioned towards her in a broad gesture, to include everything. 'Why was that necessary?'

'You are the second person to ask that in the past month or so.'

'Oh?'

'The other one was a detective in Cape Town.' She smiled as she recalled. 'Griessel. He had tousled hair. And soft eyes, but they looked right through you.'

'Did you tell him the truth?'

'I almost did.'

'Was he a . . . what do you call it?'

'A client?' She smiled.

'Yes.'

'No. He was . . . just . . . I don't know . . . lost?'

'I see,' said the minister.

There was a soft tap on the door and he had to get up to take the tea tray.

5

Detective Inspector Benny Griessel opened his eyes to his wife standing before him, shaking his shoulder with one hand and urgently whispering, 'Benny,' she said. 'Benny, please.'

He was lying on the sitting-room couch, that much he knew. He must have fallen asleep here. He smelt coffee; his head was thick and throbbing. One arm squashed under him was numb, circulation cut off by the weight of his body.

'Benny, we have to talk.'

He groaned and struggled to sit up.

'I brought you some coffee.'

He looked at her, at the deep lines on her face. She was still stooped over him.

'What time is it?' His words battled to connect with his vocal chords.

'It's five o'clock, Benny.' She sat next to him on the couch. 'Drink the coffee.'

He had to take it with his left hand. The mug was hot against his palm.

'It's early,' he said.

'I need to talk to you before the children wake up.'

The message borne on her tone penetrated his consciousness. He sat up straight and spilled the coffee on his clothes – he was still wearing yesterday's. 'What have I done?'

She pointed an index finger across the open-plan room. The bottle of Jack Daniels stood on the dining-room table beside his plate of untouched dinner. The ashtray was overflowing and a smashed glass lay in shards beside the overturned bar stools at the breakfast counter.

He took a gulp of coffee. It burned his mouth, but could not take the sick taste of the night away. 'I'm sorry,' he said.

'Sorry isn't good enough any more,' she said.

'Anna . . .'

'No, Benny, no more. I can't do this any more.' Her voice was without inflection.

'Jissis, Anna.' He reached a hand out to her, saw how it shook, the drunkenness still not expelled from his body. When he tried to put his hand on her shoulder, she moved away from his touch, and that's when he noticed the small swelling on her lip, already beginning to turn the colour of wine.

'It's over. Seventeen years. That's enough. It's more than anyone could ask.'

'Anna, I . . . it was the drink, you know I didn't mean it. Please, Anna, you know that's not *me*.'

'Your son helped you off that chair last night, Benny. Do you remember? Do you know what you said to him? Do you remember how you cursed and swore, until your eyes rolled back in your head? No, Benny, you can't – you can never remember. Do you know what he said to you, your son? When you were lying there with your mouth open and your stinking breath? Do you know?' Tears were close, but she suppressed them.

'What did he say?'

'He said he hates you.'

He absorbed that. 'And Carla?'

'Carla locked herself in her room.'

'I'll talk to them, Anna, I'll make it right. They know it's the work. They know I am not like that . . .'

'No, Benny.'

He heard the finality in her voice and his heart contracted. 'Anna, no.'

She would not look at him. Her finger traced the swelling on her lip and she walked away from him. 'That is what I tell them every time: it's the work. He's a good father, it's just his work, you must understand. But I don't believe it any more. *They* don't believe it any more . . . Because it *is* you, Benny. It is you. There are other policemen who go through the same things every day, but they don't get drunk. They don't curse and shout and break their stuff and hit their wives. It's finished now. Completely finished.'

'Anna, I will stop, you know I have before. I can. You know I can.'

'For six weeks? That is your record. Six weeks. My children need more than that. They deserve more than that. *I* deserve better than that.'

'*Our* children . . .'

'A drunk can't be a father.'

Self-pity washed over him. The fear. 'I can't help it, Anna. I can't help it, I am weak, I need you. Please, I need you all – I can't go on without you.'

'We don't need you any more, Benny.' She stood up and he saw the two suitcases on the floor behind her.

'You can't do that. This is my house.' Begging.

'Do you want us on the street? Because it is either you or us. You can choose, because we will no longer live under the same roof. You have six months, Benny – that is what we are giving you. Six months to choose between us and the booze. If you can stay dry you can come back, but this is your last chance. You can see the children on Sundays, if you want. You can knock on the door and if you smell of drink I will slam it in your face. If you are drunk you needn't bother to come back.'

'Anna . . .' He felt the tears welling up in him. She could not do this to him; she did not know how dreadfully hard it was.

'Spare me, Benny, I know all of your tricks. Shall I carry your suitcases outside, or will you take them yourself?'

'I need to shower, I must wash, I can't go out like this.'

'Then I will carry them myself,' she said, and took a suitcase in each hand.

There was an atmosphere of faint despair in the detective's office. Files lay about in untidy heaps, the meagre furniture was worn out and the outdated posters on the walls made hollow claims about crime prevention. A portrait of Mbeki in a narrow, cheap frame hung askew. The floor tiles were a colourless grey. A dysfunctional fan stood in one corner, dust accumulated on the metal grille in front of the blades.

The air was thick with the oppressive scent of failure.

Thobela sat on a steel chair with grey-blue upholstery and the foam protruding from one corner. The detective stood with his back to the wall. He was looking sideways out of the grimy window at the parking area. He had narrow, stooped shoulders and grey patches in his goatee.

'I pass it on to Criminal Intelligence at Provincial Headquarters. They put it on the national database. That's how it works.'

'A database for escapees?'

'You could say so.'

'How big would this database be?'

'Big.'

'And their names just sit there on a computer?'

The detective sighed. 'No, Mr Mpayipheli – the photos, criminal records, the names and addresses of families and contacts are part of the file. It is all sent along and distributed. We follow up what we can. Khoza has family in the Cape. Ramphele's mother lives here in Umtata. Someone will call on them . . .'

'Are you going to Cape Town?

'No. The police in the Cape will make enquiries.'

'What does that mean, "make enquiries"?'

'Someone will go and ask, Mr Mpayipheli, if Khoza's family has heard anything from him.'

'And they say "no" and then nothing happens?'

Another sigh, deeper this time. 'There are realities you and I cannot change.'

'That is what black people used to say about apartheid.'

'I think there is a difference here.'

'Just tell me, what are the chances? That you will catch them?'

The detective pushed away from the wall, slowly. He dragged out a chair in front of him and sat with his hands clasped. He talked slowly, like someone with a great weariness. 'I could tell you the chances are good, but you must understand me correctly. Khoza

has a previous conviction – he has done time: eighteen months for
burglary. Then the armed robbery at the garage, the shooting . . .
and now the escape. There is a pattern. A spiral. People like him
don't stop; their crimes just become more serious. And that's why
chances are good. I can't tell you we will catch them *now*. I can't tell
you *when* we will catch them. But we *will*, because they won't stay
out of trouble.'

'How long, do you think?'

'I couldn't say.'

'Guess.'

The detective shook his head. 'I don't know. Nine months? A
year?'

'I can't wait that long.'

'I am sorry for your loss, Mr Mpayipheli. I understand how you
feel. But you must remember, you are only one victim of many.
Look at all these files here. There is a victim in every one. And even
if you go and talk to the PC, it will make no difference.'

'The PC?'

'Provincial commissioner.'

'I don't want to talk to the provincial commissioner. I am talking
to *you*.'

'I have told you how it is.'

He gestured towards the document on the table and said softly:
'I want a copy of the file.'

The detective did not react immediately. A frown began to
crease his forehead, possibilities considered.

'It's not allowed.'

Thobela nodded his head in comprehension. 'How much?'

The eyes measured him, estimating an amount. The detective
straightened his shoulders. 'Five thousand.'

'That is too much,' he said, and he stood up and started for the
door.

'Three.'

'Five hundred.'

'It's my job on the line. Not for five hundred.'

'No one will ever know. Your job is safe. Seven-fifty.'

'A thousand,' he said hopefully.

Thobela turned around. 'A thousand. How long will it take to copy?'

'I will have to do it tonight. Come tomorrow.'

'No. Tonight.'

The detective looked at him, his eyes not quite so weary now. 'Why such a hurry?'

'Where can I meet you?'

The poverty here was dreadful. Shacks of planks and corrugated iron, a pervasive stink of decay and uncollected rubbish. Paralysing heat beat upwards from the dust.

Mrs Ramphele chased four children – two teenagers, two toddlers – out of the shack and invited him to sit down. It was tidy inside, clean but hot, so that the sweat stained his shirt in great circles. There were schoolbooks on a table and photos of children on the rickety cupboard.

She thought he was from the police and he did not disillusion her as she apologised for her son, saying he wasn't always like that; he was a good boy, misled by Khoza and how easily that could happen here, where no one had anything and there was no hope. Andrew had looked for work, had gone down to the Cape, he had finished standard eight and then said he couldn't let his mother struggle like this, he would finish school later. There was no work. Nothing: East London, Uitenhage, Port Elizabeth, Jeffreys Bay, Knysna, George, Mossel Bay, Cape Town . . . Too many people, too little work. Occasionally he sent a little money; she didn't know where it came from, but she hoped it wasn't stolen.

Did she know where Andrew would go now? Did he know people in the Cape?

Not that she knew.

Had he been here?

She looked him in the eye and said no, and he wondered how much of what she had said was the truth.

*   *   *

They had erected the gravestone. *Pakamile Nzululwazi. Son of Miriam Nzululwazi. Son of Thobela Mpayipheli. 1996–2004. Rest in Peace.*

A simple stone of granite and marble set in the green grass by the river. He leaned against the pepper tree and reflected that this was the child's favourite place. He used to watch him through the kitchen window and see the small body etched here, on his haunches, sometimes just staring at the brown water flowing slowly past. Sometimes he had a stick in his hand, scratching patterns and letters in the sand – and he would wonder what Pakamile was thinking about. The possibility that he was thinking of his mother gave him great pain, because it was not something he could fix, not a pain he could heal.

Occasionally he would try to talk about it, but carefully, because he did not want to open the old wound. So he would ask: 'How are things with you, Pakamile?', 'Is something worrying you?' or 'Are you happy?' And the boy would answer with his natural cheerfulness that things were good, he was so very happy, because he had him, Thobela, and the farm and the cattle and everything. But there was always the suspicion that that was not the whole truth, that the child kept a secret place in his head where he would visit his loss alone.

Eight years, during which a father had abandoned him, and he had lost a caring mother.

Surely that could not be the sum total of a person's life? Surely that could not be right? There must be a heaven, somewhere . . . He looked up at the blue sky and wondered. Was Miriam there among green rolling hills to welcome Pakamile? Would there be a place for Pakamile to play and friends and love? All races together, a great multitude, all with the same sense of justice? Waters beside which to rest. And God, a mighty black figure, kingly, with a full grey beard and wise eyes, who welcomed everyone to the Great Kraal with an embrace and gentle words, but who looked with great pain over the undulating landscape of green sweet veld at the broken Earth. Who shook his head, because no one did anything about it because they were all blind to His Purpose. He had not made them like *that*.

Slowly he walked up the slope to the homestead and stood again to look.

His land, as far as he could see.

He realised that he no longer wanted it. The farm had become useless to him. He had bought it for Miriam and Pakamile. It had been a symbol then, a dream and a new life – and now it was nothing but a millstone, a reminder of all the potential that no longer existed. What use was it to own ground, but have nothing?

6

From the second-storey flat in Mouille Point you could see the sea if you got the angle from the window right. The woman lay in the bedroom and Detective Inspector Benny Griessel stood in the living room looking at the photos on the piano when the man from Forensics and the scene photographer came in.

Forensics said: 'Jesus, Benny, you look like shit,' and he answered: 'Flattery will get you nowhere.'

'What have we got?'

'Woman in her forties. Strangled with the kettle cord. No forced entry.'

'That sounds familiar.'

Griessel nodded. 'Same MO.'

'The third one.'

'The third one,' Griessel confirmed.

'Fuck.' Because that meant there would be no fingerprints. The place would be wiped clean.

'But this one is not ripe yet,' said the photographer.

'That's because her char comes in on Saturdays. We only found the others on Monday.'

'So he's a Friday-night boy.'

'Looks like it.'

As they squeezed past him to the bedroom, Forensics sniffed theatrically and said, 'But something smells bad.' Then he said in a lower voice, familiarly, 'You ought to take a shower, Benny.'

'Do your fucking job.'

'I'm just saying,' he said, and went into the bedroom. Griessel heard the clips of their cases open and Forensics say to the photographer: 'These are the only girls I see naked nowadays. Corpses.'

'At least they don't talk back,' came the response.

A shower was not what Griessel needed. He needed a drink. Where could he go? Where would he sleep tonight? Where could he stash his bottle? When would he see his children again? How could he concentrate on this thing? There was a bottle store in Sea Point that opened in an hour.

Six months to choose between us and the booze.

How did she think he would manage it? By throwing him out? By putting yet more pressure on him? By rejecting him?

If you can stay dry you can come back, but this is your last chance.

He couldn't lose them, but he couldn't stay dry. He was fucked, totally fucked. Because if he didn't have them, he wouldn't be able to stop drinking – couldn't she understand that?

His cell phone rang.

'Griessel.'

'Another one, Benny?' Senior Superintendent Matt Joubert. His boss.

'It's the same MO,' he said.

'Any good news?'

'Not so far. He's clever, the fucker.'

'Keep me informed.'

'I will.'

'Benny?'

'Yes, Matt?'

'Are you okay?'

Silence. He could not lie to Joubert – they had too much history.

'Come and talk to me, Benny.'

'Later. Let me finish up here first.'

It dawned on him that Joubert knew something. Had Anna . . .

She was serious. This time she had even phoned Matt Joubert.

He rode the motorbike to Alice, to see the man who made weapons by hand. Like their ancestors used to.

The interior of the little building was gloomy; when his eyes had adjusted to the poor light, he looked through the assegais that were bundled in tins, shafts down, shiny blades pointing up.

'What do you do with all of these?'

'They are for the people with tradition,' said the greybeard, his hands busy shaping a shaft from a long sapling. The sandpaper rasped rhythmically up and down, up and down.

'Tradition,' he echoed.

'They are not many now. Not many.'

'Why do you make the long spears too?'

'They are also part of our history.'

He turned to the bundle with shorter shafts. His finger stroked the blades – he was looking for a certain form, a specific balance. He drew one out, tested it, replaced it and took another.

'What do you want to do with an assegai?' asked the old man.

He did not immediately reply, because his fingers had found the right one. It lay comfortable in his palm.

'I am going hunting,' he said. When he looked up there was great satisfaction in the eyes of the greybeard.

'When I was nine, my mother gave me a set of records for my birthday. A box of ten seven-inch singles and a book with pictures of princesses and good fairies. There were stories on them and every story had more than one ending – three or four each. I don't know exactly how it worked, but every time you listened to them, the needle would jump to one of the endings. A woman told the stories. In English. If the ending was unhappy I would play it again until it ended right.'

She wasn't sure why she had brought this up and the minister said: 'But life doesn't work that way?'

'No,' she said, 'life doesn't.'

He stirred his tea. She sat with her cup on her lap, both feet on the floor now, and the scene was like a play she was watching: the woman and the clergyman in his study, drinking tea out of fine white porcelain. So normal. She could have been one of his congregation: innocent, seeking guidance for her life. About a relationship perhaps? With some young farmer? He looked at her in a paternal way and she knew: he likes me, he thinks I'm okay.

'My father was in the army,' she said.

He sipped his tea to gauge the temperature.

'He was an officer. I was born in Upington; he was a captain then. My mother was a housewife at first. Later on she worked at the attorneys' office. Sometimes he was away on the Border for long stretches, but I only remember that vaguely, because I was still small. I am the oldest; my brother was born two years after me. Gerhard. Christine and Gerhard van Rooyen, the children of Captain *Rooies* and Mrs Martie van Rooyen of Upington. The *Rooies* was just because of his surname. It's an army thing; every other guy had a nickname. My father was good looking, with black hair and green eyes – I got my eyes from him. And my hair from my mother, so I expect to go grey early – blonde hair does that. There are photos from when they were married, when she also wore her hair long. But later she cut it in a bob. She said it was because of the heat, but I think it was because of my father.'

His eyes were on her face, her mouth. Was he listening, really hearing her? Did he see her as she was? Would he remember later, when she revealed her great fraud? She was quiet for a moment, lifting the cup to her lips, sipping, saying self-consciously: 'It will take a long time to tell you everything.'

'That is one thing we have lots of here,' he said calmly. 'There is lots of time.'

She gestured at the door. 'You have a family and I—'

'They know I am here and they know it's my work.'

'Perhaps I should come back tomorrow.'

'Tell your story, Christine,' he said softly. 'Get it off your chest.'

'Sure?'

'Absolutely.'

She looked down at her cup. It was half full. She lifted it, swallowed the lot in one go, replaced it on the saucer and put it down on the tray on the desk. She drew her leg under her again and folded her arms. 'I don't know where it went wrong,' she said. 'We were like everyone else. Maybe not quite, because my father was a soldier, and at school we were always the army kids. When the *Flossies* flew out, those aeroplanes to the border, the whole town knew about it – our fathers were going to fight the Communists. Then we were special. I liked that. But most of the time we were like all the others. Gerhard and I went to school and in the afternoon our mother was there and we did homework and played. Weekends we went shopping and barbequed and visited and went to church and every December we went down to Hartenbos and there was nothing odd about us. Nothing that I was aware of when I was six or eight or ten. My father was my hero. I remember his smell when he came home in the afternoon and hugged me. He called me his big girl. He had a uniform with shiny stars on the shoulders. And my mother . . .'

'Are they still living?' the minister asked suddenly.

'My father died,' she said. With finality, as if she would not elaborate further.

'And your mother?'

'It's a long time since I have seen her.'

'Oh?'

'She lives in Mossel Bay.'

He said nothing.

'She knows now. What kind of work I was doing.'

'But she didn't always know?'

'No.'

'How did she find out?'

She sighed. 'That is part of the story.'

'And you think she will reject you? Because now she knows?'

'Yes. No . . . I think she is on a guilt trip.'

'Because you became a prostitute?'

'Yes.'

'And is she to blame?'

She couldn't sit still any more. She stood up in a hurry, and walked over to the wall behind her to get more distance between them. Then she approached the back of the chair and gripped it.

'Maybe.'

'Oh?'

She dropped her head, letting her long hair cover her face. She stood like that, very still.

'She was beautiful,' she said at last, looking up and taking her hands off the chair-back. She moved to the right, towards the bookshelf, her eyes on the books, but she was not seeing them.

'They were in Durban on honeymoon. And the photos . . . She could have had any man. She had a figure. Her face . . . she was so lovely, so delicate. And she was laughing, on all the photos. Sometimes I believe that was the last time she laughed.'

She turned to the minister, leaning her shoulder against the bookshelf, one hand brushing the books, caressingly. 'It must have been hard for my mother when my father was away. She never complained. When she knew he was coming home, she would get the house in order, from one end to the other. Spring-cleaning, she called it. But never herself. Tidy, yes. Clean, but she used less and less make-up. Her clothes became looser, and more dull. She cut her hair short. You know how it is when you live with someone every day – you don't notice the gradual changes.'

She folded her arms again, embracing herself.

'The thing with the church . . . that must be where it started. He came back from the Border and said we were going to another church. Not the Dutch Reformed Church on the base any more; we would be going to a church in town, one that met in the primary school hall on Sundays. Clapping hands and falling down and conversions . . . Gerhard and I would have enjoyed it if our father hadn't been so serious about it. Suddenly we had family devotions at home every day and he prayed long prayers about the demons that were in us. He began to talk of leaving the army, so that he could go and do missionary work, and he walked around with the Bible all day, not the little soldier's Bible, a big one. It was a vicious circle, because the army was probably understanding at first, but later he began praying for God to drive the demons out of the colonel and the brigadier and said that God would open doors for him.'

She shook her head. 'It must have been hard for my mother, but she did nothing.'

She walked back to her chair. 'Not even when he started with me.'

7

He drove the pick-up to Cape Town, because the motorbike would be too conspicuous. His suitcase was beside him on the passenger seat. From Port Elizabeth to Knysna. He saw the mountains and the forests and wondered, as always, how it had looked a thousand years ago, when there were only Khoi and San and the elephants trumpeted in the dense bush. Beyond George the houses of the wealthy sat like fat ticks against the dunes, silently competing for a better sea view. Big houses, empty all year, to be filled perhaps for a month in December. He thought of Mrs Ramphele's corrugated iron shack on the sunburnt flats outside Umtata, five people in two rooms, and he knew the contrasts in this country were too great.

But they could never be great enough to justify the death of a child. He wondered if Khoza or Ramphele had passed this way; if they had driven this road.

Mossel Bay, past Swellendam and over the Breede river, then Caledon and eventually late in the afternoon he came over Sir Lowry's Pass. The Cape lay spread out far below and the sun shone in his eyes as it hung low over Table Mountain. He felt no joy of homecoming, because the memories this place brought lay heavy on him.

He drove as far as Parow. There was a little hotel on Voortrekker Road that he remembered, the New President, where people stayed who wanted to remain anonymous, regardless of colour or creed.

That is where he would begin.

Griessel stood in front of the Serious and Violent Crimes Unit building in Bishop Lavis and considered his options.

He could take the suitcase out of the boot and drag it past Mavis in Reception, around the corner and down the passage to one of the big bathrooms that remained after the old Police College became the new SVC offices. Then he could shower and brush his teeth and scrape off his stubble in the bleached mirror and put on clean clothes. But every fucking policeman in the Peninsula would know within half an hour that Benny Griessel had been turfed out of the house by his wife. That is the way it worked on the Force.

Or he could walk to his office just as he was, smelly and crumpled, and say he had worked through the night, but that story would only maintain the façade temporarily.

There was a bottle of Jack in his desk drawer and three packets of Clorets – two slugs for the nerves, two Clorets for the breath and he was as good as new. Jissis, to feel the thick brown liquid sliding down his throat, all the way to heaven. He slammed the boot shut. Fuck the shower; he knew what he needed.

He walked fast, suddenly light-hearted. Fuck you, Anna. She couldn't do this; he would see a fucking lawyer, one like Kemp who didn't take shit from man or beast. He was the fucking bread-winner, drunkard and all; how could she throw him out? He'd paid for that house, every table and chair. He greeted Mavis, turned the corner, up the stairs, feeling in his pocket for the key. His hand was shaking. He got the door open, closed it behind him, walked around the desk, opened the bottom drawer, lifted the criminal procedure handbook and felt the cold glass of the bottle under-neath. He took it out and unscrewed the cap. Time for a lubrica-tion, his oil light was burning red. He grinned at his own wit as the door opened and Matt Joubert stood there with an expression of disgust on his face.

'Benny.'

He stood transfixed, with the neck of the bottle fifteen centi-metres away from relief.

'Fuck it, Matt.'

Matt closed the door behind him. 'Put that shit down, Benny.'

He did not move, could not believe his bad luck. So fucking close.

'Benny!'

The bottle shook, like his whole body. 'I can't help it,' he said quietly. He could not look Joubert in the eyes. The senior superintendent came and stood next to him, took the bottle out of his hand. He let it go reluctantly.

'Give me the cap.'

Solemnly he handed it over.

'Sit, Benny.'

He sat down and Joubert banged the bottle down. He leaned his large body against the desk, legs straight and arms folded.

'What is going on with you?'

What was the use of answering?

'Now you are an abuser of women and a breakfast drinker?'

She had phoned Joubert. To kick him out was not enough – Anna had to humiliate him professionally too.

'Jissis,' he said with feeling.

'Jissis what, Benny?'

'Ah fuck, Matt, what is the use of talking? How does that help? I am a fuck-up. You know it and Anna knows it and I know it. What is there left to say? I'm sorry I'm alive?' He waited for some reaction, but none came. The silence hung in the room, until he had to know whether he would find some sympathy. He looked up carefully to see his commander's expressionless face. Slowly Joubert narrowed his eyes and a red glow suffused his face. Griessel knew his boss was the hell-in and he retreated. Joubert grabbed him without speaking, jerked him out of the chair by his neck and arm and shoved him towards the door.

'Matt,' he said, 'jissis, what now?' He felt the considerable power of the grip.

'Shut up, Benny,' hissed Joubert, and steered him down the stairs, the footfalls loud on the bare surface. Past Mavis and through the entrance hall, Joubert's hand hard between his shoulders. Then they were outside in the bright sunlight. Never had Joubert been rough with him before. Their shoes crunched over the parking area gravel to the senior superintendent's car. He said 'Matt' again because he could feel pressure in his guts. This mood had never been directed at him before. Joubert did not respond. He jerked open the car door, his big hand pressing the back of Griessel's neck, shoved him in and slammed the door.

Joubert climbed in at the driver's side and turned the key. They shot off with screeching tyres and this noise seemed to release a flood of anger inside Joubert. 'A martyr,' he spat out with total disgust. 'I catch you with a fucking bottle in your hand and that is the best you can do? Act the martyr? You drink and hit women and all I see is self-pity. Benny, Jesus Christ, that's not good enough. In fourteen years, the fourteen fucking years I have worked with you, I have never seen a person so completely fuck-up his life without any help from outside. You should have been a bloody director, but where are you now, Benny? Forty-three and you're an inspector – with a thirst as big as the Sahara. And you hit your wife and shrug your shoulders and say, "I can't help it, Matt." You fucking hit your wife? Where does that come from? Since when?' Joubert's hands were communicating too and spit sprayed against the windscreen while the engine screamed at high revolutions. 'You're sorry you're alive?'

They drove towards Voortrekker Road. Griessel stared ahead. He felt the Jack in his hand again, the desire inside.

When it was quiet he said: 'It was the first time, last night.'

'The first time? What kind of a fucking excuse is that? Does that make it all right? You are a policeman, Benny. You know that's no fucking argument. And you're lying. She says it has been threatening for months. Three weeks ago you shoved her around, but you were too drunk to do it properly. And the children, Benny? What are you doing to them? Your two children who have to see their drunkard of a father come home pissed out of his skull and assault their mother? I should lock you up with the scum, she should lay a fucking charge against you, but all that will achieve is more damage to your children. And what do you do? She throws you out and you run to a bottle. Just booze, Benny, that's all you think about. And yourself. What the fuck is going on inside your head? What has happened to your brains?'

For an instant he wanted to respond, to scream: 'I don't know, I don't know, I don't want to be like this, I don't know how I got here, leave me alone!' Because he was familiar with these questions, and he knew the answers – it was all pointless, it made no difference. He said nothing.

In Voortrekker Road the traffic was heavy, the traffic lights red. Joubert gave the steering wheel a slap of frustration. Griessel wondered where they were going. To the Sanatorium? It wouldn't be the first time Joubert had dropped him off there.

The senior superintendent blew out a long breath. 'Do you know what I think about, Benny? The whole time.' His voice had mellowed now. 'Of the man who was my friend. The little sergeant who came here from Parow, green and full of go. The one who showed the whole bunch of arrogant detectives at Murder and Robbery how to do police work. The little guy from Parow – where is he, where did he go? The one who laughed and had a clever answer for everything. Who was a legend. Fuck, Benny, you were good; you had everything. You had instinct and respect. You had a future. But you killed it. Drank it up and pissed it away.'

Silence.

'Forty-three,' said Joubert, and he seemed to grow angry all over again. He wove through the cars ahead. Another red light. 'And still you are a bloody child.'

Then only silence reigned in the car. Griessel no longer looked where they were going; he was thinking of the bottle that had been so close to his mouth. Nobody would understand; you had to have been there where he was. You had to know the need. In the old days Joubert had also been a drinker, partied hard, but he had never been to *this* place. He didn't know and that's why he didn't understand. When he looked up again they were in Bellville, Carl Cronjé Street.

Joubert turned off. He was driving more calmly now. There was a park, trees and grass and a few benches. He pulled up. 'Come, Benny,' he said and got out.

What were they doing here? Slowly he opened the door.

Joubert was striding ahead. Where were they going – was he going to beat him up behind the trees? How would that help? The traffic on the N1 above droned and hissed, but no one would see a thing. Reluctantly he followed.

Joubert stopped between the trees and pointed a finger. When Griessel reached him he saw the figure on the ground.

'Do you know who that is, Benny?'

Under a heap of newspapers and cartons and an unbelievably grimy blanket a figure moved when it heard the voice. The dirty face turned upward, a lot of beard and hair and two little blue eyes, sunken in their sockets.

'Do you know him?'

'It's Swart Piet,' said Griessel.

'Hey,' said Swart Piet.

'No,' said Joubert. 'Meet Benny Griessel.'

'You gonna hit me?' the man asked. A Shoprite supermarket trolley stood parked behind his nest. There was a broken vacuum cleaner in it.

'No,' said Joubert.

Swart Piet looked askance at the big man in front of him. 'Do I know you?'

'This is you, Benny. In six months. In a year.'

The man extended a cupped hand to them. 'Have you got ten rand?'

'For what?'

'Bread.'

'The liquid version,' said Joubert.

'You must be psychic,' said the man, and laughed with a toothless cackle.

'Where are your wife and children, Swart Piet?'

'Long time ago. Just a rand? Or five?'

'Tell him, Piet. Tell him what work you used to do.'

'Brain surgeon. What does it matter?'

'Is this what you want?' Joubert looked at Griessel. 'Is this what you want to be?'

Griessel had nothing to say. He only saw Swart Piet's hand, a dirty claw.

Joubert turned around and headed for the car.

'Hey,' said the man. 'What's his case?'

Griessel looked at Joubert's back as he walked away. He wasn't going to hit him. All the way out here for a childish lesson in morality. For a moment he loved the big man. Then he grasped something else, turned back and asked: 'Were you a policeman?'

'Do I look like a fool to you?'

'What were you?'

'A health inspector in Milnerton.'

'A health inspector?'

'Help a hungry man, pal. Two rand.'

'A health inspector,' said Griessel. He felt anger ignite inside him.

'Oh hell,' said Swart Piet. 'Are you the guy from Saddles steakhouse?'

Griessel spun around and set off after Joubert. 'He was a health inspector,' he shouted.

'Okay, one rand, my friend. A rand between friends?'

The senior superintendent was already behind the steering wheel.

Griessel was running now. 'You can't do that,' he shouted. Right up to the window. 'You want to compare me with a fucking health inspector?'

'No. I'm comparing you with a fuck-up who can't stop drinking.'

'Did you ask him why he drinks, Matt? Did you ask him?'

'It makes no difference to him any more.'

'Fuck you,' said Griessel, the weariness and the thirst and the humiliation working together. 'I won't be compared with the cockroach patrol. How many bodies has he had to turn over? How many? Tell me. How many child victims? How many women and old ladies beaten to death for a cell phone or a twenty-rand ring? You want the old Benny? Are you looking for the fucker from Parow who was scared of nothing? I'm looking for him too. Every day, every morning when I get up, I look for him. Because at least he knew he was on the right side. He thought he could make a difference. He believed that if he worked long enough and hard enough, we would win, some time or other, to hell with rank and to hell with promotion; justice would triumph and that is all that mattered because we are the white hats. The guy from Parow is dead, Matt. Dead as a doornail. And why? What happened? What's happening now? We are outnumbered. We aren't winning; we are losing. There are more and more of them and there are less of us. What's the use? What help is all the overtime and the hardship? Are we rewarded? Are we thanked? The harder we work, the more we get shat upon. Look here. This is a white skin. What does it mean? Twenty-six years in the Force and it means fuck-all. It's not the booze – I'm not stuck in the rank of inspector because of the booze. You know that. It's affirmative action. Gave my whole fucking life, took all that shit and along came affirmative action. Ten years now. Did I quit, like De Kok and Rens and Jan Broekman? Look at them now, security companies and making money hand over fist and driving BMWs and going home every day at five o'clock. And where am I? A hundred open cases and my wife kicks me out and I am an alcoholic . . . But I am still fucking *here*, Matt. I didn't fucking quit.'

Then all his fuel was burnt and he leaned against the car, his head on his chest.

'I am still fucking here.'

'Hey!' shouted Swart Piet from the trees.

'Benny,' said Joubert softly.

He looked up slowly. 'What?'

'Let's go.'

'Hey!'

As he walked around to the other door, the man's voice carried clear and shrill: 'Hey, you! Fuck you!'

8

'Your father abused you,' said the minister with certainty.

'No,' she said. 'Lots of call girls say that. The stepfather messed with me. Or the mother's boyfriend. Or the father. I can't say that. That was not his problem.'

She checked for disappointment in his face but there was none to see.

'Do you know what I would wish for if I had only one wish? To know what happened to him. I wonder about that a lot. What did he see to make him change? I know it happened on the Border. I know more or less which year, I worked it out. Somewhere in South West Africa or Angola. But what?

'If only I could remember more of how he was before. But I can't. I only remember the bad times. I think he was always a serious man. And quiet. He must have . . . They didn't all come back from the Border like that, so he must have been a certain kind of person. He must have had the . . . what is the word?'

'Tendency?'

'Yes. He must have had the tendency.'

She searched for something for her hands to do. She leaned forward and took the sugar spoon out of the white porcelain pot. It had a municipal coat of arms on the end of the curved handle. She rubbed the metal with the cushion of her thumb, feeling the indentations.

'The school held a fête every year. On a Friday in October. In the afternoon there were *Boeresport* games and in the evening there were stalls. Tombola and target shooting. *Braaivleis*. Everyone would go, the whole town. After the games you would go home and dress up nicely – for the evening. I was fourteen. I borrowed some make-up from Lenie Heysteck and I bought my first pair of jeans with my savings. I had a sky-blue blouse on and my hair was long and I think I looked pretty. I sat in front of the mirror in my room that evening, putting on mascara and eyeshadow to match my blouse, and my lips were red. Maybe I used too much make-up, because I was still stupid, but I felt so pretty. That is something men don't understand. Feeling pretty.

'What if I had taken my black handbag, walked into the sitting room and he had said, "You look beautiful, Christine." What if he had stood up, taken my hand and said, "May I have this dance, Princess?"'

She pressed the curve of the sugar spoon against her mouth. She felt the old and familiar emotion.

'That is not what happened,' said the minister.

'No,' she said. 'That is not what happened.'

Thobela had memorised the address of Khoza's brother in Khayelitsha, but he didn't drive there directly. On the spur of the moment he left his original route two off ramps west of the airport and drove into Guguletu. He went looking for the little house he had lived in with Miriam and Pakamile. He parked across the street and switched off the engine.

The little garden that he and the boy had nurtured with so much care and effort and water in the sand of the Cape Flats was faded in the late summer. There were different curtains in the windows of the front room.

He and Miriam had slept in that room.

Down the street, childish voices shrieked. He looked and saw boys playing soccer, shirt-tails hanging out, socks around their ankles. Again, he remembered how Pakamile used to wait for him every afternoon on that street corner from about half-past five. Thobela used to ride a Honda Benly, one of those indestructible little motorbikes that made him look like a daddy-long-legs on it, and the boy's face would light up when he came around the corner and then he would run, racing the motorbike the last hundred metres to their gate.

Always so happy to see him, so hungry to talk and keen to work in the front garden with its sunflowers, in the back vegetable garden full of runner beans, white pumpkins and plump red tomatoes.

He reached a hand out slowly to turn the key, reluctant to let go of the memories.

Why had everything been taken from him?

Then he drove away, back to the N2, and past the airport. He took the off ramp and turned right and Khayelitsha surrounded him – traffic and people, small buildings, houses, sand and smells and sounds, huge adverts for Castle and Coke and Toyota, hand-painted signboards for home industries, hairdressers and panel beaters, fresh vegetable stalls alongside the road, dogs and cows. A city apart from the city, spread out across the dune lands.

He chose his route with care, referring to the map he had studied, because it was easy to get lost here: the road signs few, the streets sometimes broad, sometimes impossibly narrow. He stopped in front of a house, a brick building in the centre of the plot. Building materials lay about, an extra room had been erected to window height, an old Mazda 323 stood on blocks, half covered by a tarpaulin.

He got out, approached the front door and knocked. Music was playing inside, American rap. He knocked again, harder, and the door opened. A young girl, seventeen or eighteen, in T-shirt and jeans. 'Yes?'

'Is this the home of Lukas Khoza?'

'He's not here.'

'I have a message for John.'

Her eyes narrowed. 'What sort of message?'

'Work.'

'John is not here.'

'That's a pity,' he said, 'he would have liked the job.' He turned to go, then stopped. 'Will you let him know?'

'If I see him. Who are you?'

'Tell him the guy who gives good work tips was here. He will know.' He turned away again, as if he had lost interest.

'John hasn't been here for ages. I don't even know where he is.'

He sauntered towards the pick-up and said with a shrug, 'Then I will give the job to someone else.'

'Wait. Maybe my father will know.'

'Luke? Is he here?'

'He's at work. In Maitland. At the abattoir.'

'Maybe I will go past there. Thank you.'

She did not say goodbye. She stood in the doorway, hip against the doorframe, and watched him. As he slipped in behind the wheel he wondered whether she spoke the truth.

She told the minister about the evening her father called her a whore. How he stood over her in the bathroom and made her scrub off the make-up with a face cloth and soap and water. She wept as he lectured her and said not in *his* house. There would be no whoring in *his* house. That was the night it began. When the thing happened inside her. As she recalled the tirade, she was aware of what was going on between her and the minister, because it was familiar territory. She was explaining The Reason and he wanted to hear it. They. Men looked at her, after she had done her job, after she had opened her body to them with gentle hands and caressing words and they wanted to hear her story, her tragic tale. It was a primitive thing. They wanted her really to be good. The whore with the golden heart. The whore who was so nearly an ordinary girl. The minister had it too – he stared intently at her, so ready to empathise with her. But at least with him, the other thing was absent. Her clients, almost without exception, wanted to know if it was also a sex thing – really good, but also horny. Their fantasy of the nympho myth. She was aware of all these things as she sketched her story.

'I've thought about it so much, because that is where it all began. That night. Even now, when I think about it, there is all this anger. I just wanted to look nice. For myself. For my father. For my friends. He didn't want to see that, just all this other stuff, this evil. And then the religion thing just got worse. He forbade us to dance or go to movies and sleep over at friends and visit. He smothered us.'

The minister shook his head as if to say: 'The things parents do.'

'I can't get a grip on it. Gerhard, my brother, did nothing. We had the same parents and the same house and everything, but he did nothing. He just grew quiet and read books in his room, escaped into his stories and into his head. And me? I went looking for trouble. I wanted to become exactly what my father was afraid of. Why? Why was I built like that? Why was I made like this?'

The minister watched while she talked, watched her hands and eyes, the expressions that flitted in rapid succession across her face. He observed her mannerisms, the hair she used with such expertise, the fingers that punctuated her words with tiny movements and the limbs that spoke in an unbroken and sometimes deliberate body language. He placed it alongside the words and the content, the hurt and the sincerity and the obvious intelligence, and he learned something about her: she was enjoying this. On some level, probably unconscious, she enjoyed the limelight. As if, regardless of the trash that had been dumped on it, somewhere her psyche sheltered unscathed.

At twelve o'clock, hunger pangs drew Griessel's attention away from the murder file he had been buried in. That was when he remembered that today there would be no sandwich, no lunch parcel neatly wrapped in clingfilm.

He looked up from the paperwork and the room loomed suddenly large around him. What was he going to do? How would he manage?

Thobela made an error of judgement with Lukas Khoza. He found him at the abattoir, in a blood-spattered plastic apron, busy spraying away the blood from the off-white floor tiles of the slaughterhouse floor with a fat red hosepipe. They walked outside so Khoza could have a smoke break.

Thobela said he was looking for his brother, John, because he had a job for him.

'What sort of work?'

'You know, work.'

Khoza eyed him in distaste. 'No, I don't know and I don't want to know. My brother is trash and if you are his kind, so are you.' He stood, legs apart in a challenging stance, cigarette in hand, between the abattoir building and the stock pens. Large pink pigs milled restlessly behind the steel gates, as if they sensed danger.

'You don't even know what kind of job I am talking about,' said Thobela, aware that he had chosen the wrong approach, that he had been guilty of a generalisation.

'Probably the usual work he does. Robbery. Theft. He will break our mother's heart.'

'Not this time.'

'You lie.'

'No lie. I swear. I don't want him for a criminal purpose,' he said with spirit.

'I don't know where he is.' Khoza crushed the butt angrily under the thick sole of his white gumboots and headed for the door behind him.

'Is there someone else who might know?'

Khoza halted, less antagonistic. 'Maybe.'

Thobela waited.

For a long time Khoza hesitated. 'The Yellow Rose,' he said, and opened the door. A high scream, almost human, rang out from inside. Behind Thobela the pigs surged urgently and pressed against the bars.

9

Thobela drove to the Waterfront, deliberately choosing the road that ran along the mountain so that he had a view of the sea and the harbour. He needed that – space and beauty. The role he had played had disturbed him and he couldn't understand why. Impersonation was nothing new to him. In his days in Europe it had been part of his life. The East Germans had coached him in it down to the finest detail. Living the Lie was his way of life for nearly a decade; the means justified by the goal of Liberty, of Struggle.

Had he changed this much?

He came around the bulging thigh of the mountain and a vista opened up below: ships and cranes, wide blue water, city buildings and freeways, and the coastline curving gracefully away to Blouberg. He wanted to turn to Pakamile and say: 'Look at that, that is the most beautiful city in the world,' and see his son gaze in wonder at all this.

That is the difference, he thought. It felt as though the child was still with him, all around him.

Before Pakamile, before Miriam, he had been alone; he was the only judge of his actions and the only one affected by them. But the boy had moved his boundaries and widened his world so that everything he said and did had other implications. Lying to Lukas Khoza now made him as uncomfortable as if he had been explaining himself to Pakamile. Like the day they went walking in the hills of the farm and he wanted to teach his son to use the rifle with greater responsibility, a piece of equipment to treat with care.

The rifle had awakened the hunter in the boy. As they walked he pointed the unloaded rifle at birds, stones and trees, made shooting noises with his mouth. His thoughts went full circle until he asked: 'You were a soldier, Thobela?'

'Yes.'

'Did you shoot people?' Asked without any macabre fascination: that is how boys are.

How did you answer that? How did you explain to a child how you lay in ambush with a sniper's rifle in Munich, aiming at the enemy of your ally; how you pulled the trigger and saw the blood and brains spatter against the bright blue wall; how you slunk away like a thief in the night, like a coward. That was *your* war, *your* heroic deed.

How did you describe to a child the strange, lost world you lived in – explain about apartheid and oppression and revolution and unrest? About East and West, walls and strange alliances?

He sat down with his back to a rock and he tried. At the end he said you must only take up a weapon against injustice; you must only point it at people as a very last resort. When all other forms of defence and persuasion were exhausted.

As now.

That is what he would like to tell Pakamile now. The end justifies the means. He could not allow the injustice of his murder to go unpunished; he could not meekly accept it. In a country where the System had failed them, it was now the last resort, even if this world was just as hard to explain, just as complicated to understand. Somebody had to take a stand. Somebody had to say, 'This far, and no further.'

That is what he had tried to teach the boy. That is what he owed his son.

He knocked on doors the whole afternoon, and by four o'clock Detective Inspector Benny Griessel knew the victim was forty-six-year-old Josephine Mary McAllister, divorced in 1994, dependable, unremarkable administrative assistant at Benson Exports in Waterkant Street. She was a member of the New Gospel Church in Sea Point, a lonely woman whose former husband lived in Pietermaritzburg and whose two children worked in London. He knew she was a member of the public library, favouring the books of Barbara Cartland and Wilbur Smith, owned a 1999 Toyota Corolla, had R18,762.80 in a current account at Nedbank, owed R6,456.70 on her credit card, and on the day of her death had booked a plane ticket to Heathrow, apparently planning to visit her children.

He also had, as with the previous two murders, not a single significant clue.

When he dragged his cases across the threshold of her apartment he understood the risk in what he was doing, but he told himself he had no choice. Where the hell should he go? To a hotel, where alcohol was one finger on the telephone away? Forensics had already been through here and there was no other key but the one in his pocket.

Josephine Mary McAllister's flat had no shower, only a bath. He ran it half full and lay in the steaming water, watching his heart sending delicate ripples across the surface with each rhythmic beat.

The broad connection between McAllister, Jansen and Rosen was elementary. All middle-aged, living alone in Green Point, Mouille Point. No forced entry. Each strangled with an electric cord from the victim's kitchen. How did the perpetrator pick his victims? On the street? Did he sit in a car and watch until he spotted a potential victim? And then just knock on the door?

Impossible. McAllister and Rosen's apartment blocks had security gates and intercom systems. Women didn't open up for strange men – not any more. Jansen's house had a steel gate at the front door.

No, somehow he befriended them. Then made a date for a Friday night and picked them up or brought them home. And used the electric cord, which he found in the kitchen. Did he take it into the sitting room or the bedroom? How did he manage to surprise them? Because there was not much sign of struggle – no tissue under fingernails, no other bruising.

He must be strong. Fast, and methodical.

The forensic psychologist in Pretoria said the fucker would have a record, possibly for minor offences: assault, theft, trespassing, even arson. Most likely for sexual offences, rape perhaps. 'They don't start with murder, they climb the ladder. If you catch him, you will find him in possession of pornography, sadomasochistic stuff. One thing I can tell you: he won't stop. He's getting more skilful and more and more self-confidence.'

Griessel took the soap and washed his body, wondering if she had sat in here before he fetched her. Had she prepared herself for the date, unknowing, a lamb to the slaughter?

He would get him.

Friday nights. Why Fridays?

He rinsed off the soap.

Was Friday the only night he was free of responsibilities? What professions were off on Friday nights? Or rather what professions worked on Friday nights? Only bloody policemen, that's all – the rest of the world partied. And murdered.

He climbed out of the bath, walked dripping over to his cases and took out a towel. Anna had placed one neatly on top of the clothes. She had packed carefully for him, as if she cared. But now he rummaged around in the suitcases. He would have to hang the clothes up, or they would be wrinkled.

He had to find a place to stay. For six months.

He listened to the silence in the flat, suddenly aware that he was alone. That he was sober. He chose some clothes and dressed.

Despite her anger, Anna had packed his clothes with care. She would be in the kitchen now, still in her work clothes, clattering pots and pans, radio playing on the table. Carla would be sitting at the dining-room table with her homework books, twisting the point of the pencil in her hair. Fritz would be in front of the television, remote in hand, skipping channels continuously, searching, impatient. Always on the go. He was like that too – things must happen.

Jesus, what had happened to his life?

Pissed away. With the help of Klipdrift and Coke and Jack Daniels.

Alcoholics Anonymous, Step Ten: Continue to take personal inventory and when you are wrong, promptly admit to it.

He sighed deeply. Desire pressed against his ribcage from inside. He did not want to be here. He wanted to go home. He wanted his family back, his wife and his children. He wanted his life back. He would have to start over. He wanted to be like he was before – the policeman from the Parow station who laughed at life. Could one begin again? Now. At forty-three?

Where would you begin, to start over?

You don't have to be a genius to work that one out. He wasn't sure whether he had said that out loud.

He must buy a newspaper and look for a place in the classified ads, because this fucking flat gave him the heebie-jeebies. But first he must phone. He found Mrs McAllister's phone directory in a drawer of the cupboard by the phone. He opened it near the front, and slid his finger down the list, turned a page, looked again until he found the number.

He would try one more time. One last fucking time.

He rang the number. It did not ring for long.

'Alcoholics Anonymous, good afternoon,' said a woman's voice.

By chance Thobela bought the *Argus*. It was something to do while he ate fish and chips from a cardboard carton, the seagulls waiting like beggars on the railing for alms. He spread the paper open on the table before him. First he read the main article without much interest – more political undercurrents in the Western Cape, allegations of corruption and the usual denials. He dipped the chips in the seafood sauce. That was when he spotted the small column in the right bottom corner.

COPS CALLED 'INCOMPETENT' –
BABY RAPIST CASE DISMISSED

He read. When he had finished, he pushed the remains to one side. He gazed out over the quiet water of the harbour. Pleasure boats with sunburned tourists on board cruised out in a line to serve cocktails off Llandudno and Clifton when the sun went down. But he was blind to the scene. He sat there staring and motionless for a long time with his big hands framing the article. Then he read it again.

There was a knock on the study door and the minister said, 'Come in.'

The woman who put her head around the door was in her middle years, her black hair cut short against her head and her nose long and elegant. 'Sorry to disturb you. I have made some snacks.'

The two women summed each other up with a glance. Christine saw false self-assurance, subservience, a slim body hidden by a sensible frock. A busy woman with able hands that only laboured in the kitchen. The sort of woman who had sex in order to have children, not for pleasure. A woman who would turn away stiffly if her husband's mouth and tongue slid lower than the small, worn breasts. Christine knew her type, but she didn't want to let on and tried to seem inconspicuous.

The minister stood up and crossed to his wife to take the tray from her. 'Thank you, Mamma,' he said.

'It's a pleasure,' she said, smiling tight-lipped at Christine. Her eyes said, for the tiniest moment, 'I know your kind,' before she softly closed the door.

In a detached way the minister placed the tray on the desk – sandwiches, chicken drumsticks, gherkins and serviettes.

'How did you meet?' she asked. He had gone back to his chair.

'Rita and I? At university. Her car broke down. She had an old Mini Minor. I was passing on my bicycle and stopped.'

'Was it love at first sight?'

He chuckled. 'It was for me. She had a boyfriend in the army.'

Why, she would have liked to ask. What did you see in her? What made you choose her? Did she look like the ideal rectory wife? A virgin? Pure. She imagined the romance, the propriety, and she knew it would have bored her to death at that age.

'So you stole her away from him?' she asked, but wasn't really interested any more. She felt an old jealousy rising.

'Eventually.' He smiled in a self-satisfied way. 'Please, have something to eat.'

She wasn't hungry. She took a sandwich, noting the lettuce and tomato filling, the way the bread was cut in a perfect triangle. She placed it on a plate and put it on her lap. She wanted to ask how he had managed to wait, how he had suppressed his urges until after the wedding. Did student ministers masturbate, or was that a sin too in their world?

She waited until he began to eat a drumstick, holding the leg bone in his fingers. He leaned forward so that he ate above the plate. His lips glistened with fat.

'I had sex the first time when I was fifteen,' she said. 'Proper sex.'

She wanted him to choke on his food, but his jaw only stalled a moment.

'I chose the boy. I picked him out. The cleverest one in the class. I could have had anyone, I knew that.'

He was helpless with the chicken half eaten in his hand and his mouth full of meat.

'The more my father prayed about the demons in me, the more I wanted to see them. Every night. Every night we had to sit in the lounge and he would read from the Bible and pray long prayers and ask God to cast the Devil out of Christine. The sins of the flesh. The temptations. While we held hands and he sweated and talked till the windows rattled and the hair on my neck stood up. I would wonder, what demons? What did they look like? What did they do? How would it feel if they came out? Why did he focus on me? Was it something I couldn't help? At first I didn't have a clue. But then boys at school began to look at me. At my body.'

She didn't want the plate on her lap any more. She plonked it down on the desk and folded her hands under her breasts. She must calm down; she needed him, perfect wife and all.

Her father would inspect her every morning like one of his men. He would not let her out of the door until he had approved the length of her skirt. Sometimes he would send her back to tie up her hair or to wash off some barely visible mascara, until she learned to leave a little earlier and apply her make-up in the mirror of the school toilets. She did not want to forgo the newly discovered attention of boys. It was a strange thing. At thirteen she had been just one of the crowd: flat-chested, pale and giggly. Then everything began to grow – breasts, hips, legs, lips – a metamorphosis that made her father rabid and had an odd effect on all the men around her. Matric boys began to greet her, teachers began to linger at her desk, Standard Sixes began to look at her sideways and whisper to each other behind cupped hands. Eventually she twigged. It was during this time that her mother began to work and Christine became part of a group who went to a parentless house after school to smoke and occasionally to drink. And Colin Engelbrecht had said to her from behind the blue cloud of a Chesterfield that she had the sexiest body in school, it was now officially accepted. And if she would be willing to show him her breasts, just once, he would do anything.

The other girls in the room had thrown cushions at him and screamed that he was a pig. She had stood up, unbuttoned her shirt, unhooked her bra and exposed her breasts to the three boys in the room. She had stood there with her big boobs and for the first time in her life felt the power, saw the enthralment in their eyes, the jaw-dropping weakness of lust. How different from her father's terrible disgust.

That is how she came to know the demons.

After that, nothing was the same again. Her display of her breasts was talked about, she realised later, because the level of interest increased and the style of their approach changed. This act had created the possibility of wildness, the chance of getting lucky. So she began to use it. It was a weapon, a shield and a game. The ones she favoured were occasionally rewarded with admission to her room and a long sweaty petting session in the midday heat of Upington, the privilege of stroking and licking her breasts while she watched their faces with absolute concentration and cherished the incredibly deep pleasure – that she was responsible for this ecstasy, the panting, the thundering heartbeat.

But when their hands began to drift downwards, she returned them softly but firmly to above the waist, because she wanted to control when that would happen, and with whom.

The way *she* wanted it, exactly as she fantasised when she lay in her bed late at night and masturbated, slowly teasing the devil with her fingers until she drove him out with a shuddering orgasm. Only to find the next night that he was back inside, lurking, waiting for her hand.

It was at the school sports day of her Standard-Eight year that she seduced the handsome, good and clever, but shy Johan Erasmus with his gold-rimmed glasses and fine hands. It happened in the long grass behind the bus shed. He was the one who was too afraid to look at her, who blushed blood red if she said hello. He was soft – his eyes, his voice, his heart. She wanted to give her gift to him because he never asked for it.

And she had.

10

'My name is Benny Griessel and I am an alcoholic.'

'Hello, Benny,' said thirty-two voices in a happy chorus.

'Last night I drank a whole bottle of Jack Daniels and I hit my wife. This morning she kicked me out the house. I have gone one day without drinking. I am here because I can't control my drinking. I am here because I want my wife and children and my life back.' While he was listening to the desperation in his voice, someone began to clap, and then the dingy little church hall resounded with applause.

He lingered in the dark outside the long, unimaginative building, instinctively taking an inventory of exits, windows and the distance to his pick-up. The Yellow Rose must have been a farmhouse once, a smallholder's home in the 1950s before the high tide of Khayelitsha pushed past.

Below the roof ridge was a neon sign with the name and a bright yellow rose. Rap music thumped inside. There were no curtains in the windows. Light shone through and made long tracks across the parking lot, joyful lighthouses on a treacherous black reef.

Inside they sat densely bunched around cheap tables. He spotted a few European tourists with the forced bonhomie of nervous people, like missionaries in a village of cannibals. He threaded his way through and saw two or three seats vacant at the pinewood bar. Two young black barmen busied themselves filling orders behind it. Waitresses slipped expertly up to them, each wearing a yellow plastic rose flapping from the thin T-shirt fabric above their chests.

'What's your pleasure, big dog?' the barman asked him in a vaguely American accent. *Biehg dawg.*

'Do you have Windhoek?' he asked in his mother tongue.

'Lager or Light, my friend?'

'Are you a Xhosa?'

'Yes.'

He would have liked to say, 'Then speak Xhosa to me,' but he refrained, because he needed information.

'Lager, please.'

The beer and a glass appeared before him. 'Eleven rand eighty.'

Eleven rand eighty? Alchemists Inc. He gave him fifteen. 'Keep the change.'

He raised the glass and drank.

'I hope you will still feel like applauding when I have finished,' said Griessel when the ovation died down. 'Because tonight I will say what I should have said in nineteen ninety-six. And you won't necessarily like what you hear.' He glanced at Vera, the coloured woman with the sympathetic smile who was chairing the meeting. A sea of heads was turned towards him, every face an echo of Vera's unconditional support. He felt extremely uncomfortable.

'I have two problems with the AA.' His voice filled the hall as if he were there alone. 'One is that I don't feel I fit in here. I am a policeman. Murder is my speciality. Every day.' He gripped the back of the blue plastic chair in front of him. He saw his knuckles were white with tension and he looked up at Vera, not knowing where else to look. 'And I drink to make the voices stop.'

Vera nodded as if she understood. He looked for another focal point. There were posters on the wall.

'We scream when we die,' he said, soft and slow, because he had to express it right. 'We all cling on to life. We hang on very tight, and when someone pries our fingers loose, we fall.' He saw his hands were demonstrating this in front of him; two fierce claws opening up. 'That is when we scream. When we realise it won't help to grab any more because we are falling too fast.'

The foghorn at Mouille Point mourned far and deep. It was deathly quiet in the church hall. He took a deep breath and looked at them. There was discomfort; the cheerfulness had frozen.

'I hear it. I can't help it. I hear it when I walk in on a scene while they are lying there. The scream hangs there – waiting for someone to hear it. And when you hear it, it gets in your head and it stays there.'

Someone coughed nervously to his left.

'It is the most dreadful sound,' he said, and looked at them, because now he did want their support. They avoided his eyes.

'I never talked about it,' he said. Vera shifted as if she wanted to say something. But she mustn't speak now. 'People will think I'm not right in the head. That's what *you* think. Right now. But I'm not crazy. If I were, alcohol would not help. It would make it worse. Alcohol helps. It helps when I walk in on a murder scene. It helps me get through the day. It helps when I go home and see my wife and children and I hear them laughing, but I know that scream lies waiting inside them as well. I know it is waiting there and one day it will come out and I am scared that I am the one who will hear it.'

He shook his head. 'That would be too much to bear.'

He looked down at the floor and whispered: 'And the thing that frightens me most is that I know that scream is inside *me*.'

He looked up into Vera's eyes. 'I drink because it takes away that fear too.'

'When last was John Khoza here?' Thobela asked the barman.

'Who?'

'John Khoza.'

'Yo, man, there are so many dawgs coming in here.'

He sighed and took out a fifty-rand note, pushing it with his palm over the bar counter.

'Try to remember.'

The note disappeared. 'Sort of a thin dude with bad skin?'

'That's him.'

'He mostly talks to the Boss Man – you'll have to ask him.'

'When last did he come to talk to the Boss Man?'

'I work shifts, man, I'm not here all the time. Haven't seen John-dawg for ages.' He moved off to serve someone else.

Thobela swallowed more beer. The bitter taste was familiar, the music was too loud and the bass notes vibrated in his chest. Across the room near the window was a table of seven. Raucous laughter. A muscular coloured man with complex tattoos on his arms balanced on a stool. He downed a big jug of beer, shouted something, although the words were lost, and held the empty jug aloft.

It was all too hollow, too contrived for Thobela, this joviality. It always had been, since Kazakhstan, although that was a long time ago. A hundred and twenty black brothers in a Soviet training camp who drank and sang and laughed at night. And longed for home, bone-tired. Comrades and warriors.

The barman came past again.

'Where can I find the Boss Man?'

'It can be arranged.' He stood there expectant, without batting an eyelid.

He took out another fifty. The barman did not move. Another one. A palm swept the money away.

'Give me one minute.'

'The second problem is with the Twelve Steps. I know them off by heart and I can understand them working for other people. Step One is easy, because I fu . . ., I know my life is out of control, alcohol has taken over. Step Two says a Power greater than ourselves can heal us. Step Three says just turn over our will and our lives to Him.'

'Amen,' said a couple of them.

'The problem is,' he said with as much apology as he could put into his voice, 'I don't believe there is such a Power. Not in this city.'

Even Vera avoided his gaze. For a moment longer he stood in the silence. Then he sighed. 'That is all I can say.' He sat down.

By the end of his second beer he saw the Boss Man approaching him from across the room, a fat black man with a shaven head and a gold ring on every finger. He would stop at a table here and there, almost shouting as he spoke to the guests – from the bar his words were drowned in the racket – until he reached Thobela. There were tiny drops of perspiration on his face as if he had exerted himself. Jewellery glittered as he offered his right hand.

'Do I know you?'

His voice was remarkably high and feminine and his eyes small and alert. 'Madison Madikiza; they call me the Boss Man.'

'Tiny.' He used a nickname from the past.

'Tiny? Then my name is Skinny,' said the Boss Man. He had an infectious giggle that screwed up his eyes and shook his entire body as he hoisted it onto a bar stool. A tall glass materialised in front of him, the contents clear as water.

'Cheers.' He drank deeply and wiped his mouth with his sleeve, waving an index finger up and down in Thobela's direction. 'I know you.'

'Ah . . .' His pulse accelerated as he focused more sharply on the man's features. He did not want to be caught unawares. Recognition meant trouble. There would be connotations, a track with a start and an end.

'No, don't tell me, it will come to me. Give me a minute.' The little eyes danced over him, a frown creased the bald head. 'Tiny . . . Tiny . . . Weren't you . . .? No, that was another fellow.'

'I don't think—'

'No, wait, I must place you. Hell, I never forget a face . . . Just tell me, what is your line?'

'This and that,' he said cautiously.

The fingers snapped. 'Orlando Arendse,' said the Boss Man. 'You rode shotgun for Orlando.'

Relief. 'That was a long time ago.'

'Memory like an elephant, my friend. Ninety-eight, ninety-seven, thereabouts, I still worked for Shakes Senzeni, God rest his soul. He had a chop shop in Gugs and I was his foreman. Orlando asked for a sit-down over division of territory, d'you remember? Big meeting in Stikland and you sat next to Orlando. Afterwards Shakes said that was clever, we couldn't speak Xhosa among ourselves. Fuck, my friend, small world. I hear Orlando has retired, the Nigerians have taken over the drug trade.'

'I last saw Orlando two or three years ago.' He could remember the meeting, but not the man in front of him. There was something else, a realisation of alternatives – if he had remained with Orlando, where would that have left him now?

'So, what do you do now?'

He could keep to his cover with more conviction now. 'I am freelance. I put jobs together . . .' What would he have done when Orlando retired? Operated a nightclub? Run something on the periphery of the law. How close to a potential truth was the story he was fabricating now?

'A broker?'

'A broker.' There was a time when it was possible, when it could have been true. But that lay in the past. What lay ahead? Where was he going?

'And you have something for Johnny Khoza?'

'Maybe.'

Shouts rang out above the music and they looked around. The strong coloured man was dancing on the table now with his shirt off. A dragon tattoo spat faded red fire across his chest while bystanders urged him on.

Boss Man Madikiza shook his head. 'Trouble brewing,' he said, and turned back to Thobela. 'I don't think Johnny is available, my friend. I hear he's on the run. They got him in Ciskei for AR and manslaughter. He did a service station – Johnny never thinks big. So when the court case went wrong, it cost him big money to buy a key, you know what I'm saying. I don't know where he is, but he is definitively not in the Cape. He would have come creeping in here long ago if he was. In any case, I have better talent on my books – just tell me what you need.'

For the first time the possibility occurred to him that he might not get them. The possibility that his search could be fruitless, that they had crept into a hole somewhere where he could not get at them. The frustration pressed heavily down on him, making him feel sluggish and impotent. 'The thing is,' he said, although he already knew it would not work, 'Khoza has information on the potential job. A contact on the inside. Is there no one who would know where he is?'

'He has a brother . . . I don't know where.'

'No one else?' Where to now? If he couldn't find Khoza and Ramphele? What then? With an effort he shook off the feeling and concentrated on what the Boss Man was saying.

'I don't know too much about him. Johnny is small time, one of many who try to impress me. They are all the same – come in here with big attitude, throw their money around in front of the girls like they were big gangstas, but they do service stations. No class. If Johnny has told you he has a contact on the inside for a serious score, you should be careful.'

'I will.' The farm was not an option. He could not go back. With this frustration in him it would drive him insane. What was he going to do?

'Where can I get hold of you? If I hear something?'

'I will come back.'

The Boss Man's little eyes narrowed. 'You don't trust me?'

'I trust nobody.'

The little laugh bubbled up, champagne from a barrel, and a marshmallow hand patted him on the shoulder. 'Well said, my friend . . .'

There was a crash louder than the music. The dancing dragon's table had broken beneath him and he fell spectacularly, to the great enjoyment of the onlookers. He lay on the floor holding his beer glass triumphantly above him.

'Fuck,' said the Boss Man and got up from the stool. 'I knew things would get out of hand.'

The coloured man stood up slowly and gestured an apology in Madikiza's direction. He nodded back with a forced smile.

'He will pay for the table, the shit.' He turned to Thobela. 'Do you know who that is?'

'No idea.'

'Enver Davids. Yesterday he walked away from a baby rape charge. On a technicality. Fucking police misplaced his file, can you believe it – a genuine administrative fuck-up; you don't buy your way out of that one. He's more bad news than the *Financial Mail*. General of the Twenty-Sevens. He got Aids in jail from a *wyfie*. More cell time than Vodacom, and they parole him and he goes and rapes a baby, supposed to cure his Aids . . . Now he comes and drinks here, because his own people will string him up, the fucking filthy shit.'

'Enver Davids,' said Thobela slowly.

'Fucking filthy shit,' said the Boss Man again, but Thobela was beyond hearing. Something was beginning to make sense. He could see a way forward.

His hands trembled on the steering wheel. They had a life of their own. He felt cold in the warm summer night and he knew it was withdrawal. He knew it was beginning – it was going to be a terrible night in the flat of Josephine Mary McAllister.

He reached out to the radio, locating the knob with difficulty, and pressed it. Music. He kept the volume low. At this time of night Sea Point's streets were alive with cars and pedestrians, people going somewhere with purpose. Except for him.

They had made a circle around him once everyone was finished. They gathered around him, touched him as if to transfer something to him through their hands. Strength. Or belief? Faces, too many faces. Some faces told a story in the rings around their eyes and mouths, like the rings of a tree. Heartbreaking stories. Others were masks hiding secrets. But the eyes, all the eyes were the same – piercing, glowing with willpower, like someone in floodwaters hanging on to a thin green branch. He will see, they said. He will see. What he did see was that he was part of The Last Chance Club. He felt the same desperation, the same dragging flood-waters.

The tremor ran through him like a fever. He could hear their voices and he turned the music up. Rhythm filled the car. Louder. Rock, Afrikaans, he tried to follow the words.

Ek wil huis toe gaan na Mamma toe,
Ek wil huis toe gaan na Mamma toe.

Too much synthesizer, he thought, not quite right, but good.
Die rivier is vol, my trane rol.

He parked in front of the block of flats, but didn't get out. He allowed his fingers to run down the imaginary neck of a base guitar – that's what the song needed, more base. Lord, it would be good to hold a base guitar again. The trembling limb jerked to a rhythm all of its own and made him want to laugh out loud.

'n Bokkie wat vanaand by my wil lê. . .

Nostalgia. Where were the days, where was the twenty-year-old little fucker who throttled a base guitar in the police dance band until the very walls shook?

Sy kan maar lê, ek is 'n loslappie.

Emotion. His eyes burned. Fuck, no, he wasn't a crybaby. He banged the radio off, opened the door and got out fast, so he could get away from this place.

II

The minister wondered if she was telling the whole truth – he searched between her words and in her body language. He could see the anger, old and new, the involuntary physical self-consciousness. The continuous, practised offering of mouth, breasts and hair. Her eyes had a strange shape, almost oriental. And they were small. Her features were not delicate, but had an attractive regularity. Her neck was not thin, but strong. Her gaze sometimes skittered away as though she might betray something: a thirst for acceptance? Or was there something rotten? Or spoilt, like a child still wanting her own way, craving attention and respect, an ego feeding on alternating current – now brave, now incredibly fragile.

Fascinating.

He phoned his wife just after ten, when he knew she would have had her bath and would be sitting on their bed with her dressing gown pulled above her knees smoothing cream on her legs, and then turning to the mirror and doing the same to her face with delicate movements of her fingertips. He wanted to be there now to watch her do it, because his memories of that were not recent.

'I am sober,' was the first thing he said.

'That's good,' she said, but without enthusiasm, so that he didn't know how to continue.

'Anna . . .'

She did not speak.

'I'm sorry,' he said with feeling.

'So am I, Benny.' Without inflection.

'Don't you want to know where I am?'

'No.'

He nodded as if he had been expecting it.

'I'll say goodnight then.'

'Goodnight, Benny.' She put the phone down and he held his cell phone to his ear for a little longer and he knew she did not believe he would make it.

Perhaps she was right.

She saw that she had entranced him and said: 'In Standard Nine I slept with a teacher. And with a buddy of my father.' But he did not react.

'What do you think?' she asked. Suddenly she had to know.

He hesitated for so long that she became anxious. Had he heard, was he listening? Or was he revolted by her?

'I think you are deliberately trying to shock me,' he said, but he was smiling at her and his tone was as soft as water.

For a moment she was embarrassed. Unconsciously, her hand flew up to her hair, the fingers twisting the ends.

'What interests me is why you would want to do that. Do you still think I will judge you?'

It was only part of the truth, but she nodded fractionally.

'I can hardly blame you for that, as I suspect experience has taught you that that is what people do.'

'Yes,' she said.

'Let me tell you that counselling from a Christian point of view distinguishes between the person and the deed. What we do is sometimes unacceptable to God, but we are never unacceptable to Him. And He expects the same from me, if I am to do His work.'

'My father also thought he was doing God's work.' The words were out in reflex, an old anger.

He grimaced as if in pain, as if she had no right to make this comparison.

'The Bible has been used for many agendas. Fear too.'

'So why does God allow that?' She knew the question was lying in wait and she had not seen it.

'You must remember . . .'

Her hands seemed to lose their grip, she seemed to have lost her footing. 'No, tell me. Why? Why did He write the Bible like that so that everyone could use it as they please?' She could hear her own voice, the way it spiralled, how it carried the emotion with it. 'If He loves us so much? What did I do to Him? Why didn't He give me an easy road too? Like you and your wife? Why did He give me Viljoen and then allow him to blow his brains out? What was my sin? He gave me my father – what chance did I have after that? If He wanted me to be stronger, why didn't He make me stronger? Or cleverer? I was a child. How was I supposed to know? How was I supposed to know grown-ups were fucked up?' The sound of the swearword was sharp and cutting and she heard it as he would and it made her stop. Angrily, she wiped the wet off her cheeks with the back of her hand.

When he did react, he surprised her again. 'You are in trouble,' he said nearly inaudibly.

She nodded. And sniffed.

He opened a drawer, took out a box of tissues and pushed it over the desk towards her. Somehow this gesture disappointed her. History – she was not the first.

'Big trouble,' he said.

She ignored the tissues. 'Yes.'

He put a big, freckled hand on the cardboard box. 'And it has to do with this?'

'Yes,' she said, 'it has to do with that.'

'And you are afraid,' he said.

She nodded.

He pressed a hand over the man's mouth and the assegai blade against his throat and waited for him to wake. It came with a jerk of the body and eyes opening wide and wild. He put his head close to the small ear and whispered, 'If you keep quiet, I will give you a chance.' He felt the power of Davids' body straining against the pressure. He cut him with the tip of the blade against the throat, but lightly, just so that he could feel the sting. 'Lie still.'

Davids subsided, but his mouth moved under the hand.

'Quiet,' he whispered again, the stink of drink in his nostrils. He wondered how sober Davids was, but he could wait no longer – it was nearly four o'clock.

'Let's go outside, you and me. Understand?'

The shaven head nodded.

'If you make a noise before we are outside, I will cut you.'

Nod.

'Come.' He allowed him to get up, got behind him with the assegai under Davids' chin, arm around his throat. They shuffled through the dark house to the front door. He felt the tension in the man's muscles and he knew the adrenaline was flowing in him too. They were outside, on the pavement, and he took a quick step back. He waited for Davids to turn to him, saw the dragon's raging red eyes, and took the knife from his pocket, a long butcher's knife he had found in a kitchen drawer.

He passed it to the coloured man.

'Here,' he said. 'This is your chance.'

At quarter-past seven when Griessel entered the parade room of the Serious and Violent Crimes building in Bishop Lavis, he did not feel the buzz.

He sat with his head down, paging aimlessly through the dossier on his lap, searching for a starting point on which to build his oral report. He was light-headed – thoughts darting like silver fish, diving aimlessly into a green sea, this way, that way, evasive, always out of reach. His hands were sweating. He couldn't say he had nothing to report. They would laugh at him. Joubert would crap him out. He would have to say he was waiting for Forensics. Jissis, if he could just keep his hands still. He felt nauseous, an urge to throw up, vomit out all the shit.

Senior Superintendent Matt Joubert clapped his hands twice and the sharp sound echoed through him. The voices of the detectives quieted.

'You have probably all heard,' said Joubert, and a reaction ran through his audience: 'Tell them, Bushy.' There was contentment in his voice and Griessel read the mood. Something was going on.

Bezuidenhout stood against the opposite wall and Griessel tried to focus on him, his eyes flickering, blink-blink-blink-blink. He heard Bushy's gravelly voice: 'Last night Enver Davids was stabbed to death in Kraaifontein.'

A joyful riot broke out in the parade room. Griessel was perplexed. Who was Davids?

The noise droned through Griessel, the sickness growing inside. Christ, he was sick, sick as a dog.

'His pals say they went drinking at a shebeen in Khayelitsha and came home to the house in Kraaifontein about one a.m., when they went to sleep. This morning, just after five, someone knocked on the door to say there was a man lying dead in the street.'

Griessel knew he would hear the sound.

'Nobody heard or saw anything,' said Inspector Bushy Bezuidenhout. 'It looks like a knife fight. Davids has slash wounds to the hands and one on the neck, but at this stage the fatal wound seems to be a stab through the heart.'

Griessel saw Davids fall backwards, mouth stretched wide, the fillings in his teeth rusty brown. The scream, at first as thick as molasses, a tongue slowly sticking out, and the scream growing thin, thinner than blood. And it came to him.

'They should have cut off his balls,' said Vaughn Cupido.

The policemen laughed and that made the sound accelerate, the long thin trail scorched through the ether. Griessel jerked his head away, but the sound found him.

Then he vomited, dry and retching and he heard the laughter and heard someone say his name. Joubert? 'Benny, are you alright? Benny?' But he was not fucking alright, the noise was in his head, and it would never get out.

He drove first to the hotel room in Parow. Davids' blood was on his arms and clothes. Boss Man's words repeated in his head: *He got Aids in jail from a* wyfie.

He washed his big body with great concentration, scrubbed down with soap and water, washed his clothes afterwards in the bath, put on a clean set and walked out to his pick-up.

It was past five when he came outside – the east was beginning to change colour. He took the N1 and then the N7 and the Table View off ramp near the smoking, burning refinery where a thousand lights still shone. Minibus taxis were already busy. He drove as far as Blouberg, thinking of nothing. He got out at the sea. It was a cloudless morning. An unsettled breeze still looking for direction blew softly against his skin. He looked up to the mountain where the first rays of the sun made deep shadows on the cliffs, like the wrinkles of an old man. Then he breathed, slowly in and out.

Only when his pulse had slowed to normal did he take from the cubbyhole, where he had stowed it yesterday, the *Argus* article, neatly torn out.

'Does someone want to harm you?' asked the minister.

She blew her nose loudly and looked at him apologetically, rolling up the tissue in her hand. She took another and blew again.

'Yes.'

'Who?' He reached under his desk and brought out a white plastic wastepaper basket. She tossed the tissues into it, took another and wiped her eyes and cheeks.

'There is more than one,' she said, and the emotions threatened again. She waited a moment for them to subside. 'More than one.'

12

'Are you sure he is guilty?' he had asked Boss Man Madikiza, because ideas had materialised in his head out of nowhere and his blood was boiling.

The fat man snorted and said Davids had been in his office before the drinking began. Boastful and smug. The police had his cum, in their hands, the dee-en-ay evidence, they could have nailed him right there with a life sentence with their test tubes and their microscopes and then they *moered* the bottle away, thick as bricks, and so the prosecutor came up to the judge dragging his feet and said dyor onner, we fucked up a little, no more dee-en-ay, no more rape charge. Did that judge *kak* them out, my bro', like you won't believe. 'What kind of person?' the Boss Man asked Thobela with total revulsion, 'what kind of person rapes a baby, I ask you?'

He had nothing to say.

'And they've gone and abolished the death penalty,' the Boss Man said as he got up.

Thobela said goodbye and left and went and sat in his pick-up. He put his hand behind the seat and felt the polished shaft of the assegai. He stroked the wood with his fingers, back and forth, back and forth.

Someone had to say, 'This far, and no further.'

Back and forth.

So he waited for them.

When the minister moved away from her and sat on the edge of the desk, she knew something had altered between them, a gap had been bridged. Maybe it was just on her side that a certain anxiety had subsided, a fear allayed, but she could see a change in his body language – more ease.

If he would be patient, she said, she would like to tell the whole story, everything. So that he could understand. Perhaps so she could also understand, because it was hard. For so long she had believed she was doing what she had to, following the only course available. But now . . . she wasn't so sure.

Take your time, he said, and his smile was different. Paternal.

The last thing Griessel could remember, before they took him to Casualty at Tygerberg Hospital and injected him with some or other shit that made his head soft and easy, was Matt Joubert holding his hand. The senior superintendent, who said to him all the way in the ambulance, over and over: 'It's just the DTs, Benny, don't worry. It's just the DTs.' His voice bore more worry than comfort.

She went to university to study physiotherapy. The whole family accompanied her on a scorching hot Free State day in January. Her father had made them all kneel in her hostel room and had prayed for her, a long dramatic prayer that made the sweat pop out on his frowning forehead and exposed the wickedness of Bloemfontein in detail.

She remained standing on the pavement when the white Toyota Cressida eventually drove away. She felt wonderful: intensely liberated, a floating, euphoric sensation. 'I felt as though I could fly,' were the words she used. Until she saw her mother look back. For the first time she could really see her family from the outside, and her mother's expression upset her. In that short-lived moment, the second or two before the mask was replaced, she read in her mother's face longing, envy and desire – as if she would have liked to stay behind, escape as her daughter had. It was Christine's first insight, her first knowledge that she was not the only victim.

She had meant to write to her mother after initiation, a letter of solidarity, love and appreciation. She wanted to say something when her mother phoned the hostel for the first time to find out how things were going. But she never could find the right words. Maybe it was guilt – she had escaped and her mother had not. Maybe it was the new world that never left time or space for melancholy thoughts. She was swept up in student life. She enjoyed it immensely, the total experience. Serenades, Rag, hostel meetings, social coffee-breaks, the lovely old buildings, dances, Intervarsity, men, the open spaces of the campus's lawns and streams and avenues of trees. It was a sweet cup and she drank deeply, as if she could never have enough of it.

'You won't believe me, but for ten months I didn't have sex. I was one hundred per cent celibate. Heavy petting, yes, there were four, five, six guys I played around with. Once I slept the whole night with a medical student in his flat in Park Street, but he had to stay above the belt. Sometimes I would drink, but I tried to only do that on a girls' night out, for safety.'

Her father's letters had nothing to do with her celibacy – long, disjointed sermons and biblical references that she would later not even open and deliberately toss in the rubbish bin. It was a contract with the new life: 'I would do nothing to make a ba . . . a mess of it.'

She would not tempt fate or challenge the gods. She vaguely realised it was not rational, since she did not perform academically, she was constantly on the edge of failing, but she kept her part of the deal and the gods continued to smile on her.

Then she met Viljoen.

In sharp criticism of the state's handling of the case, Judge Rosenstein quoted recent newspaper reports on the dramatic increase in crimes against children.

'In this country 5,800 cases of rape of children younger than 12 years old were investigated last year, and some 10,000 cases where children between 11 and 17 years old were involved. In the Peninsula alone, more than 1,000 cases of child molestation were reported last year and the number is rising.

'What makes these statistics even more shocking is the fact that only an estimated 15 per cent of all crimes against children are actually reported. And then there is the matter of children as

murder victims. Not only are they being caught in the crossfire of gangland shootings, or become the innocent prey of paedophiles, now they are being killed in this senseless belief that they can cure Aids,' he said.

'The facts and figures clearly indicate that society is already failing our children. And now the machinery of the state is proving inadequate to bring the perpetrators of these heinous crimes to justice. If children can't depend on the justice system to protect them, to whom can they turn?'

Thobela folded the article up again and put it in his shirt pocket. He walked down to the beach, feeling the sand soft beneath his shoes. Just beyond reach of the white foaming arcs spilling across the sand he stood, hands in pockets. He could see Pakamile and his two friends running in step along the beach. He could hear their shouts, see their bare torsos and the sand grains clinging to their skins like stars in a chocolate firmament, arms aloft like wings as their squadron flew in formation just above the waterline. He had taken them to Haga Haga on the Transkei coast for the Easter weekend. They camped in tents and cooked over a fire, the boys swam and caught fish with hand lines in the rock pools and played war games in the dunes. He heard their voices till late at night in the other tent, muffled giggling and chatting.

He blinked and the beach was empty and he was overwhelmed. Too little sleep and the after-effects of excess adrenaline.

He began to walk north along the beach. He was looking for the absolute conviction he had felt in the Yellow Rose, that this is what he must do; as if the universe was pointing the way with a thousand index fingers. It was like twenty years ago when he could feel the absolute rightness of the Struggle – that his origins, his instincts, his very nature had been honed for that moment, the total recognition of his vocation.

Someone had to say, 'This far.' *If children can't depend on the justice system to protect them, to whom can they turn?* He was a warrior and there was still a war in this land.

Why did it all sound so hollow now?

He must get some sleep; that would clear his perspective. But he did not want to, did not feel attracted to the four walls of the hotel room – he needed open space, sun, wind and a horizon. He did not want to be alone in his head.

He had always been a man of action, he could never stand by and watch. That is what he was and what he would be – a soldier, who faced the child rapist and felt all the juices of war flood his body. It was right, regardless how he might feel now. Regardless that this morning his convictions did not have the same impregnability.

They would start to leave the children of this land alone, the dogs, he would make sure of that. Somewhere Khoza and Ramphele were hiding, fugitives for the moment, invisible. But some time or other they would reappear, make contact or do something, and he would pick up their trail and hunt them down, corner them and let the assegai do the talking. Some time or other. If you wanted to get the prey, you had to be patient.

In the meantime there was work to do.

'I was clueless about money. There was just never enough. My father put a hundred rand a month in my account. A hundred rand. No matter how hard I tried, it would only last two weeks. Maybe three if I didn't buy magazines or if I smoked less or if I pretended I was busy when they went to movies or to eat out or chill . . . but it was never enough and I didn't want to ask for more because he would want to know what I was doing with it and I would have to listen to his nagging. I heard they were looking for students at a catering business in Westdene. They did weddings and functions and paid ninety rand for a Saturday night if you would waitress or serve, and they gave you an advance for the clothes. You had to wear black pantyhose and a black pencil skirt with a white blouse. I went to ask and they gave me a job, two sweet middle-aged gays who would have a huge falling out every fortnight and then make up just in time for the next function.

'The work was okay, once you got used to being on your feet for so long, and I looked stunning in the pencil skirt, even if I say so

myself. But most of all I liked the money. The freedom. The, the
. . . I don't know, to walk down Mimosa Mall and look at the
Diesel jeans and decide I wanted them and buy them. Just that
feeling, always knowing your purse was not empty – that was cool.

'At first I just did Saturdays, and then Fridays too and the
occasional Wednesday. Just for the money. Just for the . . . power,
you could say.

'Then in October we did the Schoemans Park golf-day party. I
went outside for a smoke after the main course, and Viljoen was
standing on the eighteenth green with a bottle in his hand and such
a knowing look on his face. He asked me if I wanted a slug.'

They must have injected him with something, because it was
morning when he woke, slowly and with difficulty, and he just
lay with his face to the hospital wall. It was a while before he
realised there was a needle and a thin tube attached to his arm. He
was not shaking.

A nurse came in and asked him questions and his voice was hoarse
when he answered. He might have been speaking too loudly,
because she sounded far away. She took his wrist and in her other
hand held a watch that was pinned to her chest. He thought it was
odd to wear it there. She put a thermometer into his dry mouth and
spoke in a soft voice. She was a black woman with scars on her
cheeks, fossil remnants of acne. Her eyes rested softly on him and she
wrote something on a snow-white card and then she was gone.

Two coloured women brought him breakfast, shifting the trolley
over the bed. They were excitable, chittering birds. They put a
steaming tray on the trolley and said: 'You must eat, Sarge, you
need the nourishment.' Then they disappeared. When the doctor
arrived it was still there, cold and uneaten, and Griessel lay like a
foetus, hands between his legs and his head feeling thick. Unwilling
to think, because all his head had to offer was trouble.

The doctor was an elderly man, short and stooped, bald and
bespectacled. The hair that remained around his head grew long
and grey down his back. He read the chart first and then came to sit
beside the bed.

'I pumped you full of thiamine and Valium. It will help with the withdrawal. But you have to eat too,' he said quietly.

Griessel just lay there.

'You are a brave man to give up alcohol.' Matt Joubert must have talked to him.

'Did they tell you my wife left me?'

'They did not. Was it because of the drink?'

Griessel shifted partially upright. 'I hit her when I was drunk.'

'How long have you been dependent?'

'Fourteen fucking years.'

'Then it is good that you stopped. The liver has its limits.'

'I don't know if I can.'

'I also felt like that and I have been dry for twenty-four years.'

Griessel sat up. 'You were an alky?'

The doctor's eyes blinked behind the thick lenses. 'That's why they sent for me this morning. You could say I am a specialist. For eleven years I drank like a fish. Drank away my practice, my family, my Mercedes Benz. Three times I swore I would stop, but I couldn't keep my balance on the wagon. Eventually I had nothing left except pancreatitis.'

'Did she take you back?'

'She did,' said the doctor and smiled. 'We had two more children, just to celebrate. The trouble is, they look like their father.'

'How did you do it?'

'Sex played an important role.'

'No, I mean . . .'

The doctor took Griessel's hand and he laughed with closed eyes. 'I know what you mean.'

'Oh.' For the first time Griessel smiled.

'One day at a time. And the AA. And the fact that I had hit rock bottom. There was no more medication to help, except disulfiram, the stuff that makes you throw up if you drink. But I knew from the literature it is rubbish – if you really want to drink, you just stop taking the pills.'

'Are there drugs now that can make you stop drinking?'

'No drug can make you stop drinking. Only you can.'

Griessel nodded in disappointment.

'But they can make withdrawal easier.'

'Take away the DTs.'

'You have not yet experienced delirium tremens, my friend. That only comes three to five days after withdrawal begins. Yesterday you experienced reasonably normal convulsions and, I imagine, the hallucinations of a heavy drinker who stops. Did you smell strange scents?'

'Yes.'

'Hear strange things?'

'Yes.' With emphasis.

'Acute withdrawal, but not yet the DTs, and for that you should be thankful. DTs is hell and we haven't found a way to stop it. If it gets really bad, you could get *grand mal* seizures, cardiac infarction or stroke, and any one of the three could kill you.'

'Jesus.'

'Do you really want to stop, Griessel?'

'I do.'

'Then today is your lucky day.'

13

She was a coloured woman with three children, and a husband in jail. She was the receptionist at the Quay Delta workshop in Paarden Island and it was never her intention to send the whole thing off at a tangent.

The *Argus* came at 12.30 every day, four papers for the waiting room so that clients could read while they waited for their cars to be finished. It was her habit to quickly scan the main news headlines of the day. Today she did this with more purpose because she had expectations.

She found it on the front page just below the fold in the newspaper. The headline already told her that all was not right.

POLICE LINKED TO KILLING OF
ALLEGED CHILD RAPIST

Quickly she read through the article and clicked her tongue.

The South African Police Services (SAPS) might have been responsible for the vigilante-style murder of alleged child rapist Enver Davids last night.

A spokesperson for the Cape Human Rights Forum, Mr David Rosenthal, said his organisation had received 'sensitive information from a very reliable source inside the police services' in this regard. The source indicated that the Serious and Violent Crimes Unit (SVC) was involved in the killing.

HIV-positive Davids, who was freed on charges of murder and child rape three days after the SVC had misplaced DNA

evidence pertinent to the case, was found stabbed to death on a
Kraaifontein street early this morning.

Senior Superintendent Matt Joubert, head of the SVC,
vigorously denied the allegation, calling the claim that two of his
detectives tracked down Davids and killed him 'malicious,
spurious and devoid of all truth'. He admits that the unit was
upset and frustrated after a judge sharply criticised their
management of the case and then dismissed it . . .

The woman shook her head.

She would have to do something. This morning when she went into her dark kitchen to get the bottle of Vicks for her child's chest she could see the movement from her window. She had been a witness to the awful dance on the pavement. She had recognised Davids' face in the streetlight. Of one thing she was absolutely sure. The man with the short assegai was not a policeman. She knew the police; she could spot a policeman a mile away. She had had plenty of them on her doorstep. Like this morning when they had come to ask if she had seen anything and she had denied any knowledge.

She looked up the telephone number of the *Argus* on their front page and dialled it. She asked for the journalist who had written the article.

'It wasn't the police who killed Enver Davids,' she said without introduction.

'To whom am I speaking?'

'It doesn't matter.'

'And how do you know this, madam?'

She had been expecting the question. But she could not say or they would get her. They would track her down if she gave too much information.

'You might say I have first-hand knowledge.'

'Are you saying you were involved in this killing, madam?'

'All I want to say is that it wasn't the police. Definitely not.'

'Are you a member of Pagad?'

'No, I'm not. It wasn't a group. It was one person.'

'Are you that person?'

'I am going to put the phone down now.'

'Wait, please. How can I believe you, madam? How do I know you are not a crank?'

She thought for a moment. Then she said: 'It was a spear that killed him. An assegai. You can go and check that.'

She put the phone down.

That is how the Artemis story began.

Joubert and his English wife came to visit him that evening. All he could see was the way they kept touching each other, the big senior superintendent and his red-headed wife with the gentle eyes. Married four years and still touching like a honeymoon couple.

Joubert told him about the allegation that the unit was responsible for Davids' death. Margaret Joubert brought him magazines. They talked about everything but his problem. When they left Joubert gripped his shoulder with a big hand and said, 'Hang in there, Benny.' After they had gone he wondered how long it had been since he and Anna had touched each other. Like that.

He could not recall.

Fuck, when last had they had sex? When last did he even want to? Sometimes, in the semi-drunken state of his day, something would prompt him to think about it, but by the time he got home the alcohol would long since have melted the lead in his pencil.

And what of Anna? Did she feel the need? She didn't drink. She had been keen in the days before he began drinking seriously. Always game when he was, sometimes twice a week, folding her delicate fingers around his erection and playing their ritual game that had begun spontaneously and they had never dropped. 'Where did you get this thing, Benny?'

'Sale at Checkers, so I took four.'

Or: 'I traded with a Jew for nine inches of boere sausages. Don't be afraid, he's bald.' He would think of something new every time and even when he was less ingenious and more banal she would laugh. Every time. Their sex was always joyous, cheerful, until her orgasm made her serious. Afterwards they would hold each other and she would say, 'I love you, Benny.'

Pissed away, systematically, like everything.

He yearned. Where were the days, Lord, could he ever get them back? He wondered what she did when the desire was on her? What had she done the past two or three years? Did she see to herself? Or was there. . . ?

Panic. What if there was someone? Jissis, he would fucking shoot him. Nobody touched his Anna.

He looked at his hands, clenched fists, white knuckles. Slowly, slowly, the doctor had said he would make emotional leaps, anxiety . . . He must slow down.

He unclenched his fists and drew the magazines closer.

Car. Margaret Joubert had brought him men's magazines but cars were not his scene. Nor was *Popular Mechanics*. There was a sketch of a futuristic aeroplane on the cover. The cover story read, *New York to London in 30 Minutes?*

'Who cares,' he said.

His scene was drinking, but they don't publish magazines for that.

He switched off the light. It would be a long night.

The woman at the Internet café in Long Street had a row of earrings all down the edge of her ear and a shiny object through her nostril. Thobela thought she would have been prettier without it.

'I don't know how to use these things,' he said.

'It's twenty rand an hour,' she said, as if that would disqualify him straight away.

'I need someone to teach me,' he said patiently, refreshed after his afternoon nap.

'What do you want to do?'

'I heard you can read newspapers. And see what they wrote last year too.'

'Archives. They call them Internet archives.'

'Aaah . . .' he said. 'Would you show me?'

'We don't really do training.'

'I will pay.'

He could see the synapses fire behind her pale green eyes: the potential to make good money out of a dumb black, but also the possibility that it could be slow, frustrating work.

'Two hundred rand an hour, but you will have to wait until my shift is over.'

'Fifty,' he said. 'I will wait.'

He had taken her unawares, but she recovered well. 'A hundred, take it or leave it.'

'A hundred and you buy the coffee.'

She put out a hand and smiled. 'Deal. My name is Simone.'

He saw there was another shiny object on her tongue.

Viljoen. He was not tall, barely half a head taller than she was. He was not very handsome, and wore a copper bracelet on his wrist and a thin gold chain around his neck that she never much liked. It was not that he was poor – he just had no interest in money. The Free State sun had bleached his eight-year-old 4×4 pick-up until you would be hard pressed to name the original colour. Day after day it stood in the parking lot of the Schoemans Park Golf Club while he coached golf, or sold golf balls in the pro shop or played a round or two with the more important members.

He was a professional golfer. In theory. He had only lasted three months on the Sunshine Tour before his money ran out because he could not putt under pressure. He got the shakes, 'the yips', he called them. He would set up the putt and walk away and line up and set himself up again but always putted too short. Nerves had destroyed him.

'He became the resident pro at Schoemans Park. I found him that night on the eighteenth green with a bottle in his hand. It was weird. It was like we recognised each other. We were the same kind. Sort of on the sidelines. When you are in a hostel, you feel it quickly – that you don't quite belong. Nobody says anything, everyone is nice to each other and you socialise and laugh and worry together about exams, but you are not really "in".

'But Viljoen saw it. He knew it, because he was like that too.

'We began to talk. It was just so . . . natural, from the beginning. When I had to go in, he asked me what I was doing afterwards, and

I said I had to catch a lift back to the hostel, so I couldn't do anything and he said he would take me.

'So when everyone had gone, he asked me if I would caddy for him, because he wanted to play a bit of golf. I think he was a little drunk. I said you can't play golf in the dark, and he said that's what everyone thinks, but he would show me.'

The Bloemfontein summer night . . . She could smell the mown grass, hear the night sounds, and see the half moon. She could remember the way the light from the clubhouse veranda reflected off Viljoen's tanned skin. She could see his broad shoulders and his odd smile and the expression in his eyes and that aura about him, that terrible solitariness he carried around with him. The noise of the golf club striking the ball and the way it flew into the darkness and him saying: 'Come, caddy, don't let the roar of the crowd distract you.' His voice was gentle, self-mocking. Before every shot they would drink from the bottle of semi-sweet white wine still cold from the fridge. 'I don't get the yips at night,' he said, and he made his putts, long and short. In the dark he made the ball roll on perfect lines, over the humps in the greens, till it fell clattering into the hole. On the fairway of the sixth hole he kissed her, but by then she already knew she liked him too much and it was okay, absolutely okay.

'He played nine holes in the dark and in that time I fell in love,' was all she told the minister. She seemed to want to preserve the memories of that night, as if they would fade if she took them out of the dark and held them up to the light.

In the sand bunker beside the ninth hole they sat and he filled in his scorecard and announced he had a 33.

So much – she teased him.

So little – he laughed. A muted sound, sort of feminine. He kissed her again. Slowly and carefully, like he was taking care to do it right. With the same care he stretched her out and undressed her, folding each piece of clothing and putting it down on the grass above. He had knelt over her and kissed her, from her neck to her ankles, with an expression on his face of absolute wonder: that he had been granted this privilege, this magical opportunity. Eventually he went into her and there was intensity in his eyes of huge emotion and his rhythm increased, his urgency grew and grew and he lost himself in her.

She had to drag herself back to this present, where the minister waited with apparent patience for her to break the silence.

She wondered why memories were so closely linked to scent, because she could smell him now, here – deodorant and sweat and semen and grass and sand.

'At the ninth hole he made me pregnant,' she said, and reached out a hand for the tissues.

14

Barkhuizen, the doctor with the thick spectacles, his long hair in a cheeky plait this time, came around again the next morning after Griessel had swallowed his breakfast without enthusiasm or appetite.

'I'm glad you're eating,' he said. 'How do you feel?'

Griessel made a gesture that said it didn't matter.

'Finding it hard to eat?'

He nodded.

'Are you nauseous?'

'A bit.'

The doctor shone a light in his eyes.

'Headache?'

'Yes.'

He put a stethoscope to his chest and listened, finger on Griessel's pulse.

'I have found you a place to stay.'

Griessel said nothing.

'You have a heart like a horse, my friend.' He took the stethoscope away, put it in the pocket of his white coat and sat down. 'It's not much. Bachelor flat in Gardens, kitchen and living room below, wooden stairs up to a bedroom. Shower, basin and toilet. One two per month. The building is old but clean.'

Griessel looked away to the opposite wall.

'Do you want it?'

'I don't know.'

'How's that, Benny?'

'Just now I was angry, Doc. Now I don't give a fuck.'

'Angry with whom?'

'Everyone. My wife. Myself. You.'

'Don't forget it's a process of mourning you are going through because your friend the bottle is dead. The first reaction is anger at someone because of that. There are people who get stuck in the anger stage for years. You can hear them at the AA, going off at everyone and everything, shouting and swearing. But it doesn't help. Then there is the depression. That goes hand in hand with withdrawal. And the listlessness and fatigue. You have to get through it; you have to come out the other side of withdrawal, past the rage to resignation and acceptance. You must go on with your life.'

'What fucking life?'

'The one you must make for yourself. You have to find something to replace drink. You need leisure, a hobby, exercise. But first one day at a time, Benny. And we have just been talking about tomorrow.'

'I have fuck-all. I've got suitcases of clothes, that's all.'

'Your wife is having a bed delivered to the flat, if you want the place.'

'Did you talk to her?'

'I did. She wants to help, Benny.'

'Why hasn't she been here?'

'She said she believed too easily last time. She said this time she must stick to her decision. She will only see you when you are completely dry. I think that is the right thing.'

'You have all worked this out fucking beautifully, haven't you?'

'The *Rooi Komplot*, the great conspiracy. Everyone is against you. Against you and your bottle. It's hard, I know, but you're a tough guy, Benny. You can take it.'

Griessel just stared at him.

'Let's talk about your medication,' said Barkhuizen. 'The stuff I want to prescribe . . .'

'Why do you do it, Doc?'

'Because the drugs will help you.'

'No, Doc, why do you get involved? How old are you?'

'Sixty-nine.'

Deon Meyer

'Fuck, Doc, that's retirement age.'

Barkhuizen smiled and the eyes screwed up behind the thick lenses. 'I have a beach house at Witsand. We were retired there for three months. By then the garden was lovely and the house was right and the neighbours met. Then I began to want the bottle. I realised that was not what I should do.'

'So you came back.'

'To make life difficult for people like you.'

Griessel watched him for a long time. Then he said: 'The medication, Doc.'

'Naltrexone. The trade name is ReVia, don't ask me why. It works. It makes withdrawal easier and there are no serious contra-indications, as long as you stick to the prescription. But there is a condition. You must see me once a week for the first three months and you must go to the AA regularly. That is not negotiable. It's an all-or-nothing proposition.'

'I'll take it.' He had no hesitation.

'Are you certain?'

'Yes, Doc, I am certain. But I want to tell you something, so you know what you are letting yourself in for,' he said, and he tapped an index finger on his temple.

'Tell me, then.'

'It's about the screaming, Doc. I want to know if the medication will help for the screaming.'

The minister's children came to say goodnight. They knocked softly on the door and he hesitated at first. 'Excuse me, please,' he said to her and then called, 'Come in.' Two teenage boys disguised their curiosity about her with great difficulty. The older one was maybe seventeen. He was tall, like his father, and his youthful body was strong. His lightning glance assessed her chest measurement and her legs as she sat there. He spotted the tissue in her hand and there was an attentiveness about him that she recognised.

'G'night, Dad,' they said one after another and kissed him.

'Night, boys. Sleep well.'

'G'night, ma'am,' said the younger one.

'G'night,' said the other, and when his back was turned to his father, he looked into her eyes with undisguised interest. She knew he saw her hurt instinctively and the opportunities that offered, like a dog on a blood spoor.

She was annoyed. 'Goodnight,' she said and turned her eyes away, unavailable.

They closed the door behind them.

'Richard will be head boy next year,' said the minister with a certain pride.

'You have these two boys?' A mechanical question.

'They are a handful,' he said.

'I can imagine.'

'Do you need anything? More tea?'

'I should go and powder my nose.'

'Of course. Down the passage, second door on the left.'

She stood up. Smoothed down her skirt, front and back. 'Excuse me,' she said as she opened the door and walked down the passage. She found the toilet, switched on the light and sat down to urinate.

She was still annoyed with the boy. She was always aware that she gave off a scent that said to men, 'Try me'. Some combination of her appearance and her personality, as if they knew . . . But even here? This little twerp. A minister's son?

She became conscious of the loud noise of her urine stream in the stillness of the house.

Didn't these people play music? Watch television?

She was sick of it. She didn't want to smell like that any more. She wanted to smell like the woman of this house, the faithful wife: an I-want-to-love-you woman. She had always wanted to.

She finished, wiped, flushed, opened the door and put off the light. She walked back to the study. The minister was not there. She stood in front of the bookshelf, looking at the bookends packed thick and thin beside each other – some old and hardbacked and others new and bright; all about God or the Bible.

So many books. Why did they have to write so much about God? Why was it necessary? Why couldn't He just come down and say, 'Here I am, don't worry.'

Then He could explain to her why He had given her this scent. Not just the scent, but the weakness and the trouble. And why He had never tested Missus Fucking Prude here with her sensible frock and able hands? Why was she spared? Why did she get a dependable carthorse for a husband? What would she do if the elders of the church came sniffing around her with those hungry eyes that said, 'My brain is in my penis'?

Probably catch her breath in righteous indignation and hand out tracts all round. The scene playing out in her head made her laugh out loud, just one short, unladylike laugh. She put her hand over her mouth, but too late. The minister was standing behind her.

'Are you okay?' he asked.

She nodded and kept her back turned until she had control.

The extent of it nearly overwhelmed Thobela.

The girl with the earrings first gave him a basic lesson on the workings of the Internet, and then she let him click the mouse on the screen. He battled because the coordination between his hand and the mouse and the little arrow on the screen was clumsy. He improved steadily, however. She showed him connections and web addresses, boxes he could type words in and the big 'Back' arrow if he got lost.

When at last she was satisfied he could manage on his own and he had solemnly handed over the agreed amount, he began his search.

'*Die Burger* and IOL have the best online archives,' she said, and wrote down the www-references for him. He typed in his key words and systematically refined his search. Then came the flood.

At least 40 per cent of all cases of child rape can be ascribed to the myth that it cures Aids.

People who exploit children for sex in many parts of the world are more likely to be local residents looking for a 'good-luck charm' or a cure for Aids than a paedophile or sexual tourist, rights activists told a UN conference on Thursday.

Thousands of schoolgirls in South Africa and the Western Cape are daily exposed to sexual violence and harassment at schools.

From April 1997 to March this year, 1,124 children who had been physically and sexually abused were treated by the TygerBear Social Welfare Unit for Traumatised Children at Tygerberg Hospital. This is only children who were brought to the hospital: the actual number is much greater.

Sexual molestation and the abuse of young children is reaching epidemic proportions in Valhalla Park, Bonteheuwel and Mitchells Plain. A spokesperson reports that 945 cases of sexual molestation and child abuse have been reported to their office.

Children as young as three years old watch social workers at the TygerBear Unit of the Tygerberg Hospital with wary eyes. Barely out of nappies, these victims of sexual assault have already learned that adults are not to be trusted.

The two domestic violence units on the Peninsula are working on more than 3,200 cases, of which the majority are complaints of serious sexual and other crimes against children.

Of every 100 cases of child abuse in the Western Cape, only 15 are reported to the police, and in 83 per cent of these cases the offender is known to the child.

Once an offender has been diagnosed as a 'confirmed paedophile', there will always be a chance that he will express his paedophilic tendencies again, said Professor David Ackerman, clinical psychologist at the University of Cape Town.

One report after another, a never-ending stream of crimes against children. Murder, rape, maltreatment, harassment, assault, abuse. After an hour he had had enough, but he forced himself to continue.

A three-year-old girl was locked in a cage while her grandparents allegedly sexually assaulted her and failed to provide for even her most basic needs, Mpumalanga police said on Wednesday. Sergeant Anelda Fischer said police recently received a tip-off from a travelling pastor that a child was being incarcerated in a compound outside White River.

Fischer said that when police went to investigate they found the girl had already been removed from the cage. However, she said there was evidence the child had been battered with sticks or other weapons and had been sexually assaulted. It also seemed the child had no clothes of her own and had to beg naked for food. She slept on bits of plastic in the cage.

Colin Pretorius, the owner and head of a crèche in Parow, is being charged on the grounds that he sexually assaulted eleven boys between the ages of six and nine years over a period of four years. He was released on bail of R10,000.

At last he stood and walked unsteadily to the desk to pay for his use of the Internet.

Viljoen and she had three months together before he blew his brains out.

'At first I was just angry with him. Not heartbroken – that came later, because I truly loved him. And I was scared. He left me with the pregnancy and I didn't know what to do or where to go. But I was dreadfully angry because he was such a coward. It happened a week after I told him I was pregnant, on a Monday night. I took him to the Spur and told him there was something I had to tell him and then I told him and he just sat there and said nothing. So then I said to him he didn't have to marry me, just help me, because I didn't know what to do.

'Then he said: "Jissis, Christine, I'm no good as a father – I am a fuck-up, a drunken golfer with the yips."

'I said he didn't have to be a father, I didn't want to be a mother yet, I just didn't know what to do. I was a student. I had a crazy father. If he had to find out about the baby, he would go off the deep end. He would lock me up or something.

'Then he said let him think about it, make a plan, and the whole week he didn't phone, and Friday night, just before I had to go to work, I decided I would phone him one last time and if he still tried to avoid me, well, then, fuck him, excuse me, but it was a very difficult time. And then they said there had been an accident, he was dead, but it wasn't an accident. He had locked the pro shop and sat down at a little table and put a revolver against his head.

'It took me two years to stop being angry and remember that those three months with Viljoen were good. It was when I began to wonder what I would tell my child about her father. Some time she would want to know and—'

'You have a child?' asked the minister; for the first time he was taken aback.

'. . . and I would have to decide what to tell her. He didn't even leave a note. Didn't even write anything for her. He didn't even say he was sorry, it was depression, or he didn't have the guts or anything. So I decided I would tell her about those three months, because they were the best of my life.'

She was quiet then and sighed deeply. After a pause the minister asked, 'What is her name?'

'Sonia.'

'Where is she?

'That is what my story is about,' she said.

15

Griessel almost missed it. Two nurses came around early in the morning with the meal trolley, when he was already dressed and packed and ready to be discharged. His mind was elsewhere and he was not listening to their chatter as they approached his hospital room.

'. . . so then when she found out it was an old trick of his, he confessed. She says he had worked out that all the middle-aged girls go and buy comfort food at the Pick and Pay on Friday nights because they will be sitting in front of the TV all evening and that's when he pushes his trolley down the aisles and picks the prettiest one to chat up. That's how he got Emmarentia. Oh, hallo, Sarge, up already? Cheese omelette this morning, everyone's favourite.'

'No thank you,' he said, taking his suitcase and heading for the door. But he stopped and asked, 'Friday nights?'

'Sarge?'

'Say that again about Emmarentia and Pick and Pay?'

'Hey, Sarge, you don't have to be so desperate, you're not bad looking,' said one.

'There's something of the Russian noble in you,' said the other. 'Such sexy Slavic features.'

'No, that's not—'

'Maybe sometimes a bad hair day, but that can be fixed.'

'Anyway, that's a wedding band I see, isn't it?'

'Wait, wait, wait,' he held up his hands. 'I'm not interested in women . . .'

'Sarge! We could have sworn you were hetero.'

He was starting to get cross, but he looked hard at their faces and saw their deliberate mischief. He laughed helplessly with them, from his belly. The door opened and his daughter Carla stood there in her school uniform. She was momentarily confused by the scene – then relieved. She embraced her father.

'I hope that's his child,' one nurse said.

'Can't be, he's queer as a three-rand note.'

'Or his boyfriend in drag?'

They had Carla laughing with her head on his chest and eventually she said, 'Hallo, Pa.'

'You will be late for school.'

'I wanted to know if you were alright.'

'I'm alright, my child.'

The nurses were leaving and he asked them to explain again about Emmarentia.

'Why do you want to know, Sarge?'

'I'm working on this case. We can't work out how the victims are selected.'

'So the sarge wants to consult us?'

'I do.'

They sketched a verbal picture as an alternating duet. Jimmy Fortuin picked up an occasional score at the Pick and Pay on a Friday afternoon, because by then it was crawling with single women.

'But middle-aged. The young ones still have the guts to fly solo in the clubs, or they gang up, strength in numbers.'

'They buy food for Friday night and the weekend: treats, you know, to spoil themselves a bit. Comfort food.'

'Between five and seven, that's hunting season for Jimmy, 'cause they're all on the way home from work. Easy pickings, because Jimmy is a motor mouth, a charmer.'

'Just at Pick and Pay?'

'That's just *his* convenience store, but Checkers would also work.'

'There's something about a supermarket . . .'

'Kind of hopeless . . .'

'Desperation . . .'

'The Lonely Hearts Shopping Club.'

'Last stand at the OK Bazaars.'

'Sleepless in the Seven Eleven.'

'You know?'

Laughing he said he understood, thanked them and left.

He dropped Carla off at school with the car that Joubert had left for him.

'We miss you, Daddy,' she said as they stopped at the school gates.

'Not as much as I miss all of you.'

'Mommy told us about the flat.'

'It's just temporary, my child.' He took her hand and pressed it. 'This is my third sober day today,' he said.

'You know I love you, Daddy.'

'And I love you.'

'Fritz too.'

'Did he say that?'

'He didn't have to say it.' She hurriedly opened her case. 'I brought you this, Daddy.'

She took out an envelope and gave it to him. 'You could pick us up at school sometimes. We won't tell Mommy.' She grabbed him around the neck and hugged him. Then she opened her door.

' 'Bye, Daddy,' she said with a serious face.

' 'Bye, my child.'

He watched her hurry up the steps. His daughter with the dark hair and strange eyes that she had inherited from him.

He opened the envelope. There were photographs in it, the family picture they had taken two years ago at the school bazaar. Anna's smile was forced. His was lopsided – not quite sober that night. But there were all four of them, together.

He turned the picture over. *I love you, Daddy*. In Carla's pretty, curving handwriting, followed by a tiny heart.

'That December I worked, pregnant or not. I phoned home and said I would be staying. I wasn't going home to Upington, or with them to Hartenbos. My father was not happy. He drove through to Bloemfontein to come and pray for me. I was petrified he would see that I was pregnant, but he didn't; he was too busy with other things in his head. I told him I would stay in an outside room at Kallie and Colin's place, as I was helping them with all the year-end functions, weddings and company do's for employees and there weren't so many students to help. I wanted to make good money, so that I would be more financially independent.

'That was the last time I saw him. He kissed me on the cheek before he left and that was the closest he ever came to his granddaughter.

'Kallie caught me throwing up one morning in January. He had brought my breakfast to the outside room and he stood and watched me vomiting in the toilet. Then he said: "You're preggies, sweetheart," and when I didn't reply he said, "What are you going to do?"

'I told him I was going to have the baby. It was the first time that I really knew it myself. I know it's weird, but with Viljoen and my father and everything . . . Until that moment only I knew. It was kind of unreal. Like a dream, and maybe I thought I would wake up, or the baby would just go away on its own or something. I didn't want to think about it, I just wanted to go on.

'Then he asked if I would put the baby up for adoption, and I said I don't know but I said I was going to Cape Town at the end of the month, so would they please give me all the shifts they could? So he asked me if I knew what I was doing and I said no, I didn't know what I was doing, because it was all rather new to me.

'They saw me off at Hoffman Square, with a present for the baby, a little blue babygro and booties and little shoes and bibs and an envelope for me – a Christmas bonus, they said. And they gave me a few names of gay friends they had in Cape Town in case I needed help.

'I cried that day, all the way to Colesberg. That was when I felt Sonia kick for the first time, as if to say, that's enough, we must pull ourselves together, we would be okay. Then I knew that I would not give her up.'

Griessel found what he was searching for in the three lab reports. He walked over to Matt Joubert's office and waited for the senior superintendent to finish on the telephone.

'The forensic report does not exclude an assegai,' Joubert was saying into the instrument, 'but they are doing more tests, and it will take time. You will have to call back in a day or two. Right. You're welcome. Thanks. 'Bye.'

He looked up at Griessel. 'It's good to have you back, Benny. How are you feeling?'

'Frighteningly sober. What was that about an assegai?'

'That Enver Davids thing. Suddenly the *Argus* has all these questions. I can see trouble coming.'

Griessel put the lab reports down in front of Joubert and said, 'The bastard is picking them up at Woolworths. Friday afternoons. Look here, I missed it because I didn't know what I was looking for, but Forensics analysed the trash cans of all three victims and in two of them there are Woolies bags and till slips and in the third one just a till slip, but all three were there, at the one on the Waterfront on the Friday of the murders between . . . er . . . half-past four and seven o'clock.'

Joubert examined the reports. 'It's thin, Benny.'

'I know, but this morning I heard expert witnesses, Matt. Seems to me only old married people like us think a supermarket is a place to buy groceries.'

'Explain,' said Joubert, wondering how long this light would keep burning in Griessel's eyes.

Thobela found a public phone in the Church Street Mall that worked with coins and thumbed through the tattered phone book for the number of the University of Cape Town Psychology Department. He called and asked for Professor David Ackerman.

'He is on ward rounds. In what connection is this?'

'I am researching an article on crimes against children. I have just a few questions.'

'With which publication are you?'

'I am freelance.'

'Professor Ackerman is very busy . . .'

'I only need a few minutes.'

'I will have to phone you back, sir.'

'I'm going to be in and out – can I call tomorrow?'

'To whom am I speaking?'

'Pakamile,' he said. 'Pakamile Nzuluwazi.'

16

At first the Cape was not good to her.

For one, the wind blew for days on end, a storm-strength southeaster. Then they stole her only suitcase at Backpackers in Kloof Nek, where for a hundred rand a night she was sharing a room with five grumbling, superior young German tourists. Flats were scarce and expensive, public transport complicated and unreliable. Once she walked all the way to Sea Point to check out a possible place, but it was a disappointing dump with a broken windowpane and graffiti on the walls.

She stayed in Backpackers for two weeks before she found the attic room in an old block of flats in Belle Ombre Street in Tamboers Kloof. What had once been a boxroom had been converted into a small, livable space – the bath and toilet were against one wall, the sink and kitchen cupboard against the other; there was a bed and table and an old rickety wardrobe. Another door opened onto the roof, from where she could see the city crescent, the mountain and the sea. At least neat and clean for R680 per month.

Her biggest problem was inside her because she was afraid. Afraid of the birth that drew nearer every day, the care of the baby afterwards, the responsibility; afraid of the anger of her father when she made the call or wrote the letter – which, she had not yet decided. Above all, afraid of the money running out. Every day she checked her balance at the autobank and compared the balance against the list of the most essential items she would need: cot, baby clothes, nappies, bottles, milk formula, blankets, pan, pot, two-plate stove, mug, plate, knife, fork and spoon, kettle, portable FM-radio. The list continued to grow and her bank balance continued to shrink until she found work as a waitress at a large coffee shop in Long Street. She worked every possible shift that she could, while she could still hide the bump under her breasts.

The numbers on the statements ruled her life. They became an obsession. Six eight zero was the first target of every month, the non-negotiable amount of her rent. It was the low-water mark of her book-keeping and the source of unrest in her dreams at night. She discovered the flea market at Green Point Stadium and haggled over the price of every item. At the second-hand shops in Gardens and in Kloof Street she bought a cot, a bicycle and a red and blue carpet. She painted the cot on the roof with white, lead-free enamel paint, and when she found there was paint left over she gave the old yellowish-green racing bike with narrow tyres and dropped handlebars a couple of coats as well.

In a *Cape Ads* that someone left in the coffee shop she found an advertisement for a backpack baby carrier. And she phoned, argued the price down, and had it delivered. It would allow her to ride the bicycle with the baby on her back along the mountain and next to the sea at Mouille Point, where there were swings and climbing frames and a kiddies' train.

Every Saturday she took twenty rand to play the Lotto and she would sit by the radio and wait for the winning numbers that she had marked on the card with a ballpoint pen. She fantasized about what she would do with the jackpot money. A house was top of the list – one of those modern rebuilt castles on the slopes of the mountain, with automatic garage doors, Persian carpets on the floor and kelims and art on the walls. A huge baby room with seabirds and clouds painted on the ceiling and a heap of bright, multicoloured toys on the floor. A Land Rover Discovery with a baby seat. A walk-in wardrobe filled with designer labels and shoes in tidy rows on the floor. An Espresso machine. A double-door fridge in stainless steel.

One afternoon, about three o'clock, she was sitting on the roof with a cup of instant coffee when she heard the sounds of sex drifting up from the block of flats below. A woman's voice, uh-uh-

uh-uh, gradually climbing the scales of ecstasy, every one a little higher, a little louder. In the first minutes the sound was meaningless, just another noise of the city, but she recognised it and was amused at the odd hour. She wondered if she were the only listener, or whether the sound reached other ears. She felt a small sexual stimulus ripple through her body. Followed by envy as the sounds accelerated, faster, louder, higher. The envy grew along with it for all that she did not have, until the shrill orgasm made her get up and bend her arm with the nearly-empty mug back in order to throw it at everything that conspired against her. She didn't aim at any specific target, her rage was too general. Rage against the loneliness, the circumstances, the wasted opportunities.

She did not throw it. She lowered her arm slowly, unwilling to pay for a new mug.

Early in March she could postpone the call no longer. She rode all the way to the Waterfront for a public phone, in case they traced the call. She phoned her mother at the attorneys' office where she worked. It was a short conversation.

'My God, Christine, where are you?'

'I dropped out, Mom. I'm okay. I've got a job. I just want to—'

'Where are you?' Her voice was tinged with hysteria. 'The police are looking for you too now. Your father will have a stroke, he phones them in Bloemfontein every day.'

'Mom, tell him to drop it. Tell him I am sick and tired of his preaching and his religion. I am not in Bloemfontein and he won't find me. I am fine. I am happy. Just leave me alone. I am not a child any more.' She couldn't tell where the anger came from. Had fear unleashed it?

'Christine, you can't do this. You know your father. He is furious. We are terribly worried about you. You are our child. Where are you?'

'Mom, I'm going to put the phone down now. Don't worry about me, Mom, I am fine. I will phone you to let you know I am okay.' Afterwards she thought she should have said something like, 'I love you, Mom.' But she had just slammed the phone down, got on her bike and ridden away.

She only phoned again when Sonia was a week old, early in June, because then she had a great need to hear her mother's voice.

Thobela was drinking a Coke at the Wimpy outside tables in St Georges. He read the front-page article of the *Argus* that speculated about the death of Enver Davids. Sensationalised by an anonymous woman's phone call.

Someone had seen him with the assegai. But had not reported him.

He had been too focused. No, he hadn't been thorough enough, not entirely calculated. There had been a witness. He should have known there would be publicity. Media interest. Screaming head-lines and speculation and accusations.

Could the killing of child rapist Enver Davids be the work of a female vigilante – and not the South African Police Services, as was previously suspected?

Strange consequences.

Would the police be able to trace the female caller? Would she be able to give them a description of him?

It didn't really matter.

He turned the page. On page three there was an article on a radio station's phone-in opinion poll. Should the death penalty be reinstated? Eighty-seven per cent of listeners had voted 'yes'.

On page two were short reports of the day's criminal activity. Three murders in Khayelitsha. A gang-related shooting took a woman's life in Blue Downs. A man was wounded in Constantia during a car hijacking. A cash in-transit robbery in Montague Gardens: two security guards in intensive care. A seventy-two-year-old woman raped, assaulted and robbed in her home in Rosebank. A farmer in Limpopo Province gunned down in his shed.

No children today.

A waitress brought his bill. He folded the paper and leaned back in his chair. He watched the people walking down the mall, some purposefully, some strolling. There were stalls, clothes and art-works. The sky was blue above, a dove came down to land on the pavement with its tail and wings spread wide.

It was déjà vu, all this, this existence. A hotel room somewhere with his suitcase half unpacked, long days to struggle through, time to wait out before the next assignment. Paris was his place of waiting, another city, another architecture, other languages; but the feeling was the same. The only difference was that in those days his targets had been picked for him in a sombre office in East Berlin, and the little stack of documents with photographs and pages of single-spaced typing was delivered to him by courier. His war. His Struggle.

A lifetime ago. The world was a different place, but how easy it was to slip into the old routines again – the state of alertness, the patience, the preparation, planning, the anticipation of the next intense burst of adrenaline.

Here he was again. Back in harness. The circle was complete. It felt as if the intervening period had never existed, as if Miriam and Pakamile were a fantasy, like an advertisement in the middle of a television drama, a disturbing view of aspirations of domestic bliss.

He paid for his cold drink and walked south to the pay phones and called the number again. 'Is Professor Ackerman available now?'

'Just a moment.'

She put him through. He used the other name again and the cover of freelance journalism. He said he had read an article in the archives of *Die Burger* where the professor stated that a fixated paedophile always reoffended. He wanted to understand what that meant.

The professor sighed and paused a while before he answered. 'Well, it sort of means what it says, Mr Nulwazi.'

'Nzuluwazi.'

'I'm sorry, I'm terrible with names. It means the official line is that, statistically, rehabilitation fails to a substantial degree. In other words, even after an extended prison sentence, there is no guarantee that they won't commit the same crime again.' There was weariness of life in the man's voice.

'The official line.'

'Yes.'

'Does that differ from reality?'

'No.'

'I get the idea you don't support the official line.'

'It is not a matter of support. It is a matter of semantics.'

'Oh?'

'Can we go off the record here, Mr Nulwazi?'

This time he ignored the pronunciation. 'Of course.'

'And you won't quote me?'

'You have my word.'

The professor paused again before he answered, as if weighing the worth of it. 'The fact of the matter is that I don't believe they *can* be rehabilitated.'

'Not at all?'

'It's a terrible disease. And we have yet to find the cure. The problem is that, no matter how much we would like to believe we are getting closer to a solution, there doesn't seem to be one.' Still the desperate, despairing weariness. 'They come out of prison and sooner or later they relapse, and we have more damaged children. And the damage is huge. It is immeasurable. It destroys lives, utterly and completely. It causes trauma you wouldn't believe. And there seem to be more of them every year. God knows, it is either a matter of our society creating more, or that the lawlessness in this country is encouraging them to come out of the woodwork. I don't know . . .'

'So what you are saying is that they shouldn't be released?'

'Look, I know it is inhuman to keep them in prison for ever. Paedophiles have a tough time in penitentiaries. They are considered the scum of the earth in that world. They are raped and beaten and humiliated. But they serve their sentences and go through the programmes and then they come out and they relapse. Some right away, others a year or two or three down the line. I don't know what the answer is, but we will have to find one.'

'Yes,' said Thobela, 'we will have to find one.'

How tedious the clergyman's day-to-day existence must be, because he was still sitting there with the same interest. He was still listening attentively to her story, his expression neutrally sympathetic, his arms relaxed on the desk. It was quiet in the house, outside as well, just the noise of insects. It was strange to her, accustomed as she was to the eternal sound of traffic, people on the move in a city. Always on the go.

Here there was nowhere to go to.

'I had no more money. If you don't have money, you must have time, to stand in long queues with your child on your hip for vaccinations or cough medicine or something to stop diarrhoea. If you have a child and you have to work, then you have to pay for daycare. If you are waitressing then you have to pay extra for someone to look after it at night. Then you have to walk back to your flat with your baby at one in the morning in winter, or you have to pay for a taxi. If you won't work at night, you miss the best shifts with the biggest tips. So you buy nothing for yourself, and this week you try this and next week you try that until you know you just can't win.'

'I couldn't cope any more – there were just too many things. Every Monday I read the _Times Job Supplement_ and handed in my CV for every possible job: secretarial, medical rep, clerk. Then, if you were lucky they would invite you for an interview. But it is always the same. No experience? Oh, you have a child. Are you divorced? Oh. Sorry, we want experience. We want someone with a car. We need someone with book-keeping.

'Sorry, it's an affirmative action position. I left the coffee shop because the tips were too small and it was still winter too and that's off-season. I worked at Trawlers, a seafood place that opened up on Kloof Street, and one night a guy said, "Do you want to make real money?" So I said, "Yes". Then he asked me "How much?" and I didn't click and I said, "As much as I can." Then he said, "Three hundred rand", and I asked, "Three hundred rand what – per day?" Then he got this smile on his face and said, "Per night, actually." He was just an average guy, about forty, with spectacles and a little paunch and I said, "What must I do?" and he said, "You know", and I still didn't click. Then he said, "Bring me a pen and I will write down my hotel room for you", and at last I clicked and I just stood staring at him. I wanted to scream at him, what did he think I was, and I stood there so angry, but what could I do, he was a customer. So I went to fetch his bill, and when I looked again he was gone. He had left a hundred-rand tip and a note with his hotel number and he had written 'Five hundred? For an hour.' And I put it in my pocket, because I was afraid someone might see it.

'Five hundred rand. When your rent is six hundred and eighty, then five hundred is a lot of money. If you have to pay four-fifty for daycare and extra on weekends, because that's where the tips are, five hundred fills a big gap. If you need three thousand to get through the month and you never know if you will make it and you have to save for a car, because when you have to pick up your child and it's raining . . . then you take that bit of paper out of your pocket and you look at it again. But who understands that? What white person understands that?

'Then you think, what difference does it make? You see it every day. A couple come in and he wines and dines her and for what? To get her into bed. What is the difference? Three hundred rand for dinner or five hundred for sex.

'They hit on me in any case, the men. Even when I was pregnant, in the coffee shop, and afterwards, at Trawlers, even worse. The whole time. Some just give you these looks, some say things like "nice rack" or "cute butt, sweetie"; some ask you straight out what you are doing on Friday night, or "are you attached, sweetness?" The vain ones leave their cell phone numbers on the bill, as if they are God's gift. Some chat you up with pretty little questions. "Where are you from?" "How long have you been in Cape Town?" "What are you studying?" But you know what they really want, because soon they ask you, "Do you have your own place?" or, "Jissie, we are chatting so *lekker*, when do you finish work, so we can chat some more?" At first you think you are very special, because some of them are cute and witty, but you hear them doing it with everyone, even the ugly waitresses. All the time, all of them, like those rabbits with the long-life batteries, never stopping; never mind if they are sixteen or sixty, married or single, they are on the lookout and it never stops.

'Then you get back to your room and think about everything and you think of what you don't have and you think there really is no difference, you think five hundred rand and you lie and wonder what it would be like, how bad could it be to be with the guy for an hour?'

17

All day Griessel had been looking for a decoy, a middle-aged policewoman to push a trolley up and down Woolworths at the Waterfront on Friday night. Hopefully the bastard would choose her. Someone eventually suggested a Sergeant Marais at Claremont, late thirties, who might fit the bill. He phoned her and made an appointment to talk to her.

He took the M5, because it was faster, and turned off at Lansdowne in order to drive up to Main Road. At the off ramp, just left of the road, was an advertising board, very wide and high. Castle Lager. Beer. Fuck it, he hadn't drunk beer in years, but the advert depicted a glass with drops of moisture running down the sides, a head of white foam and contents the colour of piss. He had to stop at the traffic lights and stare at that damn glass of beer. He could taste it. That dry, bitter taste. He could feel it sliding down his throat, but above all he could feel the warmth spreading through his body from the medicine in his belly.

When he came to his senses, someone was hooting behind him, a single, impatient toot. He jumped and drove away, realising only then what had happened and scared by the intensity of the enchantment.

He thought: what the fuck am I going to do? How do you fight something like this, pills or no pills? Jissis, he hadn't drunk beer in years.

He realised he was squeezing the steering wheel and he tried to breathe, tried to get his breath back as he drove.

Before she even stood up from behind the desk, he knew the sergeant was perfect. She had that washed-out look, more lean miles on the clock than her year model indicated; her hair was dyed blonde. She said her name was André. Her smile showed a slightly skew front tooth. She looked as if she expected him to comment on her name.

He sat down opposite her and told her about the case and his suspicions. He said she would be ideal, but he could not force her to be part of the operation.

'I'm in,' she said.

'It could be dangerous. We would have to wait until he tried something.'

'I'm in.'

'Talk to your husband tonight. Sleep on it. You can phone me tomorrow.'

'That won't be necessary. I'll do it.'

He spoke to the station commander, to ask permission, although he did not have to. The big coloured captain complained he didn't have people to spare, they were undermanned as it was and Marais was a key person: who would do her work when she wasn't there? Griessel said it was just Friday nights from five o'clock and her overtime would not appear on the station's budget. The captain nodded. 'Okay, then.'

He drove to Gardens late in the afternoon with the address to his flat on a slip of paper on the seat beside him.

Friend Street . . . what fucking kind of name was that? Mount Nelson's Mansions. Number one two eight.

He had never lived in this area. All his life he had been in the northern suburbs, since school a Parow Arrow, apart from the year in Pretoria at the Police College and three years in Durban as a constable. Jissis, he never wanted to go back there, to the heat and humidity and the stink. Curry and dagga and everything in English. In those days he had an accent you could cut with a cudgel and the *Souties* and Indians teased or taunted him, depending on whether they were colleagues or people he had arrested. *Fuckin' rock spider. Fuckin' hairyback pig. Fuckin' dumb Dutchman policeman.*

Mount Nelson's Mansions. There was a steel fence around it and a large security gate. He would have to park in the street at first and press a button on a sign that said Caretaker to get in and collect his keys and the remote control for the gate. A red brick building that had never been a mansion, maybe thirty or forty years old. Not beautiful, not ugly, it just stood there between two white-plastered apartment blocks.

The caretaker was an old Xhosa. 'You a policeman?' he asked. 'I am.'

'That is good. We need a policeman here.'

He fetched his suitcases from the car and dragged them up one flight of stairs. One two eight. The door needed varnish. It had a peephole in the centre and two locks. He found the right keys and pushed the door open. Brown parquet floor, fuck-all furniture, except for the breakfast counter with no stools, a few bleached melamine kitchen cupboards and an old Defy stove with three plates and an oven. A wooden staircase. He left the cases and climbed the stairs. There was a bed up there, a single bed, the one that had been stored in the garage, his garage. His former garage. Just the wooden bedstead and foam mattress with the faded blue floral pattern. The bedding lay in a pile on the foot of the bed. Pillow and slip, sheets, blankets. There was a built-in wardrobe. A door led to the small bathroom.

He went down to fetch his suitcases.

Not even a bloody chair. If he wanted to sit down, it would have to be on the bed.

Nothing to eat off or drink from or to boil water. He had fuck-all. He had less than when he went to police college.

Jissis.

In his hotel room, Thobela searched under 'P' in the telephone directory. There was the name, *Colin Pretorius*, written just like that, and the address, *122 Chantelle Street, Parow*. He drove to the Sanlam Centre in Voortrekker Road and bought a street guide to Cape Town in CNA.

As the sun disappeared behind Table Mountain, he drove down Hannes Louw Drive and left into Fairfield, right into Simone and, after a long curve, left into Chantelle. The even numbers were on the right. Number 122 was an inconspicuous house with burglar bars and a security gate. The neat garden had two ornamental cypress trees, a few shrubs and a green, mowed lawn, all enclosed by a concrete wall around the back and sides. No signs of life. On the garage wall above the door was a blue and silver sign: *Cobra Security. Armed Rapid Response.*

He had a problem. He was a black man in a white suburb. He knew the fact that he was driving a pick-up would help, keep him colour-free and anonymous in the dusk. But not for ever. If he hung around too long or drove past one time too many, someone would notice his skin colour and begin to wonder.

He drove once around the block and past 122 again, this time observing the neighbouring houses and the long strip of park that curved around with Simone Street. Then he had to leave, back to the shopping centre. There were things he needed.

Griessel sat on the still unmade bed and stared at the wardrobe. His clothes could not fill a third of the space. It was the empty space that fascinated him.

At home his wardrobe was full of clothes he hadn't worn in years – garments too small or so badly out of fashion that Anna forbade him to wear them.

But here he could count on one hand each type of garment she had packed for him, excepting the underpants – there were probably eight or nine, which he had piled in a heap in the middle rack.

Laundry. How would he manage? There were already two days' worth of dirty clothes in a bundle at the bottom of the cupboard, beside the single pair of shoes. And ironing – hell, it was years since he had picked up an iron. Cooking, washing dishes. Vacuuming! The bedroom did have a dirty brown wall-to-wall carpet.

'Fuck,' he said, rising to his feet.

He thought of the beer advertisement again.

God, no, that was the sort of thing that had got him into this situation. He must not. He would have to find something to do. There were the files in his briefcase. But where would he work? On the bed? He needed a stool for the breakfast bar. It was too late to look for one now. He wanted coffee. Maybe the Pick and Pay in Gardens was still open. He took his wallet, cell phone and the keys to his new flat and descended the stairs to the bare living room below.

Thobela bought a small pocket torch, batteries, binoculars and a set of screwdrivers and sat down in a restaurant to study the map.

His first problem would be to get into the suburb. He could not park near the house as the pick-up was registered in his name. Someone might write down the number. Or remember it. He would have to park somewhere else and walk in, but it was still risky. Every second house had a private security company's sign on the wall. There would be patrol vehicles, there would be wary eyes ready to call an emergency number. 'There's a black man in our street.'

Chances were better by day – he might be a gardener on his way to work – but at night the risks multiplied.

He studied the map. His finger traced Hannes Louw Drive where it crossed the N1. If he parked north of the freeway, using the narrow strip of veld and parkland . . . That was the long, slow option, but it could be done.

In the case in which Colin Pretorius stands accused of child molestation and rape, an eleven-year-old boy yesterday testified how the accused called him to his office three years ago and showed him material of a pornographic nature. The accused locked the door and later began to fondle himself and encouraged the boy to do the same.

His next problem would be getting into the house. The front was too visible, he would have to get in the back where the concrete wall hid him from the neighbours. There were the burglar bars. The security contract meant an alarm. And a panic button.

The woman, whose name may not be made public, testified that her five-year-old son's symptoms of stress, which included acute aggression, bedwetting and lack of concentration, obliged his parents to consult a child psychologist. In therapy the boy revealed the molestation over a period of three months by Pretorius, owner of a crèche.

There were two alternatives. Wait for Pretorius to come home. Or try to gain entry. The first option was too unpredictable, too hard to control. The second was difficult, but not impossible.

He paid for his cold drink. He was not hungry. He felt too much anticipation, a vague tension, a sharpening of his senses. He fetched his pick-up from the parking area and left.

During his arrest, police seized Pretorius's computer, CD-ROM material and videos. Inspector Dries Luyt of the Domestic Violence Unit told the court the quantity and nature of the child pornography found was the 'worst this unit has yet seen'.

He flowed with the traffic.

He thought of being with Pakamile, the week before his death, in the mountain landscape of Mpumalanga beyond Amersfoort. On their motorbikes together with the six other students in the bright morning sun, between the pretty wooden houses, his son's eyes fixed on the instructor who spoke to them with such fervour.

'The greatest enemy of the motorbike rider is target fixation. It's in our blood. The connection between eyes and brain unfortunately works this way: if you look at a pothole or a rock, you will ride into it. Make sure you never look directly at the obstruction. Fighter pilots are trained to look ninety degrees away from the target the moment they press the missile-firing buttons. Once you have spotted an obstacle in the road, you know it's there. Search for the way around it; keep your eyes on the line to safety. You and your motorbike will follow automatically.'

He had sat there thinking this was not just a lesson in motorbike riding – life worked like that too. Even if you only realised it late or nearly too late. Sometimes you never did see the rocks. Like when he came back after the war. Battle ready, cocked, primed for the New South Africa. Ready to use his training, his skills and experience. An alumnus of the KGB university, graduate of the Stasi sniper school, veteran of seventeen eliminations in the cities of Europe.

Nobody wanted him.

Except for Orlando Arendse, that is. For six years he protected drug routes and collected drug debts, until he began to notice the rocks and potholes, until he needed to choose a safer line in order not to smash himself on the rocks.

And now?

He parked beside Hendrik Verwoerd Drive, high up against the bump of the Tygerberg, where you can see the Cape stretched out in front of you as far as Table Mountain, glittering in the night.

He sat for a moment, but did not see the view.

Perhaps the motorcycle instructor was wrong: avoiding the obstacles of life was not enough. How does a child choose a line through all the sickness, all the terrible traps? Maybe life needed someone to clear away the obstacles.

When Griessel returned to the flat with both hands full of Pick and Pay bags, Dr Barkhuizen was standing at his door, hand raised to knock.

'I came to see if you were okay.'

Later they sat cross-legged on the kitchen floor, drinking instant coffee from brand new floral mugs, and Griessel told him about the beer advertisement. The doctor said that was just the beginning. He would begin seeing what had been invisible before. The whole world would conspire to taunt him, the universe encourage him to have just one little swallow, just one glass. 'The brain is a fantastic organ, Benny. It seems to have a life of its own, one that we are unaware of. When you drink long enough, it begins to like that chemical balance. So when you stop, it makes plans to restore the balance. It's like a factory of cunning thoughts lodged somewhere, which pumps the best ones through to your conscious state. "Ach, it's just a beer." "What harm can one little drink do?" Another very effective one is the, "I deserve it, I have suffered for a week now and I deserve a small one." Or, even worse, the, "I have to have a drink now, or I will lose all control."'

'How the fuck do you fight it?'

'You phone me.'

'I can't do that every time . . .'

'Yes, you can. Any time, night or day.'

'It can't go on like this for ever, can it?'

'It won't, Benny. I will teach you the techniques to tame the beast.'

'Oh.'

'The other thing I wanted to talk about was those voices.'

He sat in the deep night-shadows of neglected shrubs, in the park that bordered on Simone Street. The binoculars were directed at Pretorius's home, three hundred metres down Chantelle Street.

A white suburb at night. Fort Blanc. No children playing outside. Locked doors, garages and security gates that opened with electronic remote controls, the blue flicker of television screens in living rooms. The streets were silent, apart from the white Toyota Tazz of Cobra Security that patrolled at random, or an occupant coming home late.

Despite these precautions, the walls and towers and moats, the children were not even safe here – it only took one intruder like Pretorius to nullify all the barriers.

There was life in the paedophile's house, lights going on and off.

He weighed up his options, considered a route that would take him away from the streetlights through back gardens up to the wall of Pretorius's house. Eventually he decided the fastest option was the one with the biggest chance of success: down the street.

He stood up, put the binoculars in his pocket and stretched his limbs. He pricked his ears for cars, left the shadows and began to walk with purpose.

'Doc, they are not voices. It's not like I hear a babble. It's . . . like someone screaming. But not outside, it's here inside, here in the back of my head. "Hear" is not even the right word, because there are colours too. Some are black, some are red; fuck, it makes me sound crazy, but it's true. I get to a murder scene. Let's say the case I am working on now. The woman is lying on the floor, strangled with the kettle cord. You can see from the marks on her neck that she has been strangled from behind. You begin to reconstruct how it happened – that's your job, you have to put it all together. You know she let him in, because there is no forced entry. You know they were together in the room because there is a bottle of wine and two glasses, or the coffee things. You know they must have talked, she was at ease, suspecting nothing, she was standing there and he was behind her saying something and suddenly there was this thing around her neck and she was frightened, what the fuck, she tried to get her fingers under the cord. Perhaps he turned her around, because he is sick, he wanted to see her eyes, he wanted to watch her face, because he's a control freak and now she sees him and she knows . . .'

He had to make a quick decision. He walked around the house and past the back door and saw that it was the best point of entry, no security gate, just an ordinary lock. He had to get in fast: the longer he remained outside, the greater the chance of being spotted.

He had the assegai at his back, under his shirt, the shaft just below his neck and the blade under his belt. He lifted his hand and pulled out the weapon. He raised a booted foot and, aiming for the lock, kicked open the door with all his strength.

The verdict in the case against crèche owner Colin Pretorius on various charges of child rape and molestation and the possession of child pornography is expected tomorrow. Pretorius did not testify.

The kitchen was dark. He ran through it towards the lights. Down the passage, left turn, to what he assumed was the living room. Television noise. He ran in, assegai in hand. Living room, couch, chairs, a sitcom's canned noise. Nobody. He spun around, spotted movement in the passage. The man was there, frozen in the light of a doorway, mouth half agape.

For a moment they stood facing each other at opposite ends of the passage and then the prey moved away and he attacked. The alarm must be in the bedroom. He had to stop him. The door swung shut. He dropped his shoulder, six, five, four paces, the door slammed, three, two, one, the snick of a key turning in the lock and he hit the door with a noise like a cannon shot, pain racking his body.

The door withstood him.

He was not going to make it. He stepped back, preparing to kick the door in, but it would be too late. Pretorius was going to activate the alarm.

'The picture in my head, Doc . . . It's like she's hanging from a cliff and clinging to life. As he strangles her, as the strength drains out of her, she feels her grip loosen. She knows she must not fall, she doesn't want to, she wants to live, she wants to climb to the top, but he squeezes the life out of her and she begins to slip. There is a terrible fear, because of the dark below; it's either black or red or brown down below and she just can't hold on any more and she falls.'

He felt a moment of panic: the locked door, the sharp pain in his shoulder, knowledge that the alarm would sound. But he drew a deep breath, made his choices and kicked the door with his heel. Adrenaline coursed thickly. Wood splintered. The door was open now. The alarm began to wail somewhere in the roof. Pretorius was at the wardrobe, reaching up, feeling for a weapon. He bumped him against the cupboard, the tall, lean figure, bespectacled with a sloppy fringe. He fell. Thobela was on him, knee to chest and assegai against his throat.

'I am here for the children,' he said loudly over the racket of the alarm, calm now.

Eyes blinked at the assegai. There was no fear. Something else. Expectation. A certain fatalism.

'Yes,' said Pretorius.

He jammed the long blade through the man's breastbone.

'It's when they fall that they scream. Death is down there and life is up here and the scream comes up, it always comes up to the top, it stays here. It moves fast, looks like a . . . like water you throw out of a bucket. That is all that is left. It is full of horrible terror. And loss . . .'

Griessel was quiet for a while; when he continued, it was in a quieter voice. 'The thing that scares me most is that I know it's not real, Doc. If I rationalise it, I know it's my imagination. But where does it come from? Why does my head do this? Why is the scream so shrill and clear and so loud? And so bloody despairing? I am not crazy. Not really – I mean, isn't there a saying that if you know you are a little bit mad you are okay, because the really insane have no idea?

Barkhuizen chuckled. It caught Griessel by surprise, but it was a sympathetic chuckle and he grinned back.

He sprinted through the house as the alarm wailed monotonously. Out the back door, around the corner of the house to the lighted street. He swerved right. He could see the park over the way, the security of the dark and the shadows. He felt a thousand eyes on him. Legs pumped rhythmically, breath raced; instinctively he pulled his head into his shoulders and tensed his back muscles for the bullet that would come, his ears pricked for a shout or the noise of the patrol car as his feet pounded on the tar.

When he reached the shrubbery, he slackened his pace as his night vision was spoiled by the streetlights. He had to plot his course carefully and not fall over anything. He could not afford a twist or sprain.

'You know where it really comes from,' said Barkhuizen.

'Doc?'

'You know, Benny. Think about it. There are contributing factors. Your job. I think you all suffer from post-traumatic stress syndrome – with all the murder and death. But that is not the actual source. It's something else. The thing that makes you drink, too, that made me drink as well.'

Griessel stared at him for a long time and then his head bowed. 'I know,' he said.

'Say it, Benny.'

'Doc . . .'

'Say it.'

'I am afraid to die, Doc. I am so afraid to die.'

He sat behind the wheel. He was still breathing hard, sweat dripped, his heart pounded. Jesus, he was forty – too old for this shit.

He pressed the key into the ignition.

There was one difference. His seventeen targets for the KGB . . . mostly he was detached, mechanical, even reluctant if it was some pallid pen-pusher with stooping shoulders and colourless eyes.

But not this time. This was different. When the assegai pierced the man's heart, he had a feeling of euphoria. Of absolute rightness.

Perhaps he had, at last, found his true vocation.

18

It was the following morning before she phoned him in his hotel room. From a public phone booth with Sonia on her shoulder.

'Five hundred rand,' was how she identified herself in an even voice that did not betray her anxiety.

It took only a few seconds for him to work it out and he said: 'Can you be here at six o'clock?'

'Yes.'

'Room 1036, in the Holiday Inn opposite the entrance to the Waterfront.'

'Six o'clock,' she repeated.

'What is your name?'

Her brain seemed to stop working. She didn't want to give her own name, but she couldn't think of any other one. She must not hesitate too long or he would know it was a fabrication – she said the first word that came to her lips.

'Bibi.'

Later she would wonder why that? Did it mean anything, have any psychological connotation, some clue by which to understand herself better? From Christine to Bibi. A leap, a new identity, a new creation. It was a birth, in some sense. It was also a wall. At first thin, like paper, transparent and fragile. At first.

'I have thought about it a lot,' she said, because she wanted to get the story right this time.

'The money was a big thing. Like when you play the Lotto and think of what you would do with the jackpot. In your imagination you spend on yourself and your child. Sensible things: you aren't going to squander your fortune. You are not going to be like the nouveau riche. That is why you will win. Because it's owed to you. You deserve it.

'But the money wasn't the main thing. There was another aspect, something I had since my school days. When I had sex with my father's friend. And the teacher. How I felt. I controlled them, but I didn't control myself. How can I explain it? I wasn't *in* myself. Yet I *was*.'

She knew those were not the right words to describe it and made a gesture of irritation with her hands. The minister did not respond, but just waited expectantly, or maybe he was nailed to his seat.

She shut her eyes in frustration and said: 'The easy one is the power. Uncle Sarel, my father's buddy, gave me a lift one day when I was walking home in the afternoon. When I opened the car door and saw the look on his face, I knew he wanted me. I wondered what he would say, what he would do. He held the steering wheel with both his hands because he was trembling and he didn't want me to see. That's when I felt how strong I was. I toyed with him. He said he wanted to talk with me, just for a short while, and could we take a drive? He was scared to look at me and I saw how freaked out he was but I was cool so I said: "Okay, that would be nice." I acted like I was innocent, that's what he wanted. He talked, you know, silly stuff, just talking, and he stopped by the river and I kept on acting and he told me how he had been watching me for so long and how sexy I was, but he respected me and then I put my hand on his cock and watched his face and the look in his eyes and his mouth went all funny and it . . . it excited me.

'It was a good feeling to know he wanted me, it was good to see how much he wanted me, it made me *feel* wanted. Your father thinks you are nothing, but they don't think so. Some grown-ups think you are great.

'But when he had sex with me, it was like I wasn't in my body. It was someone else and I was on one side. I could feel everything, I could feel his cock and his body and all, but I was outside. I looked at the man and the girl and I thought: What is she doing? She will be damaged. But that was also okay.

'That was the weirdest part of all, that the damage was also okay.'

She found someone to stand in for her at Trawlers. She spent the day with Sonia, rode her bike along the seafront as far as the swimming pool in Sea Point and slowly back again. She thought about what she would wear and she felt anticipation and that old feeling of being outside yourself, that vague consciousness of harm and the strange satisfaction it brought.

At four o'clock she left her daughter with the childcare lady and took a slow bath, washed and blow-dried her long hair. She put on a G-string, the floral halterneck, her jeans and sandals. At half-past five she took her bike and rode slowly so as not to arrive at the hotel out of breath and sweaty. This feels almost like a date, she thought. As she wove through the peak-hour traffic in Kloof Street, she saw men in cars turn their heads. She smiled a secret smile, because not one of them knew what she was and where she was going. *Here comes the whore on her bicycle.*

It wasn't so bad.

He was just a regular guy. He had no weird requests. He received her with rather exaggerated courtesy and spoke to her in whispers. He wanted her to stroke him, touch him and lie beside him. But first she had to undress and he shivered and said, 'God, what a body you've got,' and trailed his fingers slowly over her calves and thighs and belly. He kissed her breasts and sucked the nipples. And then the sex. He reached orgasm quickly and groaning and with eyes screwed shut. He lay on top of her and asked: 'How was it for you?' She said it was wonderful, because that was what he wanted to hear.

When she rode her bicycle home up the long gradient, she thought with a measure of compassion that what he had really wanted was to talk. About his work, his marriage, his children. What he really wanted was to expel the loneliness of the four hotel room walls. What he really wanted was a sympathetic ear.

When it became her full-time profession later, she realised most of them were like that. They paid to be someone again for an hour.

That night she just felt she was lucky, because he might have been a beast. In her little flat, while Sonia slept, she took the five new hundred-rand notes from her purse and spread them out in front of her. Nearly a week's work at Trawlers. If she could do just one man a day, for only five days a week, that was ten thousand rand a month. Once all the bills were paid, there would be seven thousand over to spend. Seven thousand rand.

Three days later she bought the cell phone and placed an ad in *Die Burger's Snuffelgids*. She carefully studied the other ads in the 'adult services' section first before deciding on the wording: *Bibi. Fresh and new. 22-year-old blonde with a dream body. Pleasure guaranteed, top businessmen only*. And the number.

It appeared on a Monday for the first time. The phone rang just after nine in the morning. She purposefully did not answer at once. Then in a cool voice: 'Hello.'

He didn't have a hotel room. He wanted to come to her. She said no, she only did travelling. He seemed disappointed. Before the phone rang again, she thought: why not? But there were too many reasons. This was her and Sonia's place – here she was Christine. Safe, only she knew the address. She would keep it that way.

A pattern was established. If they phoned in the morning, it was local men who wanted to come to her. In the late afternoon and evening it was hotel business. The first week she made two thousand rand, as she would take one call per evening and then switch off the phone. Thursday her daughter had not been well and she decided not to work. In the second week she decided to do two per day, one late afternoon and one early evening. It couldn't be too bad and it would give her time to have a good bath, put on fresh perfume . . . It would double her income and compensate for evenings when there were no clients.

Clients. That wasn't her word. One afternoon she had a call, a woman's voice. Vanessa. 'We're in the same trade. I saw your advert. Do you want to go out for coffee?'

That was her initiation into what Vanessa, real name Truida, called the AECW: the Association of Expensive Cape Whores. 'Oh it's like the Woman's Institute, only we don't open with scripture reading and prayer.' Vanessa was *Young student redhead, northern suburbs. Come and show me how. Upmarket and exclusive.*

She recited her life story in a coffee shop in the Church Street Mall. A sharp-featured woman with a flawless complexion, a scar on her chin and red hair from a very expensive bottle. She came from Ermelo. She had so wanted to escape the oppression of her hometown and parents' middle-class existence. She had done one year of secretarial at technical college in Johannesburg and worked in Midrand for a company that maintained compressors. She fell in love with a young Swede whom she met at a dance club in Sandton. Karl. His libido had no limits. Sometimes they spent entire weekends in bed. She became addicted to him, to the intense and multiple orgasms, to the constant stimulus and the tremendous energy. Above all she wanted to continue to satisfy him, even though every week it took a little more, a step further into unknown territory. Like a frog in water that was getting gradually warmer. She was hypnotised by his body, his penis, his worldly wisdom. Alcohol, toys, Ecstasy, role playing. One afternoon he called in a prostitute so they could make a threesome. A month later he took her to a 'club': a lovely big house on a smallholding near Bryanston. He was not unknown at the place, a fact she registered only vaguely. The first week she had to watch while he had sex with two of them, the second week she had to take part – four bodies writhing like snakes – and eventually he wanted to watch while she had sex with two male clients in a huge bedroom with a four poster bed.

When she heard for the first time what the girls at the Bryanston place earned, she laughed in disbelief. Six weeks after Karl dumped her, she drove to the club and asked for a job. She hoped she might see him there; she wanted the money, because she had lost all direction. But she was not so lost that she was blind to the inner workings. Too many of the girls were supporting men, men who beat them, men who took their money from them every Sunday to buy drink or drugs. Too many were dependent on the perks of cocaine, sometimes heroin, which was freely available. The club kept half of their earnings. Once she had got Karl out of her system, she came to Cape Town, alone, experienced and with a purpose.

'The trick is to save, so you don't end up in ten years' time like the fifty-rand whores on the street, hoping someone wants a quick blow job. Keep off the drugs and save. Retire when you are thirty.'

And: 'Do you know about asking names?'

'No.'

'When they phone, ask who is speaking. Ask for his name.'

'What's the point of that? Most of them lie.'

'If they lie, that's good news. Only the married ones lie. I have never had trouble with a married one. It's the ones who can't get a wife that you have to watch. The secret is to use the name he gives you when you speak to him. Over and over. That's how you sell yourself over the phone. Remember, he's still window shopping and there are a lot of adverts and options and he can't claim his five hundred rand from the medical aid. Say his name, even if it is a false one. It says you believe and trust him. It says you think he's important. You massage his ego, make him feel special. That is why he is phoning. So someone will make him feel special.'

'Why are you giving me all these tips?'

'Why not?'

'Aren't we in competition?'

'Sweetheart, it's all about supply and demand. The demand from needy men in this place is unlimited, but the supply of whores who really are worth five hundred rand an hour is . . . Jesus, you should see some of them. And the men get wise.'

And: 'Get yourself a separate place to work. You don't want clients bothering you at home. They do that, turning up drunk on a Saturday night without an appointment and standing on your doorstep weeping: "I love you, I love you."'

And: 'I had a fifty-five thousand rand month once; shit, I never closed my legs, it was a bit rough. But if you can do a steady three guys a day, it's easily thirty thousand in a good month, tax free. Make hay while the sun shines, because some months are slow. December is fantastic. Advertise in the *Argus* as well, that's where the tourists will find you. And on *Sextrader* on the Internet. If he has an accent, ask for six hundred.'

And: 'It's their wives' fault. They all say the same thing. Mamma doesn't want to do it any more. Mamma won't suck me. Mamma won't try new stuff. We're therapists, I'm telling you, I see how they come in and how they go.'

Vanessa told her about the other members of the AECW – Afrikaans and English, white, brown, black and a tiny delicate woman from Thailand. Christine only met three or four of them and spoke to a few more over the phone, but she was reluctant to become involved – she wanted to keep her distance and anonymity. But she did take their advice. She found a room at the Gardens Centre and set her sights higher. The money followed.

The days and weeks formed a pattern. Mornings were Sonia's, and weekends, except for the occasional one when she was booked for a hunting weekend, but the money made that worthwhile. She worked from 12:00 to 21:00 and then collected her daughter from the daycare where they thought she was a nurse.

Every third month she phoned her mother.

She bought a car for cash, a blue 1998 Volkswagen City Golf. They moved into a bigger flat, a spacious two-bedroom in the same building. She furnished it piece by piece like a jigsaw puzzle. Satellite television, an automatic washing machine and a microwave. A mountain bike for six thousand rand just because the salesman had looked her up and down and showed her the seven-ninety-nine models.

A year after she had placed the first advertisement, she and Sonia went to Knysna for a two-week holiday. On the way back she stopped at the traffic lights in the town and looked at the sign board showing Cape Town to the left and Port Elizabeth to the right. At that moment she wanted to go right, anywhere else, a new city, a new life.

An ordinary life.

Her regular clients had missed her. There were a lot of messages on her cell phone when she turned it back on.

She had been nearly two years in Cape Town when she phoned

home once more. Her mother cried when she heard her daughter's voice. 'Your father died three weeks ago.'

She could hear her mother's tears were not for the loss alone: they also expressed reproach. Implying that Christine had contributed to the heart attack. Reproach that her mother had had to bear it all alone. That she had no one to lean on. Nevertheless, the emotion Christine experienced was surprisingly sharp and deep, so that she responded with a cry of pain.

'What was that noise all about?' her mother asked.

She didn't really know. There was loss and guilt and self-pity and grief, but it was the loss that dumbfounded her. Because she had hated him so much. She began to weep and only later analysed all the reasons: what she had done, her absence, her part in his death. Her mother's loneliness and her sudden release. The permanent loss of her father's approval. The first realisation that death awaited her too.

But she could not explain why the next thing she said was about Sonia. 'I have a child, Ma.'

It just came out, like an animal that had been watching the door of its cage for months.

It took a long time for her mother to answer, long enough to wish she had never said it. But her mother's reaction was not what she expected: 'What is his name?'

'Her name, Ma. Her name is Sonia.'

'Is she two years old?' Her mother was not stupid.

'Yes.'

'My poor, poor child.' And they cried together, about everything. But when her mother later asked: 'When can I see my grandchild? At Christmas?' she was evasive. 'I'm working over Christmas, Ma. Perhaps in the New Year.'

'I can come down. I can look after her while you work.' She heard the desperation in her mother's voice, a woman who needed something good and pretty in her life after years of trouble. In that instant Christine wanted to give it to her. She was so eager to repay her debt, but she still had one secret she could not share.

'We will come and visit, Ma. In January, I promise.'

She didn't work that evening.

That night, after Sonia had gone to sleep, she cut herself for the first time. She had no idea why she did it. It might have been about her father. She rummaged around in the bathroom and found nothing. So she tried the kitchen. In one drawer she saw the knife that she used to pare vegetables. She carried it to the sitting room and sat and looked at herself and knew she couldn't cut where it would show – not in her profession. That's why she chose her foot, the soft underside between heel and ball. She pressed the knife in and drew it along. The blood began to flow and frightened her. She hobbled to the bathroom and held her foot over the bath. Felt the pain. She watched the drops slide down the side of the bath.

Later she cleaned up the blood spoor. Felt the pain. Refused to think about it. Knew she would do it again.

She didn't work the next day either. It was the beginning of December, bonanza month. She didn't want to go on. She wanted the kind of life where she could tell Sonia: 'Granny Martie is coming to visit.' She was weary of lying to the daycare or other mothers at the crèche. She was weary of her clients and their pathetic requests, their neediness. She wanted to say 'yes' the next time a polite, good-looking man came up to her table in McDonald's and asked if he could buy them ice cream. Just once.

But it was holiday season, big-money month.

She negotiated an agreement with herself. She would work as much as she could in December. So that they could afford to spend January with her mother in Upington. And when they came back she would find other work.

She kept to the deal. Martie van Rooyen absorbed herself in her granddaughter in those two weeks in Upington. She also sensed something about her daughter's existence. 'You have changed, Christine. You have become hard.'

She lied to her mother about her work, said she did this and that, worked here and there. She cut her other foot in her mother's bathroom. This time the blood told her she must stop. Stop all of it.

The next day she told her mother she hoped to get a permanent job. And she did.

She was appointed as sales rep for a small company that manufactured medicinal face creams from extract of sea-bamboo. She had to call on chemist shops in the city centre and southern suburbs. It lasted two months. The first setback was when she walked into a Link pharmacy in Noordhoek and recognised the pharmacist as one of her former clients. The second was when her new boss put his hand on her leg while they were travelling in his car. The final straw was her pay slip at the end of the month. Gross income: nine thousand and something. Nett income: six thousand four hundred rand, sales commission included, after tax and unemployment insurance and who knows what had been subtracted.

She rethought her plans. She was twenty-one years old. As an escort she had earned more than thirty thousand rand a month and she had saved twenty thousand of it. After buying the car and a few other large expenses she still had nearly two hundred thousand in the bank. If she could just work another four years . . . until Sonia went to school. Just four years. Save two, two-fifty a year, perhaps more. Then she could afford a normal job. Just four years.

It nearly worked out. Except one day she answered the phone and Carlos Sangrenegra said: 'Conchita?'

19

He checked out of the Parow hotel. His requirements had changed. He wanted to be more anonymous, have fewer witnesses of his coming and going. He drove into the city centre where he could pass the time without attracting attention. From a public phone in the Golden Acre he called the detective in Umtata to ask for news of Khoza and Ramphele.

'I thought you were going to catch them.'

'I'm not getting anywhere.'

'It's not so easy, hey?'

'No, it's not.'

'Yes,' said the detective, mollified by the capitulation. 'We haven't really got anything from our side either.'

'Not really?'

'Nothing.'

In Adderley Street he bought *Die Burger* and went into the Spur on Strand Street for breakfast. He placed his order and shook the paper open. The main news was the 2010 Soccer World Cup bid. At the bottom of page one was an article headed, *Gay couple arrest over child's death*. He read that one. A woman had been arrested on suspicion of the murder of her partner's five-year-old daughter. The child was hit over the head with a billiard cue, apparently in a fit of rage.

His coffee arrived. He tore open a paper tube of sugar, poured it into his cup and stirred.

What was he trying to do?

If children can't depend on the justice system to protect them, to whom can they turn?

How would he achieve it? How would he be able to protect the children by his actions? How would people know: you cannot lay a finger on a child. There must be no doubt – the sentence of death had been reinstated.

He tested the temperature of the coffee with a careful sip.

He was in too much of a hurry. It would happen. It would take a little time for the message to get across, but it would happen. He must just not lose focus.

'It's not going to happen,' said Woolworth's head of corporate communication, a white woman in her early forties. She sat beside André Marais, the female police sergeant, in a meeting room of the chain store head office in Longmarket Street. The contrast between the two women was marked. It's only money, thought Griessel, and environment. Take this manicured woman in her tight grey suit and leave her at the charge desk in Claremont for three months on a police salary and then let's take another look.

There were six around the circular table: January, the Waterfront store manager, Kleyn – the communications woman, Marais, Griessel and his shift partner for the month, Inspector Cliffy Mketsu.

'Oh yes it is,' said Griessel derisively enjoying himself. 'Because you won't like the alternative, Mrs Kleyn.' He and Mketsu had decided that he would play the bad cop and Cliffy would be the peace-loving, good cop Xhosa detective.

'What alternative?' The woman's extremely red mouth was small and dissatisfied under the straight nose and over made-up eyes. Before Griessel could reply she added: 'And it's *Ms* Kleyn.'

'McClean?' asked Cliffy, slightly puzzled, and slid her business card closer across the table. 'But here it says . . .'

'*Ms*,' she said. 'As in neither Mrs or Miss. It's a modern form of address which probably hasn't yet penetrated the police.'

'Let me tell you what has penetrated the police, *Ms* Kleyn,' said Griessel, suspecting it would not be difficult to act mean with this particular woman. 'It has penetrated us that this afternoon we are

going to hold a press conference and we are going to tell the media
there is a serial killer on the loose in the shopping aisles of Woollies.
We are going to ask them to please warn the unsuspecting public to
stay away before another innocent, middle-aged Woollies customer is strangled with a kettle cord. This modus operandi has
penetrated the police, *Ms* Kleyn. So don't you tell me "it's not
going to happen", as if I came to ask if we could hold trolley races
up and down your aisles.'

Even through all that foundation he could see she had turned a
deep shade of red.

'Benny, Benny,' said Cliffy in a soothing tone. 'I don't think
we have to make threats. We must understand Ms Kleyn's
point of view too. She is only considering the interests of her
customers.'

'She is only considering the interests of her company. I say we
talk to the press.'

'That's blackmail,' said Kleyn, losing confidence.

'It's unnecessary,' said Cliffy. 'I am sure we can come to some
arrangement, Mrs Kleyn.'

'We will have to,' said January, the manager of the Waterfront
branch.

'Did I say *Mrs*? Oh, I am sorry,' said Cliffy.

'We can't afford that kind of publicity,' said January.

'It's strength of habit,' said Cliffy.

'I will not be blackmailed,' said Kleyn.

'Of course not, *Ms* Kleyn.'

'I'm going,' said Griessel, standing up.

'Could I say something?' asked Sergeant Marais in a gentle
voice.

'Naturally, *Ms* Marais,' said Cliffy jovially.

'You are afraid something might happen to customers in the
shop?' she asked Kleyn.

'Of course I am. Can you imagine what that publicity would
mean?'

'I can,' said Marais. 'But there is a way to remove the risk
altogether.'

'Oh?' said Kleyn.

Griessel sat down again.

'All we want to do is to get the suspect to make contact with me. We hope he will initiate a conversation and get himself invited to a woman's home. We can't confront him in the shop or try to arrest him: there are no grounds. So really there is no risk of a confrontation.'

'I don't know . . .' said Kleyn, and looked dubiously at her long red fingernails.

'Would it help if I was the only policeman in the supermarket?'

'Steady on, Sergeant,' said Griessel.

'Inspector, I will be carrying a radio and we know the supermarket is a safe environment. You can be outside, all over.'

'I think that's a good idea,' said Cliffy.

'I don't see why we should change good police procedure just because the Gestapo don't like it,' said Griessel and got to his feet again.

Kleyn sucked in her breath sharply, as if to react, but he didn't give her the chance. 'I'm leaving. If you want to sell out, do it without me.'

'I like your proposals,' said Kleyn to André Marais quickly, so that Griessel could hear it before he was out the door.

Thobela was standing at the reception desk of the Waterfront City Lodge when the *Argus* arrived. The deliveryman dropped the bundle of newspapers beside him on the wooden counter with a dull thump. The headline was right under his nose, but he was still filling in the registration card and his attention was not on the big letters:

VIGILANTE KILLER TARGETS 'CHILD MOLESTERS'

His pen stalled over the paper. What was written there – what did they know? The clerk behind the desk was busy at the keyboard of the computer. He forced himself to finish writing and hand the card over. The clerk gave him the room's electronic card key and explained to him how to find it.

'May I take a newspaper?'

'Of course, I'll just charge it to your account.'

He took a paper, and his bag, and headed for the stairs. He read.

One day before crèche owner Colin Pretorius (34) was to receive judgement on several charges of rape and molestation, he apparently became the second victim of what could be an assegai-wielding vigilante killer bent on avenging crimes against children.

He realised he was standing still and his heart was bumping hard in his chest. He glanced up, took the stairs to the first floor and waited until he was there before reading more.

The investigating officer, Inspector Bushy Bezuidenhout of the Serious and Violent Crimes Unit (SVC), did not rule out the possibility that the bladed weapon was the same one used in the Enver Davids stabbing three days ago.

In an exclusive report, following an anonymous phone call to our offices, The Argus *yesterday revealed that the 'bladed weapon' was an assegai . . .*

How much did they know? His eyes searched the columns.

Inspector Bezuidenhout admitted that the police had no suspects at this time. Asked whether the killer might be a woman, he said that he could not comment on the possibility (see page 16: The Artemis Factor).

He opened his room door, put the bag on the floor and spread the newspaper open on the bed. He turned to page 16.

Greek mythology had its female protector of children, a ruthless huntress of the gods called Artemis, who could punish injustice with ferocious and deadly accuracy – and silver arrows. But just how likely is a female avenger of crimes against children?

'It is possible that this vigilante is a woman,' says criminologist Dr Rita Payne. 'We are ruthless when it comes to protecting our kids, and there are several appropriate case studies of mothers committing serious crimes, even murder, to avenge acts against their children.'

But there is one reason why the suspected modern-day Artemis might not be female: 'An assegai isn't a likely weapon for a woman. In

*instances where women did use a blade to stab or cut a victim, it was a
weapon of opportunity, not premeditation,' Dr Payne said.*

However, this does not completely rule out a female vigilante . . .

He felt uncomfortable about this publicity. He pushed the
newspaper to one side and got up to open the curtain. He had
a view over the canal and the access road to the Waterfront. He
stood and stared at the incessant stream of cars and pedestrians
and wondered what was bothering him, what was the cause of this
new tension. The fact that the police were investigating as if he
were a common criminal? He had known that would happen, he
had no illusions about that. Was it because the paper made it all
sound so shallow? What did it matter if it was a woman or a man?
Why not focus on the root of the matter?

Somebody was doing something. Someone was fighting back.

'Artemis.'

He spat out the word, but it left an unpleasant aftertaste.

Since she had told him about Sonia, the minister seemed to have
grown weary. His thinning hair lay flatter on his scalp,
smoothed by the big hand that touched it every now and then.
His beard began to shadow his jaw in the light of the desk lamp,
the light blue shirt was rumpled and the rolled-up sleeves hung
down unevenly. His eyes were still on her with the same focus,
the same undivided attention, but touched now with something
else. She thought she saw a suspicion there, a premonition of
tragedy.

'You were very convincing today, Benny,' said Cliffy Mketsu as
they followed André Marais to the car.

'She pisses me off, that fucking *Ms*,' he said, and he saw
Sergeant Marais's back stiffen ahead of him.

'Now you think I have a thing against women, Sergeant,' he said.
He knew what was wrong with him. He knew he was walking on
the edge. Jissis, the pills were doing fuck-all – he wanted a drink, his
entire body was a parched throat.

'No, Inspector,' said Marais with a meekness that irritated.

'Because you would be wrong. I only have a thing about women like *her*.' He said in a falsetto voice: '*It's a modern form of address which probably hasn't yet penetrated the police.* Why must they always have something to say about the fucking police? Why?'

Two coloured men came walking towards them down the pavement. They looked at Griessel.

'Benny . . .' said Cliffy, laying a hand on his arm.

'Okay,' said Griessel, and took the keys out of his jacket pocket when they reached the police car. He unlocked it, got in and stretched across to unlock the other doors. Mketsu and Marais got in. He put the key in the ignition.

'What does she want to be a *Ms* for? What for? What is wrong with Mrs? Or Miss. It was good enough for six thousand years and now she wants to be a fucking *Ms*.'

'Benny.'

'What for, Cliffy?' He couldn't do this. He had to have a drink. He felt for the slip of paper in his pocket, not sure where he had put it.

'I don't know, Benny,' said Cliffy. 'Let's go.'

'Just wait a minute,' he said.

'If I was her, I would also want to be Ms,' said André Marais quietly from the back seat.

He found the paper, unclipped his seat belt and said: 'Excuse me,' and got out of the car. He read the number on the paper and phoned it on his cell phone.

'Barkhuizen,' said the voice on the other side.

He walked down the pavement away from the car. 'Doc, those pills of yours are not doing a damn thing for me. I can't go on. I can't do my work. I am a complete bastard. I want to hit everyone. I can't go on like this, Doc, I'm going to buy myself a fucking litre of brandy and I'm going to drink it, Doc, you hear?'

'I hear you, Benny.'

'Right, Doc, I just wanted to tell you.'

'Thank you, Benny.'

'Thank you, Benny?'

'It's your choice. But just do me one favour, before you pour the first one.'

'What's that, Doc?'

'Phone your wife. And your children. Tell them the same story.'

20

She sat looking at Sonia. The child lay on the big bed, one hand folded under her, the other a little dumpling next to her open mouth. Her hair was fine and glossy in the late-afternoon sun shining through the window. She sat very still and stared at her child. She was not looking for features that reminded her of Viljoen, she was not revelling in the perfection of her limbs.

Her child's body. Unmarked. Untouched. Holy, stainless, clean.

She would teach her that her body was wonderful. That she was beautiful. That she was allowed to be beautiful. She could be attractive and desirable – it was not a sin, nor a curse, it was a blessing. Something she could enjoy and be proud of. She would teach Sonia that she could put on make-up and pretty clothes and walk down the street and draw the attention of men and that was fine. Natural. That they would storm her battlements like soldiers in endless lines of war. But she had a weapon to ensure that only the one she chose would conquer her – love for herself.

That was the gift she would give to her daughter.

She got up and fetched the new knife that she had bought from @Home. She took it to the bathroom and locked the door behind her. She stood in front of the mirror and lightly and slowly drew the blade over her face, from her brow to her chin.

How she longed to press the blade in. How she longed to cleave the skin and feel the burn.

She took off her T-shirt, unsnapped the bra behind her back and let it fall to the floor. She held the knifepoint against her breast. She drew a circle around her nipple. In her mind's eyes she saw the blade flash as she carved long stripes across her breast. She saw the marks criss-crossed.

Just another two years.

She sat on the rim of the bath and swung her feet over. She placed her left foot on her right knee. She held the knife next to the cushion beside her big toe. She cut, fast and deep, right down to her heel.

When she felt the sudden pain and saw the blood collecting in the bottom of the bath, she thought: You are sick, Christine. You are sick, sick, sick.

'In the beginning Carlos was quite refreshing. Different. With me. I think it is more okay in Colombia to visit a sex worker than it is here. He never had that attitude of "what if someone saw me" like most of my clients. He was a small, wiry man without an ounce of fat on him. He was always laughing. Always glad to see me. He said I was the most beautiful conchita in the world. "You are Carlos's blonde bombshell." He talked about himself like that. He never said "I". "Carlos wants to clone you, and export you to Colombia. You are very beautiful to Carlos."

'He had nice hands, that's one of the things I remember about him. Delicate hands like a woman's. He made a lot of noise when we had sex, sounds and Spanish words. He shouted so loud once that someone knocked on the door and asked if everything was okay.

'The first time he gave me extra money, two hundred rand. "Because you are the best." A few days later he phoned again. "You remember Carlos? Well, now he cannot live without you."

'He made me laugh, at first. When he came to my place in the Gardens Centre. Before I started going to him, before I knew what he did. Before he became jealous.'

Before Carlos she wrote the letter.

You were a good mother. Pa was the one who messed up. And me. That is why I am leaving Sonia with you. She wanted to add something, words to say that her mother deserved a second chance with a daughter, but every time she scratched out the lines, crumpled up the paper and started over.

Late at night she would sit on the rim of the bath and stroke the knife over her wrists. Between one and three, alone, Sonia asleep in her cheerful bedroom with the seagulls on the ceiling and Mickey Mouse on the wall. She knew she could not let the knife cut in, because she could not abandon her child like that. She would have to make another plan with more limited damage.

She wondered how much blood could flow in the bath.

How great would the relief be when all the bad was out?

Carlos Sangrenegra, with his Spanish accent and his odd English, his tight jeans and the moustache that he cultivated with such care. The little gold crucifix on a fine chain around his neck, the one thing he kept on in bed, although they weren't actually in the bed much. 'Doggie, conchita, Carlos likes doggie.' He would stand with feet planted wide apart on the floor; she would be bent over the edge of the bed. From the start he was different. He was like a child. Everything excited him. Her breasts, her hair colour, her eyes, her body, her shaven pubic hair.

He would come in and undress, ready and erect, and he wouldn't want to chat first. He was never uncomfortable.

'Don't you want to talk first?'

'Carlos does not pay five hundred rand for talking. That he can get free anywhere.'

She liked him, those first few times, perhaps because he enjoyed her so intensely, and was so verbal about it. Also, he brought flowers, sometimes a small gift, and left a little extra when he went. It was her perception that it was a South-American custom, this generosity, since she had never had a Latin-American client before. Germans and Englishmen, Irishmen (usually drunk), Americans, Hollanders (always found something to complain about) and Scandinavians (possibly the best lovers overall). But Carlos was a first. A Colombian.

That origin meant nothing to her, just a vaguely remembered orange patch on a school atlas.

'What do you do?' After his theatrical orgasm, he was lying with his head between her breasts.

'What does Carlos do? You don't know?'

'No.'

'Everybody knows what Carlos do.'

'Oh.'

'Carlos is a professional lover. World heavyweight love champion. Every fuck is a knockout. You should know that, conchita.'

She could only laugh.

He showered and dressed and took extra notes from his wallet and put them on the bedside cupboard saying: 'Carlos gives you a little extra.' In that rising tone, as if it were a question, but she was used to that. Then he put his hand back in his jeans pocket and said: 'You don't know what Carlos does?'

'No.'

'You don't know what the number one export of Colombia is?'

'No.'

'Ah, conchita, you are so innocent,' he said, and he brought out a little transparent plastic packet in his hand, filled with fine white powder. 'Do you know what this is?'

She made a gesture with her hand to show she was guessing. 'Cocaine?'

'Yes, it is cocaine, of course it is cocaine. Colombia is the biggest cocaine producer in the world, conchita.'

'Oh!'

'You want?' He held the packet up towards her.

'No, thanks.'

That made him laugh uproariously. 'You don't want A-grade, super special number one uncut Colombian snow?'

'I don't take drugs,' she said, a bit embarrassed, as if it were an insult to his national pride.

Suddenly he was serious. 'Yes, Carlos's conchita is clean.'

She ascribed the early signs to his Latin blood, just another characteristic that was refreshingly different.

He would ring and say: 'Carlos is coming over.'

'Now?'

'Of course *now*. Carlos misses his conchita.'

'I miss you, too, but I can only see you at three o'clock.'

'*Tree* o'clock?'

'I have other clients too, you know.'

He said a word in Spanish, two cutting syllables.

'Carlo-o-o-o-s,' she stretched it out soothingly.

'How much they paying you?'

'The same.'

'They bring you flowers?'

'No, Carlos . . .'

'They give you extra?'

'No.'

'So why see them?'

'I have to make a living.'

He was silent until she said his name.

'Carlos will come tomorrow. Carlos wants to be first, you unnerstand? First love of the day.'

'He phoned one day and he said he was going to send someone to pick me up. These two guys that I didn't know came in a big BMW, one of those with a road map on a television up front, and they took me to Camps Bay. We got out, but you couldn't see the house, it was up on the slope. You go up in a lift. Everything is glass and the view is out of this world, but there wasn't really furniture in it. Carlos said he had just bought it and I must help him, as he wasn't very good with decorating and stuff.

'Maybe that was the night I clicked for the first time. I had been there for half an hour when I looked at my watch, but Carlos was angry and said: "Don't look at your watch."

'When I wanted to protest, he said: "Carlos will take care of you, hokay?"

'We ate on the balcony, on a blanket, and Carlos chatted as if we were boyfriend and girlfriend. The other two who fetched me were around somewhere, and he told me they were bodyguards and there was nothing to be scared of.

'Then he asked me: "How much do you get in a month, conchita?" I didn't like to say. Lots of them ask, but I never say – it's not their business. So I told him: "That's private."

'Then he came out with it. "Carlos do not want his girlfriend to see other guys. But he knows you must make a living, so he will pay what you make. More. Double."

'So I said: "No, Carlos, I can't," and that made him angry, for the first time. He smacked all the food around on the blanket and screamed at me in Spanish, and I thought he would hit me. So I took my handbag and said I had better go. I was scared; he was another person, his face . . . The bodyguards came walking out and talked to him and suddenly he calmed down and he just said: "Sorry, conchita, Carlos is so sorry." But I asked him, please, could they just take me home, and he said he would do it himself and all the way he was sorry and he made jokes and when I got out he gave me two thousand. I took it, because I thought if I tried to give it back he would be angry again.

'The next morning I phoned Vanessa and asked her what I should do, this guy thinks I am his girlfriend and he wants to pay me to be with just him and she said that is bad news, I must get rid of him, that sort of thing could ruin my whole business. So I said thanks and bye, because I didn't want to tell her this guy is in drugs and he has a terrible temper and I haven't a clue how to get rid of him.

'So I phoned Carlos and he said he was terribly sorry, it was his work that made him like that, and he sent flowers and I started to think it would be okay. But then they assaulted one of my clients, just outside the door of my room in the Gardens Centre.

The master bedroom of the Camps Bay house had a four-poster bed now. He had retained an expensive, well-known interior decorator who had begun with the bedroom and everything was in white: curtains, bedding, drapes on the bed like the sails of a ship. He showed off like a little boy, keeping his hands over her eyes all the way down the passage and then: 'Ta-daaa!' and watched her reaction. He asked her four or five times, 'You like the master's bedroom?' and she said, 'It's beautiful,' because it was.

He dived onto the bed and said, 'Come to Carlos,' and he was exuberant, even more boisterous than usual, and she tried to forget about the bodyguards somewhere in the house.

Later he lay beside her and softly traced little circles around her nipple with the tip of the little gold crucifix. 'Where do you live, conchita?'

'You know . . .'

'No, where do you *live*?'

'Gardens Centre,' she replied, hoping he would drop the subject.

'You think Carlos is stupid because he looks stupid? You work there, but where is your home, where is the place with your pictures on the fridge?'

'I can't afford another place, you pay me too little.'

'Carlos pay you too little? Carlos pay you too much. All the time the moneyman is saying: "Carlos, we are here to make a profit, remember."'

'You have a bookkeeper?'

'Of course. You think Carlos is small fish? Cocaine is big business, conchita, very big business.'

'Oh.'

'So you will take Carlos to your house?'

Never, she thought, never ever, but said, 'One day . . .'

'You don't trust Carlos?'

'Can I ask you a question?'

'Conchita, you can ask Carlos anything.'

'Did you have my client beaten up?'

'What client?' But he couldn't carry off the lie and his eyes turned crafty. He is a child, she thought, and it frightened her.

'Just a client. Fifty-three years old.'

'Why do you think Carlos beat him?'

'Not you. But maybe the bodyguards?'

'Did he buy drugs?'

'No.'

'They only beat up people who do not pay for drugs, hokay?'

'Okay.' She knew what she wanted to know. But it helped not at all.

21

Griessel and Cliffy sat in the fish restaurant a hundred metres beyond the entrance to Woolworths, each with a small earphone. They heard André Marais saying, 'Testing, testing' for the umpteenth time, but this time with a tinny voice in the background calling, 'Next customer, please.'

Cliffy Mketsu nodded, as he did every time. It irritated Griessel immensely. Marais couldn't fucking see them nod, she was in the food section of Woolworths and they were here. She was only wearing a microphone, not earphones. One-way communication only, but Cliffy had to nod.

At a table opposite, a man and a woman were drinking red wine. The woman was middle-aged, but pretty, like Farrah Fawcett, with big, round, golden earrings and lots of rings on her fingers. The man looked young enough to be her son, but took her hand every now and again. They bothered Griessel. Because they were drinking wine. Because he could taste the dark flavour in his mouth. Because they were rich. Because they were together. Because they could drink and be together and what of him? He could sit here with Nodding Cliffy Mketsu, clever Cliffy, busy with his Masters in Police Science, a good policeman, but confused, hopelessly absent-minded, as if his head was in his books all the time.

Would he and Anna ever be able to sit and enjoy themselves like that? Sit holding hands and sipping wine and gazing into each other's eyes? How did people do that? How do you regain the romance after twenty years of married life? Actually, it was fucking irrelevant, because he would never be able to sip wine again. Not if you were an alcoholic. You couldn't drink a thing. Nothing. Not a fucking drop. Couldn't even smell the red wine.

He had told Doc Barkhuizen he was going to get drunk, but the Doc had said: 'Phone your wife and children and tell them,' because he knew Griessel could not do that. He wanted to smash his cell phone on the bloody pavement, he wanted to break something but he just screamed, he didn't know what, not words. When he turned around, Cliffy and André Marais were sitting rigidly in the car pretending nothing had happened.

'Vaughn, are you receiving properly?' Cliffy asked the other team over the microphone. They were looking at Woolworths clothes on the second floor, the one above the food department.

'Ten-four, good buddy,' said Inspector Vaughn Cupido, as if it were a game. He and Jamie Keyter were the back-up team. Not *Yaymie* as the locals would say it, he called himself *Jaa-mie*. Nowadays everyone had foreign names. What was wrong with good, basic Afrikaner names? The men weren't Griessel's first choice either, as Cupido was careless and Keyter was a braggart, recently transferred from Table View Station after he had made the newspapers with one of those stories where facts do not necessarily interfere with sensation. 'Detective breaks car-theft syndicate single-handed.' With his bulging Virgin Active biceps and the kind of face to make schoolgirls swoon, he was one of the few white additions to the Serious and Violent Crimes Unit. This was the team that had to protect André Marais and catch a fucking serial killer: an alcoholic, a braggart and a sloppy one.

There was another matter on his mind; two, three things that came suddenly together: were the older woman and the young man opposite married? To each other? What if Anna had a young man who held her hand on Friday nights? He couldn't believe that she no longer wanted it, of that he was convinced. You didn't just switch off her sort of warmth like a stove plate just because her husband was a fucking alky. She met men at work – what would she do if there was a young man who was interested and sober? She was still attractive, despite the crow's feet at the corners of her eyes – due to her husband's drinking habit. There was nothing wrong with her body. He knew what men were like; he knew they would try. How long would she keep saying 'no'? How long?

He took out his cell phone, needing to know where she was on a Friday night. He rang, holding the phone to the ear without the earphone.

It rang.

He looked across at Farrah Fawcett and her toy boy.

They were gazing into each other's eyes with desire. He swore they were just plain horny.

'I thi . . . it's tha . . . . . . t,' said André Marais in the earphone.

'What?' said Griessel, looking at Cliffy, who merely shrugged and tapped his radio receiver with the tip of his index finger.

'Hello,' said his son.

'Hello, Fritz.'

'Hi, Dad.' There was no joy in his son's voice.

'How are you?'

But he couldn't hear the answer as the earphone buzzed in his ear and he only caught a fraction of what Sergeant André Marais was saying: '. . . can't afford . . .'

'What are you doing, Fritz?'

'Nothing. It's just Carla and me.' His son sounded depressed, and there was a dull tone to his voice.

'How's your reception, Vaughn?' Cupido asked. 'Her mike isn't good.'

'Just Carla and you?'

'Mom's out.'

'I usually just buy instant,' said André Marais clearly and distinctly.

'She's talking to someone,' said Cliffy.

Then they heard a man's voice over the ether, faintly: 'I can't do without a good cup of filter in the morning.'

'Dad? Are you there?'

'I'll have to call later, Fritz, I'm at work.'

'Okay.' Like he expected it.

'What . . . name?'

'. . . dré.'

'Fuck,' said Cupido, 'her fucking mike.'

'Bye, Fritz.'

'Bye, Dad.'

'We might be too far away,' said Jamie Keyter.

'Stay where you are,' said Griessel.

'Pleased to meet you,' said the policewoman below in Woolworths food hall.

'A fish on the hook,' said Cupido.

Cliffy nodded.

Mom's out.

'Just keep calm,' said Griessel, but he meant it for himself.

Thobela made a noise of frustration in his deep voice as he rose from the hotel bed in one sudden movement. He had lain down at about three o'clock with the curtains drawn to shut out the sun, closed his eyes and lay listening to the beat of his heart. His head buzzed from too little sleep and his limbs felt like lead. Weary. With deliberate breathing he tried to drain the tension from his body. He sent his thoughts away from the present, sent them to the peaceful waters of the Cata River, to the mist that rolled like wraiths over the round hills of the farm . . . to realise only moments later that his thoughts had jumped away and were pumping other information through his consciousnesses to the rhythm of the pulse in his temples.

Pretorius reaching for the weapon in his wardrobe.

Eternity in the moments before he reached the man, and the alarm wailing, wailing, to the rhythm of his heartbeat.

A heavy woman towering above a little girl and the billiard cue rising and falling, rising and falling with demonic purpose and the blood spattering from the child's head and he knew that was his problem – the woman, the woman. He had never executed a woman. His war was against men, always had been. In the name of the Struggle, seventeen times. Sixteen in the cities of Europe, one in Chicago: men, traitors, assassins, enemies, condemned to death in the committee rooms of the Cold War, and he was the one sent to carry out the sentence. Now two in the name of the New War. Animals. But male.

Was there honour in the execution of a woman?

The more he forced his thoughts elsewhere, the more they scurried back, until he rose up with that deep sound and plucked aside the curtains. There was movement outside, bright sunlight and colour. He looked over the canal and the entrance to the Waterfront. Labourers streamed on foot towards the city centre, to the taxi ranks in Adderley Street. Black and coloured, in the brightly coloured overalls of manual labourers. They moved with purpose, hasty to start the weekend, somewhere at a home or a shebeen. With family. Or friends.

His family was dead. He wanted to jerk open the window and scream: Fuck you all, my family is dead!

He drew a deep breath, placed his palms on the cool windowsill and let his head hang. He must get some sleep; he could not go on like this.

He turned back to the room. The bedspread was rumpled. He pulled it straight, smoothing it with his big hands, pulling and stretching it till it was level. He puffed up the pillows and laid them tidily down, one beside the other. Then he sat on the bed and picked up the telephone directory from the bedside drawer, found the number and rang Boss Man Madikiza at the Yellow Rose.

'This is Tiny. The one who was looking for John Khoza, you remember?'

'I remember, my brother.' The uproar of the nightclub was already audible in the background this late afternoon.

'Heard anything?'

'Haiziko. Nothing.'

'Keep your ear to the ground.'

'It is there all the time.'

He got up and opened the wardrobe. The stack of clean clothes on the top shelf was very low, the piles of folded dirty laundry were high – socks, underwear, trousers and shirts, each in their own separate pile.

He took the two small plastic holders of detergent and softener from his case, and sorted the washing into small bundles. The ritual was twenty years old, from the time in Europe when he had learned to live out of a suitcase. To be in control, orderly and organised. Because the call could come at any time. In those days he had made a game of it, the sorting of clothes according to colour had made him smile, because that was apartheid – the whites here, the blacks there, the mixed colours in their own pile; each group afraid that another group's colour would stain them. He had always washed the black bundle first, because 'here blacks come first'.

He did that now, just from habit. Pressed and rubbed the material in the soapy water – rinse once, then again, twist the clothes in long worms to squeeze out the water – until his muscles bulged. Hung them out. Next the coloured clothes, and the whites could wait till last.

Next morning he would ring reception and ask for an ironing board and iron and do the part he enjoyed the most – ironing the shirts and trousers with a hissing, hot iron till they could be hung on hangers in the wardrobe with perfect flat surfaces and sharp creases.

He draped the last white shirt over the chair and then stood indecisively in the centre of the room.

He could not stay here.

He needed to pass the time until he could attempt sleep again. And he must think through this matter of the woman.

He picked up his wallet, pushed it in his trouser pocket, took the key card for his room and went out the door, down the stairs and outside. He walked around the corner to Dock Road, where the people were still walking to their weekend. He fell in behind a group of five coloured men and kept pace with them up Coen Steytler. He eavesdropped on their conversation, following the easy, directionless talk with close attention all the way to Adderley.

It was not André Marais's fault that Operation Woollies descended into total chaos. She acted out her role as a lonely, middle-aged woman skilfully and with vague, careful interest as the man began to chat with her between the wine racks and the snack displays.

Later she would think that she had expected an older man. This one was barely thirty: tallish, slightly plump, with a dark, five o'clock shadow. His choice of clothes was strange – the style of his checked jacket was out of date, the green shirt just a shade too bright, brown shoes unpolished. 'Harmless' was the word on her tongue, but she knew appearance counted for nothing when it came to crime.

He asked her, in English with an Afrikaans accent, if she knew where the filter coffee was, and she replied that she thought it was that way.

With a shy smile he told her he was addicted to filter coffee and she replied that usually she bought instant as she could not afford expensive coffee. He said he couldn't manage without a good cup of filter coffee in the morning, charmingly apologetic, as if it were sinful. 'Italian Blend,' he said.

Oddly, she explained to Griessel later, at that moment she quite liked him. There was a vulnerability to him, a humanity that found an echo in herself.

Their trolleys were side by side, hers with ten or twelve items, his empty. 'Oh?' she said, fairly certain he was not the one they were looking for. She wanted to get rid of him.

'Yes, it's very strong,' he said. 'It keeps me alert when I am on the Flying Squad.'

She felt her guts contract, because she knew he was lying. She knew policemen, she could spot them a mile away and he was not one, she knew.

'Are you a policeman?' she asked, trying to sound impressed.

'Captain Johan Reyneke,' he said, putting out a rather feminine hand and smiling through prominent front teeth. 'What is your name?'

'André,' she said, and felt her heart beat faster. Captains did not do Flying Squad – he must have a reason for lying.

'André,' he repeated, as if to memorise it.

'My mother wanted to use her father's name, and then she only had daughters.' She used her standard explanation, although there was no question in his voice. With difficulty she kept her voice level.

'Oh, I like that. It's different. What work do you do, André?'

'Oh, admin, nothing exciting.'

'And your husband?'

She looked into his eyes and lied. 'I am divorced,' she said, and looked down, as if she were ashamed.

'Never mind,' he said, 'I'm divorced too. My children live in Johannesburg.'

She was going to say her children were out of the house already, part of the fabrication she and Griessel had discussed, but there was a voice from behind, a woman's voice, quite shrill. 'André?'

She glanced over her shoulder and recognised the woman, Molly, couldn't recall her surname. She was the mother of one of her son's school friends, one of those over-eager, terribly involved parents. Oh God, she thought, not now.

'Hi,' said André Marais, glancing at the man and seeing his eyes narrow, and she pulled a face, trying to communicate to him that she would rather not have this interruption.

'How are you, André? What are you doing here? What a coincidence.' Molly came up to her, basket in hand, before she realised that the two trolleys so close together meant something. She read the body language of the man and the woman and put two and two together. 'Oh, sorry, I hope I didn't interrupt something.'

André knew she had to get rid of the woman, because she could see in the clenching of Reyneke's hands that he was tense. The whole affair was on a knifepoint and she wanted to say: 'Yes, you are interrupting something' or 'Just go away'. But before she could find the right words, Molly's face cleared and she said: 'Oh, you must be working together – are you also in the police?' and she held out her hand to Reyneke. 'I'm Molly Green. Are you on an operation or something?'

Time stood still for André Marais. She could see the outstretched hand, which Reyneke ignored, his eyes moving from one woman to the other in slow motion; she could actually see the gears working in his brain. Then he bumped his trolley forward in her direction and he shouted something at her as the trolley collided with her and she lost her balance.

Molly screamed incoherently.

André staggered against the wine rack, bottles fell and smashed on the floor. She fell on her bottom, arms windmilling for balance, then she grabbed at her handbag, got her fingers on it and searched for her service pistol while her head told her she must warn Griessel. Her other hand was on the little microphone that she held to her mouth and said, 'It's him, it's him!'

Reyneke was beside her and jerked the pistol from her hand. She tried to rise, but her sandals slipped in the wine and she fell back with her elbow on a glass shard. She felt a sharp pain. Twisting her body sideways she saw which way he ran. 'Main entrance!' she shouted, but realising her head was turned away from the microphone, she grabbed it again. 'Main entrance, stop him!' she screamed. 'He has my firearm!' Then she saw the blood pouring from her arm in a thick stream. When she lifted up her arm to inspect it she saw it was cut to the bone.

Griessel and Cliffy leapt up and ran when they heard Molly Green scream over the radio. Cliffy missed the turn, bumping against a table where two men were eating sushi. 'Sorry, sorry,' he said and saw Griessel ahead, Z88 in hand, saw the faces of bystanders and heard cries here and there. They raced, shoes slapping on the floor. He heard Marais's voice on the microphone: 'Main entrance, stop him!'

Griessel arrived at the wide door of Woolworths, service pistol gripped in both hands and aimed at something inside the store, but Cliffy was trying to brake and he slipped on the smooth floor. Just before he collided with Griessel, he spotted the suspect, jacket flapping, big pistol in his hand, who stopped ten paces away from them, also battling not to slip.

But Cliffy and Griessel were in a pile on the ground. A shot went off and a bullet whined away somewhere.

Cliffy heard Griessel curse, heard high, shrill screams around them. 'Sorry, Benny, sorry,' he said, looking around and seeing the suspect had turned around and headed for the escalator. Cupido and Keyter, pistols in hand, were coming down the other one, but it was in fact the ascending escalator. For an instant it was extremely funny, like a scene from an old Charlie Chaplin film: the two policemen leaping furiously down the steps, but not making much progress. On their faces, the oddest expressions of frustration, seriousness, purposefulness – and the sure knowledge that they were making complete idiots of themselves.

Griessel had sprung up and set off after the suspect. Cliffy got to his feet and followed, up the escalator with big leaps to the top. Griessel had turned right and spotted the fugitive on the way to the exit on the second level. He heard Griessel shout, glanced back. Griessel could see the fear on the man's face and then he stopped and aimed his pistol at Griessel. The shot rang out and something plucked at Cliffy, knocked him off his feet and threw him against Men's Suits: Formal. He knew he was hit somewhere in the chest, he was entangled in trousers and jackets, looking down at the hole near his heart. He was going to die, thought Cliffy Mketsu, he was shot in the heart. He couldn't die now. Griessel must help. He rolled over. He felt heavy. But light-headed. He moved garments with his right arm; the left was without feeling. He saw Griessel tackle the fugitive. A male mannequin in beachwear tottered and fell. A garish sunhat flew through the air in an elegant arch, a display of T-shirts collapsed. He saw Griessel's right hand rise and fall. Griessel was beating him with his pistol. He could see the blood spray from here. Up and down went Griessel's hand. It would make Benny feel better; he needed to release that rage. Hit him, Benny, hit him – he's the bastard who shot me.

Thobela Mpayipheli was waiting for the traffic lights on the corner of Adderley and Riebeeck Street when he heard a voice at his elbow.

'Why djoo look so se-ed?'

A street child stood there, hands on lean, boyish hips. Ten, eleven years old?

'Do I look sad?'

'Djy lyk like the ket stole the dairy. Gimme sum money for bred.'

'What's your name?'

'What's *djor* name?'

'Thobela.'

'Gimme sum money for bred, Thobela.'

'First tell me your name.'

'Moses.'

'What are you going to do with the money?'

'What did I say it was for?'

Then there was another one, smaller, thinner, in outsize clothes, nose running. Without thinking Thobela took out his handkerchief.

'Five rand,' said the little one, holding out his hand.

'Fokkof, Randall, I saw him first.'

He wanted to wipe Randall's nose but the boy jumped back. 'Don' touch me,' said the child.

'I want to wipe your nose.'

'What for?'

It was a good question.

'Djy gonna give us money?' asked Moses.

'When did you last eat?'

'Less see, what month is this?'

In the dusk of the late afternoon another skinny figure appeared, a girl with a bush of frizzy tangled hair. She said nothing, just stood with outstretched hand, the other holding the edges of a large, tattered man's jacket together.

'Agh, fock,' said Moses. 'I had this under control.'

'Are you related?' asked Thobela.

'How would *we* know?' said Moses, and the other two giggled.

'Do you want to eat?'

'Jee-zas,' said Moses. 'Just my luck. A fokken' stupid darkie.'

'You swear a lot.'

'I'm a street kid, for fuck's sake.'

He looked at the trio. Grimy, barefoot. Bright, living eyes. 'I'm going to the Spur. Do you want to come?'

Dumbstruck.

'Well?'

'Are you a pervert?' asked Moses with narrowed eyes.

'No, I'm hungry.'

The girl jabbed an elbow in Moses' ribs and made big eyes at him.

'The Spur will throw us out,' said Randall.

'I'll say you are my children.'

For a moment all three were quiet and then Moses laughed, a chuckling sound rising through the scales. 'Our daddy.'

Thobela began to walk. 'Are you coming?'

It was ten or twelve paces further on that the girl's small hand clasped a finger of his right hand and stayed there, all the way to the Spur Steak Ranch in Strand Street.

22

She sat staring at the window without seeing.

'I thought I was cutting myself because of my father, at first,' she said softly, and sighed, deeply, remembering. 'Or because of Viljoen. I thought I was handling the work and that I was okay with it.'

She turned and looked at him, back in the present. 'I never clicked it was the work that made me like that. Not then. I had to get out of it first.'

He nodded, slowly, but did not respond.

'And then things changed, with Carlos,' she said.

Carlos phoned early, just after nine, to say he wanted to book her for the whole night. 'Carlos does not want money fight. Three thousand, hokay? But you must look sexy, conchita. Very sexy, we are having a formal party. Black dress, but show your tits. Carlos wants to brag. My guys will pick you up. Seven o'clock.' He put the phone down.

She waited for her anger to rise and fade. She sat on the edge of the bed, with the cell phone still to her ear. She felt the futility, knew that her anger was useless.

Sonia came up to her, doll in hand. 'Are we going to ride bicycle, Mamma?'

'No, my love, we are going shopping.' The child skipped off towards her room as if shopping was her favourite activity.

'Hey, you.'

Sonia halted in the doorway and peeped over her shoulder mischievously.

'Me?' She knew her part in this ritual.

'Yes, you. Come here.'

She ran across the carpet, still in her green pyjamas, into her mother's arms.

'You're my love,' Christine began their rhyme and kissed her neck.

'You're my life,' giggled Sonia.

'And your beauty makes me shiver.'

'You're my heaven, you're my house.' Her head was on Christine's bosom.

'You're my only paradise,' she said and hugged the child tight. 'Go and get dressed. It's time to shop till we drop.'

'Shoptill hedrop?'

'Shoptill hedrop. That's right.'

Three years and four months. Just another two years, then school. Just another two years and her mother would be done with whoring.

She phoned Carlton Hair and Mac for late-afternoon appointments and took Sonia along to Hip Hop across Cavendish Square. The sales people paid more attention to the pretty child with blonde ringlets than they did to her.

She stood in front of the mirror in a black dress. The neckline was low, the hem high, bare back.

'That is very sexy,' said the coloured shop assistant.

'Isn't,' said Sonia. 'Mamma looks pretty.'

They laughed. 'I'll take it.'

They were too early for her hair and make-up. She took her daughter to Naartjie in the Cavendish Centre. 'Now you can choose a dress for yourself.'

'I also want a black one.'

'They don't have black ones.'

'I also want a black one.'

'Black ones are just for grown-ups, girl.'

'I also want to be grown-up.'

'No you don't. Trust me.'

★　　★　　★

The carer looked in disapproval at her outfit when she dropped Sonia off.

'I don't know how late the function will finish. It's best if she sleeps over.'

'In that dress it will finish very late.'

She ignored the comment, hugged her daughter tight. 'Be good. Mamma will see you in the morning.'

'Tatta, Mamma.'

Just before the door closed behind her, she heard Sonia say: 'My mamma looks very pretty.'

'Do you think so?' said the carer in a sour voice.

It was a weird evening. In the entertainment area of the house in Camps Bay, inside and outside beside the pool, were about sixty people, mostly men in evening suits. Here and there was a blonde with breasts on display or long legs showing through split dresses and ending in high heels. Like décor, she thought, pretty furniture. They hung on a man's arm, smiled, said nothing.

Quickly she grasped that that was what Carlos expected of her. He was ecstatic over her appearance. 'Ah, conchita, you look perfect,' he said when she arrived.

It was the United Nations: Spanish-speaking, Chinese, or Oriental at least, small men who followed her with hungry eyes, Arabs in togas – or whatever you called them – who ignored her, each with his moustache. Two Germans. English. One American.

Carlos, the Host. Jovial, smiling, joking, but she felt sure he was tense, nervous even. She followed his example, held a glass, but did not drink.

'You know who these people are?' he asked her later, whispering in her ear.

'No.'

'Carlos will tell you later.'

Food and drink came and went. She could see the men were no longer sober, but only because the conversation and laughter were a bit louder. Ten o'clock, eleven, twelve.

She stood alone at a pillar. Carlos was somewhere in a kitchen organising more food to be sent. She felt a hand slide under her dress between her legs, fingers groping. She froze. The hand was gone. She looked over her shoulder. A Chinese man stood there, small and dapper, sniffing deeply at his fingers. He smiled at her and walked away. All she could think of was that Carlos must not see that.

Two Arabs sat at a glass table arranging cocaine in lines with credit cards and sharing it with a companion whose nipple showed above the neckline of her black dress. One of the men inhaled deeply over the table, leaned back in his chair and slowly opened his eyes. Languidly he stretched out a hand towards her and took the nipple between his fingers. He squeezed. The woman grimaced. He's hurting her, thought Christine. She was transfixed.

Late that night her bladder was full. She went upstairs looking for the privacy of Carlos's en-suite bathroom. The bedroom door was shut and she opened it. A blonde in a blood-red dress was gripping one of the posts of the bed and her dress was rucked up to bare her bottom. Behind her stood one of the Spanish men with his trousers around his ankles.

'You want to watch?'

'No.'

'You want to fuck?'

'I'm with Carlos.'

'Carlos is nothing. You kiss my girl, yes?'

Quietly she closed the door and heard the man laugh inside the room.

Even later. Only a small group of guests remained in the swimming pool – two women, six or seven men. Extremely drunk. She had never seen group sex before and it fascinated her. Four men were with one of the women.

Carlos came and stood behind her. 'What do you think?'

'It's weird,' she lied.

'Carlos not for groups. Carlos is a one conchita man.' He put his arms around her, but they continued to watch. Small, rhythmic waves lapped at the edge of the pool.

'It looks sexy,' he said.

She put her hand on his crotch and felt it was hard. Time to earn her pay.

'First Carlos drinks,' he said, and went to fetch a bottle.

She didn't know whether to blame the drink, but Carlos was different in bed – desperate, urgent, as if he wanted to prove himself.

'I want you to hurt me,' she said.

Maybe he did not hear. Maybe he did not want to. He just went on.

When he had finished and lay wet with his own perspiration beside her, head between her breasts, he asked: 'Carlos was good for you?'

'You were great.'

'Yes. Carlos is a great lover,' he said in all seriousness. Then he was quiet, for so long that she wondered if he was asleep.

Suddenly he rose to his feet, crossed to where he had dropped his trousers on the floor and took out a packet of cigarettes. He lit two and passed one to her before sitting down beside her, with his feet folded under him. His eyes were bloodshot.

'These people . . .' he said with venom and a deep furrow of distaste on his forehead. She knew him well enough to know he was not sober.

She drew on the cigarette.

'They did not even thank Carlos for the party. They come, they drink and snort and eat and fuck and then they leave, no goodbye, no "thank you, Carlos, for your hospitality".'

'It was a good party, Carlos.'

'*Sí*, conchita. Cost a lot of money, famous chef, best *licores*, best *putas*. But they have no respect for Carlos.'

'Carlos is nothing,' the man in his bedroom had said.

'You know who they are, conchita? You know? They are *banditos*. They are shit. They make money with drugs. Mexicans!' He spat out the word. 'They are nothing. They are *burros*, *mulas* for the Yankees. Cubans. What are they? And the Afghans. Peasants, I tell you.'

'Afghans?'

'*Sí*. Those arses holes in the dresses. *Conchas!*'

So the Arabs were Afghans. 'Oh.'

'And the China and the Thai, and the Vietnam, what are they? They are *mierda*, Carlos tell you, they have nothing but chickens and bananas and heroin. They fuck their mothers. But they come to Carlos, to this beautiful house and they have no manners. You know who they are, conchita? They are drugs. The Afghans and the Vietnam and the Thai, they bring heroin. They bring here, because here is safe, no police here. They take cocaine back. Then Sangrenegra brothers take heroin to America and to Europe. And the South Americans, they help supply, but little, because Sangrenegra brothers control supply. That is Carlos and Javier. My big brother is Javier. He is biggest man in drugs. Everybody know him. We take heroin, we give cocaine, we give money, we . . . we *distribuya*. We take to whole world. Carlos will tell Javier about the disrespect. They think Carlos is little brother, Javier is not here, so they can shit on me. They cannot shit on me, conchita. I will shit on *them*.' He squashed the cigarette disdainfully in the ashtray.

'Come, conchita, Carlos show you something.' He took her arm and drew her along. He picked up his trousers, took out a bunch of keys, took her hand and led her down the passage, down the stairs, through the kitchen, down more stairs to a pantry. The house was completely deserted by now. He opened a half-concealed door at the back of the pantry. There were three locks, each with its own key.

'Carlos show you. Sangrenegra is not small time.' He pressed a light switch. Another door. A small electronic number pad on the wall. He typed in a number. 'Oh, eight, two, four, four, nine, you know that number, conchita?'

'Yes.' They were the first six numbers of her cell phone number.

'That is how much Carlos love you.'

It was a steel door that opened automatically. A fluorescent light flickered on inside. He pulled her inside. A space as large as a double garage. Shelves up to the ceiling. Plastic bags on the racks, from one end to the other, all filled with white powder.

Then she saw the money.

'You see, conchita? You see?'

'I see,' she said, but her voice was gone and it came out as a whisper.

They were in the pool, just Carlos and her. She sat on the step with her lower body in the water. He was standing in the water with his arms around her and his face against her belly.

'Conchita, will you tell Carlos why you become . . . you know.'

'A whore.'

'You are not a whore,' he said distastefully. 'An escort. Why did you become an escort?'

'You don't want to know the truth, Carlos.'

'No, conchita. I do. The real truth.'

'Sometimes I think you want me to be this good girl. I am not a good girl.'

'You are. You have a good heart.'

'You see, if I tell you the truth you don't want to hear it.'

He straightened his arms so he could look at her. 'You know what? That is not the way Carlos thinks. Look at me, conchita. I am in drugs. I have killed guys. But I am not bad. I have a good heart. You see? You can be good, and you can do things that are not so good. So tell me.'

'Because I like to fuck, Carlos.'

'*Sí?*'

'*Sí*,' she said. 'That is my drug.'

'How old were you? When you fucked first?'

'I was fifteen.'

'Tell Carlos.'

'I was at school. And this boy, he was sixteen. He was very beautiful. He walked home with me every afternoon. And one day he said I must come home with him. I was very curious. And so I went. And he said I had beautiful breasts. He asked if he could see them. And I showed him. Then he asked if he could touch them. And I said yes. And then he started to kiss me. On my nipples. He started to suck my nipples. And then it happened, Carlos. The drug. It was . . . It was like nothing I had ever felt before. It was *intense*. I liked it so much.'

'And then he fucked you?'

'Yes. But he was not experienced. He came too quickly. He was so excited. I didn't have an orgasm. So afterwards, I wanted more. But not with boys. With men. So I seduced my teacher . . .'

'You fucked your teacher?'

'Yes.'

'And who else?'

'A friend of my father. I went to his home when his wife was away. I said I wanted to talk to him. I said I was very curious about sex, but I cannot talk to my parents about it, because they are so conservative. And I know he is different. He asked if I would like it if he showed me. I said yes. But you know what, Carlos? He was just as excited as the boy. He could not control himself.'

'Who else?'

'I fucked a lot of guys at university. For free. And then one day I thought, why for free? And that is how it happened.'

'Look,' said Carlos and pointed at his erection. 'Carlos likes your story.'

'Then fuck me, Carlos. I love it so much.'

Wasserman, the acclaimed playwright, Professor of Afrikaans and Nederlands. Fifty-three years old, with a soft body, bushy beard and a beautiful, beautiful voice. At the start of every session she would have to lie in the bath so he could urinate on her, or else he could not get an erection. But from there on he was normal, except for the reading glasses – the better to see her breasts. He would come once a fortnight at three in the afternoon, as he had a younger wife who 'might want something too'. He needed time to recharge before the evening. But his young wife would not let herself be pissed on, that was why he came to Christine.

They were waiting for him at precisely four o'clock. When he opened the door to leave her place at the Gardens Centre, they hit him with a pick handle, breaking his teeth and jaw.

She heard the commotion and grabbed a dressing gown. 'No!'

she screamed. They were wearing balaclavas, but she knew they were the bodyguards. One looked her in the eyes and kicked Wasserman where he lay. Then they both kicked him. Seven ribs broken.

'I will call the police!' One of them laughed. Then they dragged him by the feet to the stairs and down two flights and left him there, bleeding and moaning.

She grabbed her cell phone and ran down to him. She bent over him. The damage made her nauseous. She touched his broken face with her fingertips. He opened his eyes and looked at her. There was a question through the agony.

'I'm calling an ambulance,' she said, holding his hand while she spoke.

He made a noise.

'I can't stay here,' she said. 'I can't stay here.' There would be police. Questions. Arrest. She, Sonia could not afford that.

He just moaned, lying on his side in a pool of blood around his face.

She heard doors opening.

'The ambulance is on its way.' She squeezed Wasserman's hand and then ran upstairs to her room and locked the door behind her. Feverishly she dressed herself. Carlos. What was she to do?

When she went out quietly, she went down first. She saw there were security personnel with Wasserman at the foot of the stairs. They did not see her. She walked up one flight of stairs, trying to keep calm. She walked slowly so as not to attract attention. She pressed the button for the lift, waited. Voices below. The lift took an eternity to arrive.

Carlos.

She phoned him once she reached the street. He did not answer his phone.

She went to her flat, sat on a chair in her sitting room with her phone in her hand. What was she going to do?

Later she phoned the ambulance services. They had taken Wasserman to City Park. She phoned the hospital. 'We can't give out information.'

'This is his sister.'

'Hold on.'

She had to listen to synthesised music, sounding tinny in her ear.

Eventually Casualty answered. 'He's in Intensive Care, but he should be okay.'

Carlos. She phoned again. It just kept on ringing. She wanted to get in her car and drive to his house. She wanted to hit him, smash his skull with a pick handle. He didn't have the right. He couldn't do this. She wanted to go to the police, she wanted to blow him off the earth. Rage consumed her. She looked for her telephone book and got the number of the police.

No. Too many complications.

She wept, but from frustration. Hate.

When she had calmed down she went to fetch Sonia. When she crossed the street holding her daughter's hand, she saw the BMW on the other side, back window rolled down. He sat there watching, but not her. His eyes were on the girl and there was a strange expression on his face. It felt as if someone had their fist around her heart and were squeezing her to death.

The BMW pulled up alongside her when she was helping Sonia into her car.

'Now I know everything, conchita.' He looked at Sonia, looked at her child. If she had had a gun at that moment, she would have shot him in the face.

PART TWO

Benny

23

Griessel was never uncomfortable with the bosses, mainly because he could drink them under the table singly or as a group. Or outwork them. He maintained a higher case solution rate than any one of them had in their days as detectives, alcoholic or not. But tonight he was not at ease. They stood in the little sitting room outside the Intensive Care Unit of City Park Hospital, although there were chairs available: Senior Superintendents Esau Mtimkulu and Matt Joubert, first and second in command of SVC, Commissioner John Afrika, the provincial head of detection, and Griessel. Cupido and Keyter sat just out of hearing. Their ears were pricked but they could not hear anything. When a member lay in Intensive Care, the big guns spoke in muffled tones.

'Give me that Woolworths man's number, Matt,' said Commissioner Afrika, a coloured veteran who had come up through the ranks in Khayelitsha, the Flats and the old Murder and Robbery Units. 'I hear they are running to the minister, but to hell with them. I'll deal with him. That is the least of our problems . . .' Here it comes, thought Griessel. He should never have hit the bastard, he knew that; never in his life had he carried on like that before. If they were to throw out the case because he had lost control, if a fucking serial murderer were to walk because Benny Griessel was angry at the entire world . . .

'Benny,' said Commissioner Afrika, 'you say it was the tackle that caused his face to be injured like that?'

'Yes, Commissioner.' He looked into the man's eyes and they knew, all four of them in the circle, what was happening now. 'There was this shop mannequin standing just in the wrong place.

Reyneke's face hit the face of the mannequin. That's where the cuts came from.'

'He must have hit it fucking hard,' said Superintendent Mtimkulu.

'When I tackled him, I held his arms down because he had a firearm. So he couldn't shield his face with his hands. That's why he hit it so hard.'

'And then he confessed?'

'He lay there bleeding, and then he cried, "I can't help it, I can't help it", but with Cliffy wounded my attention was . . . er . . . divided. Only later under interrogation did I ask him what he meant. What it is that he can't help.'

'And what did he say then?'

'At first he didn't want to say anything. So . . . I asked Cupido and Keyter to leave, so that I could talk to him alone.'

'And then he confessed?'

'He confessed, Commissioner.'

'Will it stand up in court?'

'The whole sequence in the interrogation room is on video, Commissioner. I just asked to be alone with the suspect and, once they had left, I just looked at him. For a long time. Then I said: "I know you can't help it. I understand." And then he began to talk.'

'Full confession.'

'Yes, Sup. All three of the women. Details that were not in the newspapers. We've got him, whoever he gets as his lawyer. And there's a previous conviction. Rape. Four years ago in Montagu.'

'And the only witness of the mannequin incident is Cliffy Mketsu?'

'That's right, Matt.'

All four looked across at the double doors that led to the ICU.

'Okay,' said the head of Investigation. 'Good work, Benny. Really good work . . .'

The double doors opened. A doctor approached them; such a young man that he looked as if he should still be at university. There were bloodstains on his green theatre overalls.

'He will be alright,' said the doctor.

'Are you sure?' asked Griessel.

The doctor nodded. 'He was very, very lucky. The bullet missed nearly everything, but badly damaged the S4 area of his left lung. That is the tip of the upper lobe, anterior segment. There is a possibility that we will have to remove it, just a small piece, but we will decide once he has stabilised.'

We, thought Griessel. Why did they always talk about *us*, as if they belonged to some secret organisation?

'That's good news,' said the commissioner without conviction.

'Oh, and we have a message for a Benny.'

'That's me.'

'He says the guy fell badly against the cash register.'

All four stared at the doctor with great interest. 'The cash register?' asked Griessel.

'Yes.'

'Do me a favour, Doc. Tell him it was the mannequin.'

'The mannequin.'

'Yes. Tell him the man fell against the mannequin and the mannequin fell on the cash register.'

'I will tell him.'

'Thanks, Doc,' said Griessel, and turned to the commissioner, who nodded and turned away.

He bought a Zinger burger and a can of Fanta Orange at KFC and took them home. He sat on his 'sitting-room' floor eating without pleasure. It was the fatigue, the after-effects of adrenaline. Also, the things waiting in the back of his mind that he did not want to think about. So he concentrated on the food. The Zinger didn't satisfy his hunger. He should have ordered chips, but he didn't like KFC's chips. The children ate them with gusto. The children even ate McDonalds's thin cardboard chips with pleasure, but he could not. Steers's chips, yes. Steers's big fat barbeque-seasoned chips. Steers's burgers were also better than anything else. Decent food. But he didn't know where the nearest Steers was and he wasn't sure if they would still be open at this time. The Zinger was finished and he had sauce on his fingers.

He wanted to toss the plastic bag and empty carton container in the bin, but remembered he didn't have a bin. He sighed. He would have to shower – he still had some of Reyneke's and Cliffy's blood on him.

You have six months, Benny – that is what we are giving you. Six months to choose between us and the booze. Would you buy furniture for just six months? He couldn't eat on the floor for six fucking months. Or come home to such a barren place. Surely he was entitled to a chair or two. A small television. But first, get out of these clothes and shower and then he could sit on his bed and make a list for tomorrow. Saturday. He was off this weekend.

Terrifying. Two whole days. Open. Perhaps he ought to go to the office and get his paperwork up to date.

He washed his hands under the kitchen tap, put the carton and the can and the used paper serviette into the red and white plastic packet and put it in a corner of the kitchen. He climbed the stairs while unbuttoning his shirt. Thank God they didn't have to wear jacket and tie any more. When he started with Murder and Robbery it was suits.

Where was Anna tonight?

The plastic shower curtain was torn in one corner and the water leaked onto the floor. It had a faded pattern of fish. He would have to get a bathmat as well. A new shower curtain too. He washed his hair and soaped his body. Rinsed off in the lovely hot, strong stream of water.

When he turned off the taps he heard his cell phone ringing. He grabbed the towel, rubbed it quickly over his head, took three strides to the bed and snatched it up.

'Griessel.'

'Are you sober, Benny?'

Anna.

'Yes.' He wanted to protest at her question, wanted to be angry, but he knew he had no right.

'Do you want to see the children?'

'Yes, I would very—'

'You can collect them on Sunday. For the day.'

'Okay, thank you. What about you? Can I also—'

'Let's just keep to the children, for now. Ten o'clock? Ten to six?'

'That's fine.'

'Goodbye, Benny.'

'Anna!'

She did not speak, but did not cut him off.

'Where were you this evening?'

'Where were you, Benny?'

'I was working. I caught a serial murderer. Cliffy Mketsu was shot in the lung. That's where I was.' He had the moral high ground, a little heap, a molehill, but better than nothing. 'Where were you?'

'Out.'

'Out?'

'Benny, I sat at home for five years while you were drunk or out and about. Either drunk or not at home. Don't you think I deserve a Friday night out? Don't you think I deserve to watch a movie, for the first time in five years?'

'Yes,' he said, 'you deserve that.'

'Goodbye, Benny.'

Did you watch the movie alone? That's what he wanted to ask, but the moral contours had shifted too quickly and he heard the connection go dead in his ear. He threw the towel to the floor and took a black pair of trousers from the cupboard to put on. He fetched pen and paper from his briefcase and sat down on the bed. He stared at the towel on the floor. Tomorrow morning it would still be lying there and it would be damp and smelly. He got up and hung the towel over the rail in the bathroom, went back to the bed and arranged the pillow so he could lean against it. He began his list.

Laundry.

There was a laundromat at the Gardens Centre. First thing tomorrow.

Rubbish bin.

Iron.

Ironing board.

Fridge?

Could he manage without a fridge? What would he keep in it? Not milk – he drank his coffee black. On Sunday the children would be here and Carla loved her coffee; always had a mug in her hand when she did her homework. Would she be content with powdered milk? The fridge might be necessary, he would see.

Fridge?

Shower curtain.

Bath mat.

Chairs/sofa. For the sitting room.

Bar stools. For the breakfast nook.

How the hell was he going to support two households on a police salary? Had Anna thought of that? But he could already hear her answer: 'You could support a drinking habit on a police salary, Benny. There was always money for drink.'

He would have to buy another coffee mug for the children's visit. More plates and knives, forks and spoons. Cleaning stuff for dishes, dusty surfaces, the bathroom and the toilet.

He made fresh columns on the page, noted all the items, but he could not keep the other things in his head at bay.

Today he had made a discovery. He would have to tell Barkhuizen. This thing about being scared of death was not entirely true. Today, when he charged at Reyneke on the top level of Woolworths with the pistol pointed at him and the shot going off, the bullet that had hit Cliffy Mketsu because Reyneke could not shoot for toffee . . .

That is when he had discovered he was not afraid of dying. That is when he knew he wanted to die.

He woke early, just before five. His thoughts went to Anna. Did she go to the movies alone? But he didn't want to play with those thoughts. Not this early, not today. He got up and dressed in trousers, shirt and trainers only, and went out without washing.

He chose a direction; three hundred metres up the street he saw the morning, felt the languor of the early summer, heard the birds and the unbelievable silence over the city. Colours and textures and light of crystal.

Table Mountain leaned towards him, the crest something between orange and gold, fissures and clefts were pitch-black shadows against the angle of the rising sun.

He went up Upper Orange Street, turned into the park and sat on the high wall of the reservoir to look out. To the left Lion's Head became the curves of Signal Hill, and below a thousand city windows were a mosaic of the sun. The sea was deep blue beyond Robben Island, far off to Melkbos Strand. Left of Devil's Peak lay the suburbs. A 747 came in over the Tyger Berg and its shadow flashed over him in an instant.

Fuck, he thought, when had he last seen this?

How could he have missed it?

On the other hand, he pulled a face, if you are sleeping off your hangover in the morning, you won't see sunrise over the Cape. He must remember this, the unexpected advantage of teetotalism.

A wagtail came and perched near him, tail going up and down, dapper steps like a self-important station sergeant. 'What?' he said to the bird. 'Your wife left you too?' He received no reply. He sat until the bird flew up after some invisible insect, and then he rose and looked up at the mountain again and it gave him a strange pleasure. Only he was seeing it this morning, nobody else.

He walked back to the flat, showered and changed and drove to the hospital. Cliffy was resting, they told him. He was stable, in no danger. He asked them to tell him Benny had been there.

It was just before seven. He drove north with the N1, on a freeway still quiet – the Cape only got going by about ten o'clock on a Saturday. Down Brackenfell Boulevard and the familiar turnoffs to his house. He drove past the house only once, slowly. No sign of life. The lawn was cut, the postbox emptied, the garage door closed. A policeman's inventory. He accelerated away because he did not want his thoughts to penetrate the front door.

He drank only coffee at a Wimpy in Panorama, because he had never been one for breakfast, and waited until the shops opened.

He found a two-seater couch and two armchairs at Mohammed

'Love Lips' Faizal's pawnshop in Maitland. The floral cover was slightly bleached. There were faint coffee stains on the arm of one chair. 'This is too much, L.L.,' he said over the R600 price tag.

'For you, Sarge, five-fifty.'

Faizal had been in Pollsmoor for eighteen months for trafficking in stolen goods and he was reasonably certain three-quarters of the car radios had been brought in by the drug addicts of Observatory.

'Four hundred, L.L. Look at these stains.'

'One steam clean and it's good as new, Sarge. Five hundred and I don't make a cent.'

Faizal knew he was no longer a sergeant, but some things will never change. 'Four-fifty.'

'Jissis, Sarge, I have a wife and kids.'

By chance he saw the bass guitar, just the head protruding from behind a steel cabinet of brand new tools.

'And that bass?'

'You into music, Sarge?'

'I have tickled the neck of a bass in my day.'

'Well bless my soul. It's a Fender, Sarge, pawned by a wannabe rapper from Blackheath, but his ticket expires only next Friday. Comes with a new Dr Bass times two-ten-b cabinet with a three-u built-in rack, two-two-fifty watt Eminence tens, and a LeSon tweeter.'

'I don't know what the fuck you're talking about.'

'It's a bloody big amp, Sarge. It'll blow you away.'

'How much?'

'Are you serious, Sarge?'

'Maybe.'

'It's a genuine pawn, Sarge. Clean.'

'I believe you, L.L. Relax.'

'Do you want to start a band now?' The suspicion was still there.

Griessel grinned. 'And call it Violent Crimes?'

'So what then?'

'How much are you asking for the guitar and amp, L.L.?'

'Two thousand, for sure. If the wannabe doesn't return the ticket.'

'Oh.' It was too much for him. He had no idea what these things cost. 'Four-fifty for the sitting-room suite?'

Faizal sighed. 'Four seventy-five and I'll throw in free delivery and a six-piece coaster set with tasteful nudes depicted thereupon.'

He got the three bar stools at the place in Parow that sold only pine furniture and he paid R175 apiece, a scary amount, but he loaded them in the car, two on the back seat and one in front, and took them to his flat, because tomorrow his kids would be here and at least there was something for them to sit on. By eleven he was sitting with a newspaper at the laundromat, waiting for his clothes to be clean and dry so he could pack them in his new plastic laundry basket and iron them on his new ironing board with his new iron.

Then Matt Joubert phoned and he said: 'I know you are off, Benny, but I need you.'

'What's up, Boss?'

'It's the guy with the assegai, but I'll explain when you arrive. We are at Fisantekraal. On a smallholding. Come via Durbanville on Wellington Avenue, right on the R three-one-two and just opposite the railway bridge go left. Phone me when you get there and I will direct you.'

He checked the cycle on the washing machine. 'Give me forty,' he said.

It was an equestrian establishment. *High Grove Riding School. Riding lessons for adults and children. Outrides.* He drove past the stables before he reached the house. Everything was in a state of partial dilapidation, as all these places were, never enough money to fix everything. Police cars, a SAPS van, Forensic's little bus. The ambulance must have left already.

Joubert stood in a circle of four other detectives, just two from their unit, the other two probably from Durbanville station. When he stopped there were dogs, barking, tails wagging, two little ones and two black sheepdogs. He got out to the smell of manure and lucerne hay.

Joubert approached him with outstretched hand. 'How's it going, Benny?'

'Sober, thank you.'

Joubert smiled. 'I can see. Are you suffering?'

'Only when I don't drink.'

The commander laughed. 'I respect your tenacity, Benny. Not that I ever doubted . . .'

'Then you must be the only one.'

'Come, so we can talk first.'

He led him to an empty stable and sat on a bale of hay. The sun projected perfect round dots on the floor through holes in the corrugated iron roof. 'Sit down, Benny, this will take some time.'

He sat.

'The victim is Bernadette Laurens. She was released on Thursday on bail of fifty thousand rand. Charged with the murder of her partner's five-year-old daughter. They lived together as a couple. Partner's name is Elise Bothma. Last weekend the child was hit on the head with a billiard cue, one blow . . .'

'Lesbetarian?'

Joubert nodded. 'Last night the dogs began to bark. Laurens got up to see what was going on. When she did not return to bed, Bothma went to look for her. Fifteen metres from the front door she found the body. One stab wound to the heart. I am waiting for the pathology report, but it could be the assegai man.'

'Because she killed a child.'

'And the stab wound.'

'The papers say it is an assegai woman.'

'The papers are full of shit. There's no way a woman could have murdered the previous two victims. Enver Davids was a jailbird, well built, strong. According to the scene, Colin Pretorius had time to defend himself, but he didn't stand a chance. Laurens was a strong woman, round about one point eight metres tall, eighty kilograms. And women shoot, they don't stab with a blade. In any case, not multiple victims. As you know, the chance that a woman is involved in multiples is one per cent.'

'I agree.'

'One of the sheepdogs is limping this morning. Bothma believes it might have been kicked or hit in the process. But apart from that, not much. The Durbanville people will come and help to question the neighbours.'

Griessel nodded.

'I want you to take charge of the whole investigation, Benny.'

'Me?'

'For many reasons. In the first place, you are the most experienced detective in the unit. In the second, in my opinion, you are the best. Third, the commissioner mentioned your name. He's very pleased with your work yesterday and he knows big trouble when he sees it. We have a circus on our hands, Benny. With the media. An avenging murderer, punishment for crimes against children, death penalty . . . you can imagine.'

'And fourth, I have the time, now that I no longer have a wife and kids.'

'That was not part of my reasoning. But I must say this: I thought it might help – keep you too busy to think of drink.'

'Nothing could keep me that busy.'

'The last thing that made me ask you is that I know you enjoy this kind of thing.'

'That's true.'

'Are you in?'

'Of course I'm fucking in. I was in the moment you said "assegai". You could have saved the rest. You know that "positive feedback" shit never worked with me.'

Joubert stood up. 'I know. But it had to be said. You must know you are appreciated. And, oh, the commissioner says you have all the manpower you need. We must just let him know where we need help. He will do the necessary. For the present, Keyter is your partner. He's on his way . . .'

'Not a fock.'

'Cliffy is in hospital, Benny, and there is no one else available full-time . . .'

'Keyter is an idiot, Matt. He is a little braggart station detective with an attitude and a big head. He knows fuck-all. What happened to the manpower you just promised me?'

'For foot work, Benny. I can't spare men from the unit. You know everyone is snowed under with work. And Keyter is new. He has to learn. You will have to mentor him.'

'Mentor him?'

'Make an investigator of him.'

'It's times like this,' said Griessel, 'that I know why I'm an alcoholic.'

24

Griessel, Keyter and the dogs sat in Elise Bothma's sitting room. Keyter, in a loose white shirt, tight jeans and new bright blue Nike Crosstrainers, asked the questions as if he were the senior investigator. 'What sort of dog is this, ma'am? Looks like a Pomeranian cross, but don't they bark a lot at night? I hear they bark so much, the genuine Pomeranians . . . looks like there is a bit of Dachshund in this one. You say you heard the dogs and then Miss Laurens went out to look?'

She was a fragile woman. Her eyes were red-rimmed and her voice gentle and she hadn't been expecting the question at the tail end of the dog speech. 'Yes,' she said. She sat hunched up and did not raise her head. Her fingers were entangled in a tissue. The room smelt strongly of dogs and rooibos tea.

'Do you know what time that was?' asked Keyter.

She said something, but they couldn't hear it.

'You need to speak louder. We can't hear a word you say.'

'It must have been just before two,' said Elise Bothma, and sank back, as if the effort was too great.

'But you are not sure?'

She just shook her head.

'Do we know what time she phoned the station?' Keyter asked Griessel.

He felt like getting up right there and taking the little shit outside to ask him who the fuck did he think he was, but this was not the time.

'Two thirty-five,' said Griessel.

'Okay,' said Keyter. 'Let us say the dogs began barking just before two and she got up then to look. Did she take something with her? A weapon? Snooker stick or something?'

Bothma shuddered and Griessel decided this was the last one he would stand before taking Keyter outside. 'A revolver.'

'A revolver?'

'Yes.'

'What revolver?'

'I don't know. It was hers.'

'And where is the revolver now?'

'I don't know.'

'Did anyone find a revolver with the body?'

Griessel just shook his head.

'So the revolver is missing now?'

Bothma nodded slightly.

'And then, when did you get up to go and look?'

'I don't know what time it was.'

'But why did you go out? What made you?'

'She was too long. She was gone too long.'

'And you found her lying there?'

'Yes.'

'Just as she was when we came?'

'Yes.'

'And nothing else?'

'No.'

'And then you phoned the station?'

'No.'

'Oh?'

'The emergency number. One zero triple one.'

'Oh. Then you waited in the house until they came?'

'Yes.'

'Okay,' said Keyter. 'Okay. That's the story.' He stood up. 'Thank you very much and sorry for the loss and all that.'

Bothma made the slight nod of her head again, but still no eye contact.

Griessel stood and Keyter moved towards the door. He was taken aback when he saw Griessel sitting down on the sofa next to the woman. He didn't turn back but stood there in the doorway looking impatient.

'How long were you together?' Griessel asked her, gently and sympathetically.

'Seven years,' said Bothma, and pressed the tissue against her cheeks.

'What?' said Keyter from the door. Griessel looked at him meaningfully and held a finger to his lips. Keyter came back and sat down.

'She had a temper.' A statement. Bothma nodded.

'Did she sometimes hurt you?'

Nod.

'And sometimes hurt your child?'

The head said 'yes' and tears ran.

'Why did you stay?'

'Because I have nothing.'

Griessel waited.

'What could I do? Where could I go? I don't have a job. I worked for her. Did the books. She looked after us. Food and clothing. She taught Cheryl to ride. She was good with her most of the time. What could I do?'

'Were you angry with her over what she did to Cheryl?'

The thin shoulders shook.

'But you stayed with her?'

She put her small hands over her face and wept. Griessel put a hand in his pocket and took out a handkerchief. He held it out to her. It was a while before she saw it.

'Thank you.'

'I know it's hard,' he said.

She nodded.

'You were very angry with her.'

'Yes.'

'You thought of doing something to her.'

Bothma paused before she said anything. On the carpet a sheepdog scratched itself. 'Yes.'

'Like stabbing her with a knife?'

Bothma shook her head at that.

'The revolver?'

Nod.

'Why didn't you?'

'She hid it.'

He waited.

'I didn't kill her,' said Elise Bothma and looked up at him. He saw she had green eyes. 'I didn't.'

'I know,' said Griessel. 'She was too strong for you.'

He waited until Keyter was in his car and then he stood at the window and he talked quietly, because there were still other policemen in the yard. 'I want you to understand a few things fucking well,' he said, and Keyter looked up at him in surprise.

'Number one. You will not open your mouth again during questioning, unless I give you permission. Do you understand?'

'Jissis. What did I do?'

'Do you understand?'

'Okay, okay.'

'Number two. I did not ask for you. You were given to me. With the instruction that I must teach you to be a detective. Number three. To learn, you will have to listen. Do you understand?'

'I *am* a fucking detective.'

'You are a fucking detective? Tell me, mister fucking detective, where do you start a murder investigation? Where is the first place you look?'

'Okay,' said Keyter reluctantly.

'Okay what, Jaaa-mie?'

'Okay, I get it.'

'Get what?'

'What you said.'

'Say it, Jaaa-mie.'

'Why do you keep calling me, Jaaa-mie? I get it, okay? First you look near the victim.'

'Did you look there?'

Keyter said nothing, just held his steering wheel in the ten-to-two position.

'You are not a wart on a detective's backside. Two years at Table View Station says nothing. Burglaries and vehicle theft don't count here, Jaaa-mie. You button your lip and listen and learn. Or you can go to Matt Joubert now and tell him you can't work with me.'

'Okay,' said Keyter.

'Okay what?'

'Okay, I won't talk.'

'And learn.'

'And learn.'

'Then you can get out again, because we are not finished here.' He took a step back to make room for the door. Keyter got out, shut the door and folded his arms on his chest. He leaned back against his car.

'Are we sure that she didn't do it?' asked Griessel.

Keyter shrugged. When he saw that was not sufficient, he said 'No', cautiously.

'Did you hear what I said inside there?'

'Yes.'

'Do you think she could have done it?'

'No.'

'But she wanted to?'

'Yes.'

'Now think, Jaaa-mie. Put yourself in her shoes.'

'Huh?'

'Think the way she would think,' said Griessel, and suppressed the impulse to cast his eyes heavenwards.

Keyter unfolded his arms and pressed two fingers to his temples. Griessel waited.

'Okay,' said Keyter.

Griessel waited.

'Okay, she is too small to stab Laurens.' He looked at Griessel for approval. Griessel nodded.

'And she can't get her hands on the revolver.'

'That's right.'

The fingers worked against his temples.

'No, fuck, I don't know,' said Keyter with an angry gesture and straightened up.

'How would *you* feel?' said Griessel, patience dragging at his voice like lead. 'Your child is dead. And it's your lover who did it. How would you feel? You hate, Jamie. You sit here in the house and you hate. She is sitting in the police cells and you know she will get out on bail, some time or other. And you wish you could beat her to death for what she has done. You imagine it in your head, how you shoot her, or stab her. And then on the radio you hear about this man who has his knife in for people who mess with children. Or you read the papers. What do you do, Jamie? You weep and you hope. You wish. Because you are small and weak and you need a superhero. You think: what if he comes with his big assegai? And you like thinking about it. But the week is too long, Jamie. Later you start thinking: what if he doesn't come? Bothma said the revolver was hidden. So ten to one she had looked for it. Why, Jamie? In case the assegai man didn't come. And then, what is the next logical step? You look for the assegai man. And where do you begin to look? Where do you look for someone who has it in for Laurens just as much as you? Because she had a temper. A hard woman. Where do you look?'

'Okay,' said Keyter and kicked at a clump of grass with a Nike Crosstrainer. 'Okay, I get it. You look here, on the plot.'

'There's hope for you, Jamie.'

'The labourers?'

'That's right. Who cleans the stables? Who cuts the feed? Who did Laurens shout and swear at when they came to work late? Who will do a little favour for five hundred rand?'

'I get it.'

'I want you to go and talk, Jamie. Watch the body language, look at the eyes. Don't make accusations. Just talk. Ask if they saw anything. Ask if Laurens was a difficult employer. Be sympathetic. Ask if they have heard of the assegai man. Give them a chance to talk. Sometimes they talk easily and too much. Listen, Jamie. Listen with both your ears and your eyes and your head. The thing with a murder investigation is, first you look at it from a distance, look at everything. Then you come a step closer and look again. Another step. You don't charge in – you stalk.'

'I get it.'

'I'm going in to the office. We need the other case files. I am going to ask the investigating officers to tell me everything about Davids and Pretorius. Phone me when you are finished, then you come in.'

'Okay, Benny.' Grateful.

'Okay,' he said, turning to go to his car and thinking: fuck, I'm starting to talk like him too.

25

He was still in conference with the other two investigating officers when Cloete, the liaison officer, phoned and said the media had heard there was another Artemis murder.

'A what?'

'You know, the assegai thing.'

'Artemis?'

'The *Argus* started that crap, Benny. Some or other Greek god that went around stabbing with a spear or something. Is it true?'

'That a Greek god went around . . .'

'*No, man*, that the Laurens woman who beat the child to death is the latest victim?'

The media. Fuck. 'All I can say now is that Laurens was found dead outside her house this morning. The post mortem is not finished yet.'

'They will want more than that.'

'I don't have more than that.'

'Will you phone me when there is more?'

'I will,' he lied. He was definitely not intending to feed information to the press.

Faizal phoned him just before he went to the mortuary, to ask if he could deliver the sitting-room suite. He drove to the flat to open up and then raced to Salt River where Pagel was waiting for him.

He heard the music as he closed the door of the state mortuary behind him and it made him grin. That is how you could tell Professor Phil Pagel, chief pathologist, was at work. For Pagel played only Beethoven on his ten-thousand rand hi-fi system in his office, as loud as was necessary.

'Ah, Nikita,' said Pagel with genuine pleasure when Griessel looked in his door. He was seated behind a computer and had to get up to turn the music down. 'How are you, my friend?'

Pagel had been calling him 'Nikita' for twelve years. The first time he had met Griessel he had remarked: 'I am sure that is how the young Khruschev would have looked.' Griessel had to think hard who Khrushchev was. He had always had immense respect for highly educated and cultured people, he who had only his matric and police examinations. Once he had said to Pagel: 'Damn, Prof, I wish I were as clever as you.' But Pagel had looked back at him and said: 'I suspect you are the clever one, Nikita, and you have street smarts, too.'

He liked that. Also the fact that Pagel, who featured so often on the social pages, Friends of the Opera, Save the Symphony Orchestra, Aids Action Campaign, treated him as an equal. Always had. Pagel didn't seem to age – tall and lean and impossibly handsome, some people said he looked like the star of some or other television soap that Griessel had never seen.

'Well, thank you, Prof. And you?'

'Splendid, my dear fellow. I have just finished with the unfortunate Miss Laurens.'

'Prof, they have given me the whole show – Davids, Pretorius, the works. Bushy and them tell me you think this is also an assegai.'

'Not think. I am reasonably sure. What is different about you, Nikita? Have you cut your hair? Come, let me show you.' He walked ahead down the passage and opened the swing doors of the post mortem laboratory with a deft thump of his palms. 'It's a long time since we saw an assegai – it's no longer a weapon of choice. Twenty years ago it was more common.'

There was the smell of death and formalin and cheap air freshener in the room and the air conditioning was set quite low. Pagel unzipped the black body bag. Laurens's remains lay there naked, like a cocoon. There was a single wound in the middle of her torso between two small breasts.

'What was not present with Davids,' said Pagel as he snapped on a pair of rubber gloves, 'is the exit wound. Entry wound was wide, about six centimetres, but there was nothing behind. My conclusion was a very broad blade, or two stabs with a single, thinner blade – most unlikely, however. But I didn't think "assegai". With Pretorius we have the exit wound, two point seven centimetres wide, and the entry wound of six point two. That's when the penny dropped.'

He turned Laurens's body on its side. 'Look here, Nikita. Exit wound right behind, just beside the spinal column. I had to cut the entry wound for chemical analysis, so you can no longer see, but it was even wider – six point seven, six point seven five.'

He lowered the body carefully on its back again, and covered it again.

'It tells us a couple of things which you will find interesting, Nikita. The blade is long; I estimate about sixty centimetres. We see a great deal of stab wounds inflicted with butcher's knives – you know, the kind you can buy at Pick and Pay, about a twenty-five centimetre blade. Those wounds display clearly only one cutting edge and sometimes an exit wound, but never wider than a centimetre. Entry wounds usually three, occasionally four centimetres. Here we have two cutting edges, much like a bayonet, but wider and thinner. Considerably wider. A bayonet also does more damage internally – designed for it, did you know? So we have a blade sixty centimetres long, with a narrow piercing point growing steadily wider towards the back where it is just under seven centimetres. Do you follow, Nikita?'

'I'm with you, Prof.'

'It's the classical assegai, nothing else approaches that description. Not even a sword wound. Sword wounds are naturally very rare, I think I have seen two in my life. Swords have a much wider exit wound and the wound widths are much more uniform. But that is not the only difference. The results of the chemical analysis produced a few surprises. Microscopic quantities of ash, animal fats and a few compounds we could not identify at first, but had to go through the tables. It appeared it was Cobra. You know, the polish people use to shine their floors. Animal fats were of bovine origin. You don't find that on swords. I began to look around,

Nikita, as it has been a long time since we had an assegai, one tends to forget. Let's go to my office, the notes are there. Something different about you. Wait, let me guess . . .' Pagel went ahead to his office.

Griessel looked down at his clothes. Everything was as usual, he couldn't see anything different.

'Sit, dear fellow, and let me get my story straight.' He removed a black lever-arch file from the shelf and paged through it.

'The ash. They use it to polish the blade, the blacksmiths. I suppose they are assegai smiths as they only make those. Ancient method, they used it to polish Cape silver in the old days, sometimes you see pieces in the antique shops, the wear is distinctive. This tells us the assegai was made in the traditional way. But we will come back to that. The same applies to the beef lard and the Cobra polish. That is not for the blade but for the shaft. The Zulus use it to treat the wood, to make it smooth and shiny. To preserve the wood and prevent warping.

'All very well, you will say, but that isn't much help in catching the fellow – with Cobra polish? I made some calls, Nikita, I have some friends in the curio business. They say there are three kinds of assegai on the market today. The ones we can ignore are the ones they sell at the flea market on Greenmarket Square. Those come from the north, some from as far away as Malawi and Zambia – poor workmanship, with short, thin blades and metal shafts and lots of African baroque wirework. They are made for the tourists and are replicas of some or other ritual assegais of various African cultures.

'The second kind is the so-called antique or historical spear or assegai – either the short stabbing assegai or the long throwing spear. Both have blades which match our wound profile, but there is one major difference: the antique assegai blade is pitch black from ox-, sheep's or goat's blood, as the Zulus use it for slaughtering. To kill the animal. The ash residue will also be visible under the microscope in much greater quantities. Do you know, Nikita, they sell the old assegais for five or six thousand apiece? Up to ten thousand if there is good evidence of age.

'But none of your victims had traces of animal blood, which means your assegai is either antique but very well cleaned, or it is one of the third kind: exactly the same form and manufacture as the antiques, but recently made. And the rust tells us it is the latter. I asked them to look for oxidation deposits in the wound under the spectrometer and there were practically none. No rust, no age. Your assegai has been made in the last three or four years, more likely in the last eighteen months.

'Oh, and one more thing: I suspect the assegai is not thoroughly cleaned after every murder. We found traces of the first two victims' blood and DNA in Laurens's wound. Which means it is the same weapon and most likely the same murderer.'

There went his theory that Bothma had been involved with the murder of Laurens. He nodded at Pagel.

'The thing is, Nikita, there are not many people making traditional assegais any more. Demand is small. The craft mostly survives in the rural areas of KwaZulu where the traditions are still practised and they still slaughter oxen in the old way. Where they still use beef lard for the shafts and buy Cobra to polish their *stoeps*. I also don't believe we are dealing with the long throwing spear. The entry angle of the wound is not high enough. I think this is a stabbing assegai, made by a blacksmith somewhere on the Makathini plains, in the past year. Naturally the question is, how on earth did it get from there to here, in the hands of a man who has a bone to pick with people who do harm to children? An odd choice of weapon.'

'A man, Prof?'

'I believe so. It's the depth of the wound. To push an assegai through a breastbone is not so hard, but to thrust one right through the body, breaking a rib on the way and protruding four or five centimetres out the back takes a lot of power, Nikita. Or a lot of rage or adrenaline, but if it is a woman, she is an Amazon.'

'It's a good choice of weapon, Prof. Quiet. Efficient. You can't trace it like a firearm.'

'But even the assegai is not small, Nikita. Metre and a half, maybe longer.'

Griessel nodded. 'The question is: why an assegai? Why not a big hunting knife or a bayonet? If you want to stab there is plenty of equipment.'

'Unless you want to make a statement.'

'That's what I'm thinking too, but what fucking statement? What are you saying? I am a Zulu and I love children?'

'Or maybe you want the police to think you are a Zulu while all the time you are a Boer from Brackenfell.'

'Or you want to attract attention to your cause.'

'You can't deny, Nikita, that it's a good cause. My first impulse is to let him go his way.'

'No, fuck, Prof, I can't agree with that.'

'Come on, you must admit his cause has merit.'

'Merit, Prof? Where's the merit?'

'Much as I believe in the justice system, it is not perfect, Nikita. And he fills an interesting gap. Or gaps. Don't you think there are a few people out there who will think twice before they hurt their children?'

'Prof, child abusers are lower than lobster shit. And every one I ever arrested I felt like killing with a blunt instrument. But that's not the point. The point is, where do you draw the line? Do you kill everyone that can't be rehabilitated? Psychopaths? Drug addicts who steal cell phones? A Seven–Eleven owner who grabs his forty-four Magnum because a manic-depressive klep-tomaniac steals a tin of sardines? Does his cause have merit too? Shit, Prof, not even the psychiatrists can agree on who can be rehabilitated or not; every one has a different story in court. And now we want every Tom, Dick and Harry with an assegai to make that call? And this whole thing about the death penalty . . . Suddenly everyone wants it back. Between you and me, I am not by definition against the death penalty. I have put fuckers away who more than deserved that. But about one thing I can't argue, it was never a deterrent. They murdered just as much in the old days, when they were hanged or fried in the chair. So, I see no merit in it.'

'Powerful argument.'

'Chaos, Prof. If we allow bush justice. It's just the first step to chaos.'

'You're sober, Benny.'

'Prof?'

'That's what's different about you. You're sober. How long?'

'A few days, Prof.'

'Good heavens, Nikita, it's like a voice from the past.'

26

Before he reached his car, Jamie Keyter phoned to report, and without thinking Griessel said, 'Meet me at the Fireman's.' As he drove down Albert Street in the direction of the city his thoughts were on assegais and murders and the merits of a vigilante.

'Powerful argument,' the prof had said, but where had it all come from? He hadn't stopped to think. Just talked. He could swear a part of him had listened in amazement to his argument and thought, 'What the fuck?'

Suddenly he was this great crime philosopher. Since when?

Since he had given up the booze. Since then.

It was like someone had adjusted the focus so he could see the past five or six years more clearly. Was it possible to have stopped thinking for so long? Stopped analysing things? Had he done his work mechanically, by rote, according to the rules and the dictates of the law? Crime scene, case file, footwork, information, handing over, testimony, done. Alcohol was like a golden haze over everything, his buffer against thought.

What he was now and the way he thought, wasn't how it had been in the beginning. In the beginning he had operated in terms of 'us' and 'them', two opposites, two separate groups on either side of the law, sure in his belief that there was a definite difference, a dividing line. For whatever reason. Genetic, perhaps, or psychological, but that was how it was; some people were criminals and some were not and it was his job to purify society of the former group. Not an impossible task, just a huge one. But straightforward mostly. Identify, arrest and remove.

Now, on this end of the alcohol tunnel, in his rediscovered sobriety, he realised he no longer believed in that.

He now knew everyone had it in them. Crime lay quiescent in everyone, a hibernating serpent in the subconscious. In the heat of avarice, jealousy, hatred, revenge, fear, it reared up and struck. If it never happened to you, consider it luck. Lucky if your path through life detoured around trouble so that when you reached the end and the worst you had done was steal paperclips from work.

That was why he had told Pagel that a collective line must be drawn. There had to be a system. Order, not chaos. You couldn't trust an individual to determine justice and apply it. No one was pure, no one was objective, no one was immune.

Albert Street became New Market became Strand and he wondered when he had begun thinking like that. When had he passed the turning point? Was it a process of disillusionment? Seeing colleagues who had given in to temptation, or pillars of the community that he had led away in handcuffs? Or was it his own fall? Discovery of his own weaknesses. The first time he had realised he was drunk at work and could get away with it? Or when he raised his hand to Anna?

It didn't matter.

How do you catch a vigilante? That mattered.

Murder equals motive. What was the assegai man's? The why?

Was there even a simple motive here? Or was he like a serial killer, motive hidden somewhere in the short circuits of faulty neural wiring? So that there was fuck-all, no spoor leading to a source, no strand you could twiddle with and tug on until a bit came loose and you get hold of it and start unravelling.

With a serial murderer you had to wait. Examine every victim and every murder scene. Build a profile and place every bit of evidence alongside the rest and wait for a picture to form, hoping it would make sense, hoping it would reflect reality. Wait for him to make a mistake. Wait for his self-confidence to bloom and for him to become careless and leave a tyre track or a smear of semen or a fingerprint. Or you were just lucky and overheard two nurses chatting about supermarkets. You took a big gamble and the very first Friday you put out the bait, hit the jackpot.

In the old days they used to talk about Benny's Luck, shaking their heads: 'Jissis, Benny, you're so fuckin' lucky, my friend,' and it would make him fed up. He was never 'lucky' – he had instinct. And the courage to follow it. And in those days he had been given the freedom to do so. 'Carry on, Benny,' his first Murder and Robbery CO, Colonel Willie Theal, had said. 'It's the results that count.' Skinny Willie Theal, of whom the late fat Sergeant Nougat O'Grady had said: 'There but for the grace of God, goes Anorexia.' In those days the Criminal Procedure Act was a vague sort of guideline that they used as it suited them. Now O'Grady was buried and Willie Theal in Prince Albert with lung cancer and a police pension and if you didn't read a scumbag his rights before you arrested him they threw the fucking case out of court.

But it was part of the system and the system created order and that was good; if only he could create order in his life, too. That ought to be easy, as the Criminal Procedure Act of the alcoholic was the Twelve Steps.

Fuck. Why couldn't he just follow it blindly? Why couldn't he become a disciple without thinking, without a feeling of despair in the pit of his stomach when he read the Second Step which said you must believe that a Power greater than yourself is going to heal your drinking madness?

He turned right in Buitengracht, found parking, got out and walked in the early evening to the neon sign: *Fireman's Arms.* The southeaster plucked at his clothes as if trying to hold him back, but he was through the door and the tavern opened up before him, the safe, warm heart, musty with the smell of cigarette smoke and beer that had been spilt drop by drop on the carpet over the years. Camaraderie in the bowed shoulders hunched over glasses, television in the corner showing the Super Sport cricket highlights. He stood still a moment, allowing the atmosphere to settle over him.

Homecoming. He felt the yearning to sit at the wooden bar counter with its multitude of stains. The yearning to order a brandy and Coke. To settle in for the first deep draught and feel the synapses in his brain tingle with pleasure and the warmth glide through him. Just one drink, his head said to him, and then he fled, banged open the door and strode out. A tremor travelled through his body, because he knew that chorus: just one drink. He walked hastily to his car. He had to get in and lock the door and leave. Now.

His phone rang. He gripped it in a hand already shaking. 'Griessel.'

'Benny, it's Matt.'

'Jissis.' Out of breath.

'What?'

'Good timing.'

'Oh?'

'I . . . uh . . . I was just on my way home.'

'I am at the provincial commissioner's office. Could you come by here?' His tone of voice said: Don't ask, I can't talk now.

'Caledon Square?'

'Yes.'

'I'll be there now.'

He phoned Keyter and said something had come up.

'Okay.'

'We'll talk tomorrow.'

'Okay, Benny.'

There were four people in the commissioner's office. Griessel only knew three of them – the provincial commissioner himself, head of investigations, John Afrika, and Matt Joubert.

'Inspector, my name is Lenny le Grange and I am a member of Parliament,' said the fourth with an outstretched hand. Griessel shook it. Le Grange had on a dark blue suit and bright red tie like a thermometer. His grip was cool and bony.

'I am truly sorry to bother you at this time of the evening – I hear you've had a long day. Please sit down; we won't detain you long. How is the investigation proceeding?'

'As well as can be expected,' he said, glancing at Joubert for help.

'Inspector Griessel is still familiarising himself with the case files,' said Joubert as they all found places around the commissioner's round conference table.

'Naturally. Inspector, let me go straight to the point. I have the dubious privilege to be the chairman of the Parliamentary Portfolio Committee of Justice and Political Development. As you may have gathered from the media, we are busy developing a new Sexual Offences Bill.'

Griessel had gleaned nothing from the media. But he nodded.

'Very good. Part of the bill is a proposed Register of Sexual Offenders, a list of names of everyone who has been convicted of a sexual offence – rapists, sex with minors, you name it. Our recommendation is that the register be made available to the public. For instance, we want to prevent parents handing their child over to a paedophile when they enrol the child in a crèche.

'To be honest, this aspect of the new bill is controversial. There are people who say it is a contravention of the constitutional right to privacy. It is one of those cases that create division across party lines. At this stage it looks as if we are going to push the bill through, but our majority is not large. I am sure you're beginning to understand why I'm here.'

'I understand,' said Griessel.

The MP took a white sheet of paper from his jacket pocket.

'Just to make matters more interesting, I would like to read an extract from *Die Burger* of two weeks ago. I gave a press conference and they quoted me thus: *"If there are consequences for the sexual offender, such as vigilante attacks on him or inability to find work, then let it be so. A sexual offender forfeits the right to privacy. The right to privacy is not more important than a woman or child's right to physical integrity," the chairman of Portfolio Committee for Justice and Political Development, Advocate Lenny le Grange, said yesterday.*'

Le Grange looked pointedly at Griessel. 'Me and my big mouth, Inspector. One says these things because one believes with such passion that our women and children must be protected. One says it out of reaction to what one perceives as far-fetched scare stories dreamt up by the Opposition. I mean, a vigilante . . . Perhaps I thought it would never happen. Or if it did happen, it would be an isolated incident where the police would rapidly step in and make an arrest. One never foresees . . . not what is going on at the moment.'

Le Grange leaned over the table. 'They are going to make me eat my words. But that goes with the job. It's the risk I run. I don't care about that. But I do care about the bill. That's why I am asking you to stop this vigilantism. So we can protect our women and children.'

'I understand,' he said again.

'What do you need, Benny?' asked the commissioner, as if they were old friends.

He hesitated before answering. He looked from the politician to the Western Cape chief of police and then he said: 'The one thing that is no longer available, Commissioner. Time.'

'And apart from that?' His tone said that was not the answer he had wanted.

'What Benny is saying is that this sort of case is complicated. The problem is lack of an obvious motive,' said Matt Joubert.

'That's right,' said Griessel. 'We don't know why he is doing it.'

'Why would anyone do it?' asked le Grange. 'Surely it's to protect children. That's obvious.'

'Motive,' said John Afrika, 'is usually an identifier, Mr le Grange. If the assegai man's motive is purely to protect children, that identifies him as one of about ten million concerned men in this country. Everyone wants to protect children, but only one is committing murder to do so. What makes him different? Why did he choose this way? That is what we need to know.'

'There are a few things that would help,' said Griessel.

Everyone looked at him.

'We need to know if Enver Davids was the first one. As far as we know, he is the first in the Western Cape. But crime against children is everywhere. Perhaps he started somewhere else.'

'What would that help?' asked le Grange.

'The first one could be significant. The first one would be personal. Personal vengeance. And then he decides he likes it. Maybe. We must consider it. The second thing that could help is other assegai murders or attacks. It's a unique weapon. The state pathologist says they don't see them any more. You don't buy a new assegai at the Seven–Eleven. Why did he go to the trouble of getting one? Then there is the question of where he got it. Professor Pagel says Zululand. Could our colleagues in Durban help? Do they know who makes and sells them? Could they ask the questions? And the last thing we can do is draw up a list of all the reported crimes against children in the past eighteen months. Particularly those where the suspects have not been appre-hended.'

'Do you think he's taking revenge?' asked Advocate le Grange.

'Just another possibility,' said Griessel. 'We must consider them all.'

'There are hundreds of cases,' said the commissioner.

'That is why Benny said time is the one thing he needs,' said Matt Joubert.

'Damn,' said le Grange.

'Amen,' said John Afrika.

The southeaster was blowing so hard they had to run doubled over to their cars.

'You did well in there, Benny,' shouted Joubert above the roar of the wind.

'So did you.' And then: 'You know, if you drank more, you too could have been an inspector now.'

'Instead of a senior superintendent that has to deal with all this political shit?'

'Exactly.'

Joubert laughed. 'That's one way to look at it.'

They reached Griessel's car. 'I'm going to look in on Cliffy quickly,' he said.

'I'm coming too. See you there.'

Gently he pushed open the door of the hospital room and saw them sitting there – the woman and two children around the bed, all bathed in the yellow pool of the bedside lamp. Mketsu's wife holding his hand, the children on either side, their eyes on their wounded father. And Cliffy lying there with a soft smile, busy telling them something.

Griessel stopped, reluctant to intrude. And something else, a consciousness of loss, of envy, but Cliffy saw him and his smile broadened and he said, 'Come in, Benny.'

On the threshold of his flat was a small glass vase with a single, unfamiliar red flower. And a small note under the vase, folded twice.

He picked it up, opened the letter and hope welled up in him. Anna?

Welcome to our building. Pop in for tea when you have the time.
At the bottom. *Charmaine. 106.*

Fuck. He looked down the passage in the direction of 106. All was quiet. Somewhere he could hear a television. He unlocked his door quickly and went in, closing it softly. He placed the vase on the breakfast bar. He read the note again, crumpled it up and tossed it in his new rubbish bin. Not the sort of thing he wanted his children to see lying around tomorrow.

His sitting-room suite. He stood back and inspected it. Tried to see it through his children's eyes. The place looked less barren at least, more homely. He sat down in a chair. Not too bad. He stood up and went and lay down on the couch with a faint stirring of pleasure. He felt weary, felt like closing his eyes.

Long day. The seventh since he had last had a drink.

Seven days. Only a hundred and seventy-three to go.

He thought of the Fireman's Arms and his mind cajoling him: just one drink. He thought about Cliffy's family. The fucking thing was that he couldn't be sure his family would ever be like that again. Anna and himself and Carla and Fritz. How did you get that back? How did you build that sort of bond?

That made him remember the photo and he got up on impulse to find it. He found it in his briefcase and went and lay down again with the light on. He studied the photo. Benny, Anna, Carla and Fritz.

Eventually he got up, went up to the bedroom and put it on the windowsill above the bed. Then he took a shower. His cell phone rang when he was lathered with soap. He made a wet trail to the bed and answered it. It might be Anna.

'Griessel.'

'It's Cloete, Benny. The Sunday papers are driving me crazy,' the liaison officer said.

'Well, tell them to go to hell.'

'I can't. It's my job.'

'What do those vultures want?'

'They want to know if Laurens is Artemis.'

'If *she* is Artemis?'

'You know, whether it was Artemis that murdered her.'

'We don't know what the fucker's name is.'

Cloete was annoyed. 'Is it the same murder weapon, Benny?'

'Yes, it's the same murder weapon.'

'And the same MO?'

'Yes.'

'And I can tell them that?'

'It won't make any difference.'

'It will make a hell of a difference in *my* life,' said Cloete. 'Because then they will stop fucking phoning me.' He put the phone down.

27

At three minutes to ten he knocked on the door of his own house like some stranger. Anna opened up and then she asked, 'Are you sober, Benny?' and he said, 'Yes.'

'Are you sure?'

He looked in her eyes to let her know the first 'yes' was enough. She was looking pretty. She had done something with her hair. It was shorter. Her face was made up, lips red and shiny.

She took her time before reacting. 'I'll get the children.' When he lifted a foot to enter, she shut the door in his face. He stood there dumbstruck and then the humiliation descended on him. He lowered his head in case the neighbours were outside and saw him like this. Everyone would know he had been kicked out. This street was like a village.

The door opened and Carla charged at him, threw her arms around his neck and squeezed him saying, 'Daddy,' like she did when she was little. Her hair smelled of strawberries. He held her close and said, 'My child.'

He saw Fritz in the doorway with a rucksack in his hand.

'Hi, Dad.' Uneasy.

'Hello, Fritz.'

'Bring them back at six,' said Anna who stood behind her son.

'I will,' he said.

She closed the door.

Why was she looking so nice? What was she planning today?

Carla talked too much, too gaily, and Fritz, sitting in the back, said not a word. In the rear-view mirror, Griessel could see the boy gazing out of the car window expressionlessly. In Fritz's profile he saw echoes of Anna's features. He wondered what Fritz was thinking. About that last night his father had been at home and had hit his mother? How could he fix that? And Carla babbled on about the upcoming Matric Farewell and the intrigues of who had asked whom to go with them, as if she could make a success of the day single-handed.

'I thought we might eat at the Spur,' he said when Carla stopped for breath.

'Okay,' she said.

'We're not at prep school any more,' said Fritz.

'The Spur is a *family* restaurant, stupid,' said Carla.

'The Spur is for little kids,' said Fritz.

'Well, you choose, Fritz,' said Griessel. 'Anywhere.'

'It doesn't matter.'

As they walked up the stairs to his flat, he thought it would be awful for the children. This small bare space: Dad's penitentiary. He opened up and stood aside so they could enter. Carla disappeared up the stairs straight away. Fritz stood in the door and surveyed the place.

'Cool,' he said.

'Oh?'

'Bachelor pad,' said his son in answer and went in. 'Haven't you got a TV, Dad?'

'No, I . . .'

'You've got a *sweet* place, Dad,' said Carla from the top of the stairs. Then his cell phone rang, he unclipped it from his belt and said, 'Griessel,' and Jamie Keyter said, 'I thought I should come over to you and report. Where do you live?'

He would have to talk to Keyter even though he didn't want him here. He gave directions and said goodbye.

'I'll have to do a little work today,' he said to the children.

'What kind of work?'

'It's a case. My shift partner is coming round.'

'What case, Dad?' asked Carla.

'It's a guy who's stabbing people with an assegai.'

'Cool,' said Fritz.

'Artemis? You're working on the Artemis case?' asked Carla in excitement.

'Yes,' he said, and wondered if he had ever discussed his work with his children before. When he was sober.

Carla dived onto the new couch with the anonymous stains and said: 'But that's not a guy. The television says it's a woman. Artemis. She's taking revenge on everyone who messes with children.'

'It's a man,' said Griessel, and sat down on one of his new chairs, opposite his son. Fritz's legs hung over the armrest. He had taken a magazine out of his rucksack. *New Age Gaming.* He flipped through it.

'Oh,' said Carla deflated. 'Do you know who it is, Dad?'

'No.'

'So how do you know it's a man?'

'It's highly improbable that it's a woman. Serial killers are usually men. Women almost never use—'

'Charlize Theron was a serial murderer,' said Carla.

'Who?'

'She got an Oscar for it.'

'For the murders?'

'Dad doesn't know who Charlize Theron is,' said Fritz from behind his magazine.

'Dad knows,' said Carla, and they both looked at him to settle the argument and he knew the time had come to say what he must say, the words he had composed in his head while he drove to Brackenfell that morning.

'I am an alcoholic,' he said.

'Dad . . .'

'Wait, Carla. There are things we must talk about. Sooner or later. It's no use pretending.'

'We know you're an alky,' said Fritz. 'We know.'

'Shut up,' said Carla.

'What for? That's all we did and what use was that and now they're getting divorced and Dad drinks like a fish.'

'Who says we're getting divorced?'

'Dad, he's talking rubbish . . .'

'Did your mother say we're getting divorced?'

'She said you could come back when you stop drinking. And we know you can't stop drinking.' Fritz's face was hidden behind the magazine again, but he could hear the anger in his son's voice. And the helplessness.

'I have stopped.'

'It's eight days already,' said Carla.

Fritz sat motionless behind *NAG*.

'You don't think I can stop?'

Fritz clapped the magazine shut. 'If you wanted to stop, why didn't you do it long ago? Why?' The tears were close. 'Why did you do all those things, Dad? Why did you hit Mom? Swear at us. Do you think it's funny seeing your father like that?'

'Fritz!' But she couldn't shut him up.

'Putting you in bed every night when you pass out? Or finding you in a chair in the morning, stinking and you never even remembered what you did? We never had a father. Just some drunkard who lived with us. You don't know us, Dad. You don't know anything. You don't know we hide the liquor away. You don't know we take money out of your wallet so you can't buy brandy. You don't know we can't bring our friends home because we're ashamed of our father. We can't sleep over at our friends because we're scared you'll hit Mom when we're not there. You still think we like to go to the Spur, Dad. You think Charlize Theron is a criminal. You don't know anything, Dad, and you drink.'

He could no longer hold back the tears and he got up and rushed up the stairs. Griessel and Carla stayed behind and he could not meet her eyes. He sat in his chair and felt shame. He saw the fuck-up he had made of his life. The whole irrevocable fuck-up.

'You *have* stopped, Dad.'

He said nothing.

'I *know* you have.'

The unease had driven Thobela up Table Mountain early Sunday morning. He drove to Kirstenbosch and climbed the mountain from behind, up Skeleton Gorge, until he stood on the crest and looked over everything. But it didn't help.

He pulled and kneaded the emotion, looking for reasons, but none came.

It wasn't only the woman.

'Oh God,' she had said. He had come from the shrubs and the shadows and in the dark he grabbed the firearm in her hand and gave it a sharp twist, so that she lost her grip. The dogs were barking madly around them, the sheepdog biting at his heels with sharp teeth. He had to kick the animal and Laurens had formed her last word.

'No.'

She had shielded herself with her hands when he lifted the assegai. When the long blade went in, peace had come over her. Just like Colin Pretorius. Release. That was what they wanted. But inside him there was a cry, a shout that said he couldn't make war on women.

He heard it still, but there was something else. A pressure. Like walls. Like a narrow corridor. He had to get out. Into the open. He must move. Go on.

He walked over the mountain in the direction of Camp's Bay. He clambered over rocks until the Atlantic Ocean lay far beneath his feet.

Why did he feel this urge now? To fetch his motorbike and have a long, never-ending road stretching ahead. Because he was doing the right thing. He did not doubt any more. In the Spur with the street children he had found an answer that he hadn't looked for. It had come to him as if it were sent. The things people did to them. Because they were the easiest targets.

He walked again. The mountain stretched out to the south, making humps you don't expect. How far could you walk like this, on the crest? As far as Cape Point?

He was doing the right thing, but he wanted to get away.

He was feeling claustrophobic here.

Why? He hadn't made a mistake yet. He knew that. But something was wrong. The place was too small. He stood still. This was instinct, he realised. To move on. To hit and then disappear. That was how it was, in the old days. Two, three weeks of preparation until you did your job and you got on a plane and were gone. Never two consecutive strikes in the same place: that would be looking for trouble. That left tracks, drew attention. That was poor strategy. But it was already too late, because he had drawn attention. Major attention.

That was why he had to get away. Get in his truck and drive.

28

He put the kettle on.

'I'll make the coffee, Dad,' said Carla.

'I want to do it,' he said. Then: 'I don't even know how you take your coffee.'

'I drink it with milk and without sugar and Fritz takes milk and three sugars.'

'Three?'

'Boys,' she said with a shrug.

'Do you have a boyfriend?'

'Kind of.'

'Oh?'

'There is a guy . . .'

'Is powdered milk okay?'

She nodded. 'His name is Sarel and I know he likes me. He's quite cute. But I don't want to get too involved now, with the exams and things.'

He could hear Anna's voice in hers, the intonation and the wisdom. 'That's smart,' he said.

'Because I want to study next year, Dad.'

'That's good.'

'Psychology.'

In order to analyse her father's mind?

'Maybe I can get a bursary if I do well, that's why I don't want to get involved now. But Mom says she's put a bit of money aside for our studies.'

He knew nothing about it. He poured the water into the mugs, then the powdered milk and the sugar for Fritz.

'I want to take him his coffee.'

'Don't worry about him, Dad. He's just a typical teenager.'

'He's struggling with his father's alcoholism,' he said, climbing the stairs. Fritz lay on Griessel's bed with the photo in his hands, the photo of them together as a family.

'Three sugars,' he said.

Fritz said nothing. Griessel sat on the foot of the bed. 'I'm sorry,' he said.

Fritz replaced the photo on the windowsill. 'It doesn't matter.' He sat up and took the coffee.

'I'm sorry about everything I did to you. And to your mother and Carla.'

Fritz looked at the steam rising from the coffee mug. 'Why, Dad? Why do you drink?'

'I'm working on that Fritz.'

'They say it's genetic,' said his son, and tested the temperature of the liquid with a cautious sip.

Jamie Keyter was wearing a sports shirt and tight khaki trousers. The short sleeves of the shirt were too narrow and had shifted up above the bulging biceps. He sat on one of the bar stools at the breakfast bar and drank coffee with two sugars and milk and he glanced periodically at Carla while he spoke. That annoyed Griessel.

'And I went up to the little house, like a little *kaia*, and you couldn't see anything, hear anything but the TV show inside, the one with the crazy kaffi . . . green fellow who gives away prizes in green language and I knocked but they didn't hear me. So I opened the door and there they sat drinking. All four, glass in the hand. Cheers! But when they saw me, you should have seen them jump and it was mister this and mister that. The house was dirty and it was empty. Typical greens: they have nothing, but there's this giant TV in the corner and there are four greens living in the *kaia*, two old and two young ones. I don't know how people can live like that. And they didn't want to talk; they just sat there and stared at me. And when they did talk, they lied. The girl works in the house and it was all: "Miss Laurens was a good missus, she was good to all of us." They're lying, Benny, I'm telling you.' He looked pointedly at Carla, who lay on the couch.

'Did you ask them about her fits of rage?'

'I asked and they said it wasn't so, she was a good missus and they kept turning back to the TV and looking sideways at the wine box. Bloody drunken lot, if you ask me.' He was still looking at Carla.

'And they didn't see anything?' He knew what the answer would be.

'Saw nothing, heard nothing.'

'The pathologist says it was the same weapon. The same assegai as the previous murders.'

'Okay,' said Keyter.

'Did you ask about Bothma? What she's like?'

'Oh, no. We already know.'

He let that go. He didn't want to say something in front of the children.

'So,' said Keyter to Carla. 'What do you do?'

'I'm writing matric.'

'Okay,' he said. 'I get it.'

'What?' she asked.

'If I give you a rand, will you phone me when you're finished.'

'In your dreams,' she said. 'And what is your problem anyway?'

'My problem?'

'Greens? Only racists say things like that.'

'I haven't got a racist hair on my head.'

'Yeah, right.'

Griessel had been busy with his thoughts. He missed this exchange. 'Do me a favour, Jamie.'

'Okay, Benny.'

'The file on Cheryl Bothma, the daughter. Find out who's handling that.'

'I thought you talked to them yesterday?'

'I only talked to the guys who dealt with the assegai murders. I'm talking about the case of the child. When they arrested Laurens.'

'I get it.'

'Please.'

'No, I mean I know which one you mean. But what's the use?'

'Something is not right with this thing. I don't know what. Yesterday Bothma . . .'

'But the pathologist said it's the same guy?'

'I'm not talking about the murder of Laurens. I'm talking about the murder of the child.'

'But that's not our case.'

'It's our job.'

'He's weird,' said Carla when they eventually got rid of Keyter.

'He's a *drol*,' Fritz called down the stairs.

'Fritz!' said Griessel.

'I could use a ruder word, Dad.'

'But where does he get the money?' asked Carla.

'What money?'

'Didn't you notice, Dad? The clothes. Polo shirt, Daniel Hechter trousers. Nikes.'

'Who's Daniel Hechter?'

'He's married to Charlize Theron, Dad!' yelled Fritz from upstairs. 'But he's not a murderer.'

For the first time Carla laughed and then Griessel laughed with her.

In the Ocean Basket in Kloof Street, while they waited for their food, Carla asked him about the Artemis case. He suspected that was her way of avoiding the silences. Out of the blue, in the middle of the discussion, she asked: 'Why did you become a policeman, Dad?'

He had no ready answer. He hesitated and saw Fritz look up from the magazine and knew he had to get this right. He said, 'Because that is who I am.'

His son raised an eyebrow.

Griessel rolled his shoulders. 'I just knew I was a policeman. Don't ask me why. Everyone has a vision of himself. That is how I saw myself.'

'I don't see myself,' said Fritz.

'You're still young.'

'I'm sixteen.'

'It will come.'

'I am not a policeman. And besides, I'm not going to drink. Policemen drink.'

'Everyone drinks.'

'Policemen drink more.'

And with that he went back to his magazine and took no further part in the conversation. Until they had eaten and Griessel asked Carla casually if she knew an Afrikaans song with the words: ''n Bokkie wat vanaand by my kom lê, sy kan maar lê, ek is 'n loslappie.' A babe who wants to lie with me tonight, can lie with me, I'm free and easy.

She was still pointing her thumb at her brother when Fritz, without looking up, asked: 'What recording?'

'I don't know, I just heard it the other night over the radio.'

'Was it a medley or a whole song?'

'A whole song.'

'Kurt Darren,' said Fritz.

Griessel had no idea who Kurt Darren was but he wasn't going to admit it. He didn't need another Charlize Theron quip.

'Kurt Darren needs to get himself a decent bass guitarist,' said Griessel.

Something changed in his son's face. It was as if the sun came up. 'Yeah right, that's right, his whole mix is wrong. It's an ancient song, but it has to rock. Theuns Jordaan does it better. He's the guy who does the medley with "*Loslappie*", but he's just as scared of proper bass. There is only one oke in Afrikaans who makes good use of bass, but he doesn't sing that song. It's a helluva pity.'

'Who's that?'

'Anton Goosen.'

'I know Anton Goosen,' said Griessel with relief. 'He's the guy who sang that thing about the donkey cart?'

'A donkey cart?'

'Yes, what was the name of the song? *Kruidjie-roer-my-nie?*'

'That's like, a hundred years ago, Dad,' said Fritz in amazement. 'The Goose doesn't sing stuff like that any more. He rocks now. He's got the Bushrock Band.'

'Unbelievable.'

'No, you know what's really unbelievable, Dad? The guy who plays bass for the Bushrock Band is the same guy who backed Theuns Jordaan with his "*Loslappie*" medley. And he had Anton L'Amour on lead, but Theuns is too middle-of-the-road. Not bad, but he doesn't want to rock. He doesn't want to badass. Diff-olie is badass. And . . .'

'Diff-olie?'

'Yes. And—'

'Diff oil is the name of a *band*?'

'With all due respect, how long were you drunk, Dad? There's Diff-olie and Kobus and Akkedis and Battery 9 and Beeskraal and Valiant Swart and they all kick butt. There's every type of rock in Afrikaans now, from heavy metal to Country. But you have to listen to Anton live in concert if you want to hear bass and genuine rock. Anton likes heavy bass, he turns it on. The only downside of that concert is the flippin' audience.'

'The flippin' audience?'

'Yup. That will teach the Goose to play in the State Theatre. They did this awesome rock and instead of the people going ape, they clapped. I ask you. It's not a flippin' school concert, it's rock, but they gave him these self-conscious ovations. Flippin' Pretoria.'

'Mister Boere Rock,' said Carla, and cast her eyes up to heaven.

'It's better than that Leonard Cohen crap that *you* listen to.'

Griessel was beginning to form a reproof when he began to laugh. He couldn't help himself and he knew why: he was in total agreement with his son.

When he had stopped laughing Fritz said, more to himself than to Griessel: 'That's the one way I see myself.'

'How?'

'Bass guitarist.'

'For Karen Zoid, I suppose,' said his sister.

He pulled up his nose at Carla. 'Only the uninformed think she's into rock only. You read too much *You* magazine. Zoid is closet ballad queen, not a rock chic. But she *is* awesome and that's a fact.'

'And you have an enormous crush on her.'

'No,' said Fritz with regret. 'Karen is spoken for.' Then he turned to his father. 'So you like bass too, Dad?'

'A little,' said Griessel. 'A little.'

Cloete phoned again when they were on their way to Brackenfell.

'I thought you had a thing about the media, Benny.'

'What?'

'Last night. Then it was "vultures" and "tell them to go to hell" and this morning I see you prefer to speak to them direct.'

'What are you talking about?'

'Front page of the *Rapport*, Benny. Front fucking page: "A source close to veteran Detective Inspector Benny Griessel of the Peninsula Unit for Serious and Violent Crimes (SVC) says that the team is still investigating the possibility that the vigilante was not responsible for the murder of Laurens." I know I didn't fucking say that.'

'I did not f . . .' He realised the children were in the car with him. 'It wasn't me.'

'Must have been the ghost girl of Uniondale.'

'I'm telling you, it wasn't me . . .' Then he fell silent because he knew who it was. Biceps Keyter. That's who.

'Doesn't matter. Thing is, the dailies want a follow-up, because everyone has an opinion now. Even the politicians. The DP says the ANC is to blame, the Death Penalty Party say it's the voice of the people and the *Sunday Times* ran an opinion poll and seventy-five per cent of the nation say the assegai man is a hero.'

'Jissis.'

'Now the dailies are phoning me like crazy. So I thought, while you're doing my job, you can handle the enquiries yourself.'

'I told you, Cloete, it wasn't me.'

Cloete was quiet for a moment, then asked, 'What's new?'

'Since yesterday?'

'Yes.'

'Nothing.'

'Benny, you have to give me something. The dailies want blood.'

'One thing, Cloete, but you have to clear it with Matt Joubert.'

Cloete said nothing.

'Do you hear?'

'I hear.'

'We were with the commissioner last night. The plan is to put together a task team tomorrow. We're bringing people in from the stations.'

'To do what?'

'I'm not telling the press that.'

'That's fuck-all, Benny. A task team. So what?'

'Talk to Joubert.'

'I prefer to talk to the source close to veteran Detective Inspector Benny Griessel,' said Cloete, and put the phone down in his ear.

'What was that all about?' asked Fritz from the back.

'The media,' said Benny and sighed.

'They're like a bunch of hyenas,' said Fritz.

'Vultures,' said Griessel.

'Yup,' said Fritz. 'When there's a carcass they start circling.'

He dropped them off at his wife's at three minutes to six. Fritz said: 'Hang on just a minute,' and jumped out of the car.

'It was a lovely day, Dad,' said Carla and hugged him.

'It was,' he said.

'Bye, Dad. See you next week.'

'Bye, my child.'

She got out and went into the house. Fritz came out of the door with an object in his hand. He came up to Griessel's window and held it out.

Griessel took it. It was a CD case. anton & vrinne & die bushrockband. Anton & friends & the bushrockband.

'Enjoy,' said Fritz.

His flat was silent. Suddenly empty. He sat down on the couch where Carla had sat. He turned the CD case over and over in his fingers. He had fuck-all to play it on.

He needed to do something. He couldn't just sit here and listen to the silence. There was too much trouble in his head.

Where had Anna been today? Why was she all dolled up? What for?

Why did Fritz think they were getting divorced? Had she said something? Made some remark? 'Your father won't stop drinking anyway.' Is that what his wife believed?

Of course she fucking believed that. What else, with his record? So, if she knew how it would end, what stopped her from filling the vacuum in the meantime? Why not allow some or other young, handsome and sober shit to take her out. And what else did she allow him? What else? How hungry was she? Anna, who always said, 'I like to be touched.' Who was doing the fucking touching now? God knows it wasn't veteran Detective Inspector Benny fucking Griessel.

He got up from the couch, his hands searching for something.

What a day. His children. His wonderful children. That he barely knew. His son with his base guitar genes and accusing words. Carla, who tried so desperately to pretend everything was normal, everything would work out right. As if her sheer will-power would keep him sober, if only she believed strongly enough.

We never had a father. Just some drunkard who lived with us.

Shit. The damage he had done. It burned him inside, the extent of it, all the multiple implications. It gnawed at him and he looked up and realised he was searching for a bottle, his hands itching to pour, his soul needing medication for this pain. Just one drink to make it better, to make it manageable, and that was when he realised he didn't stand a chance. Here he was with all the shit of his life suffocating him, the shit his boozing had created – and he wanted a drink. He knew with absolute certainty that if there had been a bottle in the flat he would have opened it. He had already ticked off the possibilities in his mind – where he could go to get a drink, what places would still be open on a Sunday evening.

He made a noise in the back of his throat and kicked one of his new secondhand armchairs. What the fuck was it about him that had made him such an absolute shit? What?

He felt for the cell phone with trembling hands. He typed the number and when Barkhuizen answered he just said: 'Jissis, Doc. Jissis.'

29

At half-past six the next morning he walked to the reservoir and he knew the feeling he had was vaguely familiar, but he did not yet recognise it. First he looked at the mountain. And the sea. He listened to the birds and thought about one more day he had survived without alcohol. Even if yesterday had been touch and go.

'What is it about me, Doc?' he had asked Barkhuizen in despair. Because he needed to know the cause. The root of the evil.

The old man had talked about chemistry and genes and circumstance. Long, easy explanations, he could hear how Barkhuizen was trying to calm him down. The oppression and the gnawing anxiety slowly ebbed away. At the end of the discussion the doctor told him it didn't matter where it came from. What counted was how he went on from here, and that was the truth. But when Griessel lay in bed with a great weariness upon him, he still searched, because he could not fight a thing he could not understand.

He wanted to go back to the source, wanted to remember how things were when the drinking began. Sleep overcame him before he got there.

By five o'clock he was awake, fresh and rested, with the assegai affair occupying him and his mind full of ideas and plans. It drove him out of bed, here to the park in shorts and T-shirt and he felt that pleasure again. The morning and the view belonged only to him.

'My name is Benny Griessel and I am an alcoholic and this is my ninth day without alcohol,' he said out loud to the morning in general. But that was not the reason he felt a certain rush. Only once he was on the way to work did he realise what it was. He shook his head because it was like a voice from his past, a forgotten friend. Today the race was on. The search was about to begin. It was the first tingle of adrenaline, expectation, a last short silence before the storm. What surprised him most was how hungry he was for it.

Matt Joubert told the detectives on morning parade that Griessel would lead the assegai case and through the tepid applause he heard the jokesters calling, 'Klippies and Coke squad' and, 'So, we don't really want to catch him.'

Joubert held up a hand. 'The officers who will assist him are Bushy Bezuidenhout, Vaughn Cupido and Jamie Keyter.'

Fantastic, thought Griessel. Now he had the sloppy one and the braggart and the semi-useful detective. Where the fuck were all the stalwarts? He did an involuntary stocktaking. Only Matt Joubert and himself remained from the old days. And Joubert was at least the commanding officer, a senior superintendent. The rest were new. And young. He was the only inspector over forty.

'This morning the commissioner is pulling in four people from the Domestic Violence Unit and ten uniformed people from the Peninsula to help with research,' said Joubert. Here and there people whistled. The political pressure had to be intense because it was a big team. 'They will use the old lecture hall in B-block as a centre of operations. Some of you are storing stuff there – please remove it directly after parade. And give Benny and his team all the cooperation you can. Benny?'

Griessel stood up.

'Drunk, but standing,' someone said in an undertone. Some muffled laughs. There was an air of expectation in the room, as if they knew he was going to make a fool of himself.

Fuck them, he thought. He had been solving murders when they were investigating how to copy their Science homework without getting caught.

At first he just stood there, until there was complete silence. Then he spoke. 'The greatest single reason that we have case discussions at morning parade is because thirty heads are better than one. I want to tell you how we are going to approach this case. So that you can blow holes in my argument. And make better suggestions. Any ideas are welcome.'

He saw he had their attention. He wondered for an instant if it was astonishment that he could string five sentences together. 'The bad news is the similarity between the assegai vigilante murders and serial murders. The victims are, I believe, unknown to the murderer. The choice of victims is relatively unpredictable. The motive is unconventional and, although we can speculate about it, still reasonably unclear. I don't know how many of you remember the red ribbon murders about six years ago: eleven prostitutes murdered over a period of three years. Most were from Sea Point, the murder weapon was a knife, and all the bodies were found with mutilated breasts and genitalia and a red ribbon around the neck. We had the same problem then. The choice of victim was limited to a specific category, the motive was psychological, sexual and predictable and the murder weapon consistent. We could build a profile, but not one definite enough to identify a suspect.

In this case we know he has a hang-up about people who molest or murder children. That is our category, regardless of race or gender. From that we can more or less deduce the motive. And the weapon of choice is an assegai that is used in a single fatal stab. The psychologists will tell us that indicates a highly organised murderer, a man with a mission. But let us focus on the differences between the typical serial murderer and our assegai man. He does not mutilate the victims. There are no sexual undertones. The single wound is deep. One terrible penetration . . . There is anger, but where does it originate? The only reasonable conclusion is that we are dealing with revenge. Was he personally molested as a child? I think the possibility is very strong. It fits. If that is the motive we are in trouble. How do you track down such a suspect? However, there is another possibility. Perhaps he lost a child through some crime. Perhaps the system failed him. We will have to look at the baby that was raped by Enver Davids. Is there a father who wants revenge? The families of the children molested by Pretorius. But it's possible that he was not directly affected by any of these crimes.

As far as his race goes, we must not be blinded by the assegai. It could be a deliberate ploy to mislead us. Here is a man who found Davids in a coloured neighbourhood just as easily as he got into Pretorius's house in a white neighbourhood in the early evening. We must keep our options open. But I swear the assegai means something. Something important. Any comments?'

They sat and listened in absolute quiet.

'We can approach this thing from four perspectives. The first is to find out if we can identify any suspects close to the original child victims. The second is to look at all unsolved crimes against children. We must begin in the Western Cape, since that is where he's operating. If we find nothing, we must expand the search. A long process, I know. Needle in a haystack. But it must be done. The third thing is the murder weapon. We know it's a typical Zulu assegai. We know it was made by hand in the traditional way, most likely in the last year or so. That means we might determine *where* it was made. How it was distributed and sold. But why would someone choose an assegai? We will talk to the forensic psychologists too. Everyone with me so far?'

He saw Bushy Bezuidenhout and Matt Joubert nod. The rest just sat and stared at him.

'The problem with all three of these strategies is that they are speculative. We must go on with them and hope they produce results, but there are no guarantees. They will take time too – the one thing we don't have. The media is on fire and there are political aspects . . . That is why I want to try a fourth approach. And for that I need your help. The question I ask myself is how he selects a victim. I think there can only be two methods: he is part of the system, or he sees it in the media. All three victims were in the news. Davids when he was acquitted, Pretorius when he was in court, Laurens when she was arrested. So he is either part of the justice system, a policeman, prosecutor, court orderly or something –' they shifted around for the first time since he had begun to speak '– or he's just a member of the public with time to read the papers or watch the news on TV. That's more likely. But one or the other – that is how we are going to catch him. I want to know of every serious crime against children in the next week or so. We want something we can blow up in the media. We want something that will get everyone talking.'

Jamie Keyter's voice came from somewhere near the wall: 'You want to set a trap for him, Benny?'

'That is correct. We want to catch him in a snare.'

'Sup,' said Bushy Bezuidenhout, 'there's something I want you all to know from the start.'

Griessel, Keyter, Bezuidenhout and Cupido sat in Joubert's office while they waited for the lecture hall to be cleared.

'Go on, Bushy,' said Joubert.

'I don't have a problem with this guy.'

'You mean the assegai man?'

'That's right.'

'I am not sure I understand you, Bushy?'

'Benny says he's like a serial killer. I don't see it like that. This guy is doing what we should have done a long time ago. And that is to take these evil fuckers who do things to children and hang them by the neck. Christ, Sup, I worked on the original Davids case. Lester Mtetwa and I stood and cried over that baby's body. When we arrested Davids, I had to hold Lester back, because he wanted to blow that fucking animal's head away, he was that upset.'

'I understand, Bushy. We all felt like that. But the big question is: will it prevent you doing your work? From bringing him in?'

'I will do my best.'

'Benny?'

He could not afford to lose Bezuidenhout. 'Bushy, all I ask is: if you feel there is something you can't do, just tell me.'

'Okay.'

'I don't know what your problem is,' said Keyter to Bezuidenhout.

'Jamie,' said Griessel.

'What? All I said was—'

'I agree,' said Cupido. 'He's a murderer, end of story.'

'Listen,' said Bezuidenhout. 'You're still wet behind the ears and you want to—'

'Bushy! Leave it.' Griessel turned to Cupido and Keyter. 'Everyone has the right to feel what he feels. As long as it doesn't affect the investigation, we respect each other. Do you understand? I don't need any trouble.'

They nodded, but without conviction.

'Talking of trouble,' said Joubert. Their heads turned to him. 'The trap, Benny . . .'

'I know. It's a risk.'

'I don't want another Woolworths episode, Benny. I don't want people in hospital. I won't have civilians in danger. If there is any chance it could turn into a fiasco, walk away. I want your word on that.'

'You have it.'

Keyter told him it was Inspector Tim Ngubane who had investigated the murder of Cheryl Bothma. Griessel found Ngubane in the tearoom.

'Tim, I need your help.'

'Impressive speech this morning, Benny.'

'Oh, I . . . er . . .'

'You've got all the angles on this one.'

'I hope so.'

'What can I do for you?'

'The Bothma child . . .'

'Yes.'

'You handled that.'

'Anwar and I did.'

'An easy one?'

'Open and shut. When we got there, Laurens was already waiting with her wrists together, ready for the cuffs. Crying a river, "I didn't mean to do it", that sort of thing.'

'She admitted it?'

'Full confession. Said she was drunk and the kid was going on and on, being disgusting, disobedient, a real little terror. Ignored her mother . . .'

'Bothma.'

'Yes, the mother. And then Laurens lost it. Grabbed the pool cue, actually wanted to hit the kid on the backside, but because she was drunk . . .'

'Fingerprints on the pool cue?'

'Yes.'

'Only *her* prints?'

'What are you saying, Benny?'

'I'm not saying anything.'

'It was open and shut, Benny. She confessed, for fuck's sake. What more do you want?'

'Tim, I don't want to interfere. I'm just curious. I thought Bothma—'

'You're not just curious. What do you have that I don't know about?'

'Did you test her blood?'

'What for?'

'For alcohol.'

'Why the fuck would I need to do that? I could smell the booze. She fucking confessed. And then the prints came back and they were hers on the pool cue. That's enough, for fuck's sake. What's your story?'

'I don't have a story, Tim.'

'You fucking whiteys,' said Ngubane. 'You think you're the only people who can do detective work.'

'Tim, it's nothing to do with that.'

'Fuck you, Benny. It has everything to do with it.' Ngubane turned and walked away. 'At least I was able to smell the booze on her breath,' he said. 'Not everyone in this building could have done that.'

He disappeared down the corridor.

By eleven the assegai task team were still waiting for computers and extra telephone lines, but Griessel couldn't wait any longer.

He called the team together and began to allocate work. The most senior officer of the Domestic Violence Unit was a coloured woman, Captain Helena Louw. He made her group leader of research into previous cases where minors were the victims. He gave Bezuidenhout five uniformed men to help with the reinvestigation of the first two assegai victims. He took Cupido aside and spoke to him seriously and at length about his responsibility to investigate the assegai background. 'Even if you have to fly to Durban, Vaughn, but I want to know where it comes from. Make yourself the greatest expert on assegais in the history of mankind. Do you understand?'

'I understand.'

'Well then. Get going.' Then he raised his voice so that everyone could hear him. 'I will move between teams and check out a lot of the stuff myself. My cell phone number is up on the board. Anything, day or night. Call me.'

He walked out, down the stairs. He heard steps behind him, knew who it was.

Keyter stopped him just outside the main entrance.

'Benny . . .'

Griessel stood.

'What about me, Benny?'

'What about you, Jamie?'

'I haven't got a group.'

'How do you mean?'

'You haven't given me anything to do.'

'But that's not necessary. You already are the unofficial media liaison officer, Jaaa-mie.'

'Uh . . . I don't get it.'

'You know what I mean, you little shit. You talked to the papers behind my back. That means I can't trust you, Jaaa-mie. If you have a problem with me, talk to the sup. Tell him why I haven't given you anything to do.'

'It's this chick at the *Burger*, Benny. I've known her since the car syndicate case. She phones me non-stop, Benny. The whole day. You don't know what it's like . . .'

'Don't tell me I don't know what it's like. How long have I been a policeman?'

'No, what I mean . . .'

'I don't give a fuck what you mean, Jaaa-mie. You only drop me once.' He turned on his heel and strode to his car. He thought about self-control. He could not afford to hit a colleague.

He drove through Durbanville and out along the Fisantekraal road. He could never understand why this piece of the Cape was so ugly and without vineyards. Rooikrans bushes and Port Jackson trees and advertising hoardings for new housing developments. How the hell would the Cape handle all the new people? The road system was already overloaded – nowadays it was rush hour from morning till night.

He turned right on the R312, crossed the railway bridge and stopped on the gravel road that turned off to the left. There was a small hand-painted sign that read *High Grove Riding School. 4 km*. Assegai man would have seen it in the dark and begun to look for a place to leave his car. How far was he prepared to walk?

He drove slowly, trying to imagine what a person would see in the night. Not much. There were no lights nearby. Plenty of cover, the rooikrans grew in dense ugly thickets. He stopped awhile, took out his cell phone and rang Keyter.

'Detective Sergeant Jamie Keyter, Serious and Violent Crimes Unit.'

'What's with all that, Jamie?'

'Er . . . hello, Benny,' in a cautious tone. 'It's just in case.'

'In case of what?'

'Oh . . . um . . . you know . . .'

He didn't, but he left it at that. 'Do you want to help, Jamie?'

'I do, Benny.' Keen.

'Phone the weather office at the airport. I want to know what the phase of the moon was on Friday night. Whether it was overcast or not. That night, specifically, let's say between twelve and four.'

'The phase of the moon?'

'Yes, Jamie. Full moon, half moon, understand?'

'Okay, okay, I get it, Benny. I'll call you just now.'

'Thanks, Jamie.'

Roads turned off to other smallholdings with ridiculous names. *Eagle's Nest*. But an eagle wouldn't be seen dead here. *Sussex Heights* but it was flat. *Schoongesicht*. More like a dirty view. *The Lucky Horseshoe Ranch*. And then *High Grove Riding School*. If it were him, he would have driven past the turnoff. Gone quite a bit further on, perhaps, to check out the area. Then turned around.

He did exactly that. Nearly a kilometre beyond High Grove the road ended at a gate. He stopped twenty metres in front of the gate and got out. The southeaster blew his hair up in the air. There was an old gravel pit beyond the gate, desolate, obviously long out of use. The gate was locked.

If it were him, he would have parked here. You wouldn't want to turn into the High Grove driveway. Not if you had never been there before. You wouldn't know what to expect, or who would see you.

His phone rang.

'Griessel.'

'It's Jamie, Benny. The guy at the weather office said it was half moon, Benny, and zero per cent cloudy.'

'Zero per cent.'

'That's right.'

'Thank you, Jamie.'

'Is there anything else I can do, Benny?' Sucking up.

'Just stand by, Jamie. Just stand by.'

A clear night, light of a half moon. Enough to see by. Enough to keep your headlights switched off. He would have parked here. Somewhere around here, since this section of road would have no traffic, a dead end. The road up to the gate was too hard to show tracks. But he would have to have turned around if he came this far. Griessel began to walk down the boundary fence on the High Grove side of the road, searching for tracks on the sandy verge. Where would he have parked? Perhaps over there, where the rooikrans bushes leaned far over the fence. Bleached white grass tufts and sandy soil beside the fence.

Then he spotted the tracks, two vague rows of tyre marks. And in one spot the unmistakeable hollow where a tyre had stood still for a while.

Got you, you bastard!

He walked with care, building the picture in his mind. Assegai man had driven to the gravel-pit gate and turned around. Then the car would be facing in the direction of the High Grove turnoff. He would see the rooikrans thicket in the moonlight even with his lights turned off. He left the road about here and pulled up close to the fence. Opened the door and put a foot on the ground. Griessel searched for the footprint.

Nothing. Too much grass.

He squatted on his haunches. Only one cigarette butt, that was all he needed. A little trace of saliva for DNA testing. But there was nothing to find, only a fat black insect that scurried through the faded grass.

Still squatting, he phoned Keyter.

'I have another job for you.'

30

He knew it would be an hour or two before Forensics turned up. He wanted to determine assegai man's route to the house. Had he climbed through the fence, here, without knowing where the homestead was? Possible, but unlikely. Along the road would be better. He could see headlights coming from far off and have enough time to duck into the shadows.

Griessel walked slowly along the road. The wind blew from diagonally in front. The sun shone on his back, his shoes crunched on the gravel. He scanned the ground for footprints. He became aware of a pleasurable feeling. Just him here. On the trail of the murderer. Alone. He never had been a team player. He had done his best detection work on his own.

Now he was a task team leader.

Joubert was hiding Benny's alcoholism from the Area and Provincial Commissioners. Maybe he was lying about that because, despite the recent appointments of the top structures, the Force was like a small village. Everyone knew everything about everybody.

But why? Did Joubert feel sorry for Anna? Or was it loyalty to an old colleague who had come through the wars with him? The last two old soldiers, who had survived the antics of the old regime and affirmative action of the new era. Who had survived without becoming entangled in politics or monkey business.

No. It was because there was no one else. This morning he had sat and watched them. There were good people, enthusiastic young detectives, clever ones and hard workers and those with ambition, but they didn't have the experience. They didn't have twenty years of hard-grind policing behind them. Task team leader because he was a drunk-but-standing veteran.

But it was neither here nor there. He had better make it work, because it was all he had. *Last stand at the High Grove corral.*

He walked as far as the smallholding's driveway. No footprints. He turned up the drive, the wind now at his back. He knew the house was four hundred metres north. The question was, how long was it before the dogs had heard assegai man in the quiet of the night? He would have stopped, moved off the road and into hiding, at a place where he could overlook the yard.

The stables were ahead, on his left. A coloured man was busy with a pitchfork. The man didn't notice him. He kept on walking and could see the house now, two hundred metres further on. The place where Laurens had fallen.

The dogs began to bark.

He stopped. The workman looked up.

'Afternoon, sir,' said the man warily.

'Good afternoon.'

'Can I help you, sir?'

'I'm from the police,' he said.

'Oh.'

'I just want to look around.'

'Okay, sir.'

The garden began here, shrubs and bushes in old overgrown beds. He would have jumped in behind the shrubbery when the dogs started barking in the night. Then made his way through the plants till he was closer to the house. Plenty of camouflage. He followed the imaginary route searching for tracks. He estimated the distance and built a picture. You could survey the whole yard from behind the garden plants. You could watch a woman in her nightclothes, with a firearm in her hand. You could see the dogs that barked nervously in the darkness. Now you were close to the house, close to her. You ignore her shouts. 'Who's there?' Or perhaps a more threatening, 'Come out or I'll shoot!' You wait until her back is turned and then you rush out of the shadows. Grab the firearm. Raise the assegai. The dog bites at your trousers. You kick.

Something like that.

He looked for footprints in the flowerbed.

Nothing.

How likely was that? Or was the fucker cool and calm enough to wipe them out?

The labourer was still standing and watching.

'What is your name?'

'Willem, sir.'

He walked over to the man and put out his hand. 'I'm Benny Griessel.'

'Pleased to meet you, sir.'

'Bad business this, Willem.'

'A very bad business, sir.'

'First the child and then Miss Laurens.'

'Ai, sir, what will happen to us?'

'What do you mean, Willem?'

'It was Miss Laurens's place. Now it will be sold.'

'Maybe the new owners will be good people.'

'Maybe, sir.'

'Because I hear Laurens could be quite difficult.'

'Sir, she wasn't so difficult. She was good to us.'

'Oh.'

'The people around here pay minimum wage, but Miss Laurens paid us a thousand clean and we didn't have to pay for the house.'

'I believe she drank, Willem.'

'Hai, sir! That's not true.'

'And had a terrible temper . . .'

'No, sir . . .'

'No?'

'She was just strict.'

'Never got angry?'

Willem shook his head and glanced at the house. Elise Bothma stood there in her dressing gown just outside the homestead door.

It was late afternoon by the time he got back to the SVC building. He found Matt Joubert in his office with a stack of files in front of him.

'Do you have ten minutes, boss?'

'As much time as you need.'

'We have a possible tyre print of the assegai man's car.'

'From the smallholding?'

'Just outside, along the fence. Forensics have made a plaster mould. They will let us know. If you could hurry things up, I would be glad.'

'I'll give Ferreira a ring.'

'Matt, the Bothma child . . .'

'I hear you have a problem with it.'

'You hear?'

'Tim was here, just after lunch. Upset. He says you're a racist.'

'Fuck.'

'Relax, Benny. I talked to him. What's the problem?'

'It wasn't Laurens, Sup.'

'Why do you say that?'

'When we questioned Bothma on Saturday . . . There was something – I knew she was lying about something. I thought at first it was about Laurens's death. But then I got to thinking. Keyter questioned the labourers. This morning I went myself. And I don't think it was Laurens.'

'You think it was Bothma?'

'Yes.'

'And Laurens took the blame to protect her? Hell, Benny . . .'

'I know. But it happens.'

'Do you have proof?'

'I know Bothma is the one with the temper.'

'That's all?'

'Matt, I know it's too thin for the courts . . .'

'Benny, Laurens made a statement. She admitted guilt. Her fingerprints are on the billiard cue. And she's dead. We don't have a snowball's chance.'

'Give me an hour with Bothma . . .'

Joubert sat back in his chair and tapped a ballpoint pen on the folder in front of him. 'No, Benny. It's Tim's case. The best I can do is ask him to look at it carefully again. You have the assegai case.'

'It's the same thing. If Laurens was innocent, it means the vigilante punished the wrong one. It changes everything.'

'How so?'

Griessel waved his arm. 'The whole fucking world out there is on his side – the guy who reinstated the death penalty. The noble knight who is doing the pathetic police force's work. Even Bushy says we should leave him; let him get on with it . . . Say there is a witness somewhere. Someone who saw him. Or knows something. He could have a wife or a girlfriend, people who support him because they think he is doing the right thing.'

Joubert tapped his pen again. 'I hear what you're saying.'

'I hate that expression.'

'Benny, let me talk to Tim. That's the best I can do. But they will kill us in court.'

'We don't need the court. Not yet, in any case. All I want is for the media to know we suspect Bothma. And that Laurens might have been innocent.'

'I'll talk to Tim.'

'Thanks, Matt.' He turned to go.

'Margaret and I want to ask you to dinner,' said Joubert before he reached the door.

He stopped. 'Tonight?'

'Yes. Or tomorrow, if that suits you. She'll be cooking anyway.'

He realised that he had only had a tearoom sandwich since that morning. 'That would be . . .' But he envisioned himself at Joubert's family table surrounded by Matt's wife and children. He, alone. 'I . . . I can't, Matt.'

'I know things are crazy here.'

'It's not that.' He sat down on the chair opposite the command-ing officer. 'It's just . . . I miss my family.'

'I understand.'

He suddenly needed to talk about it. 'The children . . . I had them yesterday.' He felt the emotion well up. He didn't want that now. He raised a hand to his eyes and dropped his head. He didn't want Joubert to see him like this.

'Benny . . .' He could hear the awkwardness.

'No, Matt, it's just . . . shit, I fucked up so much.'

'I understand, Benny.' Joubert got to his feet and came around the desk.

'No, fuck. Jissis. I mean . . . I don't know them, Matt.'

There was nothing Joubert could say, just put a hand on Griessel's shoulder.

'It's like I was away for fucking ten years. Jissis, Matt, and they are good children. Lovely.' He dragged a sleeve under his nose and sniffed. Joubert patted his shoulder rhythmically.

'I'm sorry, I didn't mean to bloody cry.'

'It's okay, Benny.'

'It's the withdrawal. Fucking emotional.'

'I'm proud of you. It's already, what, a week?'

'Nine days. That's fuck-all. What's that against ten years of damage?'

'It's going to be okay, Benny.'

'No, Matt. I don't know if it will ever be okay.'

He walked into the task group office in the old lecture hall. They were all sitting waiting for him. He was tired. It was as if the tears he had shed with Joubert had drained him. Captain Helena Louw motioned him closer. He went to her. 'How's it going, Captain?'

'Slowly, Inspector. We have—'

'My name is Benny.'

She nodded and pointed at the computer in front of her. 'We have started a database of all the unsolved cases where children were the victims. There are a lot . . .' She had a peaceful manner, a slow way of speaking. 'We start with the most serious. Murder. Rape. Sexual abuse. So far one hundred and sixty.'

Griessel whistled softly through his teeth.

'Yes, Inspector, it's bad. This is only the Peninsula. Lord knows how many in the whole country. We put in the names of the children, the next of kin and the suspects. We include the nature of the crime and the location. If it's gang-related, we mark it "B" because those are a bit different. We indicate the weapon, if there is one. And the dates of the offences. That's about it. Then we can start cross-referencing. As new information comes in, we can plot it against what we have.'

'Sounds good.'

'But will it help?'

'You never know what will help. But we can't afford not to do something.'

He didn't know if he had convinced her. 'Captain, we need two more items.'

'Call me Helena.'

'I want another field in the database. For vehicles. We have a tyre print. Maybe we'll get something from it.'

'That's good.'

'I'm not sure how we will handle the last thing. I wonder how he makes his choices. The murderer. How does he decide who the next victim will be?'

She nodded.

'There are two possibilities. One is that he is part of the system – policeman or prosecutor or something. But if you say there are more than a hundred and sixty . . . and the victims are too disparate regarding their location and their offences. I have a feeling he is using the media. Radio, or newspapers. Maybe TV. My trouble is I don't read the papers and I don't listen to the radio much. But I want to know when the victims were in the news. I want to know the date of the reports compared to the date of the assegai murders. Am I being clear?'

'Yes. Is it okay if we draw up a table on this blackboard?' She pointed at the front wall of the old lecture hall.

'That would work,' he said. 'Thanks.'

Griessel stood up. Jamie Keyter sat in the corner at the back and watched him in expectation. Cupido and Bezuidenhout sat beside each other, each at his own desk. He drew up a chair and sat down opposite them.

'The assegai is a stuff-up,' said Cupido. He leaned back and from behind him picked up a wrapped parcel, long and thin. He unrolled the brown paper and let the assegai drop onto the desktop. The shiny blade gleamed in the fluorescent light.

'Wallah!' he said. He pronounced the 'W' like 'Willy'.

'Voilà,' Bezuidenhout corrected him with a fake accent. 'It's a fucking French word. It means "check me out".'

'Since when are you the great language expert?'

'I'm just helping you not make a fool of yourself.'

Griessel sighed. 'The assegai . . .' he said.

'On loan from Pearson's African Art. In Long Street. Six hundred rand, VAT included. Imported from Zulu Dawn, a distributor in Pinetown. I talked to Mr Vijay Kumar, the sales manager at Zulu Dawn. He says they have agents who drive around and buy them up, there must be at least thirty places in KwaZulu that make them.'

'That's not *art*,' said Bezuidenhout.

'Bushy . . .' said Griessel.

'I'm just saying. Nowadays everything is art. I wouldn't pay fifty rand for that thing.'

'But you're not a German tourist with euros, pappa,' said Cupido. 'The fact of the matter is, our suspect could have bought it on any street corner. Pearson's say there are five or six chaps in the city alone who peddle them. And then there's another place or two on the Waterfront, two in Stellenbosch and one in the southern suburbs. The whiteys from Europe like them and the African masks like nobody's business. And ostrich eggs. They sell ostrich eggs for two hundred rand apiece. And they're empty . . .'

'I want Forensics to look at the thing, Vaughn . . .'

'Sorted. They're busy already. I took two on loan; I wanted to bring one in for you to see, Benny. Forensics will compare it with the chemical results of the three stab wounds.'

'Thanks, Vaughn. Good work.'

'You said it. But it doesn't look like I'm going to score a trip to Durbs.'

'You'll let me know what Forensics say?'

'Absolutely. Tomorrow I'm going to all the places that sell

assegais. See if they have sales records we can trace. Credit-card slips, tax invoices, anything. See what I can find.'

'I want those names in the database, please. They must be compared with the names Captain Louw has.'

'You got it, chief.'

Griessel turned to Bezuidenhout. 'Anything, Bushy?'

Bezuidenhout pulled a pile of files closer with an air of getting to the important stuff at last. 'I don't know.' He pulled them one by one off the pile. 'The Enver Davids rape,' he said. 'Strongest possibility so far. The baby's parents live in the informal settlement on the corner of Vanguard and Ridgeway. Residents call it Biko City; municipality doesn't call it anything. Father is unemployed, one of those men who stand on Durban Road in the morning and raise their hands if the builders come to pick up cheap labour. The mother works at a paper recycling plant in Stikland. They buy old cardboard boxes and turn them into toilet paper. Dawn soft. What the "dawn" has to do with "soft" who the fuck knows, but then I'm just a policeman. Anyway, they say they were together in their shack in Biko City the night of Davids' murder. But the father says, and I quote, "good riddance" about Davids' death. He says if he had known where to find the bastard, he would have stabbed him himself. But he says it wasn't him and he doesn't own an assegai. Their neighbours say they know nothing about that night. Saw nothing, heard nothing.'

'Hmm,' said Griessel.

Bezuidenhout took another file off the heap. 'Here's a list of all the children that were molested by Pretorius. Eleven. Can you believe it! Eleven that we know of. I have started phoning. Most of the parents are in the Bellville area. I'll start with them tomorrow. It will be a long day. I'll get the names onto the database too.'

'Use the uniform guys, Bushy.'

'Benny, I don't want to be funny, but I prefer to talk to them myself. The uniforms are very green.'

'Let them talk to neighbours or something. We have to use them.'

'What about Jamie?'

'What about him?'

'He's doing fuck-all.'

'Do you want him?'

'I could use him.'

'Bushy . . .' Then he changed his mind. 'Jamie,' he called in Keyter's direction.

'Yes, Benny?' Keyter responded eagerly. He leapt up, almost knocking his chair over.

'Tomorrow you go with Bushy.'

He had reached them. 'Okay, Benny.'

'Do the first few interviews with him. Is that understood?'

'Okay.'

'I want you to learn, Jamie. Then Bushy will let you know which you can do on your own.'

'I get it.'

'Jamie . . .'

'Yes, Benny.'

'Don't say that.'

'Don't say what?'

'Don't say "I get it". It irritates the hell out of me.'

'Okay, Benny.'

'It's Amerikaans anyway,' said Bezuidenhout.

'Amerikaans?' asked Cupido.

'Yes, you know. The way they say it in America.'

'An Americanism,' said Griessel wearily.

'That's what I said.'

Griessel said nothing.

'You said "Amerikaans" you clot. You're not a language expert's backside,' said Vaughn Cupido, getting up to leave.

31

He wanted to go home. Not to the flat, but to his *home*. Where his wife and children were. He had a pounding headache and a sluggishness as if his fuel had run out. But he steered the car towards the city. He wondered what the children were doing. And Anna.

Then he remembered. He wanted to phone her. About the thing that had been bothering him since yesterday. He took out his phone while driving and looked up her number on the list. He pressed the button and it rang.

'Hello, Benny.'

'Hello, Anna.'

'The children say you are still sober.'

'Anna . . . I want to know. Our agreement . . .'

'What agreement?'

'You said if I could stop drinking for six months . . .'

'That's right.'

'Then you'll take me back?'

She said nothing.

'Anna . . .'

'Benny, it's been barely a week.'

'It's been nine fucking days already.'

'You know I don't like it when you swear.'

'All I'm asking is if you are serious about the agreement?'

The line was quiet. Just as he was about to say something, he heard her. 'Stay off the booze for six months, Benny. Then we can talk.'

'Anna . . .' but she had disconnected him.

He didn't have the energy to lose his temper. Why was he

putting himself through this? Why was he fighting the drink? For a promise that was suddenly no longer a promise?

She had someone else. He knew it. He was a bloody detective; he could put two and two together.

It was her way of getting rid of him. And he wasn't going to fall for that. He wasn't going through this hell for fuck-all. No, damnit, not the way he felt now. One glass and the headache would be gone. Just one. Saliva flooded his mouth and he could already taste the alcohol. Two glasses for energy, for gas in the tank, for running the assegai task force. Three, and she could have as many toy boys as she liked.

He knew it would help. It would make everything better. Nobody need ever know. Just him and that sweet savour in his flat and then a decent night's rest. To deal with this thing with Anna. And the case. And the loneliness. He looked at his watch. The bottle stores would still be open.

When he arrived at his door with the bottles of Klipdrift and Coke in a plastic bag, there was a parcel on the threshold wrapped in aluminium foil. He unlocked the door first and put the bottles down before picking up the package. There was a note stuck to it. He unpeeled the sticky tape.

For the hard-working policeman. Enjoy. From Charmaine – 106.

Charmaine? What was the woman's case? He unwrapped the foil. It was a Pyrex dish with a lid. He lifted the lid. The fragrance of curry and rice steamed up to his nostrils. Boy, it smelt good. His hunger overcame him. Light-headed, he grabbed a spoon and sat down at the counter. He dug in the spoon and filled his mouth. Mutton curry. The meat was tender under his teeth; the flavour seeped through his body. Charmaine, Charmaine, whoever you are, you can cook, that's for sure. He took another spoonful, picked out a bay leaf with his finger, licked it off and put it aside. He took another mouthful. Delicious. Another. The curry was hot and fine beads of perspiration sprang out on his face. The spoon fell into a rhythm. Damn, he was hungry. He must make a plan about eating. He must take a sandwich to work.

He looked at the bottle of Klippies on the counter beside him. Soon. He would relax in his armchair with a full belly and take his drink as it should be: slowly, with savour.

He ate like a machine down to the last spoonful of curry, carefully scraped up a morsel of meat and a last bit of sauce and brought it to his mouth.

Damn. That was good. He pushed the dish away.

Now he would have to take it back to Charmaine at 106. He had a mental picture of a plump young woman. Why was that? Because her food was so good? Somewhat lonely? He got up to rinse the dish in the sink, then the lid and his spoon. He dried it off, found the foil, folded it neatly and placed it inside the dish. He fetched his keys, locked the door behind him and walked down the passage.

She knew he was a policeman. The caretaker must have told her. He would have to tell her he was a married man. And then he would have to explain why he was living here alone . . . He stopped in his tracks. Did he really need to go through all that shit? He could just leave the dish at her door.

No. He must thank her.

Perhaps she wouldn't be in, he hoped. Or asleep or something. He knocked as softly as possible, thought he could hear the sound of a television inside. Then the door opened.

She was small and she was old. The wrong side of seventy, he judged.

'You must be the policeman,' she said, and she smiled with a snow-white set of false teeth. 'I'm Charmaine Watson-Smith. Please come in.' Her accent was very British and her eyes were large behind the thick lenses of her spectacles.

'I'm Benny Griessel,' he said and his intonation sounded too Afrikaans to him.

'Pleased to meet you, Benny,' she said and took the dish from him. 'Did you enjoy it?'

'Very much.' The inside of the flat was identical to his, just full. Crammed with furniture, lots of portraits on the walls, full of bric-a-brac in display cabinets, on bookshelves and small coffee tables:

porcelain figurines and dolls and framed photographs. Crocheted cloths and books. A giant television set with some or other soapie on the go.

'Please take a seat, Benny,' she said and turned the sound of the television completely off.

'I don't want to interrupt your programme. I've actually just come to say thank you very much. It was very nice of you.' He sat down on the edge of a chair. He didn't want to stay long. His bottle awaited him. 'And the curry was fantastic.'

'Oh, it was a pleasure. You not having a wife . . .'

'I, uh, do. But we are – ' he searched for the word – '. . . separated.'

'I'm sorry to hear that. I sort of assumed, seeing your children yesterday . . .'

She didn't miss much. 'Yes,' he said.

She sat down opposite him. She seemed to be settling in for a long discussion. He didn't want . . .

'And what sort of policeman are you?'

'I'm with the Serious and Violent Crimes Unit. Detective Inspector.'

'Oh, I'm delighted to hear that. Just the right man for the job.'

'Oh? What job is that?'

She leaned forward and stage-whispered conspiratorially: 'There's a thief in this building.'

'Oh?'

'You see, I get the *Cape Times* every morning,' she said, still in that exaggerated whisper.

'Yes?' A light began to go on for him. There is no such thing as a free curry and rice.

'Delivered to my postbox at the entry hall. And somebody is stealing it. Not every morning, mind you. But often. I've tried everything. I've even watched the inner door from the garden. I believe you detectives would call it a stakeout, am I right?'

'That's right.'

'But the perpetrator is very elusive. I have made no headway.'

'My goodness,' he said. He had no idea what else to say.

'But now we have a real detective in the building,' she said with immense satisfaction and sat back in her chair.

Griessel's phone rang in his shirt pocket.

'I'm sorry,' he said. 'I have to take this.'

'Of course you do, my dear.'

He took the phone out. 'Griessel.'

'Benny, it's Anwar,' said Inspector Anwar Mohammed. 'We've got her.'

'Who?'

'Your assegai woman. Artemis.'

'Assegai woman?'

'Yup. She's made a complete statement.'

'Where are you?'

'Twenty-three Petunia Street in Bishop Lavis.'

He got up. 'You'll have to direct me. I'll phone you when I'm nearby.'

'Okay, Benny.'

He switched off the connection. 'I'm really sorry, but I have to go.'

'Of course. Duty calls, it seems.'

'Yes, it's this case I'm working on.'

'Well, Benny, it was wonderful meeting you.'

'And you too,' he said on the way to the door.

'Do you like roast lamb?'

'Oh, yes, but you mustn't go to any trouble.'

'No trouble,' she said with a big white smile. 'Now that you're working on my case.'

Petunia Street was in uproar. Under the streetlights stood a couple of hundred spectators, so that he had to drive slowly and wait for them to open a path for him. In front of number 23 rotated the blue lights of three police vans and the red ones of an ambulance. Forensics and the video team's two Toyota minibuses were parked halfway up the pavement. In front of the house next door were two minibuses from the SABC and e.tv.

He got out and had to push his way through the bystanders. On the lawn a coloured constable in uniform tried to stop him. He showed his plastic ID card and instructed him to call in more people for crowd control.

'There aren't any more, the entire station is here already,' was the reply.

Griessel walked through the open front door. Two uniformed members sat in the sitting room watching television.

'No, damnit,' Griessel said to them. 'The crowd is about to come in the door and you sit here watching TV?'

'Don't worry,' one answered. 'This is Bishop Lavis. The people are curious, but decent.'

Anwar Mohammed heard his voice and came out of an inner room.

'Get these people outside, Anwar, this is a fucking crime scene.'

'You heard the inspector, hey?'

The men stood up reluctantly. 'But it's *Frasier*,' said one, pointing at the screen.

'I don't care what it is. Go and do your work,' said Mohammed. Then, to Griessel: 'The victim is here, Benny.' He led the way to the kitchen.

Griessel saw the blood first – a thick gay arc of red starting on the kitchen cupboard door and sweeping up, all the way to the ceiling. To the right against the fridge and stove was more blood in the distinctive spatters of a severed artery. A man lay in a foetal position in the corner of the smallish room. The two members of the video team were setting up lights to film the scene. The light made the reddish-brown blood on the victim's shirt glisten. There were a few rips in the material. Beside him lay an assegai. The wooden shaft was about a metre long, the bloodied blade about thirty centimetres long and three or four centimetres wide.

'This is not the assegai man,' said Griessel.

'How can you know?'

'Whole MO is different, Anwar. And this blade is too small.'

'You better come talk to the girl.'

'The girl?'

'Nineteen. And pretty.' Mohammed gestured with his head to the door. He walked ahead.

She was sitting in the dining room with her head in her hands. There was blood on her arms. Griessel walked around the table and pulled out the chair beside her and sat down. Mohammed stood behind him.

'Miss Ravens,' said Mohammed softly.

She raised her head from her hands and looked at Griessel. He could see she was pretty, a delicate face with deep, dark, nearly black eyes.

'Good evening,' he said.

She just nodded.

'My name is Benny Griessel.'

No reaction.

'Miss Ravens, this inspector has been working on the assegai case. Tell him about the others,' said Mohammed.

'It was me,' she said. Griessel saw her eyes were unfocused. Her hands trembled slightly.

'Who is the man in there?' he asked.

'That's my dada.'

'You did that?'

She nodded. 'I did.'

'Why?'

She slowly blinked her big eyes.

'What did he do?'

She was looking at Griessel but he wasn't sure she was seeing him. When she spoke there was surprising strength in her voice, as if it belonged to someone else. 'He would come and sleep with me. For twelve years. And I wasn't allowed to tell anyone.'

Griessel could hear the anger.

'And then you read about the man with the assegai?'

'It's not a man. It's a woman. It's me.'

'I told you,' said Mohammed.

'Where did you get this assegai?'

'At the station.'

'Which station?'

'The station in Cape Town.'

'At the station flea market?'

She nodded.

'When did you buy it?'

'Yesterday.'

'Yesterday?' queried Mohammed.

'And then you waited for him to come home tonight?'

'He wouldn't stop. I asked him to stop. I asked him nicely.'

'Did you two live here alone?'

'My mother died. Twelve years ago.'

'Miss Ravens, if you only bought the assegai yesterday, how could you have killed the other people?'

Her black eyes moved over Griessel's face. Then she looked away. 'I saw it on TV. Then I knew. It's me.'

He put out a hand and rested it on her shoulder. She jerked away and in her eyes he saw momentary fear. Or hate, he couldn't differentiate. He dropped his hand.

'I called SS,' said Mohammed quietly behind him.

'That's good, Anwar,' he said. Social Services could handle her better. He rose and led Mohammed out by the elbow. In the kitchen, beside the body, he said: 'Watch her. Don't leave her alone.'

Before Mohammed could reply, they heard Pagel's voice in the door. 'Evening, Nikita, evening, Anwar.'

'Evening, Prof.'

The pathologist was in evening wear with his case in his hand. He shuffled past the video team and squatted down beside the man on the floor.

'This is not our assegai, Nikita,' he said as he opened his case.

'I know, Prof.'

'Benny,' a voice called from the sitting room.

'Here,' he said.

Cloete, the officer from Public Relations, walked in. 'Hell, but it's busy here.' He looked at the victim. 'He's copped it.'

'Oh, so now you're a pathologist too?' asked one of the video men.

'Look out, Prof, Cloete's after your job,' said the other.

'That's because Benny's sober now. One less job opportunity for Cloete.'

'But Benny doesn't *look* better.'

'Shit, but you're funny tonight,' said Griessel. To Cloete: 'Come, we'll talk in there.' He saw Mohammed following them. 'Anwar, get someone to watch the girl before you come.'

'Will she try to escape?' asked Cloete.

'That's not what I'm afraid of,' said Griessel, and sat down on a chair in the sitting room. The television was still showing a situation comedy. Laughter sounded. Griessel leaned forward and turned it off.

'Did you see the television people outside?'

Griessel nodded. Before he could say more the cell phone in his pocket rang. 'Excuse me,' he said to Cloete as he took the call: 'Griessel.'

'It's Tim Ngubane. Joubert says you're looking for bait. For the assegai thing . . .'

'Yes.' A little surprised at the friendly tone.

'How does a Colombian drug lord who's got a thing for little girls grab you?'

'It sounds good, Tim.'

'Good? It's perfect. And I've got it for you.'

'Where are you?'

'Camps Bay, home to the rich and famous.'

'I'll come as soon as I can.'

Before he could put the phone away, Cloete forged ahead. He pointed outside: 'Someone told them it was Artemis. The papers are here too. I had to hear it from them.' Accusing.

'I just got here myself.'

'I didn't say it was you, but the fuck knows . . .'

'Cloete, I'm sorry about yesterday. It was one of my team members that talked to the media. It won't happen again.'

'What do you want, Benny?'

'What do you mean?'

'The day you apologise is the day you want something. What's going on here?'

'This is a difficult one. Nineteen-year-old girl stabbed her father with an assegai because he molested her. But she didn't commit the other murders.'

'Are you sure?'

'Absolutely.'

'How do you want me to handle this?'

'Cloete, there are politics involved with the assegai thing. Between you and me, the girl in there was partly inspired by our murderer, if you know what I mean. But if you tell the media that, the commissioner will have a stroke, because he's under pressure from above.'

'The minister?'

'Parliamentary Commission.'

'Fuck.'

'You must talk to Anwar, too, so we all have the same story. I feel we should only mention a domestic fight and a sharp instrument. Don't let on about the weapon for now.'

'That's not the thing you want from me, Benny, is it?'

'No, you're right. I need another favour.'

Cloete shook his head in disbelief. 'The fuck knows, I am nothing but a whore. A police prostitute, that's what I am.'

32

The town was too small.

He couldn't reconnoitre. This afternoon when he drove down the long curve of the main street there were eyes on him. The eyes of coloured people in front of a few cafés, the eyes of black petrol attendants at the filling station, which consisted of a couple of pumps and a dilapidated caravan. The eyes of Uniondale's few white residents watering their dry gardens with hosepipes.

Thobela knew he had only one chance to find the house. He wouldn't be able to look around; he wouldn't be able to drive up and down. Because here everyone knew about the Scholtz scandal and they would remember a black man driving a pick-up – a strange black man in a place where everyone knew everybody.

He had to be content with a signboard in the main street indicating the road. It was enough. He took the R339 out of the town, the one running east towards the mountain. As the road curved around the town, he saw there was a place to park with pepper trees and clefts in the ridges beside the road where he could leave the vehicle in the dark. He drove on, through the pass, along the Kamannasie River, and at twelve kilometres he filled up with petrol beside the cooperative at Avontuur.

Where was he going? asked the Xhosa petrol attendant.

Port Elizabeth.

So why are you taking *this* road?

Because it is quiet.

Safe journey, my brother.

The petrol attendant would remember him. And that forced him to drive back to the main road and turn right. Towards the

Langkloof, because the man's eyes could follow him. If he deviated from that route, the man would wonder why and remember him even better.

In any case he had to pass the time until dark. He made a long detour. Gravel roads, past game farms and eventually back via the pass. To this spot above Uniondale where he stood beside the pick-up in the moonlight and watched the town lights below. He would have to walk through the veld and over the ridge. Sneak. Between the houses. He would have to avoid dogs. He must find the right house. He must go in and do what he had to do. And then come back and drive away.

It would be hard. He had too little information about the lay of the land and the position of the house. He didn't even know if they would be home.

Leave. Now. The risk was too great. The town was too small.

He took the assegai from behind the seat. He stood on a rock and looked over the town. His fingertips stroked the smooth wooden shaft.

He had all night.

Between Bishop Lavis and Camps Bay his cell phone rang twice.

First it was Greyling from Forensics: 'Benny, your man drives a pick-up.'

'Oh, yes?'

'And if we are not mistaken, it's a four-by-two with diff lock. Probably a double cab. Because the imprint is from a RTSA Wrangler. A Goodyear 215/14.'

'What make is the pick-up?'

'Hell, no, it's impossible to say, the whole lot come out of the factory with the Wrangler – Ford and Mazda, Izuzu, Toyota, you name it.'

'How do you know it's not an ordinary pick-up?'

'Your ordinary one comes out with the CV 2000 from Good-year, which is a 195/14, the G 22, they call it. Trouble is, nearly every minibus-taxi comes out with the same tyre, so it's chaos. And your four-by-four is a 215/15. But this print is definitely a

215/14, which is put on the four-by-twos. And eighty per cent of your four-by-twos are double cabs or these other things with only two doors, the Club Cabs. Which also means our suspect is not a poor man, because a double cab costs the price of a farm these days.'

'Unless it's stolen.'

'Unless it's stolen, yes.'

'Thanks, Arrie.'

'Pleasure, Benny.'

Before he had time to ponder the new evidence, the phone rang again.

'Hi, Dad.' It was Fritz.

'Hi, Fritz.'

'What're you doing, Dad?' His son wanted to chat?

'Working. It's a circus today. Everything is happening at once.'

'With the vigilante? Has he nailed someone else?'

'No, not him. Someone else who thinks they are the assegai man.'

'Cool!'

Griessel laughed. 'You think it's cool?'

'Definitely. But I actually wanted to know if you listened to the CD, Dad.'

Damn. He had completely forgotten about the music. 'I only realised last night that I didn't have a CD player. And there wasn't time today to get one. It was a madhouse . . .'

'It's okay.' But he detected disappointment. 'If you want it, I've got a portable CD player. The bass isn't too great.'

'Thanks, Fritz, but I must get something for the flat. I'll make a plan tomorrow, I promise.'

'Great. And then let me know.'

'The minute I have listened to it.'

'Dad, don't work too hard. And Carla sends her love and says yesterday was cool.'

'Thanks, Fritz. Give her my love too.'

'Okay, Dad. Bye.'

'Sleep well.'

He sat behind the wheel and stared into the dark. Emotion welled up in him. Maybe Anna didn't want him any more, but the children did. Despite all the harm he had done.

The dramatic difference between the crime scenes at Bishop Lavis and Camps Bay was immediately apparent. In the wealthy neighbourhood there were practically no onlookers, but at least twice as many police vehicles. The uniformed officers huddled on the sidewalk as if they expected a riot.

He had to drive down the street a bit to find parking and walk back up the slope. All the houses were three storeys high to see the now invisible view of the Atlantic Ocean. They were all in the same style of concrete and glass – modern palaces that stood empty most of the year while their owners were in London or Zurich or Munich busy raking in the euros.

At the steps a uniform stopped him. 'Sorry, Inspector Ngubane only wants key personnel inside,' the constable said.

He took out his identity card from his wallet and showed it. 'Why are there so many people here?'

'Because of the drugs, Inspector. We have to help move them when they are finished.'

He walked up to the front door and looked in. It was as big as a theatre. Two or three sitting areas on different levels, a dining area and, to the right, on the balcony side, a sparkling blue indoor swimming pool. Two teams of Forensics were busy searching for bloodstains with ultraviolet lights. On the uppermost level, on a long leather couch, four men sat in a neat row, handcuffed and heads bowed as if they felt remorse already. Beside them stood uniformed policemen, each with a gun on his arm. Griessel went up.

'Where is Inspector Ngubane?' he asked one of the uniforms.

'Top floor,' one indicated.

'Which one of these fuckers messed with the girl?'

'These are just the gofers,' said the uniform. 'The inspector is busy with the big chief. And it's not just about *messing* with the kid.'

'Oh?'

'The child has disappeared . . .'

'How do I get up there?'

'The stairs are there,' pointed the constable with the stock of his shotgun.

In the first-floor passage, Timothy Ngubane stood and argued with a large white detective. Griessel recognised him from the faded blue and white cloth hat sporting a red disa flower emblem and the word *WP Rugby*: Senior Superintendent Wilhelm 'Boef' Beukes, a former member of the old Murder and Robbery and Narcotics branches and now a specialist in organised crime.

'Why not? The girl is not in there.'

'There might be evidence in there, Sup, and I can't risk . . .' He spotted Griessel. 'Benny,' he said with a degree of relief.

'Hi, Tim. Boef, how are you?'

'Crap, thanks. Drugs haul of the decade and I have to stand in line.'

'Finding the child has priority, Sup,' said Ngubane.

'But she's not here. You already know that.'

'But there might be evidence down there. All I'm asking is that you wait.'

'Get your butts moving,' said Beukes and stalked off down the passage.

Ngubane sighed deeply and at length. 'It's been an amazing night,' he said to Griessel. 'Absolutely amazing. I've got everybody down there—'

'Down where?'

'There's this storeroom in the basement with more drugs than anyone's ever seen, and the entire SAPS is here – the commercial branch and organised crime and the drugs guy from Forensics, and they all have their own video teams and photographers, and I can't let them in, because there might be leads to where the girl is.'

'And the suspect?'

'He's in here.' Ngubane pointed at the door behind him. 'And he's not talking.'

'Can I go in?'

Ngubane opened the door. Griessel looked in. It was not a big room. Untidy. A man sat on a cardboard box. Thick black hair, drooping black moustache, white shirt unbuttoned, the breast pocket seemed torn. A red bruise on the cheekbone.

'*Sy naam is Carlos,*' began Ngubane deliberately in Afrikaans so that Sangrenegra would not understand and took a small notebook from his trouser pocket. 'Carlos San . . . gre . . . ne . . . gra,' he carefully enunciated the syllables.

'Fuck you,' said Sangrenegra with venom.

'Did someone beat him up?' Griessel spoke Afrikaans.

'The mother. Of the little girl. He's a Colombian. His visa . . . expired long ago.'

'What happened, Tim?'

'Come in. I don't want to leave the cunt alone.'

'You curse very prettily in Afrikaans.'

Ngubane moved into the room ahead of Griessel. 'I'm well coached.' He closed the door behind him. It looked as if it was meant to be a study. Shelves against the wall, dark glowing wood, but empty. Boxes on the floor.

'What's in the boxes?' Griessel asked.

'Look,' said Ngubane and sat down on the single chair, an expensive piece of office furniture with a high back and brown leather.

Griessel opened one of the boxes. There were books in it. He took one out. *A Tale of Two Cities* was printed in gold lettering on the spine of the book.

'Look inside.'

He opened it. There were no pages – just a plastic filler with sides that looked like paper.

'Not a great reader are you, Carlos?' said Griessel.

'Fuck you.'

'A woman phoned Caledon Square about eight o'clock.' Ngubane continued in Afrikaans. 'She was crying. She said her child had been abducted and she knew who it was. They sent a team to the flat in Belle Ombre Street and found the lady. She was confused and bleeding from the head and she said a man had assaulted her and taken her child. She was . . .' he searched for the Afrikaans word.

'Unconscious.'

Ngubane nodded. 'She gave the man's name and this address and she said he had raped her too. She said she knew him and he liked children . . . you know? And then she told us he's a drug lord.'

Griessel nodded and turned to look at Sangrenegra. The brown eyes smouldered. He was a lean man, veins prominent on his forearms, dressed in blue denim and trainers. His hands were cuffed behind his back.

'The uniforms phoned the station commander and the SC phoned us and I was on call and talked to Joubert and got the task force. Then we were all here and the task force arrived by helicopter and the works. We found five men here. Carlos and those four downstairs. They found the drugs in the basement and the girl's clothes in this one's room. Then they found blood in his BMW and a dog, one of those stuffed toys, but no child and this cunt won't talk. He says he knows nothing.'

'The child. It's a little girl?'

'Three years old. Three.'

Griessel felt a red flood of revulsion. 'Where is she?' he asked Carlos.

'Fuck you.'

He jumped up and grabbed the man by the hair, jerked his head back and kept pulling the dark locks. He shoved his face close up to Sangrenegra. 'Where is she, you piece of shit?'

'I don't know!'

Griessel jerked his hair. Sangrenegra winced. 'She lie. The whore, she lie. I know nothing.'

'How did the girl's clothes get in your room, you cunt?' He jerked again as hard as he could as frustration gnawed at him.

'She put it there. She is a whore. She was *my* whore.'

'Jissis,' said Griessel with disgust and gave the hair one last pull before he left him. His hand felt greasy. He wiped it off on Sangrenegra's shirt. 'You lie. You cunt.'

'I've been through that process,' said Ngubane behind him in a calm voice, as if nothing had happened.

'Ask my men,' said Sangrenegra.

Griessel laughed without humour. 'Who gave you this?' he asked and shoved a finger hard onto the bruise on Carlos's cheek.

The Colombian spat at him. Griessel drew his hand back to slap him.

'He said he visited the complainant today,' Ngubane said. 'He says she is a prostitute. She invited him to her flat. The child wasn't there. Then she hit him for no reason. So he hit her back.'

'That's his story?'

'That's his story?'

'And the mother?'

'Social Services are with her. She's . . . traumatised.'

'What do you think, Tim?' Griessel realised he was out of breath. He sat down on a box.

'The child was in his car, Benny. The blood. And the dog. She *was* there. He drove somewhere with her. We have two hours from the assault on the complainant until we got here. He took the child somewhere. He thought because the mother is a call girl, he could do what he wanted. But something happened in the car. The child got scared, or something. So he cut her. That's what the blood looks like. It's against the armrest of the back seat. Looks like an – ' he searched for the Afrikaans word again – '. . . artery. Then he knew he was in trouble. He must have got rid of the kid.'

'Jissis.'

'Yes,' said Ngubane.

Griessel looked at Sangrenegra. Carlos stared back, with disdain.

'I don't think we should be optimistic about the child. If she was alive, this cunt would want to bargain.'

'Can I try something?' Griessel asked.

'Please,' said Ngubane.

'Carlos,' said Griessel, 'have you heard of Artemis?'

'Fuck you.'

'Let me tell you a story, Carlos. There is this guy out there. He has a big assegai. Do you know what an assegai is, Carlos? It's a spear. A Zulu weapon. With a long blade, very sharp. Now, this guy is a real problem for us, because he is killing people. And do you know who he kills, Carlos? He is killing people who fuck with children. Sure you haven't heard about this, Carlos?'

'Fuck you.'

'We are trying to catch this guy. Because he is breaking the law. But with you we can make an exception. So this is what I'm going to do. I'm going to tell all the newspapers and the television that you have abducted this beautiful little girl, Carlos. I will give them your address. And we will publish a photograph of you. And I'm going to see to it that you make bail. And I'm going to keep all your friends in jail, and leave you here, in this big house, all alone. We will sit outside to make sure you don't go back to Colombia. And we will wait for the guy with the spear to find you.'

'Fuck you.'

'No, Carlos. You are the one who is fucked. Think about it. Because when he comes, we will look the other way.'

Sangrenegra said nothing, just stared at Griessel.

'This assegai guy, he has killed three people. One stab, right through the heart. With that long blade.'

No reaction.

'Tell me where the girl is. And it can be different.'

Carlos just stared at him.

'You want to die, Carlos? Just tell me where the girl is.'

For a moment Sangrenegra hesitated. Then he shouted, in a shrill voice: 'Carlos don't know! Carlos don't fucking know!'

33

When they shoved Sangrenegra into the back of a police van and clanged the door shut, Ngubane said: 'I owe you an apology, Benny.'

'Oh?'

'About this morning.' Griessel realised he had already forgotten the incident; it had been a long day.

'We get a little paranoid, I suppose,' said Ngubane. 'Some of the white cops . . . they think we're shit.'

Griessel said nothing.

'I went to visit Cliffy Mketsu. In hospital. He says you're not like that.'

Griessel wanted to add that no, he wasn't like that. His problem was that he thought *everyone* was crap. 'How's Cliffy doing?'

'Good. He says you have more experience than the rest of us combined. So I want to ask you, Benny, what more can I do here? How do I find this kid?'

He looked at Ngubane, at the neat suit, the white shirt and red tie, at the man's ease with himself. In the back of his mind a light began to shine.

'Are there other properties, Tim? These drug guys, they have more than one place. They have contingency plans.'

'Right.'

'Talk to Beukes. They must have known about Sangrenegra. They will know about other places.'

'Right.'

'Has Forensics been to the mother's place?'

He nodded. 'They got his prints there. And they drew the mother's blood. For DNA comparison with the blood in the car. They say that way they can tell if it belongs to the kid.'

'I don't think she's alive, Tim.'

'I know.'

They stood in silence a moment. 'Can I go and see the mother?'

'Sure. Are you going to use this guy as bait?'

'He's perfect. But I have to talk to the mother. And then we'll have to talk to the sup, because Organised Crime is involved, and I can tell you now, they won't like it.'

'Fuck them.'

Griessel chuckled. 'That's what I was thinking too.'

When he drove through the city towards Tamboerskloof, his thoughts jumped between Boef Beukes and Timothy Ngubane and the children he saw in Long Street. At half-past eleven at night there were children everywhere he looked. Teenagers on a fucking Monday night at the top end of Long Street, at the clubs and restaurants and cafés. They stood on the pavements with glasses and cigarettes in their hands, small groups huddled beside parked cars. He wondered where their parents were. Whether they knew where their children were. He realised he did not know where his own children were. But surely Anna knew. If she were at home.

Beukes. Who had worked with him in the old days. Who had been a drinking partner. When his children were small and he was still whole. What the hell had happened? How had he progressed from drinks with the boys to a full-blown alcoholic?

He had started drinking when Murder and Robbery was still located in Bellville South. The President in Parow had been the watering hole, not because it was anything like a presidential hotel, but there would always be a policeman leaning on the long mahogany bar, no matter what time of the day you turned up there. Or that other place beyond Sanlam in Stikland that made those delicious pizzas, the Glockenberg or something, Lord, that was a lifetime ago. The Glocken*burg*. There was a Spur Steak Ranch there now, but in those days it had been a colossal tavern. One night, thoroughly drunk, he had climbed on the stage and told the band they must cut the crap and play real rock 'n' roll and give me that bass, do you know 'Blue Suede Shoes'? His colleagues at the big table had shouted and kicked up a row and clapped and the four-piece band had nervously said yes, they knew it, young Afrikaner fuckers with soft beards and long hair who played 'Smokie' and he put the bass around his neck and got behind the mike and sang 'One for the money . . .' and they were off and rocking, between the commotion from the floor and the orchestra's relief that he was not hopeless. They were cooking; they thrashed that fuckin' song and people came in from the bar and from outside. And that Benny Griessel had run his fingers up and down the neck of the bass guitar and he laid down a fucking carpet of bass for the rock 'n' roll and when they had finished everybody screamed for more, more, more. So he let rip. Elvis songs. And he sweated and played and sang till who knows what time, and Anna came looking for him, he saw her at the back of the Glock. At first angry with arms folded tight, where was her husband, look at the time. But the music melted her too, she loosened up and her hips began to sway and she clapped too and screamed: 'Go, Benny, go!' because that was *her* Benny up there on the fucking stage, *her* Benny.

Lord, that was a lifetime ago. He hadn't been an alky then, just a hard-drinking detective. Like the rest of them. Just like Matt Joubert and Boef Beukes and fat Sergeant Tony O'Grady, the whole damn lot of them. They drank hard because, hell, they worked hard, back then in the late eighties. Worked like slaves while the whole world shat on them. Necklace murders, old people murdered, gays murdered, gangs, armed robbery wherever you turned. It never stopped. And if you said you were a policeman, the room would fall silent and everyone looked at you as if you were lower than lobster crap, and that, they always said, was as low as you could go.

Then he had been as Tim Ngubane was now. At ease with himself. Lord, and he *could* work. Hard, yes. But clever. He nailed them, murderers and bank robbers and kidnappers. He was ruthless and enthusiastic. He was light of foot. That was the thing – he had danced when the others plodded. He was different. And he thought he would be like that always. But then all the shit had a way of overwhelming you.

Maybe that was the problem. Maybe the booze only got the dancers; look at Beukes and Joubert, they don't drink like fish, they plod along still. And he? He was fucked. But there in the back of his mind the germ of an idea remained that he was better than them all, that he was the best fucking detective in the country, end of story.

Then he laughed at himself there behind the steering wheel, at the top end of Long Street near the swimming baths, because he was a wreck, a drunkard, a guy who had bought a bottle of Klippies an hour ago after nine days of sobriety and only half an hour ago had lost control with the Colombian because he was carrying so much shit around with him and here he was, thinking he was the be-all and end-all.

So what had happened? Between Boef Beukes and the Glockenburg and now? What the fuck happened? He had reached Belle Ombre Street and there was no parking so he pulled half onto the pavement.

Before he opened the door, he thought about the body tonight in Bishop Lavis. There had been no death screams in his head. No dreadful voices.

Why not? Where had they gone? Was it part of his drinking; was it the alcohol?

He paused a few moments longer and then pushed open the door, because he had no answers. The building had ten or twelve floors so he took the lift. There were two black policemen in civilian clothes at the door, each with a shotgun. Griessel asked who they were. One said they were from Organised Crime and that Boef Beukes had sent them, since she would be a target now.

'Did you know about Sangrenegra before this happened?'

'You should talk to Beukes.'

He nodded and opened the door. A young woman jumped up in the sitting room and came over to him. 'Did you find her?' she asked, and he could hear the hysteria just below the surface. Behind her on the couch sat two police officers of the gentler sort, smaller and thinner, with caring hands folded sympathetically on their laps. Social Services. The members of the Force who appear on the scene when all the shit is already cleared away. A man and a woman.

'Not yet,' he said.

She stood in the middle of the room and uttered a sound. He could see her face was swollen and there was a cut that someone had treated. Her eyes were red with weeping. She balled her fists and her shoulders drooped. The coloured woman from SS got up and came over to her and said: 'Come and sit down, it's better if you sit.'

'My name is Benny Griessel,' he said and held out his hand.

She shook it and said, 'Christine van Rooyen.' He thought that she didn't look like your usual whore. But then he smelt her, a mixture of perfume and sweat; they all smelt like that, it didn't wash out.

But she looked different from the ones he knew. He searched for the reason. She was tall, as tall as he was. Not scrawny, strongly built. Her skin was smooth. But that wasn't it.

He said he worked with Ngubane and he knew it was a difficult time for her. But perhaps there was something she knew that could help. She said he must come through and she went over to a sliding door and pushed it wider. It led onto a balcony and she sat on one of the white plastic chairs. He got the idea that she wanted to get away from the SS people and that said something. He joined her on another of the chairs and asked her how well she knew Sangrenegra.

'He was my client.' He noticed the unusual shape of her eyes. They reminded him of almonds.

'A regular client?'

In the light from the sitting room he could only see her right hand. It was on the arm of the chair, finger folded into the palm, the nails pressing into the flesh.

'At first he was like the rest,' she said. 'Nothing funny. Then he told me about the drugs. And when he found out I had a child . . .'

'Do you know what we found at his house?'

She nodded. 'The black man phoned.'

'Did Carlos ever take you to other places? Other houses?'

'No.'

'Have you any idea where he would have taken . . . er . . . your daughter?'

'Sonia,' she said. 'My daughter's name is Sonia.'

The fingers moved in her palm, the nails dug deeper. He wanted to reach out to her. 'Where would he have taken Sonia?'

She shook her head back and forth. She did not know. Then she said: 'I won't see her again.' With the calm that only absolute despair can bring.

In the early hours it was only five minutes' drive from Belle Ombre to his flat. The first thing he saw when he switched on the light was the brandy bottle. It stood on the breakfast counter like a sentry watching over the room.

He locked the door behind him and picked up the bottle and turned it in his hands. He examined the clock on the label and the golden brown liquid within. He imagined the effect of the alcohol in his fibres, light-headedness, and effervescence just under his skull.

He put down the bottle as if it were sacred.

He should open the bottle and pour the brandy down the sink.

But then he would smell it and he wouldn't be able to resist it.

Get control first. He rested his palms on the counter and took deep breaths.

Lord, it had been close, earlier that evening.

Only his hunger had stopped him getting drunk.

He took another deep breath.

Fritz was going to phone him to find out if he had listened to the CD and he would have been drunk and his son would have known. That would have been bad. He considered his son's voice. It wasn't so much the boy's interest in his opinion about the music. Something else. A craving. A longing. A desire to make contact with his father. To have a bond with him. *We never had a father.* His son wanted a father now. So badly. He had been so close to fucking it up. So close.

He drew another deep breath and opened a kitchen cupboard. It was empty inside. He quickly picked up the bottle and put it inside and shut the door. He went upstairs. He didn't feel so tired any more. Second wind, when your brain gets so busy you just keep on going, when your thoughts jump from one thing to another.

He showered and got into bed and shut his eyes. He could see the prostitute and he felt a physical reaction, tumescence and he thought, hello, hello, hello? He felt guilty, as she had just lost her child and this was his reaction. But it was odd because whores had never done it for him. He knew enough of them. They were in a profession that was a magnet for trouble; they worked in a world that was just one small step away from serious crime. And they were all more or less the same – regardless of the fee they charged.

There was something about Christine van Rooyen that set her apart from the others he knew. But what? Then when he lined her up against the rest he identified it. Prostitutes, from the Sea Point streetwalkers to the few who serviced the tourists for big money in the Radisson, had two things in common. That distinctive bitter-sweet smell. And the damage. They had an atmosphere of depression. Like a house, a neglected house, where someone still lives, but you can see from the decay that they don't really care any more.

This one was not like that. Or less so. There was a light still burning.

But that wasn't what was giving him an erection. It was something else. The body? The eyes?

Hell, he had never once been unfaithful to Anna. Except by boozing. Maybe Anna reasoned like that: he was unfaithful to her because he loved alcohol with an all-encompassing passion. So she was justified in looking elsewhere. His head said she had the right, but the green monster sprang to life, made him writhe in the bed. He would pulp the fucker. If he caught them. If he should walk into his house and bedroom and they were busy . . . He saw the scene too clearly. He turned over violently; pulled up the sheet, thrust his head under the pillow. He did not want to see. Some or other handsome young shit pumping his wife and he could see Anna's face, her ecstasy, that small private sublime smile that told him she was in her own little world of pleasure and her voice, he remembered her voice, the whispering. Yes, Benny, yes, Benny, yes, Benny. But now she would be saying someone else's name and he leapt up and stood beside the bed and he knew: he would shoot the fucker. He had to phone her. *Now*. He had to drink. He must get the bottle out of the kitchen cupboard. He took a step toward the wardrobe. He clenched his fist and stopped himself.

Get a hold of yourself, he said out loud.

He felt the absence below. His erection was gone.

No fucking wonder.

It was an old stone house with a corrugated iron roof. He climbed a sagging wire boundary fence and had to deviate around the carcass of a Ford single cab pick-up on blocks before he could make out the number on one of the pillars of the veranda. The seven hung askew.

It was dark inside. Thobela retraced his steps to the back door. He turned the knob. It was open. He went in, closing the door quietly behind him, assegai in his left hand. He was in the kitchen. There was an odour in the house. Musty, like fish paste. He allowed his eyes to grow accustomed to the deeper dark inside. Then he heard a sound from the next room.

Once the two from the police force's Social Services had gone, she took a big flask of coffee and two mugs to the armed men on guard outside her door. Then she locked the door and went out onto the balcony.

The city lay before her, a creature with a thousand glittering eyes that breathed more slowly and deeply in the depths of night. She gripped the white railing feeling the cold metal in her hands. She thought about her child. Sonia's eyes pleading with her.

It was her fault. She was responsible for her child's fear.

From the sitting room he heard a snore like the grunt of a boar: short, crude and powerful.

Thobela peered around the doorframe and saw the man on the couch under a blanket.

Where was the woman?

The Scholtzes. Their two-year-old son had died in hospital in Oudtshoorn two weeks ago from a brain haemorrhage.

The district surgeon had found lesions on the tiny organs and thin fragile ribs and ulna, cheekbones and skull. From them he had reconstructed a jigsaw of abuse. 'The worst I have seen in fifteen years as coroner,' the Sunday paper had quoted his testimony.

He walked closer to Scholtz over the bare floor. In the dark the silver half-moons of rings gleamed in the visible ear. Across the bulky arm was a spider web of black tattoo, the pattern unclear without light. The mouth was open and at the peak of every breath he made that animal noise.

Where was the woman? Thobela smoothed the cushion of his thumb over the wooden shaft of the assegai as he slipped past, deeper into the house. There were two bedrooms. The first one was empty, on the wall hung a child's drawings, now without colour.

He felt revulsion. How did these people's minds work? How could they display the child's art on his bedroom wall and moments later smash his head against it? Or batter him until the ribs splintered.

Animals.

He saw the woman in the double bed of the other room, her shape outlined under the sheet. She turned over. Muttered something inaudible.

He stood still. Here was a dilemma. No, two.

Christine let go of the railing and went back inside. She closed the sliding door behind her. In the top drawer in the kitchen she found the vegetable knife. It had a long narrow blade, slightly curved with a small, sharp point. It was what she wanted now.

He didn't want to execute the woman. That was his first problem.

A war against women was not a war. Not *his* war, not a Struggle he wanted to be involved in. He knew that now, after Laurens. Let the courts, imperfect as they were, take responsibility for the women.

But if he spared her, how would he deal with the man? That was his second problem. He needed to wake him. He wanted to give him a weapon and say: 'Fight for your right to crack a two-year-old skull, and see where justice lies.' But the woman would wake up. She would see him. She would turn on lights. She would get in the way.

Christine sat on the edge of the bath after closing the bathroom door. She took the cap off the bottle of Dettol and dipped the blade of the little knife into the brown fluid. Then she lifted her left foot onto her right knee and chose the spot, between her heel and the ball of her foot. She pressed the sharp point of the blade gently against the soft white skin.

Sonia's eyes.

He walked around the door of the bedroom where the woman lay, right up close. That's when he saw the key in the lock and knew what he must do.

He pulled the key out of the lock. It made a scraping sound and he heard her breathing become shallow. Quickly he closed the door. It creaked. He pushed the key in from the outside. In haste he struggled to get it in.

He heard her say something in the room, a bleary, unrecognisable word.

At last the key went in and he turned it.

'Chappie?' called the woman.

The man on the couch stopped snoring. Thobela turned towards him.

'Chappie!' she shouted, louder now. 'What are you doing?'

The man sat up on the couch and threw the blanket aside.

'I am here about the child,' said Thobela.

He noted Scholtz's shoulders. A strong man. It was good.

'There's a kaffir in the house!' the man shouted to his wife.

*   *   *

She jabbed the blade into her foot, as hard as she could. She could not help the cry that fell from her lips.

But the pain was intense. It burned the hurt away; it covered over everything, just as she had hoped.

34

He dreamed wild, mixed-up dreams that drove him from his sleep
and made him get up twice before he finally dropped off again at
three in the morning. He was busy talking to Anna, a conversation
of no use or direction, when the cell phone woke him. He grabbed
it, missed, the handset fell from the windowsill and landed somewhere on the bed. He found it by the light of the screen.

'Yes?' He couldn't disguise his confusion.

'Inspector Griessel?'

'Yes.'

'Sorry to wake you. Tshabalala here, from Oudtshoorn detective
branch. It's about your assegai murderer.'

'Yes?' He felt for his watch on the windowsill.

'It seems he was in Uniondale last night.'

'Uniondale?' He found his watch and checked it. 04:21.

'We have a child batterer here, Frederik Johannes Scholtz, out
on bail with his wife. Stabbed to death in his house last night.'

'Uniondale,' he repeated. 'Where is Uniondale?'

'It's about a hundred and twenty kilos east of here.'

It made no sense. Too far from the Cape. 'How do you know it's
my assegai man?'

'The wife of the deceased. The suspect locked her in the
bedroom. But she could hear what was going on . . .'

'Did she see him?'

'No, he locked the door while she was asleep. She heard Scholtz
shout from inside the house. And he said the guy had an assegai.'

'Wait, wait,' said Griessel. 'He locked her in the bedroom? How
did he get the man out of the bedroom?'

'The woman says they don't share a bed any more, since the

child died. He slept in the sitting room. She woke up when Scholtz began shouting. She heard him say: "He's got an assegai." But there's something else . . .'

'Yes?'

'She said he shouted it was a black man.'

'A black man?'

'She said he shouted: "There's a kaffir in the house."'

It didn't fit. A black man? That's not how he had pictured the assegai man in his head.

'How reliable that is, I'm not sure. It seems they were fighting in the dark.'

'What does the wound look like?'

'The fatal wound is in the chest, but it looks like he was trying to fend it off with his hands. There are some cuts. And there is furniture overturned and broken. They obviously fought a round or two.'

'The chest wound – is there an exit wound in the back?'

'Looks like it. The district surgeon is still busy.'

'Listen,' said Griessel. 'I am going to ask our pathologist to phone him. There are a lot of forensic details they must see to. It's important—'

'Relax,' said Tshabalala. 'We have it under control.'

He showered and dressed before he phoned Pagel, who took the early call with grace. He passed on the numbers to call. Then he drove to the Quickshop at the Engen garage in Annandale Road. He bought a pile of pre-packed sandwiches and a large take-away coffee and drove to work. The streets were quiet, the office quieter still.

He sat down behind his desk and tried to think, pen in hand.

Union-fucking-dale. He opened a sandwich. Bacon and egg. He took the lid off the coffee. The steam drifted lazily upwards. He inhaled the aroma and sipped.

It would be a day or two before they knew whether it was the same assegai, regardless of how much pressure the commissioner exerted. He bit into the sandwich. It was reasonably fresh.

A black man. Scholtz wrestling with an attacker in the dark, frightened, he sees the long blade of the assegai. Had he made an assumption? Could he really see?

A black man with a pick-up. In Uniondale. Big surprises. Too big. The sudden detour to a place five hundred kilos from the Cape.

They didn't need a copycat, God knows. And this thing could easily spawn a lot of copycats. Because of the children.

He began to jot down notes in the crime report file in front of him.

'No, damnit,' said Matt Joubert and shook his head with finality.

Griessel and Ngubane were in the senior superintendent's office at seven in the morning. All three were too frenetic to sit.

'I've—' said Ngubane.

'Matt, just a few days. Two or three,' said Griessel.

'Lord, Benny, can you see the trouble if he gets away? Flees the country? These fuckers have false passports like confetti. There's no way . . .'

'I—' said Ngubane.

'We have the manpower, Matt. We can shut the whole place down. He won't be able to move.'

Joubert still shook his head. 'What do you think Boef Beukes will do? He has the biggest drug bust of his career and you want to let his big fish out on bail? He'll squeal like a skinny pig.'

'Matt, last night I—' said Ngubane.

'Fuck Beukes. Let him squeal. We won't get bait like this again.'

'No, damnit.'

'Listen to me,' barked Ngubane in frustration, and they looked at him. 'Last night I talked to one of the people from Investigative Psychology at head office. She's here in Cape Town. She's helping Anwar with a serial rapist in Khayelitsha. She says if he gets the chance, Sangrenegra will go to the child. Whether she is alive or not. She says the chances are good that he will lead us to her.'

Joubert sat down heavily on his chair.

'That makes our case very strong,' said Griessel.

'Think about the child,' said Ngubane.

'Let the commissioner decide, Matt. Please.'

Joubert looked up at the pair of them leaning shoulder to shoulder over his desk. 'Here comes trouble,' he said. 'I can see it a mile away.'

Pagel phoned him before eight to say indications were that the Uniondale assegai was the same blade, but he would have to wait for the tissue samples being brought by car from Oudtshoorn. Griessel thanked the prof and called his team together in the task team room.

'There have been a few interesting developments,' he told them.

'Uniondale?' asked Vaughn Cupido with a know-it-all smirk.

'It was on Kfm news,' said Bushy Bezuidenhout, just to spoil Cupido's moment.

'What did they say?'

'It's all Artemis, Artemis, Artemis,' said Cupido. 'Why must the media always give them a name?'

'It sells newspapers,' said Bezuidenhout.

'But this is radio . . .'

'What did they say?' asked Griessel louder.

'They said there is a suspicion that it is Artemis but that it can't be confirmed,' said Keyter piously.

'Our assegai man is black,' said Griessel. That shut them up. He described what they knew of the sitting-room battle in the small town. 'Then there is the question of the tyre tracks from yesterday. Forensics says he drives a pick-up, probably a two-by-four. Not yet a breakthrough, but it helps. It can help us focus . . .' He saw Helena Louw shaking her head. 'Captain, you don't agree?'

'I don't know, Inspector.' She got up and crossed over to the notice board on the wall. There were newspaper clippings in tidy rows, separated into sections by pinned strands of different coloured knitting wool.

'We researched the publicity surrounding each of the victims,' she said and pointed at the board. 'The first three were in all the papers, and probably on the local radio too. But when we heard about Uniondale this morning we had a look.'

She tapped a finger on the single report in a red-wool section. 'It was only in *Rapport*.'

'So what's your point, sister?' asked Cupido.

'Afrikaans, genius,' said Bushy Bezuidenhout. '*Rapport* is Afrikaans. Blacks don't read that paper.'

'I get it,' said Jamie Keyter, followed by: 'Sorry, Benny.'

'Coloured,' said Griessel. 'Maybe he's coloured.'

'We coloured chaps are always handy with a blade,' said Cupido proudly.

'Or it could just have been very dark in that house,' said Griessel.

Joubert appeared at the door with a sombre face and beckoned Griessel to come out. 'Excuse me,' he said and left. He shut the door behind him.

'You've got four days, Benny,' said the senior superintendent.

'The commissioner?'

Joubert nodded. 'It's just the political pressure. He sees the same dangers I do. But you have till Friday.'

'Right.'

'Jesus, Benny, I don't like it. The risks are too high. If it goes bad . . . If you want to get the assegai man you will have to use the media. Organised Crime is highly pissed. The child is still missing. There's just too much—'

'Matt, I will *make* it work.'

They looked each other in the eyes.

'I will make it work.'

He took ten of the uniformed members of the task team along with Bezuidenhout, Cupido and Keyter and they drove in four cars to the house in Shanklin Crescent, Camps Bay to investigate the lay of the land.

He knew the problem was the rear of the castle-like dwelling. It was built against the mountain, with a plastered wall to keep trespassers out, but it was less than two metres tall – and it was a large area.

'If he comes here and spots us, he'll disappear – we won't find him in the bushes. So the men lying here must not be seen, but must be able to see everything. If you see him, you must allow him to get over the wall. Everyone understand?'

They nodded solemnly.

'If I were him, I would come down the mountain. That's where the cover is. The street is too problematic, too open. Only two entry points and it's practically impossible to get into the house from that side. So we will deploy most of our people on the mountain.'

He checked his street map. 'Kloof Nek runs up above, on the way to Clifton. If he doesn't park there, he will at least drive up and down a few times. Which of you can handle a camera?'

Keyter raised his hand like a keen prep-school boy.

'Only Jamie?'

'I can try,' said a black constable with alert eyes.

'What's your name?'

'Johnson Madaka, Inspector.'

'Johnson, you and Jamie must find a spot where you can watch the road. I want photos of every pick-up that passes. Jamie, talk to the photography guys about cameras. If you have trouble, phone me.'

'Okay, Benny,' said Keyter, pleased with his task.

He divided them into two teams – one for day and one for night. He determined every point on the street and against the mountain that would be manned. He asked Bezuidenhout to find out if any house in the street was empty, and whether they could use it. 'I'm going to talk to Cloete. The media should start humming by tonight. All of you go home and rest, but at six I want the night shift in place.

He walked into Joubert's office and found Cloete and the senior superintendent wearing graveyard faces. Cloete said: 'I want you to know that I had nothing to do with this, Benny.'

'With what?' he asked and Cloete handed him the *Argus*.

COP SCRAP
OVER ARTEMIS

Front page.

'They haven't got news, that's the fucking problem,' said Cloete. He read the article.

Senior police officials are up in arms over the appointment of a confirmed alcoholic as leader of the task team investigating the Artemis vigilante murders in the Peninsula. A source within the senior ranks of the SAPS called it 'a huge blunder' and 'a mess-up just waiting to happen'.

The top cop in the firing line is veteran Serious and Violent Crimes Unit Detective Inspector Bennie Griessel, who was reportedly admitted to Tygerberg Hospital just a fortnight ago after an alleged drinking binge. A hospital spokesperson confirmed that Griessel had been admitted, but declined to comment on his illness.

'Fuck,' said Griessel, and all he could think about were his children.

'Benny . . .' said Joubert and Griessel knew what was coming and said: 'You're not taking me off this case, Sup.'

'Benny . . .'

'Not a fock, Matt. Not a fock, you won't take me off.'

'Just give me a chance . . .'

'Who are these cunts?' he asked Cloete. 'Who gave them this?'

'Benny, I swear I don't know.'

'Benny,' said Joubert. 'This is not my call. You know I wouldn't take you off if it was my call.'

'Then I'm coming along to the commissioner.'

'No. You have enough to do. You have to get the media sorted. Go. Let me talk to the commissioner.'

'Don't take me off, Matt. I'm telling you.'

'I will do my best.' But Griessel could read his body language.

⋆   ⋆   ⋆

He struggled to concentrate on his strategy with Cloete. He wanted to know who the shits were who had sold him out to the press. His eyes strayed back to the copy of the *Argus* lying on Cloete's desk.

Jamie Keyter, the well-known newspaper informant? He would kill him, the little shit. But he had his doubts: it was too political for Keyter, too sophisticated. It was interdepartmental. Organised Crime must have got wind of his plans. That was what he suspected. He had four people from Domestic Violence in his task team. And Domestic Violence fell under OC in the new structure, God knows why. Was Captain Helena Louw the tattle-tale? Perhaps not her. One of the other three?

When he had finished with Cloete, he drove into the city. He bought a newspaper at a streetlight and parked in a loading zone in Caledon Street. The SAPS Unit for Organised Crime was located in an old office building just around the corner from Caledon Square. He had to take the lift up to the third floor and he could feel the pressure of rage inside him and he knew he must slow down or he would stuff up everything. But what did it matter, they were going to pull him anyway.

He walked in and asked the black woman at reception where he could find Boef Beukes and she asked, 'Is he expecting you?'

'For sure,' he said with emphasis, newspaper in hand.

'I'll find out if he can see you.' She reached out for the telephone and he thought what shit this was, policemen hiding behind secretaries like bank managers, and he slapped his ID card down in front of her and said, 'Just show me where his office is.'

With wide-open eyes that clearly showed her disapproval, she said, 'Second door on the left,' and he walked out down the corridor. The door was open. Beukes sat there with his fucking ridiculous little Western Province hat. There was another detective present, seated, collar-and-fucking-tied, and Griessel threw the newspaper down in front of him and said: 'Was it your people, Boef?'

Beukes looked up at Griessel and then down at the paper. Griessel stood with his hands on the desk. Beukes read. The detective in the suit just sat and looked at Griessel.

'Ouch,' said Beukes after the second paragraph. But not terribly surprised.

'Fuck ouch, Boef. I want to know.'

Beukes pushed the newspaper calmly back to him and said: 'Why don't you sit down a moment, Benny?'

'I don't want to sit.'

'Was I ever a backstabber?'

'Boef, just tell me – do you guys have anything to do with this?'

'Benny, you insult me. There are only ten or twelve of us left from the old days. Why would I nail you? You should look for traitors at Violent Crimes. I hear you are one big happy family there after all the affirmative action.'

'You are pissed, Boef, about Sangrenegra. You have the motive.' He glanced at the other detective sitting there with a taut face.

'Motive?' Beukes queried. 'Do you think we really care if you keep Sangrenegra busy for a few days? Do you think it makes a difference to us . . . ?'

'Look me in the eyes, Boef. Look me in the eyes and tell me it wasn't you.'

'I understand that you're upset. I would have been too. But just calm down so you can think straight; was I ever a backstabber?'

Griessel examined him. He saw the mileage on Beukes's face. Police miles. He had them too. They had been together in the dark days of the eighties. Copped the same deal, ate the same shit. And Beukes had never been a backstabber.

Griessel sat in the back of the courtroom and waited for the moment when the state prosecutor said, 'The state does not oppose bail *per se*, your honour.' He watched Sangrenegra and saw his surprise, how he stiffened beside his lawyer.

'But we do ask that it be set at the highest possible figure, at least two million rand. And that the defendant's passport be held. We also ask the court to rule that the defendant reports to the Camps Bay Police Station every day before twelve noon. That is all, Your Honour.'

The magistrate shuffled papers around, made some notes, and

then he set bail at two million rand. Lawyer and client conferred under their breath and he wished he knew what was said. Just before Sangrenegra left the court, his eyes searched the public benches. Griessel waited until the Colombian spotted him. And then he grinned at him.

Sangrenegra's shoulders sagged, as if a great burden had come to rest on them.

He was on the way to Faizal's pawnshop in Maitland when Tim Ngubane phoned him.

'The blood in Sangrenegra's BMW belongs to the kid. The DNA matches,' he said.

'Fuck,' said Griessel.

'So you'll have to watch him very carefully, Benny.'

'We will,' he said and he wanted to add: if I am still on the case by tonight. He thought better of it.

'Tim, I have a suspicion Organised Crime have been after Sangrenegra longer than they let on. Just a feeling. I have just come from Beukes. He knows something. He's hiding something.'

'What are you saying, Benny?'

'I wonder more and more whether they were following Sangrenegra before he abducted the child.'

Ngubane paused before he answered. 'Are you saying they know something? About the kid?'

'I'm not saying anything. I'm just wondering. Perhaps you can try and find out. Talk to Captain Louw. She's from Domestic Violence, but she's working on my task team. Maybe her loyalty will be to the child. Maybe she can find out.'

'Benny, if they do know something . . . I can't believe it.'

'I know. I'm also having trouble with it. But see it from their point of view. They are messing about with Nigerian syndicates distributing crack in Sea Point when suddenly they come across something a hundred times bigger. Something that makes them look like real policemen. Colombia. The Holy Grail. There was a shithouse full of drugs in that storeroom. If it were me, I would have gone to the national commissioner and made a stink about jurisdiction. But they just sit there. Why? They know something. They're busy with something. And I think they have been busy with it for quite some time.'

'Geeeeez,' said Ngubane.

'But we'll have to see.'

'I'll go talk to the captain.'

'Tim, the number of that shrink . . . do you still have it?' asked Griessel.

'The one who was down here from Pretoria? The profiler?'

'Yes.'

'I'll text it.'

35

Faizal said the base guitar was not in the market; the rapper from Blackheath had paid up and collected it. Griessel said what he was looking for now was a CD player, nothing fancy, just something for listening to music at home.

'Car, portable, or hi-fi component?' asked Faizal.

Griessel thought about it and said portable, but with good bass.

'Portable with speakers or portable with headphones?'

Headphones would be better in the flat. Faizal took a Sony Walkman out and said: 'This is the D-NE seven-ten, it can also play MP threes, sixty-four-track programmable, but the most important thing is, it has an equaliser and bass boost, the sound quality is awesome, Sarge. Great headphones. And just in case you are chilling in the bath and it falls off the soap dish, it's waterproof too.'

'How much?'

'Four hundred, Sarge.'

'Jissis, L.L., that's robbery. Forget it.'

'Sarge, this is brand new, slightly shop-soiled, no previous owner. Three fifty.'

Griessel took out his wallet and held two hundred-rand notes out to Faizal.

'Think of my children, Sarge,' groaned the shopkeeper. 'They must eat too.'

He stood in the street beside his car with his new CD player in his hand and felt like going home, locking the door and listening to the music his son had lent him.

Because they *were* going to pull him off the case. He knew it. It was too political to keep an alky in charge. Too much pressure. The image of the Service. Even though he and the other dinosaurs like Matt Joubert talked about the Force, it was the Service now. The politically correct, criminal-procedures-regulated, emasculated and disempowered Service, where an alcoholic could not be the leader of a task team. Don't even talk about the fucking constitutional protection of criminals' rights. So let them pull him, let them give the whole fucking caboodle to someone else, one of the Young Turks, and he would watch from the sidelines as chaos descended.

He unlocked his car and got in. He opened the box of the CD player, shifted the plastic flap and pushed in the batteries. He leaned across and took the CD out of the cubbyhole. He scanned the titles on the back of the jewel case. Various artists performing Anton Goosen's songs. He knew almost none of them. '*Waterblommetjies*'. Lord, that took you back. Twenty years? No. Thirty! Thirty years ago, Sonja Herholdt sang '*Waterblommetjies*' and the whole country sang along. He had a crush on her, then. A vague teenage desire. I will cherish-and-protect-and-regularly-service-you. She was so . . . pure. And innocent. Darling of the people, the Princess Di of the Afrikaners before the world knew Princess Di. With those big eyes and that sweet voice and the blonde hair that was so . . . he didn't know what the style was called, but it was seventies cool, if anything could be 'cool' back then.

He had been sixteen. Puberty in Parow. All he could think about in those days was sex. Not always about the deed itself, but how to get some. With the girls in Parow in the seventies it was well nigh impossible. Middle-class Afrikaners, the iron grip of the Dutch Reformed Church and girls who didn't want to make the same mistakes as their mothers, so that the best a guy could do was perhaps some heavy petting in the back of the bioscope. If you were lucky. If you could draw the attention of one. So he began to play bass guitar to get their attention, since he was no athlete or academic giant, he was just another little fucker with a sprinkling of pimples and an ongoing battle with school rules to grow his hair long.

In Standard Nine at a garage party there was this four-man band, guys of his age from Rondebosch. English speaking *Souties*, not very good, the drummer was so-so and the rhythm guitarist knew only six chords. But the girls didn't care. He saw how they looked at the band members. And he wanted to be looked at like that. So he talked to the leader when the band took a break. He told him he played a bit of acoustic and a bit of piano by ear, but the guy said get a bass guitar, china, because everyone played six-string and drums, but bass guitarists were hard to find.

So he began to look into it and he bought a bass for a knockdown price from an army guy in Goodwood whose Ford Cortina needed new rings. He taught himself in his room, with the help of a book that he bought in Bothners in Voortrekker Road. He dreamed dreams and he kept his ear to the ground until he heard of a band in Bellville that was looking for a bass. Five-piece: lead, rhythm, drums, organ and bass. Before he knew what happened he was on the stage of an English-medium primary-school hall laying down a foundation of Uriah Heep's 'Stealin'' and he sang the fucking song – he, Benny fucking Griessel, stood in front of the teen girls in an undersized T-shirt and his Afrikaans haircut and he sang, 'Take me across the water, 'cause I got no place to hide, I done the rancher's daughter and it sure did hurt his pride', and they all looked at him, the girls looked at him with those eyes.

It only brought him one sexual experience while he was at school. What he hadn't known was that while the band played, the guys who were dancing had the advantage. By the time the party broke up, all the girls had to go home. But it had given him the music. The deep notes he picked off the strings and via the amplifier, resonating through his whole body. The knowledge that his bass was the basis of every song, the substructure, the defining foundation from which the lead guitarist could deviate or the organist could drift away, always to return to the steadfast form that Benny laid down. Even though he knew he would never be good enough to go pro.

Unlike the police work. He knew from the start that was his

thing. That was the place where all the connections came together, that was how his brain was wired.

Now they were going to pull him off the assegai case and he put the CD down and took out his phone, because he wanted to talk to the psychologist before they posted him. He wanted to test a few of his theories before they took him off.

She met him at the Newport Deli in Mouille Point, because she was 'mad about the place'. They sat outside on the pavement at a high, round table.

Captain Ilse Brody, Investigative Psychology Unit, Serious and Violent Crime, Head Office, he read on the card she passed across the little table. She was a smoker, a woman in her thirties with a wedding ring and short black hair. 'You're lucky,' she said, 'I fly back tonight.' Relaxed, self-assured. Accustomed to the man's world she worked in.

He remembered her. He had been on a course she presented two or three years ago. He didn't mention it, as he couldn't remember how sober he had been.

They ordered coffee. She ordered a flat biscuit with chocolate on top and nuts underneath with some Italian-sounding name that he didn't quite catch.

'Do you know about the assegai murders?' he asked.

'Everyone down here is talking about them, but I don't have the details. I hear the media first speculated that it was a woman.'

'Couldn't be a woman. The weapon, the MO, everything . . .'

'There's another reason too.'

'Oh?'

'I'll get to that. Tell me everything first.'

He told her. He liked the intense way she listened. He began with Davids and finished with Uniondale. He knew she wanted details of the crime scene. He gave her everything he knew. But two things he withheld: the pick-up and the fact that the suspect might be black.

'Mmm,' she said, and turned her cigarette lighter over and over in her right hand. Her hands were tiny. They made him think of an old person's hands. There were fine grey hairs between the black at her temples.

'The fact that he confronts them in their own homes is interesting. The first deduction is that he is intelligent. Above average. And determined. Orderly, organised. He has guts.'

Griessel nodded. He agreed with the guts part, but the intelligence was a surprise.

'It will be difficult to determine a vocational group. Not a labourer, he's too clever for that. Something that allows him to be alone so he doesn't have to explain how he spends his time. He can drive to Uniondale without anyone asking questions. Sales? His own business? He must be quite fit. Reasonably strong.'

She took a cigarette from a white packet with a red square on it and put it in her mouth. Griessel liked her mouth. He wondered what effect her work had on her. To use the gruesomeness of death to paint a mental picture of the suspect, until she could see him, vocation and all.

'He's white. Three white victims in white neighbourhoods. It would be difficult if he wasn't white.' She lit the cigarette.

Exactly, he thought.

'In his thirties, I would say.' She drew on the cigarette and blew a long white plume into the air. It was windless here where the mountain blocked the southeaster. 'But what you really want to know is why he is using an assegai. And why he is killing people.'

He wondered why he was so conscious of her mouth. He shifted his eyes to a point on her forehead, so that he could concentrate.

'I think the assegai is one of two things. Either he is trying to convince you he is not white, to put you off the trail. Or he is looking for media sensation. Is there any indication that he has made contact with the media yet?'

Griessel shook his head.

'Then I would go with the first option. But I'm guessing.'

'Why doesn't he just shoot them? That's what I'm wondering.'

'I think it must be connected to the why,' she said, and drew again on the cigarette. There was a masculine manner to her smoking, probably because she always smoked with men. 'It definitely isn't because he was molested or abused himself. In that case the victims and the MO would have been very different. That's another reason it has to be a man. When men are damaged, if they are abused or molested, they want to do the same to others. Women are different. If there is damage from a young age, they don't do it to others. They do it to themselves. Therefore not a woman. If it had been a man who was damaged, his target would have been children. But this one is going for the ones who are doing the damage. And he is psychologically strong. What makes more sense to me is that a child of his has been a victim. Or at least a close member of his family. A younger sister or brother perhaps. A personal vendetta. A pure vigilante. They are rare. In our country it is usually a group with a very specific dynamic.'

'And the assegai?'

'I have to admit the assegai bothers me. Let's think about stabbing versus shooting. Stabbing is much more personal. Intimate and direct. That fits a personal loss. It makes him feel that he himself is exacting retribution. There's no distance between him and the victim, he isn't acting on behalf of a group, he represents only himself. But he could have done that with a knife. Because he is smart, he knows a knife can be messy. Also less effective. He wants to get it over quickly. There is no pathology of hanging about at the scene. He leaves no messages. But maybe he wants to intimidate them with the assegai; maybe it's a tool to gain immediate control, so that he can do his work and be done with it. Now I'm speculating freely, because I can't be sure.' She stubbed out the cigarette in the small glass ashtray.

He told her he also thought the suspect was white. And he still thought so, but there was evidence to the contrary. He told her about Uniondale and the fact that the child abuse report only appeared in *Rapport*. She pressed the tip of a finger on the biscuit crumbs in her plate and licked them off. She did it again. He wondered if she knew it made him think of sex, and then he was faintly surprised that he was thinking of sex at all and eventually he said: 'If he is black, you have much bigger problems.'

A third time the finger went to the plate and then to her mouth and he looked at her mouth again. An eyetooth, just the one, was canted to the inside.

'I would also put more check marks against intelligence and motivation. And that puts another light on the assegai. Now we start to talk of symbolism, of traditional values and traditional justice. He's sophisticated, at home in a city environment. He's not a country boy – it takes too much skill to execute three white victims in white neighbourhoods without being seen. He reads Afrikaans newspapers. He is aware of the police investigation. That's possibly why he went to Uniondale. To divide attention. You should not underestimate him.'

'If he's black.'

She nodded. 'Improbable but not impossible.' She looked at her watch. 'I will have to finish up,' she said and opened her handbag.

Quickly he told her about Sangrenegra and asked if she thought the ambush would work.

She held her purse in her hand. 'It would have been better if you could have set your trap outside Cape Town. He feels the pressure here.'

'I'm paying,' he said. 'But will he come?'

She took out a ten-rand note. 'I'll pay half,' she said and put the money under the saucer with the bill. 'He will come. If you play your cards right with the media, he will come.'

He drove along the coast, because he wanted to go to Camps Bay again. He saw the new developments on the sea front in Green Point. Big blocks of flats under construction, with advertising boards romantically depicting the finished product. *From R1.4 million.* He wondered if it would revive this part of the city. What would they do with the *bergie* hobos that lived on the commonage behind? And the old, dilapidated buildings in between, with paint peeling off in long strips and the rooms rented out by the hour?

That made him think of Christine van Rooyen and that he should tell her what they were planning, but he would have to pick his words carefully.

Along Coast Road through Sea Point. It looked a lot better here by the sea. But he knew it was a false front – further inland was erosion and decay, dark corners and dirty alleys. He stopped at a traffic light and saw the scaffolding on a sea-front building. He wondered who would win this battle. It was Europe against Africa – rich Britons and Germans against Nigerian and Somalian drug networks, the South Africans marginalised as spectators. It depended on how much money poured in. If it was enough, the money would win and crime would find another place, southern suburbs, he thought. Or the Cape Flats.

The money ought to win, because the view was stunningly beautiful. That's what money did. Reserved the most beautiful for the rich. And shunted policemen off to Brackenfell.

At the traffic circle he turned left in Queens, then right in Victoria, all along the sea, through Bantry Bay. A Maserati, a Porsche and a BMW X5 stood side by side in front of a block of flats. He had never felt at home here. It was another country.

Clifton. A woman and two young children walked over the road. She was carrying a big beach bag and a folded umbrella. She was wearing a bikini and a piece of material around her hips, but it blew open. She was tall and pretty, long brown hair down the length of her back. She looked down the road, past him. He was invisible to her in his middle-class police car.

He drove on to where Lower Kloof Street turned up left and then took the road round the back, to Round House. He drove up and down three times and tried to assess it as the assegai man would. He couldn't park here, it was too open. He would have to walk a long way, above maybe, from the Signal Hill Road side. Or below. So that, when he had finished with Sangrenegra, he could flee downhill.

Or would he choose not to come through the bushes? Would he chance the street?

He has guts, Ilse Brody had said. He has guts *and* he's clever.

He phoned Bushy Bezuidenhout and asked him where he was. Bezuidenhout said they had found a house diagonally opposite Sangrenegra's. Belonged to an Italian who lived overseas. They had got the keys from the estate agent. They were not allowed to smoke in the house. Griessel said he was on his way.

His cell phone rang almost immediately. 'Griessel.'

'Benny, it's John Afrika.'

The commissioner.

Fuck, he thought.

36

He wanted to shower, eat and sleep.

Thobela was driving down York Street in George when he spotted the Protea Forester's Lodge. It was nameless enough for him. He parked in front of the building and had already put a hand on his bag when the newsreader began to talk about the Colombian and the child over the radio.

He listened with one hand still on the carry straps of his bag, the other on the door latch and his eyes on the front door of the hotel.

He sat like this for three or four minutes after he had heard everything. Then he let go of the bag, started the pick-up and put it in reverse. He made a U-turn and drove down York Street, turned right into C.J. Langenhoven Street. He headed for the Outeniqua Pass.

The policemen who should have been guarding Christine van Rooyen's door were not there. Griessel knocked and assumed they would be inside.

'Who's that?' her voice sounded faint from the other side of the door. He gave his name. The guards were not inside, or she would not have answered. As the door opened he saw her face first. It didn't look good. She was pale and her eyes were swollen.

'Come in.' She was wearing a jersey, although it wasn't cold. Her shoulders were hunched. He suspected she knew she would not see her child again. She sat down on the couch. He saw the television was showing a soapie, the sound muted. Is that how she got time to pass?

'Do you know he was granted bail?'

She nodded.

'Do you know we arranged it?'

'They told me.' Her voice was toneless, as if she was beyond caring.

'We think he will lead us to Sonia.'

Christine just stared at the television, where a man and woman stood facing each other. They were arguing.

He said: 'It's a possibility. We have forensic psychologists helping us. They say the chances are good he will go to her.'

She turned her eyes back on him. She knows, he thought. She knows now.

'Would you like coffee?' she asked.

He considered a moment. He was hungry. He hadn't eaten since breakfast. 'Can I go and buy food? Take aways?'

'I'm not hungry.'

'When did you last eat?'

She didn't answer.

'You have to eat. What can I get you? Even if it's something small.'

'Whatever.'

He stood. 'Pizza?'

'Wait,' she said and went into the kitchen. A Mr Delivery booklet was stuck to the door of the big two-door fridge with a magnet. 'They can deliver,' she said and brought the booklet to him. She sat down again. 'I don't want you to leave now.'

'Where are the two policemen that were at the door?'

'I don't know.'

He flipped through the booklet. 'What do you like?'

'Anything. Just not garlic or onion.' Then she reconsidered. 'It doesn't matter. Anything.'

He took out his cell phone, phoned and placed an order. He hesitated when asked for the address and she provided it. He said he had an official call to make and asked if he could go out on the balcony. She nodded. He slid the door open and went out. The wind was blowing. He closed the door behind him and found Ngubane's number on the cell phone.

'Tim, are you aware that Organised Crime's people aren't guarding the mother any more?'

'No. I haven't been there today. I called, but she didn't say anything.'

'Jissis, they're idiots.'

'Maybe they think she isn't in danger any more.'

'Maybe they think it's not their problem now.'

'What can we do?'

'I haven't any spare people. My entire team is busy in Camps Bay.'

'I'll talk to the sup.'

'Thanks, Tim.'

He gazed out over the city. The last rays of the sun reflected off the windows of the hotels in the Strand area. Was she in danger? His SVC team was watching Sangrenegra. His four henchmen were still in the cells.

Boef Beukes would know. He would know how big Sangrenegra's contingent was. How many there were who did not live at the Camps Bay place. There had to be more. Local hangers-on, assistants, people involved: you don't run such a big drug operation with only five people. He called SVC and asked if Captain Helena Louw was still there. They put him through and he asked her if she had Boef Beukes's cell phone number.

'Just a minute,' she said. He waited until she came back and gave it to him.

'Thanks, Captain.' Could he trust her? With Domestic Violence part of the Organised Crime structure? Where did her loyalties lie?

He called Beukes. 'It's Benny, Boef. I want to know why you withdrew Christine van Rooyen's protection.'

'It's your show now.'

'Jissis, Boef, don't you think you might have told us?'

'Did you tell us anything? When you decided to hang Carlos up for bait. Did you have the decency to consult with us?'

'You feel fuck-all for her safety?'

'It's a question of manpower.' But there was something in his voice. He was lying.

'Fuck,' said Griessel. He ended the call and stood with his handset in his hand thinking, that's the problem with the fucking

Service, the jealousy, the competition, everyone had to fucking PEP, everyone was measured by Performance Enhancement Procedure and everyone's balls were on the block. Now they were stabbing each other in the back.

Commissioner John Afrika had phoned him while he was on his way to Christine van Rooyen. Benny, are you sober? he had asked. He had said yes, Commissioner, and John Afrika had asked him, Are you going to stay sober and he said yes, Commissioner. Afrika said, I will get the people who ran to the papers, Benny. Matt Joubert tells me you are the best he has. He says you are on the wagon and that's good enough for me, Benny, you hear? I will stand by you and I'm going to tell the papers that. But, fuck, Benny, if you drop me . . .

Because if he dropped the commissioner, then the commissioner's PEP was blown to hell.

But he appreciated it that the man was standing by him. A coloured man. He was thrown on the mercy of a coloured man who had to swallow so much crap from the whites in the old days. How much mercy had John Afrika received, then?

He had said: 'I won't drop you, Commissioner.'

'Then we understand each other, Benny.' There were a few beats of silence over the air, then John Afrika sighed and said, 'This backstabbing gets me down. I can't get a grip on it.'

Griessel thought over his conversation with Beukes. Organised Crime were on to something. He knew it. That's why they went to the papers. That's why they withdrew the guard detail.

What?

He opened the sliding door; he couldn't hang around out there for ever.

Before he came in, while he was putting his phone away, he tried to think like Boef Beukes. Then he understood and he froze. Christine van Rooyen was OC's bait. They were using *her* as an ambush. But for whom? For Sangrenegra?

His visit to Beukes's office. The other detective there, the one in the suit and tie. Nobody dressed like that any more. Who the fuck was that? The Scorpions, the special unit for the public prosecutor?

Never. Beukes and Co. would rather slit their wrists in the lavvy than work with the Scorpions.

He became aware that Christine had got up and was standing watching him.

'Are you okay?'

'Yes,' he said. But would *she* be okay?

In the sultry late afternoon of a Highveld summer, at the New Road filling station between the old Pretoria Road and Sixteenth Avenue in Midrand, the stolen BMW 320d stopped in front of the Quickshop. John Khoza and Andrew Ramphele got out and walked through the automatic glass doors. They walked casually up to the fast-food counter in the back of the shop.

While Ramphele ordered two chicken burgers, Khoza inspected the four corners of the large room. There was only one security camera. It was against the eastern wall opposite the cash register.

He murmured something to Ramphele, who nodded.

Griessel's phone rang while they waited for the pizzas.

'Benny, the boss says we can give her Witness Protection, but it's going to take time,' said Ngubane.

'How much time?'

'Probably only tomorrow. That's the best we can do.'

'Okay, Tim. Thanks.'

'What are you going to do? For tonight?'

'I'll make a plan,' he said.

Khoza waited until the last of the four clients in the shop had paid and left. Then he walked up to the woman behind the cash register, shoved his hand in the back of his denim jacket and drew out a pistol. He shoved it against her face and said, 'Just open it up, sister, and give us the cash. Nobody will get hurt.'

'I'll have to sleep on your couch tonight,' said Griessel.

Christine looked up at him and nodded.

'We will place you in Witness Protection tomorrow. They are organising it now, but it takes a little time.'

'What does that mean?' she asked.

'It depends.'

There was a knock on the door. Griessel got up and took out his Z88 service pistol. 'That must be our pizzas,' he said.

The Toyota Microbus of the South African Police Services Task Force Unit stopped at the filling station for petrol. The nine policemen were stiff from hours of sitting and thirsty. They had last stretched their legs at Louis Trichardt. They all got out. The young black constable, the sharpshooter of the team, knew it was his duty as the youngest to take the orders for cool drinks.

'What do you want to drink?' he asked.

That was when two men came out of the Quickshop, each carrying a pistol in one hand and a green, purple and red plastic bag in the other.

'Hey,' said the sharpshooter and dropped a hand to the firearm on his hip holster. The other eight members of the Task Force team looked instinctively at what the constable had seen. For a moment they could hardly believe their eyes. For a very short moment.

'Just now, you said you did not want me to leave. Why?' asked Griessel, but her mouth was full of pizza and she had to finish chewing before she answered.

'You are the first person I have seen today,' she said and left it at that. He could see she was struggling not to cry.

He understood. He visualised her day. Her child was missing, probably dead. The awful worry and doubt. Fear perhaps, because the guards were gone. Alone, between these four walls. 'I'm sorry,' he said.

'You needn't be sorry. It's my fault. Only mine.'

'How can you say that?'

She closed her eyes. 'If I wasn't a whore, I would never have met him.'

The first thing that popped into his head was to ask her why she had become a whore. 'It doesn't work like that,' he said. She just shook her head, keeping her eyes closed. He wanted to get up and go over and put his arm around her shoulders.

He stayed where he was. 'It's a psychological thing,' he said. 'We see it often. Victims or their families blame themselves. You can't be responsible for someone else's behaviour.'

She didn't react. He looked down at the pizza on the plate in front of him and pushed it away and wiped his hands on a paper serviette. He looked at her. She was wearing jeans. She sat on the chair with her bare feet folded under her. Her long blonde hair was half covering her face. What could he say to her? What could anyone say to him if it had been his child?

'I actually came to tell you about something else.'

She opened her eyes. 'I don't want to hear bad news.'

'I don't think it is bad news. It's just that I think you have the right to know. You know about the Artemis affair the papers are writing about?'

With a sudden movement of her head she tossed her hair back and said, 'Yes. And I wish he would come and kill Carlos.' She said it with hate he could understand.

'It's my case. The assegai man. I want to use Carlos to catch him.'

'How?'

'We know he picks his victims when the media writes about them. About their crimes. Today we gave the media a lot of information about Carlos. About how he . . . abducted Sonia. About his drug-dealing background. We think it will lure the assegai man.'

'And then?'

'That's another reason we're watching Carlos so carefully.'

It was some time before she answered. He saw the process in her face, the eyes narrowing, the lips thinning. 'So it's not about Sonia,' she said.

'It *is* about her. All the indications are that he will lead us to her.' He tried hard to be convincing, but he felt guilty. He had told

Sangrenegra what they were going to do. This morning in court he had looked Carlos in the eyes and reinforced the message: you are bait. He knew Carlos was going nowhere, because Carlos knew the police were watching him. The chances that the Colombian was going to lead them anywhere were nil.

'I don't believe you.'

Could she hear from the tone of his voice that he was lying? 'My black colleague talked to the psychologist this morning. She said people like Carlos go back to their victims. I give you my word. It's true. It's a chance. It's possible. I can't swear it will happen, but it's possible.'

Her face altered, the venom dissolved and he saw she was about to cry. He said: 'It's possible,' again, but to no avail.

She put her face in her hands and said: 'Leave him. Let him kill Carlos.' Then her shoulders heaved. He couldn't take it any more. Guilt and pity drove him to her. He put a hand on her shoulder. 'I understand,' he said.

She shook her head.

'I have children too,' he said, and inhaled her smell, perfume and the faint scent of perspiration.

He sat on the arm of the chair. He put his hand behind her neck onto her far shoulder. His fingers patted her comfortingly. He felt a bit of an idiot because she was unyielding under his touch. 'I understand,' he repeated.

Then she moved and he felt her soften and she pressed her head against him. With her arm around his hip she wept.

37

He thought many thoughts while she leaned against him, shrunken under his arm. For the first time since Anna had kicked him out, some sort of calm came over him. A kind of peace.

He looked around the flat. The sitting room and kitchen were one big room separated by a white melamine counter. A passage led off to the right behind him. To the bedrooms? He noted the large fridge and big flat-screen television. New stuff. A child's drawings of multicoloured animals were stuck up on the fridge with magnets. A crocodile and a rhinoceros and a lion. He noted the coffee machine in the kitchen, shiny chrome, with spouts and knobs. But the chairs at the counter were scuffed; one sitting-room chair was old and worn. Two worlds in one.

Leaning against the wall to the left of him was a painting. Large and original. A rural landscape, a blue mountain in the distance and a green valley, the grass in the veld growing high and verdant. A young girl was running through the grass. She was a tiny figure on the left, dwarfed by the landscape, but he could distinguish the blonde hair bouncing up behind. Four or five steps ahead of her there was a red balloon, with a string hanging down, a thin, barely visible black stripe against the blue of the mountain. The girl's hand was stretched out to it. The grass bent away from her. It must be the wind, he thought. Blowing the balloon away from her. He wondered if she were running fast enough to catch it.

He had a partial erection.

She wouldn't be able to feel it, as she wasn't in contact there. Her breathing was quieter now, but he couldn't see her face.

He crossed his legs to hide his state. He couldn't help it; there were a lot of things affecting him here. Knowing that sex was her

job. She was attractive. And vulnerable. Hurt. Something in him
that responded to that. Something that somewhere in his brain did
surveys and sent out primitive orders: take your chance, the time is
right. He knew that was how his head worked. He – and the other
members of his sex. Also the mentally ill, those for whom it was
more than just an opportunity for sexual victory. Like serial
murderers. They searched out the weak, soft targets for their dark
deeds. Often prostitutes. Not always deliberately, with precon-
ceived reasoning and planned strategy. Instinct. Somewhere, in the
pre-alcoholic period a memory stirred, something he had worked
out for himself. He was a good policeman because he understood
others through self-knowledge. He could use his own weaknesses,
his own fears and instincts, because he knew them. He could
magnify them, amplify them like turning up an imaginary volume
control to the level where they made other people commit murder
or rape, lie or steal. As he sat there he realised it was one of the
things that had made him start drinking. The slow realisation that
he was like them and they were like him, that he was not a better
man. As he had felt last night or the previous, he couldn't
remember which, when he had seen Anna and her young, imaginary lover in his mind and the jealousy had turned on the
switches with an evil hand and he had wanted to shoot. If he
were to find them like that and he had his service pistol on his hip,
he would shoot the fucker, between the eyes, no fucking doubt
about that.

But that was not the main reason he drank. No. It was not the
only reason. There were others. Large and small. He began to
realise it all now. He was a rough stone and he was cut with a
thousand facets and it was his bad luck that this shape fitted so well
into the crooked hole of alcoholism.

The thing that he was had consequences. The way in which the
fine wiring of his brain made connections, had implications. It
enabled him to view a crime scene and *see* things; it also wakened
an urge in him to hunt. It made the search sweet; inside his skull he
experienced an addictive pleasure. But the selfsame wiring made
him drink. If you wanted to hunt and search, you had to look death

in the eye. And what if death frightened you? Then you drank, because it was part of you. And if you drank long enough, then the alcohol created its own wiring, its own thoughts, its own justification. Its own thick glasses through which you saw yourself and the world.

What do you do about it? What do you do about the consequences, the opposite sides of the coin, if it fucked up your life? Leave the police and go and drive a white Toyota Tazz for Chubb Security around Brackenfell's streets at night and leave notes under people's doors? *You left your window open. Your alarm went off.* Or do you sit behind the small black-and-white screens of a shopping centre's closed-circuit television and watch the dolled-up mommies spending the daddies' money?

And you never hunt again and you die here inside.

He experienced a sudden feeling of despair, like someone trapped in a labyrinth. He needed to think of other things – of the woman leaning against him and the fact that it satisfied a need. The need to be held. That he needed to be touched. Ever since he had been thrown out of his house, he had an increasing need for it.

He wondered about her.

Why had she found it necessary to become a whore? An *Afrikaner* girl. Not as beautiful as a model. Attractive rather, sexy.

Did all women have this potential? Did it lie hidden until circumstances arose? Or was it, like his own polished facets, connected to a specific combination of angles and surfaces?

It hadn't been necessary for him to come around here tonight. But it had been in the back of his mind all day: he wanted to look in.

Was it coincidence that he had recalled his first experience of sex with such clarity on his way here? At the same time he had been wondering how alcohol and memory interacted. He had a mental image of synapses submerged in brandy; while he stayed sober the level kept dropping and, like a dam drying up, exposed old, rusty objects.

Not all the memories were pleasant, but he focused on those from long ago: the one of the girl with the gold chain around her neck and her name in gold letters against her throat. YVETTE.

She was wearing jeans and a T-shirt with blue-and-white horizontal stripes and she had used too much perfume. But it smelt heavenly.

There were odd details that he had remembered this afternoon. They had a gig in Welgemoed against the Tygerberg at the sixteenth birthday party of some or other rich man's son. They set up beside the swimming pool on imported ceramic tiles. The rich wanker had kept hanging around and asking, 'Have you got rubbers for the feet of the drums?' When he was a distance away, the drummer said, 'I have rubbers for your daughter,' and they all laughed. The rich wanker, one of those men who dress as if they were still sixteen too, stopped and asked, 'What did you say?' The drummer said: 'I said I have rubbers,' but with a smirk. The rich man stood there knowing he was making a fool of himself, but there was not a lot he could do about it.

When they played, the girl was there. She moved at the edge of the big group, half in the twilight. She wasn't truly part of it. Or didn't want to be. Sometimes she danced on her own. She looked at him and he noticed her eyes first, big brown eyes that looked sad. Long straight brown hair. Then he noticed her neat little breasts and pretty round bottom and he saw a potential opportunity and began to play to her.

The prospect was nearly too much for him. He was afraid his hopes were unrealistic. He waited until late that night, until their very last break. He went over to her and said 'Hi' and she said 'Hi' and looked at him with that lost smile as if to say I know what you're thinking. Then the strangest thing happened. She took his hand and led him past the house into the shadows. She opened a door low down at the side of the house. It was a storeroom of sorts. She closed the door and it was pitch-dark. He could see fuck-all. Then she was against him, hands around his neck and kissing him. He tasted alcohol on her tongue and Spearmint Beechies and smelt her perfume. Lust took hold of them in the dark, they kissed and undressed each other with searching hands and he felt her body – he ran his palms over her face and neck and breasts and hips and bottom. They bumped into invisible garden tools and somehow or other found a place to lie, a canvas tarpaulin over some sacks – not soft, but not as hard as the floor. He remembered the smell of turpentine and old paint, but above all, her perfume. The only sounds were their breathing and urgency. She took his dick and put it in her mouth. Lord, he would never forget that. For a moment she was nowhere to be found and then her hand was around his thing and then there was something warm and wet around it and it hit him like a sledgehammer, his dick was in her mouth. The realisation of every masturbatory dream. He wanted to see it. He wanted terribly to capture it in his mind, so that he could know what it looked like and remember, but there was no light, absolutely none. He groaned partly from frustration and partly from ecstasy and he stretched out his hand until he found her bush, slid his finger in and felt her heat like glowing coals inside.

Afterwards she opened the door for light so they could find their clothes and dress. He watched her silhouette faintly etched against the little light from outside. That was the last he saw of her. He went back, self-conscious and worried he hadn't dressed properly in the storeroom. He hadn't been missed. He looked around for her, but she was gone.

Yvette. That was all he knew. That night he had lain in bed with a strange melancholy. Her smell was on his fingers and on his body. But the next morning it was gone. Just like her.

While she was in the bathroom, he walked quickly out to his car and fetched the music and the CD player.

When she came out her hair was clean and wet. She made up a bed on the couch for him. She put out a big blue towel for him and said he was welcome to use the bathroom. He said he would like to shower. He was aware of the awkwardness between them. Or was it just him?

Tonight he was going to share a house with a whore. He couldn't look at her and forced a polite smile.

'Well, I'll say goodnight, then.'

'Sleep well,' he said.

'You too.' She went down the passage and shut her door. He went to the bathroom. It was still steamy from her shower and filled with her fragrances, soap and shampoo and lotion. It smelt different from Anna's bathroom. Fuller. Richer.

He undressed and neatly folded his clothes and put them on the toilet lid, on top of his service pistol. He looked down at his body. Naked in a whore's bathroom. He looked at the chest hairs already turning grey and the middle age slackening of his belly. His penis was in that no-man's land between indifference and desire, a half-smoked cigar. Not exactly your Greek God. Not exactly seductive in Christine van Rooyen's eyes. He smiled wryly at himself in the steamy mirror.

He showered using her semi-transparent soap that was the colour of red wine, and shampoo from a white bottle. He rinsed off and towelled. Put only his trousers on and carried the rest of his clothes and his firearm to the sitting room. He stacked them in a neat pile beside the couch and sat. He examined his bed. It was a big, wide couch. Long enough. He took out the Anton Goosen jewel case and had another look at it. He took out the second disc of the double set and put it in the player. Earphones on. He switched off the standard lamp beside the couch, swung his feet up and placed the player on his stomach. Pressed Play.

Only once the nine members of the Task Force had grown tired of laughing and jesting and gone on their way did the detective in Midrand get a chance to take the fingerprints of the two suspects. Then he had them locked up in the cells again.

He sat down at his desk and began to go through the evidence systematically. In one of the transparent plastic evidence bags he saw the identity documents that the Task Force men had found in the BMW. He took them out and looked at the names.

Let's see, he thought, and picked up the phone. The number he keyed was that of the SAPS Criminal Records Centre in Pretoria.

As the applause after the last cut faded, he lay with closed eyes and a light heart. He wondered what he had lost in the past few years.

He was the drinking equivalent of Rip van Winkel with this huge hole in his life, a black hole of unconsciousness. Everything had grown up. His children, the music of his culture . . . his fucking country. Everything except him. In his mind he was being exposed to the alternatives, how different things might have been. He didn't want to see that now. He took the earphones off.

City sounds penetrated faintly from outside. His eyes were adjusted to the dark now. Streetlights illuminated the room sufficiently through the gauzy curtains. The outlines of the furniture, the dark shape of the painting against the wall. Small red and green lights shone from the fridge and the TV.

He wanted to tell Fritz. Reaching over the little table he found his cell phone and scrolled through the menu to text messages. He struggled a bit with the tiny pads of the keyboard. CD IS BASS HEAVEN. THANKS. DAD.

He sent the SMS and put the CD player and phone on his pile of clothes. He must sleep. He didn't want to think, enough thinking for one day. He shifted around on the couch, struggling to be comfortable. It was best with his back against the backrest. Too hot for the blanket. Sleep.

He thought once of Christine lying in the bedroom, but he put her out of his mind and tried to think of Anna. That brought no peace so he thought about the music and he did what he used to do when he was seventeen: he visualised himself on stage. At the State Theatre. With Anton & friends. He was playing bass guitar. Playing without effort, going with the flow of the music, letting his fingers run where they would and he heard the bedroom door open and soft footfalls on the carpet. She must be going to the bathroom. But here she was beside him. She lay down on the couch. Her back was against him. She shifted up close to him so they lay like two spoons. He hardly dared breathe. He must pretend to be asleep. Keep his breathing even and calm. He could smell her, her shoulder right by his nose.

She wanted comfort. She just needed a person. She didn't want to be alone, she missed her child, she was raw and hurting. He knew all that.

He made a sound that he hoped would sound like a person asleep and put a hand on her hip. A comforting gesture. Half on thin material and half on bare flesh.

He felt the heat of her body. Now he was getting a fucking erection, it blossomed irreverently and there was no way to stop it. He had to think of something. He made another vague noise and shifted his hips back. Lord, she mustn't know. He should have put his underpants on, that would have kept it reined in. Perhaps she wasn't fully awake. He tried to listen to her breathing, but all his senses returned to him were her heat and her scent.

She shifted back against him. Right against him. Up here. Down there.

He wanted to apologise. He wanted to mumble 'I'm sorry' or something, but he was too scared. She was half asleep and that would make it all worse. He lay very still. Thought about the music. Played bass guitar along with '*gee die harlekyn nog wyn, skoebiedoewaa, skoebiedoewaa, rooiwyn vir sy lag en traan en pyn, skoebiedoewaa, skoebiedoewaa . . .*' Give the harlequin more wine, scoobydoowaa, scoobydoowaa, red wine for his laughter and tears and pain . . .

She moved her arm, her hand, put it over his. She held it on her hip a moment and then drew it up under her nightie, oh fuck, up to her breast, her palm on the back of his hand and he felt her, felt the softness and she sighed deeply and pressed his hand tightly and roughly against her. Moved again, her hips away from his pelvis and her hand came down there, behind her back and undid the clip of his trousers, how he had no idea. Unzipped his trousers. Slipped in her hand and grasped him. Lust was one high perfect note in his head, a lead guitar that took flight to the rhythm of his heart's bass and then she pushed him into her from behind.

Long after his orgasm they lay still like that, belly to back, still inside her, though spent and flaccid now. The first words she spoke, barely aloud, were: 'You are broken too.'

He thought for a long time before answering. He wondered how she knew. How she could see it. Or feel it. Why had she come to him? Her need? Or her gift to him? A comfort?

So he told her. About Anna. About his children. The drinking. Without plan or structure, he let it flow as it came into his head, his arm tight around her now, and his hand softly on the fullness of her breast. Her face against his, the fine hairs against his stubble.

He told her how he had been, in the days before the booze. He had been an optimist, an extrovert. A joker. He was the one who could make everyone laugh, at the funniest moments. In the parade room, when tensions ran high and tempers were stretched, he could spot the silly side of the matter and cut through all the crap with a phrase and leave them helpless with laughter. He was the one everyone phoned first when they wanted to throw some meat on the griddle for a *braai*. Two or three times a month he would join Murder and Robbery for an impromptu barbecue, a *braai*. Three o'clock on a Friday afternoon, just to relieve the never-ending pressure, at Blouberg or Silvermine or even at the office itself in Bellville South. Beer and meat and bread, laughter, chat and drink, he would be first on the list, because he was Sergeant Benny Griessel, instinctive investigator and unofficial, cynical chief clown who could ridicule the job and the bureaucracy and affirmative action but with compassion. So that they could all face up to it again.

Now, this side of the booze, they still had their *braais*. But no one called him. No one wanted him there, the sot who staggered and couldn't string two coherent words together. The oaf who bumped into others, swore and fought and had to be taken home to a wife who opened the door reluctantly. Because she didn't want that drunkard or the humiliation.

He told Christine he had been sober for eleven days now and he didn't know the man this side of the booze.

Everything had changed around him. His children, his wife, his colleagues. Jissis, he was an old has-been amongst all the *Sturm und Drang* of the young policemen in the Service.

But the main thing was, he believed he *had* changed. He wasn't sure how. Or how much. A strange fellow in his forties with a gaping hole in his life.

He told her all this and somewhere in the telling she asked: 'Why do you want your wife back?' He wondered about that before he answered. He said the thing was, he had been happy then. They had. She was the woman he had begun his life with. They had nothing, just each other. Set up house together, suffered together. Laughed together. Shared the same wonder at the magic of Carla and Fritz's births. Celebrated together when he was promoted. They had history, the sort of history that mattered. They were friends and lovers and he wanted that back. He wanted the bond and the camaraderie and the trust. Because that was a great part of who he had been, what made him what he had been.

And he wanted to be that again.

If he couldn't get Anna back, he had fuck-all. That was it.

She said: 'A person can never be like that again,' and before he could react, she asked, 'Do you still love her?' It made no difference how long he thought about that one, he could not answer her. He wanted to talk shit about 'what is love', but he kept quiet and suddenly felt weary of himself, so he asked, 'What about you?'

'What about me?'

'Why was it necessary . . . to become a prostitute?'

'A sex worker,' she said, but in quiet self-mockery.

She moved slowly and he slipped out of her. A small moment of loss. She turned over so her face was towards him and his hand was off her breast.

'Would you have asked me that if I was selling flowers?' There was no confrontation in her voice. Her words were flat and without emotion. She didn't wait for an answer. 'It's just a job.'

He drew a breath to answer, but she went on: 'People think it's this dreadful thing. Bad. Damaging. Your work brings you damage too. That's what you just said. But it's okay to be a policeman. Just don't be a whore.'

He thought if she hadn't been a sex worker, Sonia would have been safe at home, but he knew he could never say it.

'When I began, I also wondered what was different about me. All my clients ask the same thing. "Why did you become an escort?" It makes you think there's something wrong with you.

Then you think, but why should it be something *wrong*? Why can't it be something *right*? Why can't it just be that I think further than most people? What is sex? Is it so bad? What makes it such a bad thing?'

She got up and walked away from him and he was sorry he had asked her. He didn't mean to upset her. He should have thought. He wanted to say he was sorry, but she had disappeared down the passage. He became aware of his trousers still unfastened so he zipped them up.

She came back. He saw her shadowy figure moving and here she was, but this time she sat at his feet.

'Do you want a cigarette?'

'Please.'

She put two cigarettes in her mouth and clicked the lighter. In the light of the flame he could see her breasts and face and bare shoulders.

She passed one to him. He drew deeply.

'I was always different,' she said and blew a plume of smoke that cast a ghostly shadow on the opposite wall. 'It's hard to explain. When you are small, you understand nothing. You think there's something wrong with you. My parents . . . I come from a good home. My father was in the army and my mother was mostly at home and they were okay with that. With their little world. With that kind of life. The older I got the harder it was for me to understand. How could that be all? How could that be enough? You go to school, you find a husband or a wife, you raise kids, you retire by the sea and then you die. You never upset anyone, you do the right thing. Those are my father's words. "My child, you do the right thing." Whose right thing? The people's? Who are they to decide what the right thing is? You pay your parking money and you never drive too fast and don't make a noise after ten at night. And you do your duty. That's another of my father's classics. "People must do their duty, my child." To your family, to your town, to your country. What for? What did they get for doing their duty? My father did his duty to the army and he was dead before he took his pension. My mother did her duty to us and she has never been to Cape Town or Europe or anywhere. After all the duty, there was never money for anything. Not for clothes or cars or furniture or holidays. But it was okay for them, because people mustn't be flashy, that's not the right thing to do.

'Everyone wants you to be ordinary. Everything everyone teaches you, is just so you won't be different. But I was different. I couldn't help it. It's the way I am. If my parents or the school or whoever said that is what you should do, then I wondered what it felt like to do the opposite. I wanted to see what it looked like from the other side. So I did. I smoked a bit and I drank a bit. But when you are fifteen or sixteen, almost all the rules are about sex. You mustn't do this and you mustn't do that, because you must be a decent girl. I wanted to know why you had to be a decent girl. What for? So you could get a decent man? And a decent life, with decent children? And a decent funeral with lots of people? So I did things. And the more things I did, the more I realised the other side is the interesting one. Most people don't want to be decent, they've all got this stuff inside that wants to be different, but they don't have the guts. They are all too scared someone will say something. They are afraid they will lose all the boring things in their lives. There was this teacher, he was so dutiful. I worked on him. And I slept with him on the Students Christian Association camp at The Island. He said, God, Christine, I've wanted you so long. So I asked him why he hadn't done something about it. He couldn't answer me. And this friend of my father. When he came to our house he would look at me sideways but then go and sit next to his wife and hold her hand. I knew what he wanted. I worked on him and he said he liked young girls but that it was his first time.'

She stubbed the cigarette out and half turned to him.

'He was as old as you,' she said, and for a second he thought he heard scorn in her voice.

She leaned her back against his feet. She folded her arms below her breasts.

'Do you know why my parents sent me to university? To find a husband. One with education. And a good job. So I could have a good life. A good life. What does a good life help? What use is it when you die and you can say to yourself I had a good life? Boring, but good.

'At varsity this guy was visiting me, third-year medical student. His parents lived in Heuwelsig and they had money. I saw how they lived. I saw if you have money you don't have to be dutiful and ordinary and good. Having money means more than being able to buy things. You can be different and no one says anything. Then I knew what I wanted. But how to get it? You could marry a rich man, but it's still not your money. I got a job working weekends for a catering business. One night at a golf course I stood having a smoke and this man comes up to me. He had a car business in Zastron Street, and he asked me, "How much do you earn?" When I told him he said, "Wouldn't you rather make a thousand rand a night?" and I asked, "How would I do that?" and he said, "With your body, love." He gave me his card and he said "Think about it." I phoned him that Monday. And I did it. In a flat, they were seven guys who had a flat in Hilton, and sometimes at lunchtime or sometimes in the evening they would phone me at the hostel and I would go.

'But then, just before final exams, I got pregnant,' she said. 'I was on the pill, but it didn't work. When I told them they said they would pay for the abortion, but I said no. So they gave me money and I came to Cape Town.'

38

Orlando Arendse had a fixed routine every morning. In his large, pretty house in West Beach, Milnerton, he got up at six without the help of an alarm clock. He put on slippers and a burgundy dressing gown. He picked up his reading glasses from the kitchen table, left his wife sleeping and went to the kitchen. He put the spectacles on the kitchen table and ground a 50/50 mix of Italian and Mocca Java coffee beans – enough for four large mugs. He filled the coffee machine with water and carefully poured in the ground coffee. Then he pressed the switch.

He walked to the front door, opened it and went out. He looked up to see what the weather was doing today, then crossed the paved driveway to the big, automatic security gate. He walked briskly erect, despite his 66 years, most of them lived on the Cape Flats. To the right of the gate was the postbox. He opened it and took out *Die Burger*.

Without unfolding the newspaper he glanced at the headlines. He had to hold the paper at arm's length, as he was not wearing his glasses.

He walked back to the house and just before he went through the door he looked left and right. It was instinctive behaviour, no longer functional.

He spread the paper open neatly on the Oregon pine table in the kitchen. He put on his reading glasses. His right hand drifted down to the dressing gown pocket. It was empty and he clicked his tongue in exasperation. He no longer smoked. His wife and doctor were conspiring against him.

He only read the front page. By now the coffee machine ended its burbling with a final sigh. Orlando Arendse sighed with it as he did every morning. He got up and fetched two mugs from the cupboard above the machine and placed them on the counter. First he filled one cup and inhaled the aroma with pleasure. No milk or sugar. Just as it was. He poured the rest of the coffee into a flask so it would stay fresh. Mug in hand, he sat down at the paper again. He turned the page and inspected the small photo of the page-three editor, a lovely woman. Then he shifted his gaze to page two and began to read in earnest.

Usually at seven he would pour coffee from the flask into the other mug and take it to his wife. But at ten to seven, while he was reading the cricket report on the sports page, the electronic box in the entrance hall made its irritating noise.

Orlando stood up and crossed to the hall. He pressed a button and held his mouth close to the microphone. 'Yes?'

'Orlando?'

He knew that deep voice, but couldn't place it at the moment. 'Yes?'

'It's Thobela.'

'Who?'

'Tiny. Tiny Mpayipheli.'

He ran down a green valley through knee-high grass, chasing a red balloon. He stretched out a hand to the string but stumbled and fell and it shot up into the air. He woke in Christine van Rooyen's sitting room and smelt the sex on his body. What the fuck have I done?

He swung his legs off the couch and rubbed his eyes. He knew he hadn't slept enough, could feel the lethargy in his mind and body, but that was not what lay so heavily. He didn't want to think about it. He stood up a little unsteadily. He pushed his Z88 pistol and cell phone under the couch and took the little pile of clothes and shoes with him to the bathroom. He would have liked to brush his teeth, but that would have to wait. He got under the shower and opened the taps.

Jissis. Drunkard and adulterer. Whore-fucker. Fucking weakling who couldn't control himself, telling her his entire life story. What the fuck was wrong with him? He wasn't a fucking teenager any more.

He scrubbed himself with the soap, washing his genitals two, three, four times. What was he going to do with her now? How far was Witness Protection? He would have to call them. How had the night gone for Bushy Bezuidenhout and company out at Camp's Bay? While he lay in the embrace of a prostitute. With premeditation, that was the fucking thing – he had come here looking for it. Wanting her to touch him because he needed someone to touch him so fucking much. Because he thought a whore would find it easier to touch him. Because he couldn't wait six fucking months for his wife, just maybe, to touch him.

He got out of the shower and towelled himself aggressively. Jissis, if only he could brush his teeth, his mouth tasted as if a mongoose had shat in it. He smelt his trousers. They still smelt of sex, he couldn't go to work like that. Better phone Tim Ngubane and find out if Witness Protection could come and collect her.

Why did she have to come and lie with him? And then to tell him her story as if it was *his* fucking fault?

He was still standing like that holding his trousers up to his nose, when she opened the bathroom door and said in a frightened voice: 'I think there is someone at the door.'

Arendse had last seen Tiny Mpayipheli five years ago. Sitting together at the Oregon table, he could see that the Xhosa had changed. Still a very big man with a voice like a cello. Still the pitch-black eyes that made him shiver the first time he looked into them. But the lines in the face were a bit deeper and the short-cropped hair had acquired a little grey at the temples.

'Tell me about Carlos Sangrenegra,' said his visitor, taking a swallow of his coffee.

Arendse looked down at the front page of the newspaper before him and then up at the big man. He saw absolute intent. He was on the point of saying something, asking a lot of questions, while the tumblers dropped slowly but surely. He looked down at the newspaper again, back at Tiny and it all became clear. Everything.

'Jesus, Tiny.'

The Xhosa said nothing, just looked back with that eagle's eye.

'What happened?' asked Arendse.

Thobela looked at him for a long time, then shook his head, left and right, once only.

'I am retired,' said Arendse.

'You know people.'

'It's all different now, Tiny. It's not like the old days. They've marginalised us coloured people. Even in the drug trade.'

No reaction.

'I owe you. That's true.' Arendse stood and crossed over to the coffee machine. 'Let me just take my wife her coffee or I'll never hear the end of it. Then I'll make a few calls.'

Griessel tried to pull his trousers on, but he was in too much of a hurry. He lost his balance while he was standing on one leg. In the fall he knocked his head against the edge of the washbasin with a dull thud. He swore, jumped up and got the trousers on and fastened the clip only and strode out of the bathroom to the couch under which his weapon lay.

As he bent to retrieve the Z88 he felt dizzy. He got a hand on the pistol and went to the door.

'Who's there?' He pressed down the safety clip of the pistol.

At first he heard nothing and then only the sound of the footsteps of more than one person. Footsteps receding down the passage. He turned the key with his left hand, jerked the door open and swung the barrel of his pistol into the passage. To the right he saw a figure disappearing into the lift. He ran that way. His head was still not clear.

The door to the lift had closed. He hesitated just a fraction then ran for the stairs and down, two steps at a time.

Six bloody storeys. With his left hand on the rail, firearm in the right, just his trousers on, down, down. On the third floor his legs couldn't keep up and he slipped and it was only his hand on the stair rail that prevented a headlong fall. He saw a pair of legs in front of him and looked up. A very fat woman in a bright purple tracksuit stood staring with a mouth like an 'O', her face glowing with perspiration.

'Excuse me,' he said and dragged himself upright, squeezing past her and taking the next set of stairs.

'You're bleeding,' he heard the fat woman say. Instinctively he touched a hand to his forehead to check and it came away wet, warm and red. Run. What was he going to do when he reached the bottom if there were more than one? His breath laboured, chest burned, legs complained.

Second storey, first storey, ground.

He went in pistol first, but the entrance hall was empty. He jerked the glass door open and sprinted out into the morning sun just as below at the corner of Belle Ombre and Kloof Nek Road a white Opel turned the corner with screeching tyres.

When the call came from Midrand, the detective had to find the file in a forgotten pile against the wall.

Then he began to remember the two who had shot the boy at the garage. And the father who had bought the contents of the file.

He tapped a middle finger on the cover of the file. He wondered if he would still be interested. Whether there might be another opportunity here.

He looked up the father's details in the documents. He found a number with a Cathcart code. Pulling the phone nearer he keyed them in. It rang for a long time. Eventually he put the phone down.

He would try again later.

She had heard someone trying to open the door, she said as she cleaned the wound on his forehead with a warm, damp facecloth. His nose was full of the smell of Dettol. She stood up against him where he sat on the couch. She was wearing a thin dressing gown. He didn't want her this close.

At first she hadn't been certain. She had gone to put the kettle on in the kitchen while he was showering when she heard it. She saw the door latch move. That was when she went to the door and called: 'Is anyone there?' It had been quiet a second and then someone had rattled the door. She had run to him in the bathroom.

'You have a bump and a cut.' She stepped back to view her handiwork.

She was gentler this morning, but he didn't want to think about it.

'Witness Protection will be here soon,' he said. He had called them before she had started on the cut.

'I'll get ready.'

'They will take you to a safe house. You must pack clothes.'

He looked up at her face. She was watching him with an unreadable expression. She stretched out a hand to his face, touched her fingertips to his chin. Softly. She stroked up across his cheekbone to the plaster she had put over his wound.

There was a foil-wrapped parcel at his door. He picked it up, unlocked the door and went inside. The room felt dead, as if no one lived there. He put the food on the counter and went up the stairs. His legs were stiff from the earlier exercise. He brushed his teeth long and thoroughly. Washed his face. He found clean clothes, dressed in a hurry and jogged down the stairs. He was out of the door when he remembered the food parcel. He went back. Charmaine had left a note again. It read:

> *Care of your food and living; and believe it,*
> *My most honour'd lord,*
> *For any benefit that points to me,*
> *Either in hope or present, I'd exchange*
> *For this one wish, that you had power and wealth*
> *To requite me, by making rich yourself.*
>
> Timon of Athens.

He hadn't the faintest idea who that Greek was.

Bushy Bezuidenhout looked pointedly at his watch as Griessel entered the house opposite Sangrenegra's.

'Sorry, Bushy. It's been a rough morning.'

'Very rough, I see. What happened to your head?'

'It's a long story,' he said and he could read the drunkenness question in his colleague's bloodshot eyes.

'How's it going here?'

'The other night-shift people have already gone. I've been waiting for you.'

He felt extremely guilty and for a moment considered telling him where he had been. But he had already given one version of his night over the phone to Matt Joubert. He didn't want to go through it again. 'Thanks, Bushy.'

'Nothing happened here. No suspicious vehicles, no pedestrians except an old girl taking her dogs for a walk this morning. Carlos's last lights went off at a quarter-past twelve.'

'Any sign of him this morning?'

'Nothing. But he has to report to the police station before twelve, so he will probably start moving around soon.' Then, as an afterthought. 'We should have bugged his phone.'

Griessel thought it over. The chances that the assegai man would phone him were slim. 'Maybe.'

'I'll be off then.'

'I'll stay until eight tonight, Bushy.'

'No, it's okay. I won't be able to sleep that long anyway.'

Vaughn Cupido was on the third floor with a large pair of binoculars.

'*My moer*, Benny, what happened to your head?'

'It's a long story.'

'I'm not going anywhere.'

Griessel put his dish of food on a chest of drawers and went to stand next to Cupido. He held out his hand for the binoculars. Cupido handed them over and Griessel aimed them at Sangrenegra's house.

'There's not much to see,' said Cupido.

That was true. Most of the windows had reflective glass. 'He has to go to the police station.'

'Fielies will follow him in a car.' Cupido tapped the radio on his hip. 'He'll keep us informed.'

Griessel handed the binoculars back. 'I don't think he'll come in daytime.'

'The assegai man?'

Griessel nodded.

Cupido sat in an armchair that had a view outside. 'You never know. I try putting myself in his shoes, but I can't. What's in the package?'

Griessel leaned back against the wall. He would have preferred to lie down on the double bed behind them. 'Lunch.'

'Are you back with the missus, Benny?'

'No.'

'Made it yourself?'

'Do I question you about your fucking eating arrangements, Vaughn?'

'Okay, okay, I'm just making conversation. Stakeout was never my idea of high excitement. So, tell me about the knob. Or is that also off limits?'

'I bumped my head on a washbasin.'

'Sure.'

'Jissis, Vaughn, what do you think? That I was pissed? Do you want to smell my fucking breath? So you can run to the papers and tell the fucking journalists what a fuck-up I am? Here, use my cell phone. Call them. Go on, take it. Do you think I care? Do you think it still bothers me?'

'Jeez, Benny, take it easy. I'm on *your* side.'

Griessel folded his arms. The radio on Cupido's hip beeped. 'Vaughn, its Fielies, come in.'

'I'm standing by.'

'Do we have someone in number forty-eight?'

'Not that I'm aware of.'

'There's a man with a huge pair of binoculars on the second floor. I don't think he knows I can see him.'

'Is he watching Carlos?'

'Yep.'

'Tell him I'll check it out,' said Griessel.

'Wait,' said Cupido. 'Here comes King Carlos.'

Griessel looked at Sangrenegra's house. The door of the double garage was slowly opening. 'Fuck,' he said, 'give me the radio.' He took it from Cupido. 'Fielies, this is Benny. Does the guy have *only* binoculars?'

'That is all that I can see.'

'Carlos is on his way. Look carefully at the window . . .'

'Only the binoculars. There, they've gone now . . .'

Please not a sniper, thought Griessel. 'Is everyone on this frequency?' he asked Cupido, who nodded.

'Everyone, stand by.'

'The binoculars are back,' said Fielies.

'Follow Carlos, Fielies.' To Cupido: 'Who is his back-up?'

'He's on his own. You know we don't have enough manpower for back-up.'

'Fielies . . .'

'Standing by.'

'Don't lose him.'

When Carlos's BMW disappeared down the road, Griessel left the house and crossed the street. It was hot outside and windless in the lee of the mountain. The heat reflected up from the ground and perspiration sprang out on his skin. He worried that the smells of last night would come out again. Number 48 was another rich man's house, white-painted concrete filling the entire plot. No-where for children to play. A playground for adults only. He looked up at the windows of the second floor. There was a room overlooking the street and Sangrenegra's house and the curtains were parted. There was no one there now.

He approached the front door and rang the bell. He couldn't hear it ring. He never could understand why people didn't make their doorbells audible. How were you supposed to know if it was working or not? You stand there pressing like crazy, and most of the time it's out of order and you wait like a fool at the door, but no one knows you're there.

Irritably he pressed again. Once, twice, three times.

Nothing happened. Not a sound.

Fielies had clearly seen something. The binoculars. Appearing and disappearing.

He hammered on the door with the base of his fist. Boom, boom, boom, boom, the sound echoed inside. Open up, fuckers.

No reaction, no sound of footsteps.

He took out his phone and looked up Boef Beukes's number that he had called last night. Pressed the green key. It rang unanswered. Boef knew who was calling. And he probably knew why, because the chump with the binoculars up there had probably phoned his boss and said the SVC people were at the door.

He banged one last time on the door, more out of frustration than expectation.

Then he turned and left.

39

He had fetched himself a chair from the luxurious sitting room, carried it up the stairs and positioned it next to Cupido's. They watched Sangrenegra return and listened while Fielies reported. The Colombian had been to the police and directly home again.

They sat and waited and had meaningless chats. They tried to keep the attention of the team, the detectives down the street, and the others hidden in the veld behind the house.

It was 15:34 now and the sleepiness felt like lead inside him. He must have been asleep with his eyes open, because when Cupido said with an edge, 'Benny . . .,' he jumped in fright. Looking down at the street he saw a panel van parked at Carlos's door. There was a big blue cross on the side. *First Aid for Pools. Intensive Care Unit.*

A black man got out. Big. Blue overalls.

Griessel picked up the radio. 'Stand by, everyone.'

The man walked around to the back of the panel van and took out pipes, nets and other paraphernalia.

'That's their sign on the wall,' said Cupido, binoculars to eyes. 'What?'

'On the wall of Carlos's house. There, beside the garage door. "Swimming pool care by First Aid for Pools". And a number.'

The swimming-pool man approached the front door. He pressed the intercom and waited.

'The number is four eight seven double-o, double-o.'

Griessel called it and waited.

The door across the street opened. They could see Carlos. He held the door open. The black man picked up all his things and went in.

'The number you have dialled does not exist,' said the woman's voice in his ear. 'Fuck,' he said. 'Are you sure of that number?'

'Four eight seven double-o, double-o.'

'That's what I . . .' He realised he hadn't added the Cape Town code and he swore and pressed 021 and then the number again. At the fourth ring a woman answered.

'First Aid for Pools, good afternoon. This is Ruby speaking. How may I help you?'

'This is Detective Inspector Benny Griessel here from Serious and Violent Crimes. Can you tell me whether you have a San-grenegra on your books? Forty-five Shanklin Crescent in Camps Bay.' He tried to communicate urgency in his voice so she wouldn't fuck around.

'I'm sorry, sir, we cannot give you that information over the telephone . . .'

He stayed calm with effort and said: 'Ruby, this is a police emergency and I do not have the time to . . .' He wanted to say 'fuck around' and had to think of other words. '. . . Please, Ruby, I'm asking you really nicely here.'

She was quiet at the other end and perhaps it was the despera-tion in his voice, because eventually she said: 'What was that name again?'

'Sangrenegra.' He spelt it out for her. Across the street the front door was still shut.

He faintly heard Ruby tapping her keyboard. 'We have no Sangrenegra on our records, sir.'

'Are you sure?'

'Yes, sir, I am. Our computer doesn't lie.' Sharply.

'Okay. Now we have to be sure here. Do you have a forty-five Shanklin Crescent in Camps Bay?'

'One moment.'

'Postman,' said Cupido, pointing down the street. A man in uniform was riding a bicycle from postbox to postbox. At Carlos's house all was quiet.

'Sir?'

'I'm here,' said Griessel.

'We do have a forty-five Shanklin Crescent, Camps Bay on our books . . .'

He felt extremely relieved.

'The client is a company, it seems.'

'Yes.'

'The Colombian Coffee Company.'

'Okay,' said Griessel. The tension began to ebb.

'Here he comes,' said Cupido. The big black man exited the front door. He was holding only a white plastic pipe.

'They seem to be good clients. All paid up,' said Ruby.

'He must be fetching something from the van,' said Cupido.

Griessel's eyes followed the black man in the blue overalls. The clothes looked a bit tight on him. The man opened the driver's side door.

'We service them . . .'

The man tossed the swimming-pool pipe into the front of the van.

'. . . on Fridays,' said Ruby.

The man got into the van.

'What?' said Griessel.

'Something's not right,' said Cupido. 'He's leaving . . .'

'We service them on Fridays.'

'. . . and his tools are still inside.'

Griessel grabbed his radio: 'Stop him! Stop the swimming-pool man, everybody!' He rushed down the stairs, phone in one hand and radio in the other. Ruby said 'Excuse me?' faintly over the phone as he screamed into the radio: 'Fielies, turn your car around and stop the swimming-pool man!'

'Are you there, sir?'

'I'm on my way, Benny.'

He nearly fell as he turned the corner on the last set of stairs and the thought crossed his mind that the world was a fucking funny place. For years you don't climb stairs and then all of a sudden you are faced with more stairs than your fucking legs can manage. 'Hello?' said Ruby over the cell phone. 'He's around the corner!' shouted Fielies over the radio.

'Go, Fielies, drive, man!'

Griessel sprinted across the street to Carlos's house. He heard feet slapping behind him, and half turning he saw Cupido and two constables running across the tar.

'Sir, are you there?'

The postman on his bicycle was in front of him, wide-eyed and mouth agape. Griessel sidestepped and for a second he thought they were going to collide.

'Hello?'

His knee bumped the rear tyre of the bicycle and he thought if he fell now the cell phone and the radio would be buggered. He regained his balance. He shoved the door open and ran in and saw the Colombian lying by the swimming pool, blood everywhere. He reached him, he lay on his face and Benny turned him over and saw he was stone dead, a huge hole in his chest. He said: 'Fuck, fuck, fuck,' and Ruby said: 'That's it!' and the cell phone made three beeps and the three policemen behind him skidded to a halt and then everything went quiet.

On the corner of Shanklin and Eldon, Detective Constable Malcolm Fielies wondered whether the swimming-pool man had turned left or right. He turned left, guessing, and ahead saw the panel van turning right and he put his foot flat on the accelerator and the tyres screeched.

He turned right down Cranberry after the man and he saw on the sign that it was a crescent and he thought, got you, mother-fucker, let's see you get out of this one! But the road ran straight as an arrow and he saw the brake lights go on ahead and the van turned left and Fielies cursed and shouted into the radio: 'I'm after him!' but he knew they only worked over short distances and he didn't know whether they heard him.

He threw the radio down on the seat beside him and turned left. Geneva Drive. He suspected it was the street leading up to Camps Bay Drive, the one leading into the city, and he changed the Golf down to a lower gear and listened to the engine scream as he drove.

He was catching up, slowly but surely he was catching the motherfucker, although this motherfucker could drive.

He grabbed the microphone of the police radio off its hook and called Control and said he needed back-up, but then Geneva curved sharply to the right, so fucking unexpectedly, and he felt the back of the Golf go and he grabbed the steering wheel with both hands. The tyres screeched and he saw he was going to hit the kerb. Look *through* the turn, that was what they were taught. He looked *through* the fucking turn. Too fast. There went the back end and he spun, 360 degrees, and the engine stalled on him. He said 'motherfucker' very loudly. He turned the key and it whined and whined and then it took and the Golf and Detective Constable Malcolm Fielies pulled away with screaming tyres. At the T-junction with Camps Bay Drive he stopped and looked left and right and left again, but there was no sign of the panel van.

The swimming-pool floor of the house was filled with policemen and forensic people. Griessel sat to one side with his cell phone in his hands. He felt he had robbed Christine van Rooyen of her last chance to know her daughter's fate. He thought, if the child was still alive somewhere, they would never find her now.

He knew that Senior Superintendent Esau Mtimkulu and Matt Joubert, first and second in command of SVC, and Commissioner John Afrika, the provincial head of Investigation, were arguing about his future down there beside the pool. If they sent him down the tubes, it was only right, because he had continued to believe the assegai man was white, even after he had had good evidence to the contrary. That was why he had been so slow to react to the swimming-pool van. That was why he had phoned first.

His fault. Too much fucking faith in his instinct, too cocky, too self-assured – and now he would pay for it.

The phone rang.

'Griessel.'

'Inspector, the helicopter has found the swimming-pool company's van on Signal Hill Road. We are sending a patrol vehicle.'

'And the suspect?'

'He's gone. It's just the vehicle.'

'Explain to me where it is.'

'It's the road that turns off Kloof Nek Road to the lookout points on Signal Hill, Inspector. About half a kilometre in there is a clump of trees on the right-hand side.'

'No one goes near the vehicle, please. They must just secure the area.' He was on his feet and walking over to Cupido. 'Vaughn, they found the van on Signal Hill. I want you to think carefully – was he wearing gloves?'

'No fucking way. I checked him out thoroughly.'

'So you're sure?'

'I'm sure.'

Griessel crossed over to the three senior officers. They stopped arguing when he approached. 'Superintendent,' he said to Joubert, 'the helicopter has found the van on Signal Hill. We think we have a good chance of getting fingerprints. He wasn't wearing gloves. I want to take Forensics immediately . . .'

He could see from the three faces that it was coming now.

'Benny,' said John Afrika, quietly so that only the four of them could hear. 'You will understand if Superintendent Joubert takes over now?'

He fucking well deserved it, but it hurt and he didn't want to show that. He said: 'I understand, Commissioner.'

'You are still part of the team, Benny,' said Matt.

'I . . .' he began, but didn't know what to say.

'Take Forensics, Benny. Call if you find something.'

They found nothing.

The assegai man had wiped the steering wheel and gear lever and the door catch with a cloth or something. Then Griessel recalled he had taken stuff out of the back and the forensic examiner sprayed his spray and dusted with his brush and said: 'We have something here.'

Griessel came around to look. Against the outer panel of the rear door a fingerprint showed up clearly against the white paint.

'It's not necessarily his,' said the man from Forensics.

Griessel said nothing.

He sat at the breakfast counter of his flat and ate some of the thinly carved roast leg of lamb from Charmaine Watson-Smith's dish. But his mind was on the bottle of Klipdrift in the cupboard above.

Why not? He couldn't think of a single good answer to his question.

He had no appetite, but ate because he knew he must.

Last night he had had big theories about why he drank. Griessel the philosopher. It was *this* and it was *that* and everything but the truth. And the truth was: he was a fuck-up. That's all. Whore-fucking wife-beating drunken sot fuck-up.

Where was that jovial fellow who used to play the bass guitar? That's where he had been last night and now he knew. That guy was already a fuck-up, he just didn't know it. You can fool some of the people some of the time . . . But you can't fool life, pappa. Life will fucking catch you out.

He stood up. So weary. He scraped the last of the food into the bin. He washed and dried the dish. He didn't feel like taking it to the old girl now. He would leave it at her door in the morning with a note.

You can't fool life.

His cell phone rang in his pocket.

Let the fucking thing ring.

He took it out and checked the screen.

ANNA.

What did she want? Can you fetch the kids on Sunday? Are you sober? Did she really care whether he was sober or not? Really? She didn't believe he had it in him in any case. And she was right. She knew him better than anyone. She had watched the whole process, lived through it. She was witness number one. Life had caught him out and she had had a ringside seat. She knew in six months' time she would phone an attorney and say let us put an end to this marriage with my alcoholic husband who still drinks. The six months were just to show the children she wasn't heartless.

Let her call. Let her go to hell.

1 MISSED CALL.

1 MISSED LIFE.

The phone rang again. It was the number from work. What did they want?

'Griessel.'

'We've got him, Benny,' said Matt Joubert.

40

They were all in the task team room at SVC when he walked in. He could feel the excitement, saw it in their faces, heard it in their voices.

Joubert sat beside Helena Louw where she was working on the computer. Bezuidenhout and his night team were there too. Keyter stood talking to a constable; the fucking camera he had borrowed was still hanging from his neck, zoom lens protruding.

Griessel sat down at one of the small tables.

Joubert looked up and saw him, beckoned him closer. He got up and went over. 'Sit here with me, Benny.'

He sat. Joubert stood up. 'May I have your attention, please?'

The room quietened.

'We have identified a suspect, thanks to fingerprints that Inspector Griessel and his team recovered from the vehicle of the swimming-pool company. His name is Thobela Mpayipheli. He is a Xhosa man in his forties from the Eastern Cape. His registered address is Cata, a farm in the Cathcart district. That is in the Eastern Cape. Earlier this year Mpayipheli lost his son during an armed robbery at a filling station. Two suspects were arrested, but escaped from detention during the trial. It seems as if that is where it all began. By the way, he owns an Izuzu KB pick-up, which fits with the tyre print that Inspector Griessel found, and we must assume that that is the vehicle with which he travelled to Cape Town and Uniondale. That is all the information we have at this time.'

Griessel's cell phone rang again and he took it out of his pocket. ANNA.

He switched it off.

'So,' said Joubert. 'Since I am going to ask Griessel to go to the Eastern Cape, I will hold the fort at this end.'

He didn't want to go anywhere.

'We are going to search the Cape with a fine-tooth comb for Mpayipheli. He must be staying somewhere. Benny will find out if he has any family or friends here, but in the meantime we will have to visit or contact every establishment that offers accommodation. We are waiting . . .'

Joubert's eyes turned to the door and everyone followed suit. Boef Beukes had come in. Behind him was the man in the suit that Griessel had seen in Beukes's office. Joubert nodded in their direction.

'We are waiting for good photos from Home Affairs and you will each get one, along with the best description we can compile. There already is a bulletin out for the pick-up and we are putting up roadblocks on the N-one, N-two, N-seven, R-twenty-seven, R-forty-four and four places on the R-three hundred around Mitchells Plain and Khayelitsha. We will also provide details to the media and ask the public to cooperate. In an hour or so we should have a timetable drawn up, so that you can begin phoning places of accommodation. Stand by until we are ready for you.'

Joubert came to sit beside Griessel directly. 'Sorry about that, Benny. There was no time to warn you.'

Griessel shrugged. It made no difference.

'Are you okay?'

He wanted to ask what that meant, but he just nodded instead.

'We've booked you onto the nine o'clock flight to Port Elizabeth. It's the last one today.'

'I'll go and pack.'

'I need you there, Benny.'

He nodded again. Then Boef Beukes and Mr Red Tie came up to them. The unknown man was holding a big brown envelope.

'Matt, can we have a word?' Beukes said, and Griessel wondered why he was speaking English.

'Things are a bit mad here,' said Joubert.

'We have some information . . .' said Beukes.

'We're listening.'

'Can we talk in your office?'

'What's with the English, Boef? Or are you practising for when the *Argus* phones?' Griessel asked.

'Let me introduce you to Special Agent Chris Lombardi of the DEA,' said Beukes and turned to Red Tie.

'I work for the United States Drug Enforcement Agency, and I've been in your country now for three months,' said Chris Lombardi. With his bald pate and long fleshy ears, Griessel thought he looked like an accountant.

'Superintendent Beukes and I have been part of an inter-agency operation to investigate the flow of drugs between Asia and South America, in which South Africa, and Cape Town in particular, seems to play a prominent part.' Lombardi's accent was strongly American, like a film star's.

Three months, thought Griessel. The fuckers had been watching Carlos for three months.

Lombardi took an A4-size sheet of paper from his brown envelope and placed it on Joubert's desk. It was a black-and-white portrait photograph of a clean-shaven man with dark curly hair. 'This is César Sangrenegra. Also known as *El Muerte*. He is the second in command of the Guajira Cartel, one of the biggest Colombian drug-smuggling operations in South America. He is one of the three infamous Sangrenegra brothers, and we believe he arrived in Cape Town early this morning.'

'Carlos's brother,' said Griessel.

'Yes, he is the brother of the late Carlos. And that's part of the problem. But let me start at the beginning.' Lombardi took another photograph from the envelope. 'This is Miguel Sangrenegra, a.k.a. *La Rubia*, or *La Rubia de la Santa Marta*. "Rubia" means "blond", and as you can see, the man isn't blond at all. He is the patriarch of the family, seventy-two years old, and has been retired since nineteen ninety-five. But it all started with him. In the nineteen-fifties Miguel was a coffee smuggler in the Caribbean and was perfectly positioned to graduate to marijuana in the sixties and seventies. He hails from the town of Santa Marta in the Guajira province of Colombia. Now, the Guajira is not the most fertile of the Colombian districts, but it has one strange advantage. Due to soil quality and chemistry, it produces a very popular variant of marijuana, called Santa Marta Gold. It is much sought-after in the US, and the street price is considerably higher than any other form of weed. In the Guajira, they refer to Santa Marta Gold as *La Rubia*. And that is what Miguel started smuggling, hence his nickname.'

Lombardi took a map out of the envelope and unfolded it on the desk.

'This is Colombia, and this area, on the Caribbean coast, is the Guajira. As you can see, what the province lacked in soil fertility, it made up for in geographic location. Just look at this length of coastline. If you wanted to smuggle marijuana to the US, you either sent a boat to the Guajira coast, or you sent a cargo plane. Miguel knew the farmers who grew the stuff in the mountains, and he knew the coast like the back of his hand. So he became a *marimbero*. A smuggler of marijuana. The Colombians refer to it as *marimba*. Anyway, he made a killing in the seventies. But then, in the late seventies and eighties, cocaine became the drug of preference internationally. And the balance of drug power, the money, and the focus of law enforcement, moved to central Colombia. To people like Pablo Escobar and the Medellín Cartel. Carlos Lehder, the Ochoa brothers, José Rodríguez-Gacha . . .

'Miguel did not like cocaine, and he didn't have the natural contacts for it, so he stuck to *marimba*, made good money, but he never reached the dizzy heights of wealth and power like Escobar or Lehder. However, in the long run, this was to his great advantage. Because when we started hunting the big cartels, Miguel was quietly going about his business. And in the nineties, his family stepped into the vacuum after the removal of the big guns.'

Another photograph came out of the brown envelope.

'This is Miguel Sangrenegra's eldest son, Javier. He is short and stocky, like his mother. And we think he has the old lady's brains and ambition too. He was the one who put pressure on his father to expand the family business into cocaine. Miguel resisted, and Javier sidelined the old man. Not immediately, but slowly and quietly retired him in a way that meant everybody's respect remained intact.

'Now let's talk about Carlos.' Another photograph, this time of the youngest brother. Grainy black and white. In a sunny street in a South American town, a younger Carlos was getting out of a Land Rover Discovery.

Griessel checked his watch. He still had to pack. He wondered what the point of this story was.

'Carlos was the runt of the litter. The least intelligent of the brothers, bit of a playboy, with a taste for young girls. He managed to get a fourteen-year-old girl from the neighbouring town of Barranquilla pregnant and Javier shipped him off to Cape Town to avoid trouble. He needed someone here he could trust. To oversee his operations. Because, by 2001, the Guajira Cartel, as they are now known, had gone truly international. And they had branched out into the whole spectrum of drugs.

'Carlos was doing okay. He kept out of trouble, managed his side of the business reasonably well with the help of a team very loyal to Javier – the four guys we have in custody. And then he got into the mess with the prostitute's daughter. And now, as you know, Carlos is dead.

'Enter César Sangrenegra. *El Muerte*. The Death, they call him. If Javier is the brains of the cartel, César is its strong arm. He is a killer. Rumour has it that he has executed more than three hundred people in the last ten years. And we're not talking about ordering the death of opponents. We're talking about personally twisting the knife.'

The last photographs came out of the envelope. Lombardi spread them over the desk. Men with amputated genitals pushed into their mouths. The bodies of women with breasts removed.

'And this is the necktie method. See how the tongue is pulled through the slit throat. *El Muerte* is one sick puppy. He is big and strong and very, very fit. He is totally ruthless. Some say he is a sociopath. When his name is whispered in Guajira, people tremble.'

'So what's he doing in Cape Town?' Matt Joubert asked.

'That's why we're here,' said Boef Beukes.

'You see, there is a simple code in the Guajira,' said Lombardi. 'When someone takes from you – money, possessions, or whatever – it is said that he walks with *culebras* on his back. It means "snakes". He walks with a snake on his back, a poisonous thing that can strike at any time, which keeps him looking over his shoulder in fear. The *guajiro* unconditionally believe in *justicia*. Justice. Revenge.'

'So what are you saying?' asked Griessel.

'I am saying that you, Inspector Griessel, will be held responsible for Carlos's death. You, the spearman and the prostitute. You are all walking with *culebras* on your backs.'

The detective inspector with the snake on his back was going to be late. He packed his suitcase in too much of a hurry and when he reached the kitchen he grabbed the brandy bottle from the cupboard and put it in as well.

He tore a sheet of paper from his notebook and wrote a thank-you note to Charmaine Watson-Smith in an untidy scrawl. For a moment he thought that the only rhyme he knew began with, 'There was a young man from Australia . . .' He couldn't remember the rest, but it didn't matter, as it wasn't exactly relevant.

He put the clean dish down at her door and hurried to the entrance of the block of flats. As he walked he realised what was happening to Charmaine's newspaper to make it disappear. He stopped in his tracks, turned and jogged back to her door and knocked. He picked up the dish.

It was a while before she opened.

'Why, Inspector . . .'

'Madam, I'm sorry, I have to catch a flight. I just wanted to say thank you. And I know what happens to your newspaper.'

'Oh?' she said and took the dish.

'Someone takes it when they are going out. They take it with them. In the morning.'

'My goodness . . .'

'I have to run. I will look into it when I get back.'

'Thank you, Inspector.'

'No, madam, thank you. That . . .' and for a moment he couldn't think what the English word was. He wanted to say 'sheep's meat' although he knew it was incorrect. '. . . Lamb, that lamb was wonderful.' He jogged back to the front entrance and thought he had better hurry, because now he *was* late.

When the second brandy and Coke flooded through him like a heavenly heat wave, he leaned back in the seat of the plane and sighed deeply in pleasure. He was a fuck-up, a drunk, but that was that – he was born to drink, made for drink. That was what he did best, that was when he felt whole and right and one with the universe. Then the rhyme came back to him.

> *There was a young man from Australia*
> *Who painted his arse like a dahlia.*
> *The colours were bright,*
> *And the look was all right*
> *But the smell was a hell of a failure.*

He grinned and wondered how many others he could remember, now that his brain was working again. He could rattle them off in his jokester days. *There was a young man from Brazil, who swallowed a dynamite pill . . .* Perhaps he should compose one about himself. *A detective inspector who drank. . . .*

He took another swallow from the bloody small plastic airline cup with its two blocks of ice and thought, no,

> *There was a dumb cop from the Cape,*
> *Who let a black spearman escape.*

The stewardess approached from the front and he held his glass up and tapped an index finger on it. She nodded, but didn't seem extremely friendly. Probably afraid he would get paralytically drunk on her plane. She with her hair combed back and little red mouth, she could relax; he might be a wife-beating, whore-fucking fuck-up of a policeman, but he could hold his drink, daddio. That was one thing he could do with great, well-oiled skill.

> *He thought he was white,*
> *And that's not all right.*

But what the fuck rhymed with 'Cape' and 'Escape'? All he could think of was 'rape'. Maybe he should start over; here came the stewardess with his next drink.

> *On his back's not a snake, but an ape.*

'Sir, are you all right?' asked the woman at Budget Rent-a-Car with a slight frown and he said: 'As right as rain,' and he signed flamboyantly next to every fucking cross she made on the document. She gave him the keys and he walked out into the windy evening in Port Elizabeth. He thought he ought to turn on his bloody cell phone, but, first, find the car. Then again, why turn on the phone? He was relieved of his responsibilities, wasn't he?

They had given him a Nissan Almera, that's what it said on the tag on the keys. He couldn't find the fucking car. Suitcase in hand he walked down the rows of cars. The whole lot were white, almost. He couldn't recall what an Almera looked like. He used to have a Sentra, a demonstration model he had bought at Schus in Bellville for a helluva bargain, never had any shit with that car. Jissis, it was a lifetime ago. Here was the fucking Almera, right here under his nose. He pressed the button on the key and the car said 'beep' and the lights flashed. He unlocked the boot and put his suitcase away. Maybe turn on the phone, they might have caught the guy by now.

He had to lean against the car. He had to admit he was a bit tipsy.

YOU HAVE THREE MESSAGES. PLEASE CALL 121.

He pressed the tabs. A woman's voice. 'You have three new voice messages. First message . . .'

'Benny, it's Anna. Where are you? Carla isn't home yet. We don't know where she is. If you are sober, phone me.'

What time had Anna phoned? It was sometime in the afternoon that he had switched the phone off. Why did she sound so panicky?

'This is Tim Ngubane. The time is now twenty forty-nine. Just wanted to let you know Christine van Rooyen is missing, Benny. Witness Protection called me. She walked out on them, apparently. They kept her in a house in Boston, and she's just gone. Will keep you posted. Bye.'

She walked out on them? Now why would she do that? He pressed seven to delete the message.

'Benny, it's Anna. I talked to Matt Joubert. He says you have gone to PE. Call me, please. Carla is still not home. We have phoned everyone. I am very worried. Call me when you get this message. Please!'

There was despair in Anna's voice that penetrated through his alcoholic haze, that made him realise this was trouble. He pressed nine and cut the connection. He leaned against the Almera. He couldn't phone her, because he was drunk.

Where was Carla? Jissis, he had to get some coffee or something, he had to sober up fast. He got in the car. The driver's seat was shifted right up to the steering wheel, he had to feel around for the lever underneath before he could get in. At last he got the car going.

Not so very drunk, he just had to concentrate. He pulled away, must get to the hotel. Drink some coffee. And walk, keep walking until the haze lifted, then he could phone Anna; she mustn't hear he had been drinking. She would know. Seventeen fucking years' experience – she would catch him out at the speed of white light. He should never have had those drinks. He had even packed the bottle. He was ready to start drinking full bore again and now Carla was missing and a suspicion began to grow in him and he didn't want to think of it.

Cell phone rang.

He checked. It wasn't Anna.

Who was phoning him at eleven at night?

He would have to pull over. He wasn't sober enough to drive and talk.

'Griessel.'

'Is that Detective Inspector Benny Griessel?' The 'g' was spoken softly and in a vaguely familiar accent.

'Yes.'

'Okay. Detective Inspector Griessel, you will have to listen very carefully now, because this is very important. Are you listening very carefully?'

'Who is this?'

'I will ask again: are you listening very carefully?'

'Yes.'

'I understand you are hunting the killer of Carlos Sangrenegra. This is so?'

'Yes.' His heart was racing.

'Okay. This is good. Because you must bring him to me. You understand?'

'Who are you?'

'I am the man who has your daughter, Detective Inspector. I have her here with me. Now, you must listen very, very carefully. I have people who work with you. I know everything. I know if you do a stupid thing, you understand? When you do a stupid thing, I will cut off a finger of Carla, you understand? If you tell other police I have your daughter, I will cut her, you understand?'

'Yes.' He forced out the words with great effort; thoughts were scrabbling through his brain.

'Okay. I will call you. Every day. In the morning and in the afternoon, I will call you, for three days. You must find this man who kill Carlos, and you must bring him to me.'

'I don't know where you are . . .' Panic overflowed into his voice, he couldn't stop it.

'You are scared. That is good. But you must be calm. When I call you and you tell me you have this man, I will tell you where to go, you understand?'

'Yes.'

'Three days. You have three days to get this man. Then I will kill her. Okay, now I have to do something, because I know people. Tomorrow, you think you are more clever than this phone man. So I have to do something to let you remember tomorrow, okay?'

'Okay.'

'Carla is here with me. We take her clothes. Your daughter has a good body. I like her tits. Now, I will put this knife in her tit. It will hurt, and it will bleed. But I want you to listen. This is the thing I want you to remember. This sound.'

PART THREE
Thobela

41

'I will leave you to it,' said Sangrenegra and walked away from him.

Thobela said his name. 'Carlos.' The lone word echoed around the interior of the large room. The Colombian turned.

Thobela swiftly and deftly drew the assegai by the shaft out of the white swimming-pool pipe. 'I am here about the girl,' he said.

'No,' said Carlos.

He said nothing, just stepped closer to where the man stood beside the pool.

'She lie,' said Carlos walking backwards.

He adjusted his grip on the assegai.

'Please,' said Carlos. 'I did not touch the girl.' He raised empty hands in front of him. Terror distorted his face. 'Please. She lie. The whore, she lie.'

Fury washed over him. At the man's cowardice, his denial, everything he represented. He moved fast, raised the assegai high.

'The police . . .' said Carlos, and the long blade descended.

Christine saw the minister's eyes were red-rimmed and tired, but she knew she still held his attention.

She rose from her chair and leaned over the desk. When she stood like that, slightly bent over, arms stretched out to the cardboard carton, her breasts were prominent. She was aware of it, but also that it didn't matter any more. She pulled the box to her side of the desk and folded the flaps open.

'I have to explain this now,' she said and reached into the carton. She took out two newspaper clippings. She unfolded one. She glanced briefly at the photograph and article on it, specifically at the young girl emerging from a helicopter with a man. She put the clipping down on the desk and smoothed it with her hand.

'This is my fault,' she said, and rotated the article so that the minister could see better. She tapped a fingertip on the photo. 'Her name is Carla Griessel,' said Christine.

While the minister looked she reached for the second clipping.

He came out of Sangrenegra's front door and in the corner of his eye he spotted a movement. Opposite, in the big house, behind a window. The discomfort of Carlos's reaction, the Colombian's choice of words and the overwhelming feeling of being watched unfolded in his belly.

Something wasn't right.

Five objects lay on the desk in an uneven row. The two newspaper clippings were on the far right. Then the brown and white dog, a stuffed toy with big, soft eyes and a little red tongue hanging out of the smiling mouth. Next the small white plastic container with medicinal contents. And last on the left, a large syringe.

Christine shifted the box to the left again. It was not yet empty.

'The next morning, after Carlos had seen Sonia for the first time, I phoned Vanessa.'

He braked with screeching tyres next to his pick-up, grabbed the white pipe holding his assegai and leapt out.

Slowly, his head told him. Slowly. Do the right thing.

He unlocked his pick-up, tilted the backrest forward and put the pipe behind it. He unzipped his sports bag, looking for an item of clothing. He took out a blue and white T-shirt. He had bought it at the motorbike training centre at Amersfoort. One each for himself and Pakamile. He walked back to the swimming-pool van.

A siren approached, he wasn't sure from which side, not sure how close. Adrenaline made his heart jump.

Slowly. He wiped the panel van's steering wheel with the T-shirt. The gear lever.

The siren was closer.

The inside door handle. The window winder.

What else?

Another siren, from somewhere in the city.

What else had he touched? Rear-view mirror? He wiped but he was in a hurry, didn't do it properly.

Slowly. He wiped it again, back and front of the mirror.

His eye caught the speck of the helicopter in the blue sky where it came around Devil's Peak.

They were after him.

When he raced away from Sangrenegra's house, just before he turned the corner at the bottom of the street, he had seen something in the rear-view mirror. Or had he?

They were on to him.

He cursed in Xhosa, a single syllable. A walker came around the bend, down the slope from the Signal Hill side.

He took four long strides to get to his pick-up.

'I didn't know how the whole thing would end,' she said to the minister, to try and justify what she was yet to tell him. She listened to the lack of intonation in her voice. She was aware of her fatigue, as if she didn't have the strength for the final straight. It was because she had gone through it so many times in her head, she told herself.

The first time she had seen the clipping, the eyes of Carla Griessel and the terrible knowledge that it was all her fault and also the relief that she still had the ability to feel guilt and remorse. After everything. After all the lies. After all the deception. All the years. She could still feel someone else's pain. Still feel compassion. Still feel pity for someone besides herself. And the guilt that she felt that relief.

She took a deep breath to gather her strength, because this explanation was the one that mattered.

'I was afraid,' she said. 'You have to understand that. I was terrified. The way Carlos looked at Sonia . . . I thought I knew him. That was one of the problems. I know men. I *had* to know them. And Carlos was the naughty child. Sort of harmless. He was nagging and possessive and jealous, but he wanted so much to please. He had my clients beaten up, but he never did the hitting himself. Up to that moment I still thought I could control him. That's the main thing. With all the men. To be in control without them knowing it. But then I saw his face. And I knew, everything I had thought was wrong. I didn't know him. I had no control over him. And I panicked. Totally.

'I . . . It wasn't like I worked out a plan or anything. There was just all this stuff in my head. The Artemis guy and the stuff in Carlos's house, the drugs and all, and the panic over the way he looked at Sonia. I think if a person is really scared, like terrified, then a part of your brain starts working that you don't know about, it takes over. I don't know if you understand that, because you have to *be* there.

'I phoned Carlos and said I wanted to talk to him.'

He drove with the radio on. He deliberately chose alternate routes and drove instinctively east, towards Wellington and through Bains Kloof, over Mitchells Pass to Ceres and via gravel roads to Sutherland.

At first he rejected the possibility that Sangrenegra might be innocent.

It was the other elements that came together first – the movement in the house opposite, the man he thought he saw running across the road in his rear-view mirror. The newspaper reports that taunted him. Carlos's words, 'The police . . .' He wanted to say something, something he knew.

They were waiting for him. They had set up an ambush and he had walked into it like a fool, like an amateur – unconcerned, overconfident.

He wondered how much they knew. Did they have a camera in that house across the street? Was his photograph on its way to the newspapers and television right now? Could he risk going home?

But he kept coming back to the possibility that Carlos was innocent.

His protestations. His face.

The big difference between Carlos and the rest, who welcomed the blade as an escape. Or justice.

Lord. If the Colombian was innocent, Thobela Mpayipheli was a murderer rather than an executioner.

Thirty kilometres west of Fraserburg, over a radio signal that came and went, he heard the news bulletin for the first time.

'A task team of the police's Serious and Violent Crime Unit was just too late to apprehend the so-called Artemis vigilante . . . set up various roadblocks in the Cape Peninsula and Boland in an apparent attempt . . . a two-thousand-and-one model Isuzu KB two-sixty with registration number . . .'

That was the moment when self-recrimination evaporated, when he knew they knew and the old battle fever revived. He had been here before. The prey. He had been hunted across the length and breadth of strange and familiar continents. He knew this, he had been trained for it by the best; they could do nothing he hadn't experienced before, *handled* before.

That was the moment he knew he was wholly back in the Struggle. Like in the old, old days when there was something worth protecting to the death. You see furthest from the moral high ground. It brought a great calm over him, so that he knew precisely what to do.

She met Carlos at the Mugg & Bean at the Waterfront. She watched him coming towards her with his self-satisfied strut, arms swinging gaily, head half cocked. Like an overgrown boy that has got his own way. Fuck you Carlos; you have no idea.

'So how's your daughter, conchita?' he said with a smirk as he sat down.

She had to light a cigarette to hide her fear.

'She's fine.' Curtly.

'Ah, conchita, don't be angry. It is your fault. You hide things from Carlos. All Carlos wants to do is to know you, to care for you.'

She said nothing, just looked at him.

'She is very beautiful. Like her mother. She have your eyes.' And he thought that would make her feel better?

'Carlos, I will give you what you want.'

'What I want?'

'You don't want me to see other clients. You don't want me to hide things from you. Is that right?'

'*Sí*. That is right.'

'I will do that, but there are certain rules.'

'Carlos will take good care of you and the leetle conchita. You know that.'

'It's not the money, Carlos.'

'Anything, conchita. What you want?'

He drove from Merweville across the arid expanses of the Great Karoo to Prince Albert as the sun set in spectacular colours.

According to the radio they thought he was still in the Cape.

In the dark of night he crossed the Swartberg Pass and cautiously descended to Oudtshoorn. On the odd one-lane tarred road between Willowmore and Steytlerville he recognised that fatigue had the better of him and he looked out for a place to turn off and sleep. He shifted into a more comfortable position on the front seat and closed his eyes. At half-past three in the morning he slept, only to wake at first light, stiff-limbed, scratchy-eyed, his face needing a wash.

At Kirkwood, in the grimy toilets of a garage, he brushed his teeth and splashed cold water on his face. This was Xhosa country and no one looked twice at him. He bought take-away chicken portions at Chicken Licken and drove. Towards home.

At half-past ten he crossed the Hogsback Pass and thirty-five minutes later he turned in at the farm entrance and saw the tracks on the reddish-brown dirt of the road.

He got out.

Only one vehicle. Narrow tyres of a small sedan. In. Not yet out. Someone was waiting for him.

'My daughter's name is Sonia.'

'That is very beautiful.' Like he really meant it.

'But I will not bring her to your house, Carlos. We can go somewhere together. Picnic, or the movies, but not to your house.'

'But, conchita, I have this pool . . .'

'And you have these bodyguards with guns and baseball bats. I will not allow my daughter to see that.'

'They are not bodyguards. They are my crew.'

'I don't care.'

'Hokay, hokay, Carlos will send them away when you come.'

'You won't.'

'No? Why not?'

'Because they are with you all the time.'

'No, conchita, I swear,' he said, and made the sign of the cross over his upper body.

'When my daughter is with me, I don't sleep with you and we don't sleep over. That is final.'

'Carlos unnerstand,' he said, but couldn't hide his disappointment.

'And we will take it slowly. I have to talk to her about you first. She must get used to you slowly.'

'Hokay.'

'So, tomorrow night, we will see if you are serious. I will come to your house and it will only be you and me. No bodyguards.'

'*Sí*. Of course.'

'I will stay with you. I will cook for you and we will talk.'

'Where will Sonia be?'

'She will be safe.'

'At the nanny's place?' Pleased with himself, because he knew. 'Yes.'

'And maybe the weekend, we can go somewhere? You and me and Sonia?'

'If I see I can trust you, Carlos.' But she knew she had him. She knew the process had begun.

42

Thobela left his pick-up behind the ridges at the Waterval Plantation and walked along the bank of the Cata River towards his house, assegai in his left hand.

A kilometre before the homestead came into view he turned northeast, so he could approach from the high ground. They would be expecting him from the road end.

He sat watching for twenty minutes, but saw only the car parked in front of the house. No antennae, nothing to identify it as a police vehicle. Silence.

It made no sense.

He kept the shed between him and the house, checking that the doors were still locked. Crouching, he approached the house, below window level, to where the car was parked.

There was one set of footprints in the dust. They began at the driver's door and led directly to the steps of the front veranda.

One man.

He ran through alternatives in his head while he squatted on his haunches with his back to the veranda wall. Something occurred to him. The detective from Umtata. Must have heard the news. Knew him, knew everything, from the start.

The detective had come for more money.

He stood, relieved and purposeful, and strode up his veranda steps and in at the front door, assegai now in his right hand.

The man was sitting there on the chair, pistol on his lap.

'I thought you would come,' said the white man.

'Who are you?'

'My name is Benny Griessel,' he said and raised the Z88 so that it pointed straight at Thobela's chest.

Christine took the stuffed toy dog from the desk and held it in her hands. 'I had a battle to get the right dog,' she said. 'Every year there are different toys in the shops.'

Her fingers stroked the long brown ears. 'I bought her one when she was three years old. It's her favourite, she won't go anywhere without it. So I had to get another and switch them, because the one she played with had her genetics on it. The police computers can test anything. So I had to take the right one along.'

He stood in front of the white man weighing up his chances, measuring the distance between the assegai and the pistol, and then he allowed himself to relax, because now was not the moment to do anything.

'This is my house,' he said.

'I know.'

'What do you want?'

'I want you to sit there and be quiet.' The white man motioned with the barrel of the Z88 towards the two-seater couch opposite him. There was something about his eyes and voice: intensity, a determination.

Thobela hesitated, shrugged and sat down. He looked at Griessel. Who was he? The bloodshot eyes, a hint of capillaries on the nose that betrayed excessive drinking. Hair long and untidy – either he was trying to keep the look of his youth in the seventies alive, or he didn't care. The latter seemed more likely, since his clothes were rumpled, the comfortable brown shoes dull. He had the faint scent of law enforcement about him and the Z88 confirmed it, but policemen usually came in groups, at least in pairs. Police waited with handcuffs and commands, they didn't ask you to sit down in your own house.

'I'm sitting,' he said, and placed the assegai on the floor beside the couch.

'Now you just have to be quiet.'

'Is that what we are going to do? Sit and stare at each other?'

The white man did not answer.

'Will you shoot me if I talk?'

No response.

'The pills were easy,' said Christine. She indicated the white medicinal container on the desk. 'And the dress. I don't have it; it's with the police. But the blood . . . I couldn't do it at first. I didn't know how to tell my child I had to push a needle into her arm and that it would hurt and the blood would run into the syringe and I had to spray it on the seat of a man's car. That was the hardest thing. And I was worried. I didn't know whether the blood would clot. I didn't know if it would be enough. I didn't know if the police would be able to tell it wasn't fresh blood. I didn't know how they did all those genetics. Would the computer be able to tell the blood had been in the fridge for a day?'

She held the dog against her chest. She didn't look at the minister. She looked at her fingers entangled in the toy's ears.

'When Sonia was in the bath, I went in and I lied to her. I said we had to do it, because I had to take a little bit of her blood to the doctor. When she asked, "Why?" I didn't know what to say. I asked her if she remembered the vaccination she had at play school so she wouldn't get those bad diseases. She said, "Mamma, it was sore", and I said, "But the sore went away quickly – this sore will also go away quickly, it's the same thing, so you can be well." So she said, "Okay, Mamma" and she squeezed her eyes shut and held out her arm. I have never drawn blood from someone before, but if you are a whore, you have your AIDS test every month, so I know what they do. But if your child says, "Ow, Mamma, ow", then you get the shakes and it's hard and you get a fright if you can't get the blood . . .'

'What are we waiting for? What do you want?' he asked. But the man just sat and looked at him, with his pistol hand resting on his lap, and said nothing. Just the eyes blinking now and again, or drifting off to the window.

He wondered whether the man was right in the head. Or on drugs, because of that terrible intensity, something eating him. The eyes were never completely still. Sometimes a knee would jerk as if it were a wound spring. The pistol had its own fine vibration, an almost unnoticeable movement.

Unstable. Therefore dangerous. Would he make it, if he could pull himself up by the armrest and launch himself over the little more than two metres between them? If he picked a moment when the eyes flicked to the window? If he could deflect the Z88?

He measured the distance. He looked into the brown eyes.

No.

But what were they sitting here and waiting for? In such tension?

He had partial answers later when the cell phone rang twice. Each time the white man started, a subtle tautening of the body. He lifted the phone from his lap and then just sat dead still, and let it ring. Until it stopped. Fifteen, twenty seconds later it beeped twice to show a message had been left. But Griessel did nothing about it. He didn't listen to his messages.

They were waiting for instructions; that much Thobela gathered. Which would be delivered via the cell phone. The intensity was stress. Anxiety. But why? What did it have to do with him?

'Are you in trouble?'

Griessel just stared at him.

'Can I help you in some way?'

The man glanced at the window, and back again.

'Do you mind if I sleep a bit?' asked Thobela. Because that was all he could do. And he needed it.

No reaction.

He made himself comfortable, stretched his long legs out, rested his head on the cushion of the couch and closed his eyes.

But the cell phone rang again and this time the white man pressed the answer button and said; 'Griessel' and, 'Yes, I have him.' He listened. He said: 'Yes.'

And again: 'Yes.' Listened. 'And then?'

Thobela could hear a man's voice faintly over the phone, but couldn't make out any words, just the grain of a voice.

Griessel took the cell phone away from his ear and stood, keeping a safe distance.

'Come,' he said. 'Let's go.'

'I'm very comfortable, thank you.'

A shot thundered through the quiet of the room and the bullet ripped a hole beside him in the couch. Stuffing and dust exploded from it, falling back to the floor in slow motion. Thobela looked at the white man, who said nothing. Then he got up, keeping his hands away from his body.

'Easy now,' he said to Griessel.

'To the car.'

He went.

'Wait.'

He looked back. Griessel stood beside the assegai. He looked at it, looked at him, as if he had to make a decision. Then he bent and picked it up.

Thobela drew his own conclusions. The man didn't want to leave any evidence. And that was not good news.

He was supposed to pick her up at half-past four, but at a quarter past there was a knock on the door; when she opened up, there stood Carlos with a big smile and a bunch of flowers.

He came inside and said, 'So, conchita, this is where you live. This is your place. It is nice. Very nice.'

She had to remain calm and friendly, but the tension was overwhelming. Because the toy dog was lying in sight and the syringe of blood was still in the fridge.

She wanted to hide it in the shopping bags along with the ingredients for the meal she was going to cook. Sonia's dress was folded up in her handbag. Carlos wanted to see where she slept, where her daughter's room was. He was impressed with the big television screen (Carlos will get you one like this, conchita. For you and Sonia.') He wandered over to her fridge. 'Now dees ees a freedge,' he said in awe, and as he reached for the handle and pulled, she said, 'Carlos,' sharply, so that the sound of her voice gave her a fright and he looked around like a child who had been naughty.

'Will you help me to get the groceries to the car, please?' She could send him down to the car with a few of the plastic bags.

'*Sí*. Of course. What are you going to cook for us?'

'It's a surprise, so don't open the fridge.'

'But I want to see how big it is.'

'Another time.' There wouldn't be one.

The white man sat in the left back seat of the car and let Thobela drive.

'Go.'

'Where?'

'Just drive.'

Thobela took the farm road out. He couldn't see in the rear-view mirror what was happening on the back seat. He turned his head, as if he had seen something outside the car. At the edge of his vision he saw Griessel with a roadmap on his lap.

He added up what he knew. He was reasonably certain Griessel was a policeman. The Z88, the attitude. The white man had known where the farm was and that Thobela would be on his way there. More important: no other policemen had shown up. The law considered the farm covered.

Griessel had waited for the right call to come over the cell phone. *Yes. I have him.* But that was not police procedure. Couldn't be.

Who else was after him? To whom else did he have value?

'Go to George,' said Griessel. Thobela looked around, saw the roadmap was folded now.

'George?'

'You know where it is.'

'It's nearly six hundred kilometres.'

'You drove more than a thousand yesterday.'

The policeman knew he had left the Cape yesterday. He had access to official information, but he wasn't official. It didn't make sense. He would have to try something. He could do something with the car on the gravel road because he was wearing a seatbelt and Griessel was not. He could brake suddenly and grab the man when he was thrown forward. Try and get the pistol.

Not without risks.

Was the risk necessary? George? What was at George? If the policeman had been official they would have been on the way to Cathcart or Seymour or Alice or Port Elizabeth. Or Grahamstown. To the nearest place with reinforcements and cells and state prosecutors.

He was a high-profile suspect; he knew that. If you were SAPS and you caught the Artemis vigilante, then you called the guys with guns and helicopters, you didn't get off your cell phone until you had your detainee in ten sets of handcuffs.

Unless you were working for someone else. Unless you were supplementing your income . . .

He considered the alternatives and there was only one logical conclusion.

'How long have you been working for Sangrenegra?' He turned the mirror with his left hand. Bloodshot eyes stared back. He got no response.

'That's the problem with this country. Money means more than justice,' he said.

'Is that how you justify your murders?' said the policeman from behind.

'Murder? There was only one murder. I didn't know Sangrenegra was innocent. It was you people who used him for an ambush.'

'Sangrenegra? How do you know he was innocent?'

'I saw it in his eyes.'

'And Bernadette Laurens? What did her eyes tell you?'

'Laurens?'

The policeman said nothing.

'But she confessed.'

'That's what they all keep telling me.'

'But it wasn't her?'

'I don't think it was. I think she was protecting the child's mother. Like others would protect their children.'

The unexpectedness of it left Thobela dumb.

'That's why we have a justice system. A process. That is why we can't take the law into our own hands,' said Griessel.

Thobela wrestled with the possibility, with rationalising and acceptance of guilt. But he couldn't tip the scales either way.

'So why did she confess then?' he asked himself, but aloud.

There was no response from the back seat.

43

While they carried the shopping bags into Carlos's kitchen, she could think of nothing but the syringe of blood.

The house was unnaturally quiet and empty without the bodyguards; the large spaces echoed footsteps and phrases. He embraced her in the kitchen after they had put the groceries down. He pressed her to him with surprising tenderness and said: 'This is right, conchita.'

She made her body soft. She let her hips flow against his. 'Yes,' she said.

'We will be happy.'

In answer she kissed him on the mouth, with great skill, until she could feel his erection developing. She put her hand on it and traced the shape. Carlos's hands were behind her back. He pulled her dress up inch by inch until her bottom was exposed and slipped his fingers under the elastic of her panties. His breathing quickened.

She moved her lips over his cheek, down his neck, over the cross that hung in his chest hair. Her tongue left a damp trail. She freed herself and dropped to her knees, fingers busy with his zipper. With one hand she pulled his underpants down and with the other she pulled his penis out. Long, thin and hairy, it stood up like a lean soldier with an outsized shiny helmet.

'Conchita.' His voice was a whispering urgency, as she had never done this without a condom before.

She stroked with both hands, from the pubic hairs to the tip.

'We will be happy,' she said and softly put it in her mouth.

Thobela Mpayipheli and his white passenger, sitting in the back like a colonial property baron, drove past Mwangala and Dyamala, where fat cattle grazed in the sweet green grass. They turned right onto the R63. Fort Hare was quiet over the summer holidays. Five minutes later they were in busy Alice. Fruit vendors on the pavements, women with baskets on their heads and children on their backs who walked stately and unhurried across the road and down the street. Four men were gathered around a board game on a street corner. Thobela wondered if the policeman saw all this. If he could hear the Xhosa calls that were exchanged across the broad street. This was ownership. The people owned this place.

Thirty kilometres on was Fort Beaufort and he turned south. Four or five times he spotted the Kat River on the left where it meandered away between the hills. It had been one of his plans to bring Pakamile here: just the two of them with rucksacks, hiking boots and a two-man tent. To show his boy where he had grown up.

Thobela knew every bend of the Kat. He knew the deep pools at Nkqantosi where you could jump off the cliff and open your eyes deep under the greenish-brown water and see the sunbeams fighting against the darkness. The little sandy beach below Komkulu. Where he had discovered the warrior inside him thirty years before. Mtetwa, the young buffalo who was a bully, an injustice he had to correct. The first.

And far over that way, out of sight, his favourite place. Four kilometres from the place where it flowed into the Great Fish River, the Kat made a flamboyant curve, as if it wanted to dally one last time before losing its identity – a meander that swept back so far that it almost made an island. It was about ten kilometres from the Mission Church manse where he lived, but he could run there in an hour down the secret game paths around the hills and through the valleys. All so he could sit between the reeds where the chattering weaverbirds in brilliant colour lured females to their hanging nests. To listen to the wind. To watch the fat iguana warming itself in the sun on the black rocky point. In the late afternoon the bushbuck came out of the thickets like phantoms to dip their heads to the water. First the grace of the does in their red glowing coats. Later the rams would come two by two, dark brown in the dusk, sturdy, short, needle-sharp horns that rose and dipped, rose and dipped.

He had wondered if they were still there. Whether he and his son would see the descendants of the animals he had waited for with bated breath as a child. Did they still follow the same paths through the reeds and bulrushes?

Would he still know the paths? Should he stop here, take off his shoes and disappear between the thorn trees? Search out the same paths at a jogtrot; find that rhythm when you felt you could run for ever, as long as there was a hill on the horizon for you to climb?

While Carlos was seated in front of the TV with a glass and a bottle of red wine, she took the syringe of blood out of her handbag and hid it deep in a cupboard where pots and pans were stacked, bright, new and unused.

She looked for a hiding place for the toy dog before she took it out from under packs of vegetables in the shopping bags.

Her hands shook because she would not hear Carlos coming before he was in the room.

They drove in silence for two hours. Beyond Grahamstown, in the dark of early evening, he said: 'Did you ever hear of Nxele?' His tongue clicked sharply pronouncing the name.

He did not expect an answer. If he did get one he knew what it would be. White people didn't know this history.

'Nxele. They say he was a big man. Two metres tall. And he could talk. Once he talked himself off a Xhosa execution pyre. And then he became chief, without having the blood of kings.'

He didn't care if the white man was listening or not. He kept his eyes on the road. He wanted to shake off his lassitude, say what this landscape awakened in him. He wanted to relieve the tension somehow.

'Exceptional in that time, nearly two hundred years ago. He lived in a time when the people fought against each other – and the English too. Then Nxele came and said they must stop kneeling to the white God. They must listen to the voice of Mdalidiphu, the

God of the Xhosa, who said you must not kneel before Him in the dust. You must live. You must dance. You must lift your head and grab hold of life. You must sleep with your wife so we can increase, so we can fill the earth and drive the white man out. So we can take back our land.

'You could say he was the father of the first Struggle. Then he gathered ten thousand warriors together. Did you see where we travelled today, Griessel? Did you see? Can you imagine what ten thousand warriors would look like coming over these hills? They smeared themselves red with ochre. Each had six or seven long throwing spears in his hand and a shield. They ran here like that. Nxele told them to be silent, no singing or shouting. They wanted to surprise the English here at Grahamstown. Ten thousand warriors in step, their footsteps the only sound. Through the valleys and over the rivers and hills like a long red snake. Imagine you are an Englishman in Grahamstown waking up one morning in April and looking up to the hills. One moment things look as they do every day, and the next moment this army materialises on the hilltops and you see the glint of seventy thousand spears, but there is no sound. Like death.

'Nxele moved through them. He told them to break one of their long spears over their knees. He said Mdalidiphu would turn the British bullets to water. They must charge the cannons and guns together and throw the long spears when they got close enough. And they could throw, those men. At a range of sixty metres they could launch a spear through the air and find the heart of an Englishman. When the last long spear had been thrown, they must hold the spear with the broken shaft. Nxele knew you couldn't use a long spear when you could see the whites of your enemy's eyes. Then you needed a weapon to stab open a path in front of you.

'They say it was a clear day. They said the English couldn't believe the way the Xhosa moved up there on the crest. Deathly quiet. But each knew exactly where his place in line was.

'Down below, the Redcoats erected their barriers. Up there, the red men waited for the signal. And when the whites sat down at their tables laid for midday dinner, they came down.

'From the time I first heard that story from my uncle I wanted to be with them, Griessel. They said that when the warriors charged, a terrible cry went up. They say that cry is in every soldier. When you are at war, when your blood is high in battle, then it comes out. It explodes from your throat and gives you the strength of an elephant and the speed of an antelope. They say every man is afraid until that moment, and then there is no more fear. Then you are pure fighter and nothing can stop you.

'All my life I wanted to be a part of them. I wanted to be there at the front. I wanted to throw my spears and keep the short assegai for last. I wanted to smell the gunpowder and the blood. They said the stream in town ran red with blood that day. I wanted to look an Englishman in the eyes and he must lift his bayonet and we must oppose each other as soldiers, each fighting for his cause. I wanted to make war with honour. If his blade was faster than mine, if his strength was greater, then so be it. Then I would die like a man. Like a warrior.'

He was quiet for a long time. A distance past the turnoff to Bushmans River Mouth he said: 'There is no honour any more. It makes no difference what Struggle you choose.'

Again silence descended on the car, but it felt to Thobela as if the character of the silence had changed.

'What happened, that day?' Griessel's voice came from the back.

Thobela smiled in the darkness. For many reasons.

'It was a tremendous battle. The English had cannon and guns. Shrapnel shells. A thousand Xhosa fell. Some of them they found days later, miles away, with bunches of grass pushed into their gaping wounds to stem the bleeding. But it was a close thing. There was time in the battle when the balance began to swing in favour of the Xhosa. The ranks of Nxele were too fast and too many, the English could not reload quickly enough. Time stood still. The battle was on a knife edge. Then the Redcoats got their miracle. His name was Boesak, can you believe it? He was a Khoi big-game hunter turned soldier. He was out on patrol with a hundred and thirty men and they came back, on that day. At just the right time for the English, when the British captain was ready to sound the retreat. Boesak and a hundred and thirty of the best marksmen in the country. And they aimed for the biggest warriors, the Xhosa who fought up front, who ran between the men and urged them on. The heart of the assault. They were shot down one by one, like bulls from the herd. And then it was all over.'

She tried to grind the pills in a flour sifter, but they were too hard.

She took the breadboard and a teaspoon and crushed the pills – some pieces shot over the floor and she began to panic. She used more pills, pressed. The teaspoon banged on the breadboard.

Would Carlos hear?

She wiped the yellow powder off the breadboard into a small dish she had set on one side. Was it fine enough?

She set the table. She couldn't find candles or candlesticks so she just put the place mats and cutlery on the table. She called Carlos to come to the table and then she brought out the food: fillet of beef stuffed with smoked oysters, baked potatoes and *petit pois*.

Carlos couldn't compliment her enough, although she knew the food wasn't that special. He was still buttering her up. 'You see, conchita, no crew. Just me and you. No problem.'

She said he must save room for dessert, pears in wine and cinnamon. And she was going to make him real Irish coffee and it was very important to her that he drink it because she had made it the way she had been taught, long ago when she worked for a caterer in Bloemfontein.

He said he would drink every drop and then they were going to make love, right here on the table.

Somewhere on the N2, fifty kilometres before Port Elizabeth, Griessel made him stop.

'Do you need a piss?'

'Yes.'

'Now's the time.'

When they had finished, standing four metres apart, the white man holding his organ in one hand and the pistol in the other, they went on their way.

At the outskirts of the city they stopped for petrol without getting out of the car.

When they passed the turnoff to Hankey and the road began to descend down to the Gamtoos Valley, Griessel spoke again: 'When I was young I played bass guitar. In a band.'

Thobela didn't know if he should respond.

'I thought that was what I wanted to do.

'Yesterday night I listened to music my son gave me. When it was finished I lay in the dark and I remembered something. I remembered the day I realised I would never be more than an average bass guitarist.

'I had finished school, it was December holidays and there was a battle of the bands at Green Point. We went to listen, the guys from my band and me. There was this bassist, short with snow-white hair in one or other of the rock bands that played other people's songs. Jissis, he was a magician. Standing stock-still, not moving his body in the slightest. He didn't even look at the neck, just stood there with closed eyes and his fingers flew and the sounds came out like a river. Then I realised where my place was. I saw someone who had been born for bass guitar. Fuck, I could tell we felt the same. The music did the same inside; it opened you up. But feeling and doing are not the same thing. That is the tragedy. You want to be like *that*, so fucking casually brilliant, but you don't have it in you.

'So I knew I would never be a real bass guitarist, but I wanted to be like that in something. That good. So . . . skilful. In something. I began to wonder how you found it. How did you start to search for the thing you were made for? What if there wasn't one? What if you were just an average fucker in everything? Born average and living your average life and then you fucking die and no one knows the difference.

'While I was searching I joined the police, because what I didn't know is that you know without knowing. Something deep in your head directs you to what you *can* do. But it took me a while.

Because I didn't think being a policeman was something you could feel, like music.

'Also, it doesn't happen just like that. You have to pay your dues, you have to learn, make your own mistakes. But one day you sit with a case file that makes no sense to any other fucker, and you read the statements and the notes and the reports and it all comes together. And you feel this thing inside. You hear the music of it, you pick up its rhythm deep inside you and you know this is what you were made for.'

Thobela heard the white man sigh. He wanted to tell him he understood.

'And then nothing can stop you,' said Griessel. 'Nobody. Except yourself.

'Everyone thinks you're good. They tell you. "Fuck it, Benny, you're the best. Jissis, pal, you're red hot." And you want to believe it, because you can see they are right, but there is this little voice inside you that says you are just a Parow Arrow who was never really good at anything. An average little guy. And sooner or later they will catch you out. One day they will expose you and the world will laugh because you thought you were something.

'So, before it happens, you have to expose yourself. Destroy yourself. Because if you do it yourself, then you at least have a sort of control over it.'

There was a noise behind, almost a laugh. 'Fucking tragic.'

44

He fell asleep at the table. She saw it coming. Carlos's tongue began to drag more and more. He switched over to Spanish, as if she understood every word.

He leaned heavily on his place mat, eyes struggling to focus on her.

The scene played out as if she had no part in it, as if it were happening in another space and time. He had a stupid smile on his face. He mumbled.

He lowered his head interminably slowly to the tabletop. He put his palms flat on the surface. He said one last, incomprehensible word and then his breath came deep and easy. She knew she couldn't leave him like that. If his body relaxed he would fall.

She rose and came around behind him. She put her hands under his arms, entwining the fingers of her hands with his. Lifted him. He was as heavy as lead, dead weight. He made a sound and gave her a fright, not knowing if he was deeply enough asleep. She stood like that, feeling she couldn't hold him. Then she dragged him, step by step, over to the big couch. She fell back into a sitting position with Carlos on top of her.

He spoke, clear as crystal. Her body jerked. She sat still a moment, realising he was not conscious. She rolled him over her with great effort, so that he lay skew on the couch. She squirmed out from under him and stood beside the couch, breath racing, perspiration sprung out on her skin, needing badly to sit to give her legs time to recover from their trembling.

She forced herself to continue. First she called a taxi, so they could arrive sooner; she didn't know how much time she would have.

She made sure the plastic container of pills was in her handbag. She took the dog and the syringe and went down the stairs to the garage.

The BMW was locked. She swore. Went up again. She couldn't find the keys. Panic overcame her and she was conscious of how her hands shook while she searched. Until she thought to look in Carlos's trouser pocket and there they were.

Back to the garage. She pressed the button on the key and the electronic beep was sudden and shrill in the bare space. She opened the door. She shoved the toy dog under the passenger seat. Taking the syringe, she put her thumb on the depressor and aimed the point at the backrest of the rear seat. Her hand shook badly. She made a noise of frustration and put her left hand on her right wrist to stabilise it. She must get this part right. She squeezed the syringe quickly and jerked it from right to left. The dark red jet hit the material. Fine drops spattered back onto her arms and face.

She inspected her handiwork. It didn't look right. It didn't look real.

Her heart thumped. There was nothing she could do. She climbed out looking back one last time. She had forgotten nothing. Shut the door.

There were still a couple of drops in the syringe. She must get them on the dress. And put the garment somewhere in his cupboard.

He weighed up the policeman's words. He assumed the man was trying to explain why he had become corrupt. Why he was doing what he was doing.

'How did they find you?' he asked later, beyond the turnoff to Humansdrop.

'Who?'

'Sangrenegra. How did you come to work for them?'

'I don't work for Sangrenegra.'

'Who do you work for, then?'

'I work for the SAPS.'

'Not at the moment.'

It took a while for Griessel to grasp what he had said. He repeated that ironic laugh. 'You think I'm crooked. You think that's what I meant when I said . . .'

'What else?'

'I drink, that's what I do. I booze my fucking life away. My wife and children and my job and myself. I never took a cent from anyone. I never needed to. Alcohol is efficient enough if you want to fuck yourself up.'

'Then why are we driving this way – why am I not in a cell in Port Elizabeth?'

It burst out and he heard the rage and the fear in the man's voice: 'Because they've got my daughter. The brother of Carlos Sangrenegra took my daughter. And if I don't deliver you to them, they will . . .'

Griessel said no more.

Thobela had all the pieces of the jigsaw now and he didn't like the picture they made.

'What is her name?'

'Carla.'

'How old is she?'

Griessel took a long time answering, as if he wanted to ponder the meaning of the conversation. 'Eighteen.'

He realised the white man had hope, and he knew he would have, too, if he were in the same position. Because there was nothing else you could do.

'I will help you,' he said.

'I don't need your help.'

'You do.'

Griessel did not respond.

'Do you really believe they will say, "Thank you very much, here is your daughter, you may leave"?'

Silence.

'It's your decision, policeman. I can help you. But it's your decision.'

*   *   *

Eleven minutes past seven in the morning he hammered on her door, as she knew he would. She opened up and he rushed in and grabbed her arm and shook her.

'Why you do that? Why?' The pressure of his fingers hurt her and she slapped him against the head with her left hand, as hard as she could.

'Bitch!' Carlos screamed and let go of her arm and hit her over the eye with his fist. She nearly fell, but regained her balance.

'You cunt,' she screamed as loud as she could and hit out at him with her fist. He jerked his head out of the way and smacked her on the ear with an open hand. It sounded like a cannon shot in her head. She hit back, this time striking his cheekbone with her fist.

'Bitch!' he shouted again in a shrill voice. He grabbed her hands and pulled her off her feet. The back of her head hit the carpet and for a moment she was dizzy. She blinked her eyes; he was on top of her now. 'Fucking bitch.' He slapped her against the head again. She got a hand loose and scratched at him.

He grabbed her wrist and glared at her. 'You like, bitch, Carlos see you like this.'

He pinned her down with both hands above her head. 'Now you will like even more,' he said and grabbed her nightie at the bosom and jerked. The garment tore.

'Are you going to fuck me good?' she said. 'Because it will be the first time, you cunt.'

He slapped her again and she tasted blood in her mouth.

'You can't fuck. You are the world's worst fuck!'

'Shut up, bitch!'

She spat at him, spat blood and saliva on his face and shirt. He grabbed her breast and squeezed until she shrieked in pain. 'You like that, whore? You like that?'

'Yes. At least I can feel you now.'

Squeezed again. She screamed.

'Why you drug me? Why? You steal my moneys! Why?'

'I drugged you because you are such a shit lover. That's why.'

'First, I will fuck you. Then we will find the moneys.'

'Help me!' she shouted.

He pressed a hand over her mouth.

'Shut the fuck-up.'

She bit the soft part of his palm. He yelled and hit out at her again. She jerked her head away, screaming with all her might. 'Help me, please, help me!'

One of her hands came free; she struggled and punched, scratched and screamed. A man's voice came from somewhere outside, or down the corridor, she couldn't be sure. 'What's going on?'

Carlos heard. He bumped her with both hands on her chest. He stood up. He was out of breath. There was a swelling on his cheek.

'I will come back,' he said.

'Promise me you will fuck me good, Carlos. Just promise me that, you shitless cunt.' She lay on the ground, naked, bleeding and gasping. 'Just once.'

'I will kill you,' he said and stumbled towards the door. Opened it. 'You take my moneys. I will kill you.' Then he was gone.

Beyond Plettenberg Bay he asked Griessel: 'Where must you take me?'

'I will know when we get to George. They will phone again.'

She examined herself in the mirror before calling the police. She was bleeding. The left side of her face was red. It had begun to swell. There was a cut over her eyes. There were dark red finger marks on her breasts.

It looked perfect.

She took her cell phone and sat down on the couch. She looked up the number she had saved in the phone yesterday. Her fingers worked precisely. She looked down at the phone. She was rock steady.

She dropped her head, trying to feel the pain, the humiliation, the anger, hate and fear. She took a deep breath and let it out tremulously. Only a single tear at first, then another and another. Until she was crying properly. Then she pressed the call button.

It rang seven times. 'South African Police Services, Caledon Square. How can we help you?'

The policeman's phone rang while they were stopped at yet another traffic light in Knysna.

Griessel spoke quietly, swallowing his words, and Thobela could not hear what he said. The conversation lasted less than a minute.

'They want us to keep driving,' he said at last.

'Where to?'

'Swellendam.'

'Is that where they are?'

'I don't know.'

'I need to stretch my legs.'

'Get out of town first.'

'Do you think I want to escape, Griessel? Do you think I will run away from this situation?'

'I think nothing.'

'They have your daughter because I killed Sangrenegra. It's my responsibility to fix it.'

'How can you do that?'

'We'll see.'

Griessel ruminated on that, then said, 'Stop when you like.'

Seventy kilometres on, on the long sweeping curves the N2 makes between George and Mossel Bay, something dropped onto the front seat beside Thobela. When he looked down, the assegai lay there. The blade was dull in the lights of the instrument panel.

45

First came police in uniform and she was hysterically crying and screaming: 'He's got my child, he's got my child!' They got the information out of her and tried to calm her down.

More policemen arrived. They sent for an ambulance for her. Suddenly her flat was full of people. She wept uncontrollably. A first-aid man was cleaning her face while a black detective questioned her. He introduced himself as Timothy Ngubane. He sat beside her and she told her story between sobs while he wrote in his notebook and said earnestly: 'We will find her, ma'am.' Then he called out orders and then there were fewer people around.

Later the two from Social Services arrived, and then a large man with a Western Province cap. He showed no sympathy. He asked her to repeat her story. He did not take notes. There came a moment in the conversation when she realised he didn't believe her. He had a way of looking at her with a faint smile that only lasted a moment. Her heart went cold. Why wouldn't he believe her?

When she had finished he stood up and said: 'I am going to leave two men here with you. Outside your door.'

She looked at him in inquiry.

'We don't want anything to happen to you, do we?'

'But didn't you arrest Carlos?'

'We did.' The faint smile again, like someone sharing a secret.

She wanted to phone Vanessa to hear how Sonia was and she wanted to get away from here. Away from all the people and the fuss, away from the gnawing tension, because it was not over yet.

Another detective. His hair was too long and ruffled. 'My name is Benny Griessel,' he said, and he held out his hand and she took it and looked into his eyes and looked away again because of the intensity in them. As if he saw everything. He took her out onto the balcony, and asked her questions in a gentle voice, with a compassion she wanted to embrace. But she couldn't look him in the eye.

They turned off the N2 and drove into Swellendam. There was a filling station deep in the town, past a museum and guesthouses and restaurants with small-town Afrikaans names, deserted at this late hour.

When Griessel got out Thobela saw the Z88 was not in his hand. He got out too. His legs were stiff and there were cramps in the muscles of his shoulders. He stretched his limbs, feeling the depth of his fatigue, his red, burning eyes.

Griessel had the Nissan filled up. Then he came to stand next to Thobela, not speaking, just looking at him. The white man looked rough. Shadows around the eyes, deep lines in his face.

'The night is too long,' he said to Griessel.

The detective nodded. 'It's nearly over.'

Thobela nodded back.

'I want you to know we got Khoza and Ramphele,' said Griessel.

'Where?'

'They were arrested yesterday evening in Midrand.'

'Why are you telling me this?'

'Because no matter what happens tonight, I will make sure they don't get away again.'

She lay on her bed and told herself she must suppress the urge to go and lie with the detective who was asleep on her couch, because it would be for all the wrong reasons.

Griessel's cell phone rang and he answered and said, 'Yes' and 'Yes' and 'Six kilometres' and 'Yes' and 'Okay'.

Then Thobela heard him say: 'I want to hear her voice.'

Silence on the street in Swellendam. 'Carla,' said Griessel. Thobela felt a hand squeeze his heart because of the awful emotion in the white man's voice when he said: 'Daddy is coming to fetch you, you hear? Daddy is coming.'

She needed to be held. She wanted him to hold her because she was afraid. Afraid of Carlos and of the detective in the rugby cap and afraid that the whole scheme was going to collapse in on her. Afraid that Griessel would see through her with those eyes of his, that he would expose her with that energy of his. It wasn't right, because she wanted to lie with him to make him blind.

She must not do that.

She got up.

'Infanta,' said Griessel. 'Six kilometres outside town the road to Infanta turns off. There will be a car there. They will drive behind us from there.'

They got back into the Nissan, Thobela in front and Griessel behind.

'Infanta,' he heard the man say, as if the name made no sense to him.

On the instrument panel the numbers of the LCD display of the clock glowed yellow. 03:41.

He drove out of town, back to the N2.

'Turn right. Towards Cape Town.'

Over a bridge. *Breede River*, the signboard read. Then he spotted the road sign. *Malgas. Infanta.*

'This one,' said Griessel.

He put the left indicator on. Gravel road. He saw the vehicle parked there, chunky in the lights of the Nissan. A Mitsubishi Pajero. Two men stood beside it. Each with a firearm, shading eyes from the headlights with their free hands. He stopped.

Only one man approached. Thobela wound his window down. The man did not look at him, but at Griessel. 'Is this the killer?'

'Yes.'

The man was clean-shaven, including his head. There was just a small tassel of hair below his lip. He looked at Thobela. 'You die tonight.'

Thobela looked back, into his eyes.

'You the father?' Shaven Head asked Griessel and he said: 'Yes.' The man smirked. 'Your daughter has a nice little cunt.'

Griessel made a noise behind him and Thobela thought: not *now*, don't do anything now.

Shaven Head laughed. Then he said: 'Hokay. You ride straight. We will be somewhere behind you. First, we will look if you brought some friends. Now go.'

They were in control, he realised. Didn't even look for weapons, because they knew they held the trump card.

Thobela pulled away. He wondered what was going on in Griessel's head.

The two detectives from Witness Protection were carrying shot-guns when they came to collect her.

She packed a suitcase. They accompanied her down in the lift and they all got in the car and drove away.

The house was in Boston, old and quite shabby, but the windows had burglar proofing and there was a security gate at the front door.

They showed her around the house. The master bedroom was where she could 'make herself at home', there were groceries in the kitchen, the bathroom had towels. There was television in the sitting room and piles of magazines on the coffee table, old issues of *Sports Illustrated*, *FHM* and a few copies of *Huisgenoot*.

'That's how they bring in the drugs,' said Griessel when they had been on the gravel road for half an hour.

Thobela said nothing. His mind was on their destination. He had seen the weapons of the two in the Pajero. New stuff, hand carbines, he guessed they were Heckler & Koch, family of the G36. Costly. Efficient.

'Infanta and Witsand. Every fucker with a ski boat goes there to fish,' said Griessel. 'They are bringing the stuff in small boats. Probably off ships . . .'

So that was how the detective was keeping his mind occupied.

He didn't want to think of his child. He didn't want to imagine what they had done to his daughter.

'Do you know how many there are?' asked Thobela.

'No.'

'You will want to reload your Z88.'

'I only fired one shot. In your house.'

'Every round will count, Griessel.'

She was in the sitting room when there was a knock on the door. The two detectives first looked through the peephole and then opened the series of locks on the front door.

She heard heavy steps and then the big man with the Western Province rugby cap stood there and he said: 'You and I must talk.'

He came to sit on the chair closest to her and the two Witness Protection detectives hung around in the doorway.

'Let's not make her nervous, chaps,' said Beukes.

Reluctantly, they retreated down the passage. She heard the back door open and close.

'Where is the money?' he asked when the house was quiet.

'*What* money?' Her pulse beat in her throat.

'You know what I'm talking about.'

'I don't.'

'Where is your daughter?'

'Ask Carlos.'

'Carlos is dead, you slut. And he never had your daughter. *You* know it and *I* know it.'

'How can you *say* that?' She began to weep.

'Save the fucking tears. They won't work on me. You should just be fucking grateful I was following him yesterday morning. If it had been one of the others . . .'

'I don't know what you're talking about . . .'

'Let me tell you what I'm talking about. The team that was on duty day before yesterday said you went to his house in his BMW. And in the middle of the fucking night you take a taxi from the front of his house and you have all these Pick and Pay bags and you're in a helluva hurry. What was in the bags?'

'I cooked dinner for him.'

'And took everything home again?'

'Just what I didn't use.'

'You're lying.'

'I swear.' She wept and the tears were genuine, because the fear was back.

'What I don't know is where you went with the fucking taxi. Because my fucking so-called colleagues didn't think to send someone after you. Because their job was to watch *him*. That's what you get when you work with the policeman of today. Fucking black rubbish. But yesterday was another story, because I was in the saddle, my dear. And Carlos drove out of there as if the devil was on his tail, straight to your little flat. Ten minutes later he comes out with this big red mark on his face, but there's no child anywhere. But the next minute the whole fucking radio is full of Sangrenegra and before I could do anything the Task Force was there and SVC and who knows what. But one thing I do know: your child was not with him. Not the night before last, and not yesterday morning. Of all the money in that strong room of his, there is a shithouse full of rands missing. Only rands. Now why, I ask myself, why of all the dollars and euros and pounds would someone only take South African rands? I guess it was an amateur. Someone who doesn't want to bother with foreign exchange. Someone who had time to think about what she wanted to steal. What she could use. That she could carry in Pick and Pay shopping bags.'

She realised something and without further thought she asked: 'How do you know there are rands missing?'

'Fuck you, whore. I'm telling you now; this thing is not over yet. Not for *you*, anyway.'

Griessel's cell phone rang. He answered and told Thobela: 'They say we must drive slower.'

He reduced speed. The Nissan rattled on the dirt road. Behind them the Pajero's headlights shone dim through the cloud of dust. The lights of Witsand twinkled on the Breede River off to the left.

'He says we must turn left at the road sign.'

He slowed even more, spotted the sign that said *Kabeljoubank*. He put on his indicator and turned. The road narrowed between two boundary fences. It ran down to the river. In the rear-view mirror he saw the Pajero was behind them.

'Are you calm?' Thobela asked the detective.

'Yes.'

He felt the fizz inside him, now that they were close.

In the headlights he saw three, four boats on trailers. And two vehicles. A minibus and a pick-up. Figures moving. He stopped a hundred metres away from the vehicles. He turned the key and the Nissan's engine fell silent. He deliberately kept the lights on.

'Get out and hide that pistol of yours,' he said, and picked up the assegai, pushed it down behind his neck, under his shirt. There was barely enough room in the car, the angle was too tight. He heard the blade tear the material of his shirt, felt the chill of the blade against his back. It would have to do. He opened the door and got out. Griessel stood on the other side of the Nissan.

Four men approached from the minibus – one was tall and broad, considerably bigger than the others. The Pajero pulled up behind them. Thobela stood beside the car, aware of the four in front, the two behind. He heard their footsteps on the gravel, smelt the dust and the river and the fish from the boats, heard the waves in the sea beyond. He felt the stiffness throughout his body, but the weariness was gone, his arteries were full of adrenaline. The world seemed to slow down, as if there were more time for thinking and doing.

The quartet came right up to him. The big one looked him up and down.

'You are the spearman,' he said as if he recognised him. He was as tall as Thobela, with long straight black hair down to his massive shoulders. He wasn't carrying a firearm. The others had machine pistols.

'Where is my daughter?' asked Griessel.

'I am the spearman,' said Thobela. He wanted to keep the attention; he didn't know how stable Griessel was.

'My name is César Sangrenegra. You killed my brother.'

'Yes. I killed your brother. You can have me. Let the girl and the policeman go.'

'No. We will have *justicia*.'

'No, you can—'

'Shut the fuck up, black man.' Spit sprayed from César's lips, the drops making shiny arcs in the light from the Nissan. '*Justicia*. You know what it means? He made the trap for Carlos, this policeman. Now I have to go back to my father and say I didn't kill him? That will not happen. I want you to know, policeman, before you die. I want you to know we fucked your daughter. We fucked her good. She is young. It was a sweet fuck. And after you are dead, we will fuck her again. And again. We will fuck her so long as she can be alive. You hear me?'

'I will kill you,' said Griessel, and Thobela could hear his breaking point was close.

He laughed at Griessel, shaking his head. 'You can do nothing. We have your kid. And we will find the white whore too. The one who tells lies about Carlos. The one who steals our money.'

'You are a coward,' Thobela said to César Sangrenegra. 'You are not a man.'

César laughed in his face. 'You want me to attack you? You want me to lose my temper?'

'I want you to lose your life.'

'You think I did not see the spear you put behind your back? You think I am stupid, like my brother?' He turned around, to one of his henchmen. '*Déme el cuchillo*.'

The man drew a knife from a long sheath on his hip. César took it from him.

'I will kill you slowly,' he said to Thobela. 'Now take out that spear.'

46

When Superintendent Boef Beukes had gone, she went to the bedroom where her things were.

She opened her handbag, took out her identity document and put it on the bed. She took out her purse, cigarettes and a lighter. She clipped the bag shut and lifted up her dress. She pushed the ID book and the purse down the front of her panties. She carried the cigarettes in her hand.

She walked to the front of the house and said: 'I'm going outside for a smoke.'

'At the back,' gestured the one with the moustache. 'We don't want you to go out the front.'

She nodded, went through the kitchen and out the back door. She closed it behind her.

There were fruit trees in the backyard. The grass was long. A concrete wall surrounded the property. She walked straight to the wall. She put her cigarettes on the ground and looked up at the wall. She drew a deep breath and jumped. Her hands gripped the top of the wall. She pulled herself up, swung one leg over. The top of the wall felt sharp against her knee.

She dragged her whole body up onto the wall. Beyond was another garden. Vegetables in tidy rows. She jumped, landing in the mud of a wet vegetable bed. She got up. One of her sandals stayed behind in the mud. She pulled it out and put it on again. She walked around the house to the front.

She heard the animal's paws on the cement path before it appeared around the corner. A big brown dog. The animal barked deeply and feinted back a little, as much in fright as she was. She kept her hands protectively in front of her. The dog stood square, growling, exposing big sharp teeth.

'Hello, doggy, hello,' she said.

They stood facing each other, the dog blocking her way around the house.

Don't look scared, she knew, she remembered that from some-where. She let her hands drop and stood up straight.

'Okay, doggy.' She tried to keep her tone caressing, while her heartbeat rocked her.

The animal growled again.

'Easy, boy, good dog.'

The dog shook his head and sneezed.

'I just want to come past, doggy, just want to come past.'

The hairs on the dog's neck dropped. The teeth disappeared. The tail gave one uncertain wag.

She took one step forward. The dog came closer, but didn't growl. She put out her hand to his head.

The tail wagged more vigorously. He pressed his head against her hand. The dog sneezed again.

She began to walk slowly, the dog following. She could see the front garden gate. She walked faster.

'Hey,' came a voice from the front veranda.

An old man stood there. 'Can I help you?' he asked.

'I'm just walking through,' she said, one hand on the gate. 'I'm just passing through.'

He reached for the assegai behind his neck and César Sangre-negra's movement was subtle and rapid and the long knife cut through Thobela's shirt and across his ribs, a sharp, red-hot pain. He felt the blood run down his belly.

He took a step back and saw the grin on the Colombian's face. He held the assegai in his right hand and bent his knees for better balance. He moved to the right, watching César's eyes; never watch the blade, there are no warnings there. César stabbed. Thobela jumped back and the knife flashed past in front. He stabbed with the assegai. César was no longer there. The knife came again. He jerked back his arm, the blade sliced over his forearm. Another step back. The man was fast. Light on his feet, ten kilograms lighter than he was. Moved again, this time to the left, César feinted right, moved left. Thobela dodged, up against the front of the Nissan, he must not be trapped against the car, three, four short steps to the right, the knife flashed so fast, it missed him by millimetres.

Thobela knew he was in trouble; the big man with the long hair was skilled. Faster than him. Lighter, younger. And he had another great advantage – he could kill, Thobela could not. Carla Griessel's life depended on him not killing César.

He must use the length of the assegai. He adjusted his grip, held it by the end of the shaft and swung it with a whooshing noise through the night, back and forth, back and forth. He felt the wound in his arm; saw an arc of blood spray as he swung. César moved back, but calmly. The henchman widened the circle. One made a remark in Spanish and the other four laughed.

The opponents looked into each other's eyes. The Colombian darted forward, the knife flashed, then he was back.

The man was toying with him. César was aware of his superior speed. Thobela would have to neutralise that. He would have to use his power, his weight, but against a knife that was impossible.

The Colombian's eyes betrayed his attack. Thobela pretended to move back, but came forward, he must keep the knife away, forward again, within the sweep of the knife arm, stabbed with the assegai. César grabbed at it, grasping the blade in his left hand and unexpectedly jerked it towards him, Thobela lost his balance. Saw the blood on César's hand where the assegai had cut deeply, here came the knife, jerked his own left hand up to block it, got hold of Cesar's arm, forced it back. César adjusted his grip on the assegai, getting his hand on the shaft.

They stood locked in that grip. The knife bowed down, the point entered Thobela's biceps, deep. The pain was intense. He would have to move his grip close to the wrist. Would have to do it swiftly and efficiently. He shifted suddenly; the knife cutting through his biceps saved him, because it kept the hand static for a split second.

He knew the injury was serious. He had César's wrist, all his strength behind it. His forearm shrieked. Brought up his knees, kicked César as hard as he could in the belly. Saw in his eyes it was a good contact.

Would have to finish now, in this moment of slight advantage. Pushed the knife hand back. His left arm would not last; the muscle was deeply cut. Shifted his point of balance, jerked the assegai free from the grasp, let it drop in the dust. Both hands on the knife-arm, bent it behind César's back. Lord, he was strong. Straining, he kicked him at the back of the knee and César began to fall; he twisted the arm the last centimetres and César made a sound. The henchmen called out. Swinging weapons from their shoulders, they moved too late. He twisted the arm until something popped and the knife came free from the fingers.

His right hand pressed César's arm against his back, the left hand had the knife, arm around the throat, pressing the point into the hollow of the neck. Deep. César screamed and jerked and struggled. Strong. Would have to neutralise that. Turned the arm another bit, until ligaments tore. César's knees buckled. He kept the man upright, as a shield in front of him.

He pressed the point of the knife deeper into the neck. Felt the blood run over his hand. He felt his own pain shrill in his arm. He didn't know how much blood he was losing. His entire left side was soaking, warm.

'You are very close to death,' he said softly into César's ear. The henchmen had carbines and machine pistols aimed at them.

The Colombian was frozen against him.

'If I move the knife, I will cut an artery,' he said. 'Do you hear me?'

A noise.

'Your men have to put down their weapons.'

No reaction. Was it going to work? He thought he understood the hierarchy of the drug industry. The autocracy.

'I will count to three. Then I cut.' He tightened the muscles of his arm as if in readiness but it didn't work so well. He knew there were sinews cut.

'One.'

César jerked again, but the arm was bent too far back, the pain must be dreadful.

'Two.'

'*Coloque sus armas.*' Practically inaudible.

'Louder.'

'*Coloque sus armas.*'

The henchmen did nothing, just stood there. Thobela began to move the knife point slowly, deeper into the throat.

'*¡Ahora!*'

The first one moved slowly, putting his weapon carefully down on the ground. Another one.

'No,' said one of the Pajero men, the one with the shaven head.

He stood beside Griessel, the Heckler & Koch against the detective's temple. 'I will shoot this one,' said Shaven Head.

'Shoot,' said Thobela.

'Let César go.'

'No.'

'Then I shoot this one.'

'Do I care? He is a policeman. I am a murderer.' He turned the knife in César's throat.

'*¡Ahora!*' The cry was hoarse and high and desperate and he knew the blade had scraped against something.

Shaven Head looked at César, back at Griessel and spat out a word. He threw the carbine in the dust.

'*Now,*' said Thobela in Afrikaans. 'Now you must get your daughter.'

At a stop sign in Eleventh Avenue she knocked on the window of a woman's Audi and said: 'Please, ma'am, I need your help.'

The woman looked her up and down, saw the mud on her legs and drove off.

'Fuck you!' Christine yelled after her.

She walked in the direction of Frans Conradie Avenue, looking back often. By now they must know she was gone. They must be looking for her.

At the traffic lights she looked left and right. There were shops across the street. If she could just get there. Unseen. She ran. A car braked and hooted at her. She kept on running. Oncoming traffic. She stood on the traffic island waiting. Then it was clear. Jogged across. The sandals were not made for this sort of thing.

Turned left, up the hill. Not far now. She was going to make it. She must phone Vanessa. No taxis. They would follow those up; know where she was dropped off. Vanessa would have to fetch her. Vanessa and Sonia. Take them to a station. Catch a train, anywhere. Get away. She could buy a car, in Beaufort West or George or wherever. She must just get away. Disappear.

Griessel crossed in front of him where he held César in an embrace. The policeman walked slowly, with empty hands. Thobela wondered where the pistol was. Wondered what the expression in the white man's eyes meant.

Griessel walked to the minibus.

He opened it. Thobela saw movement inside. He heard Griessel speak. Lean inwards. Saw two arms encircle Griessel's neck.

He looked at the henchmen. They stood still. Uneasy. Ready, their eyes on César.

He made sure of his grip on the Colombian. He didn't know whose blood was running over him. Looked back at the minibus. Griessel stood half in the minibus, his daughter's arms around him. He thought he heard the detective's voice.

'Griessel,' he said, because he didn't know how long he could hold out.

A henchman shuffled his feet.

'You must be quiet. I will cut this man's throat.'

The man looked at him with an unreadable expression.

'Shoot them,' said César, but the words came out with blood, unclear.

'Shut up, or I will kill you.'

'Shoot them.' More audible.

The henchmen inched closer. Shaven Head stepped towards his firearm.

'I will kill César *now*.' The pain in his upper arm reached new heights. There was a buzzing in his head. Where was the policeman? He looked quickly. Griessel stood there, with the Z88, and his daughter, hand in hand.

They all looked at Griessel. He shuffled up to the first henchman.

'Did he?' he asked his daughter.

She nodded. Griessel raised the pistol and fired. The man flew over backwards.

Father and daughter approached the next one. 'And he?'

She nodded. He aimed at the man's head and pulled the trigger. The second shot thundered through the night and the man fell. Shaven Head dived for his weapon. Thobela knew it would all happen now and he pulled the knife across César's throat and let him fall. He knew where the nearest machine pistol lay, threw his body that way, heard another shot. He kept his eyes on the firearm. Hit the gravel, stretched out, heard another shot. Got his finger on the steel. Dizzy, a lot of blood lost. His left arm wouldn't work. Rolled over. Couldn't see well in the lights of the Nissan. Tried to get up, but had no balance.

Got onto one knee.

Shaven Head was down. César lay. Three others as well. Griessel had the Z88 trained on the last one. Carla was close to Thobela now. He saw her face. He knew in that moment he would never forget it.

Her father turned to the last one.

'And this one?'

His daughter looked at the man and nodded her head.

PART FOUR
Carla

47

Beyond Calvinia he saw the clouds damming up against the mountains, the snow-white cumulus towers in late morning sun, the straight line they formed over the dry earth. He wanted to show Carla. He wanted to explain his theory of how the contours of the landscape created this weather.

She was asleep in the passenger seat.

He looked at her. He wondered if it was a dreamless sleep.

A huge plain opened up ahead of them. The road was as straight as an arrow, to Brandvlei – a pitch-black ribbon stretching to the point of invisibility.

He wondered when she would wake up, because she was missing everything.

The minister looked at the newspaper clipping. There was a photo of two people getting out of a helicopter. A man and a young woman. The man's hair was dark and untidy, with a hint of grey at the temples. A somewhat Slavic face, with a severe expression. His head was turned towards the young woman in concern.

There was a resemblance between them, a vague connection between brow and the line of the chin. Father and daughter, perhaps.

She was pretty, with an evenness of feature below her black hair. But there was something about the way she held her head, how she looked down. As if she were old and unattractive. Maybe the minister got the impression because the jacket over her shoulders was too big for her. Maybe he was influenced by the headline of the report.

ABDUCTION DRAMA ENDS IN BLOODBATH

John Afrika, Matt Joubert and Benny Griessel were sitting in the spacious office at Serious and Violent Crimes. Keyter came in and greeted them. They did not reciprocate.

'I am only going to ask you once, Jamie,' said Griessel, and his voice was quiet but it carried across the room. 'Was it you?'

Keyter looked back at them, nervously from one to the next.

'Uh . . . um . . . What are you talking about, Benny?'

'Did you give Sangrenegra the information?'

'Jesus, Benny . . .'

'Did you?'

'No. Never.'

'Where do you get the money, Jamie? For the clothes. And that expensive cell phone of yours? Where does the money come from?' Griessel had risen halfway from his chair.

'Benny,' said John Afrika, his voice soothing.

'I . . .' said Jamie Keyter.

'Jamie,' said Joubert. 'It's better if you talk.'

'It's not what you think,' he said and his voice shook.

'What is it?' asked Griessel, forcing himself to sit.

'I moonlight, Benny.'

'You moonlight?'

'Modelling.'

'Modelling?' said John Afrika.

'For TV ads.'

No one said a word.

'For the French. And the Germans. But I swear, I'm finished with that.'

'Can you prove it, Jamie?'

'Yes, Sup. I have the videos. Ads for coffee and cheese spread. And clothes. I did one for the Swedes for milk, I had to take my shirt off, but that's all, Sup, I swear . . .'

'TV ads,' said John Afrika.

'Jissis,' said Griessel.

'Was this about my clothes, Benny? Did you suspect me just because of my *clothes*?'

'There was a fax, Jamie. It was sent from here. From SVC's fax machine. With Mpayipheli's photo.'

'It could have been anyone.'

'You were the dresser, Jamie.'

'But it wasn't me.'

Silence settled over the room.

'You may go, Jamie,' said Joubert.

The detective constable dallied. 'I thought, Benny . . .'

They looked at him impatiently.

'I thought about how they got your daughter's address. And your cell phone number. All that stuff . . .'

'What are you trying to say?'

'They must have phoned him. Carlos's brother. Not just sent faxes.'

'Yes?'

'He must have had a cell phone, Commissioner. The brother. And you get missed calls and received calls and dialled numbers.'

It took them a while to grasp what he meant.

'Fuck,' said Griessel and got up.

'Sorry, Benny,' said Keyter and ducked, but Griessel was already past him, heading for the door.

By 12:30 they had reached Brandvlei and he decided to stop at a café with a concrete table under a thatched roof. Coloured children played barefoot in the dust.

Carla woke up and asked him where they were. Griessel told her. She looked at the café.

'Do you want to eat something?'

'Not really.'

'Let's have something to drink.'

'Okay.'

He got out and waited for her. It was boiling hot outside the car. She put on trainers before getting out, stretched and came around the car. She was wearing a short-sleeved blouse and bleached jeans. His lovely daughter. They sat at one of the concrete tables. It was slightly cooler under the thatch.

He saw her watching the coloured children with their wire cars. He wondered what she was thinking.

'How far is it to Upington still?'

'About a hundred and fifty to Kenhardt, another seventy to Keimoes and then maybe fifty to Upington. Just under three hundred,' he quickly added up.

A coloured woman brought them single-page menus. At the top of the white laminated page was printed *Oasis Café*. There was an amateurish palm tree alongside the words. Carla ordered a white Grapetiser. Griessel said: 'Make that two.'

As the woman walked away he said, 'I've never had Grapetiser before.'

'Never?'

'If it didn't go with brandy, I wasn't interested.'

She smiled, but it didn't extend further than the corners of her mouth.

'This is another universe, here,' she said and looked up the main street.

'It is.'

'Do you think you will find something in Upington?'

'Perhaps.'

'But why, Dad? What's the use?'

He made a gesture with his hand that said he didn't know himself. 'I don't know, Carla. It's the way I am. That's why I am a detective. I want to know the reasons. And the facts. I want to understand. Even if it won't necessarily make a difference. Loose ends . . . I don't like them.'

'Weird,' she said. She put out her hand to him and wiggled her fingers under his. 'But wonderful.'

He called the numbers on César Sangrenegra's received calls list on the speakerphone in Joubert's office. With the first three he got voice mailboxes in Spanish. The fourth rang and rang and rang. Eventually it switched over to a cell phone messaging service.

'Hello, this is Bushy. When I've caught the crooks, I will phone you back.'

'I won't go to hell for Carlos,' said Christine. 'Because I saw the look in his eyes when he saw Sonia. And I know God will forgive me for being a sex worker. And I know he will understand that I had to draw the blood. And take the money.' She looked at the minister. He didn't want to assent to that.

'But He punished everyone for Carla Griessel.' She opened the second newspaper clipping. The headline read: MASSIVE COP CORRUPTION SCANDAL.

'Carlos's brother and his bodyguards. The Artemis man. All dead. And these policemen are going to jail,' she said, and tapped the two photos with the report. 'But what about me?'

'I didn't even know them,' said Bushy Bezuidenhout.

'But you gave them the information,' said Joubert.

'For money, you piece of shit,' said Griessel.

Joubert put his big hand soothingly on the inspector's arm.

Bezuidenhout wiped the perspiration from his forehead and shook his head. 'I'm not going down alone for this.'

'Give us the others, Bushy. You know, if you cooperate . . .'

'Jissis, Sup.'

'Give me five minutes alone with this cunt,' said Griessel.

'Jissis, Benny, I didn't know what they were going to do. I didn't know. Do you think I would—?'

Griessel shouted him down. 'Who, Bushy? Tell me who!'

'Beukes, fuck it. Beukes with his bloody cap brought me this shitload of money in a fucking brown envelope . . .'

Matt Joubert's voice was sharp in the room. 'Benny, no. Sit. I will not let you go.'

Fourteen kilometres beyond Keimoes he saw the sign and turned right to Kanoneiland. They crossed the river that flowed peaceful and brown under the bridge, and between green vineyards heavy with giant bunches of grapes.

'Amazing,' said Carla, and he knew what she meant. This fertility here, the surprise of it. But he was also aware that she was observing, that she was less turned in on herself, and it gave him hope again.

They drove up the long avenue of pines to the guesthouse and Carla said, 'Look,' and pointed a finger at his side of the road. Between the trees he could see the horses: big Arabians, three bays and a magnificent grey.

When Christine van Rooyen walked down the street in Reddersburg, the sun came up over the Free State horizon, a giant balloon breaking loose from the hills and sweeping over the grassland.

She turned off the main street, down an unpaved street, past houses that were still dark and silent.

She looked intently at one of them. The babysitter said a writer lived here, a man hiding away from the world.

It was a good place for it.

The secretary at the high school shook her head and said she had only worked here for three years. But he could ask Mr Losper. Mr Losper had been at the school for years. He taught Biology. But it was holidays now; Mr Losper would be at home. She gave him precise directions and he drove there and knocked on the door.

Losper was somewhere in his fifties, a man with smoker's wrinkles and rough voice who invited him in, since it was cooler in the dining room. Would he like a beer? He said no thanks, he was fine.

When they were seated at the dining-room table and he asked his question, the man shut his eyes for a moment, as if sending up a quick prayer to heaven, and then he said, 'Christine van Rooyen.' Solemnly, he put his arms on the table and folded his hands together.

'Christine van Rooyen,' he repeated, as if the repetition of the name would open up his memory.

Then he told Griessel the story, regularly inserting admissions of guilt and rationalisation. Of Martie van Rooyen who lost her soldier husband in Angola. Martie van Rooyen, the blonde woman with the big bosom and the small blonde daughter. A woman the community gossiped about even when her husband was still alive. Rumours of visits when Rooies was away on training courses, or on the Border.

And after Rooies' death there was very soon a replacement. And another. And another. She lured them home from the ladies' bar at the River Hotel with red lipstick and a low neckline. While the child wandered around the yard with a stuffed dog in her arms, an object that later became so filthy it was scandalous.

The gossipmongers said the substitute for Rooies used to hit Martie. And sometimes played around with more than just the mother. But in Upington, many watch but few act. Social Welfare tried to step in, but the mother sent them packing and Christine van Rooyen grew up like that. Sad and wild. Earned a reputation of her own. Loose. Easy. There was talk when the girl was a teenager. About an old friend of her father's who . . . you know. And an Afrikaans teacher. There were goings-on at the school. The child was difficult. Smoking and drinking with the rough crowd, the school had always had one, it was a funny town, this, with the Army and all.

Losper had heard the story that when Christine had finished school she walked out of the house with a suitcase while her mother was in bed with a substitute. Went to Bloemfontein, apparently, but he didn't know what became of her.

'And the mother?'

She had also left, he had heard. With a man in a pick-up. Cape Town. Or the West Coast: there were so many stories.

She walked past. Three houses down she turned in at a garden gate that creaked on opening. It needed oiling.

The garden was overgrown with weeds. She took the box and put it down on the veranda. It was light now.

In the minister's study she had pulled it towards her one last time and taken out the cash. Four hundred thousand rand in one-hundred-rand notes.

'This is a tenth,' she said.

'You can't buy the Lord's forgiveness,' he had answered wearily, but couldn't keep his eyes off the money.

'I don't want to buy anything. I just want to give. It's for the Church.'

She had waited for his response and then he walked her to the door and she could smell the odour of his body behind her, the smell of a man after a long day.

She came back off the veranda and stooped to pull out a weed. The roots came free of the reddish soil and she thought it looked fertile here.

She went over to the steps. She reached for the sign to the right of them, the one that said *Te Koop/For Sale*. She pulled. It had been hammered in deep and had been there a long time. She had to wiggle it back and forth before it slowly began to shift and eventually came out.

She carried it up, put it down on the veranda. Then she took her keys out and quietly unlocked the door. On the new couch the large black babysitter was reclining. She was fast asleep.

Christine went down the passage to the master bedroom. Sonia lay there in a foetal position, her whole body curled around the toy dog. She lay down gently beside her daughter. Later, when they had finished breakfast, she would ask Sonia if she would like to exchange the stuffed animal for a real one.

Griessel thought about Senior Superintendent Beukes as he drove back to the guesthouse. Three weeks ago, they confronted him.

They would not allow him to be present at the interrogation – Joubert had put his foot down. He had to sit with the disillusioned American, Lombardi. Tried to explain to him that not *all* the police in Africa were corrupt. But afterwards Joubert came to tell him. Beukes would admit nothing. Right till the end when they got his bank statements through a court order and spread them out in front of him. And Beukes had said, 'Why don't you try and find the whore? She's the one who stole money. And lied about her daughter.'

He didn't know whether it was true or not. But now, after Losper's story, he hoped it was. Because he recalled the words of the forensic psychologist. *Women are different. When there is damage at a young age, they don't do to others. They do to themselves.*

He only hoped she used the money well. For herself and her daughter.

His cell phone rang while he was driving up the avenue of pine trees. He pulled over.

'Griessel.'

'This is Inspector Johnson Mtetwa. I am phoning from Alice. I wonder if you could help me?'

'Yes, Inspector.'

'It's about the death of Thobela Mpayipheli . . .'

'Yes?'

'The trouble is, I had some people here. The missionary priest from the Knott Memorial between us and Peddie.'

'Yes?'

'He told me the strangest thing, Inspector Griessel. He said he saw Mpayipheli, yesterday morning.'

'How strange.'

'He said he saw a man walking, from the Kat River hills to near the manse. He went out to see who it might be. When he came close, the man turned away. But he could swear it was Mpayipheli, because he knew him. In the old days. You see, Mpayipheli's father was also a missionary.'

'I see.'

'I went out with the people from Cathcart station to Mpayipheli's farm. They have to deal with things there. And now they tell me there is a motorbike missing. A . . . Hang on. . . . A BMW R eleven-fifty GS.'

'Oh?'

'But the people in the Cape say you were a witness to his death.'

'You must request the file, Inspector. They did search the river for his body . . .'

'Strange,' said Mtetwa, 'that someone would steal only the motorbike.'

'That's life,' said Griessel. 'Strange.'

'That's true. Thank you, Inspector. And good luck there in the Cape.'

'Thank you.'

'Thank *you*.'

Benny Griessel put the cell phone back in his breast pocket. He put his hand out to the ignition key but, before starting the car, he saw something that made him wait.

Between the trees, there in the horse paddock, Carla stood by a large grey. She was leaning against the magnificent beast, her face in the horse's mane, her hand gently stroking the long muzzle.

He got out of the car and went over to the fence rail. He had eyes only for her, and a tenderness that might just overwhelm him.

His child.

ACKNOWLEDGEMENTS

More than any of my previous books, *Devil's Peak* is to a great extent the product of the astounding goodwill, unselfishness, readiness to share knowledge – and unconditional support of a large number of people.

I wish to thank them:

Even now I don't know her real name, but as a sex worker she went by the name of 'Vanessa'. In two long morning interviews she talked intelligently, openly and honestly about her work and life. When I had finished the book, I tried to contact her to thank her. The message on her cell phone said 'I am no longer in the business . . .' May all her dreams be realised.

The three other nameless sex workers who made time to talk to me in coffee shops and tell me their stories.

The personnel of Sex Worker Education and Advocacy Taskforce (SWEAT) in Cape Town, and specifically the director, Ms Jayne Arnott.

Ms Ilse Pauw, a clinical psychologist, who shared hours of her knowledge of and insight into sex workers.

Captain Elmarie Myburgh of the South African Police Service's Psychological Investigation Unit in Pretoria. Her incredible insight, experience and knowledge of the psychology of people in general and specifically crime and criminals, her enthusiasm for the project and many hours of patience left me deeply in her debt. She is any author's research dream and a wonderful ambassador for her unit and the SAPS.

Inspector Riaan Pool, SAPS Liaison Officer in Cape Town.

Superintendent Mike Barkhuizen of the SAPS Serious and Violent Crimes Unit in Cape Town.

Gerhard Groenewald of Klipbokkop, for his knowledge of tyres.

Dr Julie Wells of Rhodes University History Department, for the background of the Xhosa stabbing assegai.

All the wonderful curio-shop people of Cape Town city centre who provided information on assegais so freely, even when they knew I did not wish to buy.

Professor Marlene van Niekerk of the Department Afrikaans and Nederlands of the University of Stellenbosch, for her compassion, understanding, patience, great knowledge, intellect and creativity. She is a national treasure, in every sense of the word.

All the members (the veterans and the young ones!) of the US MA class in Creative Writing. That dinner is coming . . .

My editor, Dr Etienne Bloemhof, for his eagle eye, his enthusiasm, support and depth of knowledge.

My agent Isobel Dixon, to whom I owe so much – and all her colleagues at Blake Friedmann, especially David Eddy and Julian Friedmann.

My wife, Anita, who gets up and has coffee with me before dawn and never stops supporting and believing and reading and loving. And the children who wait so patiently for the writing door to open.

The ATKV, for the financial support that made so much of the research possible.

One of the great joys of researching a manuscript is finding and reading relevant books – and hunting down relevant information on the Internet. I am grateful for the following:

Smokescreen by Robert Sabbag, Canongate, London, 2002.

Killing Pablo by Mark Bowden, Atlantic Books, London, 2002.

With Criminal Intent, Rob Marsh, Ampersand Press, Cape Town, 1999.

Frontiers by Noel Mostert, Pimlico, London, 1992.

www.alcoholicsanonymous.org.au

www.alcoholics-anonymous.org.uk

www.fda.gov

www.digitalnaturopath.com
www.heckler-koch.de
www.dieburger.com
www.iol.com

Translated by K. L. Seegers, October 2005

KER

WHO'S WHO IN
The Archers
2004

To Steve and Catherine, who led me astray

This book is published to accompany the BBC Radio 4 serial *The Archers*.
The editor of *The Archers* is Vanessa Whitburn

Published by BBC Books, BBC Worldwide Ltd, Woodlands,
80 Wood Lane, London W12 0TT
First published 1999
This new edition published 2003
Copyright © BBC 2003

ISBN: 0 563 48766 6

Commissioning Editor: Emma Shackleton
Project Editor: Cath Harries
Designer: Sarah Ponder
Production Controller: Belinda Rapley
Text set in Garamond Light
Printed and bound in Great Britain by Martins of Berwick Ltd
Cover printed by Belmont Press

Events in Ambridge are constantly changing, but we have done our best to make *Who's Who in The Archers 2004* accurate at the time of publication.

Official Archers Website: www.bbc.co.uk/radio4/archers
for *Archers* episodes in Real Audio, including an audio archive of the last seven days. The site also features daily plot synopses, news, information, a map of Ambridge, quizzes and chat.
Official Fan Club: Archers Addicts 0121 683 1951
Web site:www.archers-addicts.com

THE AUTHOR
A character in search of a cliché, after 11 years in Ambridge Keri Davies gave up the role of senior producer of *The Archers* to spend more time with his family. He now runs the BBC's Archers website and writes scripts for the programme. He lives in Birmingham with his wife and three sons, who think that having a father who is a part-time DJ is pretty cool. They don't mind about *The Archers*, either...

WELCOME TO AMBRIDGE

I am delighted that our handy guide to the characters and locations in *The Archers* is now in its fifth year.

While originally designed to help newcomers take their first steps down the byways of Ambridge, we have found that the book is used by more established listeners too; as a quick reference guide, or even an entertaining means of passing time in the smaller rooms of the house.

So when you are wondering who is the older, Eddie Grundy or Mike Tucker, this book is for you. What it can't tell you is why Eddie sometimes behaves like an overgrown schoolboy. That would require several large volumes.

Vanessa Whitburn
Editor, The Archers

In December 2002, even people who didn't listen to *The Archers* knew that something big was happening. They'd read it in the papers. An affair between wealthy Brian Aldridge and some Irish woman? And wasn't there a baby involved? In the last three months of the year our listening figures had increased by a quarter of a million. There was a fantastic climax as first Brian's daughter, then his wife, discovered the truth. The acting and writing was praised from all sides.

Of course, by then, regular listeners had been enjoying the story for a year. And it was by no means the end of the tale. Through 2003, with listening figures still increasing, we followed Brian and Jennifer's attempts to mend their marriage, sympathised with Debbie's inability to forgive her step-father, and held our breath as Siobhan returned in a last-ditch attempt to win back the father of her child.

So far, the story has run for nearly two years. And, although we never divulge the future in Ambridge, we can be sure that the affair and its aftermath will influence events for many years to come. Compare this with our younger cousins, the television soaps, who seem to measure storylines in weeks at best, and whose characters are often blessed with remarkable amnesia about what's gone on in their lives. This real-time story telling is one of the great strengths of *The Archers* – and one of the reasons for its longevity.

The creator of *The Archers,* Godfrey Baseley, devised the programme as a means of educating farmers in modern production methods when Britain was still subject to food rationing. Five pilot episodes were broadcast on the BBC's Midlands Home Service in Whit Week 1950, but *The Archers'* official birthday was on 1 January 1951, when for the first time the lively 'dum-di-dum' of Arthur Wood's maypole dance 'Barwick Green' introduced episode one to a national audience. Episode 14108, broadcast on 1 January 2004 makes this comfortably the world's longest running radio drama.

The Archers lost its original, educational, remit in the early 1970s, but it still prides itself on the quality of its research and its reflection of real rural life. The Editor, Vanessa Whitburn, leads a nine-strong production team and ten writers as they plot the complicated lives of the families in Ambridge, looking ahead months or sometimes years in biannual long-term meetings. The detailed planning is done at monthly script meetings about two months ahead of transmission. Each writer produces a week's worth of scripts in a remarkable fourteen days. To retain listeners' attention in the early years, *Archers* writers drew on the tradition of the 'cliffhanger' which was so much part of its predecessor, the thriller serial *Dick Barton, Special Agent*! The modern equivalent is a blend of stories carefully planned and structured to captivate today's sophisticated audience.

Actors receive their scripts a few days before recording, which takes place every four weeks in Studio 3 at BBC Pebble Mill in Birmingham, although in 2004 a move is planned to the Mailbox complex in Birmingham's city centre. Twenty-four episodes are recorded in six intensive days, using only two hours of studio time per thirteen minute episode. This schedule means that being an *Archers* actor is by no means a full time job, even for major characters, so many also have careers in film, theatre, television or other radio drama. The episodes are transmitted three to six weeks after recording. But listeners are occasionally intrigued to hear topical events reflected in that evening's broadcast, a feat achieved through a flurry of rewriting, re-recording and editing on the day of transmission. With nearly five million listeners every week in the UK alone, *The Archers* is the most popular non-news programme on BBC Radio 4 (92-95 FM, 198 LW). It can also be heard world-wide via the *Archers* website:www.bbc.co.uk/radio4/archers.

The website has been a particular baby of mine, and in 2003 I went part-time to run it, being lucky enough to combine this role with writing *Archers* scripts. Given my usually low boredom threshold, I'm slightly surprised to be working for the same programme after eleven years. But if *The Archers* suits you, it suits you very well. And, thank goodness, that goes for the listeners too.

Keri Davies

Web Producer, *The Archers*

Transmission times: 7pm Sunday to Friday, repeated at 2pm the next day (excluding Saturdays). Omnibus edition of the whole week's episodes every Sunday at 10am. The website also holds an archive of episodes from the previous seven days.

John Archer m Phoebe

John Benjamin (Ben) m Simone Delamain
27.5.1898-2.8.1972   1900-1929

Frank m Laura Wilson
1.6.1900-   29.8.1911-
30.5.1957   14.2.1985

John (Jack) m Margaret (Peggy) Perkins
17.12.1922-   b. 13.11.1924
12.1.1972

m (2) Jack Woolley
b. 19.7.1919

Philip Walter m (1) Grace Fairbrother
b. 23.4.1928   2.4.1929-22.9.195.

m (2) Jill Patterson
b. 3.10.1930

Jennifer m (1) Roger Travers-Macy
b. 7.1.1945   b. 9.3.1944
div. Feb 1976

Adam
b. 22.6.1967
(by Paddy Redmond)

Deborah m Simon Gerrard
b. 24.12.1970
div. 5.2003

m (2) Brian Aldridge
b. 20.11.1943

Lilian m (1) Lester Nicholson
b. 8.7.1947   7.6.1946- 18.3.1970

m (2) Ralph Bellamy
26.2.1925-18.1.198●

James Rodney Dominic
b. 30.3.1973

Katherine Victoria (Kate) m Lucas Madikane
b. 30.9.1977   b. 1972

Alice Margaret
b. 29.9.1988

Phoebe
b. 28.6.1998
(by Roy Tucker)

Noluthando Grace
b. 19.1.2001

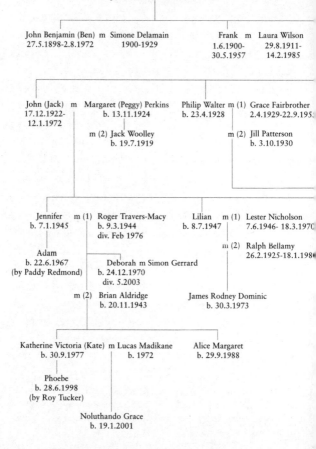

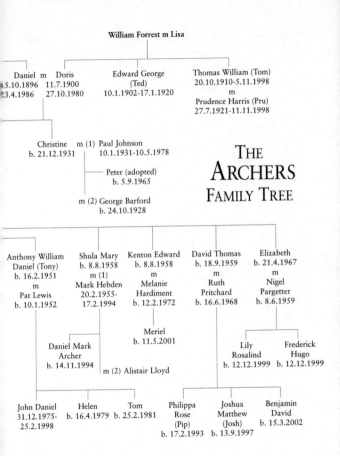

William Forrest m Lisa

Daniel m Doris
5.10.1896 11.7.1900
3.4.1986 27.10.1980

Edward George
(Ted)
10.1.1902-17.1.1920

Thomas William (Tom)
20.10.1910-5.11.1998
m
Prudence Harris (Pru)
27.7.1921-11.11.1998

Christine m (1) Paul Johnson
b. 21.12.1931 10.1.1931-10.5.1978

Peter (adopted)
b. 5.9.1965

m (2) George Barford
b. 24.10.1928

THE
ARCHERS
FAMILY TREE

Anthony William
Daniel (Tony)
b. 16.2.1951
m
Pat Lewis
b. 10.1.1952

Shula Mary
b. 8.8.1958
m (1)
Mark Hebden
20.2.1955-
17.2.1994

Kenton Edward
b. 8.8.1958
m
Melanie
Hardiment
b. 12.2.1972

David Thomas
b. 18.9.1959
m
Ruth
Pritchard
b. 16.6.1968

Elizabeth
b. 21.4.1967
m
Nigel
Pargetter
b. 8.6.1959

Meriel
b. 11.5.2001

Daniel Mark
Archer
b. 14.11.1994

m (2) Alistair Lloyd

Lily
Rosalind
b. 12.12.1999

Frederick
Hugo
b. 12.12.1999

John Daniel
31.12.1975-
25.2.1998

Helen
b. 16.4.1979

Tom
b. 25.2.1981

Philippa
Rose
(Pip)
b. 17.2.1993

Joshua
Matthew
(Josh)
b. 13.9.1997

Benjamin
David
b. 15.3.2002

ALICE ALDRIDGE

Home Farm • Born 29.9.88
(Hollie Chapman)

Alice was delighted when her father **Brian** bought Spearmint, a full size horse to replace her old pony, Chandler. She didn't realise it was a product of his guilty conscience following the affair with **Siobhan Hathaway**, because mercifully she remained unaware of the cause of the arctic relations between Brian and her sister **Debbie Travers-Macy**. None of the family wanted to scupper Alice's promising prospects as she started working towards her GCSEs as a day girl at a local private school, but Debbie must be seriously tempted to explain the real reason for her departure to France. Alice's second cousin **Shula** took over Debbie's role as riding mentor, but Alice missed her sister badly as she dealt with the angst and anguish – real and imagined – of her mid-teen years.

BRIAN ALDRIDGE

Home Farm • Born 20.11.43
(Charles Collingwood)

Wealthy and charming, Brian has had affairs in the past, most notably with **Caroline Pemberton.** But he entered new territory when a fling with **Siobhan Hathaway** turned into something much more serious. And serious was far too small a word when she had his son – Ruairi. It was an impossible secret to keep, and Brian's daughter **Debbie Travers-Macy** was the first to collapse the house of cards. Agonised Brian attempted to mend his marriage with **Jennifer**, losing contact with Ruairi as a consequence. Losing Debbie too because, unable to forgive him, she took a job in France. Then in September 2003, Siobhan returned from Ireland with fresh temptation. Although torn, Brian stuck to his decision, and as they fought in his car he lost control. The slow recovery from his injuries made for difficult times at **Home Farm**.

JENNIFER ALDRIDGE

(Formerly Travers-Macy, née Archer)
Home Farm • Born 7.1.45
(Angela Piper)

Although outwardly a respectable farmer's wife, observing a comfortable orbit from food hall to clothes shop to elegant farmhouse kitchen, Jennifer's history reads like, well… a soap opera. Unmarried and pregnant by a local farm hand, she gave birth to Adam (now **Macy**) in 1967. She later married Roger Travers-Macy, who adopted Adam. They had a daughter **Debbie**, but the marriage didn't last, and Jennifer wed **Brian** in 1976. They had more daughters: **Alice** and **Kate** (now **Madikane**) who by the age of 20 was taking after her mother, with two children by two different fathers (Jennifer regularly looks after **Phoebe**). Once a teacher and writer, Jennifer's interest in local history led her to set up the **Ambridge** website in 2002. Although devastated by Brian's affair with **Siobhan Hathaway**, she fought determinedly to save her marriage.

Willow Farm
Born 28.6.98

Product of a short-lived relationship between **Roy Tucker** and **Kate Madikane** (née Aldridge), this little mite was born in a tepee at the Glastonbury Festival, prevented from leaving the country by a court order, subjected to DNA testing and named in a New Age ceremony on Lakey Hill. Roy bravely cared for Phoebe following Kate's departure to Africa. But when Kate had eventually 'found herself' – and a husband, **Lucas** – she swanned back expecting to collect the child like a piece of left luggage. Largely thanks to wise Lucas, Kate eventually accepted that Phoebe's home was with her father now. But she still plays the mother card on her occasional visits to **Ambridge**, which can only confuse Phoebe, who sees Roy's wife **Hayley** as her mother, and Kate as a rather exotic Aunty figure.

'...*Stand on the village green, trying to ignore the ghastly seventies cul de sac and the hideous faux-Georgian estate (c2003), and you can still get an echo of an England painted in watercolour by ladies called Clarissa. If you're the sort who thinks the Met Bar is getting a bit parochial, then Ambridge be may not be for you, even though* **The Bull** *Upstairs can get quite lively when local heroes pull in the crowds on a Friday night. But from Saxon church to duck pond, country house hotel to half-timbered pub, this place holds an addictive charm. Some have passed through, lingering for fifteen minutes on the way to somewhere else, and to their surprise ended up regulars for life...*'

The Rough Lonely Guide to the UK, £12.99, paperback

Early in 2002, **Lynda** and **Robert Snell** had cause to regret the river frontage which gave their home such an attractive prospect. Swollen by heavy rain, the Am broke its banks and inundated the building. Fortunately the flash flood receded after only a few hours, but it took weeks of work to restore the six-bedroomed Victorian house, and months before the landscaped gardens recovered. The gardens in particular had been the work of years for Lynda, a keen and opinionated gardener, who had established a low allergen area to which she can retreat when struck by her annual affliction – hay fever. In 2003, with the assistance of contractors, she developed a Shakespearean garden, using only plants mentioned by the Bard. Adjoining the Hall is a small paddock strikingly occupied by Constanza and Wolfgang – two llamas.

AMBRIDGE ORGANICS

Harcourt Road, Borchester

During the boom time for organics it seemed like a good idea for **Pat** and **Tony Archer** to open a shop selling the farm's vegetables, yoghurt and ice cream, pork and sausages, plus a whole range of bought-in organic produce. But what with business rates and other overheads, **Helen**, who manages this family enterprise, has found it hard to make a decent profit out of the place. She does her best to minimise costs by paying fairly modest wages to her staff – **silent** Anja and **Kirsty Miller**, the girlfriend of Helen's brother **Tom**.

MARJORIE ANTROBUS

The Laurels • Born 1922
(Margot Boyd)

In 2003, Marjorie – known to many **Ambridge** villagers as 'Mrs A' – finally faced the realisation that her independent life was at an end, and reluctantly she moved into a nursing home. She'd fought the inevitable for a long time, not just because of her self-reliant instincts but also because it meant evicting her good friends and lodgers **Roy** and **Hayley Tucker**. Marjorie is unbowed by the loss over the years of her old colonial husband 'Teddy', her beloved Afghan hounds and her role as the bastion of the parish council and PCC. Although physically frail, mentally she is as sharp as ever, even if she has replaced the boundless horizons of her African youth with the comforting care and routine of The Laurels.

Brookfield Farm
Born 15.3.02

Ben's conception – on a Brookfield hay cart on a warm June night – was blissfully bucolic. But so soon after breast cancer, the pregnancy posed additional health risks for **Ruth**. Fortunately all was well, and the labour was so quick that **David** had to draw on a lifetime's lambing and calving experience as he became an emergency midwife. **Pip** loved having a new baby to bathe and dress, although for a while **Josh** worried that he was going to be replaced. **Ruth** has found that as a mother of three she can't be as active on the farm as she was used to, which has put more pressure on **David**.

DAVID ARCHER

Brookfield Farm • Born 18.9.59
(Timothy Bentinck)

Following **Phil**'s much delayed retirement and after a bitter family squabble, David and his wife **Ruth** finally took over the running of **Brookfield Farm** in 2001. They've struggled through some difficult years, facing falling farm incomes, TB, BSE, foot and mouth and worst of all Ruth's breast cancer, but David has plugged away doggedly at every challenge that has come his way. With Phil's help now limited, **Bert Fry** getting on and Ruth busy with their young family, David struggled to keep on top of the relentless round of work, which includes raising Hereford beef for local customers and quality lamb marketed through The Hassett Hills Meat Company – in every way a 'joint' venture. No-one's quite sure where he'll find the time but in May 2003 David was elected to **Ambridge**'s parish council.

A Tied Cottage at Home Farm • Born 16.4.79
(Louiza Patikas)

Helen seemed set for early middle age when she moved in with **Greg Turner**. It's been a tricky relationship. Helen is still maturing (not unlike her Borsetshire Blue cheese, which drew on her HND in Food Technology). And Greg took an awfully long time to reveal trivial details of his past life. You know, wife, children, vasectomy... Helen has done her best to help Greg cope with the impossibilities of being an absent parent of teenage girls. But she finds his bleak moods harder to deal with. Unkind observers (like her brother **Tom**) reckon they deserve each other, because Helen can, herself, be difficult. In Helen's case, it's because she needs to be more tactful when dealing with people, as her staff at **Ambridge Organics** can confirm.

JILL ARCHER

(née Patterson)
Glebe Cottage • Born 3.10.30
(Patricia Greene)

Jill was once an unashamed townie, but through 40-plus years of marriage to **Phil** she grew to be the consummate countrywoman. Never far from the Aga at **Brookfield**, Jill brought up four children – **Kenton, Shula** (now **Hebden Lloyd**), **David** and **Elizabeth** (now **Pargetter**) – and took a full part in village affairs through the church, WI and parish council. When she and Phil moved to their retirement cottage in 2001, Jill feared that her role at the heart of Brookfield would somehow end. No chance. She continued to run holiday lets at the farm's Rickyard Cottage, and retained her bees and hens in the orchard there. Jill's caring, practical nature is always valued by her family and by other villagers, and her sense of justice means she's always ready to take a stand on a point of principle.

Brookfield Farm • Born 13.9.97

When **Ruth** went into labour, keen cricketer **David** was in the middle of the innings of a lifetime, but he was persuaded to leave the field to see his son born. Josh attends the local primary school at Loxley Barratt. He was worried when he was replaced as Ruth and David's youngest son by the arrival of **Ben**. But they managed to persuade the lad that they had no plans to send him back to the shop.

KENTON ARCHER

The flat above Jaxx Caff • Born 8.8.58
(Richard Attlee)

Kenton was saved when **Jack Woolley** threw this one-time merchant-navy officer a lifeline, agreeing that he could manage Jack's new café in **Borchester**. Kenton had been thrown out by his Australian wife Mel and, on his return to **Ambridge,** had done the rounds of all the Archer family homes. In Australia, he'd left behind a sailing business and a daughter, Meriel; in Ambridge it was a trail of exasperated relatives. Kenton has an on-off relationship with **Kathy Perks**, who has no illusions about him. He's great fun, but flakier than a *mille feuille* with a Flake on top.

MEL ARCHER

(née Hardiment)
Somewhere in Oz • Born 12.2.72

Mel isn't the first woman to fall for **Kenton Archer**'s plausible charms. But she was the first actually to marry him and the first to have his baby – at least the first he's acknowledged. Baby Meriel arrived two weeks late in May 2001 – already taking after her father – **David** quipped. But before the child's first birthday, Mel had seen through Kenton, who had borrowed money from her with little sign of it ever being repaid. She chucked him out, and he returned to **Ambridge** sadder but (this is Kenton, after all) no wiser.

PAT ARCHER

(née Lewis)
Bridge Farm • Born 10.01.52
(Patricia Gallimore)

Meeting Pat was probably the best thing that ever happened to **Tony**. Not only was she good with cows, having managed a herd of Welsh Blacks in, er, Wales, but she had the entrepreneurial spirit that he lacked. Together, they have built **Bridge Farm** into a thriving organic enterprise that produces its own yoghurt, ice cream, cheese (thanks to daughter **Helen**), pork and sausages (son **Tom**). They even have their own shop, **Ambridge Organics** in **Borchester**. Through all this, Pat has retained most of the radical principles that saw her famously replace Tony's *Daily Express* with *The Guardian* in 1984. **Clarrie Grundy** would certainly say Pat's a sympathetic employer, and she's been a good friend to **Kathy Perks**, even giving her a temporary home after her break-up with **Sid**.

PHIL ARCHER

Glebe Cottage • Born 23.4.28
(Norman Painting)

Phil is probably the only soap character to have been admired by a former Home Secretary as a fine example of British manhood. He's grown from a bright, if hot-headed, farmer's son, eventually taking over **Brookfield** during the boom years for British agriculture and passing it on to **David** and **Ruth** in much tougher times. His marriage to **Jill** has been one of the most stable relationships in the village and, all being well, they are on course for their golden anniversary in 2007. Despite retirement, Phil still lends David and Ruth a hand on the farm, but he does have more time now to indulge his passion for music; he is the organist at the parish church of **St Stephen's** and his piano playing often accompanies village productions.

PIP ARCHER

Brookfield Farm • Born 17.2.93
(Rosie Davies)

Christened Philippa after **David**'s father and Rose after **Ruth**'s aunt, the eldest **Brookfield** child is universally known as Pip. She took well to Loxley Barratt Primary School until brother **Josh** came along, when she started to play up. David eventually solved the jealousy by allowing Pip to show off her brother to her classmates. Fortunately, when **Ben** was born Pip was old enough to help out, and enjoyed having a living doll to bathe and dress. Pip loves to help with the young stock, and takes after grandfather **Phil** in another way too – she is learning to play the piano and has sung enchanting solos at carol concerts. Well . . . her family were enchanted, anyway.

RUTH ARCHER

(née Pritchard)
Brookfield Farm • Born 16.6.68
(Felicity Finch)

Ruth has always seen herself as a farmer, not a farmer's wife. She came from Prudoe in Northumberland to work at **Brookfield** as an agricultural student, and married **David** in 1988. The arrival of **Pip** and **Josh** didn't stop her working on the farm, particularly with her much-loved dairy herd, but she had to take much more of a back seat when struck by breast cancer in 2000. A mastectomy and punishing chemotherapy were successful, although the threat of a recurrence hangs constantly over her. Eager to pull her weight after her recovery, she was back in the milking parlour despite an unplanned pregnancy the following year. But when **Ben** arrived, she finally had to slow down a bit. Even Wonder Woman didn't have to save the world *and* cope with three children.

TOM ARCHER

Bridge Farm • Born 25.02.81
(Tom Graham)

Tom's cooled down a bit since his days as a notorious eco-warrior. In 1999 he was acquitted on a charge of criminal damage, despite admitting attacking a trial crop of genetically modified oil seed rape. This was on land owned by his uncle, **Brian Aldridge**, which didn't do a lot for family harmony. Tom works with his father **Tony** at **Bridge Farm**, mainly running the outdoor herd of organic Gloucester Old Spot pigs, which his brother John established before his tragic death in 1998. In 2003, despite his parents' caution, Tom drove through an ambitious expansion to supply a national supermarket with Tom Archer Sausages, although he soon found out how difficult it is to supply such a powerful customer. As with many young men, Tom's libido can lead him by the, er... lead him astray, but most of the time he remains true to his girlfriend **Kirsty Miller**.

Bridge Farm • Born 16.2.51
(Colin Skipp)

Jennifer Aldridge's brother and the only son of **Peggy Woolley** and her late husband Jack Archer. For a long time, Tony felt responsible for the loss of his elder son John in a tractor accident, but each anniversary of the death is slightly easier to bear. Tony will never be dubbed Mr Sunshine, but he gets a quiet satisfaction from producing high quality organic milk and veg. Wife **Pat** and her dairy workers turn the milk into **Bridge Farm** yoghurt and ice cream, and daughter **Helen** converts small amounts into cheese. The veg is sold to a co-op and at the farm shop, **Ambridge Organics**. What does cheer Tony up is roaring round the country lanes in his venerable MG Midget ('mid-life crisis', scoffed son **Tom**), a game of cricket or the excellent products of Shires Brewery.

This large Victorian house with a 17th century core has served as a community centre 'with soundproofed room for rock and roll' and later a field studies centre, but for a long time it remained unoccupied and unloved. The owner **Jack Woolley** eventually decided to lease it to the Landmark Trust. Architect **Lewis** supervised the building's restoration to its Victorian splendour and it is now available to holidaymakers looking for something a little different. As housekeeper, **Freda Fry** cleans the place between lets.

JEAN-PAUL AUBERT

Grey Gables • Born 1951
(Yves Aubert)

No sane person would put a highly strung, temperamental control freak in a hot room surrounded by blunt instruments and the sharpest of knives. But if they hadn't, then we would never have experienced the exquisite creations of **Grey Gables's** head chef. And he hasn't killed anyone. Yet.

BAGGY AND SNATCH

Baggy and Snatch. They go together like 'drunk and disorderly'. And, to **Clarrie**'s alarm and despondency, they often go arm in arm with **Eddie Grundy**. Unlike Baggy, Snatch admits to a surname – Foster – and while admitting to that, he'd like several other offences to be taken into consideration. When Eddie comes home drunk, with hooky gear, or with pheasants protruding from his clothing, the chances are he'll have spent the evening in the company of either or both of these gentlemen.

CHRISTINE BARFORD

(Formerly Johnson, née Archer)
The Old Police House • Born 21.12.31
(Lesley Saweard)

Phil **Archer**'s younger sister is always known in the family as Chris. She had a hard time accepting that worsening back trouble meant the end of her riding days, which had been her work and her life, and reluctantly she sold her business and house at The Stables to her niece **Shula Hebden Lloyd**. For many years Chris struggled with marriage to an airy dreamer, Paul Johnson. After his death she found happiness with the altogether more down-to-earth **George**, and they were eventually able to enjoy a companionable retirement. Christine hopes to see more of Peter, her adopted son from her first marriage. He lives away from the village, and travels a lot as an administrator with a symphony orchestra, but turned up as the star guest at her 70th birthday party.

GEORGE BARFORD

The Old Police House • Born 24.10.28
(Graham Roberts)

It's odd that George ended up in **Ambridge**'s former police house, because he spent a few years as a copper before devoting the bulk of his working life to the gamekeeping trade. A sort of gamekeeper turned gamekeeper, you might say. George has been a great help to his fellow Ambridge keepers. He recruited and trained **William Grundy**, and William's boss **Greg Turner** has often benefited from George's wisdom, which George gained the hard way through an early life that was marred by his alcoholism and divorce. Because of this, George is on his second marriage, to **Christine**. His two children, Karen and Terry, are from the first relationship. A straight-talking Yorkshireman, George plays the cornet, works voluntarily both as a tree warden and a flood warden, and makes a popular chairman of the Parish Council.

LILIAN BELLAMY

(formerly Nicholson, née Archer)
Guernsey • Born 8.7.47
(Sunny Ormonde)

Jennifer **Aldridge**'s younger sister and the widow of **Ambridge**'s last real squire figure, Ralph Bellamy, who ended his days in Guernsey. After Lilian's son James (born in 1973) moved to London, his mother seems to have found comfort mainly in gin and the company of attractive young men. The collapse of her relationship with a two-timing gold-digging bit-part actor/model called Scott led to her temporary return to Ambridge in 2001 and a bid to regain her youth via cosmetic surgery. Rich, self-centred and impatient with Ambridge's sleepy ways, she has much in common with **Matt Crawford**. Jennifer was annoyed when Lilian got into bed with Matt over **Borchester Land**'s housing development, **Grange Spinney**. It was a metaphorical bed, but we wouldn't put it past either of them to find a real one some day.

NEVILLE BOOTH

Born 1942 • Ambridge

A member of the bell ringing team at **St Stephen's**. Mr Booth's name was once linked by the **Ambridge** net-curtain twitchers with **Jolene Perks's** (then Rogers), when her car was seen parked outside his house *all night*. In reality it was because she was with **Sid** and she didn't feel it was safe for her car to be seen outside **The Bull**. Going on the speed with which the Mr Booth rumour spread, she was right to be cautious.

Welcome to the official Borchester website.

Borchester Chamber of Trade – bringing this historic market town into the 21st century

<continue running scripts on this page?>
SHOPPING: **Underwoods** (traditional department store), **Ambridge Organics** (speciality foods):
<u>Click Here</u> *<file not found>*

LEISURE: Theatre Royal, Multiplex Cinema (3 screens), Leisure Centre (gym, swimming pool)
<u>Click Here</u> *<fatal exception at E44CA965>*

AM VALE: visit the picturesque countryside that surround *<This program has performed an illegal operation and will be shut down>*

Property company owning the 1020 acre **Berrow Estate**, including business units at Sawyers Farm and one tenanted holding, **Bridge Farm**. **Brian Aldridge** thought he was moving into the big boys' playground when he became a director, but he soon found that big boys play rough games. With world prices so low, the board has been unhappy with its return on capital, and is constantly looking for ways of screwing more money out of its investment. Brian saw his contract to farm the Estate's 'in hand' land go to a more ruthless outside firm, and was unable to prevent plans for the **Grange Spinney** housing development. As the Borchester Land chairman **Matt Crawford** makes Machiavelli look like Postman Pat, Brian would be advised to take a food taster to dinner parties.

BRIDGE FARM

STOCK
75 milkers (Friesians) • 35 followers (heifers/calves)
120 outdoor reared pigs

CROPS
115 acres grassland • 22 acres barley
15 acres wheat • 6 acres potatoes • 2 acres carrots
2 acres leeks • 3 acres swedes
2 acres Dutch cabbage • 1 acre Savoy cabbage
4 acres mixed vegetable and salad crops,
including 2 polytunnels

LABOUR
Tony Archer • **Pat Archer** • **Tom Archer**
Clarrie Grundy • Colin Kennedy (dairy)
Stan Derby • **Susan Carter** (sausages)

Tenant farmers **Tony** and **Pat Archer** rent 140 acres from the **Estate**, with an extra 32 acres from other landlords. Bridge Farm converted to organic in 1984. The farm's produce – including yoghurt and ice cream made in their own dairy – is sold through a wholesaler and to local outlets including **Ambridge Organics.** In 2003, ambitious **Tom** took on a brave commitment to sell his own brand sausages to a national supermarket, renting a business unit at Sawyers Farm for the processing.

BROOKFIELD FARM

STOCK
130 milkers (Friesians) • 70 followers (heifers/calves)
90 beef cattle (Herefords) • 300 ewes
Hens (small scale)

CROPS
258 acres grassland • 115 acres cereals
34 acres oil seed rape • 15 acres potatoes
12 acres beans • 10 acres fodder beet
17 acres forage maize • 8 acres set-aside

LABOUR
David Archer • **Ruth Archer** (relief)
Phil Archer (relief) • **Jill Archer** (hens, bees, holiday cottage)
Bert Fry (general) • **Biff** (sheepdog)

Brookfield is a 469-acre mixed farm, which incorporates the old holdings of Marney's and Hollowtree. With **Phil**'s retirement in 2001, **David** contracted out the arable work to **Home Farm** so he and **Ruth** could concentrate on their livestock. Despite recurring problems with TB in the dairy herd, Brookfield is doing its best to move away from selling its products as commodities and to get closer to the customer. High quality beef from the Herefords is sold at the farm gate, and the lamb is marketed co-operatively under the Hassett Hills brand.

41

*'...Chips with your Shires Bitter? Not unusual, you might think. But The Bull on **Ambridge'**s village green now boasts two computers in their public bar, which opens at 10am for coffee and internet surfing. It's part of **Sid** and **Jolene Perks**'s drive to find new customers, supplementing the long standing attractions of the beer garden (with Eccles the peacock), the boules "piste", and the economical Family Restaurant. If, like me, you find the tapping of keyboards at odds with the olde worlde ambience of this half-timbered free house, you can escape to the quiet of the Ploughman's bar. No escape, sadly, from the caterwauling of the pop groups in the function room (the "Bull Upstairs") on Fridays and Saturdays...'*

Extract from *The **Borchester** Echo*'s 'A Word in Your Beer' column.

CHRISTOPHER CARTER

No 1, The Green • Born 22.6.88

Neil and **Susan**'s son and younger brother to **Emma**, Christopher started at **Borchester** Green secondary school in September 1999. Christopher has had the odd episode of juvenile idiocy (haven't we all), but generally gives his parents little trouble. He's a dab hand with radio controlled cars, and came a terrific second to **Alice Aldridge** at the 2001 village fete. Neil has managed to persuade Christopher into the bell tower at **St Stephen's**, and he rang his first full peal – of Grandsire Triples – at the Jubilee celebrations in 2002. But of late he's become rather more interested in mixing on his record decks. Perhaps he intends to become **Ambridge**'s answer to Paul Oakenfold (an eminent disk jockey in the field of house music, your honour).

No 1, The Green • Born 7.8.84
(Felicity Jones)

In 2003, **Neil** and **Susan**'s bright and sassy daughter had a difficult time as the apex of a love triangle. She was torn for a while between **William Grundy** and his more erratic but more exciting younger brother **Ed**, who once saved Emma's life by pulling her out of a burning car. Unfortunately, the car was William's. Ed had taken it without permission, driven it without a licence and crashed it into a tree, which hardly endeared Ed to his brother – or to Neil. In the end, Emma chose the security and undoubted love that William could offer, soon sealing the decision by getting engaged to him. Emma is assistant manager (albeit in a very small team) at **Jaxx Caff**. The job basically involves running the place while giving the illusion that **Kenton Archer** is in charge, and Emma does it very well.

NEIL CARTER

No 1, The Green • Born 25.5.57
(Brian Hewlett)

Neil worked, reluctantly, for a few years as a feed rep, but in 1998 he returned to his first love – pigs. **Susan** wasn't impressed, and not just by the words 'first' and 'love'. Neil runs an outdoor herd of Gloucester Old Spots at **Willow Farm**, and does a lot of the pig husbandry for would-be sausage baron **Tom Archer**. In 2001, Neil replaced his and **Mike Tucker**'s pick-your-own strawberry enterprise with **Betty**'s free-range hens, to Mike's annoyance. **Eddie Grundy**'s attempts to exploit Neil – or, as Eddie put it, make them both millionaires – were scuppered by **Emma**'s accident. Neil's opinion of the Grundy family has been less than zero ever since. He could have knocked seven bells out of **Ed**, but he contented himself with ringing them – as tower captain at **St Stephen's**.

(née Horrobin)
No 1, The Green • Born 10.10.63
(Charlotte Martin)

Susan's not had a lot of luck in her attempts to shake off the bad start that comes with being a **Horrobin**. In 1993 she was forced to shelter brother **Clive** when he was on the run, getting three months in prison when he betrayed her to the police. She tried to get husband **Neil** into a white-collar job, only to see him return to the land. Susan supplemented her job at the **Village Shop** with a receptionist's post at the surgery, but it closed in 2002. In September 2003 she started as a part-time school secretary at **Borchester** Green, but it was only maternity-leave cover, so she continued to pack sausages for **Tom Archer**. She hoped her children would get further up the social ladder, but daughter **Emma** went to work in a café rather than on to university. So no pressure on **Christopher**, then...

MATT CRAWFORD

Somewhere posh near Borchester
and a nice place in town
(Kim Durham)

Brian Aldridge's chairman in **Borchester Land** is a Del Trotter who really did make a million, but without that character's redeeming social features. Matt doesn't let a little thing like the planning laws get in the way of his business objectives, or the fact that he is married to Yvette get in the way of his sexual urges (as **Debbie Travers-Macy** once found out, to her horror). Brian has won some battles, but Matt still managed to get the **Grundys** evicted from **Grange Farm**, and the **Grange Spinney** housing development pushed through – albeit on a smaller scale than the mini-Milton Keynes he'd originally planned. It's clear from various clandestine house purchases that Matt has designs on **Ambridge** – and they are not the sort that the Arts and Crafts movement would appreciate.

More correctly, the Berrow Estate: see **Borchester Land**.

Building contractor Paul Blocker is a man who eats not wisely, but too well. He managed to squeeze himself into the cab of his JCB to perform a comically awful 'Disco Diggers' routine with **Eddie Grundy** at the 2001 **Ambridge** fete.

For **Ambridge** residents, Birmingham supplies the real bright lights, but this cathedral city 17 miles east of the village is a good half-way house. Lots of shops, nice places to eat and drink: a nirvana for the credit-card generation. In the evenings, Bannisters café bar is where the young and beautiful congregate until sensible people over the age of 30 have gone to bed. Then they move on to Angels club for several hours dancing, preening and 'pulling'.

DEREK FLETCHER

Glebelands

In 1979, Pat and Derek Fletcher were among the first occupants of one of the 'executive homes' in Glebelands – the **Grange Spinney** of its day. The development was not welcomed by most villagers, and they soon felt the same way about the less-than-charming Mr Fletcher. Along with **Peggy Woolley**, Derek was one of the parishioners who left **St Stephen's** for All Saints, **Borchester** on the appointment of a woman vicar. **Roy Tucker** traced a poison-pen letter back to delightful Derek, when **Hayley** had the temerity to criticise people who want to protect their rural idyll by objecting to new housing. Ironic that, because in 1979, Pat and Derek Fletcher were among the first occupants...(this is where we came in).

WAYNE FOLEY

(Ian Brooker)
Radio Borsetshire
Broadcasting throughout the county on 87.3FM

'Tune in to the Wayne Foley Afternoon Show. With news and views from around the county and a tea-time guest just after four. And play spot the personality with Wayne's Usual Suspects competition!

Something to say? Call Brenda* on the phones.

Every weekday, 2 'til 5.

Life going slowly? Tune to Foley.'

(*That's **Brenda Tucker**. Mike's so proud)

ALAN FRANKS

The Vicarage, Ambridge
(John Telfer)

Once an accountant, Alan worked as a non-stipendary minister before being appointed vicar of **Ambridge**, Penny Hassett, Darrington and Edgeley in June 2003. He's a man of passionate convictions, not all of which might be welcome to his more traditional parishioners. Alan's wife died of breast cancer in 1995, so his bonds with his daughter **Amy** are immensely strong.

The Vicarage, Darrington

The Reverend **Alan** has brought his daughter up to think for herself, and now reaps the results in occasional blazing rows, although underneath they are extremely close. Coming to the countryside was a joy for Amy, primarily because she loves riding. She hit it off very quickly with **Alice Aldridge**, who is of the same age and similarly nutty about horses.

Brookfield Bungalow • Born 1936
(Eric Allan)

To the casual observer, there's not much to set Bert apart from the general run of agricultural workers. But don't be fooled, because underneath those overalls beats the heart of a poet. Bert is the unofficial bard of Borsetshire who once had his own column in the **Borchester** *Echo*. Despite reaching retirement age in 2002, Bert kept plugging away at **Brookfield**, where **David** and **Ruth** have often been grateful for his understanding way with their children. Bert and **Freda** have one son, Trevor, and a granddaughter, Amy. Whether as cricket umpire or church-warden, Bert approaches all tasks with the same steady, dutiful approach, which can infuriate the more impatient. But my goodness it pays dividends in his garden, as demonstrated by the numerous prizes he's amassed at the annual Flower and Produce Show.

Brookfield Bungalow

Freda cleans the house and holiday cottage at **Brookfield**, and is the housekeeper at **Arkwright Hall**. She knocks out cheap-and-cheerful meals aplenty for **The Bull**'s family restaurant, and at home she keeps **Bert**'s body and soul together with large helpings of hearty traditional nosh. At the annual Flower and Produce Show her cakes and preserves are so successful that despairing competitors wonder if she's made a pact with the devil. But it's not these domestic accomplishments that make Freda seem the perfect woman to a certain sort of unreconstructed male. It's that she is never heard to speak.

SIR SIDNEY
AND LADY MERCEDES GOODMAN

A garage mechanic announcing that he's going to give Sir Sidney's Mercedes a good seeing-to might soon expect a visit from a couple of burly men. Because Mercedes is Sir Sidney's Spanish wife, whose decades of sun-worshipping and couture shopping combine to form an appearance reminiscent of a distressed leather settee swathed in an elegant throw. Goodman's Spanish interests date back to the days when he fought with Franco, and he still takes a totalitarian approach to running his food-processing empire, which includes canning factories in **Borchester**, Spain and elsewhere.

A working farm (just) until the bankrupt **Grundys** were evicted in April 2000. The bulk of the acreage was absorbed back into the **Estate** and the farmhouse sold with fifty acres to **Oliver Sterling**, who runs a few beef cattle ('hobby farming', scoffed **Joe Grundy**) with the occasional help of Joe's grandson **Ed**.

GRANGE SPINNEY

Or **Crawford**'s Folly as it might have been known. **Borchester Land**'s plans for a housing development on old **Grange Farm** land was the source of much **Ambridge** angst, but spirited opposition was only able to reduce the extent, to twelve luxury residences and six 'low cost' homes, which were built in 2003.

'Dear Dean,
As you can see from the pictures on the front, I am
staying in a really nice hotel. If you were here,
you'd be out on the golf course all day – or in the
health club, or showing off in the swimming pool.
I've taken all the money out of your jet bike
account and I've been having fantastic French
meals and beauty treatments. **Caroline**
Pemberton *(the manager) and* **Jack Woolley***,*
(he owns the place), they were really nice when I
told them what you'd done. The receptionist is
going to post this after I've gone, so you won't know
where I am. I'm not coming back Dean, never.
And if you turn up here I've asked the assistant
manager **Roy Tucker** *to set* **Higgs** *on you. You*
don't want to meet him, Dean...'

Postcard entrusted to **Lynda Snell** for delayed despatch.

ALF GRUNDY

Gloucester • Born 13.11.44

When the Grundys were farmers, they didn't need to buy any black sheep, because they had one of their own, in **Eddie**'s brother Alf. The Grundys adhere more to their own idiosyncratic moral code than the letter (or indeed word, sentence, paragraph or subsection) of the law. But after his release from prison for breaking and entering, Alf committed the ultimate offence; he stole from his family. When Joe was 80, Eddie and Clarrie arranged for him to visit Alf as a birthday treat. It was better than Alf coming back to **Ambridge**.

CLARRIE GRUNDY

Keeper's Cottage • Born 12.5.54
(Rosalind Adams)

While some people think **Eddie** should be shot, most agree that his wife Clarrie should be canonised. Only a saint could have put up with the four Grundy men (father-in-law **Joe** and feuding sons **Ed** and **William** complete the unlovely set) for so long and for such little reward. Clarrie labours night and day at **The Bull** and **Bridge Farm** dairy respectively, so you might expect the men to pull their weight around the house. You might, but stoical Clarrie gave up that expectation a long time ago... To escape her daily drudgery, she likes a nice romantic novel (not that she gets much time to read), and very occasionally she escapes to Skegness to see her sister Rosie Mabbott.

ED GRUNDY

Keeper's Cottage • Born 28.9.84
(Barry Farrimond)

Clarrie worries about Ed, and well she might. Although he's happiest playing his electric guitar, he can be a hard worker when he puts his mind to it. Father **Eddie** and **Oliver Sterling** both employ him, and he's trying to establish a small beef enterprise at **Grundys' Field**. But he all too frequently crosses the line of legality. A run of joyriding led to his crashing his brother **William**'s car and injuring **Emma Carter.** Although Ed bravely pulled Emma from the burning vehicle, the relationship between the brothers is usually dire, especially as Ed once came close to stealing Emma away from William. **Jazzer**'s ghastly experience has warned Ed off ketamine but not all drugs by any means. And he hasn't been able to resist a bit of petty thieving, either. Worry on, Clarrie…

EDDIE GRUNDY

Keeper's Cottage • Born 15.3.51
(Trevor Harrison)

Once a farmer, always... in debt, as Eddie might have said. Having lost the tenancy of **Grange Farm**, Eddie turned his back on agriculture to concentrate on his other enterprises – or 'scams', as the rest of **Ambridge** call them. He's your man for garden ornaments, compost, landscaping or (keep your voice down) a couple of trout or a brace of pheasants. This motley collection of money-earners pays the rent to landlord **Jack Woolley**, although **Clarrie**'s wages are just as vital. Eddie found he couldn't leave farming behind completely; he's often employed in his tractor or digger around the fields of Borsetshire. And in 2003 this former tenant farmer was at last able to say "git orf moi laarnd", when a windfall from his old milk quota allowed him to buy **Grundys' Field**.

JOE GRUNDY

Keeper's Cottage • Born 18.9.21
(Edward Kelsey)

The Grundys had been tenant farmers 'since time immoral', and Joe still feels the burden of being the Grundy who lost **Grange Farm** for future generations. He finds there is little that will console him, except possibly hitching up Bartleby his pony and trotting off in his trap for a pint at **The Bull** (Joe is a devout Methodist, except for the bit about not drinking alcohol. Or going to chapel.) Joe used to suffer from a complaint known as 'farmer's lung', but it's been a lot less troublesome since son **Eddie** hasn't expected him to do any work. So Joe potters around his garden and, thanks to neighbour **Robert Snell** and the computers at The Bull, has become an unlikely 'silver surfer'. He's the man who put 'bored' into message board.

WILLIAM GRUNDY

The Dower House Flat • Born 9.2.83
(Philip Molloy)

It looks like brother **Ed** inherited the Grundys' wilder traits, while **Clarrie**'s respectable Larkin genes were passed to William. The elder son takes life seriously, to the point of being slightly stolid. But **Emma Carter** found Will sufficiently attractive not only to go out with him but to choose him over Ed when she was tempted to stray. William is lucky enough to have **Caroline Pemberton** for a godmother. Even when Caroline moved to **Grange Farm**, she allowed him to stay on in his flat at her house. To his father **Eddie**'s dismay, Will works as an under-keeper with **Greg Turner** at the combined **Grey Gables**, Berrow **Estate** and **Home Farm** shoot. Sadly, William has a low opinion of both Eddie and Ed. Ever sadder, it's probably justified.

GRUNDYS' FIELD

This 3.4 acres may not look like much, but when the **Grundys** bought it in 2003 it represented their first step into land ownership after generations of being tenants. **Ed** grazes his few beef cattle there, but it's as much a storage area as a piece of productive grassland. A rough shed and a pole barn – controversially erected without planning permission – house Eddie's venerable tractor, his early Jurassic digger, and his stock in trade; of garden ornaments, materials for his landscaping business, and mounds of 'organic' compost. Don't complain about the piles of manure – that's Eddie's bread and butter, that is.

SHIV GUPTA

Coventry
(Shiv Grewal)

Accountant Shiv is **Usha Gupta**'s elder brother, and can usually be relied upon to appear at Blossom Hill Cottage when Usha needs cheering up. He didn't really approve of her partner Richard Locke, and when Richard left after that unpleasant business with **Shula Hebden Lloyd**, Shiv did his best not to say 'I told you so'. More recently, perhaps in despair of Usha finding a suitable man by her own devices, he tried to pair her up with an ex-partner of his: Ashok, who was conveniently moving to **Felpersham**. But Usha seemed to prefer the barrister Adrian Manderson, and by the time she'd realised that Adrian was not the committing type, Ashok had moved away.

USHA GUPTA

Blossom Hill Cottage • Born 1962
(Souad Faress)

Solicitor Usha is an equity partner with the **Felpersham** firm of Jefferson Crabtree. Usha's parents were unhappy when she moved to the countryside from Wolverhampton in 1991. She's been welcomed by many villagers, but integrating into the rural community brought plenty of challenges, including a very distressing series of attacks by a gang of racist thugs. Although she gets on well with **Ruth Archer**, relations with Ruth's sister-in-law **Shula Hebden Lloyd** never recovered from Shula's affair with Usha's boyfriend Richard Locke. After Richard's messy departure, Usha couldn't find a satisfactory relationship, and for a while submitted herself to the matchmaking wiles of her Auntie **Satya Khanna.** It didn't work. Seduced by the Western romantic ideal, Usha still hankered after a love match.

SIOBHAN HATHAWAY

Ireland/Germany
(Caroline Lennon)

Siobhan and former husband Tim came to **Ambridge** in 1999; he to be the local GP and she to work as a freelance translator. But the marriage foundered. Tim became close to the then-vicar Janet Fisher (to whom he is now married) and Siobhan started an affair with **Brian Aldridge**. Once she gave birth to Brian's son, Ruairi, matters accelerated rapidly and she was hurt and furious when Brian chose to stay with his wife **Jennifer**. After an unhappy sojourn in her native Ireland, Siobhan returned to Ambridge in September 2003 in a last ditch attempt to persuade Brian to start a new life with her in Germany. Rebuffed again, she fought with him and urged by him, had to walk away in shock from the car crash in which he was injured. One wonders if she's got the message now…

BUNTY AND REG HEBDEN

Bunty born 20.2.22
(Bunty - Sheila Allen)

Retired solictor Reg and wife Bunty are the parents of **Shula Hebden Lloyd**'s first husband Mark. Since her marriage to **Alistair**, Shula has been uncomfortably caught between husband and in-laws on a number of issues affecting **Daniel**, whom Mark fathered by IVF, although he died before Daniel was born (pay attention at the back). Against Reg and Bunty's wishes, Alistair was determined that Daniel would not suffer the torments of private education that he had endured. Alistair won that argument, which didn't exactly smooth the way when he wanted to adopt Daniel, thus severing Reg and Bunty's legal rights. It took the scone-assisted intervention of the other grandparents **Jill** and **Phil Archer** before they consented. And of course Shula has made sure that their relationship with Daniel is just as close, despite the adoption.

JOHN HIGGS

Grey Gables

Is Higgs – as he is invariably known – the strong, silent type? Silent, certainly and as for strong... well, all right, perhaps he could wash a little more frequently, but he has a dirty job, as general handyman and gardener at **Grey Gables**. He does spruce up when required to drive **Jack Woolley**'s vintage Bentley.

Although the bus service around **Ambridge** is pretty dire, just six miles west of the village is a railway station, which means it's easier to get to Birmingham or London (via Paddington) than it is to get to some of the surrounding villages. Ah, the wonderful logic of 21st century public transport...

HOME FARM

STOCK
600 ewes • 110 hinds, stags, calves

CROPS

954 acres cereals • 136 acres grassland
75 acres oil seed rape • 100 acres sugar beet
80 acres linseed • 75 acres peas • 2 acres strawberries
80 acres woodland • 58 acres set-aside, including:
40 acres industrial rape • 10 acres willow (game cover)

OTHER
25 acre riding course • Fishing Lake

LABOUR
Brian Aldridge (managing and relief)
Adam Macy (deputy) • **Greg Turner** (gamekeeper)
William Grundy (under keeper)
Andy, Jeff (general workers) • Fly (sheepdog)

With 1585 mainly arable acres, Home Farm is the largest in **Ambridge**. It has made the most of its huge machinery by carrying out contract farming for **Brookfield** and other local farms. And as a partner with Brookfield and others in the Hassett Hills Meat Company, it raises and supplies high quality lamb to butchers and caterers. Since **Adam**'s arrival, it started selling its venison at local farmers' markets and entered the soft-fruit business.

RT REVEREND CYRIL HOOD

Felpersham
Peter Howell

Bishop Cyril? Decent bloke, most people think. The Bishop of **Felpersham** is a firm supporter of women priests. He was a great help to **Ambridge**'s previous vicar Janet Fisher over the untidy emotional mess caused by her attraction to the local doctor Tim Hathaway, who was at the time married to the adulterous **Siobhan**. Although Tim and Janet had to move away – to Southampton – they were still able to follow their respective vocations and were married in May 2003. **Shula Hebden Lloyd** and husband **Alistair** were among the parishioners who attended the wedding, which, despite rumours, was not sponsored by the Clerical Medical insurance company.

CLIVE HORROBIN

Coming soon to a prison near you
Born 9.11.72
(Alex Jones)

Honour among thieves? (Pause for hollow laughter.) Clive demonstrated quite the opposite when he was on the run following an armed raid on the **Village Shop**. He forced his big sister **Susan** to harbour him, and then when eventually caught, he shopped her to the police. Nice… When he returned to **Ambridge** after his prison sentence, it wasn't long before ex-copper **George Barford** correctly suspected that Clive was linked to a series of burglaries in the area. Although George took a beating for his good citizenship, that wasn't enough revenge for our Clive. After his release from another prison term, he started a terror campaign by slashing horses at The Stables, tragically not realising that the Barfords had meanwhile sold the place to **Shula Hebden Lloyd**. Even his family's stomachs were turned at how twisted Clive had become.

6, The Green, and elsewhere

Three ex-cons out of six children is going some, particularly in a relatively law-abiding manor like **Ambridge**. **Clive**, Keith and **Susan** (now **Carter**) have all known the jangle of keys and the slamming of doors, although to be fair Clive was really to blame for Susan's incarceration. Their brothers Stewart and Gary aren't exactly feckful, and Tracy has exhausted the patience of numerous local employers, including the **Bridge Farm** dairy and the café at **Lower Loxley**. Bert is a lengthman by trade (it's something to do with road building) and Ivy cleans for **Usha Gupta** at Blossom Hill Cottage. The phrase 'where did we go wrong?' is a rather over-used one chez Horrobin.

JASON

🌳 🌳

Borchester
(Brian Miller)

Jason, an ebullient Brummie builder, had three children with his ex-wife, but has lived for many years with his girlfriend in **Borchester**. He's a good craftsman, although prone to taking on too many jobs and so spreading himself thinner than the skim on a partition wall.

JAXX CAFF

Borchester

One-time greasy spoon bought in 2003 by **Jack Woolley** and reopened with a retro 1950s feel. **Kenton Archer** practically begged Jack to give him the job of managing it, partly because it came with a flat upstairs, but the real assets are the chef Frank – a prince in the bacon-butty department – and assistant manager **Emma Carter**.

JAZZER

Borchester • Born 1984

(Ryan Kelly)

Jack 'Jazzer' McCreary was in **Ed Grundy**'s class at school, and left with a similar lack of qualifications. He originally played drums and later sang in the band *Dross*, with his elder brother Stuart on bass and Ed and **Fallon Rogers** on guitar, but in 2002 his hopes of rock stardom were shattered. Always equipped with a dangerously wild streak, he took enthusiastically to a drug called ketamine. After one session with this living death he woke up a week later in hospital. Permanent brain damage left him clumsy and with memory problems, and his shocked friends tried their best to rehabilitate him. He worked as their roadie for a while, until the group broke up in 2003. Ed's dad **Eddie** finds work for Jazzer occasionally, but it's probably best not to ask where most of his money comes from.

Lower Loxley

What's that stunning bird often seen on the hunt at **Lower Loxley**? No cheap jokes here, please. That's probably a Harris Hawk, in the care of the resident falconer Jessica. She is self-employed, with a *quid pro quo* arrangement whereby she uses premises at Lower Loxley and they are able to offer falconry displays and 'experience days'. She is a good looking woman, though, so it's as well that **Elizabeth Pargetter** is confident that **Nigel**'s interest is purely ornithological.

SATYA KHANNA

Wolverhampton
(Jamilla Massey)

When **Usha Gupta**'s family fled from Uganda in the 1970s, they ended up in Wolverhampton, and they really wished that Usha had stayed closer to them rather than moving to **Ambridge**. It falls to Auntie Satya to act as go-between. She has a knack of sensing when Usha needs a bit of support – or something to eat that doesn't involves piercing a plastic lid and four minutes on 'high'. When Usha asked for help in finding a mate, enterprising Satya went into matchmaking overdrive, but to her frustration even her best efforts couldn't find Usha a 'suitable boy'. Satya always gets on well with **Marjorie Antrobus**, who has seen something of the world and has similar attitudes on many subjects – like the importance of a hot meal on the table.

LEWIS

(Robert Lister)

Life was tricky for **Nigel** and **Elizabeth Pargetter** until Lewis came along. At last, someone who could get the better of the otherwise indomitable **Julia**, who is remarkably meek in his company. When not on pleasant outings, Lewis and Julia often take charge at **Lower Loxley**'s art gallery, and occasionally look after **Lily and Freddie**. Lewis is an architect, officially retired, but he still does the occasional job that interests him, like the conversion of **Lower Loxley**'s shop and café, the refurbishment of **Arkwright Hall**, or the extension of buildings at The Stables to form **Alistair Lloyd**'s new veterinary surgery.

ALISTAIR LLOYD

The Stables
(Michael Lumsden)

In 2002, Alistair was aghast to find that his partner Theo was stealing drugs from their veterinary practice to fund a cocaine habit. Bruised Alistair dissolved the partnership to set up in converted buildings at his home, where wife **Shula** runs a riding school. Alistair's first marriage ended when his wife had an affair, and Shula's fling with Richard Locke meant that she and Alistair might not have made it to the altar themselves. But his love for her and her son **Daniel** won out, and he's been a wonderful father to the boy, whom he adopted in 2000. In his spare time, Alistair keeps wicket for – and captains – the **Ambridge** team, and enjoys a game of poker.

DANIEL HEBDEN LLOYD

The Stables • Born 14.11.94
(Dominic Davies)

Daniel is fascinated by animals, and you might think that he takes after his father **Alistair**, a vet. But Alistair is actually Daniel's adoptive father. The boy's blood father Mark died never knowing that his and **Shula**'s second IVF attempt had been successful, and the pregnancy gave despairing Shula something to live for. In 1998, a mysterious illness was eventually diagnosed as juvenile arthritis, and Daniel is subject to occasional 'flares' of this debilitating condition. No surprise then that Shula can sometimes be too indulgent of her miracle child, who certainly takes after his mother in his enjoyment of horse riding.

SHULA HEBDEN LLOYD

(formally Hebden, née Archer)
The Stables • Born 8.8.58
(Judy Bennett)

Phil and **Jill Archer**'s elder daughter and **Kenton**'s twin. Shula married **Alistair** in 1998, after an unwise dalliance with the then local GP Richard Locke, which lost Shula the friendship of Richard's partner **Usha Gupta**. It was an uncharacteristic aberration for Shula, a regular churchgoer, bellringer and church-warden. Shula's first husband Mark was killed in a car crash in 1994, never knowing that after years of disappointment and treatment for infertility Shula was finally pregnant with **Daniel**. Shula has always loved horses and after twenty years as a qualified chartered surveyor she took over The Stables – as a home and a business – on the retirement of her aunt **Christine Barford**. It soaked up all her capital and is hard work for limited financial reward, but she doesn't regret the move.

LAWRENCE LOVELL

A rather sad little bed-sit in Felpersham
(Stephen Hancock)

'...my greatest moment was when I was understudying the Red Shadow in a West End production of The Desert Song. *I still remember the thrill when the director told me that Maurice's irritable bowel syndrome had flared up and I was to go on...'*

'...I know from my experience as a model for knitting patterns the importance of the pose. I have often been dubbed a great poseur...'

*'...In **Ambridge** they still talk of the courageous casting of my 1998* Aladdin, *which I might say found gold among dross...'*

'...one's leading ladies do have a tendency to fall for one. It's an occupational hazard. Are you doing anything later, by the way...'

Reporter's notes from a press interview to publicise a production of *Grand Hotel* by the Felpersham Light Opera Society, directed by Laurence Lovell.

To the casual observer, Lower Loxley oozes the luxury of a grander age. But, as **Elizabeth Pargetter** would testily explain, a 300-year-old building takes more than Handy Andy and a bit of MDF to maintain. So to earn its keep, the Hall hosts conferences and takes sightseers; Elizabeth's husband **Nigel** runs falconry courses and displays with **Jessica**; and the grounds boast a vertiginous tree-top walk, rare breeds, cycle trails and an art gallery. Ancient retainers **Titcombe** and **Mrs Pugsley** have been joined over the years by numerous additional employees. Among others, **Kathy Perks** runs the shop and the Orangery café, employing the culinary talents of Owen the chef. **Hayley Tucker** nannies for the Pargetter twins **Lily and Freddie**, and for Kathy's little boy **Jamie**, and runs occasional activity visits for local schoolchildren.

Home Farm
Born 22.6.67

Adam's arrival in **Ambridge** in 1967 caused quite a stir. **Jennifer** (now **Aldridge**) was unmarried and refused to name the father, although Adam's shock of red hair implicated Paddy Redmond, **Phil Archer**'s cowman. Adam was later adopted by Jennifer's first husband Roger Travers-Macy. For many years, Jennifer saw only the occasional card or email from her son who, after graduating in agricultural economics, settled in Africa, working on farming development projects. Eventually the hard life of the development worker – and an unhappy love affair – took its toll on Adam, who returned to **Home Farm** in 2003. He rapidly made himself indispensable, especially after the departure of half-sister **Debbie Gerrard**. Thanks to Adam's energy and new ideas, **Brian** thought his stepson was the wasp's whiskers – until he discovered that Adam was gay, that is.

KATE MADIKANE

(née Aldridge)
Johannesburg • Born 30.9.77
(Kellie Bright)

Kate's packed a lot into her first quarter-century. In her teenage years she graduated from straightforward mischief to out-and-out rebellion against her wealthy parents, **Brian** and **Jennifer Aldridge**. She took up with travellers and for a while was something of an eco-warrior. She had a daughter, **Phoebe Aldridge**, initially fighting **Roy Tucker**'s attempts to prove himself the father. But eventually she had to leave Phoebe with Roy when she travelled to Africa to 'find herself'. In 2001, she returned to **Ambridge** to give birth to her second daughter **Noluthando**, later marrying the child's father **Lucas** in his native South Africa. Kate's occasional visits to her home village are always fraught with tension, because she still feels herself to be Phoebe's mother, even if in reality the role has passed to Roy's wife **Hayley**.

LUCAS MADIKANE

Johannesburg • Born 1972
(Connie M'Gadzah)

The father of **Kate**'s baby **Noluthando** proved his commitment to mother and child when he spent a large sum of money flying to be with them in **Ambridge** after the birth. Caught in the middle of the parental struggle over Kate's other daughter **Phoebe Aldridge**, Lucas eventually managed to achieve the impossible; making Kate see sense. She reluctantly accepted that Phoebe was settled with her father **Roy Tucker** and returned to South Africa, marrying Lucas in June 2001. They are making a success of married life in Johannesburg, where Lucas is a radio journalist with the South African Broadcasting Corporation. They make the occasional (and often slightly fraught) visit to Ambridge, usually funded by Lucas's mother-in-law **Jennifer**.

❦ NOLUTHANDO (NOLLY) MADIKANE ❦

Johannesburg • Born 19.1.01

Lucas and **Kate**'s daughter was born in **Borchester** General Hospital, ironically with Kate's arch rival **Hayley Tucker** in attendance. **Noluthando** means 'one who is loved' in Xhosa, the language of Lucas's tribe. In June 2001 Nolly's grandparents **Jennifer** and **Brian Aldridge** flew to South Africa for the christening, where Kate's half-brother **Adam Macy** became Nolly's godfather.

KIRSTY MILLER

Borchester
(Anabelle Dowler)

Kirsty's relationship with **Tom Archer** is like an ageing fluorescent tube: on again, off again... Initially drawn together by environmental concerns – they both attacked fields of GM crops in 1999 – she and Tom were prevented from seeing each other for months while Kirsty's trial was pending. Once the charges were dropped she reappeared on the scene to win Tom back from the girlfriend he'd found in the interim. Tom's obsession with his sausage business led Kirsty briefly into the arms of Chaba, a Hungarian student who'd been working at **Brookfield**, but she and Tom were again reunited at the 2003 Glastonbury Festival. Kirsty enjoys hearing embarrassing stories about Tom's youth from his sister and her boss **Helen**, who manages **Ambridge Organics**, where Kirsty now finds a more legal outlet for her environmental enthusiasms.

A farm in name only, this farmhouse with outbuildings and half an acre of gardens was home to **Marjorie Antrobus** before she reluctantly had to sell it to finance her move to The Laurels nursing home. The self-contained flat had been occupied by a variety of **Ambridge**'s young people before their first steps into home ownership, notably **Neil** and **Susan Carter** and **Ruth Archer**. The most recent tenants were **Roy** and **Hayley Tucker** and Roy's daughter **Phoebe**, who had to move in with Roy's parents following the sale of the farm to **Matt Crawford**.

ELIZABETH PARGETTER

(née Archer)
Lower Loxley Hall • Born 21.4.67
(Alison Dowling)

Never afraid to make waves, Elizabeth unleashed a tsunami when she objected to father **Phil**'s plans to pass **Brookfield Farm** on to **David**. (Elizabeth was to receive a mere token; half a £200,000 house.) She protested that running **Lower Loxley** was like knitting submarines out of fifty pound notes, and anyway she was thinking only of **Lily and Freddie**. To be fair, Elizabeth hasn't had it easy in the past. Before her marriage to Nigel, she had an abortion after being dumped by swindler Cameron Fraser, and her congenital heart problem required a valve-replacement operation after the birth of the twins. Recruiting **Hayley Tucker** as a nanny, Elizabeth threw herself into keeping the Hall afloat. Despite her spikiness, Nigel owes a lot to his 'Lizzie'.

JULIA PARGETTER

Lower Loxley Hall • Born 17.8.24
(Mary Wimbush)

Grande dame Julia resents letting hoi polloi into her home, even though **Lower Loxley Hall** wouldn't survive without them. Julia would have preferred **Nigel** to marry better than a 'farmer's daughter' (**Elizabeth**), which is ironic as Julia's true past was as a greengrocer's daughter and dancer in wartime variety. Julia has fallen prey to addiction, to alcohol and later to gambling. But in recent years, having **Lewis** on hand has helped to curb her excesses, and she's mainly restricted herself to being annoying. Julia was pleased by the arrival of a son and heir in the shape of **Freddie**, seeing **Lily** as rather incidental. But when, in 2002, Nigel's sister Camilla and her husband James produced a son – Piers – Julia's delight knew no bounds. At last, a grandchild with breeding on both sides of the family...

🐄 LILY AND FREDDIE PARGETTER 🐄

Lower Loxley Hall • Born 12.12.99

Elizabeth Pargetter's heart condition would have made even a simple pregnancy daunting, but with twins the pressure was really on. Happily, both were born safely (if early) by caesarean section and soon became troublesome toddlers (what other sort is there?). Freddie (the second and smaller child) used to be the particular favourite of grandmother **Julia**, until **Nigel**'s sister Camilla gave birth to her son, Piers, in 2002.

NIGEL PARGETTER

Lower Loxley Hall • Born 8.6.59
(Graham Seed)

Nigel shares the eccentric streak which can make the English upper classes so entertaining to watch. In his youth it manifested itself in high jinks in a gorilla suit, and in recent years in a fascination with the sport of falconry, which, thanks to the expertise of **Jessica**, he has made a particular attraction at **Lower Loxley**. In 2003 an over-enthusiasm for good wine led to a conviction for drink driving, to wife **Elizabeth**'s fury. But having to cycle everywhere soon made Nigel a convert for the two-wheeled life (note Lower Loxley's new cycle trails and bike hire), and he developed a growing enthusiasm for the natural world.

CAROLINE PEMBERTON

(née Bone)
Grange Farm • Born 3.4.55
(Sara Coward)

Arelation of Lord Netherbourne and best friend to **Shula Hebden Lloyd**, Caroline has been bringing a touch of class to Ambridge since 1977. It's a measure of **Jack Woolley**'s respect that he trusts her completely to manage his biggest asset, **Grey Gables** hotel. In fact Caroline's career progression has been one steady upward slope, in contrast to the boulder-strewn byway of her romantic life. After twenty years of serial disasters (including an affair with **Brian Aldridge**), she married landowner Guy Pemberton. But his heart attack only six months later left her a grieving widow, albeit a wealthy one, with the **Dower House** and a majority share in **The Bull**. Caroline was lucky enough to get a second chance though, meeting **Oliver Sterling** through her love of hunting, and moving in with him in 2003.

JAMIE PERKS

April Cottage • Born 20.7.95
(Ben Ratley)

Don't traumatise the child by telling him, but if Jamie hadn't been born, it's possible **Sid** and **Kathy** might still be together. Trying to keep up with a lively toddler, Sid – by then in his early fifties – decided to get fit. But what he also got was the amorous attention of Jolene Rogers – now **Jolene Perks**, so you'll get the gist of what it led to. Jamie still sees his father regularly, often staying over at **The Bull**. As for the other men in his life, he's quite fond of eccentric **Joe Grundy** and his tearaway grandson **Ed** next door. And Jamie gets on brilliantly with Kathy's occasional boyfriend **Kenton** (call me irresponsible) **Archer**. Oh dear...

JOLENE PERKS

(neé Rogers)
The Bull
(Buffy Davis)

Jolene's lively personality and generous assets shout 'lock up your husbands' to many Ambridge women, particularly **Clarrie Grundy**, who once saw this singer and keyboard player make beautiful music – well, all right, Country and Western Music – with **Eddie**. But it's **Kathy Perks** who should have been riding shotgun, because she lost her husband **Sid** to the one time 'Lily of Layton Cross'. Jolene (real name Doreen) is a natural behind the bar. Much of **The Bull**'s success in recent years has been down to her, with innovations including a cyber-area with internet access. Jolene runs line-dancing sessions and still does occasional gigs with her band *The Midnight Walkers*. She's proud that her daughter has followed in her musical footsteps, although **Fallon**'s preferred genre is a long way from Nashville.

KATHY PERKS

(formerly Holland)
April Cottage • Born 30.1.53
(Hedli Niklaus)

There's no doubt that Kathy came off the worse from her divorce. **Sid** kept his home and business at **The Bull**, and married warm, voluptuous **Jolene**. Kathy faced the isolation of being a single mum and the attentions – although attention deficit would be a better description – of **Kenton Archer**. With experience as a Home Economics teacher and at The Bull, at least Kathy is happy managing the café and shop at **Lower Loxley**. Having **Hayley Tucker** as a workplace nanny helps considerably with son **Jamie**, too. And Kathy is not completely without support at home. Her friend **Pat Archer** has been a rock in times of trouble. And the **Grundys** next door are... well, next door.

SID PERKS

The Bull • Born 9.6.44
(Alan Devereux)

Despite approaching the age of 60, Sid takes pride in keeping fit and is manager of the **Ambridge** cricket team. Many men envy him, but whether more for his 49 percent share of **The Bull** (with **Caroline Pemberton**), or the fact that he is married to the lovely **Jolene** is open to question. Sid's first wife Polly died in 1982. Their daughter Lucy lives in New Zealand and in 2003 made Sid a grandfather, while the much younger **Jamie** – his son from his second marriage – lives with his ex-wife, **Kathy**. Sid is usually the classic genial host but on certain topics – like homosexuality – he can be pretty reactionary. He clashed with the more liberal Jolene when his step-daughter **Fallon Rogers** started dabbling in drugs, and felt that **Jazzer**'s downfall proved him right.

HEATHER PRITCHARD

Prudoe, Northumberland
(Joyce Gibbs)

After Heather's husband Solly died in 2002, she spent several months with daughter **Ruth Archer** at **Brookfield**. Heather found that being resident granny to the children (and to Ruth and **David** too, if we're honest) was occupational therapy to help her through her loss, although it did lead to some friction with **Jill**. Ruth urged Heather to make the move permanent, but she vigorously resisted, eventually returning to her life and friends in Northumberland.

MRS PUGSLEY

Lower Loxley

Like her colleague, the admirable **Titcombe**, **Lower Loxley**'s housekeeper has seen the staff at the Hall grow considerably to service its various business activities, from conferences to falconry. She has accepted all these changes with a stoic resignation, and we have heard not one word of complaint from her. In fact, we have never heard *any* words from her.

Manorfield Close • Born 13.7.15

When people say Manorfield Close is next to Paradise, they aren't praising the facilities but reflecting on the imminent destination of most of the residents. When the last trumpet sounds for the **silent** and weak-bladdered Mr Pullen, he'll probably have to pay one last call before entering those pearly gates.

ELLEN ROGERS

Denia, Costa Blanca.
Born 1926
(Rosemary Leach)

Not a typing error for **Fallon Rogers** (no relation), but **Julia Pargetter**'s younger sister. A very merry widow, Ellen owns a bar in Spain and is only rarely seen in **Ambridge**. She was at one time a source of great embarrassment for Julia, who had tried to hide her humble past, having jumped several social strata on her marriage to Gerald, **Nigel**'s father. Julia had even dropped her original *déclassé* name, but she'll always be 'Joan' to her sister.

FALLON ROGERS

The Bull • Born 19.6.85
(Joanna van Kampen)

Fallon has an uninhibited streak that males find dangerously attractive, but she tempers it with a degree of common sense. She has more or less come to terms with her mother **Jolene** marrying **Sid Perks**, even though she used to think the relationship 'gross'. Fallon's father is the guitarist Wayne Tucson, and she has inherited her parents' musical talents, although her tastes are more for metal and indy than their country and western. She plays guitar and sings, and is studying for a HND in popular music performance at **Borchester** College. **Ed Grundy** and **Jazzer** thought they'd never forgive Fallon for winning a song competition, which led to the break-up of their band *Dross*, but she was not suddenly catapulted to stardom, and they eventually realised that she was much better to have as a mate than an enemy.

GRAHAM RYDER

Borchester
(Malcolm McKee)

As a land agent working for the **Borchester** firm of Rodway and Watson, which manages the **Estate** for **Borchester Land**, Graham is often to be found in the estate office at Sawyer's Farm. He is conscientious and courteous, and takes his professional duties very seriously, even when he's required to do the unpopular. Most villagers see him as **Matt Crawford**'s puppet, and when Graham stood for the **Ambridge** parish council in 2003 everyone suspected that Matt was pulling the strings. Or depending on what sort of puppet Graham was, Matt could have had his hand up... well, anyway, Graham didn't get in.

ST STEPHEN'S CHURCH

Established 1281

This fine old church dates back to Saxon times. **Shula Hebden Lloyd** and **Bert Fry** (churchwardens), **Neil Carter** (captain of the bell ringers) and **Phil Archer** (organist) have seen some controversy over the years: the installation of a lavatory; clandestine attempts to kill off the bats in the roof; and the politics of the flower rota, which make the Florentine court look like, well, a church flower rota. But perhaps the greatest alarms were caused in 1995 when the parish was merged with three others – Darrington, Penny Hassett and Edgeley – under the charge of a *woman* vicar. Janet Fisher left in January 2003. We wonder if her successor **Alan Franks** knew what he was letting himself in for.

One of the delights of **Ambridge** is that coterie of characters whom the listener knows well and can picture clearly, but who are never actually heard to speak. A large but obviously rather quiet band, they include the ageing **Mrs Potter** and **Mr Pullen** at Manorfield Close, **Lower Loxley**'s talented chef Owen and resident falconer **Jessica**, the quite delectable **Mandy Beesborough**, the rather less delectable **Baggy and Snatch**, not to mention **Fat Paul**, exotic East European Anja at **Ambridge Organics**, Frank, who flips the burgers at **Jaxx Caff**, **Freda Fry** who performs a similar function at **The Bull**, bellringer **Neville Booth**, **Tom Archer**'s butcher Stan Derby, many of the Horrobins, and the king of them all, the wonderful **John Higgs.**

LYNDA SNELL

Ambridge Hall • Born 29.5.47
(Carole Boyd)

Ambridge would be a poorer, if less irritated, place without Lynda. Despite living in the village since 1986, she's still viewed as an incomer by many, especially near-neighbours and thorns-in-flesh the **Grundys**. Lynda doesn't help by regularly lecturing the locals on her latest environmental bonnet-bee. She's a keen gardener, when her hayfever allows, and producer of amateur theatricals, when her cast allows. She's known for bizarre enthusiasms but she excelled herself in 2003 with her 60th birthday present to long-suffering husband **Robert**: two llamas; Constanza and Wolfgang. When January 2002 brought floods to **Ambridge Hall**, the Snells were touched at the practical support that villagers gave. However, soon the bramble bushes on her way to work (as a receptionist at **Grey Gables**) were once more full of desperate people, diving in to avoid being recruited to her latest project.

ROBERT SNELL

Ambridge Hall • Born 5.4.43
(Graham Blockey)

What accolade is sufficient to reward Robert Snell? A knighthood? No, a sainthood, surely, because this is a man who can live with **Lynda** and like it. Robert is a computer expert, although he wasn't expert enough to keep his previous software business afloat, which forced Lynda to take a job at **Grey Gables**. Robert puts up with a lot, but when he's reached his threshold he's implacable, as Lynda found out when she objected to his helping Leonie – his daughter from his first marriage – buy a flat. Leonie has always been difficult, while relations with the younger Coriander ('Cas') are fortunately more amicable. Robert and Lynda have no children of their own. Wolfgang and Constanza are llamas, so don't really count.

Grange Farm
(Michael Cochrane)

A single man in possession of a good fortune? It is a truth universally acknowledged that Oliver's arrival in **Ambridge** created quite a stir. He sold a large farm in the north of the county to fund his divorce settlement with wife Jane, and bought **Grange Farm** with 50 acres to do a bit of hobby farming. That work – with occasional help from former Grange Farm resident **Ed Grundy** – left him plenty of time to pursue his passion for hunting, as joint master of the South Borsetshire. Through the hunt, it was inevitable that he would meet staunch horsewoman **Caroline Pemberton**, which soon led to passion of a different sort. Although at first Oliver wasn't used to a woman of such independent spirit, they grew to love each other, and Caroline moved into Grange Farm in April 2003.

TITCOMBE

Lower Loxley Hall

Who is that enigmatic figure atop **Lower Loxley**'s mighty ride-on mower? None other than head gardener Titcombe. He's seen a lot of goings-on at the Hall in his time, particularly in the wilder, party-throwing heyday of **Julia Pargetter**. But he never talks about it.

DEBBIE TRAVERS-MACY

(formerly Gerrard, formerly Aldridge)
Rheims, France • Born 24.12.70
(Tamsin Greig)

The daughter of **Jennifer Aldridge** and her first husband Roger Travers-Macy, Debbie used to work as deputy to her stepfather **Brian** at **Home Farm**, but in 2002 her happy life fell apart. Still emotionally raw, having unmasked her (now former) husband Simon as a serial adulterer, she discovered that Brian was cut from the same philandering cloth. As Brian and Jennifer tried to mend their marriage, unforgiving Debbie descended into a vortex of loathing and depression, turning on all who tried to help her – even her brother **Adam Macy**. Then one day she stunned her family by announcing that she had taken a job with a French agribusiness firm, and was gone the following week. Her sister, **Alice**, visits her occasionally, but Debbie can't play happy families, and so has chosen to play solitaire.

BETTY TUCKER

Willow Farm • Born 4.8.50
(Pamela Craig)

As manager of the **Village Shop** and a staunch WI member, Betty gets to hear most of what goes on in **Ambridge**. And she's got a few tales of her own she could tell, if she'd a mind to. Once a cleaner at **Home Farm**, she's still not quite adjusted to being linked to the **Aldridge** family (she and **Mike** are grandparents to **Phoebe** through their son **Roy**). Mike has had some pretty erratic times in the past, not to mention the results of **Brenda**'s pitiful taste in men and Roy's brief involvement with fascists. In 2001 Betty started an organic egg enterprise in partnership with **Neil Carter**, who owns some land adjoining the Tucker residence. Mike wasn't impressed. But then very little impresses our Michael.

BRENDA TUCKER

Willow Farm • Born 21.1.81
(Amy Schindler)

When torn between two brothers – **Ed** and **William Grundy** – **Emma Carter** took a lot of advice from Brenda. Which is ironic, as Brenda's romantic career has been not so much chequered as houndstooth. The older men she has fallen for are fascinatingly varied in their unsuitability: duplicitous gigolo (**Lilian Bellamy**'s former-toy boy Scott); adulterous slimeball (**Debbie Gerrard**'s ex-husband Simon); or admirable but gay (**Adam Macy**). Brenda works with **Wayne Foley** as a journalist at Radio Borsetshire, where her enthusiasm for a story about **Matt Crawford** and a corrupt local councillor once nearly got her sacked. Her parents **Mike** and **Betty** would like Brenda to learn a bit of wisdom as she gets older, but we hope she doesn't; it's much more entertaining this way.

HAYLEY TUCKER

🌱   🌱

(née Jordan)
Willow Farm • Born 1977
(Lucy Davis)

Bubbly Hayley is a qualified nursery nurse, working as a nanny at **Lower Loxley**. She originally descended on **Ambridge** in 1995 in a hormone-driven search for **Pat** and **Tony Archer**'s son John. After John's death in 1998 (she wasn't responsible . . . well, only indirectly by refusing to marry him), Hayley grew close to John's friend **Roy**. They were married in May 2001 and Hayley took on the role of mum to Roy's daughter **Phoebe Aldridge**. This is not something that warms the heart of the child's real mother **Kate Madikane**. Very much a Brummie, Hayley still can't tell a cattle crush from a creep feeder. Nonetheless the little family has been very happy in Ambridge, although in 2003 they lost their flat at **Nightingale Farm** and had to move in with Roy's parents.

MIKE TUCKER

Willow Farm • Born 1.12.49
(Terry Molloy)

What's your impression of a typical milkman? A whistling early-morning visitor cheerily dispensing the fruits of the dairy? Well, you can forget that baloney. Meet Mike 'Miserable' Tucker. A once-bankrupt would-be farmer who lost an eye in a forestry accident, Mike had years of chasing casual farm and forestry work, until eventually supplementing the milk round with a more regular job at a turfing company. Mike's also had occasional business ventures with **Neil** 'Cautious' **Carter** and **Eddie** 'Godawful' **Grundy**. You'll gather that Mike isn't the first person you'd invite to a party. But in 2002 he surprised everyone – especially himself – by learning ballroom dancing so that he could treat **Betty** to a night out in true Fred and Ginger style.

ROY TUCKER

Willow Farm • Born 2.2.78
(Ian Pepperell)

To look at him now, you'd never guess that Roy was once part of a gang of racist thugs who terrorised **Usha Gupta**. Penitent Roy eventually realised the horror of what he was involved in. He ended the persecution, suffering a severe beating for his confession (from the gang, not from Usha, although she was sorely tempted). After a business studies degree from **Felpersham** University, casual work at **Grey Gables** led to formal training and an assistant manager's position there. He enjoys the work, but the money's not brilliant. Roy, wife **Hayley** and daughter **Phoebe Aldridge** (from ex-girlfriend **Kate Madikane**) used to be happy tenants of **Marjorie Antrobus**. But when she sold **Nightingale Farm** in 2003, they found they couldn't afford a place of their own and had to move back in with **Mike** and **Betty**.

GREG TURNER

A Tied Cottage at Home Farm
(Marc Finn)

A former design technology teacher and outdoor activities leader, Greg arrived to look after the expanded **Home Farm**/Berrow **Estate** shoot in 1998. Widely read, he is a useful member of the pub quiz team, but for a long time his private life was a closed book. Eventually, people discovered that he'd become involved with **Helen Archer**. And even Helen took months before uncovering some big truths about Greg's past life: he'd had a vasectomy, for example, and he was divorced, his family having moved to France. In recent years his ex-wife Michelle has become more demanding, particularly as their elder daughter Sonja started to go off the rails (the younger, Annette, has been less trouble, but give it time...). The frustration of being an absent father of a difficult teenager did nothing to improve Greg's already surly demeanour.

UNDERWOODS

Well Street, Borchester

UNDERWOODS - Borchester's most varied store

* *Up-to-the-minute fashions and classic tailoring*
* *Everything your kitchen needs*
* *A treasure trove for the gift buyer*

We think our Food Hall is the finest in the county – see if you agree.

And take the weight off those feet in our self-service restaurant, with a lite bite or one of our naughty-but-nice pastries.

UNDERWOODS – look no further.

Advertisement in *The **Borchester** Echo*.

Ambridge is fortunate in still having a village shop and post office, due in great part to the philanthropy of the owner **Jack Woolley**. **Betty Tucker** manages it, with the part-time help of **Susan Carter**. So for a pint of milk, book of stamps or a video – and especially for the low-down on the latest in Ambridge – you know where to go.

Fortunately the farmhouse is quite big, as it's home not only to **Mike** and **Betty Tucker** and their daughter **Brenda**, but also son **Roy**, Roy's wife **Hayley** and their daughter **Phoebe Aldridge**. Like **Nightingale Farm**, Willow Farm's land was bought up by others long ago. **Neil Carter** owns eight acres, on which he keeps his outdoor breeding herd of pigs, and an organic free-range egg enterprise, run jointly with Betty.

HAZEL WOOLLEY

Last seen in Soho
(Jan Cox)

Adopted daughter of **Jack Woolley** and his first wife Valerie, the wayward Hazel seldom visits **Ambridge**, to the great relief of all who work at **Grey Gables** and not a few Ambridge residents. Hazel works in the film business, making (according to doting Jack) 'proper films, for the cinema'. No-one is on record as actually seeing any of them, though. Hazel claimed she was too busy to attend her father's 80th birthday, but stepmother **Peggy** suspects that when Jack is finally called to that nineteenth hole in the sky, Hazel will be there faster than you can say 'last will and testament'.

JACK WOOLLEY

The Lodge, Grey Gables • Born 19.7.19
(Arnold Peters)

Jack still harks back to his humble beginnings in the Birmingham suburb of Stirchley, a sharp contrast to the business empire he built up in and around **Ambridge**, including **Grey Gables** hotel, the **Village Shop** and *The **Borchester** Echo* newspaper. Even at 83, he was still ready to expand, buying **Jaxx Caff**, to wife **Peggy**'s exasperation and **Kenton Archer**'s relief. Jack has one adopted daughter, **Hazel**, from his first marriage. Although into his eighties, he still enjoys shooting, a brisk eighteen holes on Grey Gables' golf course or a slow foxtrot with Peggy, whom he recruited as his assistant at Grey Gables in 1972. Slow courtship, too: they were married in 1991.

PEGGY WOOLLEY

(formerly Archer, née Perkins)
The Lodge, Grey Gables • Born 13.11.24
(June Spencer)

Peggy is one of the wealthiest women in **Ambridge**, but it wasn't always so. Originally from London's East End, she came to the village having married **Phil Archer**'s elder brother Jack. But with the country air and the glorious views came years of struggle, coping with Jack's get-rich-quick schemes and the alcoholism, which eventually caused his death. In **Jack Woolley**, Peggy found a rich man for her second husband, as did her daughters **Jennifer Aldridge** and **Lilian Bellamy**. This couldn't be said for her son **Tony Archer**. His wife **Pat** is neither rich, nor a man. Peggy is conservative with all he usual 'C's. She was delighted at the appointment of **Alan Franks** as vicar of **St Stephen's**. Not by him as a person, you understand; by the fact that he was male, allowing her to return to the fold.